PIMLICO

368

ONE DAY IN A
VERY LONG WAR

John Ellis was born in Bradford and
educated at the Universities of Sussex and
Manchester. He was a lecturer in the
latter's Department of Military Studies
before becoming a full-time writer. His
books include *The Sharp End: The Fighting
Man in World War II; The Social History of
the Machine Gun* (both available in
Pimlico); *Eye-Deep in Hell*, an account of
trench life in the Great War; *Cassino: The
Hollow Victory*; and *Brute Force: Allied
Strategy and Tactics in the Second World War*.

ONE DAY
IN A
VERY LONG
WAR

Wednesday 25th October 1944

JOHN ELLIS

PIMLICO

To Aidan and Peta
who saved my bacon,
and Sally and Caity
who made it worth saving.

Published by Pimlico 1999

2 4 6 8 10 9 7 5 3 1

First published in the Great Britain by
Jonathan Cape 1998
Pimlico edition 1999

Pimlico
Random House, 20 Vauxhall Bridge Road,
London SW1V 2SA

Random House Australia (Pty) Limited
20 Alfred Street, Milsons Point, Sydney,
New South Wales 2061, Australia

Random House New Zealand Limited
18 Poland Road, Glenfield,
Auckland 10, New Zealand

Random House South Africa (Pty) Limited
Endulini, 5A Jubilee Road, Parktown 2193, South Africa

Random House UK Limited Reg. No. 954009

A CIP catalogue record for this book
is available from the British Library

ISBN 0-7126-7465-9

Papers used by Random House UK Limited are natural,
recyclable products made from wood grown in sustainable forests.
The manufacturing process conform to the environmental
regulations of the country of origin.

Typeset in Bembo and Ehrhardt by MATS, Southend-on-Sea, Essex
Printed and bound in Great Britain by
Mackays of Chatham PLC, Chatham, Kent

Contents

*

The photographs that appear in the plates section are reproduced
with permission from the following sources: AKG London, numbers
1, 5, 6, 9, 11; Corbis, 16 and 17 (by Stanley Trautman); Hulton Getty,
2 and 13; Imperial War Museum, London, 3, 4, 7, 8, 10, 14 and 15.
The author has been unable to trace Frank Cancellare, who took
photo no. 12.

Respectively British, American, Allied,
Soviet and German Army Groups
(Figures in brackets denote their total
number of divisions/number of which
were armoured, including panzer-
grenadier. Russian figure denotes number
of armies.)

●■ Army group boundaries

■── Front Line, 25th October 1944

------ Frontiers, end of August 1939

▤ Lost by Rumania, 1940

NORTH SEA

ATLANTIC OCEAN

MEDITERRANEAN SEA

IRELAND

UNITED KINGDOM

London

Caen

Paris

R. Loire

FRANCE

R. Seine

R. Garonne

Bordeaux

R. Rhone

SPAIN

PORTUGAL

Madrid

Marseille

Nice

SWITZERLAND

Turin

Milan

Salò

La Spezia

R. Po

Belfort

Metz

Luxembourg

BELGIUM

Brussels

Antwerp

Aachen

Cologne

Koblenz

Frankfurt

Essen

Arnhem

Rotterdam

NETHERLANDS

Bremerhaven

Hamburg

Kiel

DENMARK

NORWAY

20
MOUNTAIN
ARMY
(11)

AOK
NORWAY
(7)

B
(35/7)

21
(20/6)

12
(21/7)

G
(17/2)

6
(13/3)

R. Meuse

R. Moselle

R. Rhine

THE WAR
AGAINST
GERMANY
25th October
1944

KARELIA (2)

FINLAND

Oslo •

SWEDEN

Leningrad •
LENIN-
GRAD (2)
Narva •

Stockholm •

ESTONIA

Moscow •

Copenhagen •

BALTIC SEA

Riga •
NORTH (37/2)
2 Balt. (5)
LATVIA

Dvina

U.S.S.R.

1 Balt. (7)
Memel •
LITHUANIA
Kaunas •
3 Byel. (4)

Tilsit •
Königsberg •
GERMANY
(EAST PRUSSIA)
R. Niemen

Danzig •

Stettin •

Berlin •

CENTRE (50/11)
R. Vistula
Warsaw ■
2 Byel. (4)

Pinsk •
R. Pripyar

1 Byel. (8/2)

POLAND

Kiev •

(31/9)
Forming,
Refitting,
Strategic
Reserve
GERMANY

R. Elbe
Dresden •

A (39/4)

1 Ukr. (5)

R. Oder

Prague •

4 Ukr. (3)

BOHEMIA-MORAVIA

SLOVAKIA

R. Dniester

R. Danube

Bratislava •
Vienna •

SOUTH (35/8)

Munich •

(AUSTRIA)

Budapest •
HUNGARY
Debrecen •

2 Ukr. (7)

R. Prut

Cluj •

RUMANIA

Zagreb •

Trieste •
(31/4)
Venice •
C

Bologna •
Ravenna •

F (9)

Belgrade •
3 Ukr. (5)

Bucharest •

BLACK SEA

R. Danube

Florence •
15 (23/4)

YUGOSLAVIA

BULGARIA

ITALY

ADRIATIC SEA

E (9)

Sofia •

Rome •

Salonica •

ALBANIA

TURKEY

GREECE

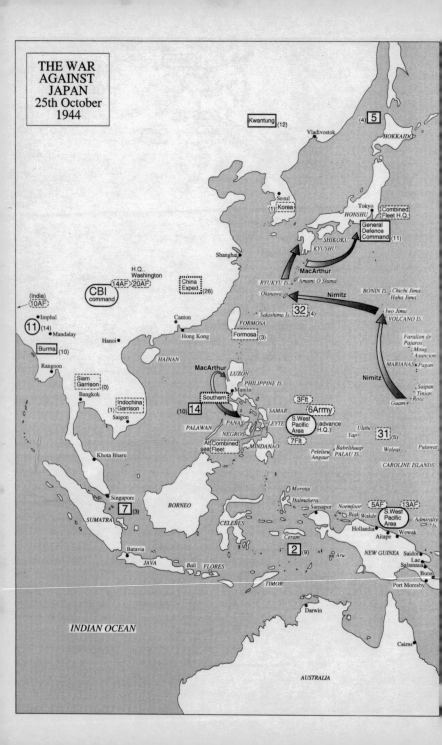

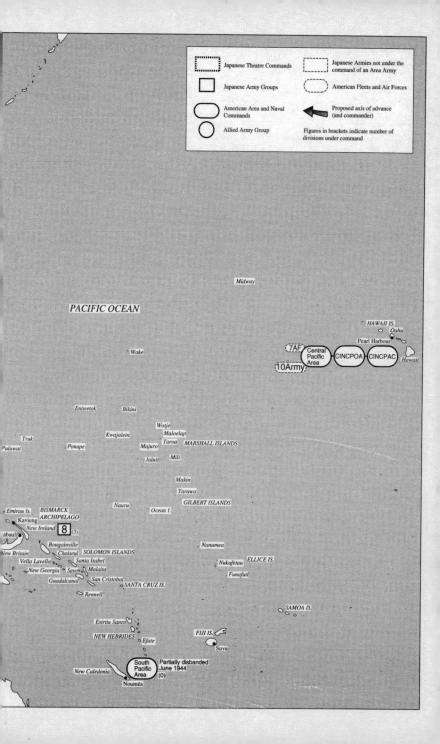

		Japanese Theatre Commands		Japanese Armies not under the command of an Area Army
		Japanese Army Groups		American Fleets and Air Forces
		American Area and Naval Commands		Proposed axis of advance (and commander)
		Allied Army Group		Figures in brackets indicate number of divisions under command

Midway

PACIFIC OCEAN

HAWAII IS.
Oahu
Pearl Harbour

7AF — Central Pacific Area — CINCPOA — CINCPAC
Hawaii

10Army

Wake

Eniwetok   *Bikini*

Wotje
Maloelap
Truk   *Kwajalein*   *Taroa*
Puluwat   *Ponape*   *Majuro*   *MARSHALL ISLANDS*
Jaluit   *Mili*

Makin
Tarawa
Nauru   *Ocean I.*   *GILBERT ISLANDS*

Emirau Is.   *BISMARCK ARCHIPELAGO*
Kavieng
New Ireland   8 (3)
Rabaul   *Bougainville*
New Britain   *Choiseul SOLOMON ISLANDS*
Vella Lavella   *Santa Isabel*   *Nanumea*
New Georgia   *Savo*   *Malaita*   *Nukufetau*   *ELLICE IS.*
Guadalcanal   *San Cristobal*   *Funafuti*
Rennell   *SANTA CRUZ IS.*

SAMOA IS.

Esiritu Santo
NEW HEBRIDES   *Efate*   *FIJI IS.*
Suva

South Pacific Area   Partially disbanded June 1944 (0)
New Caledonia
Nouméa

Preface

Despite the fact that the events of 1939–45 are generally acknowledged to constitute a World War, appreciation of the actual nature of the conflict is still subject to much chauvinistic distortion and misunderstanding. In this country and many others there has been a persistent failure to appreciate the truly global extent of the war and the enormous efforts and sufferings of millions of people throughout the world. American, Russian, Canadian, Indian, French, Polish, Czech, Chinese, Australian, New Zealand, Rumanian, Italian, Finnish and Brazilian troops all took part in the struggle against fascism, as did Yugoslav, Greek, Bulgarian, Albanian, Chinese, Vietnamese, Burmese and Filippino guerrillas, and in many of these countries, notably Poland, the USSR, Yugoslavia and China, as well as Germany and Japan in the last months of the war, vast numbers of civilians were killed, had their homes and livelihoods destroyed or were dragged off into slave labour. Much of this epic story still seems well beyond the ken of much popular history or any national curriculum. No one, it seemed to me, had attempted to describe properly the sheer extent of human suffering during the Second World War, not just in the front lines but also among whole populations, and it was this that prompted me to attempt a survey that would look beyond these very parochial icons – the Spitfire, St Paul's in the Blitz, Churchill's V-for-Victory, thumbs-up from a grinning Tommy – that sum up the war for the British.

A straightforward narrative history of the whole conflict would either oversimplify or become bogged down in detail, so I decided to concentrate on just one day in the whole six years of war and to build up a series of historical snapshots from every front, military and civilian, that would together give a real feeling of the panorama of suffering from one side of the world to the other. The choice of possible days was much more limited than might be supposed. Every writer seeks an element of drama and good drama demands some sort of resolution. In the Second World War, however, very little was ever resolved in a single day and most so-called battles were accretions of lesser battles that went on for days, weeks, sometimes even months. The only battles that were usually resolved within twenty-four hours were those at sea, and it was one of these that would have to serve as the dramatic focus for the book. The greatest of all naval battles, involving almost every conceivable type of naval action, was the Battle of Leyte Gulf, mostly fought and decided on 25th October 1944, and so this day became my template upon the war as a whole.

Although military events dictated the choice of my particular day, I have made every effort not to dwell solely on the war as combat. Indeed, another reason for choosing the 24-hour template was to allow me to move more easily from foxhole and cockpit, tank turret and warship's bridge to look at the experiences of those millions behind the front. In this book a day of war is taken to include also the effects of economic dislocation, inflation and food shortages; the destruction of property and the growing number of refugees and displaced persons; the enormous concentration of labour in war-related industries; the surge of scientific activity to devise more effective ways of killing people; the social and political effects of occupation and liberation and popular aspirations for a better postwar world. Inevitably, a book like this can only be an assembly of fragmentary impressions but it is to be hoped that their very variety, combined with the way they have been assembled, offers the reader a meaningful mosaic of a whole world at war.

The reader will accept, I hope, that even a book such as this cannot deal exclusively with one 24-hour period. For one thing, military events make little sense without some introductory explanation and scene-setting. For another, very few accounts of the war – be they general and unit histories, diaries and memoirs, or interviews – have much space to focus on individual days. Even newspapers, harried by the censors, tend to be irritatingly vague about linking events to particular dates, units and places. Thus, while the book is always able to offer a detailed account of what happened on 25th October 1944, all over the world, it has sometimes been necessary to use actual eye-witness testimony that generalises about a period as a whole or describes very similar events that occurred on other days, weeks or even months. Be that as it may, not one of the hundreds of personal accounts presented here is not strictly pertinent to the events on my chosen day. In striving to give humanity its myriad voices, I have been careful to ensure that all precisely echo the attitudes, doubts, aspirations and sufferings of this one day in a very long war, a day by which the historian will tell us the war was virtually decided, but which for those at the time marked only another 24 hours of accumulated anguish and fears for the future. Having myself once written a book which described the Allied victory as an inevitable consequence of their enormous material superiority, I am glad to have had this extended opportunity to show that the inevitability discerned by hindsight has precious little to do with the anxieties and tribulations of the moment.

Researching and writing this book has been beset by various delays and crises. That it has appeared at all owes a great deal to the forbearance and consistent support of the publishers, notably Dan Franklin, Tony Colwell and Will Sulkin, and of my agent John Parker. I am particularly grateful to Tony Colwell, my editor, who has worked long and hard on a rather unwieldy manuscript, heavily barnacled with ugly excrescences of tactical and technical quotidian detail. Whatever shapely lines the narrative now presents are due in no small part to his tireless chipping away and repair.

I am also very grateful to Andras Bereznay who, at extremely short notice, produced the maps from my erratically sketchy originals; to Joanne Hill who so meticulously 'mopped up' the proofs; to Phil McCarty, Jeff Brider and Mark Axworthy who gave invaluable assistance tracking down various obscure titles; to Mike Cox, omniscient as ever with regard to orders of battle; and to Andy Callan, Hugh Dent and Martin Wallace whose valued friendship prompted them to take an interest in the events of 25th October 1944 that must at times have seemed like being trapped inside the *Tardis*.

John Ellis
Manchester 1998

"A bad day is bad to the end."

Admiral Matome Ugaki, 23rd October 1944

Prologue
The Big Three

WHEN Joseph Stalin was told that he, President Franklin Roosevelt and Prime Minister Winston Churchill, the three great leaders allied against Hitler's Germany, were often dubbed the Big Three, and sometimes the Holy Trinity, he suggested that Churchill must be the Holy Ghost because he flew about so much. Certainly, on Wednesday 25th October 1944, Churchill had not long returned from a trip to Moscow where he met the Russian leader. He had landed back in England on the previous Sunday and gone straight to Chequers, his weekend retreat, before arriving back in Downing Street on Monday, where he fell straight into his usual daily routine. He would wake and breakfast between 8 and 9 a.m. and then remain in bed as he perused official papers. Some of these came direct from British and Allied commanders, or from senior statesmen, but many were one-page distillations of Whitehall memos and reports prepared by his personal Chief-of-Staff, General Sir Hastings Ismay, and his staff. All this reading matter frequently provoked a response, almost always written, and for some time, still abed, he busied himself with fountain pen, foolscap sheet, his 'klop' for punching tag-holes in the paper, and his little stacks of special labels inscribed 'Action This Day' and 'Action Within One Week'. These sometimes abrupt communications were known in Whitehall as 'prayers' for they almost always began with the word 'Pray . . .'.

He rose between 10 and 11 o'clock and, if not attending the House (which this week would not be until the 27th), he carried on working, usually breaking at around 1 p.m. for lunch with one or two guests. Then it was time for a siesta and, tying on a black blindfold, he would fall asleep almost as soon as his head touched the pillow. Rising again soon after five, he was now suitably refreshed for another punishing round of work. Normally this consisted of a Cabinet meeting from 6 until 8 or 9 p.m. and, after dinner, attendance at one of the numerous committees he chaired. These often did not begin until after 10 p.m., and even when they were over Churchill was still alert and eager for discussions with whichever generals, admirals, politicians, under-secretaries and the like were still to hand. These might go on until 2 or 3 o'clock in the morning before the Prime Minister finally turned in for the night.

On the 25th Churchill spent much of the afternoon working on the speech he was to deliver at the House of Commons on Friday, reporting on the results of his trip to Moscow. One of the main reasons for the visit had been to come to an agreement about the future of Poland, now partially liberated by the Red Army, and writing the speech only served to rekindle his anger at the attitude adopted by the London-based Polish government-in-exile. Its leader, Stanislaw Mikolajczyk, who had accompanied Churchill in Moscow, adamantly refused to accept the new Russo–Polish frontier proposed by Stalin which would have kept the disputed city of Lwow as part of the Ukraine. Mikolajczyk had in fact been bound by undertakings to his colleagues in London, but Churchill had little patience with Polish notions of their 'natural' frontiers and, eager to reach agreement with Stalin about the future of Eastern Europe as a whole, he had urged the Poles to accept the proposed 'Curzon Line'. At one private meeting he had lectured the Polish premier in the most humiliating terms. Happily, the impasse did not seem to have troubled Stalin unduly, no doubt because his sponsored provisional government, dominated by Polish communists, was already in the country, based at Lublin and backed up by the formidable Soviet forces that had already battled their way to the upper Vistula.

So while Stalin had remained as intransigent as Mikolajczyk over their common frontier, he had proved remarkably amenable about other countries now wholly or partly liberated by the Red Army. Though he could hardly brandish it in the House, Churchill had with him a sheet of paper, duly inscribed with Stalin's blue-pencilled tick, which allocated zones of relative Soviet and Anglo–American influence. The hastily scribbled list stipulated that Greece was to be 90 per cent Allied and 10 per cent Soviet, Yugoslavia and Hungary 50/50, Bulgaria 75 per cent and Rumania 90 per cent in the Soviets' favour. In the notes for his speech Churchill wrote that he and Stalin had "reached a very good working agreement about all these countries, singly and in combination, with the object ... of providing, as far as possible, a peaceful settlement after the war is over".[1] Nevertheless, Churchill clearly did not attach as much confidence to pieces of paper as his predecessor, Chamberlain, for British troops had already landed at Athens on the 15th. The Germans were in the process of withdrawing from Greece and the Aegean and the British force was to dog their heels, at the same time ensuring that the powerful Greek Communist Party did not attempt to take advantage of the political vacuum.

Churchill's interest in Greece was consistent with his geopolitical perspective which had focussed throughout the war upon the Mediterranean as a key theatre. As the war progressed his original priorities of guarding Britain's Imperial links through the Suez Canal and assailing the Axis via its vulnerable Italian and Balkan flanks were complemented by his urgent desire to get Allied troops into south-eastern Europe before the Soviets. The Americans on the other hand had remained committed to making the main attack across the Channel. They had grudgingly acceded to Allied landings in North Africa, Sicily and mainland Italy, but kept these commitments to a minimum and later insisted on withdrawing several divisions to support the cross-Channel invasion with landings in southern France. Churchill had bitterly opposed this transfer and now grumpily noted that forces had become pinned down in the Vosges mountains while the denuded armies in Italy had also proved too weak to break through the German defence line in the Appenines. Allied generals were already predicting that their men would have to spend the whole winter ahead shivering in their mountain outposts.

Churchill must also have felt considerable disappointment over the front in North-West Europe, or the European Theater of Operations as the Americans called it. The D-Day landings in June had been followed by brutal fighting to break out of the Normandy beachheads, but by the first week of September the Allies had been able to make sweeping advances across the River Seine, right through Belgium and up to the Meuse in the south. The Germans seemed in total disarray, yet within a couple of weeks they had formed a new solid defence line. As the whole front became mired in one of the wettest autumns on record, this line seemed more and more likely to thwart the Allies right through to the following spring. Another major constraint on the Allies was a supply shortage, especially of fuel and ammunition, caused by failure to open up the port of Antwerp and its enormous, undamaged docks. The port itself had been taken during the headlong Allied advance, but by the time commanders realised that this meant nothing without seaborne access via the Scheldt estuary, the Germans had burrowed into both banks of the river, amidst the waterlogged Dutch polders, and soon slowed the Allied advance to a crawl. By late October, however, thanks to heroic efforts on the part of First Canadian Army and a forthcoming amphibious assault on the key bastion of Walcheren Island, the opening up of Antwerp seemed imminent. But even so, it was already apparent to the Allied commander in North-West Europe, General Dwight Eisenhower, that opportunities for strategic exploitation thereafter were slight. He settled instead on a measured timetable of limited offensives up and down the whole front, from the Vosges mountains to the Scheldt, and held out no real prospect of any immediate war-winning breakthrough. The one commander who still hoped for such a breakthrough was the British General, Bernard Montgomery who, along with some of his Army patrons and acolytes, never ceased to agitate, and irritate, for a concentration of all available supplies and several extra U.S. divisions for one narrow, concerted thrust across the Rhine under his command. As Montgomery had already badly botched one such thrust, towards Arnhem in September, he was finding it difficult to muster much high-level support.

Problems on the Continent were also affecting British operations on the other side of the world, in Burma. The latest Japanese offensive, the self-styled 'March on Delhi', had foundered irredeemably at Imphal and Kohima in June, and the Japanese were now in full disease-wracked retreat. At the beginning of October, however, Churchill was forced to accept his Chiefs-of-Staff's recommendation that a long-cherished project to capitalise upon any Japanese defeat – an amphibious assault on Rangoon known as Operation DRACULA – could not now be attempted before November 1945. Because of manpower demands in North-West Europe, the three divisions mooted for DRACULA would have to remain in Eisenhower's theatre. Churchill could take some comfort, however, from the fact that the Americans had recently agreed (although without much enthusiasm) that a Royal Navy carrier task force would be allowed to operate alongside the mighty U.S. Pacific Fleet during the final advance towards Japan. Thus, Churchill hoped, might the prestige of the British Empire be restored again in the Far East.

On the naval front generally, and in the air, prospects seemed much brighter than on land. One of Britain's severest trials, the Battle of the Atlantic, seemed to have been won for the time being. Despite disturbing rumours of new types of U-boat with all manner of advanced weaponry, as well as of old types made much more elusive by using a schnorchel to remain submerged, actual statistics showed that submarine attacks had fallen away dramatically during 1943 and 1944. Continued vigilance was essential and large numbers of ships and Coastal Command aircraft would still be required to screen Allied convoys, but food, raw materials and military supplies to the United Kingdom and both European theatres now seemed relatively secure.

Victory seemed even more assured in the skies above Germany. After a long battle of attrition against the Luftwaffe, the Allied Combined Bombing Offensive – with RAF Bomber Command flying by night and Eighth U.S. Air Force by day to pound German cities, industries and rail communications – was finally beginning to deliver significant tonnages of bombs on target. German fighter pilots, especially at night, remained a tenacious foe, but month by month their reserves of aircraft and skilled pilots dwindled and Allied bomber losses dropped accordingly to what the statisticians asserted were 'acceptable' rates. Few, and certainly not Churchill, argued that bombers alone could win the war but it did now seem that they might significantly hasten Hitler's defeat by terrorising his civilians and choking the flow of munitions to his soldiers at the front.

The one blemish in the air situation was that Britain itself was being blitzed once more. Although the Luftwaffe had largely been chased out of British skies in 1940, unmanned weapons had now appeared. V1 and V2 rockets were falling constantly on south-east England, and while they hardly threatened major dislocation of military or civilian activity, especially as both types were extremely inaccurate, the effect on morale was undeniable. Lord Beaverbrook, the Lord Privy Seal, an intimate of Churchill's and a press baron with his ear to the ground, wrote on 23rd October to an American friend: "Here we are somewhat in the doldrums. The rockets come to us in London at the rate of six a day. I do not know how much injury we shall have to sustain before the winter is over. The slogan of 'London can take it' will prevail. But there may be quite a lot to take."[2] Moreover, the threat of the V1s meant that Anti-Aircraft Command continued to tie up enormous material and human resources. Antwerp and Brussels were also coming under fire and beginning to clamour for their own AA defences. These attacks by mobile German rocket batteries also raised the awful prospect of concerted missile attacks on military positions. A yet more dreaded possibility was that the Germans might be making progress on their own version of TUBE ALLOYS, what the Americans called the MANHATTAN PROJECT – the development of an atomic bomb, with as yet unquantifiably terrible destructive potential. Very little hard evidence about such a development had come to light, and Churchill knew that the American effort had encountered various seemingly intractable problems. Yet the Germans had once been world leaders in the field of experimental nuclear physics, and was not Hitler continuing to trumpet the unveiling of new and awesome secret weapons?

There was much besides Poland, then, to give Churchill pause for thought. Just how widely his mind roamed on the 25th we can never know, but if he did get the chance to emerge from the routine detail and to ruminate on the broader picture, beyond the prospects for eventual military victory, beyond even the Soviet threat to postwar stability, then he may well have gloomily pondered his nation's own future role in the world. Britain had entered the war as a major imperial power, but now the war was costing her people dear, with gold and foreign reserves draining away, enormous Lend Lease debts piling up, and production seriously distorted by the demands of the war effort. An immediate worry was the ability to reshape postwar production and make a swift transition to an economy that could satisfy the public's legitimate yearning for an end to rationing and austerity generally. In September, at the Octagon Conference with Roosevelt in Quebec, Churchill had argued hard for an extension to Lend Lease, commonly referred to as Lend Lease II, which would provide the same credit facilities for civilian goods after the war as had been available for munitions and food since 1941.

Although Roosevelt had seemed enthusiastic in Quebec, when a British delegation, including Lord Cherwell and Lord Keynes, arrived in Washington in October to negotiate terms, they found the Americans pretty hard-nosed and had no choice but to persist. Cherwell pleaded that food credits be maintained because "we can't grow more food than we are growing . . . [and] are already down to 80 per cent of pre-war [consumption]." He went on to state that food was not the only "wearisome shortage. We must build. We can't let the soldiers come home if they haven't got any houses. If they have no place to live there will be a riot." Clothing stocks were less than 60 per cent of normal, as were household goods. There was need, too, for more gasoline, especially for doctors and professional men. "Our civilians", he continued, "have been very hard pressed for a long time." Cherwell also repeated that "British exports had dropped 30 per cent in terms of production and 50 per cent in terms of price [and] that the British had growing external debts . . ."[3]

The delegation's arguments cut little ice. The whole Lend Lease organisation was now a part of the Foreign Economic Administration, a relentlessly bureaucratic little empire, totally devoid of the early 'hands across the water' idealism. With both the State and Treasury Departments also vying to be the tough guy on the postwar block, no firm decisions were taken, but Churchill could see that there were few in Washington with any deep commitment to mollycoddling the British economy. Had he but known, the U.S. Joint Chiefs of Staff had already led the way, recommending to the President on 24th October that Lend Lease provisions not be extended to cover any new non-military items.

Despite his immense prestige as a war leader, Churchill must also have worried about the future for his party, the Conservatives, in postwar Britain. There was still in place a coalition government which on the whole had achieved a remarkable consensus on major issues. The first signs of renewed division were now becoming apparent in the passage of the Town and Country Planning Bill, soon to be voted upon in the Commons. The Bill, which dealt with the compulsory acquisition of land for development by local authorities, outraged many Tories with both its compulsory provisions and the inadequate levels of compensation offered, based on 1939 prices. Although Churchill himself was fiercely anti-socialist, even he was angered and depressed by this resurgence of Tory mean-mindedness and the total lack of commitment to any conception of postwar social harmony. On 24th October, he had written to Lord Cranborne, the Dominions Secretary, regretting that "nothing will be more detrimental to Conservatism . . . than for our Party to forget all the great issues still at stake for the sake of wrangles about occupying and investing owners while leaving so many other cases of outstanding hardship untouched and untouchable." This point was also picked up by Lord Beaverbrook in his letter to America in which he reported that the British "parties are squaring up for an election. In my view it should not be delayed too long. For the Government is now unable to deal with postwar issues, the limit of their capacity to compromise has been reached."[4]

Elections were also in the offing in the United States when, in November, voters would decide whether to back President Franklin D. Roosevelt for an unprecedented fourth term. For several weeks the President had seemed not to have his heart in yet another contest, this time against Governor Thomas E. Dewey of New York, but he had none the less declined to join Churchill on the Moscow trip, pleading domestic pressures. As October progressed he appeared to his intimates to be gaining a renewed zest for the fight ahead. On the 24th, Averell Harriman, reporting back to Roosevelt on the results of the

Moscow Conference, which he had attended instead of the President, remarked that he looked older and thinner than he had six months ago but was "vigorous and determined in spirit . . . He told me that he had never become so bitter about any opponent as Dewey . . . because of Dewey's dirty tactics. He said he had become much more determined as a result."[5] With the schedule of election appearances now being stepped up, speeches were arranged in Philadelphia on progress in the war, for the 27th, Navy Day; in Chicago the day after, on postwar domestic issues; and a general summary speech in Boston on Saturday, 4th November. This was a punishing routine for a man who had been stricken with polio 23 years earlier and who had experienced great difficulty in standing and walking ever since. After the Teheran Conference in November 1943, Roosevelt had made hardly any speeches while not sitting down and his hip and leg muscles had atrophied markedly. Yet, with the help of his redoubtable wife, Eleanor, he was now working to a strict exercise regime and was able, with something to grip on to and in considerable pain, to stay upright during speeches lasting up to half-an-hour.

On the 25th, the President was back in the White House, having returned from Hyde Park, his weekend retreat in New York State, late on the 23rd. He was due to board his campaign train on the morning of the 26th and spent some of his day working on the Philadelphia speech. The bulk of his daily routine, like Churchill's, was taken up with running the war. The mornings were the busiest time and were orchestrated by his personal Chief-of-Staff, Admiral William Leahy. At about 9.45 a.m. Leahy would meet Roosevelt outside his elevator and follow his wheel-chair into either his study or the map room.

> The President kept himself informed minutely on the progress of the war. The maps in the map-room were so hung that he would not have to get out of his wheel-chair to look at them. There were flags and pins of various colours showing the disposition of our land, naval and air forces over the entire globe . . . There were a number of young officers assigned to the White House map-room who received military dispatches twenty-four hours a day. The President could have instant information any time he needed it. From this map-room also messages could be sent by him all over the world, as there was a relay from this point in the White House to the Communications Center in the Pentagon Building.[6]

Leahy himself always arrived with a slim tan portfolio of documents selected by him as the most pertinent items in the previous night's signals traffic. These were arranged by colour, an agreed scheme by which incoming dispatches from field commanders were pink, copies of outgoing despatches to these commanders yellow, Joint Chiefs of Staff papers green, Joint Staff Planners blue, Combined Chiefs of Staff white, and Atomic Energy Commission orange. The Joint Chiefs' papers were less interesting on Wednesdays as this was when they themselves met, beginning with luncheon, and Leahy's digest of their discussion would appear the following morning. The Joint Chiefs also had formidable bureaucratic back-up, and sprouted numerous sub-committees which produced reams of documentation daily, all of which Leahy had to summarise for the President.

In distilling Leahy's own distillation, the President's main military concerns would have been very much the same as Churchill's. The slowing down of Eisenhower's advance was a matter of keen regret and was not helped by the growing shortage of combat troops. On 16th October, Roosevelt had informed Churchill of the need "to give some rest to our front-line soldiers, who have been the spearpoint of battle since the first days in Normandy . . . We are now taking the very drastic step of sending the infantry regiments of the divisions ahead of the other units in order that General Eisenhower may be able to rotate some of our exhausted front-line soldiers." The same telegram also informed the Prime Minister that the Americans deemed it essential for all reinforcements to be sent to Eisenhower's front. As far as the Joint Chiefs were concerned, "we cannot now expect to destroy Kesselring's army [in Italy] this winter and . . . the terrain and conditions in the Po Valley will prevent any decisive advance this year."[7]

Above all, the Pacific was the real focus of attention on the 25th. Ever since turning back the Japanese tide in 1942, on New Guinea, Guadalcanal, and in the carrier battle off Midway, the Americans had been doggedly advancing back towards Japan. They were following a twin axis: to the south was General Douglas MacArthur, who had come via the Solomon Islands, the Bismarck Archipelago and New Guinea, while north of him was the mass of the U.S. Pacific Fleet, under Admiral Chester Nimitz, supporting U.S. Marine and some Army divisions as they 'hopped' from one cluster of tiny islands to another through the Marshalls, the Carolines and the Marianas. At the heart of this amphibious armada were the powerful carrier task groups of Admiral 'Bill' Halsey's Third Fleet, ranging far and wide to contain and eliminate Japanese air bases throughout the Central Pacific. The ground troops were still mopping up on many islands but the cutting edge of both MacArthur's and Nimitz's forces was now concentrated against Leyte, an island in the central Philippines. Army troops had gone ashore on 21st October and were slowly forcing their way inland. During these first days they were screened by Halsey's fleet carriers and battleships, and on the 25th jumbled reports began to reach Washington of a series of battles off Leyte against what seemed to be the main elements of the Imperial Japanese Navy. Preliminary indications were that significant damage had been inflicted on each of the Japanese groupings, though at no small cost to the Americans.

Other news from the Far East was important for its political rather than its military ramifications. For most of the war the Americans had set great store by helping Chiang Kai-shek's Nationalist regime in China to pursue their own war against the Japanese. To this end they had flown in Lend Lease aid over 'the Hump', had based brand new bombers in southern China, and had provided the Chinese army with a senior American staff officer, General Joseph Stilwell. By the autumn of 1944 the Americans had grown tired of this commitment, wearied by official corruption, military incompetence, and the debilitating effects of a spluttering civil war against communist guerrillas under Mao Tse-tung. A decision was taken to switch heavy bombers from China to the Marianas and some of the bases for medium bombers and fighters had already fallen to a major Japanese ground offensive. Relations between Chiang and Stilwell had never been good, and when the former began to demand the American be removed, Roosevelt, not wishing to alienate the Chinese completely, and so lose the assistance of several of their best divisions fighting in Burma, had bowed to the inevitable and recalled Stilwell on 20th October. By the 25th, the General had got only as far as Delhi on his way home, but strict instructions had gone out that 'minders' should be on hand once he reached the USA to keep him out of reach of the media until the election was over.

Also prominent in Roosevelt's thoughts at this time was a series of telegrams from Churchill about the Moscow Conference, especially those dealing with "the obvious resolve of the Soviet Government to attack Japan on the overthrow of Hitler . . . their detailed study of the problem and . . . their readiness to begin inter-Allied preparations on a large scale".[8] On the 21st, Harriman amplified this report with news of Stalin's assurance to him that the necessary Soviet preparations could be completed within three months of Hitler's surrender.

There was much that had not been resolved, however, and Roosevelt was keen to arrange another 'Big Three' meeting at which real progress might be made towards arranging the postwar settlement and devising an effective international system for maintaining world peace. On 24th October he cabled Stalin about the exact venue for a proposed November meeting. He had already suggested a Black Sea port, for Stalin's convenience, and now added: "I have been thinking about the practicability of Malta, or Athens, or Cyprus, if my getting into the Black Sea on a ship should be impracticable or too difficult. I prefer travelling and living on a ship."[9]

Two of the main items he hoped to tackle were the future of Germany and the role of the Soviets in any proposed international peace-keeping organisation. The Americans and the British had already agreed their respective occupation zones in Germany, at the OCTAGON Conference. The demarcation line was to run east from the Rhine through Coblenz and then along the northern borders of Nassau and Hessen. The British would be north of this line and the Americans to the south. Control of the ports of Bremen and Bremerhaven would also be under an American commander. But it was still unsettled how far east their zones would stretch. This was the province of the European Advisory Commission which included Soviet representatives. It had been meeting for most of the year and had produced a draft report on 12th September, but this confirmed only that Berlin would remain well inside the Soviet zone, whatever its exact borders. Access routes to the city for the British and Americans had also been specified but there was no acknowledgement from the Soviets that their Allies actually had a right to such access. Another question still unresolved was what sort of Germany the Allies would be dividing between themselves. At Quebec, Roosevelt and Churchill had suddenly taken it upon themselves to adopt an especially harsh policy towards the defeated Germans, following proposals drawn up by Henry Morgenthau. Many were already having second thoughts but the British and Americans were still committed on paper to overseeing the complete dismantling of the Saar and Ruhr industrial regions and were "looking forward to converting Germany into a country primarily agricultural and pastoral in its character."[10] The only good news for the millions of prospective *Bauern* was that it was recognised that such an economy would be unable to afford to pay any financial reparations.

The Soviet role in world peace-keeping was perhaps the most vexed question of all. A conference had been held at Dumbarton Oaks, in Washington, to try to work out the basic framework of a collective security organisation that would undertake to impose economic and military sanctions on any 'rogue' states. Again a draft resolution had been signed but it was longer on pious hope than collective resolve. Still undecided, in large part because of dilatory but invariably intransigent

instructions from Moscow to the Soviet delegation, were the vital
questions of Security Council unanimity (the Soviets insisted in
retaining a veto, even in a minority of one); the ability to vote on a
dispute in which one was involved oneself (the Soviets saw no reason
why not); and a Soviet claim that their sixteen Socialist Republics
entitled them to sixteen places on the Council. This latter point was
regarded by Roosevelt as being so outrageous, and so likely to turn
public opinion against the whole notion of attempting to establish a
new League of Nations, that he dubbed it the 'X-Matter', to be
shrouded in even greater secrecy than the hapless General Stilwell.

Many Americans were nevertheless still confident that the USSR
would emerge from the war to take a responsible place at the great
power council table. James Forrestal, the Secretary of the Navy, wrote
to Harriman just before the latter left Moscow: "Dumbarton Oaks I
think has done well . . . I think there is general agreement that England,
Russia and ourselves have got to play together . . . There is great
admiration here for the Russians and, I think, an honest desire, even on
the part of the so-called 'capitalist quarters', to find an accommodation with them." Essentially, however, Stalin's own ambitions and
view of the postwar world remained shrouded in mystery, despite
the Moscow meeting seeming to offer some grounds for optimism.
Harriman noted in his dispatches "the extraordinary courtesies" shown
to Churchill by Stalin and that the Soviet leader had openly "doubted
whether Germany could have been defeated without the full weight of
the United States on the side of the Allies."[11] Churchill could also point
to Stalin's tick on the list of respective spheres of influence, which
seemed to indicate a measure of Soviet self-restraint in the Balkans and
Greece. Moreover, towards the end of the conference Stalin had
elaborated upon his vision of postwar eastern Europe. According to
Churchill, in a telegram to Roosevelt on the 22nd: "U[ncle] J[oe] wants
Poland, Czecko, and Hungary to form a realm of independent, anti-
Nazi, pro-Russian States, the first two of which might join together . . .
He would be glad to see Vienna the capital of a federation of South
German States, including Austria, Bavaria, Wurttenberg, and Baden
. . . As to Prussia, U.J. wished the Ruhr and the Saar detached and put
out of action and probably under international control, and a separate
state formed in the Rhineland."[12]

The trouble was that everyone was obliged to take Stalin at his
word, for so secretive was he, so much power had he gathered to
himself, and such was the fear he inspired in his subordinates, that
there were simply no alternative channels of communication, even

informed rumour, through which to test the Soviet leader's own pronouncements. It was well known that he had the power to do whatever he said, but there was no reliable way of gauging his intention to carry it out. One of Stalin's biographers offers a good insight into his total grip on power, and one that also highlights the punishing daily routine involved:

> Many visitors who called at the Kremlin during the war were aston-ished to see on how many issues, great and small, military, political. or diplomatic, Stalin personally took the final decision. He was in effect his own commander-in-chief, his own minister of defence, his own quartermaster, his own minister of supply, his own foreign min-ister, and even his own *chef de protocole*. The *Stavka*, the Red Army's G.H.Q., was in his offices in the Kremlin. From his office desk, in constant and direct touch with the commands of the various fronts, he watched and directed the campaigns in the field . . . In later days the number of foreign visitors, ambassadors, and special envoys from all parts of the world grew enormously. He entertained them, usually late at night and in the small hours of the morning. After a day filled with military reports, operational decisions, economic instructions, and diplomatic haggling, he would at dawn pore over the latest dis-patches from the front or some confidential report on civilian morale from the Commissariat of Home Affairs, the N.K.V.D.[13]

This organisation would often include a report on British attitudes to the Soviet Union that was authoritative and most interesting as the NKVD had for some years been eavesdropping on General Burrows, head of the British Military Mission in Moscow, via powerful bugs hidden in every room of the old Czechoslovak Legation building in which they were housed.

Usually it was military affairs that dominated Stalin's thoughts. Having surrounded himself with superbly competent staff officers, as well as exceptional field commanders and *Stavka* delegates in the field, Stalin nevertheless had to approve all operational and strategic decisions and was quite capable of ordering fundamental alterations to any plan submitted. It was certainly difficult to gainsay his achievements by late 1944. Despite a momentary panic in the first month of the war, and some costly premature offensives in 1942 and 1943, it was the Red Army above all which had stretched Hitler's generals on the rack. Pressed back to the gates of Moscow in 1941, and again to Stalingrad the following year, the Red Army had each time rallied and inflicted costly defeats on the Germans. A final German offensive against Kursk in 1943 had been absorbed with ease and thereafter the Soviet steamroller, backed by burgeoning production of supremely functional tanks, aircraft and artillery, and driven with considerable finesse, had forced the enemy out of Russia, Byelorussia and the Ukraine, and now stood on the shores of the Baltic, along the upper reaches of the Vistula, and south to Belgrade and Bulgaria. German troops were already fighting hard on their own soil in East Prussia, while Budapest, another ancient bastion against threats from the east, was also in danger.

Stalin's daily routine betrayed no hint of complacency and, like Roosevelt and Churchill, he insisted on being kept completely up-to-date. He lived and worked in the Kremlin, maintaining a modest, four-roomed apartment run by his daughter and a very old housekeeper. One room was a study but most of Stalin's business was conducted in a separate office suite two or three hundred yards away. This comprised a signals room, containing a bewildering array of telephones and teleprinters, and then a sort of cubby-hole occupied by the commander of his NKVD bodyguard, which led into the main office, a large room with a vaulted ceiling and panelled in light oak. One wall had a window and near the wall opposite was a long table with seating for twenty or so. At the end of this table was a large globe with its stand resting on the floor. The overall impression, according to one distinguished British visitor, was of a station waiting-room.

For much of the time the room was thronged with busy senior politicians and *Stavka* members. The General Staff had to report to Stalin and these luminaries three times a day, by telephone at around 10 a.m. and in person in the late afternoon and at night. During the actual meetings, "the members of the Politbureau usually sat along one side of the table by the wall, facing us military people, and two large portraits of Suvorov and Kutuzov, which hung on the opposite side of the room. Stalin would listen to the report, stalking up and down on our side of the table. Occasionally he would go to his desk, which stood at the back of the room on the right, take out two Hercegovina Flor cigarettes, break them up and pack the tobacco into his pipe. To the right of the desk on a special stand lay a white plaster death mask of Lenin, under a glass cover."[14]

Detailed maps were prepared for each of these reports, one showing the situation on the Eastern Front overall, and another set giving the details for each army group. Accompanying these maps were three bulky reports, one on the state of the reserves, one listing all movements of men and materiel that day, and one giving the strength of the army in the field down to regimental level. The morning report by telephone could be the most unnerving of all, even when things were going well. The Chief of Operations, General Sergei Shtemenko, who normally delivered it, moved around his office with these maps and reports spread over several tables and tried to remain as matter-of-fact as possible. "If our troops were doing well, the report was not usually interrupted. An occasional cough or smacking of the lips characteristic of a smoker sucking his pipe were all that could be heard." The face-to-face reports had much in common with Admiral Leahy's presidential briefings, with all relevant material being carefully sorted and filed in advance. According to Shtemenko, three files were used. "Top-priority documents, which were to be reported first, went into a red folder. Most of these were orders, directives, instructions, and arms distribution plans for the army in the field and the reserves. A blue folder was kept for papers of secondary importance, usually various requests [which] were dealt with selectively, as far as possible, but usually every day . . . The green folder contained recommendations for promotion and decorations, and proposals and orders concerning appointments and reappointments . . . dealt with only in favourable circumstances."[15]

Stalin, then, spent most of his waking hours at work, rising at about 9.30 a.m. and not getting to bed until 3 or 4 in the morning. Shtemenko gives an account of such relaxation as the Soviet leader might have allowed himself on the 25th, and it would hardly qualify as sybaritic excess. Stalin's main evening meal would, as like as not, have been a working dinner, served buffet-style and comprising fish or cabbage soup and then various meat dishes. Bread, spices, salt, herbs, vegetables and mushrooms were usually laid out in advance, along with bottles of dry wine, vodka and brandy. "As a rule there was nothing in the way of ham, smoked sausage or other hors d'oeuvres. Stalin could not bear tinned food." Nor was there usually a dessert, tea being served instead from a pot kept warm over the samovar of boiling water. On the rare occasions Stalin allowed himself to be alone he preferred simply to listen to "music from the radio and phonograph records. Of the new phonograph records delivered to him, he tried out the greater part himself, and immediately rated them. Each record was labelled in his own hand as 'good', 'tolerable', 'bad' or 'trash'. Only records bearing the first two labels were left on his night table and on the table in the living room near a Russian-made phonograph with a crank. The boss himself carried it to where he wanted it."[16] What remained to be seen was whether the Boss intended to do the same with the Red Army.

PART ONE

North-West Europe

1

Eisenhower and Montgomery

IN LATE October 1944, from General Dwight D. Eisenhower's Supreme Headquarters Allied Expeditionary Force (SHAEF) to the almost ninety subsidiary army, corps and divisional headquarters spread throughout France and the Low Countries, the dominant mood was one of intense disappointment. Only six or seven weeks earlier commanders and staffs had been confidently predicting imminent German collapse in the West, yet now, despite the Allies lining up vastly superior forces along Germany's western frontiers, few could discern any real possibility of a decisive breakthrough. Having overcome the Wehrmacht in a dour slogging match in Normandy, they had caused the whole German front to unravel as German divisions began a pell-mell retreat back towards the Fatherland. By 25th August the British were across the River Seine, by 2nd September they were in Brussels and two days later in the great port of Antwerp. The Americans had swept directly eastwards and by mid-September had taken Luxembourg, Lunéville and Epinal and were across the German frontier at several points between Aachen and the southern tip of Luxembourg. Below Lunéville the Normandy armies had linked up with other American and French forces that had landed in the south of France in August, and by mid-September Eisenhower was commander of an unbroken front stretching from just south of Breskens, in south-western Holland, to the French Riviera. By late October the eight Allied divisions that had sailed and parachuted into Normandy on D-Day had been expanded to 56, of which 53 were actually in the line or in local reserve. Thirty of these divisions were American, eleven British and the rest Canadian, French and Polish.

Unfortunately, even as the Germans in the West had seemed in complete disarray, they too managed to rush fresh troops to the front. At their point of deepest crisis they frantically organised the transfer of almost new and reconstituted divisions to the western front. In only a few weeks, aided by the recall of Field-Marshal Gerd von Runstedt to command OB West and the insertion of a brand new army head-quarters, First Parachute Army under General Kurt Student, the Germans had stopped the rot and turned to face their pursuers. Now they awaited renewed Allied attacks from behind a fairly solid defensive line running from the flooded polders of Holland, along the Maas and the West Wall and then south as far as Belfort, making best use of whatever advantages the terrain offered between the Eifel and the Vosges mountains. Despite grievous losses during the retreat, by 25th October the Germans had amassed 57 divisions in the West, most in the line or in local reserve but with some elite panzer formations held back in Army Group or High Command reserve. Of the 50 divisions in the line or local reserve, just over half were newcomers to this front, having arrived in September and October. Even in its hour of greatest peril the German military machine was never less than supremely efficient.

Yet only a few weeks before the Allies had been convinced that the war was almost over. In late August 1944, the Intelligence Committee of the Combined Chiefs of Staff in Washington had written: "The German strategic situation has deteriorated to such a degree that no recovery is now possible . . . We consider that organised resistance is unlikely to continue beyond 1st December 1944 and that it may end even sooner." The British Director of Military Operations had been even more optimistic and in September noted that "if we go at the same pace as of late, we should be in Berlin by the 28th." The British in the field shared the general euphoria. Field Marshal Bernard Montgomery, commanding 21st Army Group, began to lose his habitual caution. On 4th September, as his vanguards entered Antwerp, he confided to General William Simpson, commanding Ninth U.S. Army, that "he expected to be in Berlin in two to three weeks."[1] And on that same day SHAEF issued orders for the immediate capture of the Saar and the Ruhr and an advance as far as Frankfurt. On the 16th they were still of the opinion that "no force can be built up in the west sufficient for a counter-offensive or even a successful defence."[2]

Before the month was out, however, the optimism had vanished completely. "The Miracle in the West", as it began to be known in Berlin, soon became equally apparent, and not much less miraculous, to the Allies. German extemporisation, amounting at times almost to *legerdemain*, and greatly assisted by increasingly foul weather, ground the once rampant Allied armoured columns to a halt. On 20th October Eisenhower replied to a friend who had told him of the widespread conviction at home that things should still 'be over by Christmas'. "One thing that puzzles me," wrote Eisenhower, "is where anyone finds any factual ground on which to base a conviction that this battle is over, or nearly over. We have chased the Hun out of France, but he is fighting bitterly on his own frontiers and there is a lot of suffering and sacrificing for thousands of Americans and their Allies before the thing is finally over."[3]

Similarly gloomy thought now permeated Montgomery's head-quarters. Their latest Intelligence Review, in the middle of October, concluded that "the enemy has effected comparative stabilisation with formation of a crust thicker than had been thought possible in previous issues of this review."[4] Nevertheless, as Montgomery sat in his sparse personal caravan on the 25th, at his tactical headquarters in the municipal gardens in Eindhoven, in Holland, it is difficult to imagine that he did not savour a little *Schadenfreude* over Eisenhower's plight. Montgomery had come to Normandy as commander of all Allied land forces but had been obliged, on 1st September (one day after being promoted to Field Marshal), to hand over his Supreme Command to Eisenhower. That this transfer would take place had long been agreed, but it had still come as a considerable blow to Montgomery, who "had always believed that he would be in control up to the very end. It was for him a severe shock to be 'relegated' to 21st Army Group. He withdrew into a shell . . ."[5]

To some extent Montgomery's reaction was merely the pain of a very bruised ego, and his was more easily bruised than most. Yet it also reflected his sincere conviction that Eisenhower's strategic concept for future western European operations was seriously flawed and was conducive to just the sort of operational and tactical impasse that now threatened. Eisenhower's plan, in essence, was to advance into Germany on a broad front and, despite temporary concentrations of effort in one sector or another, to push the whole Allied front slowly forwards at the same pace. For Eisenhower there was no absolutely decisive *Schwerpunkt* in the German defences, and a concentration along one touted axis or another could only lead to the creation of exposed salients, vulnerable to German counter-attack. It is difficult to deny the merit of Eisenhower's attritional strategy. The Allies had an enormous preponderance of firepower along the whole front and it was well known that German operations, at every level from platoon to army group, revolved around the counter-attack. How much more sensible, then, to let the Germans wear themselves down attacking organised gun-lines, advancing slowly and methodically, than to invite them to concentrate against a narrow salient in which it was rarely possible, at least whilst advancing, to achieve any useful weight of defensive firepower.

Indeed Montgomery's own military doctrine right through North Africa, Italy and Normandy had consisted in amassing an over-whelming balance of force for a set-piece offensive that could hardly fail to steamroller through the enemy lines. But the Montgomery of late summer 1944 became a quite different sort of general, at least in his own mind. He began to object strenuously to Eisenhower's gradualist approach and to advocate a bold, concentrated thrust into Germany, supported by the greater part of Allied logistical resources. The Germans, he felt, were off-balance. Dissipating resources and fire-power along the whole front would only help them to regain it, by failing to maintain concerted pressure against one selected sector. Instead Montgomery recommended a concentrated thrust north of the Ardennes, under his personal command. On 18th August he had spoken of "a solid mass of some 40 divisions which would be so strong that it need fear nothing." Four days later he reiterated that "the quickest way to win this war is for the great mass of the Allied armies to advance northwards . . . into the Ruhr. The force must operate as one whole, with great cohesion, and be so strong that it can do the job quickly . . . This is a *whole time* job for one man . . . To change the system of command now, after having won a great victory, would be to prolong the war."[6]

On the next day he had bearded Eisenhower personally and demanded that one U.S. army be halted to conserve fuel, another be put under his command, and the SHAEF airborne strategic reserve be also put at his disposal. By the beginning of September his plans had become yet more grandiose and he urged Eisenhower in a letter: "We have now reached a stage where a really powerful and full-blooded thrust towards Berlin is *likely to get there* and thus end the German war. We have not enough maintenance resources for two full-blooded thrusts. The selected thrust must have all the maintenance resources it needs without any qualification . . . [Of the] two possible thrusts, one via the Ruhr and the other via Metz and the Saar . . . [the] one likely to give the best and quickest results is the northern one via the Ruhr." On 7th September, after Eisenhower had revealed himself less than enthused with the idea of putting much of the American Army at

Montgomery's beck and call, the Field Marshal remained unabashed, insisting in a telegram that "a reallocation of our present resources of every description would be adequate to get one thrust to Berlin."[7]

Eisenhower's reaction to these persistent entreaties is admirably summed up in a telegram sent to Montgomery on 5th September, in which he repeated his view that a broad front advance was the only sure way ahead: "While we are advancing we will be opening the ports of Havre and Antwerp, which are essential to sustain a powerful thrust deep into Germany. No re-allocation of our present resources would be adequate to sustain a thrust to Berlin."[8] His position was firmly restated at a meeting between the two generals, on 10th September when, according to Montgomery himself, Eisenhower clearly "disagreed with my analysis. He repeated that we must first close to the Rhine and cross it on a wide front; then, and only then, could we concentrate on one thrust."[9]

In Montgomery's eyes, German dispersal was a one-off opportunity. It had to be exploited immediately, and to the full, concentrating the maximum strike force in one sector and relying on the shock of its eruption into the enemy rear to dissuade him from mounting his own attacks into thinly-held or static Allied sectors. Montgomery, in other words, was quite uncharacteristically advocating that the Allies take a chance on mesmerising the Germans with one swift thrust. Both generals knew that the longer their lines of communication grew, with no new ports opened up, the more they would be walking a logistical tightrope. Yet while Eisenhower favoured crossing with the greatest deliberation and carrying the longest possible pole, the impatient Montgomery wanted to dispense with the pole entirely and get to the other side through sheer momentum. He wrote to the Secretary of State for War, Sir James Grigg, adopting a fairly strident 'I told you so' tone. "I cannot feel happy about things out here . . . We have lost flexibility on the front as a whole. We are now unlikely to get to the Ruhr, *or* the Saar, *or* Frankfurt. In fact it is my opinion that we have 'mucked' the whole show . . . It is a great tragedy."[10]

The Allies faced other difficulties too, notably the delay in getting supplies forward from the Normandy beachhead and such Channel ports as they could use, to the troops at the front. The solution to this problem was obvious to all – the opening up of the port of Antwerp. Unfortunately, though the port itself had been in Allied hands for several weeks, local commanders had made no immediate effort to also secure the banks of the Scheldt estuary through which all shipping must pass. So the Germans still occupied both banks which meant that they not only could block the passage of Allied shipping but also had a good escape route for 86,000 troops, from eight divisions, who would otherwise have been trapped south of the estuary. As it was, most of these divisions were now entrenched along the Maas as one of the main obstacles to Montgomery's further progress.

It was he, however, who had remained woefully careless of the need to open up Antwerp, insisting that Allied success depended mainly on his being allowed to lead a concentrated, forty-division thrust across the Rhine, utilising all available supplies and aimed at slashing through to Berlin itself. Eisenhower remained sceptical about such a venture but eventually gave Montgomery his head with Operation MARKET GARDEN, an extremely narrow push towards the Rhine bridge at Arnhem. This was a sorry failure but Montgomery persisted in pressing for another "rapier-like thrust".

Eisenhower had made his mind up. Now he had just two main priorities: that future Allied operations would only be undertaken on a broad front, with armies attacking simultaneously or in rotation all along the line, and that Antwerp must be opened up. On 9th October, tiring of Montgomery's continual shilly-shallying, be "sent off the most imperative order, and snub, of the whole campaign". Unless Antwerp were taken, he said, the Allies' entire operations were likely to grind to a halt by the middle of November. "Our intake into the Continent will not repeat not support our battle. I must emphasise that of all our operations on the entire front . . . I consider Antwerp of first importance and I believe that the operations designed to clear up the entrance require your personal attention."[11] In officialese these last four words meant nothing more or less than "get your finger out".

Montgomery continued to kick, even trying to turn the issue into one of Eisenhower's suitability as Allied ground forces commander, but after another sharp rejoinder from Ike he finally bowed to the inevitable on 16th October, assuring him: "You will hear no more on the subject of command from me. I have given you my views and you have given me your answer. That ends the matter . . . I have given Antwerp top priority in all operations in 21 Army Group and all energies and efforts will now be devoted towards opening up that place."[12] All attacks eastwards towards the Ruhr were closed down and two extra divisions were transferred from Second British Army to First Canadian. The latter was relieved of any responsibility for the British left flank and was to concentrate on clearing the Breskens Pocket and South Beveland on either side of the Scheldt. South Beveland was also to be completely isolated by a double thrust, north towards Bergen op Zoom and Breda by I Corps, and west along the south bank of the Maas by XII Corps, through s'Hertogenbosch and Tilburg.

No longer the ground forces supremo, and without his compact mass of forty divisions, Montgomery was now not even attacking towards Germany. Instead, with a mere eleven divisions actually advancing, he was engaged in mopping-up operations leading back towards the North Sea. Largely through his own tardiness in dealing with the problem of the Scheldt estuary he was now condemned to thrash around in flooded Dutch backwaters whilst American and French divisions to the south girded themselves for the broad push into Germany. There is no evidence to suggest just what was going through Montgomery's mind on 25th October, as he sat in his Tactical HQ, located for the moment in the Municipal Gardens in Eindhoven. Much of his attention would have been devoted to the actual attacks along the Scheldt and the Maas but it is difficult to believe that he did not anxiously wonder whether his brand-new Field Marshal's baton was but a sham and that the real baton of command had already been passed to other hands.

2

That Quagmire of Misery

FIRST CANADIAN ARMY ON THE SCHELDT

THE CANADIAN contribution to the Allied offensive in North-West Europe in 1944 was three divisions, two infantry and one armoured, and their struggle so far had been one of the hardest in the whole theatre. That summer they had fought alongside the British in the great attritional battles around Caen, and in the drive south of Caen, especially the attacks to close the Falaise Gap and cut off the retreating German Army. Although the Gap was finally closed on 20th August, First Canadian Army played little part in the subsequent dash to Brussels, Antwerp and the Dutch frontier. Their forces did pursue as far as Elbeuf, on the Seine, but were then directed to clear the Channel coast, most of whose ports Hitler had directed should be held to the last man, so as to deny them to Allied supply ships. By the end of October all the ports had been taken, with the exception of Dunkirk, the siege of which had just been handed over to the Czechoslovak Armoured Brigade. Much of this fighting had been bitter, with Le Havre holding out to 12th September and Calais to the 30th. The Canadians' next task was no easier, for it was they who had to clear up the mess after Montgomery's failure to seize the banks of the Scheldt estuary. After the Germans had been allowed to extricate several divisions across the estuary, leaving two of them behind, one on either bank, to deny the Allies access to Antwerp, Canadian efforts to dislodge them began in earnest in early October, with one of their own infantry divisions allotted to each bank of the estuary, the South Beveland peninsula to the north and the Breskens Pocket to the south.

The attack against South Beveland, by 2 Canadian Division, stalled for much of the month around the village of Woendsdrecht, where the German Battle Group Chill, including some very tough paratroopers, inflicted very heavy losses on the attackers, one battalion losing 183 men in a single day. On the 23rd, however, 2 Division's attack became part of a general 21st Army Group offensive all along the Maas and the threat to General Chill's rear obliged him to pull back on the following day. The Canadians followed hard on their heels, with two of their brigades shielding the north-eastern shoulder of the narrow isthmus and the third advancing westwards along it. By the evening of the 25th this brigade had taken the village of Rilland and had troops just east of Krabbendijke, about seven miles beyond Woensdrecht and four miles short of their first main objective, the Beveland Canal. The brigade was on a two-battalion frontage, with the Royal Hamiltons on the left and the Essex Scottish on the right, mainly around a railway embankment that ran along the peninsula.

It had been far from easy going. The departure of Chill's Battle Group had relieved the brigade of fears about their own rear but they still faced a capable enemy to their front in the shape of 70 Infantry Division. This unit had been mustered in South Beveland in May 1944, with a view especially to strengthening the defences around Walcheren at the western end of the peninsula. Always under strength, it had also had one of its regiments transferred away in September. It was nick-named the "White Bread Division" because most of its soldiers suffered from stomach ailments and required special diets. At sixty, the divisional commander was probably too old for such an assignment, and certainly one German naval officer who came in contact with the division in October claimed in his war diary that "the men appeared apathetic, an undisciplined mob. If this is not set right by energetic leadership, I forsee a black future for the defence of Walcheren."[1]

Nevertheless, it would have been difficult to persuade 4 Canadian Brigade of such a dismissive assessment. Only one single German battalion, from 1020 Regiment, was positioned east of the Beveland Canal yet it did a remarkably fine job of slowing the Canadian infantry. Even the least regarded German units, it seemed, could be relied upon to put in an exemplary defensive performance, especially when the terrain was so much to their advantage. For the Canadians were now deep into polder country, rich agricultural land reclaimed from the sea and requiring an elaborate network of dykes to keep the small fields adequately drained. In September the Germans had begun partial flooding of Beveland and Walcheren, and on 16th October Field Marshal von Runstedt sanctioned further breaches in some of the main dykes. The aim was not total flooding, which would have simply given

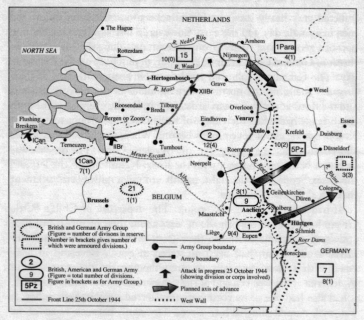

The Western Front: Holland and Belgium 25th October 1944

the whole area back to the Scheldt and demolished the very approaches which made it defensible. As the acting commander of First Canadian Army, General Guy Simonds, explained, the intention was to use "grand saturation" to impede any Allied advance. "This denies to us the use of the ground for movement to exactly the same extent as if it were completely flooded, but allows the enemy the use of his roads, [and] avoids the flooding of buildings, stores and many works which must be of importance to him. Attacking across a 'saturated' area, movement is possible only on top of dyked roads. We sacrifice every advantage which we normally possess in the offensive."[2]

All of these advantages, in fact, passed to the defenders who had only to zero their machine guns, mortars and artillery in on the inter-sections of these dyke roads to prevent any freedom of movement whatsoever. To hedge their bets the Germans also set up strongpoints at the intersections of the twelve-foot-high dykes and dug slit trenches into the reverse sides which were virtually immune to Canadian fire, even from artillery. The dyke roads were cratered at regular intervals – one on the main road along the isthmus measured 70 feet across, totally defeating the bulldozers – and felled trees and wire entanglements were liberally strewn down their whole length. All approaches were also liberally sowed with Teller mines, to incapacitate vehicles, and Schu-mines, a new anti-personnel weapon in an undetectable wooden casing containing a charge just big enough to blow off a man's foot. Every feature still standing now had a malevolent purpose. Pill-boxes were painted to look like houses while the houses and barns had numbers painted on the roofs and rear walls so that German guns and mortars could quickly bring down pre-plotted fire. Even tree-stumps were suspect, especially those with a good view of the approaches. Often these were carefully hollowed out and contained a German soldier carefully logging Canadian movements or spotting for the mortars and artillery.

Most movement, then, had to be across the sunken fields, or polders, themselves, or by edging along the banks of the dykes. In the polders, usually about 400 to 500 metres square, sometimes up to 1000, 'saturation' was nothing like a water-logged garden or a sodden cricket outfield, but meant, at best, thick mud and, at worst, several feet of icy water covering a glutinous bed that made every step forward a tremendous physical effort. For even without German interference with the sluice-gates and the dykes, the water was constantly replenished by the pouring rain. According to one journalist with the Canadians the fighting was "a monotone of mud, fire, water and mines. The phrase 'relentless rain' occurs in a half-a-dozen [war] diaries, as though the rain itself had reached a pitch when only this 'relentless', among quotable words, might describe it." He went on to describe the isthmus itself, only a mile wide at its narrowest point, with the railway embankment along its northern shore. "There is nothing else but a road, deeply cratered and heavily mined, and water. The secondary roads make geographical patterns round the flooded polders, leading to nowhere. Tanks were useless. Clinging to the banks of the dykes the Canadian infantry of the 4th Brigade waded, crawled, even swam in bitter sardonic humour, beyond cursing . . . Frankly one would have thought that these Canadians would have had enough, too much. They had been waist deep in water, many of them (I do not exaggerate) for two weeks. Impossible to overstate their discomfort."[3] In fact, exaggeration is barely possible when it comes to describing the atrocious conditions endured by the Canadians in the campaign in the Scheldt estuary and even the soberest of writers have waxed grimly eloquent. A Royal Marine who fought alongside the Canadians in South Beveland wrote: "If not chest deep in some [polder] as they tried to advance, [they] were flattened on the sodden ground and inching forward under the pelting rain, cautious of trip wires, booby traps and mines. For them time had ceased to exist and place was only an infinite grey misery of pain, discomfort and the ever-present threat of death or injury – grey from the leaden sky with its relentless, chilling downpour, grey from the glutinous quagmire of the dykes and polders, grey from the flat reaches of murky water covering flooded ground, now churned incessantly by driving rain."[4]

In the attack along the isthmus on the 24th it had been intended that once the first line of German defences were penetrated by the Royal Regiment, then the advance would be taken up by lorried infantry from the Essex Scottish, supported by some attached tanks and armoured cars. But this mobile group had only advanced 600 yards or so when its two columns were brought to an abrupt halt by a well-placed anti-tank gun. At this stage they were still moving up to pass through the Royals and had not yet even crossed their start line. The Essex Scottish infantry wearily dismounted and on foot they and the whole brigade "stayed, for 48 hours of plodding through the salt marshes in the icy, relentless rain, hammering at each fierce crossroad with no cover and no space to manoeuvre for any form of protection from the enemy's defensive fire. The child's game of leapfrog had become a necessary wartime tactic as each battalion . . . [made] hard-earned gains before handing over its position to the battalion coming up from behind. There simply was not room in the narrow entrance to the peninsula for any more troops than one or two companies to lead the pursuit."[5] So wrote Lieutenant-Colonel Denis Whitaker, looking back on his experiences as commander of the Royal Hamilton Light Infantry. Another historian of this battle was R. W. Thompson, a journalist who had attached himself to the Canadian forces, and he relied on his own memories, interviews at the time, and battalion war diaries to give some picture of 4 Brigade's grim passage along the Beveland isthmus. "Absurd to attempt to recount in detail that waterlogged progress. In individual minds it lives merely as discomfort, a blurred memory, of men's feet blown off in a grey futuristic landscape, something of Dali's. Waves of 20-mm fire held men tight against dyke banks and made others thankful even of the water. Air bursts from '88s' worked in with the hideous barrage of the mortars with a sound like green seas on iron decks, a drenching sound, horribly threatening . . . stretcher-bearers picked men out of mud and silt and water and bore them back to Regimental Aid Posts, to regain feeling, to know pain."[6] And all this pain was attributable to the rearguards of one battalion, plus artillery support, of a gastrically challenged, 'undisciplined mob' of a division.

The Canadians were also enduring appalling conditions in their other main attack along the Scheldt estuary against the Germans defending the Breskens Pocket and guarding its southern bank. The latter were the men of 64 Infantry Division, another scratch formation only recently formed from men on leave from the Eastern Front. It had fought hard in the retreat from France, and in October had only 2,000 of its original infantrymen left, the remaining 70 per cent of its troops coming from support and service units. Nevertheless, 64 Division was selected to hold the south bank of the Scheldt to the last man, and its commander was resolved to follow these instructions to the letter.

He at least had all the advantages of the terrain. The attacking troops, 3 Canadian Division, who had begun their attack against the Pocket on 6th October, had expended enormous effort just penetrating the moat-like perimeter, along the Leopold Canal and east to Braakeman's Inlet. Most of the Pocket was reclaimed polder, similar to that in the Beveland peninsula and made up of "entirely low-lying land . . . none of it more than a few feet above sea level. On a map where contours are shown by lines at 10-metre intervals, there are no contours whatever within the Pocket." R. W. Thompson saw the battlefield for himself, just before the offensive opened and shared the general apprehension that "in the intricate pattern of its dykes and major waterways, its individual fields and floods, its exposed causeways, and its entire absence of cover for attacking troops, it presented perhaps the grimmest piece of 'ground' over which men have ever been called to fight."[7] The terrain was possibly even worse than that in the Beveland isthmus for not only were there the usual dykes draining the polders but these were criss-crossed with cuttings, called *kreeks* or *vliets*, some almost as wide as the Leopold Canal, which served as alternative highways to the various hamlets and farms. The whole area was in a way reminiscent of Venice, but after most of it had already sunk beneath the waves.

The fighting in the Pocket, therefore, was just as tough as in South Beveland, and by the 25th the Canadians had still not fully cleared it. Two brigades were in the line on this day. To the west was 8 Brigade, driving towards Zeebrugge but still bogged down in house-to-house fighting in Oostburg. Fighting along the north-east coast was 9 Brigade. They had taken Breskens itself on the 21st but had endured another four days of close-quarter combat before Schoondijke finally succumbed on the 24th. Other troops in the Brigade had been held up on the outskirts of Breskens, around the ancient Dutch fastness of Fort

Frederik Hendrik. Nothing much remained of the original fort except the double moat, but the Germans had since added substantial concrete bunkers and it now served as a formidable bastion in which to die for the Führer. Such, indeed, seemed the occupants' intentions, and the moat continued to prove its military value on the 23rd and 24th, when two attacks by the North Nova Scotia Highlanders were repulsed. The defenders, however, seem to have got rather carried away by the similarity to sieges of earlier centuries when, on the 25th, they decided in the best Vauban tradition that they had done quite enough to preserve their honour and that discretion was now the better part of valour. One of their number slipped out of the fortress early that morning and gave himself up to Canadian troops in Breskens, informing them that the German garrison now numbered only 23 men, all eager to surrender. He was dispatched back to the fort, his ears ringing with dire ultimatums about impending bombardment and bombing, and the defenders meekly gave themselves up.

Such meekness was not typical of the rest of the German defenders. For R. W. Thompson, "the week from October 18th to the 25th was, I think, the worst week of Operation *Switchback* . . . [and] the enemy fought for territory yard by yard to the bitter end, and with a resolution that would have commanded admiration and respect for a foe less steeped in evil, less prone to self-pity, and open to shame."[8] The commander of the Queen's Own Rifles of Canada, part of 8 Brigade, included his memories of the Breskens fighting in the regimental history he wrote and recalled "the utter misery of the conditions and the great courage required to do the simplest things. Attacks had to go along dykes swept by enemy fire. To go through the polders meant wading, without possibility of concealment, in water that at times came up to the chest. Mortar fire, at which the Germans were masters, crashed in at every rallying point. Spandaus sent their whining reverberations across the marshes . . . It was peculiarly a rifleman's fight in that there were no great decisive battles, just a steady continuous struggle."[9] These riflemen, moreover, could only operate in very small numbers, usually sections or small patrols, at most a platoon, and a company's whole attention in a particular attack might be devoted to taking just one dug-out or machine-gun post. Two or three such attempts to edge forward might be made in any 24-hour period. One officer wrote of "desperate slogging matches between platoons . . . [with] the Germans . . . dug into the crossroads where two dykes intersected. One platoon, two at most, with some carriers or flame-throwers, would be sent in to clear them out."[10]

R. W. Thompson has one of the most vivid descriptions of this particularly hazardous and vicious form of petty warfare, where "again and again by day and night strong fighting patrols crawled forward over the sodden polders, squelching in mud and water, meeting the enemy literally hand-to-hand to smash and strangle and kill in the sodden dug-outs, to gain perhaps a score of yards as the prize of those who prevailed . . . [in] that quagmire of misery." The War Diary of the Toronto Scottish cursed the terrain and the torrential rain. "Water and soil make mud. Mud sticks to everything. Boots weigh pounds more. Rifles and Brens operate sluggishly. Ammunition becomes wet. Slit trenches allow one to get below ground level but also contain several inches of thick water. Matches and cigarettes are wet and unusable." It was also extremely difficult to get any kind of supplies forward, including rations. And even when these got through, the all-pervasive wetness made it well-nigh impossible to heat the food. "Only at night", according to one officer, could tinned "rations, heated in vats of hot water, be ferried over by crews from the quartermaster's store. To troops isolated in sodden trenches, a tin of hot food tossed from a passing rowboat was a welcome break."[11]

A telling summary of the Canadians' catalogue of suffering on either side of the Scheldt is given by R. W. Thompson, certainly the ablest contemporary chronicler of these terrible battles. Right to the end of the campaign, he wrote:

the rain, driven by winds blowing half a gale, had seemed to join the dark evil sky to the dark evil land, so that the small space that had been won resembled the inside of a tureen squelching with mud and water like some foul stew. Even the dykes had lost their lines, crushed and churned into the grey muck heap of the featureless wilderness. There were no fires. There was no rest . . . Men . . . lived and died and slept always wet and caked with ooze. The first respect for the enemy had given way to a bitter hatred, growing to an absolute loathing, for the Germans had mined and booby-trapped the bodies of their dead. The bloated bodies in the mud of the polders, and lolloping face down like filthy grey bags in the dark waters of the dykes, had proved as dangerous dead as alive. Bodies exploded at a touch to destroy men in their rare moments of compassion . . . [So they] rotted and stank where they had fallen, of less account than the swollen carcasses of oxen with their legs sprouting stiffly upwards, symbols of the misery of that terrible land reclaimed from the sea.[12]

By the 25th, then, both Canadian divisions were beginning to feel the grievous effects of this prolonged ordeal. Casualties were fearsome. Polder warfare was even more of a drain on riflemen and company officers than had been the dour fighting in Normandy. There were two key variables. One was that most attacks had to be platoon-sized. or less, often advancing on a one-man front. "That meant," pointed out an officer of the North Nova Scotias, "somebody had to lead, and that job was always given to an NCO or platoon commander. The result of it was I lost every lieutenant I took in, and I lost every NCO." Eventually the battalion began to run out of lieutenants and, according to its second-in-command, was eventually reduced to a single lieutenant, and even he was killed by a blast of machine-gun fire on 15th October. Moreover, "almost every company commander that went into that Breskens battle became a casualty – not wounded, killed."[13] The padre of the Highland Light Infantry drew attention to the second variable. Unlike the Normandy fighting where most casualties were from mortar fire, the majority of those in the polders were caused by the interlocking machine-gun fire and the percentage of fatalities was much higher, upwards of 50 per cent instead of the usual 25 to 30 per cent.

Casualties were high among the 'other ranks' too. After only a week's fighting in the Breskens Pocket, 7 Brigade had lost 533 men, of whom 111 had been killed. In the fighting in the Pocket as whole to 2nd November, 3 Canadian Division lost 2,077 men, of whom 544 were killed or missing. One historian has made an extremely pertinent comparison between Canadian casualties at the Third Battle of Ypres (Passchendaele) in 1917 and those suffered during the Battle of the Scheldt in October 1944. In 29 days in Flanders, in October and November 1917, four Canadian divisions lost 15,654 men killed, wounded and missing, a ratio of 119 men per division per day. On the Scheldt, in 33 days, 2 Canadian Division alone lost 3,650 men, a ratio of 111 men per day.[14] The conclusion is clear, and still bears emphasising even fifty years after the end of the Second World War: the lot of the infantryman in that war was often just as arduous, horrific even, as that of his predecessors on the more notorious Western Front.

Because of these dreadful casualty figures on the Scheldt, Canadian battalions at the end of October were either terribly understrength or – almost as bad – had their numbers made up with untrained soldiers from the rear echelons. Towards the end of the battle, according to the commander of the Stormont, Dundas and Glengarry Regiment, "we were damn short. Our platoons, which were supposed to be thirty-three or thirty-four men, were all down to about sixteen men. We were down to twenty-five at one point in a couple of companies." An officer in the Queen's Own Rifles recalled, "We were so thin on the ground at the Scheldt that most of the time the company I commanded could do nothing but man the automatic weapons. We didn't have enough men left to have a rifleman. At one time I had one officer and only twenty-nine other ranks in the company."[15]

Because the Canadian authorities, like the western Allies generally, had seriously underestimated the likely scale of casualties in the rifle companies, there were few properly trained replacements available to fill the gaps. In the Canadian Black Watch, on a typical day in late October, of the 379 personnel of all ranks only 42 per cent had training of three months or more. Of the rest, 46 had two months, 131 one month, 29 less than a month, and 14 none at all. According to the second-in-command: "Very few men arrive with knowledge of the PIAT, or elementary section and platoon tactics. Some reinforcements have never fired the Bren LMG or handled grenades." Lieutenant-Colonel Whitaker of the Royal Hamiltons complained that "nearly all reinforcements reaching the battalion of late have been men transferred from other arms, armoured corps, artillery, ordnance and service corps. They have very little infantry training and are difficult to control."[16]

The influx of such men presented a double strain for the officers and NCOs, undermining the fighting efficiency of platoon and company, creating pangs of guilt when they were forced to use raw replacements as little more than cannon fodder. A French-Canadian officer wrote: ". . . reinforcements weren't plentiful so they were coming up pretty fast, with no break-in period. These poor buggers were being sent up and popped into a slit trench in the evening, and they were attacking the next morning. They never got to know their neighbour or the other guys in the platoon." The commander of another battalion was sent anti-aircraft officers who had had a mere ten days of battle school before being sent forward to command rifle platoons. "It was inexplicable and inexcusable . . . I'm not exaggerating when I say they had no notion of war, let alone at the infantry battalion level . . . They kept coming in and God – if they lasted twenty-four hours they were lucky. They just came in, went out on the line, and zap – they were either wounded or killed. They were nice guys, but they were no use to me wounded or dead."[17]

By the end of October the strain was telling equally on all those in the infantry battalions, on veterans and tyros, officers and men, and was indeed becoming a considerable worry for divisional, corps and Army commanders. The clearest testimony to a serious drop in morale came from the Canadian Casualty Clearing Stations and military hospitals where psychiatric battle casualties were appearing in ever-increasing numbers. In a report on psychiatric cases during the autumn, Major Dancey, stationed at Number 1 Neurological Hospital, at Basingstoke, observed that while several cases were men new to battle who broke down almost immediately, "we are handling an increasing number of men who have carried on under considerable stress for long periods of time. These individuals, on examination, show a minimum of objective findings ... The principal complaint, which is almost invariably present, consists of a realisation that they will never again be able to face front line service." A report by Dr Robert Gregory, the psychiatrist with 3 Canadian Division, expressed particular alarm at the casualties for October 1944, noting that fully 90 per cent of them were among men who had more than three months' combat experience. He feared morale was beginning to crack generally and commented: "There was one thing to note among all troops admitted for exhaustion [that month] – lack of morale or lack of volition to carry on. The foremost cause of this seemed to be futility. The men claimed there was nothing to which to look forward to (*sic*) – no rest, no leave, no enjoyment, no normal life and no escape. The only way one could get out of battle was death, wounds, self-inflicted wounds and going nuts."[18]

3

A Showground for Desolation

THE BRITISH ADVANCE TO THE MAAS

THE FRONT LINE held by 21st Army Group on 25th October was pretty much the same as that at the end of Field Marshal Montgomery's failed drive across the Rhine in September. Its most prominent feature remained the deep salient thrusting north towards Arnhem, flanking the road from Eindhoven, through Grave and Nijmegen. At first Montgomery had hoped to mount another major offensive, this time eastwards to clear the Reichswald and then open up a route to the south-east towards Krefeld and the Ruhr, but the objective had to be abandoned when in October he was ordered to make Antwerp his absolute priority. The co-ordinated British and Canadian offensive to clear the Scheldt estuary began on the 23rd and involved seizing the major towns of Bergen op Zoom, Roosendaal, Breda, Tilburg and s'Hertogenbosch and then pushing the Germans back behind the lower Maas. In this way, not only would the sea approaches to Antwerp be secured but also a buffer zone north of supply routes inland from the city, which might otherwise be exposed to German counter-attacks.

British Second Army was to play an important role in this offensive, deploying three of its infantry divisions, one armoured division and three powerful independent armoured brigades. All these were under the command of XII Corps, whose part in the overall battle had been code-named Operation ALAN. The opening days of the advance were fairly low-key and, despite the considerable mass of armour involved, had little in common with the set-piece, hell-for-leather tank assaults in Normandy. What struck observers was the dispersal of individual units and the almost desultory tempo of operations. This was a reflection not so much of the attitude of the attacking troops or the competence of their commanders, as the nature of the country, the dispersal of German units to take maximum defensive advantage of every potential strongpoint, the prevalence of waterways, the sodden ground, and the necessity to engage in house-to-house fighting in the towns. The nature of the ground was well described by a British officer and historian who himself fought in Holland. From Tilburg to s'Hertogenbosch was a distance of 15 miles or so and the northern half of that front

> . . . consisted mainly of thick woods, alternating with large stretches of pine-covered sand-dunes up to within three miles of s'Hertogen-bosch. To the south it was slightly more cultivated with woods and fields dropping imperceptibly into polder . . . The roads were few and liable to collapse under the weight of armoured vehicles and heavy traffic. Dykes of an average width of four yards, some four feet deep and with an average depth of water of three feet, criss-crossed the whole area. The large canals and lakes, the embanked railways and roads and the boggy nature of the ground made it impossible for tanks and indeed any tracked vehicle to operate off the roads . . . The country was dead flat: finding an observation post presented the gunner with almost insoluble problems.[1]

The extensive flooding was engineered by the Germans and, to-gether with the incessant rain, this made movement extremely difficult. Average October rainfall in Holland was 53mm, but 81mm fell in 1944, making it one of the wettest months ever known. Terrain and weather combined to slow down the attackers and to give an enormous advantage to the defenders. A British war correspondent commented: "I have never seen such a desolate battlefield, not even in the last war. Conditions for both sides were terrible, and the men lived in acute discomfort. Shallow foxholes filled with water were the only refuge they had from the weather. The Nazis fighting with their usual toughness, held every wood, copse and ditch. Spurts of fire would come from every tiny vantage point as we advanced and our casualties mounted."[2]

A history of 5 Black Watch, part of 51 Highland Division, noted that the scattered but resolute German outposts and strongpoints turned any attack into "a series of small fights, small moves, and very close co-operation between infantry, tanks and artillery."[3] War correspondents gave particularly telling descriptions of this type of warfare and its impact on offensive operations. "From the Scheldt to the Maas the battles became as ferocious as those around Caen [in July and August]. The battle was not one of big sustained advances but a series of irregular hops taken by little groups of men who would later link up with similar adventurous groups until some sort of front position was made."[4] Another journalist gave a superb elaboration on this type of warfare, which underlines the utterly parochial nature of the fighting no matter how many divisions, brigades or battalions were involved in a particular 'set-piece'. The Germans avoided major fire-fights yet left snipers and anti-tank guns, at every farm, culvert or crossroads. Mortars and machine guns withdrew five or six hundred yards at a time, always keeping their pursuers in range but always withdrawing again before they could be attacked.

> There were few mines, but it was dangerous to take a yard of ground for it was the 'small change' of war with payment made in single lives and wounds from day to day . . . Day after day and night after night the Battalion Commanders considered a feature, a hill or hollow, a village, a group of farmsteads, strongpoints, battery sites, one thousand yards of land. The Company Commanders divided it up, and gave it to the Platoon Commanders, and the Platoon Commanders held their tiny "O" groups with their Platoon Sergeants and Corporals, studying one hundred yards of mud or sand, dyke and culvert, on 1/25,000-in. maps, pitting themselves and thirty men with rifles, grenades and three Brens and a 2-in. mortar, against it . . .
>
> The vast canvas of the campaign in North-West Europe broke down into these tiny fragments, and built up again from them, day after day, night after night, a kind of unending turbulence of death and renewal, platoons, companies, battalions, brigades, divisions, revolving in and out of battle, a wheel of death, two up, one back, in support, in reserve.[5]

It does seem, however, that this account somewhat exaggerates the severity of the fighting. The advance towards Tilburg, for example, was made by men from 15 Scottish Division, in front of which the Germans melted away, while their "rearguard activity remained slight, and consisted mainly of the delaying effects of blown bridges and the evil deployments of anti-tank mines, whose violent plumes of death took chance vehicles by surprise with stunning suddenness."[6] The experience of 51 Highland Division, pushing forward in the direction of Vught, was similar and some battalions encountered no opposition at all. Lieutenant-Colonel Martin Lindsay, commanding 1 Gordon Highlanders, wrote in his diary that between 22nd and 25th October the only hold-ups all the way to Boxtel, his Brigade's objective, were attributable to other British units in front of them. His entry for the 25th reads: "It did not take us long to choose company areas [north of Boxtel], based on some very nice houses from which the Hun had hurriedly withdrawn during the night. Soon after the Battalion arrived we received word that 5–7th Gordons had entered Boxtel without opposition . . . We had chosen a charming modern house for the command post, and Harry immediately gave orders for the bath water to be heated."[7]

Divisional casualties told a similar story. 53 Welsh Division, which probably had the toughest axis of advance, to s'Hertogenbosch, tabulated its casualties at fortnightly intervals and those for 19th October to 1st November, 48 killed spread over nine battalions, were some of the lowest of the campaign to date, comparing with 101, 200, 81 and 190 killed for the first four fortnights of the Division's battle in Normandy.

Given the intractable nature of the terrain in Holland, it might seem unlikely that tanks could have much of a role in the fighting. Indeed, they did find movement difficult. Even where there was no flooding, "the heathland with pine woods was divided up by sandy tracks where mines could be laid easily and remain unseen. The going in the small boggy fields was wet and treacherous."[8] Nevertheless, armour was present in quantity, with 7 Armoured Division advancing between 53 and 51 Infantry Divisions and the three independent armoured brigades closely supporting one infantry division each. Yet despite the poor terrain and the consequent fragmentation of the battlefield, it was found that the infantry often could not bring sufficient weight of fire to bear on even isolated strongpoints and were, moreover, extremely vulnerable to individual enemy tanks and tracked assault guns lurking in ambush. Only their own tanks, with individual troops of them constantly on call by the rifle companies, could provide them with the necessary fire support in attack and defence. But the infantry could also return the favour, by flushing out concealed enemy anti-tank gun and bazooka teams. By late October 1944, then, the gung-ho tactics that had characterised armoured operations in North Africa, and even in Italy and Normandy, were a thing of the past. Tanks and infantry had, perforce, recognised that each needed the other and that patient, small-unit cooperation and slow, incremental advance were the only way forward against an enemy in unpropitious terrain.

Nevertheless, the tankers only linked up with the infantry on an *ad hoc* basis and at night they would usually concentrate in their own battalion 'laager'. But not always. Ken Tout, who served with the

Northamptonshire Yeomanry, spent much of the 24th and the following night cooped up in his tank, protecting infantry positions established by the Black Watch on the River Dommel. Come daylight, "we are battle-weary, noise-crazed, body-sullied. It is more than twenty-four hours since we trod on firm, steady ground and since we washed or cleaned our mouths; and any natural functions performed have been negotiated from a cramped position into an empty brass shell-case or an ammunition box . . . and during the night we have walked the deepest darkness of soul, trying to find a mental slit-trench or dug-out in which to cower from reality and phantasms." They had little time to recover from their ordeal before the regiment set forth once more, still with the Gordons, and now advancing over a Bailey Bridge on the Dommel into the still occupied fields and woods beyond. "Behind the tanks walk platoons of relaxed Highlanders, easily keeping pace with the rear tanks. The front tanks . . . [are] venturing slowly and agonisingly towards the first, blank savage corners. Their caution filters back slowly along the column, dictating a snail's pace . . . The morning drags slowly by, the sluggish progress of the clock accentuated by our jolting, ten-yards-at-a-time advance as we wriggle about in our tight coops, like battery hens, trying to restore circulation in legs, buttocks and shoulders."[9]

Tanks had to be more circumspect still in built-up areas, with their rubble-strewn streets and numerous hiding-places for anti-tank gun and bazooka teams. Yet they were heavily relied upon in this type of fighting, especially in s'Hertogenbosch. According to the Welsh Division's historian, their assault was "perhaps the best example of modern times of a successful attack on a large town held by a resolute and skilful enemy . . . s'Hertogenbosch was defended street by street and building by building. It took the best part of a division supported by armour to subdue it."[10] Two accounts of the fighting give a good impression of the mixture of fear, confusion and the downright bizarre that characterised this sort of battle. A regimental history tells how, on 25th October, B Squadron was fighting with 7 Royal Welsh Fusiliers, moving through the eastern suburbs of the city towards one of the bridges over the Zuidwellems Canal. "As a troop of flame-throwing Crocodile tanks approached the area of the Canal lock, which was their objective, they found a confused situation." In the streets near the Canal the infantry were pinned down by heavy enemy fire, and a small Press and Army Cinema Unit also managed to get in the way. A tank commander in another troop was fighting in the outskirts of the town and advanced down "the main road past smouldering houses . . .

[and] a long line of refugees, bedraggled and dazed after the bombing
and the barrage ... Mortars began to fall uncomfortably close. I
searched the area with my binoculars and thought I could detect
movement in one of the houses away from the road on my right. We
fired a round at the house and out came a party of Germans with their
hands held high. A Flail tank fitted with chains to a roller to detonate
mines ahead now joined us. Just as it edged past me my tank received a
direct hit. The shell landed on the engine covers at the rear. It shook us
all up but did no great damage ... We decided to put down a barrier of
smoke in front of us to cover our movements."[11]

The Flails and Crocodile tanks were from 79 Armoured Division,
a unique formation deploying all the various specialised armour
developed for D-Day operations and beyond. In his Crocodile
Lieutenant Andrew Wilson, serving with the Buffs, was sent to assist
in seizing an unblown bridge where infantry and conventional armour
were being held up German bazooka and machine-gun teams. After
one of the Sherman tanks was hit and set on fire, Wilson was ordered
forward. His tank trundled cautiously down a narrow, rubble-strewn
street towards a windowless building at the far end, on the other side of
the canal. He gave the order to fire and the flame leapt out across the
canal and "splashed on the face of the building. It was wooden: the end
of a terrace of dwelling houses. The weir was just in front of it,
festooned with coils of barbed wire." An infantry corporal then leapt
forward with a pair of wire-cutters but was cut down before he reached
the weir. Several machine guns were now firing, "none of which could
actually be located, though they had to be in the houses on the other
bank. When Wilson was joined by the two other tanks from his troop,
they crowded in on either side of him, and together pumped in the
flame methodically, left and right, as far as the guns could reach." The
infantry began to cross the weir in numbers and Wilson's troop was
called back to refuel. He started to reverse back down the narrow street
until, to his amazement, he found it "blocked by a staff car. There was
some apparatus inside, and a figure with a war correspondent's tabs on
his battledress. The figure leant out and looked up. 'Excuse me, old
man, but you couldn't do a bit of that again could you? The bloody
recording machine broke down.'" [12]

Looking back on his experiences, Wilson described combat as
"mostly a series of unheroic things – little successes, little escapes, long
periods of waiting ... It just went on from day to day, and it was
enough that you were still there."[13] The constant stress of living with
the very real possibility of death day after day had an inexorably

debilitating effect on the front-line soldiers. Clearly, such fighting was never as unremittingly ghastly as that of the Canadians in South Beveland and the Breskens Pocket, yet the chance of being maimed or killed was still a wearisome psychological burden. Gunner Peter Ryder was a forward artillery spotter working with the East Lancashires during the s'Hertogenbosch battle. In a lull in the fighting on the 25th, he took brief respite with the infantry "in a cosy building on the edge of town" while one of the Welsh battalions took up the advance.

> Despite the squaddies' gaiety and bonhomie, I could tell they were almost at the end of their tether after fierce house-to-house fighting and lack of sleep. Men were slumped on the floor in awkward postures, too exhausted to move. Unshaven, dirty, with clothes torn, they would hardly have inspired confidence in a CO or a raw recruit seeking reassurance . . . Like me, few expected to survive the campaign in one piece. At best they could hope for a Blighty wound to see them safely on a boat home. And I had discovered that courage was expendable. Contrary to general belief, a soldier did not become braver the longer he stayed up front. Combat troops too long in the line became ultra-cautious, assuming their number was due up. They flinched at shadows, became tetchy, constantly on the *qui vive*, until their nerves reached breaking-point.[14]

Sobering a reminder as Ryder's account is of one of the fundamental truths of warfare, it would not do to suggest that the fighting troops were not allowed any sort of relaxation. Ken Tout, who spent much of the 25th cooped up in his Sherman tank, finally emerged when the regiment rested and regrouped that evening. Just as they were settling down, and despite being very close to the enemy lines, "a large loudspeaker van . . . bounces into the field, the music of 'Stars and Stripes' also bouncing as the needle of the gramophone takes the jolt from the van's wheels . . . The invisible NCO I/C gramophone records within the van remains impervious to our . . . [requests] and serves up what appears to be a job lot, 'Stars and Stripes' . . . 'White Cliffs of Dover' . . . an amputated section of Beethoven's [Fifth] . . . and eventually a banal song which . . . nobody . . . has ever heard of. The tinny but over-amplified music must be audible to the Germans on the other side of the railway tracks. We almost expect to hear . . . [a] distant voice requesting a Wagner extract."[15]

The experiences of Lieutenant-Colonel Lindsay transcend Tout's anecdote for sheer dottiness. Soon after settling into their command post, and setting about heating the bath water, Lindsay and another officer set out to investigate what they thought might have been a golf course they passed earlier in the day. Sure enough they found some playable links and, despite the fact that artillery and mortar shells were still landing less than half-a-mile away, they embarked on a twosome. Only four of the holes were still outside a German minefield and the enemy had also stolen all but three of the remaining golf clubs.

> There was a brigade H.Q. set up a hundred yards from the first tee, and as I teed up my ball I wondered what the penalty was for hitting a brigadier. The fairway of the second was bordered by the tanks of 7th Armoured Division, and the crews all stood on them and kept up a running commentary of criticism or advice. The third tee we shared with a charging engine. A full colonel (medical) came out of a tent, looking very pompous and displeased, and proceeded to stand in the middle of the fairway. I suppose he thought we were not taking the war seriously. "By Jove! it does me good to see golf again," said a young yeomanry half-colonel (as the Americans would say), striding by in his jodhpurs. "Very well, then I'll call you at my court-martial," I replied, before drawing breath to yell: "Fore!" at the Assistant-Director of Medical Services. But just in front of the fourth green the Divisional General was holding a conference of all his commanders and this was too much even for us.[16]

Throughout the Tilburg–s'Hertogenbosch battles, and the latter part of those on each side of the Scheldt estuary, the rest of 21st Army Group's front remained quiet. It was divided into two corps sectors, with XXX Corps holding the Nijmegen–Arnhem salient, the so-called 'Island', and VIII Corps guarding a German bridgehead over the Maas, east of Overloon. This *Maasbrückenkopf* was a painful reminder of the failure of Operation CONSTELLATION to close up to this section of the river and at Corps headquarters they continued to claim that it was only the removal of one of their divisions, 15 Scottish, to take part in Operation ALAN that had thwarted their own attack. As it was, the Corps was left holding a 50-mile front, with 3 Infantry Division in the north, from Cuijk to Venray (13 miles), 11 Armoured Division from there to just west of Horst (5 miles), and 7 U.S. Armoured Division holding the rest of the line as far as Wessem, to the north-west of Roermond (22 miles). The Americans' own right flank was held by a Belgian infantry brigade, that country's contribution to the Allied ground forces. To the north, XXX Corps held the Island with fully three divisions, with another two between the Waal and the Maas, holding the flanks of the original airborne corridor between Grave and

Nijmegen. These divisions were: on the Island 101 U.S. Airborne to the left and 50 Infantry Division to the right, with the Guards Armoured Division in reserve; and on the flanks of the corridor 82 U.S. Airborne on the left and 43 Infantry Division on the right, facing the Reichswald.

This whole sector of the front, all the way from s'Hertogenbosch, via the Nijmegen salient to Roermond, remained impervious to further Allied attacks and both sides had settled into a period of grudging static warfare. Even Holland could yield few more depressing autumnal spots than 'The Island', at the northern end of the salient, where the British clung on to the gains made during the Arnhem battle. It was just what its name implied, an area of land surrounded on three sides by the confluence of the Waal and the Maas, and on the remaining western side by a canal linking these two rivers. Unfortunately, the 'dry' land was sometimes difficult to distinguish from the waters around it. One of 50 Division's infantry battalions, 8 Durham Light Infantry, was based in a quadrant to the north of the village of Aam, itself almost due north of Nijmegen, and the Battalion's history could summon up little enthusiasm for the "flat, marshy country . . . [where] the majority of the few large villages and scattered farmsteads had already been reduced to ruins by the fighting, which meant the troops had to 'rough it' in the open." The whole area was intersected by dykes, many of which were blocked by dead cattle. The rain came down with the customary relentlessness and most of the dykes were already filled to overflowing. The area also included numerous orchards but by now all the leaves had fallen or been stripped from the trees, which offered little protection from the German artillery observers. "Men caught out in the open had to decide quickly whether an approaching shell would land close enough to make it imperative to jump into several feet of water in the nearest ditch or whether they could take a chance and merely press themselves flat in a foot of squelchy mud."[17]

The sector held by 43 Division, south-east of Nijmegen, was a little less waterlogged than the Island, consisting of sandy heathland, small farms and woods. A private with 7 Somerset Light Infantry recalled: "It was nasty, cold, eerie and wet in the middle of those woods, trees dripping with rain in that windy forest. I lost a good friend killed by an airburst from which there seemed no protection. Sounds seemed magnified, many a rifle was fired at an imaginary enemy or a flitting 'Ghost' that seemed to dodge among the trees . . . [Morale was barely] two degrees above rock bottom." And of course there was always the rain. Another soldier with this Division remembered two enemies: the

Germans and the "vile weather . . . The days and nights were wet. The
. . . rain seemed piercingly cold. After exertion when the body warmed,
the cold air and the wet seemed to penetrate the very marrow of every
bone in the body, so that the whole shook as with ague."[18] An infantry
captain, clearly aware that people back home were as ignorant of
conditions at the front as they had been in the 1914–18 war, got a
chance to speak his piece on BBC radio and gave a graphic, somewhat
indignant account of life at the 'sharp end' in the Nijemgen salient:

> Do you know what it's like? Of course you don't. You have never
> slept in a hole in the ground which you have dug while someone
> tried to kill you . . . a hole dug as deep as you can as quick as you can
> . . . It is an open grave, and yet graves don't fill up with water. They
> don't harbour wasps or mosquitoes, and you don't feel the cold,
> clammy wet that goes into your marrow.
>   At night the infantryman gets some boards, or tin, or an old door
> and puts it over one end of his slit trench; then he shovels on top of
> it as much dirt as he can scrape up nearby. He sleeps with his head
> under this, not to keep out the rain, but to protect his head and chest
> from airbursts . . .
>   When he is mortared or shelled he is deathly afraid and in the
> daytime he chain-smokes, curses, or prays, all of this lying on his
> belly with his hands under his chest to lessen the pain from the blast.
> If it is night, smoking is taboo . . . A trench is dug just wide enough
> for the shoulders, as long as the body and as deep as there is time. It
> may be occupied for two hours or two weeks. The next time you are
> near some muddy fields after a rain take a look in a ditch. That is
> where your man lives.[19]

The greater part of the British front around the Maas salient ran
through the Peel Marshes, as typically Dutch, waterlogged and
unpleasant as their name suggests. A *peel* is a flat, heather-covered
peat-bog in which trees crowd on to any few square yards that are
above average elevation. For most of it is not. The whole area, in
1944, comprised reclaimed land which was usually under water throughout late autumn and winter. Every field was surrounded by a large dyke
and there were few roads, most of these liable to rapid disintegration
under any sort of heavy traffic. The history of VIII Corps referred to it
as "a quagmire", particularly unsuitable for the two Allied armoured
divisions who guarded much of the front. "It is perhaps the worst
country in the world for armoured fighting for no tank dare leave the
track and one cleverly placed minefield can cause enormous delay."[20]

The men of 23 Hussars, part of 11 Armoured Division, had to drive white posts in along the roadside to mark it out above the water. Any tank was virtually certain to run across a mine or a German anti-tank gun sooner or later, with dire but ineluctable consequences. "Nor was it possible to live anywhere except underground or in a muddy hole underneath one's tank, 'or in a room in the right side of a very thick house with a tank drawn up to the window.' For six o'clock was the start of the German artillery 'variety programme', and 'every type of missile one could expect was employed' – the most original of which was an incendiary mortar pleasantly filled with oil."[21]

For some tankers even the worst attentions of the enemy could not compare with the sheer degradation of the physical conditions. A Grenadier Guards tank battalion, in the vicinity of Oploo, found that it was not the interminable mortaring that made life "seem like one long, bad dream . . . [but] something far more terrible – mud . . . Anything the Grenadiers did, anything they could do was dictated by this terrible concoction of Nature. Everywhere there was to be mud, bogging the tanks so deep that sometimes even the recovery vehicles could not pull them out, putrefying anything that came in contact with it, seeping into tents at night, making everybody cold and dirty and miserable from dawn to dark."[22] 2 Fife and Forfar Yeomanry, another of 11 Armoured Division's units, were stationed around Veulen, just south of Venray, in late October, and one of their Majors lamented the "never-ending rain and mud . . . As to Veulen itself as the weeks went by it became more and more battle-weary, ultimately becoming wholly repulsive. Livestock set off trip-wires in the night. The place was littered with dead horses, cattle – an awful stench."[23]

The infantry actually managed to paint an even less appealing picture of the Peel Marshes and usually restrained accounts angrily grope for a sufficiently grim vocabulary. An officer of 1 South Lancashires, part of 3 Division, recorded the aftermath of the fighting around Overloon and Venray which "marked a return to the utter devastation of the Normandy battlefields. Dead cattle strewed the landscape. The trees were stripped bare . . . and the rain had reduced . . . everything to black, slimy mud. Hardly a human soul was to be seen . . . Once more it was war stripped of any softer tones – naked and beastly." An account of infantry positions along 11 Armoured Division's front, by an officer in 5 Coldstream Guards, attains an almost poetic effect as the author strives to convey his sense of unrelieved awfulness. Mud "seemed to have been sprayed over everything like a coat of paint, and the whole dismal landscape of waterlogged heaths was of the same dreary colour ... The turning down to our command post was marked by a very battered Calvary and a row of graves, some of them marked by wooden crosses but mostly just a mound of earth with a rifle dug into the ground at the head and a steel helmet on the top of it. A sort of forlorn resignation hung over the place, as though it had been set aside from the world as a showground for desolation, for endless days of dismal, grey weather and for every mood of gloom."[24]

Nevertheless, it was unthinkable simply to throw up one's hands in despair and so the divisions, battalions and companies quietly got on with the business of imposing some sort of method on the madness. Just as in the previous war this consisted of organising a system of forward and reserve positions, with regular unit rotation, and the sending out of patrols. In the infantry divisions and brigades, with their triangular structure, the usual routine was to have two brigades/ battalions forward and one in reserve. In the battalions, which had four infantry companies, there could be two up and two in reserve, or three and one, depending on the length of the sector held. The amount of time spent forward depended on the size of the unit and its own opportunities to effect some sort of rotation. Thus a brigade might spend five, six, or even seven weeks forward but the battalions within it would usually be alternated every ten days or so, spending three or four days in reserve or rest positions. Within battalions, particularly as the weather worsened, it was customary at the front to send each day a few men back from each company to B Echelon lines, where for 36 hours or so they could at least sleep under cover, get regular hot meals and take a bath.

Companies in the line were based around mutually supporting platoon positions, each of only three or four men with rifles, light machine guns and mortars. Officers visited their platoon or company positions at first and last light "to check that everything and everyone was all right". So wrote a platoon commander with 4 Somerset Light Infantry who especially disliked the morning visits he had to make late that October. "One felt and was dirty and in the small hours of the morning, with boot-laces cutting into swollen feet, a foul-tasting mouth and an aching stomach, life had little to commend it."[25] Company officers were, if anything, even less appreciative of these responsibilities as platoon headquarters were more scattered and the whole trip took considerably longer, often up to two hours. Touring a company area meant covering every type of rough ground, always fearful of enemy mortars and artillery. "One was always subconsciously listening or expecting in a way that is hard to describe . . . To say that so many hundred shells fell on a position each day, or that we were shelled at such-and-such a time, entirely fails to convey the sense of continual uneasiness one felt, with a perpetual Father Time and his scythe walking along in one's footsteps."[26] At least company officers could enjoy a certain cautious freedom of movement at company headquarters. In the platoon positions, including those manned by the platoon commander himself, very little movement was usually possible, as they were either close to the enemy lines or directly overlooked. In such circumstances "our natural functions were severely inhibited. Newspaper or food cans were our last resort, but they brought their own disadvantages. Throwing a newspaper containing excreta from a slit trench could produce dire consequences . . . from the enemy . . . In the circumstances, we tried to become nocturnal animals, not always with success."[27]

Few commanders, especially at company level and above, were satisfied with simply manning static squad and platoon positions along their front. Around the whole of XXX and VIII Corps' perimeter the watchword was just as it had been in Flanders and Picardy thirty years before: patrols. And not just to gather information about enemy dispositions, but aggressive patrolling to "dominate no-man's land" and supposedly keep the Germans in a constant state of uncertainty. Official doctrine held that such patrols should be 12 to 20 men strong. Many junior officers felt that that was too many, difficult to control in a skirmish at night. Sydney Jary, for example, preferred just six men: himself, two men with a Bren gun, and three others with Sten guns and grenades and a pair of wire-cutters. Jary himself would carry a Colt pistol, four grenades and an umbrella. "My umbrella had been a source of amusement to the Platoon since I found it on the roadside in Mook. Apart from keeping me dry in or out of a slit trench, it was useful when prodding for mines and brought some fun and colour to our lines."[28]

Patrols were not always so compact. On the Island, 8 Durham Light Infantry carried out "vigorous patrolling . . . The majority were reconnaissance patrols; the few fighting patrols did not meet with much success. Conditions for patrolling were far from ideal as the men had to carry ladders or planks with which to span the ditches, making as little noise as possible. These ladders made movement very difficult . . ."[29] The reconnaissance patrols were to gather intelligence only and were supposed to steer clear of enemy patrols and even outlying positions. Usually comprising only three or four men, they were lightly armed and set forth dressed very much in the approved Hollywood manner. An officer with 1 Norfolks, on such a patrol in the Maas salient, was wearing "black plimsolls so that we could move without noise, our faces were blackened with burnt cork, woollen cap comforters on our heads. Over our battledress leather jerkins turned inside out so there would be no shine from the leather."[30]

Patrolling was only one of several ways of keeping the enemy off-balance. An officer with 1 Hampshires on the Island described the enormous trouble he had gone to to creep into a deserted ruin in front of his company positions at Bemmel. Afterwards he stationed a senior NCO there for 24 hours at a time, each making the 45-minute journey with infinite caution and always by a different route so as not to leave a tell-tale trail. "I visited the post once every day to check everything was in order and, though we could speak only in whispers, to give my NCOs about an hour's companionship during their lonely vigil." The point of all this surreptitious, highly dangerous activity was to provide a view across a low-lying area and to call down mortar fire if any enemy movement was detected. "It was mainly our fire from this cute observation post that enabled us to dominate no-man's land, always an important task."[31]

In this ongoing struggle for dominance divisions employed the whole gamut of their resources, from small-arms fire to artillery. Snipers were widely used during these periods of static warfare and most battalions had four or five attached to headquarters, with a very free-and-easy brief to cause what mayhem they could in the enemy front lines. Their claims, of course, were generally unverifiable but one battalion's 'Game Book' listed twelve such between 12th and 25th October. In this same battalion, 5 Seaforth Highlanders, the second-in-command "spent half his time in No Man's Land with a telescope and the other half going into a huddle with the snipers and hatching plots. His planning and the snipers' skill made a deadly combination . . . [In October] so great was our ascendancy that [one sniper] the redoubtable Fraser was seen one evening disappearing into No Man's Land on a bicycle."[32]

Just as common as the sniper's bullet was the 'stonk', bringing down artillery fire either in response to observed German movements or on predetermined locations where it was hoped they might be caught in the open or at least be deterred from assembling any patrols. In 43 Division, east of Nijmegen, 5 Wiltshires were engaged in a typical mixture of harassing activity, as described in one soldier's diary: "Although we did not attack, we kept up incessant shell and mortar fire.

Every night there was extensive patrolling co-ordinated with intricate fire-plans which kept the enemy awake and alert ... Our battalion snipers had some good times when they went out." An infantry officer stressed the effort that went into establishing observation posts and patiently drawing up maps of known enemy positions. For him this whole period of the war "was to a large extent gunner warfare, with the usual searchings after enemy gun positions for our mediums to engage, and ever growing and more intricate fire plans and harassing programmes" for the artillery and mortars as a whole.[33] An army that only five weeks earlier had been hoping to spearhead a breakthrough on the Rhine and perhaps push right through to Berlin, was now heavily mired in the same static trench warfare that had bamboozled the generals for much of the First World War.

4

The Siege

THE CZECH ARMOURED BRIGADE AT DUNKIRK

Dunkirk is as vivid a name in British military annals as Blenheim, Waterloo and El Alamein, for it was there that the second British Expeditionary Force, sent to France in 1939, extricated itself from impending destruction in May 1940. The preceding campaign had been nothing less than a military disaster but at least national morale had received something of a fillip as tens of thousands of British and French soldiers were plucked from the beaches. None the less, on 4th June, Dunkirk had surrendered to the commander of the German 18 Infantry Division and the port continued to be strongly garrisoned. By October 1944 this garrison was even larger, Hitler having given orders that all the Channel ports were to be held until the last man and laid waste to prevent their use as supply points for the advancing Allies. By the time Dunkirk had been sealed off by the Canadians, in early September, it contained some 18,000 German soldiers, mainly survivors of 226 Infantry Division, which had been formed only a few months before from men on leave from the Eastern Front who had promptly failed to hold the port of Le Havre against the Allies.

Despite the preponderance of army personnel, command at Dunkirk was given to Rear-Admiral Frisius, formerly in charge of the Pas de Calais naval installations, and the commander of 18 Division was evacuated by speedboat to take up another post, leaving Frisius with an army colonel as his chief-of-staff. Their new Dunkirk pocket was roughly 16 miles long by 5 miles wide, the perimeter of which was remarkably solid and often referred to by the Germans as *Festung Dunkirchen*. It included several outlying villages and areas that had been deliberately flooded, extensive minefields, and chains of farmhouses converted into bunkers and pill-boxes. Frisius could call

50

on 97 AA guns, 35 field guns and 40 heavy guns, some of the latter large naval weapons, all well-supplied with ammunition and accurately ranged on all the areas where the besiegers might choose to attack. A vigorous programme of training was conducted within the pocket, paying particular attention to artillery matters and to the creation of squads of shock troops for swift counter-attacks.

Because Le Havre, Boulogne and Calais had already fallen, and because at Cherbourg, St Malo and Brest the Germans had already shown their willingness to thoroughly demolish port installations held in any strength, the Allies decided not to attempt a prepared assault on Dunkirk but merely to maintain a tight siege perimeter. During September this duty had fallen to a Canadian Special Service Brigade and then to 51 Highland Division, but on 3rd October the mantle had passed to the Czechoslovak Armoured Brigade. One of their first acts was to arrange a cease-fire, in the first week of October, during which most of the remaining civilians in the pocket were allowed to leave. About 6,000 of the 25,000 civilians present at the beginning of the siege had already been evacuated during an earlier truce organised by the Red Cross, and by the end of this second truce only about 820 Frenchmen remained within the perimeter, plus some 60 British and Canadian prisoners-of-war and a few members of the French Resistance held in the town jail on the Rue du Vieux Rampart.

The mission of the Czechoslovak Brigade, under the command of General A. Liška, was to contain the enemy within the existing perimeter and to try to "induce his surrender, using reconnaissance, artillery fire, air bombardment, propaganda, and every means possible to cut his supplies, transported by sea or air".[1] At full strength the Brigade would include two tank battalions, one motorised infantry battalion and a reconnaissance battalion, though by the end of October only one of the tank battalions was available. The place of the other was taken by 7 Royal Tank Regiment, and back-up was provided by units from an AA brigade, Canadian artillery and a group of French infantry forces. "In addition to regular guard duties, patrols were dispatched into . . . 'no man's land' after dark to hold outposts protecting our positions against enemy infiltration. This task was dangerous and unpleasant. Patrols spent hours in the trenches, frequently in the rain, listening and staring into the darkness, then spending the rest of the night in the ruins of farm houses which they had to evacuate before daybreak."[2] The sector south-east of Dunkirk was completely flooded and patrolled by motor boats manned by the Brigade's engineer company.

   As their country's sole representatives among the vast Allied ground
forces, the Czechoslovaks were naturally somewhat disappointed to
be given this unglamorous task well behind the front line. They
themselves, reasonably enough, had expected to be given a vanguard
role, with their tanks helping to push through right to their own
frontiers. Nevertheless, the Dunkirk perimeter was far from inactive.
On 8th October, presumably realising that an unblooded formation had
come into the line, the Germans launched a raid in the Bergue sector
which penetrated the reconnaissance battalion's forward positions.
It was soon repulsed, with help from 7 Royal Tank Regiment, and
General Liška immediately set about organising offensive operations of
his own. The first was to take place on 28th October, Czechoslovak
Independence Day, in the Ghyvelde sector, and was to comprise a feint
by the motorised infantry battalion followed by an attack by 2 Tank
Battalion that was to overrun the enemy forward positions, demolish
them and then return to the start line. Hardly a major contribution to
their own national liberation, but it was still a welcome if belated
opportunity to avenge the dismemberment of their homeland in 1938
and 1939.

5

Liberation

BEHIND THE FRONT IN HOLLAND AND BELGIUM

IF ALLIED commanders were disappointed by the lack of progress made in Holland, Dutch civilians were also feeling let down and by October were beginning to realise that a long, hard winter lay ahead. Yet only a few weeks earlier there had been a general mood of elation among the Dutch as they watched the Germans, in seeming disarray, hastily withdrawing out of Belgium. On 4th September the BBC announced on Radio Oranje that British troops had captured Antwerp and that their spearheads had already pushed across the Dutch frontier. On the 5th pent-up anger against the Germans exploded on a day that became known as *Dolle Dinsdag*, or Mad Tuesday: "the Dutch exploded in a frenzy of celebration – and vengeance. Quiet village squares erupted as Resistance fighters joined their families in joyful reunion. The fears bred by four years of occupation turned to bravado as Germans were bodily booted out of town by unarmed citizens. Nazi collaborators were rounded up and publicly abused by indignant . . . citizens."[1] Then, all too soon, the retreating Germans halted, retook many of the villages they had evacuated, and once again strung together a firm defensive line.

For Dutch citizens on both sides of this line the war now began in earnest. There had never been any sort of puppet government in Holland, the administration remaining entirely in the hands of Reichskommissar Artur Seyss-Inquart, and in occupied areas German reprisals were visited on many of those who had appeared too enthusiastic on *Dolle Dinsdag*, including a last flurry of deportations to Auschwitz. In the province of Limburg, which had actually been annexed by Germany, all males aged between 17 and 40 were shipped off to be slave labourers. Food shortages, already acute, intensified

53

when the Germans refused to allow farmers in eastern Holland to sell their produce to the cities in the west. Coal was also now in very short supply. Throughout 1944 civilians were largely dependent on the vagaries of the climate for any warmth, and by late October the first piercing icy gusts of winter could be felt. Widespread and chronic hunger made them bite all the more keenly. Food distribution had been extremely erratic for several months, something the Germans were only too happy to blame on the Dutch railwaymen who had gone on strike after the Arnhem landing and most of whom were still in hiding. Even before the denial of the harvest was fully felt, people were suffering permanent hunger pangs. Moreover, such food as was available made for an extremely tedious diet. One diarist described what she called "'food cycles' [by which] I mean periods in which one has nothing else to eat but one particular dish or kind of vegetable. We had nothing but endives for a long time, day in, day out, endive with sand, endive without sand, stew with endive, boiled or *en casserole*: then it was spinach, and after that followed swedes, salsify, cucumbers, tomatoes, sauerkraut etc. However, we have the most delightful period of all now, because we don't get any fresh vegetables at all . . . Everything contains beans, not to mention the bread!"[2] Within a few weeks, Radio Oranje's tone changed completely. The Dutch government-in-exile in London gloomily stated in October that "the large cities were already without meat, and it was expected that supplies of bread, butter, sugar and potatoes would run out by the end of October. Occupied Holland was also short of fuel and light, and the Dutch government estimated that in the major cities sewerage, and the main supply of drinking water, would soon cease."[3]

Liberated Holland was spared most of these extremes but it would be a mistake to assume that life there was a bowl of tulips. For many the memory of *Dolle Dinsdag* now evoked only a hollow laugh. The agonisingly slow tide of the war was still causing immense dislocation throughout southern Holland and every day streams of refugees left their homes in the war zone or trickled back into those shattered towns and villages now sufficiently behind the front. In Woensdrecht, for example, the scene of one of the bitter Canadian battles in mid-October, returning civilians found that 72 houses had been totally destroyed by artillery and mortar fire, 355 too badly damaged to repair, and 235 others damaged in one way or another. The crops had been ruined when the Germans opened the Scheldt sluice-gates and those that had been salvaged and stored in a warehouse were now incinerated. One source estimated that 17 per cent of all Dutch arable land had been flooded by the Germans or through battle damage to the dykes.

Also lost was most of the farmers' livestock and their work animals, including 146 horses, 330 cattle and 1,000 pigs and goats. One typical farmer discovered his cows dead in the fields, his three work-horses likewise in the barn, still tethered in their stalls, all his chickens killed as well as most of his pigs, and his dog gone mad after the constant shelling. On the 25th itself, the villagers endured yet further hardship. In the words of one: "We were requested by the Canadians to leave again, this time due to danger from typhoid. Dead pigs, sheep, cows and horses were everywhere. The smell was sometimes unbearable."[4]

According to some accounts, the Dutch took this sort of wholesale destruction remarkably well. One village was entered by tanks of the Northants Yeomanry on the 25th, after being fought over for most of the previous day. One of the crews recognised a house they had demolished with their gun and went over to commiserate with the civilians sifting through the ruins. The tank commander apologised, explaining that Germans had been holed up inside.

The Dutchman smiled unexpectedly. "No go. We are enthusiast."

"I beg your pardon. I don't understand."

"We are all enthusiast. All Dutchmen enthusiast. You liberate us. Better you blow up our houses two years, three years, four years ago. Then we have house and Germans. Now no house and no Germans. Better no house and no Germans. Ja! We are all enthusiast. How are you?"[5]

Whether most other Dutchmen faced the destruction of their homes with such equanimity is at least open to question. Certainly other descriptions of Dutch civilians in late October lack the Brothers Cheeryble feel of the above encounter. A British trade union official, visiting Holland at this time, described driving just north of Antwerp. "It was still raining and it was still cold rain . . . Flooded fields both sides of the road. A man and a boy escorting a cow even bonier than themselves coming towards us slowed us down . . . Forlorn villages with hungry-looking men, women and children in slow motion as though they did not care what happened next. A blown-up bridge away to the right. Man and woman away to the left, standing in water up to their knees as they groped for vegetables . . . Dutch landscape, moist and grey and cold." The historian of 15 Scottish Division recalled the daily streams of homeless trudging through the British lines. "In front of us the Germans burnt down farms and villages. All day long, sad columns of refugees came our way, heading west, tired, their few belongings loaded in prams and wheelbarrows, or simply being carried on their backs, plodding through mud and rain, to us an unforgettable picture of abject human misery." But it was not only the Germans who forced out refugees. In late October it was decided that the village of Leunen, part of British 3 Division's front line, west of the Maas, would have to be evacuated. A sad procession of villagers slowly walked away from their homes, some trying to coax their livestock along. Their surviving horses and cattle posed little problem but pigs and poultry were impossible to control and had to be left behind. "The soldiers watched with mixed feelings: pity, but also the very tempting prospect of the very best food of the campaign – fresh pork and chicken breasts galore."[6]

Many refugees drifted for days on end, taking shelter in ruined farms and in the woods. Eventually most found their way to friends and relatives or, more likely, to one of the Displaced Persons (D.P.) camps set up by the Allies. For thousands of Dutchmen liberation had come to mean only a new kind of imprisonment, benign to be sure, but still marked by harsh austerity and clumsy regimentation. A novel by Colin McInnes, who served in North-West Europe, offers a vivid picture of one such camp, located outside a Dutch village and comprising a score or more of large huts and a big central square. The refugees entered their new accommodation via the reception hall where British servicemen sat behind trestle tables piled high with official forms, identity cards, labels, rubber stamps and pads, and cartons of insecticide. Registration was also a screening process and one of the forms included a column for 'Remarks', in which would be entered A, for legitimate, D, doubtful, and X, suspect. As this welcoming procedure is explained to him, McInnes's narrator asks:

> "And what's all this insecticide for?"
> "To spray new arrivals with. The Red Cross do it, of course, not us."
> "How do they do it?"
> "The sexes are split up, stripped down and the powder applied to them and their clothes with a sort of bellows."
> "And these huge labels?"
> "They're supposed to wear them round their necks. But most of them lose them."

He is then given a tour of the camp, starting again at the main square where "crowds of refugees were wandering all over it in an aimless, dejected sort of way. Of those who turned to watch me, some looked resigned, but others gave me a hostile glance of reproof. Their eyes said clearly, 'All this should be an affair between soldiers. Wars should take place far away from home.'" Most of those in the camp were from small farms and villages of the region and

> herded together in the huts with a few cooking pots and with their animals tethered outside, the villagers looked even more uprooted than townspeople might do, even further removed from their natural rhythm. Dwellers in cities may feel that they are lodgers anyway, and the camp might have been for them another inconvenient halting-place. But these farmers looked undignified and despoiled.

> I followed some of them into one of the huts. There was no furniture, but families had marked themselves out little territories on the floor. It was soon possible to see what areas were left for general congregation, and others to go into which you would have to knock at an imaginary door.[7]

Yet one should not paint too gloomy a picture or suppose that the whole population of liberated Holland was emaciated and homeless, huddled sullenly in unfenced prison camps or sloshing through the mud from one cluster of ruins to the next. Our Cheeryble Brother was not entirely in a world of his own and many others, while probably not quite so blasé about losing home and hearth, were at least prepared to pitch in and start rebuilding their lives and their small communities. Another excellent novel, this time by a British artilleryman with Second Army, paints a rather different picture of Dutch refugees that October, and invests their return home with an air almost of jauntiness.

> Back to the village came little caravans of civilians, riding in their high wooden carts, with a cow or two ambling behind the buckboard and curious, doll-like children with fair hair and blue eyes riding atop the mattresses and bedding that filled the cart . . . A policeman came first, in his dark blue shako and a white braided lanyard looped across his chest. He was wheeling a bicycle to which was strapped a great cavalry sword, and walking beside him was an old man who did not lift his eyes from his shuffling clogs. Behind them both was the farm-cart, drawn by a heavy-bowed shire horse, kicking the grey dust about its swinging head. The cart was piled with scarlet mattresses, folded blankets, a chair or two, and a child's chamber-pot slashed with painted roses. A man held the animal's bridle, looking back anxiously over his shoulder to a girl sitting high on the blankets . . . Then, as the cart drew abreast of him, she took

her hand from her lap and threw him a scarlet-coated apple which
he caught deftly. She smiled in a slow, beautiful manner and he
grinned back and flipped his hand in the air.[8]

There was also a steely resilience to be found in towns very near the
front in late October. Throughout the autumn, Nijmegen was only a
couple of miles behind the gun-lines and, according to one British
officer, it was "a very remarkable front-line town." Although the
inhabitants looked constantly thin, pale and anxious, they all managed
to carry on "with complete disregard for the war that was going on all
around them and every day you would find the streets thronged with
people going about their daily business." While most looked shabby by
this stage of the war, seemingly every other person had contrived to
endow themselves with a sort of government-issue chic by wearing at
least one "garment made of parachute silk scrounged at the time of the
air landings. Silk scarves, silk blouses, even whole dresses of it; the
mottled green and brown was almost a local uniform, and I expect they
were justly proud of it."[9]

It certainly would not do to characterise Dutch civilians as being
ungrateful for the efforts of the British and Canadian troops. Displaced
persons and those in the war zone proper might see liberation as
something of a mixed blessing, but those to the south who had been
able to stay in or return to their homes offered generous hospitality. For
21st Army Group was not just a thin khaki line stretched along the
front. Like all modern armies, it had an enormous logistical and
administrative 'tail' stretching behind it, as well as thousands of
soldiers resting out of the line, and so there was constant contact with
civilians in the rear, in more settled, partially reconstructed, or
occasionally undamaged towns and villages along the lines of communication. Here relations between soldiers and civilians were most
amicable, with the Dutch going out of their way to extend such
kindnesses as they could. Memoirs of the time abound with references
to Dutch generosity and their affection for Montgomery's men. A
Brigadier with 43 Division marvelled at "the warm-hearted welcome
given to British and Canadian troops when out of the line . . . [The
Dutch] never complained. Their generosity to the troops was
unparalleled; their menfolk were pale and drawn, their women tired
and worn, their children pale and anaemic; nevertheless, what they
had, they gave." A British soldier with the RASC component of 11
Armoured Division, stationed 10 miles north-east of Eindhoven during
October, recalled that throughout his eleven-week stay the family with
whom he was billeted, parents and children alike, enjoyed an evening

meal of one small boiled potato, half an apple and a cup of hot water each. Brigadier Essame continues: "On arrival in a village, or housing estate, allotment of individual billets was unnecessary. Companies were marched to the end of a street or block; thereafter the men billeted themselves. Above all the Dutch had the virtue of kindness as understood by the British. Where men were killed and buried by the roadside, the women and children placed flowers on their graves. When they came out of the line to rest, the women, as formidable as many of their own mothers, hurried to dry their greatcoats, mend their clothes and do their washing."[10]

Such solicitude was the gift of people who still had little else to give but shelter and their own labours. An engineer officer with this same division wrote that "almost everyone not actually in a slit-trench was taken under cover somewhere . . . The Dutch took the Tommies into their hearts as well as into their homes. Women would turn up, as it were for fatigues, to peel potatoes every day and saying that they had been ordered to do so by the Germans, but that now they did it as a pleasure." Another soldier felt that the Dutch "loved us not really for ourselves but because we were the liberators who made them feel young again." Nevertheless, the affection seemed real enough at the time and soldiers were able to "impose on . . . [this] friendliness in a hundred ways. Everyone has imagined a world in which he can open any door and be quite sure of being made welcome; and during the campaign this had really happened again and again." And this hospitality satisfied a tremendous need in soldiers so long away from home. Men had a "homing instinct for finding themselves a family who would wash their socks, cook them fried potatoes and listen admiringly to their con-versation . . . When their unit came to a new village, the men would find a fireside to which they could transfer their longing for their own. It was best if there were girls there, but other important elements were the presence of an alien version of Mum, the dispenser of cups of tea and uncritical kindness, and the measured, soothing and fuggy rhythm of a friendly family inside its home."[11]

Yet in every army there is at least a proportion of 'licentious soldiery', and on the 25th, for every battalion with its feet under welcoming tables there were a few individuals with a downright callous attitude to the meagre bounty that liberated Holland could offer. Brutalised perhaps by the sights around them and the constant fear for their own safety, some men began to adopt a thoroughly rapacious approach to any property that was not bolted down or under military guard. In theory, according to one soldier, there was an informal understanding about these things, and while "I would not like to give the impression that we were all little angels . . . there was a sort of code about looting; if it was civilian stuff and they might come back for it, and if it had any value, it was regarded as 'not on' . . ."[12]

No doubt this was the attitude, more or less, of the vast majority of Canadian and British soldiers, but it is also undeniable that the 'hard case' exceptions made a lasting impression on many Dutch civilians. Two historians have found it "sad to report that in the liberated parts of the battle area . . . looting was commonplace . . . Despite all measures, despite all signs proclaiming 'Looting Is a Serious Crime', pillage cast a shadow on the liberation."[13] They made a particular study of the village of Venray, just behind the front lines, and found that it was being systematically looted throughout the second half of October. Much of the looting was with a view to domesticating front-line billets, often in ruined cellars, barns and factories. Tables, armchairs, spring mattresses vanished by the truckload. Ordinary chairs were also in great demand, which with their seats knocked out were positioned over the latrine trench. And many items which might be thought superfluous to soldiers' daily needs also vanished, such as curtains, sheets, pillow-cases, towels and the like. It turned out that these were being taken by soldiers going on leave who hoped to solicit the favours of women in the rest areas. Others were simply after monetary value, and in many houses the floorboards were prised up to uncover radios, china, ornaments, clocks, jewellery and the like hidden there by the evacuated civilians.

Two priests who stayed on in the town offered reliable testimony to to the extent of what became known, in an almost embarrassed way, as 'English damage'. One told how "often the soldier caught red-handed in the act of looting or wanton destruction would say 'Sorry' and that you were right in reprimanding him, but as soon as the coast was clear he resumed his activities." The other found that the safe in the sacristy of his monastery had been forced open some time after the liberation of the town on 17th October. A doctor at a local psychiatric hospital was shocked by the results of the first week's looting: "Words cannot describe how appalled I was when I saw how the town had been pillaged and destroyed. I spoke to an elderly English officer whose words speak for themselves: 'I'm very sorry and deeply ashamed; the Army has lost its reputation here.' Every house I went into I found smashed furniture, drawers prised open, their contents scattered on the floors, kicked-in panels, marble mantelpieces broken to pieces, chandeliers torn from the ceilings, a piano standing in the pouring rain. Valuables had vanished. And I spoke to Englishmen who without any embarrassment told me that down in the cellars things were even worse."[14]

It bears repeating that there is no suggestion here that on the 25th the whole of liberated Holland was being systematically picked clean. Thousands of soldiers were too busy trying to stay alive and tens of thousands of others were esconced among hospitality so open-hearted that it defied them to take advantage. It would be equally misleading to picture the entire Dutch population as noble Samaritans. In the cities, most especially in the occupied zone, the universal criminal element was always present, but by late 1944 the terrible privations of occupation had provoked a much more widespread incidence of petty theft and juvenile delinquency. One account of life in Amsterdam at this time gave a depressing picture of a tide of creeping lawlessness such that

> doctors are unable to visit the sick, because if they turn their backs on their cars for a moment, they are stolen. Burglaries and thefts abound, so much so that you wonder what has taken hold of the Dutch for them suddenly to have become such thieves. Little children of eight and eleven years break the windows of people's homes and steal whatever they can lay their hands on. No one dares leave his house unoccupied for five minutes, because if you go, your things go too. Every day there are announcements in the newspapers offering rewards for the return of lost property, typewriters, Persian rugs, electric clocks, cloth, etc. Electric clocks in the streets are dismantled, public telephones are pulled to pieces – down to the last thread . . . Everyone is wearing old clothes and old shoes. A new sole costs 7.50 florins on the black market; moreover, hardly any of the shoemakers will accept shoe repairs or, if they do, you have to wait four months, during which time the shoes often disappear.[15]

*

On the whole, Holland's southern neighbour, Belgium, had suffered much less during the fighting since D-Day. Despite the heavy bombing of the railways and the suspected V1 rocket sites, there was very little ground fighting there. The Germans had been in precipitate retreat even before they reached the Franco–Belgian border and their troops were not again under proper control until they were some distance into Holland. The pursuing Allies, in fact, swept across Belgium in just two days, largely avoiding the necessity for destructive military engagements. Nevertheless, as elsewhere, German military occupation had been an extremely onerous experience, and economically the country was almost as hard hit as Holland. Imports before the war – mainly food, cattle feed and raw materials for industry – had been 2.6 million tons per month; under the Germans they had fallen to just 300,000 tons per month, and then to only 30,000 tons for the whole of 1944. A good harvest that year staved off mass starvation but stocks were being used up fast and internal wheat production as a whole was only enough for three months' consumption. Even by 21st October, Sir Alexander Cadogan, the Permanent Under-Secretary at the Foreign Office, was writing in his diary: "12.45. Cartier [the Belgian Ambassador] about starving Belgium. He gets quite worked up but *I* can't feed Belgium. But I have stirred up Dept. to stick pins into SHAEF. It's going to be their headache if they have disorders and confusion in Belgium."[16]

The political situation was indeed becoming volatile. Threats to disarm the local resistance groups, usually left-wing, were meeting with fierce resistance and there was widespread indignation at the new government's failure to stop food hoarding and black market speculation by many of the farmers. The conservative Catholic party in Hubert Pierlot's coalition government was accused of being especially soft on their traditional allies, the farmers and small businessmen. The official ration was now only 1,500 calories per day, but it was generally only the poor who had to subsist at this level. Those able to afford black market prices ate well in restaurants offering menus largely indistinguishable from those before the war. A British journalist wrote: "The black market was a roaring outrage. Prices in restaurants were stratospheric ... The French *marché noir* seemed to be an amateur business compared with the highly organised and terrifyingly expensive underground food traffic across the northern border. A decent meal for four persons cost about twenty pounds, or eighty dollars.* But what astonished us most was that people had the money to pay such outrageous bills."[17]

One measure already taken to curb the black market was an attempt to cut the amount of money in circulation. Banks had been ordered to restrict withdrawals to a fixed amount per week but it was already apparent that people with larger accounts were borrowing from the bank, prepared to pay interest for the privilege of spending their own money. Another pressing shortage was coal. A miners' strike had curtailed production, and even when working, the pits were very short-

* In 1998 this would be equivalent to £446 or 735 U.S. dollars.

handed, many young men having been taken away for forced labour in the Reich. Here again the black market flourished and, according to another British journalist, denizens "took a heavy toll of what coal was mined. Trucks vanished from railway sidings, and a full train leaving Charleroi would arrive in Brussels with only half the trucks. Coal was selling in the Black Market at £30 a ton and there were plenty of buyers. In the homes of the workers there was no coal. People will put up with a certain amount of hunger if they are warm, but if they are both hungry and cold there will always be trouble."[18]

The gap between rich and poor was widening daily. While the rich buttoned warm overcoats over full bellies and adjusted felt hat-brims above shiny pink faces, "the poor stood in queues to try to get their daily ration of bread and meat and coffee, which very often did not materialise. Lack of transport . . . helped to dislocate the even distribution of foodstuffs." A British nurse posted to Brussels saw "a city of contrasts" where smart shops displayed lingerie and fur-coats and where "old folk armed with hatchets crept out as soon as darkness fell to chop down hoardings for firewood when the gendarme was not looking", and where "sophisticated men and women in evening dress [ate] around a table sparkling with crystal and silver . . . [while] not so far away, in the poorer quarter, we had seen trespassing urchins throw down handfuls of coal from the delivery trucks to their furtive, scrambling mothers below." No wonder, with a vigorous Socialist and Communist opposition in Parliament, that one of the journalists just cited noted that "each day the dogfights in the Chamber grew more embittered, and there was an electric feeling about Brussels as though an explosion could come at any moment."[19]

Not all Britons visiting Brussels were quite so sensitive to evidence of political tension and social inequality, no matter how marked. For Brussels was the main leave centre for the British and Canadian armies, where most soldiers could hope to spend at least one 72-hour spell out of the line. On any day at least 10,000 such men, mostly accommodated in one of the 17 large hotels that Montgomery had taken over for just this purpose, could be found milling around the streets of the old and new sections of the city. Their numbers were swelled by thousands more men and women in uniform attached to the Brussels Garrison base and lines of communication staff who were permanently stationed there, and who included the 21st Army Group's Main HQ and Administrative Centre. This was not to Montgomery's liking, for he would have preferred that all his staff shared the monkish seclusion of caravan trucks and bivouacs out in the field. Still, the August advance had outstripped his main cable and line communications, and Brussels offered the nub of Belgium's own network, which had already been taken over by the military. However, Montgomery's objections did make considerable sense, and his staff in Brussels were under strict orders not to behave ostentatiously in any way. According to his Operations chief, General David Belchem, he did not want men on leave from the foremost fighting units encountering HQ personnel "shopping or taking a drink in a bar during the day, even if they were off duty, nor beating it up in the night spots, since such conduct can readily arouse antipathies between the men from the sharp end and the staff officers who can acquire a reputation of living a cushy life."[20]

Montgomery's strict rules were observed in the main, and there seems to have been no groundswell of discontent comparable to the animosity against the 'red tabs' in the First World War. But soldiers were so intent on enjoying themselves, and so well provided with the means to do so, that they had little time to scrutinise the habits of headquarters personnel. Their transition from slit-trench to civilisation was wonderfully apparent from the moment the troops checked in at their hotels. The Hôtel de Colonnes, according to one, offered "the luxury of padded chairs, soft beds with sheets, tables set with cloths and china, and not least of all BATHS . . . Putting on newly issued shirts, pants and socks and cleaned battle-dress, we emerged new men. The transformation was completed by a visit to a nearby hairdressing saloon for an excellent haircut." At the Hôtel Plaza, recalled another, "we found ourselves in Heaven . . . hot bath, afternoon tea, waiters lighting matches when you produced a cigarette."[21] Women on leave were especially thrilled by such amenities, like this nurse from a Casualty Clearing Station taking a short break from her gruelling, nomadic life:

> I heard the water running slowly in the bath, and the steam bore on its back a most delicious smell. It filled you with memories you had forgotten all about, and it was good to see things again you had been unconsciously carrying around in your mind . . . as when you lay down a cigarette you are smoking and wander around a room doing things . . . but something inside you remembers that cigarette, and you go around looking for it, to pick it up and enjoy it all over again . . . the little luxuries of living – like the monogrammed linen sheets on the beds and the chest-of-drawers with its inside lined with paper . . . and the wardrobe with its long mirror, and you still human enough to want to use it, the carpeted floors and central heating, so that you could walk across the room with nothing on and still feel warm.

Looking round the ugly room, I found it all pleasing, even the lace curtains at the window. Eagerly I caught the smallest detail of form and colour as rays of light fell on the heavy mahogany furniture, and the faded bedspreads, and the carpet caught the glow from the electric fire. There was an armchair. Privacy . . .?[22]

Once cleaned and changed, the visitors set forth to sample the fabled delights of Brussels. In reputation it was Sodom and Gomorrah with military policemen, where, according to one soldier, you could become "drunk with liberty, licence, and hero-worship of the city, drunk with women, cognac . . . Brussels became an experience . . . crowded with soldiers, noisy with sex, alcohol and the wild music of cafés and symphony orchestras, the comforting, sulphurous smell of trains at the Gare du Nord and the whine of trams down the Jardins Botaniques. It was unreal and dangerously intoxicating even through the distorting mirror which was brought down from the line."[23]

Sex and alcohol did indeed play a major part in the life of the city, but it would be misleading to suggest that every man's leave was an unending Mardi Gras. In fact, for most newcomers one of the main joys was simply the chance to glimpse normalcy again, to be part of a bustling city, clean and almost completely undamaged, where restaurants provided good food, beverages and alcohol, where the shops were well-stocked with all manner of goods, and where entertainment could simply be a 'good night out' at the cinema, the theatre, or in a friendly little bar where beer, recognisable as such, was readily available. Many spent much of their leave simply walking around the city, window-shopping, sight-seeing or ambling through the many lovely parks and the Treveuren and Soignes forests or along Wellington's road to Waterloo, now carpeted in multi-coloured beech leaves. For the real *boulevardier* there was the Avenue Louise, still a remarkably elegant and sophisticated shopping street, the tall 18th-century mansions along the Grande Place, or the open-air markets in the cobbled Sablon section. Others loved to travel on the trams, free to all service personnel, and something of a fairground experience in their own right. At times, especially in the evenings, they "were invariably packed – inside and out. That is to say that passengers clung to each other on the step below the platform in the way that bees cling to one another on the outer fringe of a swarm. The last few trams to run at night would even have troops sitting huddled together on the roof."[24] This rush hour atmosphere later in the evening was mainly a result of soldiers trying to beat the curfew. Field Marshal Montgomery turned in at 10.30 every night and could not see why his armies should not follow his example. Officially, at least, it was an offence to be found out on the streets after that time.

On the whole, however, Montgomery's was a popular name in Brussels. The requisitioning of the hotels, including the 600-bed Métropole, reputedly the largest in Europe, was attributed to him, as was the founding of the Montgomery Club, an enormous NAAFI complex housed in one of Brussels' royal palaces. This was very popular with the troops, visitors and residents alike. Its marble entrance hall was studded with potted palms and the ballroom on the ground floor had been converted into a restaurant where cheap meals, not available to the civilian population, were served by smart waitresses "while a Palm Court orchestra played tea-time music, and was superseded at night by a dance band. At the top of the imposing staircase were rest rooms, writing rooms, games rooms and a comprehensive library and reading room." There were also small rooms in which one could listen to gramophone records, including the top-name American V-discs. Full facilities were provided for a comprehensive wash and brush up, including "a number of cubicles equipped with hot and cold showers, a hairdressing salon and a room where you could get your uniform sponged and pressed while you waited. It was a common sight to see rows of men sitting on chairs in their underwear, while their trousers were being pressed, prior to dashing out to keep a date with a girl friend. You could spend many contented hours at the club, with all your legitimate needs catered for at ridiculously low prices."[25]

Other popular venues were the Eldorado cinema, in the Place de Brouckère, again reputedly the largest in Europe, and the Garrison Theatre, formerly the Théatre Royal du Parc. Both had been taken over by the army, presenting free English-language films, many of them American releases not yet seen in London, and popular plays such as Eden Philpot's *Yellow Sands*. Both were for forces personnel only, though on selected nights civilian guests were permitted. One could also, of course, watch English and American films in Belgian cinemas, if one could put up with French or Flemish subtitles, but with a back-log of four years of movies to catch up with, there was a huge programme to choose from. There were also dance halls set up specially for the troops, the largest being the 21 Dance Club which could accommodate over 3,000 patrons. These were run by the NAAFI, one of whose consultants was Billy Butlin, the holiday camp pioneer. Food was a high priority with most visiting soldiers and there was no need to pay the inflated black market prices. Numerous service clubs and canteens opened in the city, and these all served cheap and tasty meals.

Especially highly rated were the Canadian 'Maple Leaf' club, near the Gare du Nord, also open to British troops, and with waiter service, the Belgian Red Cross Society in the rue Adolfe Max, and the Jewish Servicemen's Club near the Gare du Midi which had "opened its doors to Gentile servicemen as well [and] provided first-class meals served by some very beautiful young Jewesses who gave the club their voluntary services."[26]

Baths, clean uniforms, good food, playing the tourist, losing oneself in a film, glorying in the complete absence of the enemy – all this made a three-day sojourn in Brussels a magical experience. But, with the possible exception of its commander, 21st Army Group was not a monastic order and the thought of most soldiers – healthy young men who had spent many months, even years, in barracks and billets – focussed sooner or later on sex. And Brussels, like any garrison town throughout history, was fully geared up to satisfying nature's demand. Many referred to it as not Brussels, but Brothels, a fabled flesh-pot at the end of the rainbow – though it was best to have no illusions as to what was in the pot. Two tank officers walked down the Boulevard Max through an eddying crowd of soldiers, "most of them with girls . . . lost and amazed in the back-line Babylon. In a side street girls came up from the shadows. 'Exhibition, exhibition,' said a little hunchback. 'Don't be had,' said the RTR man. 'They kid you it's the donkey, and it's only a couple of nudes.' They passed him by, looking for a bar. It appeared as a light behind a curtain. They pushed aside the curtain and went in. Music beat down from an unseen loudspeaker . . . 'Dance?' said a woman. She was large and motherly, with make-up like greasepaint."[27]

Another tankman visited a brothel recommended to him earlier in the day. "It really was a bit of a conveyor-belt factory. I went upstairs with a very striking looking girl and she simply rolled up her sweater to bare her breasts and whipped her skirt off." A visit to another brothel did involve a modicum of social intercourse. There were only four or five girls working there and "what was nice was that you were not pestered and could have a drink and a chat and when you had got your strength back you could go upstairs with one of the girls."

Not all soldiers were seeking sex. The main red-light area was around one end of the rue Nerve and included a kiosk where a Royal Army Medical Corps corporal dished out packets of contraceptives on demand. One driver/cook with a Royal Engineer company newly arrived as part of the Garrison, was amazed at this generosity. "What a turn-up for the book, eh?" he gloatingly told his mates. "I flogged four packets to a civvy in a tram. No trouble at all. Shame to take the money. You could make yourself a blinkin' fortune 'ere if you put your mind to it."[28]

Many Belgians were indeed putting their minds to it and making vast profits on the black market. Almost everything that people needed or craved had a grotesquely high premium attached. One observer drew up an index of prices in October 1944 compared to those at the beginning of the war, with April 1940 taken as 100:[29]

Macaroni	1,003	Cheese	1,853
Beef	1,248	Bacon	2,119
Bread	1,248	Salad Oil	8,259
Butter	1,351	Rice	9,660
Eggs	1,360	Chocolate	9,969
Sugar	1,844	Roast Coffee	10,770
Margarine	1,851		

Elements of the British Army also took the opportunity to enrich themselves at the taxpayers' expense. One critical item was petrol, which passed up the lines of communication in prodigious quantities and could be sold to civilians for top prices. The big drawback was that Army petrol was pinkish in colour and so was easily identifiable by the authorities. Black marketeers had to employ chemists to decolourise it, and this added considerably to the price. Towards the end of October, however, someone discovered, experimentally or accidentally, an instant method of turning the petrol white, simply by adding one mothball to a jerrycanful. The trade was now within the reach of anyone with access to army fuel and prices began to fall almost immediately.

Gangs of deserters were actively involved in peddling petrol – and that other eminently saleable Army issue, cigarettes, burrowing themselves into some of the nefarious districts of Brussels. One battalion commander felt that the Army was consistently too soft on deserters. Their crimes were "treated as comparatively minor military delinquencies, and the men had . . . every reason to think that these were not regarded as very serious offences. The maximum paper sentence was three years and few men actually served six months." Brussels, and Antwerp, were magnets to such men and the history of the Corps of Military Police makes the shrewd point that "in previous wars absentees usually gave themselves up after a week or two from shortage of funds; in this campaign, by dint of periodic pilfering at army stores and subsequent sales to civilians at fantastic prices, large numbers of absentees were enabled to maintain themselves in hiding indefinitely. This added greatly to the difficulties of apprehension and caused an abnormal growth in the numbers of absentees."[30] Certainly, the words 'absentees' and 'pilfering' do not seem to do justice to the scale of the problem. A member of the Army's Special Investigations Branch reckoned that, in Brussels in autumn 1944, 70 jeeps per day went missing. He also gave the example of one group of deserters who set themselves up as a bogus 'Field Corps Police', provided themselves with their own unit insignia and false papers, and set up a large workshop in the backstreets to handle stolen army vehicles. No wonder the word 'liberate' was already acquiring a very new, entirely venal meaning for Allied servicemen.

6

Much to Learn

FIRST U.S. ARMY AND THE HÜRTGEN FOREST

DISAPPOINTING as Montgomery's progress in Holland had been, especially in the light of his ambitious expectations, it could not be claimed that the U.S. divisions of General Bradley's 12th Army Group, to the south, had done much better by late October. Though Eisenhower had been generally suspicious of Montgomery's vision of a war-winning single thrust to Berlin, and always advocated the idea of a more measured broad front advance, even he had been hoping that post-Normandy operations would maintain enough momentum to 'bounce' the German frontier and draw up along the Rhine before there was any need to pause and regroup. In this way the Americans would overrun the West Wall frontier defences – known to the Allies as the Siegfried Line – before the Germans had the chance to man them in any strength. Even such a broad front advance to the Rhine, by First and Third U.S. Armies, would have to follow the dictates of terrain and concentrate around the traditional military routes into Germany, through the Stolberg and Monschau Gaps, south-east of Aachen, and the Lorraine Gap between Metz and Nancy.

By the end of October only First U.S. Army, under General Courtney Hodges, had managed even to reach the West Wall. In the first half of September several of his divisions had managed to penetrate the Wall at various points between the Stolberg Gap, north-west of Aachen, and St Vith, just to the north of the Belgium–Luxembourg frontier. On 15th September Bradley's aide, Major Chester Hansen, had written in his diary: "Brad and Patton agree neither will be too surprised if we are at the Rhine in a week. Prepared the general's map for next phase of operations which extend from the Rhine to the city of Berlin . . . General anxious to slam on through to

Berlin . . . Marked bullseye on Berlin."[1] Unfortunately the Germans proved just as adept here as they were north of Antwerp and the Meuse–Escaut Canal in assembling effective blocking forces from remnants of units, aged reservists, men on leave, policemen, Hitler Youth and the like. Just three days after Hansen's ebullient diary entry, First U.S. Army's offensive was halted and the divisions were ordered to dig in and consolidate.

Not that consolidation brought much relief to the troops at the front. In many places divisions were "in the delicate position of being through the West Wall in some places, being half through in others, and at some points not having penetrated at all. The line was full of extreme zigs and zags . . . [variously] too narrow to serve as springboards for further operations to the east . . . open to infiltration and counter attack [or] subject to observation from high ground."[2] Attempting to eradicate these zigs and zags occupied many units for the rest of the month, especially 9 U.S. Infantry Division which was ordered to clear the dense forested area between the Stolberg Gap and Schmidt, usually referred to as the Hürtgen Forest. By the end of September it had made only limited progress through the northern fringes of the forest.

One recent historian has claimed that the difficulties of the Hürtgen Forest should have made Allied planners think twice about the Stolberg Gap as a main axis of advance. He also maintains that they were premature in writing off the Ardennes, at that time only very thinly held by one U.S. corps, as an alternative axis. "If the SHAEF planners had not ruled out the Ardennes as an invasion route, if the Schwerpunkt of Hodges' First Army had been aimed here instead of at the heavy fortifications in the narrow Stolberg corridor, if the First Army had not been yoked to the British Second Army and the latter's weaknesses but had moved in tandem with the Third – these are probably more critical might-have-beens than the much debated ones of Field Marshal Montgomery's early-autumn frustrations."[3]

However, the Stolberg Gap remained the favoured axis and for much of October First Army operations were largely concerned with surrounding and then clearing Aachen. This offensive constituted a simple pincers movement, with XIX Corps leading off to the north of the fortified town and VII Corps to the south. In less than a week the northern pincer had pushed right through to the West Wall and was only three miles from the encirclement meeting-point at Würselen. By the evening of 9th October, VII Corps had a division firmly in control of its own objective near Würselen, but it was another seven days before

PART ONE

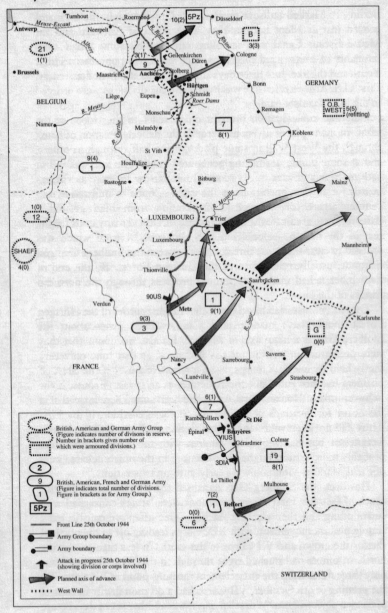

The Western Front: France and Germany 25th October 1944

XIX Corps actually closed the ring, and two days later tanks and infantry pressed forward into Aachen itself. The German garrison commander enjoined his men to fight to the last but on the 21st, having lost at least half of his surviving troops in the last five days, he decided that enough was enough and persuaded two American prisoners to lead out a white flag detail.

On the 25th the city of Würselen was a ruin, blasted apart by artillery and tactical support aircraft. To those Germans who had for many months been enduring heavy raids from the Allied four-engined bombers based in England and Italy, the sight would have been nothing new, but for Allied ground troops and observers it was an awesome novelty to see what modern firepower had done to the first major German city to be overrun. An officer on the staff of VII Corps wrote: "The city is as dead as a Roman ruin but unlike a ruin it has none of the grace of gradual decay ... Burst sewers, broken gas mains and dead animals have raised an almost overpowering smell in many parts of the city. The streets are paved with shattered glass; telephone, electric light and trolley cables are dangling and netted together everywhere, and in many places wrecked cars, trucks, armored vehicles and guns litter the streets."[4]

On the 25th, indeed, the whole of First Army's front was sinking into this same uneasy torpor born of exhaustion and desolation. All along the front both sides maintained a truculent truce, with forward units rarely called upon to mount full-scale attacks but constantly plagued by higher headquarters' insistence upon a constant level of patrol, mortar and artillery activity to 'keep the initiative' in no-man's-land. One of the rifle company commanders just inside Germany at this time, Captain Charles MacDonald, wrote: "The weather was abominable. It either rained or the skies were heavily overcast, and the ground became soggy with mud. The dirt roads became almost impassable. Day by day the weather grew colder and the daylight hours grew shorter."[5]

MacDonald's company headquarters was sited in a captured pill-box, sixteen feet square by eight feet high, in which were crammed eleven men: MacDonald himself, his executive officer, his first sergeant, the communications sergeant, the company runner/interpreter, the radio operator, three platoon and one weapons platoon runners, and the headquarters bazooka man. All the platoon commanders, of course, were out with their men. MacDonald felt nothing but sympathy for the riflemen forward of him. "I thought of the men in the forward platoons in their exposed foxholes with no protection from the elements except shelter halves stretched across their holes." As often as possible after dark MacDonald forced himself to leave the relative security of the pill-box and visit the platoon positions. But he soon found that "any idea I might have entertained that my visit might bolster the morale of these men was overshadowed by the effect . . . on my own morale. How they could smile and laugh and joke in the present conditions I could not see, but each man had a cheery word for me as I approached . . . Their courage and fortitude made me admiringly envious and brought a lump to my throat."[6]

Just as in the British lines, a regular system of rotation was operated in U.S. battalions, regiments and divisions and on any one day only a proportion of the men, perhaps no more than a third, were actually in the forward positions. MacDonald's division, like most others, had its own rest camp, and though he was not actually there on 25th October, it seems unlikely that his description of a visit a few days earlier is not equally applicable to the quota of officers and men who were passing through on my chosen day. The camp was established in a brick-built former Belgian army barracks and included a Red Cross Club "presided over by three attractive American girls in trim blue uniforms", a mess-hall, an auditorium-cum-gymnasium, where USO shows were held, and a movie theatre. "The director of the camp met our convoy and gave us a brief orientation. The men were assigned to bunks and told when they could use the showers, but there were few rules and regulations. The only roll-call formation would be held at ten o'clock in the morning . . . [on] our day of departure." The showers were a particular treat with "tiled individual compartments and steaming hot water . . . beyond the fondest dreams of any infantryman . . . The water was exhilarating . . . It had never occurred to me that I could derive so much pleasure from a bath. It was my first, other than from a helmet, for two and a half months." On his first day in the camp, Macdonald attended a movie and a USO show and the next morning went down to the village to buy wine and souvenirs. There they learnt about another shop that sold ice-cream. "We found it and a bakery nearby, and after standing in an olive-drab line, had apple-pie à la mode. We were like kids, excited with the slightest luxury."[7]

While MacDonald seems to have mixed easily with his other ranks, many enlisted men felt an enormous disparity between the way they and their officers were treated. A soldier in Seventh Army, also out of the line in late October, was deeply unimpressed with the "Red Cross Clubmobile [we had] come by with coffee and doughnuts. If the enlisted men tried to talk to the girls the officers would give them something equivalent to 'scram buddy" and take over like big operators. And so that's the way it was, a bunch of EMs standing around watching the conversation go back and forth between the RC girls and the officers. Like watching a tennis match."[8]

Such churlishness was, however, infinitely preferable to the relentlessly grim day-to-day existence all along First U.S. Army's front. In 28 Infantry Division, for example, there was a growing number of non-battle casualties. Many were trench-foot cases, also known as immersion foot, a term of First World War vintage and describing a condition very akin to frost-bite. It was the result of getting one's feet wet and not being able to dry them for hours, even days on end. The feet went numb, turned purple and in extreme cases the nerves died and gangrene set in. In such circumstances toes and sometimes the whole foot had to be amputated. The only effective way to keep trench-foot at bay was to wash and vigorously massage the feet twice daily, apply liberal amounts of talcum powder and, above all, change into dry socks. It was a cause of particular frustration. therefore, that at this time socks were one of several items of winter clothing in short supply.

Behind the divisional lines the dressing stations and field hospitals were full of such cases. "If they were lucky the medics caught the complaint in time and they would be put to bed in long lines of cots on which lay soldier after soldier, their feet sticking out from under the blankets, with a little ball of cotton wool separating each toe." One such rifleman spent fully ninety days in hospital in the autumn of 1944 after taking his boots off for the first time in two weeks. His feet appeared blue and frozen as soon as he removed his socks but he simply fell asleep while trying to rub them back to life. The next morning "my feet were like balloons, so red and swollen I couldn't put my shoes on. Some guys had big black blisters and a couple of guys had to get their feet cut off. The doc says you get that from not changing your socks when your feet are wet. Christ, what the hell you gonna do when you're living in a hole for two weeks and the water's up to here and Jerries are shooting at you so you can't go no place? Christ, I'm lucky I'm here at all."[9]

This G.I. was with VIII Corps in the Ardennes but things were no better in XIX Corps, which came under Ninth Army headquarters when the latter moved up from Luxembourg on 22nd October. Immediately afterwards the corps was reinforced by the newly-arrived 102 Infantry Division. The novices were appalled by the effect of the weather and one recalled afterwards that conditions were "terrible ... The constant rain and overcast skies seemed to prevent any evaporation. The earth was just plain mud. Our foxholes were virtual wells and the anti-tank ditches stagnant canals. No matter how careful we were our weapons became constantly clogged and jammed by the mud. It was combat under the worst possible conditions."[10]

None of these experiences can be compared with those of 9 Infantry Division, part of VII Corps, in the Hürtgen Forest. Despite the halt in operations in late September, both Hodges and General J. Lawton Collins, commanding VII Corps, were still keen that the threat to their flank be eliminated. It was also felt that by pushing through to Schmidt, on the upper Roer, an attacking force could secure the Hürtgen–Kleinhau road net, leading north-east to Duren, as well as expose the rear of defences in the secondary Monschau Gap to the south of the Forest. So 9 Infantry Division jumped off once again on 6th October, aiming to clear a whole series of valleys, village clearings and bare ridge tops through the south-east corner of the Forest, from Germeter to Schmidt.

General Louis Craig, the divisional commander, could spare only two regiments to attack, the third being needed to guard against threat to his rear from the Stolberg Gap. Of the two attacking regiments, only one could be spared for the Schmidt axis, as the other was required to swing due south to seize an important road junction which might allow the Germans to counter-attack from the Monschau Gap. Even with two-thirds of his force assigned to rear and flank protection, the single regiment carrying out the main drive still had an unprotected northern flank, and one that would extend the longer the advance went on. It was duly attacked on 12th October, and though the Germans were repulsed and the ground lost regained, and though the blocking force on the southern flank managed to seize the key road junction, the main attack was simply too weak to get more than one mile along the 2½-mile road to Schmidt. The battalion that made the best progress had to be recalled to help fight off the German counter-attack from the north, and by the 16th the whole division was ordered to go on to the defensive.

Still Hodges did not given up on the Hürtgen Forest. By mid-October planning for a November offensive was that much further along and the Forest was deemed a likely assembly point for major German counter-attacks. Unable to carry on its own attacks, 9 Infantry Division was replaced by 28 Infantry Division and the Forest passed under command of its parent V Corps. The actual relief of the front-line positions mainly took place on 25th October. Even as they approached the forest through sectors already taken, the men of 28

Division experienced a growing sense of foreboding. According to the U.S. official historian, Hürtgen Forest is "a seemingly impenetrable mass, a vast, undulating, blackish-green ocean stretching as far as the eye can see." For a while the baleful effect of this 50 square mile vista was offset by the villages and hamlets along the approaches and the brightly painted houses with pointed roofs and shuttered windows and gables adorned with wood and white plaster *Fachwerk*. Similar hamlets had been built within the Forest itself but these were now mostly just ruins. Entering the Forest in late October, "thick with dark green fir trees seventy-five to a hundred feet tall, so densely interwoven that they obscure the sky, a man might experience for the first time the stifling embrace of the kind of forests he had heard or read about in old German folk tales . . . He might be inclined to drop things behind him to mark his path . . . like Hansel and Gretel did with their bread crumbs."[11] For the thick foliage let in little sunlight, making the forest floor dark, damp and almost devoid of underbrush. Everywhere lay a dense carpet of evergreen needles that provided deadly concealment for mines and underground bunkers.

When the men approached 9 Division's lines they liked what they saw less and less. Trees were stripped and peppered by shell fragments and everywhere were craters made by artillery and mortar shells. The constant rain had long ago turned the narrow trails to mud and at the side of these and in the clearings were scattered helmets, empty ration cans, bloodied items of uniform, discarded rifles, splintered ammunition boxes and gas masks. And everywhere there were bodies. One soldier told how, when he reached his position, another rifleman "took me back in the woods to a blanket, pulled it back, and showed me a man laying there with a hole in his back, already mouldering. I thought of this guy's family with him still layin' there. That was my first contact with what combat was all about." A platoon sergeant recalled: "Graves Registration needed to remove the dead . . . many truckloads of them." Casualties had been horrendous, in all about 4,500 men from 9 Division to gain 3,000 yards of ground. By 12th October no battalion in either of the attacking regiments could field more than 300 men, and since 15th September 60 Regiment had actually experienced a 100 per cent turnover in combat troops. Another soldier noted that there were also many German bodies around and that the dead from both sides were often booby-trapped. He asked himself: "What the hell am I in? If this is what the jungle in the South Pacific is like, I don't want to be in the jungle."[12]

By the time night fell, however, the troops who took over the front-line positions might have wondered whether the jungle did not have some advantages. For they were soon wet and cold. One man remembered that the front-line foxholes were no place to spend the night. "They'd fill immediately with water. It was tough, tough going." Even in a sheltered emplacement "there was no place to get warm, so we burned these little Sterno heat blocks. We'd stand on 'em and we couldn't even feel 'em when they'd burn up through the soles of our feet."[13]

The incoming troops had dozens of questions for the outgoing veterans of 9 Division but many of the latter, dirty, unshaven and utterly exhausted, remained uncommunicative, reluctant even now to disturb memories that they knew would haunt them for the rest of their lives. Some were shattered, and according to one correspondent with Bradley's headquarters, several battalion officers "were as near gibbering idiots as men can get without being locked up for it . . . Most . . . did not talk; they just sat across the table or on the edge of your cot and looked at you very straight and unblinking with absolutely no expression whatever in their faces, which were neither tense nor relaxed but completely apathetic. They looked, unblinking, and I can see the colour of their eyes now."[14] This was what other soldiers had come to describe as the '1,000 yard stare', the fierce concentration on some distant, tiny piece of irrelevance because everything that was relevant to that man's most recent experience simply could not be assimilated.

A few officers and men were able to impart at least some of their experiences and to give a partial idea of what the incoming division should expect. This lore contained not one scintilla of encouragement. For one thing, they had little hard intelligence to impart, and while there were more than enough chilling descriptions of the strength of the German defences as a whole, there was little detail as to exactly where individual units, pill-boxes, bunkers and minefields were. That they were there in profusion was incontestable. Studded throughout the Forest were concrete pill-boxes and camouflaged log and earth bunkers, hidden machine-gun nests and miniature concrete pyramids, known as 'dragon's teeth', which served as anti-tank obstacles. Minefields extended in front of these defences, themselves skirted by double and treble rolls of booby-trapped barbed wire. Well-emplaced batteries protected all lines of approach. Each pill-box was in fact a self-contained network of outposts with a surprisingly large concrete 'keep' containing several rooms. Each pill-box had to be tackled separately and completely reduced before the attacker could move on to the next. These combats were made trebly difficult for the American infantry because the terrain and weather made it almost impossible to provide tracked gun support, the close nature of the fighting rendered conventional artillery support too hazardous, and the roof of the forest almost completely hid the fighting from supporting aircraft.

Nevertheless, 9 Division among others were well on the way to devising an effective set of tactics against pill-boxes. The first stage was to clear the outpost positions, employing mortars or allowing the attackers to fall back so that the artillery could saturate a position with a reasonable margin of safety. Once the perimeter defenders were killed or driven back into the pill-box proper, some five to eight G.I.s would inch their way forward and, as soon as the supporting fire lifted, charge in, tossing grenades, firing into embrasures and flinging or laying TNT charges to blow in the door. Sometimes a rocket from a bazooka was used instead, and on other occasions soldiers got close enough to drop phosphorus grenades down the ventilation shafts.

You did not have to be going up against a pill-box complex to confront the German Army at their most inventive. Just getting up the narrow roads and paths could be an appalling ordeal in itself, as was explained by an infantry sergeant: "The firebreaks were only wide enough to allow two jeeps to pass, and they were mined and interdicted by machine gun fire. In one break there was a teller mine every eight paces for three miles. In another there were more than 500 mines in the narrow break. One stretch of road held 300 teller mines, each one with a pull device in addition to the regular detonator . . . Hürtgen had its roads and they were blocked. The German did well by his abatis, his roadblocks cut from trees. Sometimes he felled 200 trees across a road, cutting them down so they interlocked as they fell. Then he mined and booby-trapped them. Finally he registered his artillery on them, and his mortars, and at the sound of men clearing them he opened fire."[15]

For the ordinary soldiers of 28 Division, most of the 'gen' they were given, such as it was, probably concerned personal survival. Various sources, not least the U.S. official history, have indicated the key points and from them it is possible to draw up an imaginary list of the points that might have been compiled by an alert staff officer:

1. In forested areas most shells do not burst on the ground but in the branches above. These tree bursts spray not only shrapnel but also wood chippings, snapped branches and twigs and pieces of bark which can be just as deadly.
2. Therefore foxholes are almost useless unless covered with logs and sod.

3. If you *are* caught in the open under shell-fire do not throw yourself on the ground where you present the biggest possible target for the tree-burst. Instead stand or crouch under a tree.

4. Never leave your foxhole at night. You might be caught by artillery fire. Moreover it will be pitch black. You will be unrecognisable to your buddies and might well be shot by them. Otherwise you will get lost. No-one will come looking for you.

5. At night, therefore, your foxhole will also be your latrine.

6. Aiming and firing at identified targets is impossible at night. Aiming at sounds offers the only hope. But do not use grenades as these may well hit a tree and bounce back into your foxhole.

7. Change socks and dry and vigorously rub your feet at every opportunity. Trench-foot cripples.

As the official historian wrote in his own summary of many of these points, newcomers "had to become accomplished woodsmen almost overnight, or they had no chance to survive . . . There was much to learn in the Hürtgen Forest."[16]

7

Assorted Manure Piles

THIRD U.S. ARMY BEFORE METZ

GENERAL George Patton, the commander of Third U.S. Army, had always been regarded as one of the army's more thrusting commanders. He saw his first action in North Africa, and in Sicily especially his rapid armoured advance around the north-western corner of the island seemed to compare most favourably with General Montgomery's hesitant progress to the east. Patton's headquarters, therefore, was not included in the original Normandy invasion force but was held back to take charge of the break-out force once the German reserves in northern France were fully committed. He was also to push westwards to open up the ports in Brittany for Allied shipping. Keeping Patton in England also gave extra credence to Allied efforts to persuade the Germans that a second invasion force was preparing to assault the Pas de Calais.

The breakthrough finally came in late July as First U.S. Army smashed its way out of the Cherbourg peninsula towards Coutances and Avranches. Third Army headquarters became operational on 1st August and Patton's armoured columns straight away roared into Brittany and swiftly established themselves along the south-western coast from Brest to to Saint-Nazaire. Two days later Patton was directed to turn his attention eastwards. He was now free to indulge his genius for orchestrating non-stop advance by mechanised and motorised formations and began a headlong, relentless pursuit of the retreating Germans, albeit now ill-equipped and demoralised. By 8th August he was in Le Mans and on the 16th at Chartres. On the 19th Third Army troops reached the Seine, at Mantes Granicourt, and two days later had a bridgehead over the river. This axis of advance reached Rheims on the 29th and Verdun, on the Meuse, on 1st

September. Patton's other main axis, to the south, did not reach the
Seine at Troyes until 27th August but it too had closed up to the Meuse
at Commercy by the beginning of September.

Patton was now within striking distance of one of his major strategic
objectives, Metz, long identified as the gateway into Lorraine and
thence to the Rhine. According to his G-2, Colonel Oscar Koch,
"Patton was planning to take that city as early as February 1944. Patton
had been studying a Michelin road map, from which he liked to
operate. As he said, the road map gave you 'railroads, road nets and
rivers, all that you need to know about terrain in general.' He put his
finger on Metz and said, 'I want all your planning directed here.' . . .
Colonel Koch said this was the only general directive for planning, and
that thereafter the staff was planning [thus] all the time."[1] Neither did
Patton's focus on Metz waver throughout his charge across France.
Even on 26th August he told the commander of XX Corps, still only at
Fontainebleau, to start thinking about Metz and how he was going to
take it. At a press conference shortly afterwards Patton asserted that the
Metz road net was the only useful one on the most direct route into
Germany and that advancing via Nancy to the south or Luxembourg to
the north would add at least 100 miles to his advance.

On 31st August, however, Patton's advance was abruptly halted by
a lack of petrol. The Allies had become the victims of their own success
and the remarkable advances by all their armies in northern France and
Belgium had completely outstripped the abilities of Com Z, the Allied
logistics organisation, to get adequate supplies to the front. The delay
infuriated Patton, but it does also seem to have given him pause for
thought, because when Third Army resumed its advance on 4th
September it was no longer zeroed in on Metz but deployed against the
Lorraine Gap as a whole with XII Corps in the south directed towards
the alternative approach to Germany via Nancy. The German front
was now beginning to congeal and the fighting was slow and hard. By
10th September this Corps had footholds over the Moselle and five
days later had affected a double envelopment of Nancy, trapping parts
of two German divisions within the pocket. From the 26th resistance in
the pocket began to slacken, especially after the failure of repeated
German armoured counter-attacks, and by the time the pocket was
cleared this American bridgehead across the Moselle had reached
20 miles east of Nancy, just short of the important road junction
at Château-Salins. There had also been considerable progress further
to the south where a new formation, XV Corps, had entered the
attack and pushed across the Moselle to take Lunéville and draw

up to the fringes of the Fôret de Parroy to the north-east.

None of this had prevented Patton from also hammering away at Metz. At first he tried to avoid frontal attacks and his initial effort, which jumped off on 6th September, involved attempting to envelop the city from north and south. All units soon closed up to the Moselle without too much difficulty but here the northern pincers halted, having clear sight of extremely strong German positions just across the river. To the south an attempt was made to seize a bridgehead at Dornot, but the small footholds gained were soon eliminated by the 11th. Another crossing was attempted at Arnaville and by the 17th, despite fierce fighting, this bridgehead was deemed secure.

The fortress of Metz, garrisoned by around 10,000 combat troops mainly from 462 Volksgrenadier Division, continued to mesmerise Patton and his local corps commander. A supposed diversionary frontal attack by part of 7 Armored Division was only reluctantly abandoned after a week's hard fighting. 90 Infantry Division was then moved down from Patton's northern flank and immediately commenced a series of attacks against some of the outlying Metz fortresses. An officer at the time spoke bitterly of being "thrown into suicidal attacks on the great forts of Metz . . . as we shivered in the fall rains, and slipped and slid in the ankle-deep mud."[2] Luckily these attacks were soon abandoned by the divisional commander and from 17th September the Metz front subsided into relative inactivity.

Senior commanders reacted to this differently. Patton claimed to have drawn the correct conclusions and to have realised that Nancy would now be the focal point "because it was very apparent that Nancy, and more particularly Château-Salins, was the doorway to the invasion of Germany." Moreover, as early as 20th September, "I definitely decided not to waste time capturing Metz, but to contain it with as few troops as possible and drive for the Rhine."[3] Eisenhower and the SHAEF planners also seem to have written off the Metz axis, but without the compensatory commitment to following a new one out of the Nancy bridgehead. For them, Patton's whole Lorraine offensive seemed to have foundered and on 23rd September, "one of the bad days of my military career", Patton was informed by Bradley that his offensive was being closed down to conserve supplies for 21st Army Group. Patton also lost his southernmost divisions, in XV Corps, to Seventh U.S. Army which had now linked up with Patton. It was felt that Seventh Army would find it easier to supply this corps as its supply lines came up from Marseille rather than from the overtaxed Channel ports.

So October turned out to be a bad month for Patton. For a man who firmly believed that "nobody ever successfully defended anything . . . [and] an army is defeated when it digs in", the enforced halt he had to endure right up to the 25th, and beyond, was purgatory. The fact that the halt was to allow further operations by Montgomery, a general he loathed, added more than a hint of red-hot pincers. Statistics produced by his staff served only to increase his sense of frustration. Before arriving in Nancy on 13th October, his forward headquarters had advanced to a new location on average once every three days. Moreover, in the freewheeling armoured combats of August and September Third Army tanks losses had been 303 and 200 respectively, and those of motor vehicles 1,092 in total. In October the figure for tanks was just 27 and for trucks and lorries 87. Good news for SHAEF accountants perhaps, but not for a commander totally committed to hard-hitting mobile operations. Worst of all were the figures for territory liberated by Third Army. Reckoned to total some 40,000 square miles in August and September, this was reduced to a miserable 125 square miles in October. Far from being the gateway to Germany, Lorraine had so far proved to be a strategic dead end for Patton. It is not surprising to find that in a letter to Secretary of War Henry Stimson, written at the end of October, he forgot all his earlier enthusiasm about the Metz or the Nancy–Château-Salins road nets and fumed: "I hope that in the final settlement of the war, you insist that the Germans retain Lorraine because I can imagine no greater burden than to be the owner of this nasty country where it rains every day and where the whole wealth of the people consists in assorted manure piles."[4]

By 18th October, Patton was wondering whether the war would pass him by completely, but then he received a glimmer of hope in a rather vague directive from Eisenhower which authorised a renewed offensive towards Saarbrücken and Frankfurt "when logistics permit", probably early the next month. Things looked up even more on the 21st when this was translated into detailed orders by Bradley's staff, who set a tentative date of 10th November. Patton seized upon this chance to get into the fray once more and next day, when Bradley visited his headquarters, he badgered him into putting the date forward to the 5th, though only if the weather was clear enough to permit full tactical air support.

Meanwhile, on 25th October Patton was too busy to spend much time brooding on past inactivity or speculating about future opportunities. In the morning he received General John Lee, in charge of

Com Z, at his headquarters and listened politely as he "expansively promised improvement in the supply situation."[5] The rest of the day was spent visiting the three regiments of 95 Infantry Division in the Arnaville bridgehead. During the evening, as Patton relaxed with his staff, perhaps drinking one or two of his favourite 'Armored Diesels', consisting of one-and-a-half ounces of bourbon, one tea-cup of crushèd ice, the juice of one lemon and sugar to taste, all heartily shaken, he may have felt able to look to the future with some optimism. Now he had a date for future operations and a fairly detailed plan. In essence this involved XII Corps establishing a bridgehead over the River Seille north of Château-Salins, after which the corps' two armoured divisions were to exploit, one to the east of Metz and the other towards the River Saar and in particular Saargemund. On Day Two XX Corps was to attack, with one infantry division to the south of Metz, another feinting just to the north of the city and a third attacking north of that, in the vicinity of Thionville. Here an armoured division was to pass through as quickly as possible to close the pincers east of Metz. Patton wrote: "It was hoped that the operation would eventuate in the capture of Metz and in the release of two armored divisions . . . for a rupture of the Siegfried Line and subsequent assault on the Rhine River."[6]

It seems unlikely that the troops in the line would have got much of a fillip from the prospect of renewed operations. For them the October lull had the distinct advantage of considerably reducing casualties. During August average weekly casualties were 1,300 killed and missing and 3,200 wounded, and in September 940 and 2,400 respectively. Up to the end of the third week in October, only 330 men were killed or declared missing in action each week and 940 wounded. The figures are still hardly negligible, but divided between the 51 infantry battalions in Third Army at this time, who suffered 90 per cent of the battle casualties, this was a weekly average of only 25 casualties per battalion. Clearly, static warfare had much to recommend it to the ordinary G.I. in the foxhole.

Patton was rarely content to let his line remain entirely inactive, even for a day, and throughout October he had tried to sustain a minimum tempo of operations, both to keep his troops on their toes as well as to create situations with the potential for local exploitation that would oblige SHAEF to authorise increased allocations of supplies. This Patton dubbed his 'rock soup' tactic, in the manner of a tramp who assures a housewife he is perfectly content with a soup of rocks and water that he is preparing but then gradually accumulates all the more conventional ingredients by asking for a little bit of seasoning, thickening, flavouring, garnish etc. In late September Patton had already identified his 'rock soup' objectives for the forthcoming month. As the sympathetic Bradley explained it to Eisenhower, these were "minor adjustments in . . . [Third Army's] present lines . . . localities in front of his present position which he assures me he can take from time to time as ammunition becomes available on his present allotment, and which will save many casualties in the long run."[7] These 'adjustments' involved attacks just north and south of Metz and towards Lunéville, much further to the south. In his memoirs Patton admitted what Bradley had been unable to tell Eisenhower directly, that although he and his corps commanders had "arranged a definite defensive front east of the Moselle, we also selected points along the front at which we would attack on the 'rock soup' plan, ostensibly for the purpose of securing a jump-off line – actually hoping for a breakthrough."[8]

On 25th October itself only one of Patton's corps was still engaged in this sort of operation. During early October, XX Corps had been involved in attacks on Fort Driant, an assignment which, according to one war correspondent, involved "attempting to assault a medieval fortress in a medieval manner", first against concrete walls and across a moat and later in a "weird subterranean guerrilla warfare" in the deep tunnels that led to the underground citadel at the heart of the fort's defences, tunnels partitioned off by a whole series of massive steel doors.[9] This assault, in which no more than a handful of attackers could ever assemble at any key point, was eventually called off and such gains as had been made were given up.

Attention then switched northward, beyond the defensive belt proper, to the town of Maizières-les-Metz on the main Metz–Thionville road. In fact, Maizières had already been attacked on 3rd October, when elements of 90 Infantry Division seized a prominent slag-heap overlooking the town from the north-west and four days later took much of the northern part of the town. The Germans promptly rushed in reinforcements from 19 Volksgrenadier Division and, "strengthened by these new arrivals, the garrison settled down to a long-drawn-out fight, house to house and block to block, punctuated by sorties and artillery duels. The houses in Maizières were strongly constructed, generally of stone, and strengthened by wire and sandbags so as to form a succession of miniature forts which had to be reduced one by one. The pivotal point in the Maizières *enceinte* was formed by the heavy masonry of the Hôtel de Ville, east of the railroad tracks [to Thionville], around which the fighting surged indecisively."[10]

Deploying just one battalion of infantry, the Americans pushed forward into the factory area to the west of the railroad and across the latter into the town centre. Mortars, artillery, demolition charges, flamethrowers, tank destroyers were all used, and on 11th October it was recommended that another battalion of infantry be brought in to finish the job. But it proved simply impossible to crowd two battalions into the narrow streets leading to the town hall and the Americans had to content themselves with simply replacing the weary 2nd Battalion of 357 Regiment with the relatively fresh 3rd Battalion. This turned out to be for the best as on the 13th, Army headquarters imposed drastic rationing of ammunition, actually freezing the allotment of anything above 3-inch calibre. Operations slowed right down and before long "the 3rd Battalion turned to using the town as a training ground, setting up attack problems in which a platoon, or a squad, took a house or two each day."[11]

A solution to one such problem was found when a 150mm self-propelled gun was run to within 150 yards of the town hall and twenty shells were slammed into its thick walls. The Germans, who had been quite happy to play along with the earlier low-key, pedagogic approach, now became extremely vindictive and poured in artillery of their own from the hills across the Moselle. By 25th October the Americans had still not covered the 150 yards to the town hall, although they were now only a street or so away and were confident of making the last dash the next day. The Germans, for their part, were ready for them. The perimeter of the town hall was ringed with barbed wire and minefields. Machine guns and mortars were emplaced in the town hall and all approach routes were covered by these weapons and by bazookas and anti-tank guns in adjacent strongpoints. The defenders of the town hall itself were also equipped with flamethrowers and had stacked piles of gasoline-soaked mattresses to block the hallways and corridors.

It should not be thought that just because only one American battalion was attacking on the 25th October the lot of all those others in Third Army was particularly easy. Five infantry divisions and a regimental group were holding the long stretch of front on either side of Thionville, 90 Infantry Division north-west and west of Metz, 95 Infantry Division in the Arnaville bridgehead, 80 and 35 Infantry Divisions along the River Seille, and 26 Infantry Division holding the southern perimeter of the Nancy salient. Just as in all Allied units, a regular rotation of units between front and reserve positions was in operation and on any given day perhaps no more than a third of these divisions' riflemen were actually in front-line slit-trenches and emplacements. But for them the conditions were as abysmal as anywhere else along the Allied front. In Lorraine as in the Low Countries, October 1944 was one of the wettest on record, with more than double the average rainfall for this time of year. One of Patton's staff officers complained: "Pools of water lay everywhere, some of them like good-sized lakes, and the mud was almost unbelievable. It was deep, slimy and slippery. Leather and clothing mildewed and got musty, metal began to rust. Entirely aside from fighting the enemy there was a constant battle to keep equipment clean and usable, and to keep oneself as dry as possible. It was a thoroughly miserable time for everybody."[12]

Men found some relief from the weather when the quartermasters contrived to get the first issues of winter clothing pushed through during October. By the end of the month most combat troops had been issued with at least three blankets and a heavy greatcoat. But they were still short of the most pressing requirement, protection against the teeming rain. Waterproof groundsheets and raincoats were especially elusive, the former perhaps the crucial item in making life in a flooded slit-trench remotely bearable. Also in short supply were "rubber overshoes, a critical item as the Lorraine plains turned to mire in the constant fall downpour". So scarce were they that "they could be issued only on the basis of one pair for every four enlisted men."[13] No wonder that by the end of the month, General Patton considered the weather "to be the most important [enemy], because at that moment our sick rate for the first time equalled our battle casualty rate."[14]

At the same time, most of the soldiers were given intermittent opportunities to relax behind the lines as they were rotated into reserve and rest positions. Even a division like 90 Infantry, with one of its battalions locked in fierce combat in Maizières-les-Metz, was able to take whole battalions out of the line and send them "to rest camps in the rear. For the first time since the breakout from Normandy, the men's personal comfort supplies arrived together with such items as sports equipment. There was mail from home and the chance to write letters in reply."[15] Hot baths, clean dry clothing, and adequate hot meals were provided. One of the most popular shows was given by Marlene Dietrich who spent more than nine weeks in the Third Army sector, by far the longest tour by a major artist.

Other divisions came out of the line as a whole. Prior to being relieved on 21st October, 5 Infantry Division had spent 44 days continuously in the front line. When 4 Armoured Division pulled out on the 12th, it had endured a crippling 87 days in combat. XII Corps had a fully-fledged rest centre at Nancy but XX Corps did not feel secure enough to permit such a luxury. Its resting units had to make the most of billets in some ruined village behind the lines where they could enjoy "a hot shower, coffee and doughnuts served by a Red Cross 'Clubmobile', and the chance to see a movie or a traveling 'jeep show', manned by two or three soldier-performers." In billets troops also had a chance to eat fresh bread produced in the field bakeries and to eat some of the vast quantity of German beef captured at Rheims and Briey. Roasted green coffee replaced the bitter soluble substitute found in the field rations. They also got to hear radio programmes broadcast by the Armed Services network, or to pick up the very popular swing sessions broadcast from Berlin. Reading matter was also plentiful, from the daily Army newspaper *Stars and Stripes* and the weekly magazine, with pin-up, *Yanks*, to the specially produced Armed Services Editions, cheap paperbacks of wholesome popular fiction of the day. Probably nothing boosted morale as much as mail from home and cigarettes. "Early in October, when the Third Army front began to stabilise, a special daily train loaded with 400 tons of mail was run to the army areas with the letters and packages that had accumulated on the beaches during the period of mobility."[16]

What a pity that this generally creditable effort to cater for the troops' basic comforts should have been so seriously compromised by corrupt practices in the rear. At first, most people knew only that there was an acute shortage of cigarettes and loose tobacco, especially at the front in late October, and senior commanders were as exercised about it as the troops. Only later was the full scandal brought to light when it was discovered, in Eisenhower's words, that the "fabulous prices offered for food and cigarettes" on the black market had proved too much for some Com Z personnel. "Practically an entire unit had organised itself into an efficient gang of racketeers and was selling these articles in truck- and car-load lots. Even so, the blackness of the crime consisted more in the robbery of the front lines than it did in the value of the thefts."[17]

8

Everything is Hope

SEVENTH U.S. ARMY IN THE VOSGES

IN AUGUST 1944, Seventh U.S. Army and a French force known as Army 'B' had landed in the south of France to pin down German divisions stationed there and prevent them withdrawing north to buttress the defences of the Reich or to threaten Eisenhower's exposed southern flank. Most of the Allied divisions initially involved came from the Italian theatre though these were later joined by several other newly raised French divisions or American ones just arrived in Europe. Three such joined Seventh U.S. Army, which by late October comprised five infantry divisions and one armoured, the latter a French formation which had taken part in the liberation of Paris. Its role was not a particularly glamorous one. Together with Army 'B', now renamed First French Army, it formed part of General Jacob Devers' 6th Army Group, whose main task was to provide flank protection for the 'hard hitters' of 12th Army Group to the north, especially General Patton.

Both of Devers' armies had their allotted axes along well-trodden military routes into Germany, but no one at Eisenhower's headquarters expected them to make any significant contribution to the main offensive against the German Army in the West. These axes were positioned through the Saverne and Belfort Gaps and from there to Mulhouse, Colmar, and Strasbourg, with a possible crossing of the Rhine at Rastatt, some thirty miles north of Strasbourg. The routes largely defined themselves, as the only practical ones through the formidable Vosges mountains, but by October progress along them had been much better than expected. Seventh U.S. Army, under General Alexander Patch, was directed towards the more northerly Saverne Gap and without much difficulty managed to cross the Moselle, whose middle reaches had been a stubborn barrier to Patton's Third U.S. Army. According to the official American historians, between 20th and 25th September, the Germans were "summarily ejected from good defensive terrain almost without a fight. What might have been a major combat operation . . . turned out to be an almost routine affair" for General Lucien Truscott's VI Corps.[1]

Unlike Patton's two southerly corps, Truscott's VI Corps was not immediately pinned down in its bridgehead and was able to maintain a slow steady advance with all its three divisions. On 1st October the drive was renewed and the veterans of Italy gradually forced their way forward against well-defended strongpoints and frequent counter-attacks. By the 12th all three divisions had been just about fought to a standstill. However, aware that the enemy must be feeling even more overstretched, Truscott determined not to give up the initiative. He was especially keen to create some kind of operational reserve and persuaded General Lattre de Tassigny, the commander of First French Army, to take over part of his southern flank, manned by 3 U.S. Infantry Division, to free the latter to exploit renewed advances by his other two divisions. The plan was for 3 Division to pass through 45 Division's centre and right flank on or around 23rd October as the spearhead of a final drive to St Dié. By then, it was hoped, 45 and 36 Divisions, having jumped off on 14th October, would have seized the towns of Brouvelieures and Bruyères, important road and rail centres about 12 miles south-east of St Dié.

The relief of 3 U.S. Infantry Division by 3 Algerian Infantry Division, although betraying a "lack of co-ordination between the two Allied forces [that] did not augur well for the future", was finally completed by 17th October.[2] In fact only two of 3 Division's regiments moved to the new positions, the other remaining behind near Le Tholy, opposite the Schlucht Pass, to give the impression that this was still their axis of advance. The main part of the division moved under strict radio silence while those staying behind generated radio traffic for a whole division. Troops from neighbouring 36 Division were sent out on patrol to 'lose' helmets and other gear with 3 Division identification markings. Conversely, the advance elements of 7 and 15 Regiments wore 45 Division patches on their uniforms so as not to give away their presence to German patrols. All in all, at a time when high Allied hopes had given way to grinding, constricted attacks through polders, dank forests and shattered streets, Truscott's VI Corps was doing its best to attack in strength and according to such classic military precepts as deception, manoeuvre and surprise, and the timely commitment of reserves. By late October the Allied armies in North-West Europe could be compared to a millipede shuffling sideways up to its opponent but kicking out with very few of its legs. Compared to what was happening along most of the bug's body, the activity in VI Corps' segment was a positive soft-shoe shuffle.

For the men of 45 Division, however, there was precious little dancing during the drive to Brouvelieures, a slow and tedious advance on a narrow frontage against 16 Volksgrenadier Division. The town lay in the valley of the River Mortagne and its steep western slopes were honey-combed with well-prepared German positions. Only on the 21st, after a week's bitter fighting, did German resistance in the area begin to crumble, with Brouvelieures itself falling just after dark. On the 22nd the division mopped up on either side of the town, west of the Mortagne, but an attempt to seize a bridgehead across it was repulsed.

However, two regiments from 36 Division had made better progress. By 18th October they were entering the outskirts of Bruyères from south and north, and on the following day one took over the chore of house-to-house clearance while the other secured the heights to the east and pushed on towards St Dié. The historian of 442 Regiment has given a picture of Bruyères after the Germans had been driven out. This sort of devastation had been wrought in towns and villages throughout France by late October. "During the month before the liberation of Bruyères, twenty-one townspeople had died, and more than five hundred, over ten per cent of the town's population, had been seriously wounded. According to American records 35,000 rounds of artillery had been fired at the town, and about 15,000 had been direct hits inside the town. Of 494 houses, 342 had sustained thirty per cent damage and 23 had burnt down completely."[3] Many of the townspeople made their living logging in the local forests but the trees were now so splintered or so riddled with shell fragments as to be unusable.

Truscott's original plan for the renewed advance on St Dié, now dubbed Operation DOGFACE, had called for 36 Division to hold in the Bruyères area until 45 Division was across the Mortagne. In the event some of his battalions pressed on regardless and, though a sizable gap was developing between the two divisions, Truscott was loathe to slow the momentum of the advance. He therefore asked the commander of 3 Division, General John O'Daniel, whether he would be able to funnel his men in behind 36 Division rather then 45 Division and, most important, whether this could be done from 20th October instead of from the 22nd. Instead of taking them over from 45 Division as originally envisioned O'Daniel would have to prepare his own way for the final push on St Dié. He cabled Truscott that at least one of his regiments could move immediately and by the 21st it was indeed pushing up the Brouvelieures–St Dié road (N.420).

This sudden influx of reinforcements greatly troubled the Germans, although it was not until the 23rd that General Friedrich Wiese's Nineteenth Army headquarters ascertained which troops these were. In the next days both American divisions made progress, with one of O'Daniel's regiments clearing Les Rouges Eaux, a hamlet one-third of the way along N.420, on the 25th. On that same day a second regiment ran into a stubborn road block just to the north of Les Rouges Eaux but O'Daniel's remaining regiment, the last to redeploy from the southern flank, now arrived on the scene and was fed in to the east of this strongpoint, completely outflanking it. In the meantime, to O'Daniel's rear, General William Eagles' 45 Division had finally secured crossings over the River Mortagne, and on the 25th was advancing on a revised north-easterly axis through the Rambervillers Forest to effect a more northerly swing towards the River Meurthe than had been originally planned. In the afternoon, however, all units ran into stiffening enemy resistance and were pinned down through the night by harassing mortar and artillery fire. The Americans passed the word to expect a counter-attack at first light but, in fact, the Germans, part of 21 Panzer Division, were only the rearguard for an organised withdrawal in this sector.

At the southern end of Truscott's front General John Dahlquist's 36 Division was also running into some difficulties on the 25th. Fighting its way through yet another thick forest, the Dominiale de Champ, Dahlquist was forced to focus most of his attention on a single battalion, 1/141 Regiment, cut off by the Germans near Hill 645 on the 24th and its command post overrun. Soon to become famous as 'The Lost Battalion', this unit comprised 241 men, whose only contact with the rest of the regiment was the radio of a forward artillery observer. A rescue attempt by the regiment's other two battalions made only limited headway. During the afternoon, the isolated group sent out a 36-man combat patrol to scout for a possible breakout route but they were ambushed, only five making it back to the perimeter. One did get through to American lines but only after losing his way in the woods for five days. According to a sergeant who had remained in the perimeter: "When we realised we were cut off, we dug a circle at the top of the ridge. I had two heavy, water-cooled machine guns with us at this time, and about nine or ten men to handle them. I put one gun on the right front with about half my men, and the other gun to the left. We cut down small trees to cover our holes and then piled as much dirt on top as we could. We were real low on supplies, so we pooled all of our food."[4]

Despite these setbacks, VI Corps' progress to 25th October had clearly been more impressive than anything achieved on any other American front in this theatre. This should not be taken to mean that the sector was noticeably more permeable than elsewhere. Indeed, the idea of an increased fluidity of operations in the Vosges is very much a relative concept and that sector, too, experienced a disappointing overall slow-down during October. Thus in August and September Seventh Army had advanced a little over 400 miles from their Riviera beachheads but in the next month managed to push the front less than 15 miles further forward. For in the Vosges, as in Holland and the Hürtgen Forest, the Germans were able to utilise the terrain to marshal their defensive expertise and force the Americans to fight for every inch of ground. Indeed, one explanation for such progress as the Seventh Army made in October was that the Germans were fairly happy to slowly withdraw, knowing that they had not yet reached their main line of defence. Ground gained by the Americans in October was actually only part of the German outpost line and behind it lay three more defensive lines: one behind the River Meurthe, which connected with the defences of the Belfort Gap; one along the crests of the Vosges; and lastly the West Wall itself, running along the frontier from the River Saar to Karlsruhe and thence south along the Rhine to the Swiss border. Throughout October, therefore, the German high command was grudgingly prepared to permit phased withdrawals, as on the night of 25th/26th in front of 45 Division, knowing that these were to other at least partially prepared positions.

Even so, whatever defensive position was being contested, including the outpost lines, the Germans invariably made life hard for the attackers. One of their great advantages were the thick forests that blanketed the Vosges foothills. Though perhaps not quite as grim as the Hürtgen Forest, they still presented a forbidding obstacle for advancing infantry and virtually precluded the use of tanks and self-propelled guns. As an entry in the log of the German Nineteenth Army put it: "The mountainous forests have an almost jungle-like character which swallows men . . . Visibility is often no more than 50 metres." General Truscott also emphasised the problems of fighting in the Vosges where the "rugged foothills covered with dense forests made operations most arduous. Thick woods required greater concentrations of troops to wipe out the enemy, while the Corps was extended on such a wide front that any concentration was difficult." Climate played its part, too, and between the Moselle and St Dié, as the official history explained, the ground got gradually higher as well as more densely forested as the "prevailing winds from the north and west . . . [brought] moisture-laden clouds that fed the dense forests and almost tropical vegetation."[5]

An information bulletin provided by 36 Division headquarters emphasised the difficulties of finding one's way through such dense vegetation, despite the apparent profusion of access points into even the more heavily wooded areas: "In the Vosges mountains there are a great many paths which in the heavily wooded terrain are extremely deceptive . . . Orientation by compass is vital throughout the Vosges, where paths winding through wooded areas cause even people who know the sector to lose their way."[6] The thick forests also made resupply very difficult and Truscott soon decided that mule trains, regularly used in the fighting in the Italian mountains, would be ideal to carry supplies along the narrow forest trails. A shipment of some 300 mules and their handlers was still awaited on 25th October.

One of the division's regiments drew up its own report on the Vosges forests and it, too, stressed the tropical nature of the vegetation as well as the difficulty in keeping one's bearings and accurately plotting the location of one's own and enemy units. "The fighting during the month of October was comparable to jungle-fighting . . . All commanders must report actual conditions carefully, avoiding all possibilities of errors in locations of units . . . Forest areas must be mapped thoroughly. Small well-dug-in enemy detachments, if not mopped up, will harass supply columns and present difficult problems of liquidation because of our inability to use our supporting weapons within our lines . . . Sometimes the enemy deliberately lets us get as close as seventy-five to a hundred yards to him before disclosing his presence with fire, and on occasion lets the leading elements pass by. This reduces the fight to a small arms fight with the enemy enjoying the advantage of good cover."[7]

If the Germans did not open fire it was often possible to miss their dug-outs completely unless one literally stepped into them. They were skilfully concealed with brush and painstakingly camouflaged with branches, twigs and pine-needles. The overall impression of the Vosges fighting, in fact, was of attacking a particularly intractable maze, but one inhabited by a malevolent breed of troll. Mines were scattered over all possible approaches which were also blocked by thick tangles of felled trees and barbed-wire. Such obstructions were always booby-trapped and covered by machine guns, as well as being pre-plotted for covering fire from mortars and artillery.

Troops advancing over more open terrain, usually around one of the towns or villages, were scarcely better off. The houses were characteristically stout Alsatian structures of stone and masonry, and it took only a few hours to transform one into a fully fledged pill-box. The only troops involved in serious house-to-house fighting on the 25th were the men of 179 Regiment, part of 45 Division, attacking the villages of Bru and Jeanménil, to the east and south-east of Rambervillers, on VI Corps' extreme left flank. One account tells of "most of October spent in a stationary slugfest with the 21st *Panzergrenadiers* around the twin road junction . . . villages." Another source gives a good summary of the enemy tactics employed there: "German doctrine contended that villages . . . dominated road networks, provided cover and concealment, and were natural strongholds. If defended stubbornly, small towns became breakwaters that could slow the advance of numerically superior attackers. Commanders were never to locate the M[ain] L[ine of] R[esistance] at the village's edge. Instead . . . inside a village the MLR ran through areas best suited to stop armored attacks, and German infantry platoons fought using the defensive techniques of city combat. Streets were blocked with hasty obstacles, barricades and barbed wire, and the largest buildings became strongholds."[8] In both Bru and Jeanménil, on the 25th, the MLRs held fast and the counter-attacks continued to be launched with a depressing élan.

The Americans' other great enemy, of course, was the October rain, which fell in Alsace with just the same teeming intensity as in Lorraine or Holland. In every part of the line it made day-to-day living utterly miserable. A private with the newly-arrived 44 Infantry Division soon became aware of the sheer squalor of even the 'quiet' sectors. After only a couple of days, Private William Tsuchida was "caked with mud from head to toe and my clothes are ready to be peeled off me. My underclothes are oily black and I sure would like to change."[9] Even behind the lines the rain slowly eroded morale and efficiency. A nurse with an American field hospital worked her experiences into a novel and at one stage gave a description of conditions just outside Lunéville: "Rain! Rain! October stretched drearily toward winter and each sodden day left summer further behind the slanting curtain of rain. The already dismal land was churned to a great brown waste of mud through which the ambulances floundered and stuck, the litter bearers stumbled and often fell. The eternal muck seeped into open wounds and festered in dead flesh, soaked into boots and clothing and caked the faces of the living, filled the mouths of the dead. Mud and rain! A great soggy wasteland of mud and rain where dead faces turned to oozing masks and sodden figures sank slowly in the muck. Corpses of men and horses in stinking grey castings of mud were scattered lumpishly in ditches and rubble-filled streets. And still it rained!"[10]

Tsuchida's own book, comprising letters to his parents, recalls how just the proximity of the enemy was a nerve-wracking experience, especially to a unit newly arrived at the front. Whilst his first letters make much of the fact that there are "no PXs out here so we are starved for candy, nuts and other good eats" and request "a good map of France with all the names of little towns on it", he is soon almost wholly wrapped up in the day-on-day ordeal of the ordinary rifleman. Tsuchida was in fact the medic in his rifle platoon, and though not officially entitled to wear the Combat Infantryman's Badge, he was intimately involved in their sufferings. Two letters he wrote on 23rd and 28th October provide extracts which I have elided together to give a picture of his state of mind throughout his first extended period in the line, from 22nd October to 2nd November.

What a mess this whole business is. My mind is one confused conglomeration of incidents, the basic fears of night, and the waiting for daylight. The rest of it I would just as soon forget because it is so rotten. I hope everybody with the soft war jobs realises the horrible days and nights the line company men have to spend out here. It's really awful that these young kids have to go through this sort of thing . . . And the other thing that gets me down is the B[ull] S[hit] artists back at the main aid station who don't have to risk their necks every time they go out, yet they brag the most . . . I got your V-mail letters . . . today. Let me tell you it is good to read something that has no connection with the confusion here. I get in such a daze sometimes that I force myself to read something when I can, like a magazine or an old letter. What it amounts to is you wonder whether you should eat now or later and hope you have a dry place to sleep tonight and hope that casualties will slow down. Everything is hope, hope.[11]

As for Tsuchida's concluding wish, the unwelcome fact was that, despite the relatively good progress made by VI Corps in October, casualties had not slowed down at all. By the end of the month 36 Division's rifle companies had an average complement of 121 officers and men instead of the authorised 193. Equally worrying were the disciplinary problems that were affecting all VI Corps units. Desertions among line infantry companies in combat were running at 50 to 60 cases per division in October, while stragglers were almost commonplace. In part, according to the official history, "these difficulties were a product of the heavy officer and NCO casualties sustained ... and the resulting decline in leadership", but the commander of 36 Infantry Division, writing in his diary in late October, provided a somewhat more compassionate assessment of the enormous pressures on all officers and men, veterans or novices: "It astounds me how the men are able to stand the physical and mental strain under which they are constantly living. It is almost beyond comprehension that the human can stand so much. I had a battalion commander crack the other day, and it was really pitiful."[12] For such men hope had been stretched just too far.

9

Troopships and Repple-Depples

BY THE END of October 1944 American battle casualties in North-West Europe totalled 56,260 killed in action, died of wounds and missing, and 133,100 wounded. This amounted to almost 190,000 battle casualties out of an overall strength in this theatre of 2,204,000 men. In fact, the vast majority of these casualties were inflicted on the 250 Allied infantry battalions present at that time, with an aggregate strength of approximately 214,000 men. Even when taking account of the influx of replacements these figures represent a grim casualty rate, with 17 per cent of all those riflemen serving to date killed and a prodigious 56 per cent killed, missing or wounded. Clearly, then, new blood was of the essence.

On the 25th the U.S. Army had 8 armoured divisions, 2 airborne divisions and 21 infantry divisions attached to the active armies at the front. There was also one infantry division tied down in the siege of Lorient, on the Atlantic coast, and another whose three regiments had been split between three front-line divisions. On top of this there were also a considerable number of troops en route to the front, the reinforcements and replacements to compensate for the ceaseless haemorrhage of casualties.

Most of the reinforcements consisted of two infantry divisions which had just landed at Marseille and were en route for the Seventh U.S. Army in the Vosges; two armoured, one airborne and one infantry division in England, waiting to be sent to the northern part of the American front; and another infantry division in the process of landing in England. There was also one other armoured division still at sea, having left New York on 14th October. On board was Pfc. Bruce Zorns, a soldier with 62 Armored Infantry Battalion, who has left a

99

detailed description of his crossing of the Atlantic, a phase of men's military careers that figures in very few memoirs. The whole division sailed as part of one enormous convoy and its escort carriers and large gunships, destroyers and minesweepers seemed to Zorns as though they must represent "practically every piece of weaponry the Navy owned. It was an awesome sight." He himself sailed in USS *Lejeune*, a liner captured from the Germans and converted into a Navy troopship. According to Zorns she had once plied the luxury trade but "was anything but luxurious now. Our compartment was in the hold and much too small for the large number of troops packed into it. Bunks were stacked four high in rows two feet apart. The odour was horrendous. Most of the troops began puking as soon as the ship started moving. All the four P's of troop-transport odors were prevalent – piss, puke, poop and perspiration. Most of the troops were doing all four at the same time – all the time."

As it happened, Zorns' crossing was more relaxed than some because his battalion had held a lottery to determine which companies would be spared duties during the voyage and his was one of the lucky ones. "All we had to do was eat, read, sleep, and write." The days were indistinguishable one from the other and followed the same routine of rising at 06.30 followed by breakfast at 07.15. Then out on deck to laze about for a while before returning below to read. There was no lunch but at 13.00 there was usually a band concert on deck, with the emphasis more on Tommy Dorsey and Glenn Miller than on Sousa. Back below at 15.00 and more reading until 16.30 when he joined the 'chow line', ate and went on deck again. Then "into the stinking hold" for a shower and a shave after which, at about 19.30, he would write his daily letter to his wife. "We have lights out at 21.00 and try to make it through the night to 06.30, so we can start all over again."

The predictability of the routine was matched by the monotony of most of its constituent parts. Even the daily shower was not quite the highlight one might have thought. Like everything else, it required a long period of standing in line, "a long line of naked men, each carrying a towel and a bar of brown soap. None was too eager to climb into the shower and turn on the cold salty sea water. The brown soap was supposed to lather in this water. I could never get my bar to. After every shower . . . I really felt as if I needed a bath." Meals were one hundred per cent predictable, the menu being the same for breakfast and dinner every day of the week. The only things served were "navy beans, cornbread and hot, black coffee – that's all. I ate thirty-two of these meals and survived."

Though Zorns' breakfast was served at a reasonably civilised hour, dinner came ridiculously early. This was because every compartment of the ship ate at its own pre-ordained time with serving going on continuously twenty-four hours a day. "When my compartment's time came, we fell into the sea serpentine line at least one hour before serving time – it took this long to inch our way to the hatch of the standing/dining area. Here a sailor punched a number off our green meal tickets which had been issued when we boarded." After a ludicrously petty ritual in which the Navy server endeavoured to get the food anywhere but in the proffered mess kit, "I moved out of the chow line and into the standing/dining area, where I hoped to find a shelf to hold my cup and plates while I ate." No table cloth, no serviettes – in fact, not even a table and chairs. Unless you were an officer . . .

One of Zorns' most grating memories of the trip was that of knowing what the officers were eating. They got three meals a day and had them served at tables with crisp white linen and china crockery, by deferential mess boys. He had once entered the ship's galley by mistake and seen arrayed baked hams, turkeys, candied yams, cornbread dressing, giblet gravy, mashed potatoes and green beans, not to mention chocolate cakes, pumpkin pies and cream pies. An officer soon spotted him and curtly told him to "get your ass out of here". This he did, "but I took a picture, etched deep in my mind, of the distinction between men and officers. The gap was too wide. It needed to be narrowed."[1]

Another soldier who crossed the Atlantic in October echoed this sentiment in one of his letters home. His comments also make it clear that Zorns' description of wiling his time away on deck presents a very benign version of the actual situation. According to Pfc. Keith Winston: "From what I can see the small percentage of officers on board have as much room as the troops combined. I have not seen one solitary chair where an enlisted man can sit down to write a letter . . . It has aroused a resentful feeling, not only within me, but in everyone around me . . . On this deck where we're packed like sardines, and this is no idle simile, I have to stand to write to you . . . Activity on deck consists of roving from place to place, looking for a place to sit . . . reading and card and dice games . . . Don't have the slightest desire to get into a game, but watching them is one means of passing the hours."[2]

Yet even these men, ferried from one continent to another like so many battery hens, had the presence of a few new friends around them, kindred spirits with whom they had struck up some kind of relationship during training and who would doubtless be their buddies in the line. The other main source of new blood at the front, the infantry replacements, often did not have even this solace. These men arrived from the United States unassigned to a particular unit and on landing went straight to one of the replacement depots, or 'repple depples' as most G.I.s called them, where they mixed with other unattached infantry or with men reassigned as riflemen from some rear echelon outfit. On any given day, thousands of such men wandered listlessly around their camps waiting to be sent forward, almost certainly with a bunch of men they had never even spoken to, only to be split up once again between the platoons of a battalion of yet more strangers.

All historians now agree that this system showed the U.S. Army at its worst and seriously disrupted the cohesion of units at the front, undermining the vital bonds of front-line comradeship and vitiating mutual confidence and tactical proficiency. One writer has castigated "a system that possessed a strong inherent tendency to turn men into nervous wrecks", and a staff memorandum of the time showed just how this was done. Its author trenchantly described replacements arriving in "divisional and regimental areas bewildered and disheartened . . . Field train bivouacs were usually within the sound of guns, and the replacements were acutely and nervously aware that their entry into combat was imminent." Particularly vulnerable were the reassigned riflemen who "frequently did not know how to look after themselves."[3] Neither was morale boosted by the wounded veterans who, instead of being sent back to their old units and such of their buddies as still survived, were fed back into the replacement system. An officer replacement remembered how, after listening to several platoon sergeants recount "their hair-raising experiences", exaggerated or not, "I expected confidently that I would be blown to bits within fifteen minutes after my arrival at the front."[4]

As usual, the most telling descriptions of the soulless 'repple depples' are those by the men who actually passed through them. Even the officers working there found it a deeply depressing assignment. One such at Third Army's main depot recalled: "When a man goes to a replacement depot he doesn't belong to a unit . . . that man is lost. He's being channelled like a piece of cannon fodder into some unit that has lost a dozen men. And he's going right into battle. You could tell the guys who were scared shitless and wouldn't make it."[5] Novelists gave perhaps the most incisive descriptions of all. Irwin Shaw evoked the autumnal mud of a Third Army depot near Paris, where thousands of men "milled slowly about in a restrained quiet manner that was very different . . . from the usual boisterous and loudly complaining habits of any other American soldiers he had ever seen. This camp . . . [he] thought, standing at the entrance to the tent in which he was quartered, peering out into the dull drizzle, and the men in the wet raincoats moving aimlessly and restlessly about on the long, thick streets, is not really human. The only thing it can be compared to is the stockyards at Chicago, with the beasts caught in the corrals, uneasily aware that doom is near, sniffing the scent of the waiting slaughter-house."[6] Another infantryman turned novelist, Richard Granat, also stressed the sense of impending doom but eschewed merely bovine imagery in favour of stressing the soldiers' vibrant contempt for military routine and unnecessary 'chicken shit':

There was nothing much to do but wait around for the call to the line. The most organised activity was a desultory calisthenics period in the morning, which not even the beefer in charge took seriously. The depot commander cautioned them daily about walking in fields which were probably mined, talking with Frenchmen who were probably collaborators, being absent when the next list came down, which would probably include their names. These roll calls might come at any hour, day or night, and within minutes the chosen ones were packed into trucks and gone forever. The punishment for missing a roll call was not clear – probably it was being placed on the next one.[7]

10

Soldiers of the State

FIRST FRENCH ARMY IN THE VOSGES

IF Seventh U.S. Army's was the most active American front in late October 1944, that of her sister formation within 6th Army Group, General Jean de Lattre de Tassigny's First French Army, was probably the most static. Though to be fair, this was only a recent development. Originally destined only to liberate the ports of Marseille and Toulon and then to cover General Patch's Alpine flank, de Lattre had persuaded his superiors to allow him to support the main American advance up the Rhône valley to Lyon. The situation was still not entirely satisfactory. For some weeks the five French divisions were split on either side of the Americans, with one scattered in the foothills of the Alps to provide flank protection along the Franco–Italian frontier. Nevertheless, other French units did record impressive progress beyond Lyon, through Chalon-sur-Saône to Langres, and on 12th September their patrols linked up with those of Patton's Third U.S. Army. Two days later de Lattre was given permission to unite his two divergent corps and concentrate his whole force on the eastern flank of Devers' army group.

De Lattre spent the rest of the month redeploying his divisions along their new axis towards the Belfort Gap, with the intention of outflanking its heaviest frontal defences from the north, directing his main forces against German positions between just south of Colmar and Le Thillot on the road to Mulhouse. This offensive opened on 4th October but began to stall almost from the outset. The French were jumping off from American bridgeheads across the Moselle which they found much smaller than expected. It took considerable effort just to secure the high ground overlooking the eastern bank. When finally this was taken, troops from 3 Algerian Division had to battle their way through the ubiquitous Vosges forests at Longegoutte and Gehan. After intensive fighting these were largely cleared towards the end of the month but the road to Le Thillot remained barred. Better progress was made to the north but even here the Algerians' advance was "continually hampered by foul weather and increasing supply problems. The inability of . . . II Corps to secure the road hub at Le Thillot forced the French to employ long circuitous supply routes [almost ten miles further north]. Driving across or along one forested height after another, the French gained control of high muddy mountain trails, but German artillery, mortar and anti-tank fire made it impossible for them to use the main paved roads through the valleys."[1]

The last attack took place on 16th October, when a reserve regiment from I Corps' Moroccan infantry division was committed. By the 19th the regiment had suffered over 700 casualties in a fruitless attempt to break through to the north, but by then de Lattre had already decided to close the offensive down. At a press conference about this time, the French commander gave a terse account of the problems faced by II Corps: "North-west of Belfort, the battle is hard because it is being fought in the mountains and often in woods. The forests of the Vosges are very thick and very dark. Our soldiers are already exposed to mist, rain and cold. The fighting is exhausting. It also requires large numbers of troops. Every advance costs dear. The Vosges forests eat infantry."[2] So de Lattre concluded that the state of his troops, the terrain and the weather made any strong outflanking move in the mountains impracticable and that his main effort would, after all, have to be made in the relatively easy terrain of the Belfort Gap.

The new plan de Lattre had drawn up for an assault on the Belfort Gap was issued to General Emile Béthouart, the commander of I Corps, on the 24th October. Two of the divisions involved were to carry out a frontal attack to the south, between the loop of the River Doubs and the Swiss border, and so threaten to outflank the whole Belfort position. Surprise was obviously of the essence here, not just to facilitate a rapid breakthrough into the German rear, but also to ensure that the built-up industrial areas of Montbéliard, Audincourt and Hérimoncourt at the entrance to the Gap did not become battlegrounds.

To improve the chances of surprise, the French embarked on an elaborate deception exercise to make the Germans think that First Army intended to persevere with the northern axis. Sham unit movements were continually under way and dummy command posts proliferated. Double agents 'stole' fictitious orders to pass to the Germans and various misleading directives were concocted to be 'leaked' through Swiss sources. Listening to the recriminations of those Frenchmen still under German occupation was the most difficult aspect of pretending that no Belfort offensive was to take place. De Lattre doubtless exaggerated the love of every Alsatian for *la patrie* but he was clearly right to be disturbed by many of the reports reaching him about life behind the German lines. "When we were told of the terror that reigned everywhere, of the shootings of patriots . . . and of the immense hopes fixed upon our army, which took every form in order to reach us – even to the extent of an SOS from the inhabitants of Voujeaucourt, carried to us on the side of a bottle on the waters of the Doubs – it was hard not to be able to soothe such misery, or support so much energy, by a word of confidence or a promise of early help. But such was the price of secrecy."[3]

It was also vital that the element of surprise be augmented by sufficient men and materiel to punch swiftly through the German lines, and by late October it seemed increasingly likely that de Lattre would lose some of his best divisions before the offensive actually began in the first half of November. Several other fronts were clamouring for French troops. In mid-October General Devers had told de Lattre that he wished to find more suitable employment for the 1 Airborne Task Force and withdraw these special forces hard cases from the Riviera and the Maritime Alps. Their sector would be taken over by the French who would have to extend their front right to the coast. But the most persistent solicitor of de Lattre's divisions was General de Gaulle, the French leader. De Gaulle was keen to buttress French prestige with a genuinely national army, with national responsibilities, rather than just a couple of corps under SHAEF command and manning a secondary stretch of the front. He became even more insistent when the Allied governments, after a sudden *volte-face* by President Roosevelt, agreed on 23rd October to recognise the Provisional Government in Paris as the legitimate government of France. On the same day de Gaulle signed an agreement with Eisenhower leaving SHAEF in control of 19 French *départements*, in what was known as the 'military zone', and giving the Provisional Government the remaining 'zone of the interior'. Only a week before, de Gaulle had written to his War Minister declaring that "the time has now come for France to take over management of her own military effort . . . We must start with the fact that at the present stage of the war our country must put into the field a certain number of divisions and army corps, on the basis of our real means, and constructed to our own design . . ."[4] An indication of the ambitious role such an army might have was given to de Lattre a week earlier when de Gaulle hinted at the need to send two divisions to the Far East to safeguard French interests in Indo-China once the Japanese were gone.

A more pressing commitment existed in France itself, where the Germans had left troops behind along the southern Atlantic coast, and around the Gironde estuary, so blocking access to the port of Bordeaux in just the same way as Antwerp was left in enemy hands. The opening up of Bordeaux, left largely undamaged by the Germans, was a matter of priority as most other French ports were being used to handle military supplies, which would do little to alleviate civilian hardship in the forthcoming winter. The most troublesome German pocket was that around Royan but there were also German rearguards in Rochefort, La Rochelle, Lorient and Saint-Nazaire. The whole south-west of France bounded by the Pyrenees, the Loire, the Atlantic and the Rhône had been liberated entirely by partisans from the French Forces of the Interior (FFI) and the left-wing Franc-Tireurs Partisans (FTP). But these fighters, though doing sterling work in harassing the retreating German First Army, were finding it much less easy to make any impression on prepared German defences in the Gironde estuary. So an army command was established to coordinate these operations, known as the Detachment of the Army of the Atlantic, commanded by General Edgar de Larminat. Nevertheless, throughout September and October, de Larminat's forces were mainly from the ranks of the FFI and FTP, members of the nine *maquis* columns which had converged on this part of the coast. In all they amounted to about 12,000 men. Almost all of them

> fought in precarious and demoralising conditions. Their equipment . . . was wholly rudimentary. They carried cartridges in their pockets and attached grenades to their trouser belts. They generally had a haversack in which they carried washing things, a bottle of wine, a spoon or a fork. Most of them had left without a plate, a mess tin, a blanket or a change of underclothes . . . At first . . . [their arms] consisted of a varied collection of light weapons. But the F.F.I. group commanders scrounged arms and uniforms wherever they could. In their '*gazogènes*' they toured the liberated regions . . . They raided the stocks of the Vichy Youth Camps and the American depots, each Maquis rivalling the other, sometimes to the detriment of stocks destined for the First Army, which on occasion saw its reserves of uniforms disappearing.

As for the artillery, they managed. Luckily the Wehrmacht, on leaving Bordeaux, had abandoned on the quays 150 120mm guns, which it thought useless because they lacked gun carriages. These were manufactured; and in September these guns went into action, shelling the German defenders of Royan with shells that had been destined for the Allies . . . An artillery officer of the Belgian Army . . . succeeded in transforming a regiment of F.F.I. inexperienced infantrymen into a regiment of artillery.[5]

The Germans at Royan had initially referred to their besiegers as 'terrorists', to be shot out of hand. But on 15th September talks were held, under a flag of truce, and the German commander, Admiral Michanelles, agreed to treat all opponents wearing a red, white and blue brassard on their left sleeve as a regular soldier. Talks were also held at La Rochelle, and on 20th October another German Admiral, Schirlitz, agreed to a bizarre scheme by which each side accepted a *nec plus ultra* line, behind their outpost lines, the crossing of which would negate the agreement and, on the French side, invoke a major air strike. "Between these two lines there will exist a zone of operations in which actions, which are no doubt necessary to the morale of our respective troops, can take place freely."[6]

This whole situation troubled de Gaulle, who was extremely suspicious of the political motives of many of the *maquisards*, especially the FTP, and was eager to consolidate regular army authority and where possible to replace irregular units with troops from First Army. He gave orders that FFI units should begin transferring into regular uniformed infantry battalions, and on 20th September put the whole coastal zone under direct military command. On 7th October de Lattre was informed that 1 Armoured Division was to be transferred to de Larminat at the end of the month. Strong hints were also given that 1 Free French Infantry Division might also be required, though this would be stationed in the Paris region, partly for praetorian reasons, partly to help train new regular formations. On 14th October de Larminat's headquarters was upgraded to the Command of French Forces in the West and plans were made to transfer most of II Corps headquarters and service personnel to this command, as well as the bulk of its artillery. Although de Lattre was disturbed by these developments, by the 25th he had disengaged most of the armoured division and placed it in reserve, awaiting definite orders to switch fronts. The proposed offensive to the coast now had a name, Operation HIATUS, and detailed planning had begun by combined SHAEF and French staff officers.

The amateur soldiers of the FFI were also prominent on other fronts, not least de Lattre's own in Alsace and the Alps. In the latter the Moroccan Mountain Division was able to turn many stretches of the line over to FFI groups and in October the slow process began of combining these groups into what became an Alpine Infantry Division. In the Vosges FFI members fought partly in local groups and partly as recruits sent there from all over France. On 23rd August 1944 an order laid down that all members of the *maquis* who wished to continue fighting would have to sign up for the duration. The order was not universally welcomed and something like 35 per cent of the irregulars melted away in short order, the majority of them from the FTP. A Provisional Government decree of 19th September insisted that the FFI "are an integral part of the army . . . subject to military discipline . . . under the sole authority of the Ministry of War." Moreover, these groups were now to be subjected to army "organisational rules" and were to be "regrouped at once" into regular units. A supplementary decree, issued the following day, made clear the government's mixed feelings about the existence of so many armed irregulars, patriots or not, when it declared: "No recruitment in the French Forces of the Interior may take place in any piece of territory after that territory has been liberated."[7] On 25th October, in response to a press conference question about "strange rumours" concerning the situation of the FFI in the provinces, and their political sympathies and ambitions, de Gaulle replied:

> The F.F.I. . . . came into spontaneous being, on their own ground and in their own countryside. Naturally they are not always regularly organised, which is why their appearance and leadership were frequently somewhat diverse and ill-assorted. The authority of the state is putting a stop to this. The state, as it gradually regains its power, is regularising these French forces which belong to the state alone.[8]

Some FFI groups were already earmarked to be formed into new divisions. The rest were to be absorbed into existing First French Army formations, usually as regular FFI battalions attached to existing infantry regiments. The process was generally known as 'amalgamation', a reference to the '*amalgame*' of the line army and the revolutionary militia decreed in February 1793, during the French Revolution. But this latter-day '*amalgame*' had a dual purpose, not just to regularise the *maquisards* but also to 'whiten' the regulars by allowing the transfer of blacks from tropical and sub-tropical French colonies in

Africa away from the rigours of the Vosges. In all 15,000 black troops, concentrated in two of de Lattre's original divisions, were to be transferred. In 9 Colonial Division, for example, "entire battalions of Sengalese were from one day to another replaced by F.F.I. battalions." Substitution was so general and so rapid that usually it had to be effected in the lines. "An extraordinary sight could then be seen: as far forward as the trenches, a few hundred yards from the enemy, youngsters took the place of the Sengalese and on the spot received greatcoats, helmets, arms and orders."[9] This process was still going on on 25th October, but already considerable progress had been made, with up to 8,000 black troops replaced and temporarily transferred to the more hospitable Midi.

Naturally this remarkable experiment in army reorganisation was not without its problems. A sense of mutual mistrust was prevalent among many of the amalgamated regiments, as the regular battalions and the newcomers made invidious comparisons between their respective zeal and efficiency. De Lattre himself was well aware of the very different attitudes within the Army of Africa and the FFI, though in his memoirs he took great pains not to offend either group, comparing the former's "deep brotherhood of arms . . . intimately associated with respect for the hierarchy . . . [and] traditional military virtues" with the latter's "revolutionary military virtues, those of partisans . . . whose common trait was audacity allied to the spirit of independence."[10]

Still, it was undoubtedly the FFI who bore the greater burden during this early period of amalgamation. Even where the integration of battalions was done with a minimum of rancour, the ex-*maquisards* were clearly the poor relations within First Army. A shortage of supplies meant that many units simply took over the equipment of the men they were replacing, but the following remarks by ex-FFI officers make it clear that in late October their men's patriotic fervour was costing them dear as they cowered in the autumnal rains which any day would turn to snow. A medical officer noted that 55 per cent of his unit were under 20 years of age and, already weakened by years of privation under Nazi occupation "have never done any military service, have undergone no combat training before being engaged on the Vosges front. They have undergone no proper medical examination and they have not been inoculated." Another officer, Colonel Chaval, wrote a report after a tour of FFI units at the front where he found most of them ill-equipped. Often they were wearing their own clothes which were months old and commensurately ragged and soiled.

Changes of clothing or underclothing were completely lacking, which for units in the line for several weeks resulted in numerous cases of bronchitis and sore throats, without mentioning epidemics of the itch which affect great numbers. There were too few blankets; and it was found impossible in most cases to issue more than one blanket per man, which was wholly insufficient in the weather conditions and the actual positions. Moreover, the total lack of tarpaulins made it impossible for units in the line either to organise or protect their kits and blankets against the damp. Their boots were in a very bad state owing to lack of grease. As for the American boots, which were in general issue, their leather was far from waterproof . . .[11]

Much that was happening along the Allied line in late October 1944 was reminiscent of earlier battles: of the mud of Flanders in 1917, and of the forests of the Wilderness campaign in 1864 or of the Argonne in 1918. But one hopes that American generals such as Eisenhower, Devers and Patch were also aware just how much the young citizen-soldiers of the FFI called to mind Washington's ragged and shivering Continentals during the dark days at Valley Forge.

11

The Champagne Campaign
1 AIRBORNE TASK FORCE ON THE RIVIERA

THE First French Army was not yet responsible for the whole of the Allied southern flank and de Lattre's most southerly formation was 4 Moroccan Mountain Division, whose sector extended only as far as the Col de Larche, to the east of Barcelonnette. From here to the coast the remaining 60 miles of front largely followed the mountainous Franco-Italian border high in the Maritime Alps, and was manned by the men of 1 Airborne Task Force, commanded by General Robert Frederick, which comprised 517 U.S. Parachute Combat Team and 1 Special Service Force, although there were many men "who had never seen a parachute or a glider nor heard a shot fired in anger".[1]

The Special Service Force probably contained the highest proportion of authentic hard-boiled types, being made up of British and Canadian volunteers specially trained in mountain warfare and night-fighting techniques who had already served in the Italian mountains and at Anzio. Hurriedly activated in July, in Rome, the Task Force landed Special Service troops on the offshore islands of Port-Cros and Levant in mid-August, the parachutists coming down in the Le Muy area, 12 miles inland from the nearest assault beaches between Cannes and Draguignan.

Once the beachhead was secure, by 17th August, the Task Force was directed eastwards to cover Seventh Army's right flank, firstly by taking Cannes and Nice on 24th and 29th August, and then by pushing through Grasse, the 'perfume capital' of France, into the Maritime Alps proper. General Frederick set up his headquarters in a Nice hotel and scattered his units along a line of mountain crests running from the Col de Larche, through Lantosque and peaks just west of Sospel, down to the Riviera. On 18th September 517 Parachute Combat Team extended its front slightly by seizing Mont Ventabren and the Tête de Lavina, north of Sospel, but most of the front remained static. Come October, this was pretty much obligatory as the first snows on the 5th soon turned into regular blizzards, clogging the mountain roads with knee-deep drifts.

However, this is not to say that the front became inactive. The Germans remained fearful that the Allies would use this sector as a back door into Italy and so manned it with a full division well-supplied with mountain artillery. Harassing artillery fire, in fact, was not the Allies' greatest hazard and in the last two weeks of October the front flared up in a vicious outbreak of defensive fighting around Sospel. The ridge from Col de Braus south was nicknamed 'Bloody Stump' because of the never-ending flow of casualties being evacuated from it. The trees had once been part of a heavy forest but

> now they were jagged and splintered stumps and the ground became torn and pitted from constant shelling. Any movement during the day brought a concentration of high-velocity shells from the forts on Mount Agaisen behind Sospel. Continuous and destructive patrolling was carried out by both sides, keeping everyone on the alert. These patrols were carried on under curious circumstances. Sometimes the fighting would come in tough, concentrated doses, and then there would be periods in the early morning when the sound of shells would be completely absent. The thin plumes of smoke that could be seen curling upwards through the valley from both positions would mean that coffee was being brewed over German and American campfires.[2]

This contrast between periods of intense military activity and periods lived in a much more pragmatic, even leisurely manner, typified the whole situation on this part of the Allied front. As a reporter for *Stars and Stripes* wrote: "This was the forgotten front – and it still is. The soldiers down here, suffering their losses, taking a town here and there a mountain pass don't make the headlines. They know this and they'll tell you so. Some say it with a touch of bitterness, thinking of their scanty transportation and not-too-warm clothing. Others, looking forward to glorious Nice next week-end, grin and say, 'Hope we stay forgotten.'"[3] So while most Task Force soldiers on 25th October were enduring a fairly grim time in the mountains, certainly shivering, quite likely coming under an artillery barrage, they at least had the prospect before them of leave in some of the most desirable watering holes in the whole of Europe, with Nice probably the favourite Riviera resort. In fact, these operations became known as the 'Champagne Campaign', and though the rumours of wine, women and song became much exaggerated elsewhere along SHAEF's front, there is no doubt that there were some unique distractions to be sampled.

One officer recalled a soldier who "was reputed to have dashed out of a café in Nice remarking that he had to get back in order to go on patrol." An official history speaks of paratroopers and others who "walked with the belles of the Côte d'Azur along the broad promenades by the sea to return the next day to the fighting among the trees and white shale of the Maritime Alps."

A key building in Nice was the Hôtel Negresco which had been requisitioned by 517 Combat Team as a rest and relaxation centre for the men. The management had been able to keep on their entire staff because the visiting G.I.s brought rations and cigarettes with them and these, as in many other parts of Europe cut off from normal economic activity, had become the new currency. The 517's commander, Colonel Rupert Graves, recalled: "They were willing to work if we would supply the food; you see, there was plenty of money around but no food. It was amazing; you could be up in the hills in a foxhole being shelled . . . and all the rest of it, then get into a truck and drive thirty miles to a completely different world. You'd walk into the main dining room of the Hôtel Negresco in dirty fatigues and your old jump boots and the waiters would flock around to serve you." Another soldier insisted that his first priority was having "about five baths to get clean", and that when the waiters did serve them from a silver platter, it was with army rations that the troops had handed over on arrival. The waiter would remove the cover with a flourish and "there inside you'd see an olive-drab G.I. can full of G.I. butter or whatever else we had brought. They seldom took it out of the cans because, I guess, they didn't want us to think they had kept any for themselves."

Food and cigarettes were also the currency on the streets. One sergeant reckoned that a few cans of Spam and a carton of cigarettes would, "if you watched it, carry you on for a week . . . There was also excitement in the fact that we could go out on patrol during the day, maybe getting into a little fire fight, perhaps, getting all muddy and bloody in the process, then five hours later be sitting in one of the biggest night-clubs in the world with a babe and a bottle of champagne." An officer also retained fond memories of "plenty of girls . . . plenty of champagne and cognac to go with them . . . We used to go skiing. We'd take a jeep and go up the mountains to a little resort . . . You could ski in the morning with your girl-friend, come back in the afternoon . . . go to a first-class hotel and then go swimming in the ocean. It was quite a life."

The commander of one of the independent parachute battalions emphasised the strange duality of life in the line and out of it, reminding us that not everybody went up into mountains to ski. There was combat, too, and "it was hard, it was tough, and we lost a lot of men killed and wounded. And yet the flesh-pots were close by . . . We could go back and have a bottle of wine and a bath and then go back into the mountains for another battle. It was like being in the ring where you get the sponge and the towel between rounds."

The fact remains that on any given day those sampling the flesh-pots were very much in the minority. One colonel reckoned that "there were only about two days in a hundred that we weren't actually in the lines as a unit . . . It was a rugged, physical campaign going up and down those mountains . . . They say we took light casualties, but I know that on occasion a whole platoon would be wiped out . . . It's only in the big picture that you can call losing a platoon 'light casualties'." Another commander estimated that in 317 Combat Team, numbering about 2,500 men, one hundred or so were killed and upwards of seven hundred wounded. A paratrooper in this unit said simply: "We were on the line from the middle of August to the end of November . . . We were strafed, attacked by tanks, railroad guns, 88s etc. . . . The guy who named it the Champagne Campaign got to Nice more often than I did."[4]

PART TWO

The Eastern Front

12

Sledgehammers and Nuts

ONE OF THE MANY pernicious effects of the Cold War has been the distorted yet enduring conception of the Soviet contribution to the struggle against Hitler. For most people, the Eastern Front still seems to figure as a remote theatre where German soldiers were extremely cold and did most unpleasant things to various Communists and Jews. In fact it was on the Eastern Front that the German Army fought most of its war. Throughout 1942 and 1943 they kept between 160 and 195 divisions there, with only 3 facing the Western Allies in January 1942, rising to 14 by the end of 1943. Even in October 1944, five months after the Normandy landings, the Red Army was still tying down 170 German divisions while the British and Americans engaged only 98 in the West. It was on the Eastern Front, too, that the German Army had done most of its dying. Figures up to October 1944 are not available but during the whole war German losses in the East were 4.9 million soldiers killed and wounded as opposed to 580,000 in North-West Europe, Italy and Africa. The proportion accounted for by the Soviets, then, is almost exactly 90 per cent of the total, and even when figures for missing and prisoners-of-war are included the Soviet tally is still around 80 per cent.

The Soviet Union also suffered mightily. By late October 1944, Russian victory in the East was almost inevitable, but this supremacy had been bought at enormous cost. From the very beginning blood had been the Red Army's most negotiable asset. An enormous number of casualties was suffered as Soviet infantry hurled itself against German spearheads during the great offensives towards Moscow and Stalingrad in 1941 and 1942. Both were halted, but in their aftermath, at Stalin's insistence, ill-prepared Russian offensives were launched which cost tens of thousands more lives. Nevertheless, at Stalingrad the Germans had reached their high-water mark, and even before its surrender in February 1943 the Germans were in retreat. Periodically they were able to hold one or other defensive line down their 600-mile front but each time were eventually dislodged by increasingly powerful Russian attacks. By February 1943, the Red Army was up to the Donets and by November was across the river for most of its length.

Early in 1944 the main Soviet axis was in the south, pointing towards Rumania, Hungary and Bulgaria and the new river lines of the Dniester and the Pruth. When the second of these was crossed in late March, the Red Army had established its first foothold in Rumania. Yet it was never Stalin's policy to concentrate solely on one axis and so allow the Germans to build their reserves around a single threatened sector. There were other important ancillary operations in the north, and by March consistent Soviet pressure had forced the Germans to abandon the siege of Leningrad and pull back to a line between Narva, Pskov and Revel. From the summer onwards the Soviet High Command was achieving mastery of the operational craft and delivering successive hammer blows up and down the whole Eastern Front. In the centre, the Lwow-Sandomir and Byelorussian Operations drove German Army Group Centre back to the Vistula and the borders of East Prussia. In the south, the Jassy-Kishinev Operation tore open the German front in Rumania, and just a few weeks later the same thing happened in Hungary in the Debrecen Operation. Next, in the north, the Klaipeda (Memel) Operation actually cut Army Group North off from the rest of the German front. Soviet tactical methods were still less than subtle, however, relying heavily on the massing of huge artillery forces along relatively narrow sectors of the front and on the ruthless pressing home of massed tank and infantry assaults. As one analyst has written: "In Soviet [military] thinking the concept of economy has little place. Whereas to an Englishman the taking of a sledgehammer to crack a nut is a wrong decision and a sign of mental immaturity, to a Russian the opposite is the case. In Russian eyes the cracking of nuts is clearly what sledgehammers are for."[1]

Crude tactics did not mean that the Red Army was not learning. In late 1944 individual battalions, divisions, even corps, might still crash forward rather in the manner of Kitchener's 'Tommies' against Maxim machine guns, but the timing of successive offensives, the intelligence work and selection of the point of attack, the orchestration of deception measures, the build-up of men and materiel behind the front, all was being done with an increasing deftness and self-confidence. Now

German generals were beginning to realise that time was running out. The blood of 20 million Soviet citizens spilt since 1941 had not bought the Wehrmacht victory; rather it had gained the Soviet leadership the time they needed, to design new weapons, to rebuild the factories that mass-produced them, to relearn the techniques of large-scale mechanised warfare, and to bring forth a new generation of officers to replace those lost in the Purges, while still maintaining tight Party control of the military machine.

From Lapland to Yugoslavia, therefore, with only 2.2 million men facing 5.5 Soviet soldiers, the Germans were under mounting pressure. Every portion of the front seemed to be imminently threatened. German divisions in Lithuania were now trapped in the Courland pocket; in East Prussia they were attempting to repel the first Soviet encroachments into Germany itself; along the Vistula they could only watch anxiously as guns and troops poured into the Soviet bridgeheads already across the river; and in the south they frantically tried to shore up their Balkan allies as the Red Army inexorably bored its way through the great barrier of the Carpathians.

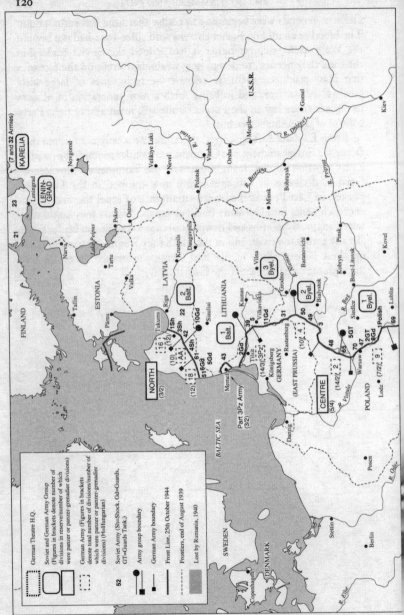

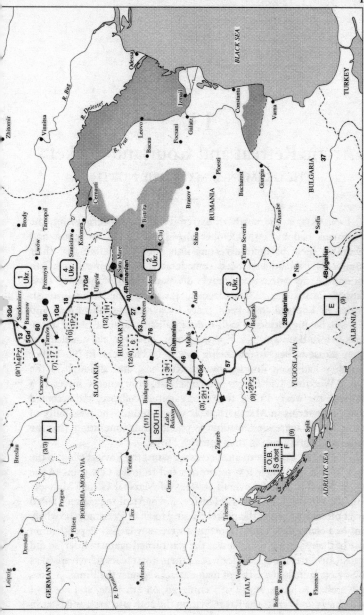

The Eastern Front 25th October 1944

13

Arctic Retreat and Courland Pocket
THE GERMAN ARMY IN THE NORTH

IN FINLAND, at the northern extremity of the Eastern Front, the Germans had by 25th October already given up the ghost and withdrawn most of their divisions into Norway. Before that their presence in Finland had been considerable, comprising Twentieth Mountain Army with a total of eight divisions, many of them top-class infantry formations. These troops, guarding the Russo-Finnish frontier in Lapland, had been there by agreement, the Finns and Germans having formed a tacit military alliance against Stalin in the weeks before BARBAROSSA. For the Finns, however, the alliance was largely a case of beggars not being able to be choosers. In November 1939 they had been invaded by the Russians, and although in the Winter War they had fought immensely superior enemy forces to a standstill, the weary Finns, fearful of eventual collapse, had accepted harsh peace terms in March 1940. It was to reduce the possibility of further Soviet aggression, leading to possible full annexation, that the Finns had then thrown in their lot with Hitler.

In the event, early German successes against the Soviets allowed the Finns to win back their lost territories and to make new gains to the east, in Karelia. Yet the overall strategy of Marshal Gustaf Mannerheim, the Finnish leader, was defensive, and in April 1942, after a failed Soviet offensive against the nickel-mining town of Petsamo, the whole front had congealed. Finnish fortunes were now largely dependent on those of their German allies and as the war turned against Hitler, so did Finnish anxieties mount. In June 1944 their worst fears were realised as the Soviets launched a series of major attacks against the Finns. Across the Karelian isthmus, north of Leningrad, on 9th June, and north of Lake Onega and across the River Svir on the 20th and 21st, and later in

July, five Soviet armies, totalling well over half a million men, 1,000 tanks and 2,000 aircraft, gave the lie to Mannerheim's obstinate belief that the Russians would only attack in Karelia. Forced to fall back, the Finns nursed their wounded pride as the city of Viipuri, at the north-western end of the isthmus, fell to the Red Army. On 21st June President Risto Ryti attempted to open peace negotiations but these got nowhere when Stalin insisted on complete surrender as a precondition for any talks. When the Germans donated a quantity of vital anti-tank weapons to the Finns, their defences stiffened and the Soviet High Command ordered its troops on the isthmus to go over to the defensive. The Karelian attacks also faltered, enabling the Finns to conduct an orderly retreat to the so-called U-Line along the 1940 frontier. By the end of July this front too had stagnated, with Stavka, the Soviet High Command, putting it on a defensive footing at the end of August. "Thus, militarily, the Russo-Finnish war ended with the Finnish army still intact and fully battleworthy, and at all points standing on the Russian side of the 1940 frontier."[1]

The Finns were still keenly aware that Soviet successes all along the rest of the Eastern Front must inevitably spell German defeat and their own total isolation. What they feared most was the prospect of the Soviets seizing all the eastern Baltic ports that were so essential for Finnish imports. After putting out renewed peace feelers, the Finns received the Soviet response on 29th August, with their conditions for a cease-fire. The Finnish parliament accepted these conditions and on 4th September an armistice was signed. Five days later a Finnish delegation travelled to Moscow, to be presented on the 16th with the stringent Soviet peace terms. Again the Finnish parliament felt that it had no option but to agree, and on the same day that it voted its acceptance the Finnish delegation signed the treaty.

The most humiliating conditions were those relating to the loss of key territories and an enormous reparations payment, but it was the purely military details that were the most pressing. These required Finnish armed forces to wind down to a peacetime level within ten weeks and in that time to ensure that all German forces had quit their country. Diplomatic relations with Germany had been broken off on 2nd September, and General Lothar Rendulic, commanding Twentieth Mountain Army, agreed to begin withdrawing his troops by 15th September. The Germans had not been unduly surprised by Finnish attempts to defect and had already drawn up a contingency plan, Operation BIRKE, to evacuate the whole of Lapland except for the vital nickel mines at Petsamo. By the 17th, therefore, Rendulic and the

Finns had drawn up a detailed schedule for German withdrawal, including specific phase lines to be reached by agreed dates. Five Finnish divisions were earmarked to follow the German forces, though not to harass or attack them. These units were grouped within III Corps, commanded by General Hjalmar Siilasvuo.

This remarkably accommodating agreement did not please the Russians. According to them, the armistice terms stipulated that the Finns were to intern all Germans within their frontiers. So irritated did they become that on 16th October Mannerheim received a letter from the Leningrad Front's political representative, General A. A. Zhdanov, "full of criticism and mistrust, concluding with threats that the Soviet military command might be compelled to take 'such measures as it considered essential', clearly implying in the last resort a possible military occupation".[2] In fact, the agreement with the Germans had already broken down and, unknown to the Soviets, several military confrontations had taken place. Tensions had been heightened on 15th September when Hitler, in a fit of pique, decided to occupy the Finnish island of Suusaari (Högland), in the Gulf of Finland, and the flash-point came on the 28th when a Finnish battalion opened fire on German troops at Pudasyärvi.

The Finns declined offers to restore the truce and on 1st October their troops guarding factories in the ports of Kemi and Tornio, at the northern end of the Gulf of Bothnia, took control of key roads and rail bridges. Rendulic ordered counter-attacks and these were intensified as Finnish 3 Division began landing at Tornio later that day. Fighting lasted until the 6th, when Finnish 11 Division landed at Kemi, and the Germans spent a further two days extricating part of one division from threatened encirclement. In the meantime, Rendulic, blaming the Finns for the breakdown of the truce, had ordered that his troops would act "without restraint" and commanded: "As of now, all cover, installations, and objects that can be used by an enemy are to be destroyed." The Germans, not unusually, were as good as their word. According to Mannerheim, they "retreated, mining roads and destroying everything in their path, even the smallest road bridges, not to mention the great railway bridges over the mighty rivers of northern Ostrobothnia."[3] Fire was a favourite weapon and farms, homesteads and villages, even the whole town of Rovaniemi, were all burnt to the ground.

Then, just as the Kemi battle was drawing to a close, another protagonist entered the fray. On 7th October, even before Zhdanov's angry note, the Soviets decided to add their weight to the 'scrum' to ensure that the Petsamo mines, ceded to them under the peace terms, would fall into their hands intact. Three Soviet armies from K. A. Meretskov's Karelian Front were involved. One was directed towards Petsamo itself, with a view to shepherding the Germans all the way across the Norwegian frontier, near the port of Kirkenes; the other two were to push due west towards Rovaniemi, supported by four Finnish divisions which were pushing up from Kemi and Tornio. In fact, Hitler had already sanctioned the abandonment of the Petsamo mines three days earlier and the German withdrawal had speeded up considerably. Their three corps were each given their own axis of retreat into Norway, one via Kirkenes, one along the Arctic Highway, and one hugging the Swedish frontier all the way to Skibatten, just south-east of Tromsö, where the battleship *Tirpitz* was bottled up. Eventually all three corps were to rendezvous at Skibatten and man the Lyngen Position, across one of the narrowest portions of the badly nibbled nail-paring that is northern Norway.

By 25th October each of the German corps had made good progress. Only occasional small rearguard actions were fought with the pursuing Finns, but for the three tough German mountain divisions, the trek was a nightmare. Often making 20 or 30 miles per day, the columns were usually soaked by autumn rains or the first snow showers as they struggled through thick forests and even thicker mud.

> . . . wet through, they would have to lie down for the night in wet uniforms on sopping ground, hoping that the gale force winds would not blow away their tiny two-man tents. When the rain finally stopped falling out of the low flying, heavy grey clouds, the soaked trees of the forest continued to drip for hours. Those damned forests whose mysterious silence drove the soldiers into fits of depression. The closeness of the trees limited all horizons and this, to men who had been accustomed to view panoramas of mountains at incredibly far distances, was the most miserable aspect of this war in the arctic regions. These mountain men were fighting just above sea level in stinking swamps. They enjoyed no vistas seen from high peaks, just the small horizons and the aching loneliness of unending forests where nothing grew but the trees and where the only wild life with which they had any close contact was vermin.[4]

It was perhaps the troops' particular loathing for their surroundings that made them so ruthless in destroying almost everything Finnish. Demolition was standard operating procedure during any German retreat, but in Finland they seemed bent on erasing all traces of civilisation in their path. One unit history gives a clear picture of the sort of thing that had already happened to most towns and villages en route. "On the 24th we passed the airfield at Nautsi, a day later the Jänikowski water barrage that supplied the nickel works with water for electricity. Spread out in the streets were large bombs from the planes at Nautsi, with which the engineers were going to undertake demolitions to block the road. The concrete dome of the Jänikowski power station, which had successfully protected it against all air attacks, was suddenly blown into the air with a tremendous explosion. Immediately afterwards, the engineers blew up the huge dam. The pent-up waters . . . gushed out over the low-lying banks on either side of the River Patsjoki."[5]

Meanwhile, to the north-east, XIX Mountain Corps withdrew completely from Finland by the 25th. There had been hopes of holding out on the River Litsa, in front of Petsamo, but Russian preparations for Fourteenth Army's offensive had been thorough. Two rifle corps had been massed in a narrow breakthrough sector, to the south of Lake Chapr, while the specially formed 126 Light Corps, able to carry all the equipment it needed on the men's own backs, was to advance through the supposedly impenetrable tundra on the German right, and a marine brigade was to land in their rear on the coastal flank. With the Light Corps soon penetrating deep into their rear, the Germans admitted to being "surprised by the scope and weight of the attack and they were hustled into a precipitate retreat . . . over the Norwegian frontier."[6]

When Meretskov proposed to Stavka (the Soviet High Command) that he should pursue the Germans across the frontier and capture their main base at Kirkenes, his suggestion was warmly endorsed by Stalin. Kirkenes, just across the Norwegian frontier, was a major German supply base and throughout October they had been frantically trying to evacuate the enormous quantities of stores there. Only 45,000 tons, about one-third, had been cleared when the nearby hydro-electric plant powering the dock facilities came under fire on the 22nd. Rendulic was given permission to abandon further loading of supplies and to evacuate the port. German rearguards fought desperately to cover this evacuation, but on the 25th the Russians entered the town, once again assailing the Germans in their southern flank in the tundra as well as their other coastal flank. General S. M. Shtemenko, Chief of Operations on the Red Army General Staff, described the difficulties of the coastal approaches:

> The cold waters of Jarfjord had blocked the approach to Kirkenes from the east. The suspension bridge had been destroyed. It was

extremely difficult to cross that deep wide fjord with its steep rocky cliffs, and with a strong and crafty enemy behind his defences on the other side. At this point Meretskov brought into play the amphibious 'ducks' with which the forces had been endowed. What with the explosions of enemy shells and the choppy water, the ducks did not always reach their destination. They would capsize, and the soldiers with their heavy equipment would sink to the bottom. When the battle had reached its critical point, low-slung, sturdy fishing boats made their appearance in the fjord. They were being operated by their owners – local fishermen who knew each stone of the fjord's rugged shores. Working under enemy artillery and machine-gun fire, the Norwegians saved Soviet soldiers who had fallen in the water; and on instruction from our officers, they ferried troops to the other side. One . . . ferried an entire battalion across in his boat . . . These valiant Norwegians also found plenty to do on shore. They put out the fires that had broken out in the town and repaired the bridges so that Soviet troops and equipment could come across . . . [Others] disarmed some bombs that had been placed in an electric power station . . .[7]

In one tiny corner of Europe at least, liberation by the Red Army proved, albeit briefly, to be a genuinely positive experience.

*

Across the Gulf of Finland lay the Baltic states of Estonia, Latvia and Lithuania. Having emerged in 1919 as independent nations from the wreckage of Imperial Russia, they succumbed once more to Russian rule in June 1940. Stalin's success was short-lived, however. During Operation BARBAROSSA the Germans succeeded in clearing the Baltic territories right to the gates of Leningrad and many of their inhabitants began to enjoy a reasonably benign and relatively prosperous period of German occupation. This was not to last. In the summer of 1944 the Red Army loomed once more on their borders and in July five Soviet army groups launched attacks along a 250-mile front from Minsk to Pskov, as well as around Narva in northern Estonia. The Narva attack had only limited objectives but in Latvia and Lithuania the Soviets made enormous gains up to the end of August.

Their armies then paused to regroup and refit, and on 14th September they stormed forward once more, now determined to clear the Baltic states of German troops and press forward into East Prussia itself. Once Tallinin had been captured on the 22nd, the Germans conducted a speedy withdrawal from Estonia, leaving the country by the end of the month. The Soviets then devoted their attentions to Latvia, most particularly to Riga where it was hoped to establish a blocking force that would cut off Army Group North from the rest of the German front. This had been briefly achieved during the first few days of August, but frenzied German counter-attacks had re-established a narrow corridor south of Riga. This was incorporated into the so-called Sigulda (Segewold) Line and fierce attacks against these concentric defences were unable to achieve a breakthrough. On 24th September the attacks were suspended and shortly afterwards a new Stavka directive ordered two Soviet Fronts to go over to the defensive while the third prepared to drive through to the coast on a new easterly axis, towards Memel (Klaipeda).

Preparations for this new offensive went on until 4th October, involving the transfer of three rifle armies, a tank army and a number of independent corps from one flank to the other. In all half a million men and 1,300 tanks and self-propelled guns were moved. The offensive opened on the next day and achieved instant success, not least because the Army Group's mobile reserve was stationed well to the north, in defiance of orders from both Hitler and the Army Chief-of-Staff, General Heinz Guderian. On 6th October, 3rd Byelorussian Front also began to attack, towards Tilsit, to pin the German Army Group Centre along the Niemen. By the time two of the Soviet armies reached the coast at Palanga, on the 10th, most of Army Group North was isolated from the rest of the German front. Recognising the danger almost as soon as the offensive opened, the Germans began evacuating Riga on the night of the 5th/6th, a desperate business that took until the 16th, as German rearguards held out tenaciously on the Sigulda Line and eventually in the outskirts of the city itself. By the 19th the Army Group North pocket had taken its final shape, occupying the bulk of the Courland peninsula in north-west Latvia. The Courland Pocket, as it is usually known, represented an impressive haul of 32 divisions, including three panzer and one panzer-grenadier. Admittedly, two of the panzer divisions had had to be grouped with an infantry division to make up the numbers, three of the infantry and *Volksgrenadier* divisions were only partial formations, and almost all the others were badly understrength. Nevertheless, this represented an impressive haul for the Soviets and dealt a grievous blow to Hitler's hopes of defending East Prussia, Poland and the Carpathians. Not that Hitler seemed to appreciate how grievous. Even as the pocket began to congeal he was proving himself implacably obstinate about redeploying these divisions further south. Despite the entreaties of the OKH, he had refused to permit the withdrawal of more than one corps headquarters, the remnants of one panzer division, and a single panzer-grenadier and infantry division. As Guderian described it after the war, once the Army Group was in serious danger of being "cut off from the rest of the front and from now on could only be supplied by sea . . . I . . . became involved in a long and bitter argument with Hitler concerning the withdrawal of these valuable troops which were essential for the defence of Germany. The sole result of this argument was further to poison the atmosphere."[8]

On 16th October the Soviets made one more attempt to liquidate the Courland Pocket by smashing through on the eastern flank, between Tukkums and Gardene. The Germans held firm, however, and after only three days' fighting Stavka ordered all units in this sector to go over to the defensive. Attacks continued against another mini-pocket in Memel, where three divisions from Army Group Centre had been trapped as 1st Baltic and 3rd Byelorussian Fronts drew up along the Lithuanian coast. While Stalin could see the merit of leaving the whole of Army Group North to rot on the vine, the Memel garrison was a constant vexation to him and Soviet troops suffered heavy losses in attempting to pinch it out. Attack after attack was repulsed, not least because among the German defenders was the elite and well-equipped *Grossdeutschland* panzer division and because "Memel had been a supply base for the Army fighting in the Soviet Union . . . There was an abundance of materials needed to withstand a long siege. The most elaborate fire plans could be worked out and any call for help by an infantry unit under pressure . . . could be answered by a rain of shells upon the advancing Red Army."

A soldier fighting with *Grossdeutschland* has described the bitter combats that flared up day after day during late October: "Memel was ringed with innumerable carcasses of Russian tanks, and there were as many anti-tank gunners as there were ordinary soldiers. Carloads of mines were driven out by civilian volunteers and placed in front of our defences by the infantry in the course of small attacks organised solely for this manoeuvre. We were defenceless only against the Russian fighter-bombers which flew over continually. To the northwest of our position the remains of several dismantled railway carriages underwent eight attacks in two days. What was left of our anti-aircraft defences was concentrated around the piers where the danger was greatest."[9] How appropriate, by this stage of the war, that *Grossdeutschland* should be penned within the ruined confines of a demolished port, brazenly annexed only five-and-a-half years earlier.

14

At the Gates of the Reich

THE RED ARMY IN EAST PRUSSIA AND POLAND

ONE EFFECT of the Soviet clearance of the Latvian coastline was to make German commanders on the River Niemen nervous about the possibility of a thrust south towards Tilsit. These fears became especially acute on 16th October when 3rd Byelorussian Front launched an attack into East Prussia, between Vilkoviski and Augustow. To the Germans, this seemed to presage a pincer movement and by the 22nd they had withdrawn their bridgeheads north of the Niemen, at Tilsit and Ragnit. In fact, no attack from the north materialised but Third and Fourth Armies, both part of General Hans Rheinhardt's Army Group Centre, found themselves sorely pressed just by the assault from the east mounted by Soviet Fifth, Thirty-First and Eleventh Guards Armies.

Their initial progress was alarming. By 20th October the Soviets were through the first German line of defences and had bridgeheads over the River Szeszuppe at Schirwindt, and were also making inroads into the Augustow Forest and the Romintener Heath. By the 23rd the Heath had been cleared and the Soviets were through the second line of German defences, linking Stillupoennen and Goldap, both of which had been stormed, as had Suwalki to the north-west of the Augustow Forest. The Soviets continued to push forward to the third German line, which ran along the River Angerapp and thence to Gumbinnen and Pilkallen. This river was reached, between Angerburg and Darknehmen, and fierce attacks were launched against Gumbinnen as other units tried to turn Pilkallen from the north. On the 25th, however, the tide turned, with some sources stating that the Soviets themselves chose to go on to the defensive and others that they were fought to a standstill. Whatever the exact truth of the matter, the

Soviets hung on to almost all the territory already conquered, having pushed their spearheads some 35 miles into East Prussia, their first gains within the Fatherland itself.

Several reasons may be adduced for the Red Army's failure to break through the final line of defences. One was the constrained nature of their axis of advance, with the left flank being barred by the Masurian Lakes, and most especially by the fortress town of Lötzen, and the right by the low-lying ground north of Pilkallen. For much of the year this ground was passable – dry enough in the summer and frozen in the winter – but in October it became extremely boggy. The "promising possibilities" of a manoeuvre north of Pilkallen "were frustrated by heavy rainfall, which made the marshy ground to the north-west of Schirwindt impracticable for the movement of tanks."[1]

Another reason for Soviet failure to make the final breakthrough was the sheer scale of the defences in East Prussia. In his memoirs, General Guderian complains of constantly being frustrated in his efforts to inject new personnel and weapons into the Eastern Front armies, and of numerous fortress battalions and artillery pieces being diverted to the West. Nevertheless, by frequently visiting the front personally Guderian had been able to boost the construction of static defence works and the imminent danger to Germany itself had even jolted some of the Gauleiters into lending a hand. "If their excessive zeal led on occasion to friction," wrote Guderian, "their desire to make themselves useful must be acknowledged nevertheless." By mid-October 1944 these defences had become enough to daunt even the Soviet steamroller. They were "deeply staggered . . . the result of skilful elaboration; and when the Russians crossed the frontier, German civilian men and even women took their place with the vast body of foreigners in digging trenches so that there should always be further positions and strong-points when one was overrun. Hills, small settlements, the causeways between the lakes that studded a great part of the eastern frontier, were all turned into strong-points, with a glacis of trenches and belts of barbed wire, minefields, and concrete pill-boxes."[2]

A final reason for the Soviet check was that the Germans had available substantial reserves with which to counter the Soviet thrust, reserves which arrived at just the time the Soviet advance was being channelled into a narrow sector towards Gumbinnen. Thus, though the original balance of forces had pitted 35 Soviet divisions and two tank corps against 15 infantry divisions and two cavalry brigades, described by one source as "half-organised remnants . . . most of which

. . . [had been] wiped out at Vitebsk", Army Group Centre was soon able to call upon a powerful armoured reserve, comprising three panzer, one panzer-grenadier and one Volksgrenadier division.[3] It was the swift commitment of these troops, who between 22nd and 24th October launched fierce counter-attacks towards the River Rominte and south-west of Goldap, that was the decisive factor in robbing the Soviets of their momentum. Upwards of 1,000 Soviet tanks and 300 guns were claimed to have been lost during these battles.

Some spearhead units were driven back on the 25th, and in the areas retaken the Germans found disturbing indications of what might lie in wait for them if the Red Army was to break through in East Prussia or along the upper Vistula. While the barbarity of German methods throughout the territories they occupied tend to minimise sympathy for their own plight, the fact remains that Soviet soldiers were determined to repay in kind. Egged on by some of their commissars, inflamed by viciously anti-German rhetoric in their Army newspapers, degraded by the brutality of pitiless infantry combat and sickened by all they had seen of German occupation methods, the ordinary soldiers sought at the very least an eye for an eye. In one village captured by the Hermann Göring Corps most of the inhabitants had been killed. According to a survivor: "In a farmyard stood a cart to which four naked women were nailed through their hands in a cruciform position. Beyond stood a barn, and to each of its two doors a naked woman was nailed through the hands in a crucified posture. In the dwellings, we found a total of 72 women, including children, and one old man dead . . . holes in their necks. Some babies had their heads bashed in. In one room, we found an old woman sitting on a sofa. Half of her head had been sheared off with an axe or a spade."[4]

There seems little use in attempting to excuse excesses of this kind, whether in terms of recent provocation or of ancient national animosities. Neither can the short and brutish life of the typical Soviet infantryman be an acceptable justification. A soldier fighting with 3rd Byelorussian Front has provided a rare description of front-line life in the Red Army, and one that above all brings out the relatively primitive nature of life in a Soviet rifle division, especially at the level of company and battalion tactics, with their reliance upon crude mass attacks. Modern studies of the Red Army have, quite rightly, drawn attention to its vastly improved operational methods during the Second World War. The selection of breakthrough sectors, the assembly of powerful combined-arms teams, and the ability to exploit properly the initial breakthrough had all been pretty well mastered by late 1944, but the fact remained that the ordinary infantryman was still as much a piece of cannon-fodder as he had been in the desperate days of 1941. As the Russian soldier tells us, throughout 1943 and 1944 "supply of arms, ammunition and equipment was . . . inadequate. Only one company in a regiment was fully equipped with automatic weapons . . . Only on the main axes of advance of an offensive were large stocks [of ammunition] built up; on the others there were only a few shells per gun . . . There were not even enough rifles for all those who were mobilised into the army . . . Tactics were very primitive. We attacked German positions mostly from the front, one wave of soldiers after another, and therefore suffered unnecessarily large casualties. Outflanking manoeuvres were hardly used at all . . . 'Forward' was the most widely used tactical command . . . When operations were local in character or on secondary axes . . . artillery or air support would be weak or lacking altogether. The soldiers then felt themselves abandoned or doomed, and would be unwilling to attack."

This ruthlessly utilitarian attitude to battle manifested itself in almost every aspect of Red Army life. Casualties, as can be imagined, were terribly high, but medical facilities were meagre. According to this same soldier: "Medical supplies could have been considerably better. We had no special ambulances – only horse-drawn carts or lorries were used to transport the wounded from the front. For those seriously wounded (especially in the head or stomach) such transportation was torture, and frequently ended in premature death." Medical equipment was also in short supply, including instruments, penicillin, medical spirits, and even bandages and cotton wool. Casualty stations near the front often had no means of artificial lighting except candles and lanterns.

Such shortages extended right to the most basic amenities of day-to-day life. Relying totally on ruthless discipline, the Soviet High Command had little time for questions of morale and resolutely ignored those little conveniences, taken for granted in most armies, that can make such a difference when out of the line or in static positions, giving the soldier a fleeting glimpse of normal life and reaffirming his reasons for fighting on. The Red Army did little to provide its soldiers the opportunity for personal hygiene. Even behind the lines there was "a lack of delousing chambers, and showers, only one or two hair clippers to a battalion, only one or two razors to a company." This list of what was not available is almost epic in its mundaneness, seeming to us in the west to cover most of the artefacts that make life tolerable. "Soldiers could not get pencils, ink, envelopes, paper, knives, scissors, razors, pocket torches, candles, spirit lamps, stoves, musical instruments, table games . . . the sort of thing that would have created a little comfort for them and raised their morale . . . Vodka was issued only in winter."[5] On the whole, then, the Soviet infantryman on 25th October, as on most other days, lived in a world of either savage combat or utter boredom, and always of relentless squalor. While most people would hardly regard this as a proper excuse for nailing Germans to walls, it does at least provide a partial explanation for the dehumanised state of mind that made such acts possible.

*

In September 1939, murder, rape and pillage had been a German speciality, and it was the violation of Poland that finally precipitated France and Britain into standing up to Hitler. Unfortunately, this belated show of resistance benefited the Poles not one jot. The country was briefly partitioned between Germany and the Soviet Union and then, after BARBAROSSA, fell entirely under German sway. Its two north-western provinces, containing many *Volksdeutsch* of German ancestry, were ethnically cleansed of Poles and everywhere the Polish professional elite and Jews from every station of life were exterminated. By October 1944 this latter process was almost complete and of the 3.3 million Jews in Poland before the war only 230,000 were left.

Also by October, the Poles were once again under dual occupation, with the Soviets in possession of all the disputed Polish portions of the Ukraine, Byelorussia and Lithuania and their armies pushed up to the Vistula from Warsaw to Baranow. These had been immense victories. The clearance of the Ukraine had been largely accomplished by May 1944, upon which the Red Army had begun final preparations for an offensive into Byelorussia and central Poland, between the Pripet Marshes and the Vistula. This campaign, which began in late June, was responsible for the destruction of 28 German divisions by mid-July. Three Byelorussian Fronts had been involved but on 11th July 1st Ukrainian Front was also unleashed, mopping up the last German footholds in the Ukraine before driving on to establish bridgeheads over the Vistula at Sandomierz and Baranow by the end of the month. Despite fierce German counter-attacks in August, the Soviets hung on, and by the end of that month had succeeded in creating a unified bridgehead along a 47-mile front and to a depth of 30 miles. This thrust to the south had been accompanied by a powerful right jab, as 1st Byelorussian Front was also directed to close to the Vistula, south of Warsaw. By the 31st Soviet troops were in the east bank suburbs of

Warsaw and by 2nd August had bridgeheads across the river though to the south of the capital, at Magnuszew and Pulawy.

All this fighting cost the Red Army dear, and in early August most of their armies in Poland went over to the defensive. This proved particularly unfortunate for the inhabitants of Warsaw who, it is claimed, were exhorted by the Soviets to start an armed insurrection to facilitate Red Army attacks towards the western half of the city. The Soviets, in their turn, claimed that they had no prior knowledge of the uprising on 1st August, and thus could only make improvised, inadequately concentrated attempts to lend military support. Whatever the truth of the matter, the Soviets failed to force their way across the Vistula. On 21st September the troops involved in these attacks were withdrawn and on 2nd October the surviving remnants of the insurrection surrendered.

By the 25th these survivors, many from the Polish Home Army which had organised the insurrection, had been rounded up. Remarkably, their surrender was accepted according to the terms of the Geneva Convention, and of the 155,000 men, women and children who were counted past the German check-points, 12,000 were recognised as *bona fide* soldiers, to be sent to prisoner-of-war camps. As for the civilians, "according to the conditions of capitulation, there were to be no collective penalties . . . nor were individual civilians to be punished for resistance activities during or before the rising." Although these conditions appear to some extent to have been observed, Warsaw civilians were sent to forced labour in Germany in considerable numbers. Some were dispatched to Oswiecim concentration camp, which was little better than a death sentence."[6] Above all, the Germans were determined to evacuate the city of all civilians. For some commanders this was seen as a means of creating a more secure *Festung* on the Vistula. Heinrich Himmler, however, had other ideas. The suppression of the uprising was a 'security' operation that had fallen under his ever more extensive aegis and on the 25th October an order of his was working its way through the labyrinthine but meticulous SS bureaucracy. Regarding military considerations as purely secondary to his monstrous vindictiveness, Himmler had decreed

Subject: New policy with regard to Poles.

Obergruppenführer von dem Bach has been entrusted with the task of pacifying Warsaw, that is to say he will raze Warsaw to the ground while the war is still going on and in so far as this is not contrary to military plans for the construction of strongpoints. Before it is destroyed, all raw materials, all textiles, and all furniture will be removed from Warsaw. The responsibility for this is assigned to the civilian administration.[7]

Home Army units were faring no better in Soviet-occupied areas. Under the terms of Operation TEMPEST, authorised by the government-in-exile in London in November 1943, once Soviet troops arrived in their area Home Army units were to quit clandestine cell activities and coalesce into 'divisional' formations, some two to three thousand strong. By late October, however, except for Home Army forces in the Baranow and Magnuszew bridgeheads, all such divisions had either been dispersed or arrested by the Soviets, notably around Kovel, Wilno, Lwow, Polesie, Lublin and Bialystok. A London representative, who had parachuted in on the night of 17th/18th October, reported back that: "There is monstrous chaos and lawlessness in the districts . . . [A leader is needed to] curtail the anarchy."[8] Indeed, October was a dreadful month overall for the Poles. Between the 9th and the 19th Churchill was in Moscow to confer with Stalin, and on the 13th a Polish delegation, led by the Prime-Minister-in-exile, Stanislaw Mikolajczyk, arrived to discuss the future shape of Poland. These discussions broke down almost at once, with Churchill urging the Poles to accept Stalin's offer of the Curzon Line as Poland's new eastern frontier while the Poles were holding out for a 'natural' frontier that would include Lwow. Their whole visit served only to make their sponsor, Churchill, much more sympathetic to Soviet allegations about Polish intransigence.

As for the Red Army, the failure to break through to support the Warsaw Uprising was not the end of the fighting in this sector. Although attacks on the city itself were suspended, some of K. K. Rokossovsky's 1st Byelorussian Front armies continued to hammer away at the German line. On either side of Ostenburg, on the River Narew, Sixty-Fifth Army made repeated attacks against two corps from German Second Army throughout the last week of October. Further south, between Modlin and Warsaw, an SS Panzer Corps, also part of Second Army, was continuously assailed by elements of three of Rokossovsky's armies. An attack on 10th October achieved some surprise and managed to drive the three German divisions back twenty miles in the first few days, but it had begun "too early and with insufficient strength [and] could not punch through the front to envelop and destroy the SS divisions." Further attacks, right up to the 25th, degenerated into "persistent and fruitless clubbing of the well-entrenched SS Panzerkorps."[9]

In fact, both Rokossovsky and the Stavka representative, Marshal G. K. Zhukov, were unhappy with these attacks and felt, even in late October, that "they were producing no results at all, except for inflicting heavy casualties on the tired and depleted Soviet armies." A report to Stalin to this effect did not please the Supreme Commander and both men were immediately summoned to Moscow. Again Rokossovsky and Zhukov made their point, the latter insisting that "our offensive will yield us nothing but casualties", and then proposing that Warsaw would be turned more effectively by a major thrust towards Lodz and Poznan, which would disrupt the whole German front on the Vistula. After directing the two generals out of the room "to think some more" – one of Stalin's favourite 'debating' tactics – he later recalled them and agreed that all Soviet forces would now go over to the defensive.[10]

One reason for Stalin's and Stavka's obvious uncertainty about the importance of Warsaw in future operations was that the Army General Staff was itself only just beginning to consider such operations in detail. Proper planning, in fact, only began on 29th October, when "the direction of each Front's attack, its zones of attack and the depth of the immediate and further objectives were exactly defined." Prior to this the existing plans "provided only the general substance of the final campaign . . . The direction of the main effort was not yet defined."[11] In short, though Berlin must have figured as a likely, certainly desirable objective, no one was as yet at all sure how it might be achieved.

Such high-level deliberations were well beyond the purview of the ordinary Soviet soldiers in Poland, most of whom were concerned simply with surviving from day to day. Along much of the front their chances were indeed somewhat better than hitherto. By late October, most Russian divisions were on the defensive, facing an enemy as exhausted as themselves and often willing to join in a grudging semi-truce, with both sides hunkered down in elaborate trench lines reminiscent of the First World War. General V. I. Chuikov commanded Eighth Guards Army in the Magnuszew bridgehead at this time and his war memoirs give a useful insight into front-line conditions. Like any modern army tied down in static warfare, the Soviets set great store by reconnaissance and patrolling, continually keeping a "careful watch on the daily timetable and habits of the German soldiers and officers. We knew when the Nazis had their dinner and supper . . . and the positions of their artillery, their six-barrelled mortars, and their tank units." There were also reconnaissance groups at Army level and these seem to have been especially audacious. It was vital for Soviet planners to "determine with the maximum accuracy what forces the enemy had in his reserve over the whole depth of his defence zone", and so groups were sent through the German lines to keep a 24-hour watch on their rear echelons and reserves "from points twenty-five to forty kilometres behind the front lines. Our reconnaissance men penetrated the Nazi dispositions for the most part on foot, passing right through the battle lines. Contact with our groups was maintained by radio, and by Po-2 planes at night."[12]

For most soldiers in their trenches and dug-outs, and in the cellars of ruined villages, October was the beginning of quiet 'defensive' life. Chuikov writes:

> In these conditions the maintenance of vigilance acquired especial importance. During a long period of manning defences men get used to the line of the front remaining unchanged, they 'settle down' with the enemy, and the two sides sometimes reach tacit agreement on letting one another live decently, so to speak. For example, they will not fire on a field kitchen coming up, will not hinder the fetching of water . . .
>
> Anyone who has had no experience of [trench life] need only go down into a damp basement or cellar with a narrow slit of a window, and then imagine men staying in conditions like that for two or three weeks, or even several months on end, just waiting for their cellar-hole to be hit by a shell and themselves crushed under logs, boards, earth and mould. Added to which the soldier has to stand long hours of look-out duty, and has to sit in his listening post whether the rain pours or the sun blazes or the blizzard howls. And to crown all this comes the uninvited guest, the louse – who is the scourge of all under such conditions . . . In a trench or shelter in a forward position, not only does the soldier suffer all manner of privations he loses his acuity of feeling, and becomes indifferent to many things.

Having so convincingly described the causes of what he calls "trench depression", Chuikov is far less credible when he hastily assures the reader that "it may sometimes be avoided altogether, as we did in the Magnuszew bridgehead, if the Party political work is properly organised at company and platoon level."[13]

Trench depression or not, political work or not, at least the Red Army still managed to hold on to a sufficient number of hardy combat veterans who could be relied upon to keep up the momentum of an attack or pass on the essential lore of trench life to the large numbers of recently conscripted, ill-armed levies from the liberated territories.

The Germans, on the other hand, were finding that heavy losses made it almost impossible to provide seasoned cadres for all the new formations raised, or even for those that had been many months in the line. Between August and October, they suffered 672,000 battle casualties but received only 201,000 replacements. The new *Volksgrenadier* divisions did tend to be built around a core of experienced NCOs and officers from a disbanded division or from several smaller units, but the latest creation, the *Volksturm*, officially brought into existence on 18th October, relied on the very oldest and youngest age-groups capable of bearing arms and was patently an almost worthless organisation. It did not help that this whole burst of recruitment activity was under Himmler's control. Several Volksturm units had already been formed even before the official decree, and Guderian was well aware of their general standard. In one, "my old comrade-in-arms General von Wietersheim was the member of the rank-and-file of a company commanded by some worthless Party functionary. As a result, the brave men of the Volksturm, prepared to make any sacrifice, were in many cases drilled busily in the proper way of giving the Hitler salute instead of being trained in the use of weapons of which they had had no previous experience." A member of the *Grossdeutschland* Division, en route to Lithuania, but in training near Lodz in October, remembered his first sight of such a unit: "Some of these troops must have been at least sixty or sixty-five, to judge by their curved spines, bowed legs and abundant wrinkles. But the young boys were even more astonishing . . . The oldest were about sixteen, but there were others who could not have been more than thirteen. They had been hastily dressed in worn uniforms cut for men, and were carrying guns which were often as big as they were. They looked both comic and horrifying, and their eyes were filled with unease, like the eyes of children at the reopening of school . . . Several of them were carrying school satchels their mothers had packed with extra food and clothes . . . A few of the boys were trading the saccharine candies which the rations allotted to children under thirteen."[14]

15

Satellites Out of Orbit

SLOVAKIA, RUMANIA AND HUNGARY

EVEN BEFORE the first shots were fired in the Second World War one European country had already been dismembered. Czechoslovakia was effectively sold out to Hitler at Munich in 1938, when he took over the Sudetenland, and then was completely betrayed in March 1939 when the German Army marched into Prague. Many Czech politicians, soldiers and others fled abroad during this period and, when war finally broke out, set up their own provisional government, first in Paris and later in London, with Eduard Benes as its premier. Their native country had all but disappeared. The provinces of Bohemia and Moravia were absorbed into the Third Reich and Ruthenia was gobbled up by the Hungarians. Only Slovakia was permitted to remain nominally independent, under the overtly fascist regime of Msg. Josef Tiso, who remained staunchly pro-Nazi, even contributing the services of the Army's Mobile Division during the invasions of Poland and the Soviet Union. Even so, internal rule was far less repressive than that of Reichsprotektor Wilhelm Frick in Bohemia-Moravia.

For most Slovaks any sort of pro-German government was an anathema, and a significant resistance movement developed within the country, some of its members specifically Slovak nationalists, others loyal to Benes' vision of a united Czechoslovakia. Armed partisan bands began to emerge, and in December 1943 a Slovak National Council was formed, bringing together a broad spectrum of political groups. There was discontent in the Army, too. The Mobile Division had fought well enough on the Eastern Front but, by 1942, it had been relegated to coastal defence duties. The protests of its men merely inspired the Germans to break it up into Construction Brigades which were packed off to Rumania and Italy. Other infantry divisions were formed inside Slovakia itself and, by August 1944, the 1st and 2nd were fully manned and equipped in barracks in eastern Slovakia, while the 3rd was still forming in the centre of the country.

By this time disaffected Slovak officers had begun planning a national uprising, working from within the Ministry of National Defence itself. Meetings with the National Council had been held in April, and in late June it set up its own Military Centre, headed by Lieutenant-Colonel Golian. He and his army co-conspirators were adherents of the London government and their planning for summer and autumn 1944 was based upon two contingencies, either of which it was hoped would provoke a general armed uprising and the speedy return of the government-in-exile, flown in by the Allies.

One contingency would be an attempt by Hitler, who already had forces along Slovakia's eastern frontier facing the Soviets, to send more troops to occupy the interior and bolster Tiso's resolve, which was already wilting as the Red Army got nearer. The closing up to the frontier by the Soviets was in fact the second contingency, so that whether or not Hitler actually invaded, the Slovak partisans would support 1 and 2 Infantry Divisions in launching diversionary attacks on German forces either in the interior or on the frontier, or both. Such a diversion would ease a Red Army breakthrough into Slovakia. Given a high degree of Soviet goodwill which the National Council seems to have taken for granted, such a breakthrough would immediately permit the return of the London government.

The Soviets, however, had their own agenda, and their own provisional government-in-waiting. While they welcomed the potential military benefits of a Slovak uprising, they feared the possibility that this might endow the Military Centre with the authority to act as Benes' Praetorian Guard. The Russians were also less than happy with the Slovak partisan movement, which was heavily under the influence of the Slovak Communist Party whose political line was not at all to Moscow's taste. Many communists also supported the return of the London government and stressed the importance of a return to a broad-based nationalist regime.

To counter this pernicious 'London concept', the Soviet leadership had determined to insinuate its own cadres into the partisan movement. In April 1944 it had set up a Slovak section of the Party-run Ukrainian Partisan Staff and from July was filtering Soviet partisan groups into the country. By early September there were more than 3,000 such personnel inside Slovakia. One historian has explained Stalin's motives here, couching his fears about the emergence of a 'bourgeois' democratic state very much in the jargon of the time. In Stalin's eyes "to allow the proponents of the 'London concept' to triumph without any challenge would have been foolish and pointless political benevolence. Once a Soviet-controlled partisan movement was entrenched on Slovak territory there was an instrument in being to 'activate' the struggle, to place the leadership of this fight firmly in the hands of the 'progressives' and to pre-empt the bourgeois nationalists by precipitating a revolt."[1]

In August the Ukrainian Staff made just such a bid to put its own partisans at the head of the liberation struggle. Without consulting the National Council or the Military Centre, it suddenly and significantly stepped up the tempo of its operations, culminating in the capture and execution of a senior German officer. This escalation took everyone by surprise. Tiso flapped around to little avail and Hitler, furious at his inability to control events, ordered in a German division on 29th August. This in turn prompted the Military Centre to issue its own call to arms that very day. The announcement took the two divisions of the East Slovak Corps by surprise and they proved quite incapable of offering any organised resistance to the other German units that now began to descend upon Slovakia. Panzer units from Hungary were the nearest troops and they disarmed and dispersed the Slovak divisions with depressing ease. The London government's projected army in being dissolved overnight.

Ironically, from the Soviet point of view, things had gone a little too well. So suddenly had the Slovak Corps disintegrated that it could provide no assistance to the Red Army's own drive into Slovakia, which began on 8th September. The main attacks fell on the right and left wings of Seventeenth and First Panzer Armies respectively, which had only four divisions covering the 70-mile front. Now largely unconcerned with the security of their rear areas, the Germans were able to concentrate upon defending the threatened portion of their Carpathian front, along the Rivers Wiskola and Wistok and through the Dukla and Lupkow Passes. Within a few days they had reinforced the original four divisions with a further two panzer and six infantry divisions. A breach had been made on the first day but this was sealed off by the 9th. Marshal I. S. Koniev, commanding 1st Ukrainian Front, then committed IV Tank Corps and was able to storm Krosno on the 11th. On the 20th the town of Dukla also fell to the Soviets, but the Pass was held and a deep penetration by a Soviet Guards Cavalry Corps, through another narrow gap north-west of the Pass, was encircled and cut off. From 30th September Soviet and Soviet-trained troops from I Czechoslovak Corps continued to hammer away at the Dukla Pass and on 6th October finally succeeded in breaking through.

The two Soviet armies involved, Thirty-Eighth and First Guards, were thrown again and again at the German defences, but though these attacks took them over the crest of the Carpathians along most of their front, they were unable to make much impression on this last line of German defences linking the southern bend of the River Wiskoda with the line of the River Ordava, south to Stropkov. The offensive had already stalled by 25th October although Stavka had not yet agreed formally to go over to the defensive. One official Soviet version admits: "The offensive deep [sic] into Slovakia was attended by enormous difficulties. One of the formidable barriers were the East Beskids, towering to a height of 850 metres above the sea level. Besides, the units committed to this operation had been engaged in the battles around Lwow and Sandomierz, with the result that they were undermanned and short of supplies . . . Very few tanks were available to support the infantry."[2] The fighting had also been extremely costly. In a campaign of which few people are now even aware, the Red Army is said to have suffered 21,000 killed and 89,000 wounded. The Czechoslovak Corps alone lost 844 officers and men killed and 4,068 wounded out of a complement of only 16,000.

Although the Red Army had not succeeded in breaking through to link up with the insurgents, they had drawn a number of German divisions to their front, divisions which might otherwise have been available for the suppression of the Uprising. In fact, this was less of a boon to the insurgents than might be thought. Insurrectional and partisan activity in areas behind the German lines were Himmler's responsibility and by October 1944 he had many troops under his direct command. Among these were the Waffen-SS divisions, which usually fought shoulder-to-shoulder with Army divisions but which owed their ultimate loyalty to Himmler. After the July 1944 Bomb Plot against Hitler, Himmler also became Head of the Replacement Army and therefore had the decisive say in the deployment of the new Volksgrenadier divisions, now being trained and equipped at a prodigious rate. Thus it was that the two waves of reinforcements sent in late August and early October to deal with the Slovak Uprising comprised in the main SS and Volksgrenadier formations. The units deployed on 25th October were a typical heterogeneous assortment of foreign volunteers and latter-day conscripts, comprising three SS divisions of Ukrainians, Hungarian Volksdeutsch and

Estonians, and two Volksgrenadier divisions rebuilt from formations smashed on the Eastern Front and in Normandy. Also present were SS Panzer Regiment 'Schill' and SS Brigade 'Dirlewanger', the latter built around a cadre of German ex-convicts and whose subsequent expansion was effected by "taking personnel from German prisons and concentration camps, SS military prisons and other human cess-pits. Its reputation for atrocity became scandalous."[3]

Unsavoury an army as these might have been, notably the SS volunteers for whom anyone not in a German uniform was a Jewish-Bolshevik horde in the making, they sufficed to slowly strangle the Uprising. From the beginning, even after the ignominious collapse of the East Slovak Corps, the insurgent commanders had tried to give their forces a semi-regularised standing. Thus they referred to themselves as the First Czechoslovak Insurgent Army and carefully distinguished between their units, containing numerous ex-soldiers from the dissolved divisions, and the ordinary partisan bands. Around 15,000 soldiers are said to have joined the Uprising, and in late September and October the National Council raised another 25,000 men through general conscription. But at the heart of this attempt to establish a regularised army was 2 Czechoslovak Parachute Brigade, another Soviet-trained formation that had been flown in at Slovak request to buttress their defence. Its effectiveness was undermined, however, by its slow arrival which was spread out over six weeks, between 13th September and 25th October. Whether this drip-feed of reinforcements was a deliberate ploy on the part of the Soviets or the result of logistic difficulties remains unclear, but there seems little doubt that Stavka persisted in trying to subvert the partisan movement. In mid-September the National Council had set up its own Main Staff for Slovak Partisans but, at the 'request' of local Party officials, the Soviets immediately began to fly in their own guerrilla commanders and commissars and at the end of September landed senior figures from the Ukrainian Staff. This marked a "significant change, for it put the Slovak partisan movement under overt Soviet command."[4]

Nevertheless, it had by now become apparent that the Soviets' grip on the partisan movement was not likely to pay them any immediate political dividends. In mid-October the insurgents still controlled a substantial chunk of central Slovakia, some fifty by ninety miles in extent, but Himmler's reinforcements were now mostly in place and his terror apparatus was hard at work in the areas already pacified. Indeed, one reason for Himmler's prompt build-up of forces had been the anger of the Führer himself, who was quite adamant that the mainspring of the Uprising must be the continued presence in Slovakia of 35,000 of the country's original 90,000 Jews. From September, hard on the heels of the Waffen-SS formations came police and security units under the command of *Obergruppenführer* Hermann Hölfe, a typical higher SS police leader. "For the special task of pacification he sent five commandos of security police under [*Obersturmbannführer* Josef] Witiska. The era of mass executions had begun . . . It took only four weeks to re-establish behind the front the perfect peace characteristic of German rule."[5] Re-established, too, were the mass deportations, which had ceased in autumn 1942, partly due to the intervention of the Slovak government. By late October a bevy of Adolf Eichmann's resettlement commissioners had arrived in Bratislava and were already busy with their file-cards and railway timetables.

The combat troops renewed their offensive on the 18th and from then until the 25th left "everywhere a trail of burning villages, mass graves or cowed civilians awaiting transportation to concentration camps."[6] The main axes of advance were those of 18 SS Division from Hungary towards Tisovec, 14 SS Division from the north-east towards Brezno, the two divisions from the west converging on Banska Bystrica, the rebel headquarters, and the Dirlewanger Brigade from the north-west. By the 25th only an ever-shrinking circle of territory on either side of the upper Hron river remained, with Brezno and Donovaly falling that very day and the Airborne Brigade pushed back to the outskirts of Zvolen. Also taken on the 25th was the Tri Duba (Three Oaks) airfield, near Banska Bystrica, while outside the River Hron enclave other groups of partisans, and some stragglers from First Insurgent Army, were still holding out on the southern slopes of the Tatras Mountains, south-east of Ruzomberok. Bystrica was where the Parachute Brigade had first landed, and it had since become the home of 1 Czechoslovak Fighter Regiment, yet another Soviet-trained and equipped unit. It provided the Slovak insurgents with the historically unique asset of air superiority over their liberated area. But within hours of these fighters leaving, German aircraft took to the air and resumed the favoured pastime of strafing refugee columns trying to make their way into the mountains.

Some accounts of the war on the Eastern Front in these months are inclined to bracket the defeat of the Slovak Uprising with that in Warsaw and to stress the failure of the Red Army on both occasions to engage with the German counter-insurgency forces. Soviet resolve before Warsaw is at least debatable, but it does seem clear that on the Slovak frontier it was the rugged Carpathian mountains, manned by ordinary but determined German Army divisions, that halted the two Soviet armies west of the Ondava. Unfortunately, the end result in Warsaw and Slovakia was much the same, and just as the Polish capital was now a desolate ruin, awaiting only Himmler's bulldozers and demolition teams, so Slovakia was fast becoming just one more charnel house in the nihilistic SS domain.

*

When Hitler had started dismantling the Versailles settlements there had been plenty of East European statesmen eager to hover around and grab chunks of their 'rightful' territory. Thus in Poland Stalin suddenly turned up for his share, while Czechoslovakia was stripped by a whole gaggle of carrion politicians. In 1940 their beady eyes had begun to turn towards Rumania. First the Soviets demanded back Bessarabia and part of Bukovina, then Hitler and Mussolini brokered, or rather imposed, a settlement by which Hungary and Bulgaria both received disputed territories. Hungary's portion was the greater part of Transylvania, the large tongue of land extending from a line Oradea–Satu Mare south-eastwards almost to the River Buzau. This Axis 'arbitration' was deeply resented in Rumania, soon leading to the accession to power of General Ion Antonescu, subsequently aided and abetted by his distant cousin Mhia. The General, who took the title 'Conducator' (Leader), was very much in the contemporary strong man mould but he had little option but to accept the territorial losses. Thereafter he was prevailed upon to sign an oil agreement with Hitler, giving Germany exclusive rights to the output from the large fields around Ploesti and, in November, to become part of the expanded Tri-Partite Pact between Germany, Italy and Japan. Hungary, under another iron-jawed autocrat, Admiral Miklos Horthy, also joined the Pact that month and in 1941 both countries were invited to another territorial feeding frenzy consequent upon the first BARBAROSSA victories. Throughout the fighting on the Eastern Front, therefore, both Antonescu and Horthy, although bitter enemies themselves over Transylvania, made available large numbers of troops to fight with the Wehrmacht. The actual numbers fluctuated alarmingly, particularly as both national contingents were susceptible to instant military collapse whenever their sectors of the front were attacked in earnest. Nevertheless, in mid-August 1944, out of 178 divisions on the Eastern Front (excluding Finland), 20 were Rumanian, 15 Hungarian and 2 Slovak, fully 21 per cent of total manpower.

In terms of quality, however, this figure of a little over one-fifth is somewhat misleading, and of the 22 panzer and panzer-grenadier divisions only two were foreign, and both had very poor equipment. The German high command was obliged to pretend otherwise and important sectors of the front were assigned to Rumanian and Hungarian divisions, though never side by side. This invariably ended in disaster, most notably in the defeat of Third and Fourth Rumanian Armies in north-west Rumania and Moldavia towards the end of August. Stationed alongside the German Sixth and Eighth Armies, they merely allowed these latter to be encircled swiftly as the Soviets ripped through the Rumanian defences between Jassy and Kishinev on 23rd and 24th August. Reformed after the Stalingrad disaster, Sixth Army had the misfortune to be almost completely destroyed yet again, and though Eighth Army did remain just about intact, though terribly depleted, it could only operate as the unwilling hinge on which the rest of the Soviet offensive swung, like a huge iron gate sweeping all before it as it closed first to the Transylvanian Alps and then to the River Tisza.

Soviet troops reached the Rumanian capital, Bucharest, on the 31st, but even before this the government had been desperately trying to extricate itself from the alliance with Germany. In April and May secret talks had been held with Allied representatives in Cairo. These came to nothing, but on the very day that the Red Army's Jassy-Kishinev onslaught began key Rumanian political and military figures, backed by young King Mihail, had steeled themselves to arrest Antonescu. German advisers, security personnel and the like were ordered out of the country and an attempted German counter-coup was thwarted. On the 26th August the new government, under General Sanatescu, declared war on Germany and on the 30th, with more evident conviction, on Hungary. Early in September a Rumanian armistice delegation arrived in Moscow and on the 12th an armistice convention was signed. It could hardly be described as a negotiated settlement. Soviet Foreign Minister Molotov had drawn up the terms without even giving the Allied co-signatories a chance to scrutinise them. "With its three signatories the convention bore some inter-Allied impress, but in practical terms Rumania was handed to the Soviet Union, lock, stock and barrel, in a very literal sense." Rumanian troops came under overall Soviet command, Bessarabia and northern Bukovina were lost once more, and over the following weeks and months the Rumanians began to meet enormous financial penalties, payable in goods and raw materials, to settle a war indemnity and to defray occupation costs. The whole Rumanian Navy had also been seized, along with a large part of the merchant fleet, much of the petroleum industry infrastructure, thousands of tons of other industrial machinery, railway rolling stock, and "every motor car to hand, all commandeered and taken into Soviet service."[7]

Considering that twenty Rumanian divisions had been steamrollered during the Jassy-Kishinev offensive, the Rumanian Army as a whole did remarkably well to get anti-German operations under way as quickly as it did. The terms of the armistice called for only twelve Rumanian divisions in all but the necessary reductions had not been made by late October. At this time there were still nineteen divisions fighting with Malinovsky, most of which had played a substantial role in the campaign to liberate Transylvania. By 25th October, Rumanian casualties in the fighting against the Germans had already reached almost 50,000 men.[8]

Fourth Army attacked in northern Transylvania, flanked by Soviet Twenty-seventh and Fortieth Armies and along an axis between Cluj and Carel. The whole offensive had begun on 9th October and on the 11th Rumanian divisions took part in the liberation of Cluj, the largest city in northern Transylvania. Thereafter the main Soviet thrust was towards Debrecen, Hungary's second city, taken on 19th/20th October, while Rumanian units continued to mop up Hungarian stragglers to the north-west. On the 25th, 9 Infantry Division had the satisfaction of liberating Carei, the most westerly town in Rumanian Transylvania. Fourth Army had had the majority of the available Rumanian divisions under its command, and had also been given the best armoured and air support, because the task of liberating lost national territory was seen as the most pressing need. First Army was much weaker, yet it was these divisions that had to fight along an axis between Arad and Budapest, the defence of which was the Germans' main priority in Hungary.

German resistance also put increasing strain on the main Soviet formation along this axis, and the Rumanian divisions were brought forward to hold three bridgeheads across the Tisza to the south of Szolnok. One of the latter was lost to a major German counter-attack on 19th October, and on the 25th two Hungarian divisions attacked a second bridgehead, held by the "raw 2nd Infantry Division. With the fate of the [first bridgehead] fresh in its memory, 2nd Division was panicked by the presence of a few tanks and allowed itself to be rapidly driven back across the river." In both Rumanian armies by the end of October it was apparent that "battle casualties were much higher than those of their opponents. This can largely be explained by their chronic equipment shortages and the inexperience of the training divisions, which led to tactical crudity in attack not displayed since Odessa [in summer 1941]."[9] For more than three years the Rumanians had found plugging the gaps in the Germans' eastern front an extremely costly, often humiliating experience. Transylvania apart, it now began to look as if fighting on Soviet coat-tails was going to be no less arduous.

*

Not the least reason for Rumania's continuing military travails was the stiff resistance put up by the Hungarian Army, which continued to fight alongside the Germans. However, despite the Magyars' natural inclination to fight Rumanians, it should not be thought that they were especially enthusiastic followers of the Nazi cause. For some months, indeed, one of the least enthusiastic had been Admiral Horthy himself. As early as March 1944, the Germans had been sufficiently worried by his lack of zeal that they had invited him for pep-talks in Berlin and then promptly marched in German troops to impose a new puppet cabinet under Prime Minister Andor Szotaj. But German anxieties persisted, leading them to move two SS Divisions close to Budapest in late August to forestall a possible anti-German coup. In the event, the new cabinet that emerged from the crisis remained loyal and in early September refused to countenance armistice negotiations with the Allies, as proposed by Horthy. Later that month the Germans moved more troops into the vicinity of Budapest and insisted that the Hungarians place their divisions directly under German army group commanders.

Horthy persisted with his peace overtures and on 1st October, little more than a fortnight after a cowed Rumanian delegation had signed over their country, Hungarian negotiators arrived in Moscow. Although terms were agreed by the 11th, or rather imposed by the Soviets, still Horthy seems to have been unable to steel himself to surrender to the Red Army and he dithered for several days. Hitler did not dither, however, and his troops seized vital communications centres on 4th October and arrested the Hungarian garrison commander in Budapest on the 8th. Thus, when Horthy did finally decide to accept Soviet terms on the 15th, he was in no position to give effect to this decision. On this same day his son was arrested, and on the 16th Horthy himself was seized when his palace was stormed by German special forces troops. He was replaced by Ferenc Szalasi who, as leader of the Arrow-Cross Party, was an ideological soul-mate of the Nazis and ardent proponent of their most rabid racial policies. One key commander, General Bela Miklos of First Army, did go over to the Soviets and offered to take his soldiers with him. "But the Germans quickly stepped in to stop the rot [and] on 24th October the Stavka issued a formal order to the commanders of the 2nd and 4th Ukrainian Fronts instructing them to treat German and Hungarian troops alike, since Hungarian troops were continuing to fight."[10]

With Soviet and Rumanian forces already advancing some way into Hungary by the 25th, Stalin was determined to 'bounce' Budapest and thus bestow more apparent legitimacy on such Hungarian politicians as could be found to form a pro-Soviet provisional government. A major offensive into Hungary had begun on 6th October, with 2nd Ukrainian Front's left wing heading for the capital and the right advancing along the axis Oradea–Debrecen–the River Tisza–Miskolc, where it would link up with 4th Ukrainian Front coming through the Dukla Pass and Uzhgorod. These last two axes were to form a pincers that would trap the northern wing of Army Group South and perhaps part of Army Group Centre's First Panzer Army. "The plan was ambitious, too ambitious. Men and materiel for an extensive build-up were not to be had at this late stage of the general summer offensive; both fronts were feeling the effects of combat and long marches; and their supply lines were overextended. Because of the difference in gauges, the Rumanian railroads, if anything, were serving the Russians less well than they had the Germans, and Second Ukrainian Front had to rely mainly on motor transport west of the Dnestr. Malinovsky's broad front deployment gave him only about half the ratio of troops to frontage usual for a Soviet offensive."[11]

The Budapest drive was the first to falter as here the Soviets were particularly short of men. Luckily, Stalin seemed prepared, at least for the moment, to accept some delay and attention was soon focussed on the Debrecen axis, where Hitler's mulish refusal to withdraw behind the Tisza seemed to offer the real possibility of a major encirclement. On 12th October, Oradea fell to the Red Army and the commander of Army Group South, General Johannes Friessner, resolved to begin withdrawing on his own authority. On the 16th, with 2nd Ukrainian Front approaching Debrecen and 4th Ukrainian Front relentlessly chipping their way through the Carpathians to the north, Hitler finally gave official sanction to this withdrawal. But substantial forces were still needed to cover the retreat and over the following days the Germans attempted to hold on a blocking line Debrecen–Nyirgyhaza–Chop. On the 20th, however, Debrecen fell, to be followed two days later by Nyiregyhaza.

The advance had been made on a very narrow front by General P. A. Pliev's Mechanised Cavalry Group, it presumably being hoped that the mere appearance of Soviet tanks and horsemen in the German rear would be sufficient to induce panic. Certainly the capture of Nyiregyhaza and the subsequent advance right up to the bend of Tisza represented something of a problem for General Otto Wöhler's subsidiary Army Group, combining Eighth and First Hungarian Armies, which was holding a bow-shaped front with an extended flank some 80 miles east of Nyiregyhaza. General Friessner's instinctive reaction was to try to disengage and reform the front to the north and east, but his chief-of-staff proposed a bolder stratagem. Sixth Army, reincarnated yet again to the south, had just received substantial armoured reinforcements and two of these divisions, 23 Panzer and 60 Panzer-Grenadier, were deployed to attack from Tokay, capital of the famous wine-growing region, into Pliev's exposed left flank. At the same time some of Wöhler's German troops were to make supporting attacks from the east, out of the rear of their own positions. The operation began late on the 22nd and "the manoeuvre worked with the flair and precision of the Blitzkrieg days. On the 23rd the two forces met and cut off three Soviet corps at Nyiregyhaza." Over the next two days fierce battles raged over these Hungarian plains, with each German pincer committing more and more men and tanks to the attack. According to one account, "the mostly treeless Hungarian plain allowed the Panzers, as in North Africa, to adopt 'warship' tactics and seek out the flanks and rear of enemy columns which kept to the roads."[12] By the 25th the Soviet armoured advance had cost them, so the Germans claimed, over 600 tanks and assault guns and upwards of 25,000 casualties.

Yet even on this day, as they closed in on and retook Nyiregyhaza, it was far from sure that the victory could have much long-term significance. To be sure the panzers had shown the panache of the old days, and even fashioned themselves an encirclement of sorts. But their units were now so understrength that encirclement was a notional term, rather than an actual staking out of a solid, aggressive perimeter. By the end of the day, the whole of Sixth Army could muster no more than 70 tanks and 60 assault guns between six panzer and panzer-grenadier divisions. German flair had, it was true, succeeded in dealing an embarrassing rebuff to Malinovsky's reckless vanguard, and one that held open a vital German escape route across the Tisza. Yet any temporary respite that the Germans had gained for themselves would only work against them in the end. Within a few weeks Soviet production lines would have replaced all their losses and more, while the Germans, already giving high priority to the forthcoming Ardennes counter-offensive, could expect only a trickle of new armoured vehicles. Ironically, the Germans' best ally in this respect was the Red Army itself. For on the 25th October "the German troops who retook Nyiregyhaza and parts of the *puszta* had ample opportunity to observe the behaviour of Soviet troops towards the Hungarian population. Women of all ages were raped and sometimes murdered. Parents were nailed to doorposts while their children were mutilated. The sights seem to have steeled the resolution in their efforts to keep the enemy out of Germany, because in Hungary German troops put up the most desperate resistance yet encountered by the Red Army."[13]

16

Communism and Revolution

BULGARIA AND YUGOSLAVIA

A T THE Moscow Conference in October 1944, when Poland was effectively handed over to Stalin, it was also agreed that Soviet influence in the Balkans should predominate in Bulgaria and be shared equally with the western Allies in Croatia, Serbia and the other small states that would eventually comprise Yugoslavia. In fact, these seem to have been Stalin's intentions even before the deal with Churchill was struck. Despite Hitler's conviction that the 'Big Three' must soon fall out over the future of the Balkans, there is little evidence that the Red Army had ever intended to move towards the Aegean or the Adriatic. By 25th October Stalin's intentions already seemed fairly clear. Most of Marshal Tolbukhin's 3rd Ukrainian Front divisions had already left Bulgaria and were assisting in the liberation of Belgrade, as well as following on the heels of the Germans retreating northwards towards Budapest.

As for Bulgaria, it cannot honestly be claimed that its forces had offered much of a challenge to Tolbukhin's troops. The Bulgarians were never whole-hearted in their commitment to Hitler's expanded Tripartite Pact and deftly avoided ever having to send troops to the Eastern Front, confining their military activities to the occupation of newly acquired territories in Macedonia and Thrace and assisting the Germans in their occupation of Serbia and Salonika. Already anxious as the Red Army began wheeling round the Black Sea coast, across the lower Bug and the Dniester, the Bulgarians had begun to feel especially exposed when Turkey broke off diplomatic relations with Germany at the beginning of August. Within days the Bulgarians had established consular relations with the Soviet Union and were soon engaged in earnest discussions at the latter's embassy in Ankara. By the end of the month they were also talking to other Allied representatives in Cairo. These talks acquired a new urgency on 2nd September when Red Army units rumbled into Guirgiu, on the Rumanian border. On the 3rd a new cabinet was sworn in, which declared its neutrality the next day. This was not enough for the Soviets, who wanted from the Bulgarians an outright declaration of war on Germany, and on the 5th they declared war themselves on Bulgaria. On the 8th they swept across the frontier but found that only a fraction of the Bulgarian Army – four out of twenty-three divisions – stood in their way and that these were not in the least interested in fighting. The rest of the Army was either assigned to occupation duties, and now busily surrendering to the Germans, or was part of the force guarding the frontier with Turkey. The Bulgarian government declared war on Germany that same day and, on the 9th, Tolbukhin halted his three armies. In the meantime, yet another government, the pro-Soviet Fatherland Front, was ushered into power in a bloodless coup backed by communist partisans and leftist elements within the armed forces.

The Bulgarians now tried to emulate, or even to surpass the Rumanians at the speed with which they turned around their forces and joined in the Soviet advance, leaving only Third Army in place on the Turkish frontier. This did not go entirely smoothly and all divisions experienced a stormy transition period, characterised by the formation of vociferous soldiers' committees and heated debates over the future role of the armed forces. Such barrack-room democracy was little to the Soviets' taste and they soon set about bringing the troops to heel. In the chillingly benign words of General Shtemenko: "More than once we argued whether the soldiers' committees . . . helped or hindered when, if they were retained, they might become an obstacle to strengthening discipline and one-man leadership in the forces and to the cause of preparing the Army for actions at the front. The committees were gradually dissolved." Soviet military advisers were attached to many of the divisions and those do seem to have had a purely military role, though there were also attached "Soviet political workers [who] greatly helped the new people's Army of Bulgaria in organising political and educational work."[1]

While this political and educational work and the "gradual dissolution" of the soldiers' committees was still going on in late October, the Bulgarian Army was coping with the absorption of 40,000 new 'volunteers'. Having crossed the Serbian border with the consent of the Yugoslav Communists, ten Bulgarian divisions were formed into three separate Armies, operating as the liberator of south-east Serbia and in

Macedonia. Though they faced little opposition from the Germans, none of these formations had managed by the 25th to fulfil their main mission of cutting off the German Army as it retreated from Greece, via Skopje and Kraljevo, to link up with the rest of the German forces in the Balkans. But they had at least helped to narrow the Germans' escape routes and by late October dominated Nis and the valley of the Morava, through which ran the other important road and rail routes northward. It was as yet uncertain just what advantage these achievements would bring to Bulgaria itself. Delegates who arrived in Moscow to discuss the details of an armistice, which the western Allies left entirely in the hands of Stalin and Molotov, were still there on the 25th, cooling their heels and waiting to be told the fate of their country.

*

The absence of any Bulgarian resistance to the Soviet invasion had quickly allowed Stavka to redeploy the armies involved to protect Malinovsky's southern flank in Transylvania and later in Yugoslavia, on both sides of the Danube, and to help guard the Turkish frontier. This enabled Tolbukhin to threaten the rear of those German forces fighting against the Communist Partisans in Yugoslavia. The nearer he got to Belgrade, the more units the Germans had to divert to its defence, which in turn permitted the Partisans to advance slowly northwards into Serbia. Commanded not to get himself tied down in operations south of Belgrade, which were the main responsibility of the 'born again' Bulgarians, Tolbukhin swung his troops north-westwards, towards much-prized Budapest, as soon as the Serbian capital was secure. Stalin was a great one for capital cities and well realised how much the occupation of Belgrade would enhance the prestige of any future Partisan government. Equally he realised that Serbia was something of a Balkan backwater when compared to Poland or Hungary, and that it would be via Budapest and Warsaw that his armies would most conveniently approach the ancient citadels of Germanic aggression, Berlin and Vienna.

Yugoslavia had been invaded by the Germans in April 1941, en route to Greece where the Italians had made a complete hash of their own invasion. The Yugoslav Army had folded within days and the nation itself did not last much longer. Many territories were simply hijacked by the Germans, Italians, Bulgarians and Hungarians but the re-emergence of a separate Croatia and Serbia was largely the work of local separatists, and very much to the taste of hundreds of thousands of *quondam* Yugoslavs. Serbia remained a German puppet regime but even in late October 1944, with the front in Serbia at last collapsing, it was still able to call upon considerable local, if somewhat heterogeneous, armed support, including I Serbian Shock Corps, the *Schützkorps* with five regiments of White Russian emigrés, several battalions of auxiliary policemen formed from the Volksdeutsch population of the Banat, and some 12,000 pro-Royalist Cetnik guerrillas based around Mount Uncjak in northern Bosnia. Croatia had been established as an autonomous state, ruled by Ante Pavelic and his Ustaci, whose creed was a sickening combination of Catholic fanaticism and SS bloodlust. But, at least on paper, they provided the Germans with considerable military support. The current OKW situation map for south-east Europe on 25th October showed 15 Croat brigades (8 Army and 7 Ustaci) stationed to the east of the River Drina and between the Drava and the Sava.

The Germans had also been successful in recruiting Yugoslavs into their own armed forces. In October there were six Waffen-SS and Army divisions in existence, mainly manned by Yugoslavs. All but one were stationed actually in Yugoslavia. The best was undoubtedly 7 SS 'Prinz Eugen' Mountain Division, mainly recruited from among the Volksdeutsch and engaged in counter-insurgency operations since October 1942. Its officers were mainly Austrian and Rumanian Volksdeutsch, despite or thanks to whom the division had a record for savage reprisals. Three other divisions, 369, 373 and 392 Infantry, were part of the regular German Army and had all been recruited in Croatia. For some months they had been stationed near the Dalmatian coast, to counter any amphibious landing by Allied forces from Italy.

The most unusual German divisions, however, were 13 and 23 SS Mountain Divisions, which were given the titles 'Handschar' and 'Kama'. A *handschar* was a type of ceremonial scimitar, and a *kama* a small dagger used by Balkan shepherds. Both divisions contained a large proportion of Bosnian Muslims, then under Croatian sovereignty. With mainly German officers, they each nevertheless flaunted the Muslim connection in the derivation of their titles, their insignia, the wearing of the traditional tasselled fez, and, most remarkably, the presence of an *imam*, or spiritual counsellor, with each battalion. In October 1944, 'Kama' Division was still stationed in Hungary, where it had gone for training, but 'Handschar' had been in northern Bosnia since February that year and had performed reasonably well during an anti-Partisan drive in June. The Muslim contingent continually fretted about their prospects should the Germans pull out of Bosnia, and when some of their number were marched off to new positions north of

Zagreb they began to desert in droves, while those remaining behind openly mutinied. The German officers suffered the further indignity of having the Divisional Security Company desert en masse, whereupon Himmler immediately ordered all Muslim units to be dissolved. On 25th October, while Muslims still in Bosnia were rounded up and disarmed, 'Kama' Division was in uproar, having learnt that it was to return to Bosnia. Why one division should revolt on having to leave Bosnia and the other on being posted there remains puzzling. But Himmler's flirtation with Muslim beliefs, and their capacity to instil fanatical loyalty, was most definitely a thing of the past.

It would be grossly misleading, however, to suggest that active collaboration had been the typical Yugoslav response to Axis occupation, for a strong guerrilla resistance movement had existed ever since the German invasion. At first concentrated in Serbia, it was later forced into the most mountainous areas of Bosnia and Montenegro, and on seven occasions German forces had launched offensives designed to flush the Partisans out. On each occasion their commander, Josip Broz Tito, despite coming close to being captured and having to evacuate successive 'liberated' base areas, escaped with enough men to keep the movement alive. Indeed, it was his willingness to give up such base areas that was one of his greatest strengths. Tito rejected the classic guerrilla tactic of concentrating upon parochial village defence while embracing an overtly revolutionary strategy of building up semi-regular forces, organised in regiments and divisions, which could engage in mobile operations against sizable German and quisling forces. In this way, when the war swung the way of the western Allies and the Soviets, and one or other of them was poised to drive the Germans out of Yugoslavia, Tito and the Communists would have available an army capable of taking advantage of any power vacuum. Their efforts in this direction were actually aided by the western Allies, who started supplying the Partisans with regular shipments of arms and equipment in September 1943, and more especially, if unwittingly, by the Italians whose general surrender that same month allowed the Partisans to seize the weaponry of fully ten of the fourteen Italian divisions in the region. By October 1944 Tito had built up an army of 400,000 men, with its best fighters divided into four armies, seventeen corps and fifty-three divisions, each of the latter comprising around 3,000 men.

The sufferings these men, and women, endured and their success in keeping alive the spirit of resistance, time and again rebuilding their units from the detritus of prolonged retreat, must rank as one of the military epics of this century. Yet the epic, as part of the prologue to the Cold War, has inevitably led to bitter controversy which seems to diminish the scale of the Yugoslav contribution to overall Allied victory in tying down German divisions. It is interesting, therefore, to tally the exact number of such divisions in Yugoslavia on our chosen day, listed in the Table below.

The German command in the Balkans was *OB Süd-Ost*, under Field Marshal Maximilian von Weichs, and this was sub-divided into Army Groups E and F. The former comprised mainly units evacuated from Greece, as well as a few 'hoovered' up as the Army Group moved into southern Yugoslavia, and the latter was in charge of the forces in Bosnia, Croatia and Serbia. Important subsidiary commands within Army Group F included Second Panzer Army, a headquarters once charged with coastal defence but now responsible for holding a line south and west of Belgrade to permit the continued withdrawal of the Greece divisions. The defence of Belgrade itself had been allocated to so-called Army Detachment Serbia. The list below, however, only distinguishes the divisions by Army Group.

Army Group E	*Army Group F*
7 SS Mountain	1 Mountain
11 Luftwaffe Field*	1 Cossack
21 SS Mountain*	13 SS Mountain
22 Airlanding*	117 Jäger (part)
41 Fortress*	118 Jäger
104 Jäger†	264 Infantry
117 Jäger (part)†	369 Infantry
181 Infantry	373 Infantry
297 Infantry†	392 Infantry
	Brandenburg
	Sturmdivision Rhodes (part)

* Divisions en route from Greece and Albania. 41 Fortress Division was in fact just on the Greek side of the border.
† As above but had served in Yugoslavia previously.

The list makes it clear why this issue became a matter of acrimonious debate. A superficial reading seems to indicate that the Partisans were tying down 18 German divisions and part of another. This number is almost exactly equivalent to the total strength that day of Army Group G, facing Patton, Truscott, *and* de Lattre de Tassigny's three armies in Lorraine and Alsace. However, several important qualifications need to be made before any sort of meaningful comparison between Yugoslavia and other theatres can be made. For one thing, as the list makes explicit, six and a half of these divisions were simply passing through Yugoslavia, having been evacuated from Greece to help shore up the critical Hungarian front. Another division, 13 SS Mountain, was beginning to implode on 25th October. The one-and-a-half Jäger divisions that were actually stationed in Yugo-slavia were not comparable to other divisions with this elite appelation, being relatively weak formations containing mostly elderly reservists. Of the nine remaining divisions, 264 Infantry was a so-called 'static' (*boständige*) division, not suitable by temperament, training or equipment for conventional mobile operations, and 1 Cossack was similarly ill-suited, being mounted on horseback and armed with sabres. That leaves just seven full divisions, of which 1 Mountain was definitely a veteran outfit, 7 SS Mountain was full of hard cases but untested in full-scale combat, the Brandenburg Division was a special Forces/SAS type of outfit, unused to working as a single formation, 181 Infantry was again untested, but would probably have stood up well in the line, and the three infantry divisions recruited in Croatia would almost certainly not have 'travelled well' to any other theatre.

Let me be clear that I have absolutely no intention of denigrating the Yugoslav achievement in the Second World War; obliging the Germans to keep eleven divisions of any kind in Yugoslavia to contain a guerrilla force built entirely from scratch was no mean achievement and far surpasses that of any other national resistance movement in Europe. Nevertheless, the value of the Yugoslav contribution to the overall Allied war effort has to be assessed with caution as it is far from clear just how effective these divisions would have been had they been deployed in a conventional role on either the Eastern or the Western Fronts.

Moreover, as so often in guerrilla wars, it was only the appearance of a friendly regular army that gave the Partisans the operational freedom to undertake significant mobile operations, in this case boldly advancing northwards through Serbia, between the Drina and the Morava. Tolbukhin's drive on Belgrade had begun on 27th September, with Fifty-third Army crossing the Bulgarian-Yugoslav frontier on 1st October. By the 8th it had a bridgehead across the Morava at Velika Plana, to provide a jumping-off point for the next stage of the offen-sive. This was spearheaded by 4 Guards Mechanised Corps which completed a twelve-day journey from south-east Bulgaria on the 11th and immediately plunged across the river. Belgrade was finally cleared of the enemy on 19th October, the Soviet troops being ably, and ostentatiously, assisted by eight Partisan divisions from General Peko Dapchevic's First Army Group. The Germans had committed 20,000 troops in the city, of whom the great majority were killed or taken prisoner.

The most direct military benefit of taking the Yugoslav capital was not the elimination of its defenders but the denial of a communications centre through which other German units could escape to the north-west. Well before the fall of Belgrade, in fact, the Soviets had seen how scattered German forces were and had deployed their own troops, along with the Partisans and Bulgarians, on several additional axes, the better to trap pockets of Germans before they could be funnelled across the Sava bridge in Belgrade. Several such pockets were created, at Krujevac, Smederovo, Pozarevac and Kucevo, to the east and south-east of Belgrade, some containing 20,000 Germans and more. Most of these pockets were largely eliminated by the 25th, one of the most telling victories being that near Smederovo, on the Danube, where 1 Mountain Division had become involved in a counter-attack to the north of the River Morava and had been cut off by armoured columns to the south heading for Belgrade.

Some troops did manage to break out and cross the Danube at Sabac, on the 19th, where they joined numerous other stragglers trying to force their way westwards between the Sava and the Drava. Second Panzer Army just about managed to avoid collapse, with units grouped in *Kampfgruppen* under particularly energetic leaders, such as the commander of 1 Mountain Division, General Walter Stettner Ritter von Grabenhofen. Frantic efforts were made to reorganise enough stragglers to man fall-back lines between Zemun and Vukovar, and one of the more positive aspects of the disarming of 'Handschar' Division was the high-quality arms and equipment that could now be redistributed to 1 Mountain Division remnants. An Army Group F staff officer noted with satisfaction on 26th October: "With the transfer of weapons . . . the absurd practice of issuing the best German weapons to [non-Germans], who in turn hand them over to the enemy, will cease. A most costly error!"[2] As the error was Himmler's and these opinions were aired in the Army Group War Diary, one can only assume that the author was past caring.

Certainly most ordinary German soldiers were fast reaching that point. As one historian notes: "In the last two weeks of October Second Panzer Army had to retreat. Its best units were smashed, and the rest were in a complete tangle." An account of the experiences of some

Brandenburg Division stragglers gives a more personalised picture of events: "Only desperate men would have attempted to break through, with a couple of Panzerfausts and their sub-machine-guns short of ammunition . . . Night march, heavy rain. It was so dark, the men tore strips off their white shirts to stick on the back of the one in front. The mud came up to their knees. When their boots got stuck, they went on in their socks . . . A gorge lit by searchlights. Partisans to right and left, possibly even Russians already. They made their way through, singly, bounding forward two or three yards at a time. Some never got up again. Others gave up, put their hands up. Bursts of gun-fire mowed them down. The others went on."[3]

Belgrade on the 25th was still recovering from the week-long battle in its streets. The devastation was not as bad as it might have been as the Germans had been denied the opportunity to complete their extensive demolition work, while the Soviets had been ordered by Tolbukhin "to avoid using their heavy weapons to blast their way through from building to building or from street to street." Moreover, as the fighting was going on and in the days following, "the Front commander ordered seven engineer battalions to demine government and official buildings and monuments, the water supply and sewage systems, power stations, the port and other buildings and installations which the enemy had intended to blow up. Soviet sappers removed mines from 845 of them, thus saving Belgrade from destruction."[4]

Yet neither the Red Army nor the Partisans could feel entirely satisfied on the 25th because they had been unable to cut off completely the German retreat. Army Group E, in particular, was managing to extricate its divisions relatively intact and a notable rearguard action by 117 Jäger Division meant that a vital subsidiary escape route through Kraljevo was still open.

Even so, no one could deny the extent of the Partisans' achievement in playing a vital role in the liberation of much of Serbia, and its capital. For most of the Russian units taking part in the victory parade in the city on the 25th it was merely the beginning of a long march to a new battlefront, as they swung right over the Sava bridge and immediately headed north for Hungary and the forthcoming battle of Budapest. For the Partisans, however, there was the feeling of having already won their major victory. As their soldiers took the salute, they were some of the first in this whole global conflict who could believe that they were not simply being delivered from one tyranny to another, and that the new prospect of freedom had been bought in great part with their own blood and heroic endeavour. Certainly at least one British observer,

Brigadier Fitzroy Maclean, leading the British Military Mission to Tito's headquarters, had come to have the greatest admiration for these self-made warriors. As he stood next to Tito at the saluting-base he found it

> impossible not to be moved by the sight of the ragged, battle-stained throng of Partisans of all sizes and ages who marched past us. Veterans . . . marched next to boys of sixteen and seventeen; here and there a girl strode along with a rifle and pack beside the men; some were tall; some were undersized. They carried an odd assortment of arms and equipment, with only this in common: that it had been captured from the enemy in battle. Their uniforms, also stripped, for the most part, from dead Germans or Italians, were torn and stained. They were slung about with water-bottles and hand-grenades and strange odds and ends of equipment . . . Their boots were worn and patched. They looked underfed and weary.
>
> And yet they marched well and held themselves proudly and smiled as they marched. They had spent the whole of the last three years fighting. Since the spring they had fought their way half across Yugoslavia. Now, after all the hazards and hardships they had endured, after the cold and hunger, the attacks and counter-attacks, the ambushes and the long night marches, after the weeks and months and years of ever-present suspense and uncertainty, they were at last entering the capital as conquerors.[5]

17

The Furnace

LABOUR AND INDUSTRY IN THE SOVIET UNION

THE great Red Army breakthrough and encirclement battles in the Baltic states and in Rumania were not achieved simply by hurling riflemen – no matter how well-equipped with machine guns and mortars – against the fiendishly engineered German defensive lines. These might stretch several miles into the rear, through a whole succession of entrenched, wired, pill-boxed and mined lines of resistance, and could only be permanently ruptured if the first waves of 'shock' troops were powerful enough to maintain the momentum of their advance through successive positions. Just as essential were adequate follow-up forces that could pass through and threaten those rear areas where the enemy was attempting to muster reserves and establish strong switch-lines. Ideally, these exploitation forces would be able to penetrate on both flanks of the breakthrough and effect a wide double envelopment of the defenders, as had happened during the Jassy-Kishinev offensive. If this were not feasible, exploitation would usually consist of a series of powerful attacks on parallel axes, one giving way to another as soon as German reserves had been attracted to it. In essence, a Red Army offensive offered two methods of demolishing the enemy dyke, either by scooping out a double armful or by punching holes to weaken it progressively.

Offensives such as these were utterly dependent on firepower and well-protected mobile reserves. Conventional artillery, the Soviets' 'Red God of Battle', was part of the answer but also vital were large numbers of sturdy armoured fighting vehicles, both tanks and self-propelled artillery.[1] Having been one of the pioneers of massed armoured formations, the Red Army wavered in the late 1930s and seriously neglected tank doctrine and training. During the great

BARBAROSSA offensive in the summer of 1941 their armour was completely overrun. Russian tank design, however, was in much better shape and two superlatively functional machines, the T34 and the KV1, were already in limited production. As the Soviets' concept of offensive operations developed they were able to turn out successive generations of ever more heavily-gunned tanks and self-propelled artillery, all based on these two chassis. By October 1944, the much improved T34/85 had an 85mm gun and the K(lementi) V(oroshilov) had become the J(oseph) S(talin) 2, with an awesome 122mm gun capable of boring through the front armour of a 'Panther', the best German medium tank, and out the back. "It delivered 3.5 times more kinetic energy on impact than the [original] 76mm round, and even in the rare case that this was not sufficient to penetrate the armour, the force of the impact and explosion of the high explosive filler was usually enough to blow the turret off almost any tank."[2] The gun was similar in size to the main armament of most navy destroyers of the time but usually firing at much closer range than at sea.

By late 1944, the Soviets had also created a huge number of armoured units, many of them grouped together in specialised tank armies, all liberally supplied with tanks and self-propelled guns. A mechanised infantry corps usually had more tanks than a tank corps. In most armies infantry normally rode in lorries or armoured personnel carriers, but as the Soviets never produced either of these in large numbers, their motorised troops went into battle clinging ten and twelve at a time to their own tanks. They were known as *tankovyi desant* troops, which might be rendered as 'tank landing', a sort of worm's eye equivalent to 'air landing' glider and parachute units.

With the Red Army again highly committed to mechanisation, very heavy demands were imposed upon the iron and steel and engineering industries in the Soviet Union. While tank armour and ammunition required some of the best high-alloy steels, industry generally had been devastated during the first months of the war. Much of Soviet mining, smelting and manufacture was concentrated in central and eastern Ukraine and around Moscow and Leningrad, and all these areas had been occupied, besieged or threatened by invading German forces. In one of the great epics of the war the Soviets managed, by November 1941, to evacuate 1,523 industrial concerns, including 1,360 major plants, and transplant them to the Volga (15 per cent), the Urals (44 per cent), Siberia (21 per cent) and Soviet Central Asia (20 per cent). The operation had been carried out mainly by rail, *na kolesakh* ('on wheels') and involved one and a half million wagon-loads. Millions of human evacuees had gone along too – some sources say as many as 16.5 million people went east in this huge migration – but the necessity to keep factory personnel in place until the last minute to help with dismantling and loading, meant that only about 40 per cent of the work force had got away with their deconstructed plant.

Most of the younger men who might have replaced these lost workers in the rebuilt and newly built factories were either called up into the army or were needed on the collective farms to help maintain food production. The authorities soon had to resort to stern measures. In June 1941, a decree of the Praesidium of the Soviet Union had extended working hours to eleven hours per day for six days a week, and replaced annual holidays with money paid into an account with the State Bank. In December workers in essential war industries (i.e. most workers) were mobilised at their posts, so that attempts to leave now constituted desertion. In the following February, all able-bodied townspeople over the age of 14 were declared mobilisable for war work, just as males of 18 and above already were for the armed forces. The industrial burden fell most heavily on the women, the old, and the young, with females making up about 60 per cent of most factories' work forces. W. L. White, a sympathetic American journalist who visited several Soviet factories in 1944, related how in all of them roughly half the workers were women while the males were either very old men or young teenagers – though age did not make them any less dependable. Absenteeism, White noted, "seems to be as rare here as it would be in the Atlanta Penitentiary, and for many of the same reasons." Chief among these was the fact that although, under socialism, the factory nominally belonged to the workers, what was more readily apparent in the Soviet Union was that "certainly the workers belong to the factory" for without it they have "nothing to eat and no place to sleep."[3]

Most of them lived in apartment blocks attached to the factories in which they worked and much of their food was obtainable only from the factory canteen, though at the very cheap rate of five roubles per day. Reports on the quality of this food varied. The American journalist poked his head unannounced into one canteen and saw workers eating a meal of buckwheat porridge, black bread and borsch, a meat and beetroot soup. The food at the foremen's table was the same plus pressed caviar, while the engineers got white bread as well as black, butter, and the more expensive loose unsalted caviar. The directors had their own dining room, where White was entertained, and where the main items on the menu included smoked sturgeon, salami, salted cucumbers, veal, tongue, and coleslaw. For dessert pastry and chocolate cake was offered, and all could be washed down with vodka, red and white wine and champagne.

It was the memory of these inequities that prompted a female electrical worker, whose factory had returned to Moscow in mid-1943, to give an altogether more spartan picture of the typical worker's meal. Throughout the rest of the war, "we lived off potatoes . . . We ate in a dining hall and then went home. But the rations weren't given out to everybody. It was a terrible thing. You sat, you ate, and people were standing behind you waiting; maybe something would be left and they would eat. They gave the men only 400 grammes of bread . . ."[4]

The main sources of food for these canteens were the factory's own vegetable gardens and animal husbandries tended by the workers, sometimes in shifts during the day and sometimes in special evening sessions after work. According to official figures, there were more than 30,000 such factory plantations by late 1944, occupying almost five million acres of land. The workers were also encouraged, individually or in mini-collectives, to cultivate their own allotments. In February 1944, the Council of People's Commissars had issued a nation-wide call for a major extension of such holdings and help was now given to factory and office workers, as well as to disabled veterans, to acquire their own hoes and forks and the necessary seeds. By October there were reckoned to be more than 16 million such holdings throughout the country. According to a British observer, some 90 per cent of Muscovites worked on their own allotments.

Rations for dependants were also issued at the factory, and throughout the war a sliding scale was applied, depending on the nature of one's work. The daily bread ration, for example, was 600 grammes (21 ounces) for those in heavy industry, 500 grammes for light, 450 grammes for office workers and 400 grammes for old people, children and the disabled. The other staples of the official ration were:

	Workers		Office		Dependants		Children
Meat/Fish	75g	(2.6oz)	40	(1.4)	20	(0.7)	20 (0.7)
Cereals	65	(2.3)	50	(1.75)	35	(1.2)	40 (1.4)
Fats	25	(0.9)	15	(0.5)	8	(0.3)	15 (0.5)
Sugar	17.5	(0.6)	10	(0.35)	3.5	(0.1)	10 (0.35)
Tea	1	(0.03)	1	(0.03)	1	(0.03)	1 (0.03)
Coffee	5	(0.2)	5	(0.2)	5	(0.2)	5 (0.2)
Salt	15	(0.5)	15	(0.5)	15	(0.5)	15 (0.5)

The other basic rations were milk and soap (for which I have not been able to find the allocation) and three boxes of matches per month. Availability of specific items varied from place to place and season to season. Soap was notoriously elusive. Bread could be black or white, "chocolate candies were sometimes given instead of sugar, the meat tickets usually bought sausage or herring, butter was often replaced by vegetable oil, and potatoes were given in the autumn for grain tickets."[5] In fact, the meat was not a particularly desirable item for the ordinary man in the queue. Factory directors might have their veal but most of the animals slaughtered were aged milkers and their carcasses yielded up little that qualified even as decent stewing steak, and were more usually turned into smoked sausages.

Nevertheless the prices of the ration allotments were very low. Russian workers were paid at piece rate and, as long they fulfilled their norms, received a basic 750 roubles for a month. Most, in fact, exceeded their norms and it was reckoned that the average wage was around 1,000 roubles per month. State prices, therefore, were more than reasonable, with bread at one rouble per kilo, sausage 12 roubles, sugar 5 roubles, butter 28 roubles, grain between 2 and 6 roubles, eggs 6 roubles for a dozen, and milk 2.2 roubles per litre. Rent was about 60 roubles per month. Workers under 18 could live for free in factory dormitories, while at the other end of the scale those greatly exceeding their production norm were entitled to more commodious apartments, though at higher rents. For those commuting to work in Moscow the subway fare was 50 kopecks.

Given that official rations were generally reckoned to supply about 90 per cent of a worker's daily, albeit very basic requirements, they were then left with an appreciable amount of money at the end of the fortnightly pay period. But here they came up against one of the major problems of the Soviet economic system, and one that was only exacerbated by the wartime demands of the armed forces. The chronic shortage of consumer goods, including many food items, left little on which to spend their surplus income. This had its inevitable effect, with the enormous pent-up demand sending prices of whatever little extras were available sky-rocketing. The authorities attempted to suppress any signs of an untrammelled, Brussels-type black market, but they did permit a flourishing 'gray market' in which the peasants on the collective farms, the *kolkhoz* sector, were allowed to sell their surplus produce in regular markets in the towns and cities, such as the sprawling Rynock in Moscow. This surplus comprised whatever extra the collective had produced over and above its official contribution to the state, as well as produce grown by the members on their small, individual plots. Typical prices at these markets in 1944 are given below, and to make them meaningful they are also expressed as a percentage of a worker's weekly earnings, again taking the average of 250 roubles per week.

Bread (lb.)	70r (28%)	Honey (lb.)	187r (75%)
Milk (pint)	17r (7%)	Calf's head & knuckles	225r (90%)
Potatoes (lb.)	13r (5%)	Matches (box)	30r (12%)
Cheese (lb.)	75r (30%)	Vodka (litre)	500r (200%)
Mutton/goat (lb.)	140r (56%)	Soap (cake)	250r (100%)
Eggs (doz.)	164r (66%)	(Soap was plentiful in public baths.)	

The terribly hand-to-mouth nature of these transactions, for both seller and buyer, is encapsulated in White's description of a Moscow-style milk-bar. One of the stalls was occupied by an old lady with an enormous pitcher of milk. This attracted a long queue of people prepared to pay her price of more than $2.50 a quart, though "of course you must bring your own bottle, except that these people can't afford more than a glassful. Is it inspected? Who knows? Maybe the old lady scalded her big pitcher and maybe not. But look closely – the customers are inspecting. The old lady pours a few drops into a customer's palm. The customer tastes it. Yes, it's fresh – so she buys. Most of the people of the milk line are holding freshly scoured American-made tin cans to carry the milk home in." Some of the goods on sale might well have gone straight into an American's trash-can, as our visitor went on to demonstrate. The calf's appendages still had "the hair on and the glassy eyes open, attracting a few flies . . . [A] wrinkled old lady is selling a bunch of peonies. Obviously, they were planted at the corner of her house, and she is selling them just before the petals get too limp. But no one is going to buy the entire bunch since she is asking (and getting) $1.60 per flower."[6] Nearby was a man selling a poorly made wooden coat-hanger, presumably his own handiwork, for which he wanted just over a dollar. In the yard outside a girl was trying to sell stockings, some of which were hardly worn at all and others carefully mended. They were cotton and cost $6.25 a pair, though for one rayon pair she wanted $25. A little further down was a man selling a spare pair of shoes which were somewhat worn but still seemed fairly serviceable. He was asking a whole month's pay.

Even at these prices, however, the *kolkhoz* markets could never satisfy the demand for extra and non-ration goods. The surpluses left after the state had taken its share were small and, like every other sector of the economy, the collectives had been largely denuded of able-bodied males. By late 1944 their population had fallen by 60 per cent, with mainly women, old men and children left to perform the arduous seasonal tasks. So the government, which fretted continually about the amount of spare roubles sloshing around and their potentially disruptive effect in a 'socialist' command economy, decided to augment the *kolkhoz* markets with some of its own, selling similar goods, especially food, and charging only slightly lower prices. These 'Commercial Stores' first appeared in April 1944. Such items as bacon, baloney, boiled ham, dressed chickens, cooked sturgeon, caviar, eggs, Swiss cheese, cream, all fresh, clean and well-packaged, were usually freely available. In capitalist terms, according to one observer, the government was "running its own black market as a state enterprise in order to skim from its workers the bulk of their war wages".[7] There were also 'commercial' clothing stores selling serviceable warm clothing at unregulated prices. These targeted the peasantry specifically, to mop up the roubles they accrued via their own *kolkhoz* markets. A third type of state enterprise were the off-ration restaurants. More than fifty had opened in Moscow during 1944, and "today you can dine and dance without coupons at the Moskva or Grand Hotels or at the Astoria in Gorki Street, which specialises in the kind of Russian gypsies who used to keep Bruce Lockhart awake all night in the old days. All this seems like intoxicating gaiety in war-time Moscow . . . [But] the new prices are extremely high. A plate of steak with vegetables costs nearly £2 and a cream cake £1."[8] These restaurants were especially popular with officers on leave from the front, who often had with them thousands of roubles in back pay.

For westerners today, used to a much higher standard of living, it is difficult to assess the perceived level of deprivation in the USSR at this time. We also live in much more cynical times and so it is also difficult to judge just how far ordinary citizens derived comfort from the knowledge that their sacrifices were in the name of Mother Russia or an authentically socialist future. Yet by any yardstick, life was extremely hard. William White, on an official tour of Soviet factories, was unlikely to have been shown anything but the best, and his descriptions of those he visited, while sympathetic, leave an indelible impression of industrial squalor. A factory making Sturmovik ground attack aircraft was

> poorly lit and unbelievably dirty. It has no production line in the American sense but rather a series of connected piles between bottlenecks, with women waiting idle at their machines for the line to start moving again. It is jammed full of the best American

machine tools, but seems to lack proper organisation. At one point, the assembly belt is a makeshift canvas affair. The floors throughout are uneven with holes in the concrete. Piles of metal shavings are everywhere. No one bothers to clean up. Many of the girls wear gunny sacks tied around their feet. Others have crude wooden sandals with a nail sticking up between the great and second toes.[9]

An armaments factory in Magnitogorsk, in the Urals, turned out everything from sheet steel to shell-cases. In the blast furnace section White and his party "stumble along for miles through piles of slag, across precarious bridges over molten metal. The white heat of boiling steel pinches our faces." In the shell-making section they see "stockingless girls with crude sandals . . . [who] stand on heaps of curled metal scrap from their machines. Occasionally they are protected from its sharp edges by crude duckboards." Desultory attempts are made to carry away the scrap on wooden litters with handles at either end, the two women carrying each one frequently stumbling and shedding part of their load. "There is no assembly belt but at one point they have devised a substitute. When one operation is finished, a shell is placed on a long, inclined rack, down which it rolls into the next room for the next operation." Such ramshackle production methods seemed to bedevil the whole of Soviet industry and White and his colleagues estimated that even in the best factory they saw, equipped with the most modern American, Swiss and German tools, production of aircraft engines took five times as many man-hours as in an American factory.

Other descriptions of life in Russian factories went beyond the merely ramshackle. The woman worker who spoke of her unrelieved diet of potatoes also recalled that at work "it was dark and cold. We burned campfires every night in the factory. It was hard . . . When we left for work it was dark, and when we came home it was dark. When the night shift started even I [a forewoman] felt like sleeping . . . and the young kids could barely stand on their feet . . . We had a thermal kiln, where the machine parts went through aging. Usually when they pulled the parts out of the kiln, we asked, 'Put them close to the machines so we can feel their warmth.' And during the dinner break everyone went to the kiln and lay down and went to sleep."[10]

There was little relaxation to be had outside work. Simply commuting to and fro could be a considerable strain, especially in the bigger cities like Moscow. According to another American journalist, "Heavy fines were imposed for being only a few minutes late for work, which meant that in Moscow most workers had to start from home one or two hours beforehand because of transport delays. It also took them an hour or more to get home at night, so it was a common sight . . . after dark to see long lines of workmen [sic] waiting for a place on a bus or street car."[11] On top of this 13- to 15-hour day, six days a week, there were, of course, the long queues at the *kolkhoz* or official markets whenever one sought some petty luxury to alleviate the daily grind. At one Commercial Store he visited, William White saw long queues stretching right round the block and another long queue to the cashier's desk. He reckoned that it would take the better part of a day just to obtain one or two items.

Most of those standing in line were mothers, eagerly seeking a little something to give their children even a scintilla of enjoyment. For they, too, endured bleak times right through the war. Those over fourteen were usually drafted for work in the factories or collective farms. Their hours were shorter, six or seven hours a day generally, but other hours were given over every day to school work. The more unfortunate children were drafted to factories, also called trade schools, or farms many hundreds of miles away from home. From late 1942, boys, and many girls, also faced the prospect of military conscription when they turned seventeen. But children under fourteen also felt the rigours of war, and a British journalist's interview with an eleven-year-old Muscovite gave a glimpse into the sense of *anomie* that was beginning to affect these youngsters and that was already being referred to in the west as 'juvenile delinquency'. According to this boy, by 1944 "there were thirty-five pupils in his form and one fearfully overworked woman-teacher for all subjects: history, geography, arithmetic, natural science and Russian. All the food the children got at school was a slice of bread with some 'nasty, bitter jam – American stuff made of oranges'; some of the kids threw this *drisnya* (diarrhoea) out of the window. Among the boys there was a great deal of lawlessness . . . and thievery . . . Most of their fathers were in the Army (or dead), and most of their mothers were working endlessly long hours in a factory. Among these youngsters there were clear signs of escapism; they no longer sang the usual patriotic songs, but an 'escapist' song from a recent film about Kostya, a swaggering beau in the docks of Odessa, or worse still, a 'hooligan' (i.e. obscene) version of the same song."[12]

Yet there were millions of Soviet citizens, not just those at the front, for whom bitter marmalade, queues for food, or for second-hand socks and wooden coat hangers would have been pure delight. Countless victims in Stalin's gulags were encouraged to make their own contribution to the war effort. On a couple of occasions, William White saw for himself long columns of ragged women on their way to a factory. Shuffling along in their makeshift sandals, they tried to maintain an orderly column four abreast as guards with fixed bayonets shouted and harried them. White also spoke to two American mining engineers assigned as advisers to a mine being opened up north of Omsk. They reckoned that of the 70,000 or so workers attached to this particular project, about half were prisoners, mostly women, kept under guard in separate huts. Even the non-prisoners were suspect, mainly evacuees from 'unreliable' frontier regions in Poland or the Baltic states. Their accommodation was uniformly appalling. The NKVD overseers had simply made them dig an enormous pit, ten feet deep and a hundred feet long, over which they spread a roof of pine logs. The floor was cold, damp earth and their thin paliasses were in direct contact. They worked 12-hour shifts, though the two Americans reckoned that even the best of them were capable of only four or five hours useful work because their diet was so inadequate. "Each prisoner was supposed to provide himself with two American tin cans that he fastened to his belt by a wire. They'd haul out one kettle of soup and one of kasha. Some days the food truck would have dried fish on it, and they'd toss this out over the tailboard like you'd throw fish to a bunch of seals." Alexander Solzhenitsyn has provided us with some further details on this diet. Usually, "the fish was mostly bones. The flesh was boiled off except for bits on the tails and the heads." The so-called *kasha* might not be buckwheat at all but "a mush made out of *magara*. It was one solid lump, and . . . [one] broke it off in pieces. When it was hot – never mind when it was cold – it had no taste and didn't fill you. It was nothing but grass that looked like millet . . . It came from the Chinese, they said. They got ten ounces of it and that was that."[13]

The historian, Robert Conquest, has given us a chilling overview of life in Stalin's political camps. At any one time there were something like 8 million people interned in them, scattered east of the Urals from Kazakhstan to the Arctic Circle. The food was often actually worse than that just described, nothing but half a pint of thin, stagnant soup twice a day and one issue of half a pound of bread. Prisoners slept two and three to a bunk, or on earth or concrete floors, and such mattresses as were provided were often packed with sawdust. The hut would be heated by a very small stove. burning a few sticks or powdery coal-dust. In "a corner would be a twenty-gallon latrine tank which prison orderlies carried off to empty daily – light work for people on the sick list."[14]

Prisoners worked as lumberjacks, miners, latter-day agricultural serfs, in factories, in construction and on the railways. Woken at around 5 a.m., they were given ten minutes for breakfast, the best meal of the day, and marched off in orderly columns, five abreast, fully aware that even stumbling momentarily out of the line might be interpreted as an attempt to escape, punishable by on-the-spot execution. They laboured for twelve hours and more each day, with only a five minute break for lunch. No matter how heavy the work, there were rarely any tractors or horses and loads were moved by teams of half-a-dozen prisoners harnessed to wooden sleds. On their return the prisoners were allowed another five minutes or so for supper before collapsing in utter exhaustion. Only those who fulfilled their norms got the 'full' ration and many therefore were already trapped in a terminally undernourished vicious circle. In most camps prisoners had Sunday off, which they largely spent sleeping. Their NKVD guards varied from the brutal to the sadistic, yet were often excelled in malevolence by the 'trusties', almost all common criminals rather than political prisoners. These preyed ruthlessly upon their fellow inmates, and in mixed camps were permitted to indulge in occasional mass-rape sessions. They invariably stole any serviceable clothes and shoes worn by new arrivals and most prisoners were soon wearing little more than a bundle of rags tied together with string and scraps of fabric. In the colder regions they also attempted to swathe all their faces, mummy-like, with strips of cloth. Their footwear was often nothing more than a length of birch-bark or rubber tyre. Disease was rife throughout the camps, especially scurvy, pellagra, pneumonia and T.B. In the farm camps there were even outbreaks of brucellosis. The death rate overall has been estimated at 30 per cent per annum. That is roughly 2.5 million men and women, which in 1944 was 750,000 more than the total Red Army and Navy fatalities that year.[15]

Yet in many parts of the war-torn USSR it was not immediately obvious that the free were much better off. In the west of the country, in the newly liberated regions, refugees were trickling back to find nothing but complete desolation. During his stay the indefatigable William White was given a glimpse of life just behind the front. The conditions he described were those at the very margins of ordered human society. From a railway carriage, looking out over a table set for another "standardised Intourist orgy" of a breakfast, including wine, champagne and caviar, he saw that people were moving back to live in dug-outs that had been burrowed into sides of the railway cutting. "They are women, barefooted and in rags, and an occasional child. Their miserable laundry, which they have washed in ditch puddles, is drying out on the barbed wire . . . We see that these ragged women, who plow barefoot through this mud, have planted little potato patches in clearings of the debris of concrete pillboxes." Further down the line they dismount and see more people, nearly all women, nearly all in rags. Three of them are picking around in the ruins of a collective farm where they seem to be trying to get some sort of roof over one end of a room to protect the stove there from the rain. "A shy, chunky, nineteen-year-old girl, dragging from another ruined house a heavy rafter, passes us on the path . . . We stand aside to let her pass. She avoids our eyes. Her hands have calluses as thick as those of a stonemason. We watch the prints which her bare feet leave in the mud path as she goes up toward the other house, dragging the beam. So Russia is built."[16]

Perhaps, in the last analysis, it is this notion of rebuilding that should predominate in any discussion of a national mood in late 1944. For the very destruction wrought by the war helped to stir up powerful popular feelings, not least a fierce loathing of the enemy and willingness to endure enormous privations to vouchsafe his defeat. Another American visitor noted that "almost everyone I knew had a father, son or brother killed, missing or wounded at the front.[17] Almost everyone had lost from fifteen to twenty-five pounds in weight. Their housing conditions were deplorable. They lacked the clothes they needed. They were tired after a day's work and cold in winter. But I can think of no sacrifice they were not willing to make for the army. They hated the Germans with everything they had, and most of them were satisfied in the knowledge that they were doing the best they could."[18]

There was also a positive aspect to this national mood, the beginnings of a belief that communist society after the war might begin to take at least some account of its citizens' well-being and of their modest aspirations. Some minor relaxation of state authority was already apparent and had led to a more relaxed attitude to religious worship. This, and the reinstatement of pre-Revolutionary national heroes and of traditional military protocols and virtues had all seemed to be possible harbingers of a less repressive postwar regime, of an end to the 'Terror' and even of the enforced collectivisation of daily life. Thus the very scale of the casualty lists, the apocalyptic extent of the enemy's depredations, the rigours of the great iron and concrete treadmills upon which the workers forged, hammered and welded the weapons of mechanised warfare, and the maelstroms of bullet and shell that had razed the land coming and going, as the enemy advanced and was then slowly forced back, all this seemed as if it might be part of a great cleansing, a purgatory of suffering in which the horrors of Stalinism might somehow melt down and be transmuted into the 'real' Russia of sturdy peasant, priest and pious autocracy.

This mood is admirably encapsulated in Boris Pasternak's *Doctor Zhivago*, when some of his characters discuss their sense of self-abandon in the face of the sheer enormity of the cataclysm. One has escaped the gulags by volunteering for service in a front-line punishment battalion. "Attack after attack, mile after mile of electrified barbed wire, mines, mortars, month after month of artillery barrage. They called our company the death squad. It was practically wiped out ... And yet – imagine – all that utter hell was nothing, it was bliss compared to the horrors of the concentration camp, and not because of the material conditions, but for some other reason." Another then chips in to point out that this sense of release, of relative bliss, "was not only felt by men in your position ... but by everyone without exception, at home and at the front, and they all took a deep breath and flung themselves into the furnace of this deadly liberating struggle with real joy, with rapture."[19]

18

The Wolf's Lair

ADOLF HITLER AT BAY

Having known little but Nazi ideology and strutting pantomime since they were born, the youngsters of Hitler's Volksturm doubtless still had complete faith in the military abilities of the Führer and complete acceptance of their sacrificial role. For them, Hitler really was the *Gröfaz*, a grotesque abbreviation, current at the time, for *der Grosster Feldheer aller Zeiten*, the greatest military leader of all time. It was not an entirely empty title. Though offering little insight into Hitler's actual strategic skills it did reflect his continued determination to be Germany's sole military leader and, as commander-in-chief of the OKW, retain a 'hands on' control of the armed forces as a whole. Moreover, he now exercised this control almost at the front itself. Ever since BARBAROSSA his eyes had been turned mainly eastwards, towards his anti-Bolshevik crusaders, and he spent much of his time at a major headquarters complex built near Rastenburg, in East Prussia. These headquarters, with their origin in headier days, were known as *die Wolfschanze*, or Wolf's Lair, and were now only a little more than thirty miles from the Soviet spearheads on the Angerapp Line.

Situated some five miles east of Rastenburg, in a state forest ringed to the south and east by a series of small lakes, the whole complex covered about 600 acres and contained three fenced *Sperrkreise*, or exclusion zones, located one inside the other. *Sperrkreis* III, the outer zone, was just dead ground, very marshy to the north and west and with a double barbed wire fence patrolled by the Army's elite Führerbegleit battalion. The headquarters staff could also call on the services of two locally stationed airborne battalions, the staff and students at a nearby SS tank training school and Army NCO school, and a district police battalion. More inert protection was offered by over 54,000 mines laid up to 150 yards beyond the perimeter wire. *Sperrkreis* II encompassed what might be called the headquarters' 'township', a 125-acre site whose southern half contained a railway station, hospital, cemetery, sauna, car park and various Luftwaffe and Kriegsmarine command posts. The inner sanctum, *Sperrkreis* I, was guarded by a special SS security unit and contained the Führer's own bunker, a fortified suite of dormitories, offices and conference rooms with its own oxygen and compressed air supplies and a U-boat air-conditioning plant. As well as additional personal bunkers for Reichsmarschall Hermann Göring, Field Marshal Wilhelm Keitel, General Alfred Jodl and Martin Bormann, there were also an SS headquarters, officers' messes, refectories, a cafeteria, a cinema, post office, guest bunker and typing pool.*

In all three zones only a few of the trees had been cut down, to clear actual building plots and roads. Both inner zones conveyed something of a sylvan holiday-camp aspect, especially where the original wooden grass-roofed huts were still extant. In many places, however, these huts had been encased in concrete. The Führer's own bunker had been virtually rebuilt into a squat two-storey structure, with windowless, sloping walls, twenty-two feet thick, looking rather like an unfinished concrete pyramid. As further protection against bomb blast or poison gas it had no through ventilation, and for Albert Speer, Hitler's Minister of Armaments, it represented a "symbol of the situation" at this time, with the appearance of "an ancient Egyptian tomb", whose impregnable walls separated Hitler "from the outside world in a figurative as well as a literal sense and locked him up inside his own delusions."[1]

Whether these were Speer's actual feelings at the time is another matter, though doubtless such views would not have gone down well with youngsters of the Volksturm. They preferred to believe that the *Gröfaz* was sharing his people's peril and was now at his post within the sound of the Russian guns. In fact, those in residence at the Wolf's Lair had begun to feel the imminence of the war even before the East Prussian offensive opened. In addition to the strengthening of many buildings, including the *Führerbunker*, an order was issued on 5th October for the installation of twelve heavy anti-aircraft batteries. Of

---

* Göring was commander-in-chief of the Luftwaffe and also had important economic powers as Plenipotentiary for the Four Year Plan, still in force after its formulation in 1936. Keitel and Jodl were OKW chief-of-staff and chief of operations respectively, and Bormann was head of the Party Chancellery, in effect Hitler's private secretary.

course, none of this would avail much if the whole area was overrun by the Red Army, and on 22nd October Keitel urged Hitler to leave for Berlin immediately. The plea was endorsed by various Party minions and personal staff, but on the 25th, displaying a certain *sang-froid*, Hitler told Bormann that he intended to stay at Rastenburg until the East Prussian situation was resolved. Bormann wrote in his diary: "We would prefer rather more safety for the Führer. After all, forty or fifty miles are nothing for modern tanks to cover. Besides, we would prefer a more congenial place for the Führer to convalesce. But the Führer commands, and we obey."[2]

Hitler's decision cannot be attributed entirely to icy resolve. Deep depression and listlessness, mainly brought on by his extremely poor health, also had a lot to do with it. From 26th September to 7th October he had been completely incapacitated by severe stomach cramps – caused as much as anything by the 'anti-gas' pills prescribed by his quack physician, which contained appreciable quantities of strychnine and atropine. The threat to East Prussia seemed to rouse him from his torpor but right up to the end of October military conferences were often cancelled and many of those that were held took place in semi-darkness in the Führer's poky bedroom, where there was hardly enough space for two or three participants and a typist. In the long pauses that regularly occurred those present were keenly aware of the chill draught from the air-conditioning system and its persistent rattling, as well as the hiss of air from the oxygen cylinder permanently at Hitler's bedside. Throw a few buckets of water down the ventilator shaft and they could well have been wallowing in the English Channel on board one of the Kriegsmarine's new *Schnorchel* U-boats.*

Occasionally Hitler was able to rouse himself sufficiently to convene a full-scale conference. One such was held on 24th October, and on the following day, as they travelled back to their respective headquarters, two senior officers who had attended found much to ponder. General Siegfried Westphal, and General Hans Krebs, Chiefs-of-Staff respectively to Field Marshal Gerd von Runstedt at OB West and to Field Marshal Walter Model at Army Group B, had been summoned to the top-secret conference at the last moment after Hitler abandoned his original plan to speak to von Runstedt and Model personally. The

---

* See Chapter oo. These bedroom conferences were often merely maudlin whingeing sessions with his personal confidants, notably Jodl, SS General Heinrich Fegelein, Himmler's liaison officer with the OKW, General William Burgdorf, an aide, and General Walter Buhle, the senior OKH officer attached to OKW headquarters.

subject of the meeting was a proposal so daring and fraught with risk that, according to another senior staff officer, Hitler decided to address the subordinates instead so as to avoid "any kind of protest on the part of Runstedt and Model."[3] Although Westphal and Krebs could not protest, they certainly felt considerable anxiety as they prepared to brief their chiefs afterwards at headquarters in Arenberg and Fischeln.

Westphal wrote later that Hitler had begun by telling them that about twenty infantry and ten panzer divisions, as well as numerous artillery corps and mortar brigades, would reach the Western Front before the end of November. Their hopes had soared. Here at last might be the means to shore up the crumbling defences in Holland and along the frontiers of the Reich. But then Hitler had gone on to stipulate that these units were to be kept concentrated behind the front and were not to be used at present. According to Westphal, Hitler made

the following disclosures. The Eastern Front had been stabilised once again [sic] . . . The forces so urgently required in the West must therefore at last be sent there. He did not, however, consider it proper that they should be tied down in defence . . . An offensive in the West could turn the tide decisively in our favour. He was therefore determined to seize the initiative once more in the West. The Wehrmacht Staff had carried out a thorough study of what were the most favourable localities and targets for an attack. He, Hitler, had decided that the offensive should be launched from the Eifel because of the weakness of the enemy forces in that region. The objective must be Antwerp . . . [from where] a mass of [Allied] troops and material would . . . [soon] pour and greatly increase the pressure on us. The attack was to proceed from the Eifel with the right wing passing through Liege. The 5th and 6th Panzer Armies were to make a frontal attack, while the 7th Army was to cover the southern flank of the wedge in the Luxembourg area. The preparation and conduct of the offensive would be the task of the Army Group Model. An operational draft would be sent by the OKW to the Western Front in the next few days.[4]

Asked by the Führer for their opinion, Westphal and Krebs had flannelled heroically, welcoming the influx of reinforcements and agreeing that a major offensive was "welcome in principle", but they had refused to be drawn into assessing the chances for success, except to affirm that without a substantial Luftwaffe presence over several days, they could not be very high. A little later they had privately shared their "initial apprehensions, namely that the forces would be inadequate for a thrust to Antwerp. If a penetration were effected over the Meuse in a north-westerly direction, the flanks of the wedge would lengthen as more ground was gained . . . Allied troops adjacent to the breakthrough front [could not] be expected to stand back politely and make way for the attackers . . . In a word: with the forces which could be expected to be at our disposal, the attack over the Meuse appeared to be too risky."

Both men were probably also apprehensive that the initial planning for the offensive and basic risk assessment were in the hands of staff officers at the Oberkommando der Wehrmacht, or OKW. Although acting as the high command for the whole German armed forces, the OKW had never involved itself in large-scale ground operations. Its deputy chief of operations, General Walter Warlimont, pointed out that his staff "was now being called upon for the first time to lay on a major offensive operation and to make all the preparations for it, something which hitherto had been the responsibility of OKH and its Operations Section." The OKH was the Oberkommando des Heeres, the Army's own high command, and for Warlimont this snubbing of the much more experienced headquarters "at this late stage of the war [meant that] the whole futility of the higher organisation of the Wehrmacht stood out starkly."[5] Still worse, the OKW were being asked to draw up their plans very hurriedly. Hitler himself had been pondering this thrust from the Eifel into the Ardennes since early September but no kind of directive was passed on to Keitel's and Jodl's staffs until 9th October.

Nevertheless, Warlimont, Westphal and Krebs need not have been entirely despondent. Because the order to begin planning was passed on so late, at least security was still tight. Even with the help of the ULTRA signals intelligence set-up at Bletchley Park, the Allies had garnered only the vaguest clues to a German offensive – hints of new fuel restrictions to build up reserve stocks, mention of some kind of forthcoming effort in the West passed on to Tokyo by the Japanese ambassador in Berlin, and news that several panzer divisions had been allocated on 22nd October to Sixth Panzer Army in OKW reserve.

Most cheering of all for Westphal and Krebs would have been the realisation of just how unconcerned the Allies were about the chosen breakthrough sector in the Ardennes. This whole portion of the front, running 80 miles as the crow flies, from Monschau to the southern Luxembourg frontier, was manned by just five American divisions, most of which had been sent there for rest and refitting. The level of immediate danger felt by these troops is clearly indicated in an anecdote from General Bradley, relating to the last days of October: "Trout streams foamed through the steep hills of this quiet middle sector and wild boar roamed its forests . . . The Luxembourg forest warden was to complain that G.I.s in their zest for barbecued pork were hunting the boar in low-flying Cubs with Thompson sub-machine guns."[6]

PART THREE

The Air War in the West

19

'Musical Wanganui'

RAF BOMBER COMMAND OVER ESSEN

THROUGHOUT the Second World War 'strategic bombing' was a central notion in the planning of the Allied counter-offensives in both Europe and the Pacific. The concept had been developed in the 1920s and 1930s and had fervent advocates in both Europe and America. The main impetus in Europe came from a realisation of just how dependent modern, machine-age armies had become on the nation's industrial base as a whole, and just how vulnerable that base might be to massed air attacks on key industries or on the civilian work-force in general. Such theories also had their proponents in America but there concern centred on their perceived vital interests in the Pacific and Latin America and the search for a weapon that could effectively project American power over long distances. It was to counter Axis and Japanese threats in these regions that the four-engined 'Flying Fortresses' and 'Superfortresses' were conceived, rather than to undertake the seemingly impossible task of getting American bombers to Europe and back. Once the war had begun, power projection also became a major consideration for the British, especially after the humiliating withdrawal from Dunkirk and the realisation that it would take years to build up an adequate invasion force. Bombers, after all, could remain based in the British Isles and even at the nadir of British fortunes maintain some sort of offensive activity over the Nazi-occupied Europe. In September 1940, Winston Churchill circulated a paper to the War Cabinet which asserted starkly: "The bombers alone provide the means of victory . . . In no other way at present visible can we hope to overcome the immense military power of Germany."[1]

By early 1942, with both the Russians and the Americans now

contributing their enormous human and material resources to the struggle against Hitler, Churchill quickly became more sanguine about the prospects for major land operations and declared in March that "bombing was not decisive, but better than doing nothing."[2] Nevertheless, by then the decision had already been taken to devote substantial resources to a bomber offensive, and a huge increase in bomber production soon made it unthinkable to try to reverse the heavy industrial, administrative and manpower commitment to strategic bombing. The creation of Bomber Command, the installation of bomber zealots like Arthur Harris, the building of a network of large bomber bases, the tooling up of aircraft factories, the organisation of a multiplicity of specialised training programmes, the expansion of bomb-making and the dedication of a large segment of the electronic industry, and the arrival of American forces already committed to large-scale deployment of bombers, all quickly meant that bombers were here to stay, almost irrespective of their proven military utility.

Even by October 1944 it was almost impossible to prove that the round-the-clock bombing of Germany was having any significant impact on their war industry or even on the morale of those German civilians who had lost homes, relatives, friends, livelihoods as part of the extensive 'collateral damage' caused, with little regret, by the Allies. It was clear, however, that the bomber offensive had mushroomed both in terms of sorties flown and tonnages of bombs dropped. In 1941 and 1942 the total tonnage dropped increased only from 32,000 to about 47,000 tons, but in 1944, to the end of October, 943,000 tons of bombs were dropped, 117,000 of them in that month alone. The number of sorties flown had shown a correspondingly dramatic increase, with the 66,000 in October representing an eightfold increase over the monthly average for the previous year.

Equally significant was the fact that the number of bombers available for operations had jumped from roughly 500 in Bomber Command in November 1941 to almost 1,500 by October 1944. American formations also burgeoned with Eighth U.S. Air Force, comprising the heavy bombers stationed in the British Isles and their fighter escorts, deploying just 214 bombers at the beginning of January 1943 and 3,818 at the beginning of October 1944. A final indication of the crescendo of airpower being produced was the fact that the Bomber Command effort one night in the middle of October had just broken a whole array of records, including the largest number of sorties yet dispatched, the largest tonnage dropped in one night over Germany, and the largest tonnage against a single target.

The exact targeting of these bombs was a matter of some dispute, and seemed likely to remain so as methods for assessing their impact on German production remained rudimentary. Even with newly installed cameras in aircraft to capture their loads exploding on the ground, the best interpreters were hard-pressed to prove that a wall knocked down there and a roof removed somewhere else actually meant that productive activity in that building was seriously affected or, indeed, that the factory's production lines had not been moved underground or dispersed out of the city altogether.

Inadequate feedback can create as much hope as doubt and many American commanders remained convinced that they could successfully pinpoint key industries such as ball-bearing or aircraft engine production, or oil and artificial fuel refineries, and effectively strangle output for the Wehrmacht. The new generation of B-17 and B-24 bombers, they felt, meant that large bomb loads could be delivered with precision, such that key industrial complexes could be bombed out of useful existence. Accuracy would be further improved by mounting the raids in daylight, an idea that had almost been abandoned in 1943 when the Flying Fortresses proved to be more like sitting ducks. Now, with the advent of long-range fighter escorts, it was feasible again, using expendable extra fuel tanks to cover a mission's whole route.

By October 1944, then, the strategic air offensive was once more high on the Allied agenda. Ever since the Casablanca Conference in January 1943, when the U.S. Army Air Force was directed to join RAF Bomber Command in mounting a Combined Bomber Offensive against Germany, efforts had been made to coordinate air attacks against supposedly vital components of the German war economy. Primary targets were nominated, which might gain or lose priority at different times, but those most consistently under attack were submarine construction yards, the aircraft industry, transportation, oil plants, and ball-bearing factories. From April 1944 to mid-September, control of British and American bombers had passed to General Eisenhower's SHAEF headquarters which could focus operations against German troop and supply movements in France. After the German collapse in Normandy, however, control reverted to the air force commanders, Marshal of the Royal Air Force Charles Portal and General Henry Arnold for the U.S. Army Air Force, and through them to Air Chief Marshal Arthur Harris at Bomber Command and General Carl Spaatz in charge of U.S. Strategic Forces in Europe. Once again discrete strategic targets were sought and oil plants were now named as the primary ones, though Eisenhower himself had permitted regular raids against such targets ever since June. Despite later accusations that the oil campaign had not been sufficiently sustained, by the end of September every important synthetic oil plant had been bombed at least twice and total German output of oil products had been cut by two-thirds. When target priorities were reassessed in late October by the newly formed Strategic Targets Committee, oil was retained as a primary target, though the German transport system was now also accorded an equal priority. Among the most important subsidiary objectives, reaffirming a decision taken by Spaatz in September, were aircraft factories known to be involved in the production of the new German jet fighters.

The Americans faithfully adhered to these strategic objectives, still retaining enormous faith in the potential of precision bombing, and being buoyant at the almost total air superiority gained by their long-range escorts over the Luftwaffe's day-fighters. In the second half of 1942, German fighter losses had been running at about 230 per month. During the whole of 1943 the monthly average was 890, while in 1944 it rose from 1,300 per month during the first quarter to just under 1,700 between June and October. The fact that the figure for October was somewhat below this average simply showed that the Germans were finding it increasingly difficult to find enough aircraft and pilots to put in the air.

In essence, Eighth U.S. Air Force had fought a brutal battle of attrition with the Luftwaffe. In 1942 and early 1943 this had cost them dear, with their bombers having insufficient escorts or, in the latter part of many missions, no escorts at all. By the second half of 1944, however, with the superb P-47 Thunderbolts and P-51 Mustangs pouring off the production lines, and with operational range extended to an arc between Stettin, Prague, Turin and Toulouse, the German day-fighters were reduced to near impotence. Again it is statistics that tell the tersest story, showing that the loss rates for U.S. daylight operations fell from an average of one bomber for every 26 sorties flown in 1943 to one for every 100 sorties in the first ten months of 1944. An equally telling comparison is that between the peak monthly loss rate, in October 1943, with 186 bombers lost for 2,117 effective target sorties (8.8 per cent), and October 1944 when 177 were lost for 17,058 sorties (1.0 per cent).[3]

Of even more interest to senior commanders was the ratio of planes lost to tons of bombs dropped, which fell from one plane for every 28 tons dropped in October 1943 to one plane for every 238 tons a year later. So economical had this rate become that by the second half of 1944 Bomber Command, too, was organising large-scale daylight raids, such sorties comprising 50 per cent of total sorties in August 1944, 60 per cent in September and 35 per cent in October. However, it was the prospect of minimal day-fighter opposition that seems to have attracted Harris rather than any possibility of enhanced bombing accuracy. Like his American partners in the Combined Bombing Offensive, Harris had been directed to concentrate his efforts against precision targets, notably oil, and a directive issued on 25th September stated: "You are to direct your strategic attacks . . . against the following systems of objectives: *First priority* (i) petroleum industry, with special emphasis on petrol (gasoline) including storage. *Second priority* (ii) The German rail and waterborne transportation systems. (iii) Tank production plants and depots. (iv) M[otor] T[ransport] production plants and depots."[4] But precision bombing had never been to Harris's taste and, for reasons which never found any cogent explanation, he continued to maintain that bombing should be directed only against large industrial and urban areas, notably the Ruhr and Berlin, where even indiscriminate raids, he claimed, would necessarily reduce output and sap the morale of the population at large. Attempts to pinpoint key industries and potential choke-points he dismissed as a search for 'panacea targets', none of which he felt were as critical or vulnerable as the 'experts' claimed.

The experts were equally disenchanted with Harris's claims and extrapolations about the value of his 'area bombing', and felt that he got far too excited about photographs of German buildings with their roofs blown off. Professor Solly Zuckerman's Bombing Survey Unit had concluded in March 1944 that "whoever it was who had done Harris's sums did not understand what he was doing . . . I said that if Bomber Command were to continue with his existing plans, his Command could not in the available time achieve more than a 7 per cent reduction in Germany's overall output."[5] But Harris retained an absolute faith in area bombing and, once the bitterly resented subordination to SHAEF was ended, he determined to resume the campaign. Moreover, his directives from Portal and the Air Staff provided him with the excuse, including as they did understandable caveats about where Harris might direct his bombers in the event of bad weather. The directive of 25th September allowed that "when weather or tactical conditions are unsuitable for operations against specific primary objectives, attacks should be delivered on important industrial areas, using blind bombing techniques as necessary." On 13th October Harris was given even more leeway in a directive which virtually contradicted itself by asserting that while the previous priorities remained in force, there was now also a need for "special operations . . . (i) In order to concentrate bombing effort on the vital areas of the Ruhr . . . [and its] great concentration of enemy economic and military resources . . . (ii) In order to demonstrate to the enemy in Germany generally the overwhelming superiority of the Allied air forces in this theatre . . . The common object of these demonstrations is to bring home to the enemy a realisation of this overwhelming superiority and the futility of continued resistance."[6] It would be difficult to find a more concise endorsement of Harris's own twin objectives of generalised industrial dislocation and the breaking of the enemy's morale through what was little more than terror bombing.

Harris was not slow to grasp the opportunity and soon stepped up the volume of attacks on German cities. During October fully two-thirds of Bomber Command's missions were for area attacks and a mere 6 per cent directed specifically against oil targets. In his autobiography, Harris himself was to note proudly that "we dropped 42,246 tons of bombs on [German] industrial cities in October, which was more than twice the weight of bombs dropped on these objectives in any previous month of the war."[7] Many of these attacks were directed against the Ruhr, and commentators frequently refer to autumn 1944 as the Second Battle of the Ruhr, the First having ended inconclusively after numerous horribly expensive night-raids between March and July 1943. During October 1944, up to the 25th, there were twelve night attacks involving more than 100 bombers, and of these four were directed against the Ruhr. Two of them were 'maximum efforts', such that in all 2,910 night bombers hit the Ruhr as opposed to 2,740 pitted against all other targets. The day raids showed a similar skew, with only six out of thirteen missions being sent against the Ruhr, but those six involving 2,520 bombers as opposed to 1,572 employed in the remainder.

In fairness to Harris it should be pointed out that three of the Ruhr raids were nominally directed against oil installations at Sterkrade, Wanne Eickel and Homberg, and even in the more generalised raids against Duisburg and Essen, Harris could justifiably point out that the Ruhr as a whole contained most of the Fischer-Tropsch synthetic oil plants, one of the two main methods by which the Germans endeavoured to compensate for their growing shortage of crude petroleum. On the other hand, it was the second type of plant, using the Bergius hydrogenation method, that produced most of Germany's synthetic aviation fuel, the prime target, and few of these were located in the Ruhr. Certainly, Portal remained unconvinced by Harris's feigned commitment to precision targeting, and during late September and October he grew increasingly annoyed about the steady reversion to area bombing. By the end of the month he was having grave doubts about Harris's claim that only bad weather forced him to fall back on area targets, and was soon to commit to paper a veiled suggestion that Harris was being economical with the truth when clearly he still hankered after indiscriminate attacks on German cities as a whole.[8]

This, then, is the background to the raids mounted on 25th October 1944, two by Bomber Command and four by Eighth U.S. Air Force. All these missions were conducted in daylight, Bomber Command mounting no raids after dark on either the 24th or the following night. The two British raids were against Essen and Homberg, the first, by far the larger, involving 759 bombers. This was an 'area raid', directed indiscriminately against factories and civilians, while the smaller raid (231 bombers) was targeted on oil installations. Oil production was also the main American target and over half of the 1,250 bombers sent out struck at synthetic oil plants in Hamburg. The remaining planes took part in three separate raids on airfields and railways. Bomber Command lost 4 planes and 28 aircrew that day, Eighth U.S. Air Force 2 and 18 respectively.[9]

At this time Bomber Command could deploy something like 1,500 front-line aircraft, the majority of them Avro Lancaster and Handley Page Halifax four-engined bombers. These aircraft were split between seven main operational groups, which are listed in the table below. It should be noted that there were also four other groups concerned with training (7, 91, 92, 93) and 26 Group handling signals and the like.[10]

Group	Base	No. of Squadrons	Type Aircraft	Specialisation (if any)	Airfield locations
1	Bawtry	14	Lancaster	–	Lincs.
3	Newmarket	11	Lancaster	–	Cambs. [Norfolk] Suffolk
4	York	13	Halifax	–	Yorks.
5	Swinderby	18	Lancaster	–	Lincs.
6	Knaresboro'	14	Halifax (12) Lancaster (2)	–	Yorks.
8	Huntington	16	Lancaster (7) Mosquito (9)	Pathfinder Force	Hunts. [Cambs.] Norfolk [Beds.]
100	E. Dereham	13	Halifax (1) Other (5)	Electronic C/measures	Norfolk

Bomber Command's squadrons were dispersed over 92 operational airfields, with either one or two squadrons assigned to each. Because of the very clear delineation of functions between aircrew and ground-crew, each squadron had its own commanding officer, distinct from the officer in charge of the airfield itself. The former had the rank of Wing Commander and the latter Group Commander. The squadron C.O.s were required to fly only one mission per month but many felt they were shirking their duty and risked losing the respect of their men if they did not get airborne on a regular basis. The ranks of both the squadron and the station C.O.s were one grade higher than their equivalents in other Commands, such as Fighter, Transport and Training, mainly because of the sheer size of their commands, not least the airfield itself. Movies about this phase of the war tend to focus on the aircrew, often of a single bomber, and to stress their sense of isolation on a remote and desolate night-bomber base. But airfields that can look on film like a dark, barren stretch of nowhere were in fact busy communities, often covering up to 600 acres and requiring the services of 2,500 RAF personnel. Of the latter, only about ten per cent were aircrew and the rest, including perhaps 400 members of the WAAF, served as airframe fitters and engineers, electricians, armourers to prepare the bombs and machine guns, radar mechanics, photographic technicians, typists, drivers and catering staff.

The first general notification of a raid came about eight hours before take-off. Battle Orders for the aircrew were posted, naming the crews to take part, while the groundcrew most in the know would be the armourers in the Bomb Dump, who had to assemble, fuse and load the particular mix of bombs for that raid. On most raids only a proportion of a squadron's aircraft were dispatched but on a near 'maximum effort', like the Essen mission on 25th October, all or most of the crews would have been alerted the night before. For some hours these crews had nothing to do but wait for the station tannoys to summon them from their Nissen huts for the pre-raid briefings. Groundcrew, however, were at work long before this. For the armourers, especially, it was punishing work, with a typical two-squadron bomb-load weighing some 190 tons. The Essen raid on the 25th was probably a little less taxing than some because the planes were each loaded with one 4,000-lb bomb, nicknamed a 'cookie', and sixteen 500-lbers. On many area missions the 'cookie' was supplemented by ten clusters of 4-lb incendiaries, especially wearisome to stow, but according to Air Chief Marshal Harris, "in Essen and many other towns almost everything that could be burnt was already reduced to ashes, and we could therefore only attack with high-explosive bombs ... Effective additional damage could only be done to the already devastated cities of the Ruhr by an enormous expenditure of [high explosive] bombs ... It was also difficult to estimate from the air photographs either the extent or the value of the damage done, since it was often a question of comparing one ruin with another that had previously stood on the same spot."[11]

If the bomb armourers had the most physically demanding job – and the most dangerous, especially when fusing bombs with long-delay, anti-removal bomb pistols or anti-disturbance fuses – others were working equally long hours. These included the armaments section, racing against time to feed tens of thousands of cartridges into the machine-gun ammunition belts, and the men at the fuel dump, filling the huge 2,500-gallon Matador petrol bowsers and driving them back and forth to the scattered aircraft dispersal pans. (A Lancaster, for example, managed about 0.8 miles to the gallon.) For a daylight raid this would have necessitated working through most of the night. Also hard at work were many of the WAAF personnel, some in the locker rooms where they "sorted out all the items of clothing and equipment needed by each member of the crew as soon as briefing ended. About fifteen articles were required ... each ... ranging from lifesaving Mae Wests to socks" and including, too, heated airsuits for the gunners and parachutes all round. "In the kitchen, WAAFs cut sandwiches for nearly 200 aircrew and parcelled up rations of chocolate, fruit, chewing gum and flasks of tea or coffee."[12]

The groundcrew with whom the fliers had the most contact were those men assigned to maintain their particular plane. These, too, were at work long before the aircrew appeared, swarming over the plane in their charge and assiduously checking each and every part. First and foremost were those parts most obviously connected with the plane's flying ability, such as engines, instruments, plugs, and hydraulics. If a fault with such a part was found, the plane had to undergo a brief test-flight after repair before it could be cleared for operations. It was not unknown for two or three test-flights to be made before clearance was obtained, nor for groundcrews to be refitting entire engines only an hour before take-off. Everyone laboured long and hard, fully aware that it was not they who would have to brave the enemy fighters and flak and thus anxious to minimise needless extra distractions and tensions for the fliers. "Carelessness by an electrician could cause a hang-up [in the bomb-bay] or a wrong T[arget] I[ndicator] being dropped and might ruin an attack. A faulty instrument would create at least anxiety among a crew working under stress and might occasion disaster. That bombsights, compasses and the whole paraphernalia of gauges and rev-counters were working correctly was vital, and not only for peace of mind. Countless small items, probably never used, or only in emergency, like fire extinguishers, had to be checked daily. A jammed gun or the wrong type of ammunition could cause the death of the gunner and even of the whole crew."[13]

The groundcrew would probably have been toiling for four or five hours before the bomber crews woke up and then made their way to the officers' and sergeants' messes for breakfast. This meal was one of the few perks of being operational aircrew and consisted of "shelled eggs and real bacon served at linen-covered tables by WAAF waitresses . . . Sometimes even a tiny vase of flowers . . . And some little tit-bit – like fresh fruit – the rest of the mess didn't have. [Before a mission] waitresses were just that little bit more polite and more cheerful. It didn't do any good. It played hell with your stomach muscles and you had indigestion all the way over. Nor did that single Benzedrine tablet, on everybody's side-plate, make for back-flips of sheer delight. The big idea was that you mustn't get bored and fall asleep over enemy territory."[14]

After breakfast most of the remaining time before take-off was taken up with briefings. Security was tight and a member of the RAF Regiment was posted on the door of the briefing room to check all identities. There were two main sessions, one for the crews as a whole outlining the purpose of the mission, strength and bomb-loads, weather conditions and likely enemy reaction, and the other bringing together the specialists within the crews, the pilots, navigators, bomb-aimers and wireless operators. The general briefing was opened by the squadron commanding officer, but probably the most important person there was the squadron intelligence officer. It was he who revealed to the assembled crews, hunched forward around their individual trestle-tables, just what the mission for the day was to be. This was kept secret to the very last minute and was usually announced by a theatrical unveiling of a huge map of Europe with the route to the target, rarely as the crow flies, marked out in half-inch red tape. An added sense of menace was provided by slabs of red and blue chinagraph hatching on the talc covering the map, the former denoting the main flak concentrations, the latter the searchlight batteries. An intelligence officer with No. 1 Bomber Group listed the full range of topics he attempted to cover, ranging over general information about the target, results of the last raid on it, flak and searchlights, enemy fighters, take-off time and phasing of the various squadrons, 'Pathfinder' details, especially the types and colours of route-markers, flares and sky-markers being used, likelihood and details of enemy decoy markers, enemy recognition signals, propaganda leaflets (if any), own fighter escort, own barrage balloons en route, location of own convoys. "That's the lot. Any questions? Nine times out of ten the crews would ask about the convoys ... Ours had a nasty habit of shooting first and then finding out what they were firing at. Nobody blamed them, but the crews always liked to be absolutely certain where the convoys were forecast to be."[15]

The meteorological officer then gave a summary of likely conditions, usually to a fairly steady barrage of groans, catcalls and whistles, and for a daylight raid he focussed on the probability of cloud over the target. For most of October this had been very heavy, usually ten tenths, and it was to be so again on the 25th. Other squadron officers might make a few brief points and then the briefing was closed, the crews splitting up into specialist huddles in the Crew Room, to be addressed at more length by the squadron officers responsible for navigation, signals, gunnery, bomb-aiming, and by the lead Master Bomber. On the way from the briefing to the Crew Room the crews picked up maps of the day's route and target, as well as escape and survival kits in the event that they should survive being shot down. After the specialist briefings, some ninety minutes since the target was first revealed, the crews reunited to hear any last-minute information and clear up outstanding queries. To this briefing the intelligence officer brought not only any updates received from Group headquarters, but also a little stack of manilla envelopes in which were placed any valuables the crew might wish forwarded to next-of-kin. They also accepted any letters written with a similar eventuality in mind.

Finally it was time for the crews to make their way to the planes. This was not quite as simple as it might sound because the bombers were widely scattered around the whole airfield, in so-called dispersal pans, to prevent their being damaged or destroyed en masse during an enemy intruder raid. Some crews had to travel as much as three miles to their aircraft and most were provided with trucks, usually unsprung Bedfords, and a WAAF driver. A few crews were close enough to walk, others were able to make the journey on bicycles. Assembly at the truck point was the last time crews met together and as each group departed they entered a very private and circumscribed world in which the next hours would be concerned solely with carrying out their allotted tasks, wrestling with their fears and fervently hoping that they did not shame themselves in the presence of their closest comrades. Once arrived at the dispersal pan, there was a temporary easing of tension as they chatted with the groundcrew but even here most conversation was concerned with the job in hand, notably the plane's readiness and the myriad points affecting each man's particular station.

Shortly after this the crew boarded the aircraft, via a door towards the rear on the starboard side. Lugging their equipment behind them, some bundled up in the bulky heated air suits, they squeezed through, took one step down into the fuselage and made their way to their stations. Lancasters had a crew of seven: the pilot (and captain), the flight-engineer, the bomb-aimer/front gunner, the navigator, the wireless operator, the upper-turret gunner and the tail gunner. The man in the rear was hunched about a cricket pitch's length away from the pilot and the lower part of this gap was taken up by the very long bomb-bay. He had no means of leaving his turret once he was shut in, while the bomb-aimer, right at the other end of the plane, could only leave his station with immense difficulty, having to wriggle underneath the flight engineer's folding seat.

Though he had to stand to operate his guns, the bomb-aimer spent much of the flight in a prone position, lying on a padded section of the floor that was also an escape hatch. To his left was the Mark XIV bombsight computer box which was connected by two drives to the sighting head just 18 inches away from his nose. To the right was the pre-selector box on which the order for releasing the bombs, singly or in salvo, could be set. This was no arbitrary procedure as it was essential to keep the aircraft balanced by correctly spreading the release from the bomb-bay. The panel on the right also contained the bomb release-button, or 'tit', with a protective guard above it to prevent it being pressed accidentally.

The flight engineer sat on the right of the pilot. His instruments were arrayed on two panels, one in front of him and one to his right, and included oil and fuel gauges, fuel tank selector cocks, booster pump switches, fuel pressure warning lights and oil dilution buttons. As for the rest of the crew,

> the navigator sat facing to port, in a little curtained office behind the pilot, and you would have to squeeze past him to reach the wireless-operator's compartment. His was the cosiest place in the aircraft, right next to the hot-air outlet. He also had the astrodome above him, for the navigator's star shots, and the wireless-op could keep a lookout there when he wasn't working on the set. Still going aft, you would climb over the wide mass of the main spar, keeping your head

down to avoid the escape hatch above it, and then past the rest-bed on your right into the long, dark fuselage. Since you left the nose, you had actually been walking on the roof of the bomb-bay, but now you came to the end of that. You stepped down on to the fuselage floor, and for the first time you could stand upright, at least until you reached the mid-upper turret, shaped like an egg, with the wide end sticking out of the roof. You wriggled past the turret and felt your way on, between the ammunition runways, past the main door and the Elsan lavatory, to reach the rear-turret entrance.[16]

Just getting to the Elsan was a fairly arduous journey and the crew forward would rarely bother just for relieving the bladder alone, which they could usually do in some sort of receptacle. One crew with 622 Squadron at Mildenhall employed a gallon-can, painted yellow and christened 'Seventh Heaven'.

As they settled down at their stations some crewmen began to wonder whether the de-luxe breakfast was such a good idea after all. For their nostrils were assailed by the pungent "smell peculiar to aircraft alone, a mixture of paint, dope, metal, oil – a smell that can play havoc with a delicate stomach even before take-off."[17] But this was usually soon forgotten during the various routines that each man had to follow, stowing parachutes, laying out documents, pre-flight checks and, perhaps most important of all, ensuring that charms and talismans were all present and correct. Most aircrew, like almost anyone facing periodic combat, carried with them some charm or other that could be thought of as being the 'reason' for their survival to date and thus the *sine qua non* of surviving future operations. Miles Tripp, of 218 Squadron, at Methwold, took part in the 25th October Essen raid and his plane seems to have been a veritable witch-doctor's surgery of superstition: "Harry . . . would never fly unless he was wearing a patterned red and blue scarf. Dig . . . wouldn't fly without his hat, and it had to be placed in a niche behind his head in the cockpit with its peak facing forward. George carried his girl-friend's brassiere on a good-luck chain; Paul always wore a yellow scarf patterned with red dragons . . . I flew with more tokens than anyone – a silk stocking, a Land Army brooch, a pink chiffon scarf and a tiny bone elephant."[18]

This time on the ground was spent on routine checks, methodical tests in addition to any already done by the groundcrew, of virtually every moving or electrical part that might malfunction during a mission. These checks were divided into three phases, one to be gone through before starting the engines, another before moving out of the dispersal pan, and the last just before take-off itself. This was sometimes known as the 'V.A.s', or vital actions. A full list of these checks, many in the first phase being done with the groundcrew, would be tediously arcane. During the final checks the engines were switched on one at a time, starting with the starboard inner, and each step was accompanied by the following ritual incantation between flight engineer and pilot:

"Ground/Flight switch." "On 'Ground'."
"Throttles." "Set."
"Pitch." "Fully fine."
"Slow running." "Idle Cut off."
"Supercharger." "'M' gear. Lights out."
"Air intake." "Cold."
"Rad shutters." "Auto."
"Number 2 tank." "Selected. Booster pump on."
"Master fuel cocks." "On."
"Ignition." "On."
"Contact!"[19]

Once all four engines were started, the starboard inner being followed by the port inner and then the two outers, the plane was ready to make its ungainly way to the marshalling point at the end of the runway. All the dispersal pans were located near what was known as the perimeter track, or peri-track, and just before leaving the pilot handed a completed Form 700 to the groundcrew chief, certifying that all pre-flight inspections had been completed and passing the plane into the temporary custody of the aircrew.

Even after the plane had left its dispersal pan the groundcrew, or 'erks', had to hang around for another hour or so in case their plane aborted its mission. This waiting around was a particular travail on a wet and wind-swept airbase in late October, though many ground-crews built themselves rickety, garden-shed type structures which offered some shelter from the elements and the chance of a 'brew-up'. Such shelters still offered little protection from the biting cold, and after their wait the crew still had to walk or cycle back to their billets which, just like the fliers', were often several thousand yards away.

The pilot gunned all four engines and the plane jerked forwards. Then, with a squeal of brakes, the pilot prepared to turn into the peri-track, now gunning only the outer engine on the side furthest away from the turn. The plane slewed round, another squeal of brakes, the opposite outer engine was gunned, and the plane straightened up to lumber round the narrow, winding track to the end of the runway, a distance of a mile or more if the dispersal pan was upwind from the marshalling point. The journey was hardly straightforward. When turning "there was a lot of inertia, and you had to anticipate each turn by ten or twenty degrees, depending on your speed. You were supposed to taxi at a fast walking-pace, but that wasn't easy to judge, sitting twenty feet above the ground. It was best to keep a ready grip on the brake-lever, in case she tried to run away with you." Especially as you were just part of a whole file of narrowly-spaced bombers. The crewman most aware of this was the upper gunner who, swivelling in his turret, could see ten, twenty and more bombers to front and rear, "a long meandering line of Lancasters weighed down by their maximum burden, appearing as clumsy as plodding elephants around a circus ring."[20]

On reaching the marshalling point, a pilot drew up behind the aircraft in front and was soon conscious of the wash from its propellers as the four Merlin engines rose to full power for take-off. As it gathered speed and disappeared down the runway some of the crew on the waiting plane looked round at what might be their very last sight of 'home', able to make out little except the caravan at the side of the runway that served as Flying Control and the little crowd of people that always gathered to see the bombers off. From the turrets there was a better view. For one bomb-aimer, seeing taxiing aircraft in front and the ambulances and rescue vehicles hovering in case of a failed take-off, the whole scene resembled nothing so much as "a car park at the end of the races." A flier at the opposite end of the aircraft had a less charitable view. "There they were. The odds and sods. Airmen and WAAFs. All sorts of ranks, all sorts of sizes and not a wing among 'em. Clerks, cooks and bottlewashers, lining the runway; waving and cheering like so many lunatics at a dog track . . . I remember the furious rage which built up inside me as we passed them. The quite genuine desire to turn all four Brownings on 'em."[21]

The pilot and flight engineer now had little time for gazing at spectators and went through their last set of checks:

"Throttles." "Set on a thousand."

"Trims, elevator two notches nose down." "Elevator and aileron trims neutral."

"Supercharger." "'M' gear."

"Pitch." "Fully fine and locked."

"Pilot-heater on. Fuel." "Contents checked, master cocks on, cross-feed off, boosters on."

"Flaps." "One third down and reading."

"Gills." "Air intake cold, rad shutters auto."

"George – clutch in, cock out. Gyro – compass set."[22]

It was now about one minute since the previous plane had taken off and at any moment a lamp in the control van would flash green and the four Merlins would begin to roar as the pilot opened them up. The plane strained against the brakes as the power increased and bucked forward as soon as they were released, bolting down the runway at ever-increasing speed. The pilot had both feet on the rudder controls, and as soon as he could he pushed the control column forward a little to raise the aircraft off the tail-wheel. As the rudders rose into the slipstream, allowing him more control over steering, the aircraft tilted forward on to the main wheels only, and the crew felt the wings flex as they took some of the weight of the tremendous fuel- and bomb-load. With his right hand, the pilot continued to push the four throttle levers towards the gate, leading with his thumb on the port outer lever to counter the plane's tendency to veer left. This was a result of the propellers' natural propensity to produce push at right-angles to their circular plane and might well be accentuated by crosswinds on the runway. Nor was this the only difficulty in keeping the plane pointed down the white centre-line. Slipstream from the propellers did not flow evenly down the fuselage but corkscrewed around it, again trying to push it out of line. Finally, there was the notorious problem of torque, the scientific explanation of an aircraft's inherent desire to make totally unwelcome responses to the force of the propellers. This had to be controlled by judicious juggling of the throttle levers. Finally all these levers were pushed through the gate and the full take-off power was achieved. As one pilot turned novelist described it: "Through the intercom he heard the level voice of the navigator reading off the speed: 'Eighty; ninety-five; hundred . . .' All the instruments were dancing, free again. '. . . hundred and five; hundred and ten . . .' He saw the end of the runway coming up and the individual lights along it melting into a golden line. He maintained a steady backward movement of the control column, and the aircraft lifted off the ground, lightly, like a leaf breaking from a parent tree."[23] After a few seconds the pilot directed the flight engineer to retract the undercarriage and set the flaps. Once this had been done, the flight engineer adjusted the engines for climbing power and everyone sat back for a while.

For a fully laden bomber, especially a Lancaster, the initial climb had to be taken very slowly. Indeed, on a relatively short trip like that to Essen, planes could not reach bombing height over the target if they set course immediately they left the ground. On such missions aircraft took off in different directions and climbed separately, in a circular mountain road fashion, until they reached an adequate height, around 10,000 feet, before climbing another 10,000 feet during the flight itself. On this second, gradual climb "the aircraft crawls upward like a heliotrope inching through the soil towards the sun. After what seems like many hours of this . . . suddenly the cockpit of the Lancaster breasts the cloud tops, and there is the sky, vast and clear and brilliantly blue. The wisps of clouds that rush past you are so white that you can't believe that you've even seen true whiteness before. It's whiter than babies' teeth and angels' wings . . . Forget the fact that the gradually decreasing atmospheric pressure is making you want to fart, close your ears to the rumble of the engines . . . This experience is something of a translation, in the biblical sense of conveyance to heaven without death."[24]

It was difficult to become fully absorbed in the sights outside the aircraft, no matter how breath-taking. Flatulence apart, the noise of the engines represented a constant mechanical din that cut out all other sounds from outside, even thunder, flak bursts and other aircraft unless they were very close. The one thing that could be heard was anything hitting the plane, though one hoped that this would be nothing worse than rain, sleet or hail, all of which drummed loudly on the canopy. Moreover, the crewmen beneath this canopy had more than enough to occupy them just doing their job. The pilot and the flight engineer had to listen to the engines constantly and the latter endeavoured to have all four going at the same r.p.m. by fiddling with the propeller pitch levers, while the pilot did his own throttle adjustments to produce a precisely harmonious sound. On a daylight raid like this one he could also try to synchronise the engines by getting the shadows on the propellers at just the same angle.

The navigator and the wireless operator also had their ongoing tasks, but the bomb-aimer and the two gunners had rather more time than they might wish to speculate on such things as fighter interception, flak over the target, and the general vulnerability of their thinly-skinned metal tube. On the 25th, however, no German day-fighters left the ground and so the possibility of falling prey to enemy action did not become an urgent reality until the aircraft approached the target.

In daylight raids most RAF bombers made little attempt to fly in formation but arrived over the target in a loose 'gaggle' strung out for some distance. The one squadron that was ordered to fly in formation on the 25th found that "the flak barrage over Essen was so intense that aircraft began to jink all over the place before spilling their bombs.

Discipline went to the winds . . ."[25] A member of another squadron described the terrible mental ordeal of flying through heavy flak. Even some way from the target one could see the sort of welcome given to the lead planes, and on this occasion the flight engineer was leading a sing-song when he suddenly yelled: "Jumping Je-e-e-sus!" The bomb-aimer bent down to see the first wave of planes hit by a dense barrage of predicted flak. The black puffs faded slowly and then were lost in a thick black cloud which had also swallowed up the first wave. The cloud was almost right over the target and he started to calculate how soon his own plane would reach it. Before long

> the cloud gave back the first wave, tremulous as through a veil, save for two aircraft losing height behind them . . . The smoke had drifted, so now it was difficult to tell where the barrage waited. We were both waiting, I thought, and soon we should fuse and spark and thunder with all the fury of a consummation. Fear was a fur on the tongue, a bitterness in the mouth, a pulse in the bowels, but the mind was bright and all-seeing . . . And then . . . there began a dull beating; bursts on either wing, poised like proffered black bouquets, shapely for a second, and then the others, below, above and beside us, as if saying: 'Take this one, or this one,' and 'This one is specially for you.' No more looking. Eyes fixed on Collins' boots. One hand on the 'chute. The lurch and upward suck and the jarring fall; the long slow ride over giant cobblestones. O'Brien's quick breathing over the intercom, the taste in the mouth, the unmistakable taste of utter fear, and then, suddenly, as if shot from a tunnel, back into a calm clear sky.[26]

The reference to 'predicted flak' denotes that the German anti-aircraft gunners were firing at where they thought the bombers should be, though in fact they were probably using radar-directed aiming techniques. In either case, the essential point is that neither the Germans nor the bombers could see each other through the ten-tenths cloud that covered the target. Although this was a daylight mission, the planes in fact adopted the techniques used by the night bombers to guide themselves over a target not visible from the air. By late 1944 these had become very sophisticated and almost any mission of note now involved the dispatch of a whole cluster of specialised aircraft to help the Main Force of bombers to deliver its payload. These 'high tech' aircraft belonged to two of Bomber Command's Groups: 8 Group, also known as the Pathfinder Force (PFF), and 100 (Special Duties) Group. The former was responsible for guiding the Main

Force to the target and providing pyrotechnic marking of the actual bombing point for the duration of the strike. The latter was concerned with what are nowadays known as electronic counter-measures (ECM), disrupting the enemy's radar by various jamming and 'spoofing' measures. These measures were a forerunner of those still widely employed, as during the 1991 Gulf War, for example.[27]

Much of 100 Group's work was concerned with disrupting the activities of the German night-fighter force, which was not called upon to respond on 25th October, but of much more direct assistance to the Essen raid were the Pathfinder Lancasters and Mosquitos which led the way to the target and marked it. The main navigational aids used in all PFF planes and a proportion of the Main Force lead bombers were 'Gee' and 'Oboe'. 'Gee' had been in use since March 1942 and allowed a navigator to plot his position via a receiver which measured time differences in receiving pulses from three separate ground transmitters. Once over Germany accuracy was only within a 6-mile margin, and so the last ten miles or so to the target were flown using 'Oboe', based on twin radar transmitters on the ground which triggered return pulses from a Pathfinder bomber. Both worked out the bomber's distance from the transmitters and when it reached a predetermined position they triggered marker and/or bomb release. It had been first used by Bomber Command in December 1942. Its range was only 270 miles, but with the retreat of the Germans out of France, forward stations were established right up to the German frontier.

Almost 7,000 of the 17,000 sorties flown that October were by daylight. The perpetual problem of cloud-cover, which could only worsen as the year drew on, meant that the PFF still had a vital role to play and they soon developed special techniques to deal with the difficulty. The basic tactic was known as sky-marking, code-named 'Wanganui', and when used in conjunction with 'Oboe' it was known as 'Musical Wanganui'.[28] The sky-markers were dropped by Mosquitos from 105 and 109 Squadrons. On the 25th it was the former that had the job and, in fact, three of its aircraft were hit by flak, one of them later having to make a forced landing at a forward fighter airfield. The markers were suspended by parachute and as they burned out quickly, the Mosquitos would drop them one load at a time, over the duration of the whole mission. At first the flares used were similar to those dropped for night-time ground marking, but these proved difficult to make out in daylight and so coloured Smoke Puffs were developed. These were 250-lb or 1,000-lb bomb-cases filled with coloured pigment which, when ejected, burned as a large ball of colour suspended in the air. The smoke was the same colour as the ball of fire and the whole conflagration lasted for about three minutes, although the smoke hung about until dispersed by the wind. Those planning a raid had recourse to red, blue, green or yellow Puffs.

Wind was the greatest problem when sky-marking, which was why the Smoke Puffs burned for only a short time before they drifted too far away from the target. Various ancillary methods were used to maintain accuracy. Sometimes the Master Bomber, in one of the PFF planes, would indicate over the radio where a marker had blown off-centre too quickly or had been dropped in the wrong place. But attempts were made to allow for drift even before the raid began, also taking into account "the normal height and airspeed of the attacking aircraft. It was most important that bombs were released on an exact heading as detailed by the briefing officer [back at the station]. If the specified headings were not maintained, very large errors could arise."[29] The bomb-aimer, therefore, set his bomb-sight for zero wind as this variable had already been taken into account. Bomb-aimers were also enjoined to drop their bombs at the estimated centre-point of the whole group of visible markers.

As each bomber flew successively over the aiming point, the bomb-aimer took temporary charge of the plane, shouting out course alterations as he waited for the selected spot between the sky-markers to creep, agonisingly slowly, down the crosspiece on his graticule. While waiting, some of the crew may have been struck by the unreality of the situation as they lumbered through the air like passengers in a very noisy, very bumpy bus that had been miraculously plucked heavenwards, with bright blue sky all around, not an enemy plane to be seen, and only dense cloud, splodges of silently exploding flak, and huge, brightly-coloured puffballs drifting below. Of Germany, the Ruhr, falling bombs, the pitiless, inexorable demolition of Essen, nothing was to be seen.

For most crews the first indication of damage caused would not come until the following day when the photographs taken at the end of each plane's bomb-run, a few seconds after release, were developed. Of course the photographs, too, depended on there being a break in the clouds. According to one historian, crews "were able to identify ground detail through a break in the cloud, confirming that the marking of their aiming point was accurate. Large explosions were reported and a good fire area was established."[30] A flyer who took part in the raid described one of the explosions as positively awesome, as "suddenly the cloud shook and rapid ripples destroyed its calm, like the smashing of clear reflections when a trout jumps in a placid pool. Instantly, every bomber in the force was shaken by a blast-wave from some mighty, as yet unseen explosion. And then, as they looked down a little fearfully, they saw the cloud-top open in a mighty billow. That endless cloud, almost two miles high, was broken open and flung aside by the flame and force of the greatest explosion that any of them had seen. A mushroom of smoke poured through the cloud and, curling and rumbling, rose to the height of the bombers themselves."[31]

Gotterdämmerung glimpsed through candy-floss.

20

'Der Grosse Schlag'

THE LUFTWAFFE AND THE DEFENCE OF GERMANY

THE LUFTWAFFE, which had once been on the cutting edge in the blitzkrieg campaigns in Poland, France and the Soviet Union, and had brought terror to the cities of Rotterdam, Belgrade and London, was by late 1944 tied down in a largely defensive role over the Reich itself. The vainglorious promises of Reichsmarschall Hermann Göring to bring England to her knees with his bombers alone and that Allied bombers would never penetrate to Berlin were now just bitter jokes as German civilians huddled in the bomb shelters and Luftwaffe fighters were sucked into a deadly battle of attrition against the waves of Allied bombers by day and by night. The protection of German cities and industries was now almost their sole task. Several of the Luftwaffe's theatre commands or air fleets providing operational and tactical support to the army groups, had been downgraded and many of their fighters were transferred. In France and Belgium, Luftflotte III was downgraded to Luftwaffe Western Command. Luftflotte V in Norway was similarly reduced in status, as was Luftflotte II in Italy which came under the command of the 'Luftwaffe General in Italy'. Only on the Eastern Front were the original air fleets, Luftflotten I, IV and VI, retained but here, too, there had been a considerable reduction in the number of fighters. In the third week of October, by far the most powerful grouping was Luftflotte Reich, originally formed in December 1943, which had under command some 900 single-engined and 800 twin-engined fighters in the front-line squadrons. There were also 90 jet- and rocket-powered fighters as well as a further 1,000 fighters with squadrons in reserve, whose crews and planes were resting, training or refitting. Of these, 500 had come from Luftwaffe Western Command, whose remaining 350 single-engined fighters were mostly prohibited from undertaking any missions except the interception of bomber formations passing through their air space. This left perhaps 300 to 400 single-engined fighters in the East and no more than a handful in northern Italy.

The Germans, moreover, were concentrating aircraft production on those fighters that were suited to bomber interception and had finally given up their own attempts to mount heavy bomber operations. Hitler was prevailed upon to moth-ball the four-engined He 177s that were supposed to pound Russian industry, as well as to forgo, at least for the time being, any thoughts of large-scale revenge raids against French ports and English cities. Fighters were now very much the top priority, and by October there had been a remarkable increase both in the number produced and in the proportion of total output they represented. Production had more than doubled in each of the previous two years, from 5,200 in 1942 to 11,800 the following year and then to 29,000 in the first ten months of 1944. In October of that year alone almost 3,000 fighters had rolled off the production lines, and this figure represented almost 83 per cent of total aircraft production, whereas in 1942 and 1943 fighters had comprised only one third and one half respectively of the annual total produced.

It was single-engined fighters, the type used mainly against daylight bomber raids, that were the most heavily produced, and data on monthly acceptances by the Luftwaffe showed just what a tremendous effort had been made during 1944. In the previous year, acceptances of single-engined types actually fell from just over 1,000 in July to only 560 in December. Yet just one month later the figure was back to more than 1,000, and by October 1944 it was up to 2,735. Despite all the Allied effort to destroy the German aircraft industry – a big enough target given that it represented some 40 per cent of total German industrial output, employing around five million workers – they were in fact unable to prevent an enormous increase in production.

Nevertheless, the Germans had long experienced serious bottlenecks on the final assembly lines. Allied bombing tended to tighten these bottlenecks and by October 1994 they were beginning to threaten the future of the final aircraft assembly. Bomber Command photo-intelligence often missed this point, thinking that a seemingly wrecked factory must have ceased production, whereas the real damage was to the ability of the Germans to transfer individual components to the final assembly lines. With this in mind, the German leadership strove to bring aircraft production, especially of fighters, under the control of the Nazi Party. On 1st March 1944, a *Jägerstab* (Fighter

Staff) had been created under the control of Karl-Otto Saur, a *Hauptdienstleiter* who had served as right-hand man to both Fritz Todt and his successor Albert Speer at the Ministry of Munitions. He was also a particular favourite of the Führer's, being possessed of a remarkable memory for dates and statistics. By October, Saur and the Party had the aircraft industry under the most stringent control, with 100,000 extra workers conscripted, and the working week increased from 50 hours to 72. Party commissioners with sweeping powers were established in every factory.

Saur did not rely on bullying alone. Rations were increased in the aircraft factories and special brigades were formed to be rushed to any plant that had been badly bombed, so as to rally management and workers. Considerable efforts were also made to eliminate the distribution bottlenecks, with hundreds of couriers employed to speed consignments of urgently needed components or equipment from one place to another. Such men became still more important as the Germans tried to thwart the Allied bombers by dispersing the aircraft industry wherever possible to underground factories and workshops. An industry that had once been concentrated in 27 main plants was now fragmented into over 700 manufacturing and assembly units. But if the number of workplaces proliferated, the Jägerstab tried hard to reduce the huge number of aircraft types and sub-types being manufactured, or requiring spare parts for refit and repair, at any one time. One source has claimed that in 1943 there were 425 such variants in production or prototype, all of which required their own inventory of special components, so making it impossible to boost overall production through standardised, albeit dispersed, production lines. By October 1944, several experimental types had been jettisoned and Messerschmitt, for example, had just rolled off the first production models of the Bf 109K, which was supposed to bring together all the best features of the numerous sub-types of the Bf 109G.[1] The production process for the plane itself was also rationalised. By breaking down a plane into a number of sub-assemblies, each produced by different teams or sub-contractors, with standard parts and within a standard time-frame, it proved possible to speed delivery of finished planes dramatically. Within a few months Messerschmitt claimed to have achieved a 53 per cent saving in production time, as well as a 25 per cent saving in raw materials used.

No wonder, then, that aircraft production in 1944 registered such a striking increase, with overall production up 58 per cent on the 1943 figure and fighter production up 146 per cent. And yet the remarkable fact remains that hardly any of these aircraft were airborne on 25th October and, indeed, they had only very rarely been encountered by Allied bombers since the 6th of that month. According to American air force sources: "For more than three weeks the Eighth's fliers seldom saw a German fighter and [our fighter pilots and bomber gunners] made no claims whatsoever."[2] A German day-fighter pilot at the time, Günther Bloemertz, noted that "the Allied bombers were staging what almost amounted to fly-past, and endless squadrons of Americans flew over our heads [while] we . . . German pilots could only stand beside our aircraft and their generally empty petrol tanks." Johannes Steinhoff of *Jagdgeschwader* (JG) 77, stationed near Berlin, spoke at more length about this bizarre truce:[3]

> It turned out to be an unexpectedly passive, almost peaceful time for us, that October. If it had not been for the continual air-raid warnings during the night and the fiery glare over Berlin one might have thought the war was over . . .
>
> The propaganda spouting from the radio sounded eerie, unreal – and was interrupted at almost regular intervals by 'early warning', 'pre-alert' and 'alert'. We had shut our ears before; on the (shrinking) periphery of the Reich we had kept our eyes turned 'frontwards' and suppressed our anxiety about the fate of our country with the therapy of combat, attack and the daily risk of death. Now there was no ducking it any longer.
>
> But our high command had given us a new goal. 'This is where you have to keep your nerve. We're going to take a bit of punishment and we mustn't let ourselves be drawn into dissipating our energies.' So, ignoring the bombers, we flew and practised and practised.[4]

What the pilots were practising for was the so-called 'Grosser Schlag', the Grand Slam that would unleash hundreds of carefully husbanded fighters against one of the big American daylight raids, probably some time in early November. The plan had been conceived by General Adolf Galland, commander of the German fighter arm, in late September, and envisioned a first mass interception by up to 2,000 fighters and then a back-up attack by a further 500 planes. In addition, 150 or so fighters from Luftwaffe Command West were to harass the bombers coming and going over France and Belgium, and in the latter phase were to be joined by 80 to 100 night-fighters which would go after crippled aircraft if they attempted to seek refuge in neutral Switzerland or Sweden. The aim was shoot down 400 to 500 bombers, fully expecting equivalent losses among their fighter squadrons, though only of a maximum of 150 pilots. Luftwaffe leaders convinced themselves that, given clear weather, this eruption of air power might actually persuade the Americans to abandon daylight operations.

For once, Galland was enthusiastically supported by his boss, Reichsmarschall Hermann Göring, who saw this as a way of reinstating the Luftwaffe in the eyes of the Führer. So disgusted had Hitler become over the wanton penetrations of German airspace by the bombers, and the huge tonnages they always managed to release, that only seven weeks earlier he had threatened to abolish the air force and rely completely on anti-aircraft guns to defend German cities. All aircraft factories would immediately switch to the production of AA weapons. The threat, like so much of Hitler's ranting bluster, was unenforceable, though that does not seem to have consoled Göring, who remained cringingly desperate to claw back some prestige as a paladin of the Reich.[5]

In the event, the idea of a mass attack was not carried over to the tactical level. The commander of one of the Jagddivisions that would take part, General Kleinrath, who had little flying experience, told his predecessor that he intended to give the *Geschwaders* full operational freedom against the bombers and let them arrive piecemeal. General Hajo Herrmann, a veteran pilot, insisted that "even if we could put 2,000 fighters in the air, it would be a mistake to fight the battle by *Geschwader* or to allow individual members . . . to choose their own approach routes and points of attack. Concentration meant bringing all one's forces together at one point . . . I spoke to him of such things as fighter concentration points, marked by smoke shells fired by the Flak; of pilot aircraft which would 'sky-mark', and so on . . . My approach was to compensate for the navigational difficulties that the lead aircraft would experience by providing visual indicators in the sky."[6]

Other pilots had still more fundamental objections to the concept of mass attack. For Johannes Steinhoff, the question of arriving en masse was secondary. What troubled him was the quality of the German aircrews. To be sure, JG 77 had been given "large numbers of new Messerschmitts" and assigned scores of new pilots to fly them. But they

> were timid, inexperienced, and scared. We flew little (fuel was in short supply) but were able to practise some formation flying and formation attacks on mock bomber flights. The young pilots were not yet ready for combat. It was hard enough leading and keeping together a large combat formation of experienced fighter pilots; with youngsters it was hopeless. They were just windy. They were

expected to fly in precise formation, stuck in the middle of an enormous unit made up of more than a hundred fighters, keeping distance, height, and spacing constant. They were supposed to watch their air space and not let themselves be lured into dogfights with enemy fighters (they had absolutely no experience of aerial combat), and when the formation attacked the bomber armada they were told they must keep in position – come what might. It could never work."[7]

Lack of training was probably the Luftwaffe's greatest problem at this stage of the war and reflected once again Hitler's and the Wehmacht's inability to foresee the enormous demands of warfare across whole continents. At the beginning of the war there had been only five fighter schools, and though this number had increased to fifteen by late 1944, these suffered from an acute shortage of competent instructors. Veteran pilots who could have fulfilled this role had increasingly to remain with the front-line squadrons where their expertise was at an absolute premium. Indeed the burden of effective combat had to be borne by an ever dwindling band of experts leading their gaggles of callow amateurs. Such skilled tuition as was available had to be spread very thin as fighter-pilot training shrank from 240 hours in 1939 to an average of only 115 by mid-1944. In comparison, 360 hours were given to flight training in the RAF and 400 hours in the U.S. Air Force.

The more the Germans felt the need to increase the number of new pilots, the worse the problem became. From April to June 1944, "the output of pilots exceeded the thousand mark, including 800 to 900 fighter pilots. The numbers could be achieved, but not the vital element of quality . . . The few flying hours allowed during training resulted in pilots on operations being too concerned with the technicalities of flying and unable to concentrate upon gunnery and tactics."[8] This was revealed in all the usual mistakes of the inexperienced pilot in combat – a preoccupation with maintaining formation and consequently a perfunctory effort to conduct proper air-search, an inability to get the best out of the aircraft, failure to jettison extra fuel tanks and arm the guns when commencing combat, and reluctance to admit unfavourable odds which would warrant breaking off combat. All these shortcomings only put further pressure on the few experienced formation leaders and detracted still more from their overall efficiency. And to cap it all, even the attempt to give the trainees a grounding in the simple technicalities of flying was hardly a total success. When they joined their squadrons the newcomers' blind-flying ability, by instrument alone, was usually negligible, a critically serious shortcoming during the frequent periods of bad weather over Germany.

By October 1944, then, the very expansion of the fighter arm was a major cause of its deterioration, as inexperienced pilots made up an ever larger proportion of those at the front. Even in that year, Field Marshal Hugo Sperrle, commanding Luftflotte 3, "found that, with rare exceptions, only group and squadron commanders had combat experience exceeding six months. A small percentage of other personnel had an average of three months combat duty, whilst the majority of pilots had seen active service for periods as low as between eight and thirty days."[9] Such tyros were, of course, extremely vulnerable, and not just to the enemy. On one fighter conversion course that followed initial flying training, 32 out of 100 were killed before they received their full thirty hours of familiarisation.

Things were not much better in operational units. Between January and September 1944, up to 50 per cent of fighter pilot casualties were attributable to flying accidents, while in the same period it was found that over half of all pilots were killed before completing their tenth sortie. Clearly the Luftwaffe was going to have to make the most of the experienced pilots it already had, as nobody else was likely to live long enough to become even a competent pilot.

No wonder Hugo Herrmann contemplated mass attack with the same lack of enthusiasm as Steinhoff. Stationed near Budapest, he and his companions spent the late October evenings "in front of a tiled stove or an open fire drinking Tokay, bitching, swearing, telling stories, exchanging views, in an attempt to discover if there was anything we could reasonably hope to do, even though the means at our disposal were insufficient. It was a complete nonsense to throw highly decorated, experienced, mature fighter leaders in with a bunch of brave beginners and send them all into the jaws of 1,000 escort fighters ready to consume all and sundry, irrespective of rank or training."[10]

The quality of the replacement pilots was probably the subject that most concerned the carousing veterans, but there were other pressing concerns to be aired, including the performance of German fighters. One of the greatest achievements of American aviation engineers during the war was to develop piston engines that could take bombers and escort fighters to hitherto impossible ceilings, where they remained relatively safe from the consistently underpowered Luftwaffe fighters. Even when pilots did manage to crawl up to the requisite height they often found themselves unable to see out of the iced-up cockpit.

American fighters had built-in de-icing equipment. To remedy this defect, Messerschmitt was working on a Bf 109H prototype designed expressly to incorporate a new engine for high-altitude combat. Kurt Tank, at Focke-Wolf, the manufacturer of the other German day-fighter, the Fw 190, had just completed the first production models of a D9 variant, featuring a distinctive long nose to accommodate the more powerful, liquid-cooled in-line Jumo 213 engine. Despite early misgivings, the few pilots who had flown these machines were most enthusiastic about their rate of climb, speed and manoeuvrability. Yet it was clear that there was no possibility of either plane being available in numbers at the front until the beginning of 1945. With the Bf 109K also in the early stages of production, the German day-fighter pilots were going to have to make do with the obsolescent 'Gustav' to provide the main strike force for any mass attacks planned for October.

The Bf 109G was not only inadequate in high-altitude performance, it also had a limited range. Aesthetically pleasing though the aircraft was, its sleek lines allowed only a small fuel tank which meant that even under the most favourable conditions range was never more than 360 miles or "an endurance of 55 minutes – quite inadequate for the prolonged combats required against the American day-bombers. Again and again fighters crashed when their pilots, having fought to the last drop of fuel, were compelled to make forced landings or even to bale out."[11] Range could be extended, of course, with the addition of drop-tanks but these further militated against high-altitude performance and inexperienced pilots often forgot to jettison them before going into combat, so dangerously compromising the performance of their planes.

Performance was also adversely affected by the 'bolt-on' weaponry that was developed to counter the firepower of the American B-17 Flying Fortresses and the P-47 Thunderbolt and P-51 Mustang fighters. One pilot, Willi Heilmann of JG 54, stated that by late 1944 the Bf 109 had "been overdesigned and deteriorated with every alteration." Once again the plane's sleek lines were part of the problem, for "in the narrow fuselage there was no longer any more room for the traditional equipment rendered imperative by improvements in the enemy machines, such as additional armaments and superchargers. Holes were cut in the sides and the projecting parts covered with streamlined plates. On its first appearance [one variant] of this outstanding aircraft was nicknamed 'The Bulge'." The addition of armour and extra 20mm and 30mm cannon was especially deleterious to performance. According to Leutnant Steigler of JG 27: "With the introduction of wing cannon in the 109, our old fighter became a truck

... They were good against bombers, but greatly hampered lateral control [and] cut speed significantly ... When we met escorting fighters of any kind we were at a mortal disadvantage. It was not worth your life to be caught flying a 109 with wing cannon against a Mustang."[12]

Herrmann and his colleagues had still more to grouse about over their Tokay, especially the shortage of aviation fuel, which imposed serious limits on both the operational readiness of the front-line squadrons and their ability to give extra tuition to the lamentably under-trained replacements. The German synthetic fuel industry had already suffered grievously at the hands of Allied air attacks. Whereas German fighter production managed to increase despite the close attentions of the Lancasters and the B-17s, the synthetic fuel industry suffered a precipitous decline in output almost as soon as Allied bombers took it in their sights. From January to April 1944, when very few raids were launched against it, total synthetic oil production averaged around 330,000 metric tons per month, of which roughly 170,000 tons was aviation fuel. In May just over 5,000 tons of bombs were dropped and this quickly rose to 26,000 tons in August. Tonnages for the next two months slumped somewhat, with only 12,500 tons dropped in October. Nevertheless, German oil plants were badly hit and overall synthetic oil production fell from almost 300,000 tons in May to 38,000 tons in October. Aviation fuel production fell equally dramatically, from 155,000 tons to just 20,000 tons over this same period.

As the figure of 170,000 tons of aviation fuel per month was regarded as the minimum that would allow a reasonable level of operations plus a certain amount of stockpiling, it is not surprising that the niggardly figures for summer and early autumn had the most drastic consequences. For a while it was possible to maintain operations by using up the stockpiles, but by October these were pretty well gone, while deliveries to the Luftwaffe in September and October were less than 30,000 tons per month. On 10th October, Göring himself admitted that the attacks on oil plants had "all the signs and portents of a major catastrophe", and it seems clear that the three weeks of almost complete Luftwaffe inactivity that followed were caused as much by fuel shortages as by the need to amass fighters for the forthcoming 'Grand Slam'.[13] Those shortages were also eroding whatever slim chances for success this onslaught might have by making it impossible to give the mass of inexperienced pilots any feel for operational flying and combat. When Munitions Minister Albert Speer visited an airfield near Berlin in October, "the commander of the training company informed me that his student pilots could have flight practice only for an hour every week. Only a fraction of the necessary fuel was being supplied to the units."[14]

A final grouse by the fighter pilots focussed on the problem of aircraft serviceability. The U.S. Strategic Bombing Survey tried to pinpoint the cause of the difficulty when, shortly after the war, it noted: "From the beginning of January through December 1944, when aggregate production of single-engined fighters was about 18,000, the actual number of single-engined fighter types in operational units increased by less than 1,000. The failure of the high level of output to be followed by a substantially increased effectiveness at the front is not easy to understand. Most Germans interviewed on this question are unable to provide plausible explanations; on the contrary, it is recognised by them as an unsolved problem."[15] The Report puts forward three possible explanations of its own. One was that a high proportion of aircraft produced had been destroyed before they could be moved from the factories. One Luftwaffe staff officer, with the O.K.W., estimated that almost the total September production of fighters was lost in this way. Another was the loss of aircraft in transit from the factories to the airfields, with various sources attributing 20 to 25 per cent of losses to the inexperienced pilots performing this task.

A third reason was the enormous disparity between the number of aircraft actually handed over to the front-line squadrons and the number available for operations at any one time. Highlighted here is the inability of Luftwaffe groundcrews to maintain and repair the first line fighters. The disaster in Normandy and the retreat through France and Belgium had put enormous strains on military manpower on the ground and in his eagerness to rush new Volksgrenadier and other infantry divisions to the front, Hitler had permitted the utter lunacy of transferring up to 15,000 groundcrew per week into these second-grade divisions. Some had been replaced by women, which definitely had a positive effect on aircrew morale, but it was going to take these newcomers some time to become fully conversant with the intricacies of an FuG16ZY homing indicator or the spark plugs in a methanol-water injection Daimler Benz DB 605AM inverted-vee engine.[16]

Even had all these women been trained to the highest standard, it is far from certain that they could have achieved a markedly better serviceability rate. Few aircraft engines had been tested properly before they left the factory, fuel shortages having reduced test running-times from two hours to half-an-hour, and that for only a sample percentage of completed engines.[17] The dispersal of the aircraft factories also prompted an urgent need for many more resident inspectors from the Ministry of Munitions, but increasingly such jobs were seen as 'cushy numbers' whose holders ought to be at the front. The *Jägerstab* was forced to rely on the service firms' own inspectors, with their inevitable loyalty to the company 'bottom line'. Spare parts were also scarce. Many were lost in the factories or in transit, and in any case, production of them was low because of the emphasis upon using all parts to make finished aircraft. Besides, dispersal and fragmentation of the aircraft industry had a serious effect on quality. Components commonly failed to meet tolerances, and as there were multiple production sources for each component, interchangeability suffered. The return of probably hundreds more damaged aircraft from mass attacks would be likely to overwhelm the groundcrews completely, even if standardised spare parts had been more readily available.

Lack of serviceability also affected two other Messerschmitt aircraft, the rocket-powered Me 163 and the turbo-jet engined Me 262. The 'jet' was very dear to Hitler's heart as an example of the new wave of German high-tech weaponry that would soon turn the tide of war. Since May 1944, therefore, it had been accorded the highest production priority and by the end of October 650 had rolled off the production lines. Unfortunately, by the same date only 40 or so were operational. "Herr Seiler, Chairman of the Board of the Messerschmitt Company, could never understand why the Me 262 was not used to a greater extent by the Luftwaffe . . . He thought that perhaps 250 were non-operational for lack of proper servicing and that the failure to provide an adequate pilot training program might be a contributory cause . . . When Saur demanded that the workers work sixteen hours a day, Herr Seiler told him firmly that there was no sense in such a demand at a time when the workers were asking, 'Where are our planes?' "[18]

The workers were entitled to wonder for both jets, rocket and turbo-jet, represented a tremendous breakthrough in aircraft development and were by several months the first such types to become operational. The jet offered a solution to the problem of any increase in an aircraft's speed involving a big increase in drag, demanding in turn a commensurate increase in engine power and weight just to compensate for the drag. To push piston-engined aircraft of the time up to speeds of 600 m.p.h. or so would have required new engines that weighed more than twice as much as the original engine and airframe. Jets, on the other hand, developed an enormous amount of thrust for a relatively modest weight, as well as obviating the problem of increased propeller inefficiency at high speeds. Thus the Germans could entertain the possibility of not only matching the high-altitude performance of the Allied escorts but of far exceeding it. The Me 262 had a top speed of 550 m.p.h. at 30,000 feet, which was about 100 m.p.h. faster than the Mustang, and a climb rate of about 4,000 feet per minute as opposed to the Mustang's 3,500. It also had terrific hitting-power, for in its nose were fitted four 30mm cannon supplied with a total of 360 shells. A 'Grand Slam' built around several groups of such aircraft might indeed be a vindication of months of loose talk about 'miracle weapons'.

One is entitled to ask how an air force that could not now produce competent piston-engined fighter pilots was going to obtain aircrew for such a dazzling high-speed interceptor. The level of realism in higher quarters about such matters is evident in the debate over another jet, the Heinkel He 162, for which finished blueprints were just about to appear. The plane, with wood and plywood wings, fins and nose-cap, was dubbed the 'People's Fighter' and was intended to be suitable for mass production by semi-skilled and unskilled labour. Its pilots – at least, according to Göring's latest suggestion – were to be drawn from Hitler Youth volunteers, one thousand of whom were to be enrolled on what we would most aptly call a crash course.

The tactical role of the jet was a matter of bitter disagreement although, as was so often the case, only one man actually endorsed the 'party line', the Führer himself. For though the Me 262 had been developed as a fighter, more specifically a hard-hitting, high-speed interceptor, and though everyone from Göring down to his pilots agreed that this was its obvious role, most of the planes produced by the end of October were destined to be designated not *Schwalben* but *Sturmvögel*, not swallows but storm petrels, bombers carrying 1,000lb of ordnance and dedicated to harrying Allied ground forces on the Western Front. Only at the end of September was Hitler prevailed upon to release Me 262s to fighter squadrons, and even then he sanctioned only one in every twenty jets produced.

By 25th October one Me 262 fighter unit had been formed, the so-called Kommando Nowotny, led by the experienced Walter Nowotny, who had 255 victories to his credit. The more numerous fighter-bombers were grouped as Kommando Schenk in *Kampfgeschwader* 51, and were deployed against the Nijmegen and Grave bridges that connected the main Allied front to the desolate bridgehead left after the Arnhem operation. The two units between them contained no more

than 60 serviceable aircraft, with roughly two-thirds of them assigned
to Schenk. The Me 163 rocket-powered fighters were concentrated at
Brandis, near Leipzig, where their job was to defend the huge synthetic
oil-plant at Leuna, 30 miles to the west. Just how many Me 163s were
operational at Brandis is uncertain but it comes as no surprise to learn
that 'operations . . . by I/JG 400 under Hauptman Rudolf Opitz
often proved somewhat abortive, mainly because of lack of servicing
facilities. Fuel had to be stored in the railway wagons that brought
it, the airfield itself was too short and the repair facilities were
inadequate."[19]

Not even the most lavish technical facilities would have made the
jets a pleasure to fly. As so often, the cutting edge of technology was as
likely to harm the user as the enemy. The Me 163 was known in its
operational B version as the *Kraft-Ei*, or power-egg, and gave a whole
new perspective on the notion of pilots being scrambled. The fuel for
the Walther 509A rocket motor combined two chemicals, codenamed
T and C Stoff, which when brought together in the combustion
chamber reacted to produce a jet of nitrogen and superheated steam
with a velocity of 6,500 feet per second, T Stoff, which comprised
three-quarters of the total, was highly concentrated hydrogen
peroxide, "an unstable compound which was liable to decompose
on contact with copper, lead, organic materials or any combustible;
on decomposition it gave out heat at a rate equivalent to that of
gunpowder. It was also highly corrosive, and not its least unendearing
feature was that it would burn away human flesh if it was in contact for
more than a few seconds. The Me 163 carried more than a ton and
a half of this vile brew in three tanks, one on either side of the cockpit
and one behind it, which can have done little for the pilot's peace
of mind."[20] They were supplied with specially formulated protective suits, but while it was found that these did inhibit flames if
in contact with T Stoff, they could not prevent it soaking through
and setting fire to the next layer of clothing, or burning the flesh.

Equally disconcerting was the fact that even if a Me 163 got within
striking distance of an American bomber formation, it was unlikely to
make an effective interception. The plane's approach speed was
between 560 and 590 m.p.h., while the bomber was some 350 m.p.h.
slower. Armed with 30mm cannon, the Me 163 had to get within 700
yards range to score a hit. A pilot flying at such speeds needed to take
evasive action no less than 200 yards short of the target, which left him
at most three seconds to get off his shots. It is hardly surprising that
only seven 'probables' had been claimed by the end of October.

Nevertheless, the Americans were considerably alarmed at the speed and jack-in-the-box appearances of the first Me 163s – until they devised a childishly simple counter. The Me 163s used up their fuel at the gluttonous rate of 20lbs per second, which gave them only a very limited radius of action. As soon as the Americans realised this all they had to do was to route their bombers around known jet bases. By 25th October JG 400 had endured much the same operational hiatus as the rest of the day-fighter force, not for lack of fuel or an attempt to conserve aircraft, but simply because the Americans knew when to leave well alone.

Pinpointing the jet bases was fairly easy. The runways had to be made of concrete as the usual asphalt was likely to catch fire during take-off. American fighters, therefore, knew just where to lie in wait, especially as the jets were most vulnerable while taking off and landing. The Me 262 was the most helpless. With three rockets beneath each wing as starting aids, the plane rose from the ground cautiously, the pilot's attention fixed on the two rev. counters for his turbo-jets. Due to the enormous demands on fuel at dangerously high temperatures, "the two turbos could only be speeded up in easy stages. As opposed to piston-engined aircraft in which the throttle is pushed well home on take-off, the pilot of a jet machine had to manoeuvre his fuel throttle slowly and gently."[21] Similar considerations applied to landing when pilots had to switch off their engines completely and glide slowly on to the runway. If they attempted to restart their engines, the chances were that only one would catch and the unbalanced thrust would almost certainly provoke a fatal accident.

By the end of October this grave shortcoming was becoming known to Allied pilots who began to hover around the jet bases like so many sparrow-hawks. Kommando Nowotny had already been assigned two squadrons of Fw 190D-9s to protect the jets around their 'nest', an unfortunate duplication of resources for a service as tightly stretched as the Luftwaffe. The ME 262s were also plagued by mechanical failures, the greatest cause of losses, and these regularly involved engine failures, undercarriage collapse, and structural faults in the tailplane caused by oscillations set up by the turbo-jets. And just to sap the pilots' confidence that little bit more, the chain-links for the 30mm ammunition were not strong enough, tending to snap during high-G manoeuvres.

By early November, Kommando Nowotny claimed to have shot down four American heavy bombers, twelve fighters and three reconnaissance aircraft. During the same period the unit had lost six

Me 262s in combat and seven destroyed on the ground or lost in accidents. At times Nowotny's unit had been reduced from an authorised complement of around thirty jets to just three serviceable aircraft. Clearly the Luftwaffe had still not found the means of offsetting the Allies' enormous superiority in numbers or in piston-engined quality, or of reversing the spiral of attrition that had all but driven them from the skies.

Der Grosse Schlag? Pass the Tokay.[22]

21

Vengeance Weapons
THE V1 AND V2 OFFENSIVE

IN OCTOBER 1944 Hitler was attempting to restage the 'Blitz' on London and pay back the Allies for their own bombing of German cities. Revenge and terror were to be the order of the day and the weapons used were dubbed the V1 and V2, denoting *Vergeltungswaffen*, or 'vengeance weapons'.

Research on these missiles had been going on since the early 1930s and had been centralised at Peenemünde on the Baltic coast, almost due north of Berlin. Most of the early work had been done by the Army which, under the direction of General Walter Dornberger, had developed a rocket known to those involved as the A-4. For many of the scientists at Peenemünde, such as Werner von Braun, the main interest was in the possibilities of space exploration, though in order to obtain funding it had been necessary to make rocketry a military project. So from the start the A-4 programme had been concerned with developing a missile that could carry a one-ton warhead. Other manned and un-manned projects were under way but what set the A-4 apart was that it remained an authentic missile in which propulsion served only to get it out of the earth's atmosphere at the correct speed and on the right bearing to follow an unpowered ballistic trajectory to its target. While the missile's original payload was fairly modest – given that the Lancaster's standard bomb load at this time was the 4,000lb, or 2 short ton 'cookie' – the technology employed to get it to the target would have seemed to most observers to be pure science fiction.

Another type of weapon was also being developed at Peenemünde, a pilotless aircraft with a built-in warhead that was supposed to navigate itself to its target. This was the V1, originally known to its developers as the Fieseler 103, after the manufacturer, and later by the code-name FZG.76. The aircraft was powered by a pulse-jet engine, which worked by boosting the air-flow through a duct in the engine with the intermittent combustion of aviation spirit. This increased the velocity of the air-flow sufficiently to provide forward thrust. As the air in the duct was exhausted the pressure fell and so the ram pressure at the front end of the duct would open a valve to allow another intake of air to be heated and blasted out. Development of this weapon was in the hands of the Luftwaffe. with successful test-firings in December 1942. The V2 remained the Army's project, and dual service sponsorship of the different programmes led to some rivalry, so that in May 1943 a 'shoot-off' was arranged to compare the two weapons. The V2 performed much better on the day but its rival's adherents argued so convincingly about mitigating circumstances that the observers from a new Long Range Bombardment Commission decided to put both weapons into production.

By this stage of the war, however, mass production in Germany was easier said than done. In June 1943, Göring had been talking blithely of producing up to 50,000 V1s per month, at Fieseler's Kassel works and the Volkswagen plant at Fallersleben, but by September the official target had sunk to only 5,000 per month. Actual monthly production for the rest of the year was a mere 25 V1s. In the following year, however, this improved dramatically, with an average monthly figure of over 2,000 and a peak of 3,419 achieved in September 1944. Mass production of V2s was undertaken at Peenemünde itself, the Zeppelin works at Friedrichshafen and an underground factory near Niedersachswerfen in the Harz mountains, known as the Mittelwerk. Later the Henschel works at Wiener-Neustadt were also brought into the picture but both these and the Zeppelin plant were bombed by the Allies and almost all production was concentrated at the Mittelwerk. Manufacture of components and sub-assemblies began there in August 1943, with Peenemünde techniques being adapted for assembly line production. In December four rockets were produced and in the following January and February 50 and 86 respectively. From March to October a more creditable 1,939 were produced. The year's monthly average was still well short of the 900 per month forecast but the totals for September and October, 629 and 628 respectively, gave some hope for further increases.

Not that increased production of the V2 was any guarantee of a reliable end-product. The output from the Mittelwerk was sent either to Peenemünde or to an Army training battery at Blizna, in Poland, for testing, and for months the trial launches were beset by rockets exploding only a few minutes after leaving the launch pad. The fault was eventually traced to the fuel tank, which was not strong enough to withstand the heat and vibration of re-entry. Some test rockets were given rivetted steel reinforcing sleeves, or 'tin trousers', and though this solved the problem, in late October the factory had still not been instructed to manufacture only sleeved rockets. Nor was this the designers' only problem. It was estimated that by the time the sleeves were first tried out, another 65,000 modifications had also been tested on the A-4. A major difficulty was the designers' inability to use computer simulation or even proper telemetry to obviate the need for continual test-firings of actual rockets. Unable to observe 'virtual' launches or to monitor properly what happened inside an actual rocket, the Germans were forced to fire "an enormous number of experimental rockets to obtain relatively little overall data on total performance . . . It was, in fact, the literally thousands of design modifications that prevented sustained, large-scale . . . assembly from beginning before August 1944. Thus, during the two preceding months some 200 test missiles had to be sent out to Heidelager [code-name for Tuchen] . . . for test flights so that 'living statistics' could be accumulated."[1]

At least production was not unduly affected by Allied bombing. The *Mittelwerk* was located in tunnels between 140 and 200 feet underground.[2] Even at Peenemünde, built mostly above ground, production was not seriously dislocated. An Allied raid on the night of 17th/18th August 1943 received much publicity but, although it did delay V2 development by perhaps three months, it failed in its main aim of killing a substantial proportion of the scientific personnel assembled there. In fact, Peenemünde was not raided again and thereafter Allied air operations against the V-weapons were mainly concerned with hindering their deployment in the field.

Hitler decreed that both weapons were to be sited in northern France from where they would be in range of London. Moreover, with just this one target in mind, he seems to have concluded that it would be better to build grandiose, fixed launching and logistical sites for both the V1 and the V2 and that a sufficient quantity of concrete could render them impervious to Allied bombing. Building the V1 sites began in August 1943, with an anticipated total of 66 main launching sites, 32 reserve launching sites and 8 huge supply dumps between Cherbourg and Calais. Two of the main launch sites, at Lotinghen and Siracourt, between Calais and the Somme, were enormous concrete structures with a 15-foot-thick steel and concrete carapace protecting a subterranean chamber more than 600 feet long. The launch platform was protected by massive steel doors that rolled along a 32-foot slot. The other V1 launch sites, known to the Allies as 'ski sites', were much smaller than these two super-bunkers but they were still fairly elaborate, built to a standardised design and comprising nine separate concrete buildings and a launch ramp.[3]

The V2s were also to have their fortress-like launch bunkers and construction of these began at the same time, first at Watten and then at Wizernes, both near Saint-Omer, and later at Brécourt. Plans for further bunker installations showed rockets being armed and fuelled in lower storeys and then either lifted mechanically to be fired through the roof or wheeled outside to a rudimentary launch platform. All the V2 sites also had their network of elaborate supply bunkers.

In the event, hardly any of this complex infrastructure, erected at enormous expense by thousands of slave and empressed labourers, was ever used. Allied intelligence, using ULTRA sources and with valuable assistance from Polish agents and the Swedish government, were able to keep abreast of the essentials of V1 and V2 development and thus devoted considerable effort to working out how and from where the weapons were to be fired. A lot of this work fell to Allied photo-reconnaissance pilots and interpreters, who in November 1943 confirmed the existence of their first 'ski site' in northern France. Most of the bunker sites had already been spotted, although it was far from clear just what part, if any, they were to play in the V-weapons offensive. Nevertheless, all sites were soon subjected to aeriel bombardment, first by twin-engined bombers and fighter-bombers and then, from late December, by the strategic bombers of Eighth U.S. Air Force and Bomber Command. By the end of the year 3,000 tons of bombs had been dropped on these targets and over the next six months a further 20,000 tons were delivered. The effects were devastating. All the big bunker sites were rendered inoperable, and of the 'ski sites' only one is known to have ever launched a flying bomb.

However, this did not signal the end of Hitler's 'vengeance' campaign'. Certain of the German commanders charged with deploying the V-weapons in the field had been consistently opposed to large, fixed launch installations and had stressed mobility and speed in setting up a battery as the most important considerations. For them, even though flying bombs and rockets were essentially strategic weapons, they should nevertheless be used as a sort of mobile artillery rather than as fixed siege guns. By January 1944 it had been generally agreed that both the V1 and the V2 should operate from much more *ad hoc* sites, the latter needing only a small wooden or concrete launch apron. Although the V1 was still reliant on the rather cumbersome ramp, that was now incorporated into a much smaller and simpler site with the minimum of outbuildings that could be constructed a few days before launching. These became known to the Allies as the 'modified' V1 sites, and their bombers found it almost impossible to put such small targets out of commission. Both the V1 and the V2 could still be launched from northern France, and by 19th September 8,564 V1s had been fired on London (53 against Southampton), while 35 V2s had also been aimed at the capital and another 21 unleashed against such continental cities as Paris, Brussels and Liège.

Fortunately, the Allies did not have to rely on airpower alone to put an end to this offensive. After the D-Day landings in northern France in June and the swift German retreat in early September, all the 'modified' sites were abandoned and the V-weapon units withdrawn into Holland and Germany, so putting ground-launched V1s out of range of English targets.

During the following weeks there was a considerable to-ing and fro-ing of units as they tried to establish secure flying bomb and rocket launcher bases that had firm logistical links by rail with the missile and fuel producers in Germany. In September and October, priority was given to sites in Holland at Enschede, north-east of Arnhem, to which V1 units had first retreated after giving up the sites in northern France, and at Zwolle, Zutphen and Almelo, all between Lake Ijsel and the German border. Others moved to sites in Germany, on the eastern side of the Rhine and the Moselle, between Bonn and Trier. When the V1 offensive finally reopened on 21st October, it was selected sites in the Eifel and the Westerwald districts in Germany that were the first to be used. The target was Brussels, whose inhabitants saw one flying bomb pass overhead on the morning of the 21st and three more crash to the south-west of the city in the next 24 hours. This bombardment, 55 V1s in all, lasted until the 24th, after which the target was Antwerp, first hit by a lone V1 on the 23rd and regularly from the 25th.

The V2s avoided such a long hiatus in their operations, and though the Allied advance had forced several units to suspend firings as they hastily withdrew into Holland and Germany, others relocated in Friesland and the Hague began relaunching against England within a week. The first of these were aimed at Norwich and Ipswich but on 4th October London, too, was brought under fire again. Up until 12th October other cities in northern France and Belgium were targeted by about 120 rockets, though V2 accuracy was never very good. With a range of about 180 miles from London, the deviation from the aim point could be more than 8 miles, and figures produced by the Ministry of Home Security showed that the missiles were especially erratic during the period 1st to 27th October, with many of them falling well short of their target.[4] Hitler objected to such dispersed targeting and ordered that in future only London and Antwerp should be attacked. By the 25th the V2 batteries' rate of fire was around 14 rockets per day in total, with about 9 of them falling on Antwerp.

Up to 25th October 99 V2 rockets exploded on British soil, one landing on the 25th itself at Rawreth, in Southend, at 12.40 a.m. The inhabitants must have begun to feel persecuted as two other V2s had hit Rawreth on 11th and 12th October. The daily average for rockets landing in or near Antwerp during October and November was nine. At the beginning of the Antwerp attacks a 7 Armoured Division Intelligence Summary noted that "something beastly fell on Antwerp today." 79 Armoured Division had its headquarters at s'Gravenwezel and the divisional history records that by the end of October this village was proving "to be about the mean Point of Impact of the V1 and V2 missiles when being directed at Antwerp. There were some casualties. . . . and eventually the houses became uninhabitable."[5] General Eisenhower was beginning to get somewhat alarmed. On 26th October he wrote to General Marshall in Washington: "We well know that the Germans appreciate the importance of Antwerp . . . [and] are quite sure that . . . [these attacks] will be intensified, and may reach a scale of considerably more than 100 a day."[6]

It is difficult to assess just what the personnel in the V1 and V2 units felt about their weapons and how aware they were of their low level of accuracy. But given the destruction of the original launch infra-structure, the confused retreat through France and Belgium, the threat of Allied reconnaissance planes and fighter-bombers, the slow rate of delivery from the factories, the desultory rate of fire, as well as the feeble payload on each missile, it can only be assumed that they were more realistic than some of the German public who listened to propaganda lauding a war-winning super-weapon.

A V1 battery was divided into two sections, each containing two firing ramps.[7] Flying bombs would arrive at the launch site in lorries or specially articulated vehicles. They were usually already fuelled but the wings and tail units were not yet attached and were stowed in with the bombs. The vehicles were unloaded by the transport squad (22 officers and men) whose job it was to move the bomb through the various operational procedures prior to launching. First stop was the assembly shop where the tail and rudder units were attached and the bomb was fitted with the detonating device that would put it into its dive. (This device measured the distance flown by the rocket by counting the revolutions of a small propeller in the nose. After a pre-set number was reached the detonator circuit was released and a spring lever in the tail put the bomb into its dive.[8]) Fuel flow and control surfaces were then checked and the compressed air spheres that operated the pneumatic controls were topped up. For the last of these steps the bomb was hoisted up by pulley and then lowered back on to the trolley that would eventually take it to the launch ramp. Before that it had to go to the non-magnetic *Richthaus*, the so-called 'square buildings' seen on reconnaissance photographs, to have its wings attached and the range and bearing of the target programmed in. These readings would have been worked out by the Calculations Squad at Battery HQ. Compass and gyroscope controls were set and the rate-of-turn clock wound and adjusted if the bomb was to alter direction after the launch. Compass setting was not a particularly high-tech procedure. Any corrections were made "by the simple expedient of putting the missile on stands in the direction of its desired course and hitting it with wooden mallets until the inherent magnetic field of the airframe was aligned with the earth's field!"[9]

As all this was going on the Launch Squad was preparing the starter trolley and the ramp. First the ramp was hosed down to remove all traces of fuel left by the previous launch and then the squad refilled the propellant tanks of the starter trolley (*Dampferzeuger*) and recharged its three compressed air cylinders. At the same time the 140-foot launch ramp was made ready. Supported by seven steel A-frames dropped into concrete foundations, the ramp sloped at six degrees so as to get the bomb airborne and flying at a sufficient speed (245 m.p.h.) to maintain the air ram effect that drove the pulse jet. The thrust to generate this speed, in less than a second, was supplied by means of a piston which was slotted into a firing tube in the base of the ramp and then attached to the belly of the bomb as it was lowered into place. After firing, the cast-iron piston fell away, landing usually some 300 yards from the end of the ramp. The weight of the bomb was supported by a metal cradle, often called the 'walking stick', which fitted between guide rails on the ramp. Before the bomb itself could be loaded on to the ramp, "a gas sealing tube was inserted into the firing tube . . . a task which needed the combined efforts of all fire crew members, and wired up by running a set of prepacked wire hangers (spaced about 10ft apart) along the entire length of the firing tube slot. The piston was inserted some 8ft into the firing tube with a wooden ram."[10] Shortly afterwards the loaded bomb trolley arrived at the end of the ramp and was manoeuvred up the ramp by means of collapsible push bars until it engaged two pawls. The bomb, with cradle attached, was then lowered through the base of the trolley on to the ramp and the trolley removed. Now the starter trolley was wheeled forward and attached to the lower end of the firing tube. Thrust was generated by compressed air forcing a solution of hydrogen peroxide and sodium or calcium permanganate at high pressure into the reaction chamber where pressures of up to 1,000lb per square inch were developed behind the piston.

Once the bomb was securely in position on the ramp, electrical tests were carried out from the firing bunker, or *Kommando Stand*, where a three-position switch on the square portable control box was turned to 'On'. Once the body of the bomb was earthed and the switch moved to '*Startfrei*', warning lights in the control box came on. Two plugs were then connected to the distributor unit and personnel retired to shelters and bunkers, where they initiated firing by pushing the switch on the control box fully towards to the 'Partial Power' position and held it there as a 'Start' button was simultaneously depressed. The first action started the Argus motor, via the ground starter unit, and the second released the compressed air that helped to trigger the catapulting of the bomb up the ramp. The three-way switch was released after three seconds or so, and it fell back into an intermediate 'Full power' position, keeping the motor running on full power for a further seven seconds. By then the pressure in the reaction chamber had built up sufficiently to shear away a 6mm steel pin holding the bomb cradle, and the bomb hurtled forward, leaving the ramp at around 360 feet per second, the thrust generating around 55,000 horsepower.

Once airborne, the bomb climbed at the angle of launch until it reached its pre-set altitude, after which it levelled off and performed any change of direction, up to 60 degrees, that had also been programmed in. It then supposedly flew straight and level until it had covered the required distance, as measured by the propeller-counter, after which it dived to the ground. To ensure that this dive was close to the target, an automatic pilot was installed. This was 'unlocked' when the bomb cradle fell away after launching, the disconnection releasing a small 'caging' pin that held the gyroscope rigid in its cradle. This was informed by the magnetic compass and was sensitive to roll as well as to pitch and yaw movements. Corrections were transmitted pneumatically to elevator and rudder altitude and heading. Next stop, Antwerp or wherever.

There were seven V2 batteries in the field on 25th October, each containing a Headquarters Troop and one Launching, one Technical and one Fuel and Rocket Troop.[11] The Launching Troop comprised three squads, each with its own launch pad, and was expected to fire two or three rockets each day. During firing trials and the first operational launches it had been found that the longer a missile was stored, the greater the chances that it would fail to launch, or abort shortly thereafter. "Because of this, the missile storage depots were abandoned in favour of rapid rail transport from Mittelwerk directly to the field units. The missile trains, once loaded, were taken to a special outfitting station where the warheads, jet vanes, fuses and containers of sodium permanganate were loaded. The trains then proceeded to the firing units."

Colonel Wilhelm Zippelius was in charge of rail transportation, and by October he was managing an average of one trainload of 20 missiles per day through the network. As he himself explained: "Trains were allocated to us and the co-operation of stationmasters assured. Since we could not display our wares to the public, we camouflaged the wagons with boxes, wood and hay. If anyone inquired what was on board our guarded trains, we would say circus elephants."[12] Obviously, then, one of the major considerations in selecting battery and launch areas was proximity to railheads, as well as the quality of any intermediate roads. With concealment a high priority, commanders tended to favour pine woods where trees made aerial detection difficult and also acted as a windbreak for the upright rockets.

When a train arrived at a railhead it was met by the *Abteilung* or Battery Quartermaster and members of the Technical and Fuel Rocket Troops. The rockets were lifted off the rail-cars by a gantry crane and placed on special trailers to be transported to the Technical Troop area between the railhead and the launch pads. This area contained several large tents and extensive parking facilities for trucks and trailers. Once in the Technical Troop area, a rocket underwent about three hours of testing – propulsion unit, steering mechanism, wiring and suchlike. Minor faults were repaired on the spot, but rockets quite often had to be sent back to the Mittelwerk. Those that were passed were next moved to the Warhead Mounting Section where the warhead, still in its oil-drum-like container, was lifted into position with a block and tackle and attached to the nose of the rocket. The exploder tube was then filled and the base fuses installed. Once everything was in position the shipping container was finally removed.

The rocket was now moved to another gantry-crane and transferred to a more robust wheeled trailer equipped with an hydraulic lift to raise the V2 from horizontal to a vertical position. The lift frame to which the rocket was attached also included three folding platforms which would provide access after it was in the launching position. When the rocket was secure, it was covered with a kind of camouflaged tent, laid over a pipe frame, and driven off to the launch site, which had already been prepared by the Launch Troop. They had been busy setting up a launch pad, positioning the fire-control vehicle about 100 yards behind the line of fire, and connecting the two with electrical cables. The fire-control vehicle, usually a converted military half-track, was dug in to the height of the tracks and slit-trenches were dug for the launch personnel still further behind the launch pad. The pad itself was remarkably unobtrusive, looking like a combination of a free-standing magnifying-glass and a lemon-squeezer. Standing about five feet high, it rested on a base of concrete, or sometimes just compacted earth reinforced with logs, the flat top of which comprised a circular cut-out, again about five feet in diameter.

The V2 rocket was driven to within 50 feet of the pad and handed over to the Firing Squad. They lifted off the camouflage frame and hand-winched the trailer to the pad, where brackets engaged lugs on the trailer to ensure proper alignment. The rocket was then raised and, once vertical, "was suspended just above the launch pad. Any final adjustments to the position of the pad were made with levers and manpower . . . The rocket stood on the launch table, which was supported by four tubular legs. Underneath the table was the blast deflector. It was made in heavy steel plate in the shape of a four-sided concave pyramid. A mast attached to the table carried an electrical cable to the missile's control compartment. The cable provided power to the rocket until launch, when it was cast off."[13] Now the launch table support plates were raised until they just touched the rocket's fins and then the three clamps securing it to the lift frame were ratchetted down until it rested firmly on the pad. Finally the clamping collars were released and moved just clear of the rocket.

Now it was time to install the four graphite jet vanes that were crucial to the rocket's viability. Designed to withstand the enormous heat of the exhaust stream, they were moved by a cybernetic servo-system, turning from side to side to deflect the rocket slightly and keep it upright during the launch phase, and then steering it over to its target trajectory. They were the only control surfaces capable of doing this during the early stages of the launch because the speed was too low to give any aerodynamic 'bite' to the fins and rudder.

Another series of checks began – on the propellant injection nozzles, steering controls and rocket motor. At the same time preparations began for fuelling the rocket. The two main propellants were alcohol, as in the V1, and liquid oxygen. These were combined and burned in the rocket's combustion chamber and the products allowed to escape through a nozzle at the base to generate the motor's thrust. The propellants were forced into the chamber by a steam-powered turbo-pump, the latter being fuelled by a combination of hydrogen peroxide and sodium permanganate. In other words, the turbo-pump, although integral to the V2, was a broadly similar device to that which gave the V1 its kick-start, though instead of a one-off boost, it was in continuous operation until the V2 rocket had begun its ballistic trajectory. Where possible, the fuels were stored well apart until moved up the launch pad itself. Each rocket required two full tankers of alcohol, 1,500 gallons in all, and one trailer-borne canister of liquid oxygen, almost 7,000 kilograms. Liquid oxygen is extremely cold and in winter or during a long delay before blast-off, a two-horsepower hot air blower was used to prevent servo-motors and valves from freezing. The hydrogen peroxide – one canister enough for 16 rockets – was also supposed to be warmed up before being pumped in, but this was deemed so perilous an activity that few crews bothered.

Now the final adjustments could be made to the rocket. The warhead was armed with extremely sensitive fuses, to prevent it from burying itself in the ground before it exploded. The integrating accelerometer was also set to prescribe at exactly what velocity the engine would cut off, leaving the rocket, in theory at least, to follow an exact ballistic trajectory to the target, much like a huge artillery shell. This complex device worked in two stages. First, when the rocket had reached 95 per cent of desired velocity, it reduced acceleration by closing one of the valves controlling the flow of hydrogen peroxide into the mixing chamber, and then a few seconds later it closed the other valve, shutting off the turbo-pump completely. The final task for the Launch Troop was to close all access hatches and lower the lift frame back on to the chassis. The trailer was towed away and, once the launch site was clear and the battery commander was satisfied that there were no enemy aircraft in the vicinity, the order was given to the fire-control vehicle. "All rockets were assumed to follow the same trajectory during powered flight. Four seconds after launch, the rocket began a pre-programmed pitch toward the target until an angle of 47° was reached about 43 seconds into the flight. After this, the elevation angle was held constant and the rocket continued to accelerate until the velocity necessary to achieve the desired range was attained."[14] Then the motor cut off, and the rocket followed an almost silent, deadly parabola which would provide it with a velocity at impact of almost 1,800 m.p.h.

Despite the fact that the V2s were much larger than the V1s, 28,000lb as opposed to less than 5,000lb, they were much more mobile. Rocket batteries were highly motorised – each employing some 5,300 personnel and almost 1,600 motor vehicles – and their simple launch pads were much more portable than the cumbersome ramps used to fling flying bombs into the air. After a few hours the whole V2 battery might pack up and move to a new location, though not necessarily very far away. Colonel Zippelius was present with batteries based in the Hague and recalled: "In the daytime we would measure off certain areas within the city and make our calculations. At night we would block off these areas and move in our convoys of Meiler-wagens, missiles and parts. After we had launched five or six V2s, we would quickly move our men and equipment away. In the morning, when the search planes flew over in a futile attempt to locate our rockets, all they would see were street-cars and motor cars."[15]

Another type of unit maintained a desultory flying bomb offensive against England, even after the over-running of sites in northern France. The Luftwaffe's *Kampfgeschwader* 53 was equipped with obsolete Heinkel He 111 bombers modified to air launch V1s. They flew their first mission from Venlo, in Holland, in July, but in September moved back to bases in Germany. Thereafter sorties were flown only about one night in two, and in the bad weather no aircraft were able to take off on 25th October. Moreover, flying bombs launched this way were wildly inaccurate. The overall hit rate against London was a mere 5.5 per cent, and only half those launched managed to cross the English coast. The bombers carried their V1s slung under the right wing, between the fuselage and the engine nascelle, lateral stability being maintained by two vertical metal struts. The V1 had to be pre-set before it was attached to the plane and thus the crew had to be sure they were at the correct launching point before release. This was done with a tachometer type of device which displayed five or six digits to be set during the flight when a given point had been reached. These digits automatically counted down, so that when they reached 100 the navigator/bombardier was alerted by a red light and at 25 he pressed a black button which ignited the bomb's motor and started the automatic pilot. At zero he pulled a lever releasing the bomb. To avoid detection by Allied radar, the Heinkels usually approached at only a little over 300 feet, the pilot taking the plane up to the requisite 1,500 feet just before release.

On those nights when SIGINT gave warning of German sorties, night-fighting Mosquitos from 25 Squadron were vectored towards their bases in the hope of making an interception. Also on stand-by throughout the autumn were the AA guns, searchlights and barrage balloons of Britain's home defences. The balloons had already made a tremendous contribution to the battle against the first V1 onslaught, and by late October there were more than 2,000 of them, using 2.6 million cubic feet of hydrogen per day, and tethered by hundreds of miles of steel cable. Guns and searchlights were deployed all along the south-east coast between Newhaven and Deal, and the balloons just south of London between Redhill and Cobham. The 25 miles or so between these two defence belts were patrolled by Fighter Command, whose planes attempted to intercept any V1s that had survived the AA barrage. These fighters had found less and less to do, as by mid-August there were 800 heavy and 1,800 light AA guns sited along the coast, as well as 700 rocket barrels, in the so-called Diver Belt. A further 200 heavy and almost 660 light AA guns were diverted to the east and north-east of London around the Thames Estuary. This was dubbed the Diver Box. When V1 raids were resumed on 16th September, the Germans launched their missiles still further to the north-east of London, in an attempt to outflank the Diver defences. General Frederick Pile, in charge of AA Command, promptly set up a new defensive line, known as the Diver Strip, between Clacton and Great Yarmouth in East Anglia, comprising 542 heavy and nearly 600 light AA guns, which were mainly redeployed from the south coast belt. They were still to be supported by the Mosquitos, as well as some Mustangs and Tempests flown by night-fighter pilots, and by mid-October 61 of the 143 V1s launched had been destroyed in flight.

Yet few in AA Command would cite the Diver Strip as one of its finest hours. For the commanders, this last major redeployment proved to be a move too far, and the logistical system that had so admirably supported earlier moves – 440 heavy and 360 light AA guns, 23,000 personnel, 30,000 tons of heavy AA ammunition were moved in just three days during the transfer to the south coast belt – suffered a serious breakdown. General Pile was especially scathing in his memoirs and spoke of a "general lassitude on the part of the staff, a great disinclination to start the whole weary business over again . . . [followed by] a panicky burst of nervous energy in which mistakes were made, tempers lost, and confusion caused . . ." Five pages later the words "chaotic", "deplorable" and "reason for shame" are all to be found. Although by the end of October all guns were finally in place "and we were achieving the same level of gratifying results that we had obtained on the South Coast", Pile could not afford to be sanguine. Though he had no reason to think that the V-weapons battle was over, he was faced with demands for huge cuts in his Command, with many units to be disbanded or transferred to the Continent. Altogether 73,000 personnel were under threat, most of them young men who could be reassigned to the depleted infantry battalions in Holland. "Now the majority of our gunners below the age of thirty had to be withdrawn and replaced by the more elderly and infirm, even while the struggle was going on: often there was not even time for a proper hand-over of equipment to be made. The fit were rushed out and the unfit were rushed in."[16]

Moreover, these elderly newcomers were not being asked just to lounge around in the gun positions. On 26th October the Command was due to start yet another mammoth task, the construction in the Diver Strip of eight new permanent 8-gun sites, all in remote areas. With no civilian labour available, Pile had to build 60 miles of road and 3,500 Nissen huts, shift 150,000 tons of hard-core, 500,000 concrete blocks and 20,000 panes of glass, organise 35 special trains and 26 large road convoys, set up 14 new railheads, find petrol for 1,000 lorries, and move 1,500 skilled and 5,000 unskilled labourers to tented camps near the new sites.

At the same time, there was nothing remotely relaxing about the existence of those still manning the guns and searchlights. Two of the best heavy AA regiments had already left for Antwerp and another six were being urgently requested. Just spotting the V1s was also a great problem. Most flew in at around 1,000 feet and it was difficult to find suitable sites for the fire-control instruments "as the need for detecting the approach of flying bombs at long ranges involved a great deal of interference when radar was working at such small elevations." Gun crews had also to be constantly alert to the possibility of firing at their own bombers, whose flight paths to and from Germany crossed over East Anglia. But perhaps the worst problems were those caused by the weather. To a cold and wet infantryman in the Dutch polders or on some Apennine mountainside, AA Command back in 'Blighty' probably sounded like a holiday in khaki, all crisp, clear nights, glowing braziers and strolls to the pub. In fact, the Diver Strip was almost as inhospitable a bit of England as the swampy lowlands, or no-lands, of Holland. The following description of a visit to a gun site at Walton-on-Naze by the Speaker of the House of Commons gives an emphatic lie to any suggestion that home service in October 1944 was necessarily a cushy billet:

> My visit to the first battery was made in a driving downpour . . . As the whole site had been hurriedly arranged within the previous fourteen days, and as it had been raining on and off for a longer period, the ground was in a very soggy state, and mud up to the knees was everywhere. It reminded me of Flanders in the last war, but the mud was not quite so sticky. The gun-crews were living in tents, the men were on the alert all night, so little could be done by day – as men must sleep – so what they had already done around the guns and by erecting duck-board passages across the mud was, I thought, highly creditable. All this was aggravated by the fact that no metalled roads run to the coastline and transport had to be taken over the muddy lanes with no foundation; added to this, the seashore is mud and not shingle, so everything had to be carried from afar in lorries . . . I do not think people realise what adverse conditions AA men serving at home have to contend with.[17]

PART FOUR

The Mediterranean

22

The Gothic Line

FIFTH U.S. AND EIGHTH BRITISH ARMIES IN ITALY

GIVEN THAT the Americans entered the Second World War on a wave of outrage over the Japanese surprise attack at Pearl Harbor, one of Winston Churchill's finer achievements was to persuade President Roosevelt and his chiefs-of-staff that victory over Germany should be the Allies' top priority. Not that Churchill's was an unalloyed success for he soon found that the Americans took this commitment quite literally and were keen to engage in a major land campaign in Europe at the earliest opportunity. Churchill and Field Marshal Brooke were more cautious. Rather than rush bald-headed across the Channel in 1942 or 1943, as the Americans were suggesting, they preferred a more circuitous route into *Festung Europa*. For them the Mediterranean offered the most promising back door into Europe and they were keen advocates of first securing its southern shores, in Libya and French North Africa, before attempting any landings in Europe itself. An Allied landing in French North Africa would confront only relatively weak German and Italian forces and would be in conjunction with the advance of Montgomery's Eighth Army from Libya. The British argued their case long and hard, and after a series of high-level conferences which occasionally degenerated into slanging matches, the Americans found, rather to their surprise, that they had acquiesced to Operation TORCH, Anglo-American landings in French North Africa in November 1942.

The Americans vowed that this Mediterranean 'dispersion debauch', as the Secretary for War called it, should go no further than Tunisia. However, by the time Tunis finally fell in May 1943, they had once again allowed themselves to be persuaded into leaving their TORCH divisions and attendant assault shipping in the Mediterranean where they would join the British in an invasion of Sicily in July 1943, and then of the Italian mainland in September. Although the Americans saved some face by bluntly insisting that some of their divisions in Italy be transferred to southern France in August 1944, nevertheless they continued to support and participate in major operations in Italy. These developed in a stand-offish, almost sulky manner, with separate American and British armies advancing up either side of Italy's mountainous central spine. The two army commanders were not the most likely to facilitate harmonious joint operations. General Mark Clark, commanding the U.S. Fifth Army on the western flank, was a deeply-committed Anglophobe, while the intensely egotistical Montgomery led the British Eighth Army up the eastern side. The situation was only made worse by the man in charge of attempting to reconcile these two abrasive personalities – Field Marshal Sir Harold Alexander, commander of 15th Army Group, who carried agreeableness to the point of vapidity.[1]

In December 1943, Montgomery returned to England to help in planning the invasion of Normandy, for which the Americans had waited so long, and command of Eighth Army was handed over to General Oliver Leese. Shortly after this Fifth and Eighth Armies came up against the Gustav Line, anchored on Monte Cassino, and were forced to make some attempt to mount a co-ordinated offensive. But considerable acrimony remained, with Clark attributing the necessarily slow progress of the later Cassino attacks on British incompetence and disinclination to fight. His growing conviction that he was the only competent commander in Italy led Clark to conclude it was he who was owed whatever honours could still be salvaged from this increasingly peripheral campaign. In late May and early June 1944, therefore, he knowingly passed up the chance to cut off German troops who were falling back from the Gustav Line and instead directed his divisions north, towards Rome, where he could take his triumphal entry.

Even as he accepted these rather tawdry laurels on 4th June, two German armies were streaming gratefully northwards prior to re-organising themselves behind one of the many natural defensive lines based on the mountain ridges and the rivers that flowed out of them, criss-crossing much of the Italian peninsula. Between 20th and 30th June, the Germans turned and fought on the Albert Line, anchored on Lake Trasimene, and later fought temporary delaying actions on the Heinrich, Georg and Paula Lines, the latter covering Florence. Their ultimate goal was the Apennines, the last barrier before the Po valley, where Allied superiority in armour, motor transport and tactical air support might finally be made to count. In these mountains, therefore, they prepared one of their most formidable *Stellungs*, the Gothic Line, under the supervision of Field Marshal Albrecht Kesselring, commander of Army Group C.[2]

In July Alexander drew up plans to break through this defence line on the run, concentrating both his armies on a central axis towards Bologna, just to the north of the Apennines. Once through, he would release a *corps de chasse* to dash across the Po valley and seize a bridgehead over that river, north of Ferrara. To ensure a severing of the German line of retreat, there was to be a sustained bombing of all 19 bridges across the lower Po. General Leese, however, was not happy with the idea of Eighth Army fighting in unaccustomed mountainous terrain. It is also frequently, and plausibly, stated that Leese could not bear the thought of fighting cheek-by-jowl with Clark, but whatever the exact reason, he prevailed upon Alexander to abandon his own conception in favour of a two-fisted offensive. Leese wanted the Eighth Army to punch first, along the coast, and make the decisive rupture in the Gothic Line, threatening the German rear with Allied armour debouching out of the Romagna plains and the vineyards of Emilia. This threat, it was hoped, would pull across some of the German divisions facing Fifth Army, still on the original Bologna axis, allowing Clark to make his own breakthrough on to Highway 9, the old Roman Via Emiliana. It also offered a lateral springboard for manoeuvre south of the Po and into Lombardy beyond.

Leese's right-hand thrust began on 25th August as II Polish Corps pushed forward through the German outpost line to Pesaro and the River Foglia. The main attack was then to pass through the Poles, across the Foglia and the Metauro. Assembling these forces had involved moving several Eighth Army divisions from the mountains to the coast, and this had been achieved in complete secrecy. The Germans had no inkling that the main blow, by I Canadian Corps, would follow hard on the heels of the Polish probing. Taking them completely by surprise, Eighth Army swept through the eastern portion of the Gothic Line and by September were up to the Gemmano and Coriano Ridges, overlooking the Po valley. After 14th September, however, the British advance slowed considerably and neither sustained infantry assaults on Gemmano nor reckless armoured attacks against Coriano were able to make much headway. Even so, these battles took a heavy toll on the Germans, and on 21st September they pulled back to the River Uso. Following close behind, Eighth Army occupied Rimini and on 26th September broke through the Uso

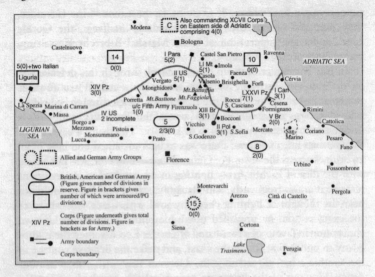

The Italian Front 25th October 1944

position and drove the enemy behind the River Fiumicino. Leese's divisions had now reached the fringes of the Emilia–Lombardy triangle, between the Apennines and the Alps, and before them, it was assumed, lay a great expanse of good tank country. Unfortunately, as everywhere else in Europe in the autumn of 1944, the weather broke early and with unaccustomed severity. Throughout late September the rains teemed down and flooded Eighth Army headquarters. It took several days to drag the caravans out of the cloying mud.

Even prolonged benign weather could not have made the Romagna the ideal setting for armoured exploitation. The area has much in common with the Dutch polders, rich agricultural land rescued from the sea by centuries of hard work and ingenuity, but requiring constant attention to prevent it from returning to its waterlogged origins. For the Romagna had once been mere swamp land around the lower courses of the many rivers that flowed down from the Apennines. By adding to these rivers connecting canals and irrigation ditches, the land had been gradually drained off, but as the water receded so the level of the ground sank, leaving river beds that were actually higher than the surrounding land. Artificial banks had to be built, up to 40 feet high, to cope with the sudden rises in water level after heavy rain or melting snow in the mountains. With surprisingly few fords and bridges, these rivers and canals offered perfect defensive positions to the Germans, while any Allied attack, mainly by infantry, involved four equally hazardous stages: approaching the near bank where enemy infantry were dug in; crossing it in the face of mortar fire and counter-attacks from infantry dug in on the opposite side; crossing the river under fire from the other bank; and finally storming that bank. When all these stages had been carried through, the bridgehead then had to be held by rifle companies alone as it required considerable extra time and effort to bring tanks or anti-tank guns across.

Even when not crossing one of the numerous rivers and canals the attackers had problems enough. The Romagna was thickly populated and the dozens of solidly-built farms and hamlets made excellent strongpoints and sniping positions for the enemy. Moreover, vines abounded, full-leafed and entwined around a veritable forest of high trellises that "cut off the view ahead, but often allowed the Germans to enfilade our advance with machine-guns sited to fire down one leafy corridor, and anti-tank guns to shoot along the one behind". As one of the first historians of the Italian campaign wrote: "There was little that generalship could do to solve the tactical problems which a masterly agricultural economy had created, and the delta suited the enemy's purpose of imposing delay upon our advance as well as had the endless mountains of the peninsula." In the Romagna, too, mud was yet another serious obstacle to offensive operations. The same historian neatly summarised the difficulties: "Between the rivers were in-numerable lesser water-courses, also canalised, and running roughly parallel to the main streams. The soil and subsoil was clay which in dry weather was quickly pulverised; under light rain became at once greasy, slippery and treacherous; and after heavy rain dissolved into a morass in which men sank to their boot-tops and wheels to their axles."[3] And heavy rain there was, malevolently abetted by German engineers who, just as in Holland, set about sabotaging the delicate drainage systems. The tanks bogged down and yet again it had to be the infantry that shouldered the burden in another slow, scuttling, costly advance from one German defence line to another.

In drawing German divisions across from Fifth Army's front, the Eighth Army's offensive was broadly successful. By late September it had attracted to it five German divisions, including the much-valued 29 and 90 Panzer-Grenadier Divisions, and these movements did much to simplify the task of General Clark's American units, which had begun driving towards Bologna earlier. Soon a seven-mile wide stretch of the Gothic Line, on either side of Il Giogio Pass, was in American hands.

Although this pass did not straddle Highway 65, the direct road between Florence and Bologna, but ran to Imola, Clark felt that this was his most promising axis, especially as Imola also lay on the highly-prized Via Emiliana. But its potential was equally apparent to the Germans, and in late September, as Eighth Army's attacks began to slacken, they transferred one of their best infantry divisions, the 44th, from the Adriatic sector just in time to halt the Americans, now 13 miles beyond Il Giogio but still 15 miles short of Imola. Although the Gothic Line had been overrun, in what Fifth Army's historian rightly described as "a brilliant achievement", the unpalatable truth was now beginning to dawn on Allied commanders.[4] Although American troops had indeed crossed the crests of the Apennines and were now descending through the foothills bordering the Po valley, they soon found that these 'foothills' were really no such thing. Instead they found another jumble of mountain peaks, narrow valleys and knife-edge ridges whose only virtue was that they were not quite as high as the ones just traversed. If Eighth Army had stormed its castle only to fall into the moat on the other side, then Fifth Army had seized the enemy keep only to see a dozen lesser fortresses stretching beyond. In another book I have described the breaching of the Gustav Line at Monte Cassino as a 'hollow victory' because the attempts to trap the retreating Germans were hopelessly botched. But the victory in the Gothic Line turned out, even more tragically, to be a mere chimera.

However, neither Alexander, Clark nor General Richard McCreery, commanding Eighth Army since 1st October, were prepared to halt operations so close to the Elysian fields of the Po valley. Throughout October both Allied armies strained towards the plains though both, ultimately, were frustrated. Clark switched his main axis back towards Bologna and committed himself to a straight slogging match against three defensive lines in the mountains on either side of Moghidoro, Loiano and Livergnano. To the right of this main thrust by the four divisions of II U.S. Corps – the only ones Clark felt he could rely upon – was XIII British Corps, also part of Fifth Army. Its task was simply to keep German divisions pinned down along its front, away from the Americans, but this involved combat almost as dour and costly as that south of Bologna. For essentially every division around Fifth Army's salient was fighting the same battle, advancing painfully, via a road or river valley, past a seemingly endless series of dominating mountain peaks that had to be cleared and then held against enemy counter-attacks.

Eighth Army's problems were also much the same from one division to another. With the exception of 5 Polish Infantry Division, on McCreery's extreme left, which was following the valley along the left bank of the River Ronco, all his other divisions had been engaged in successive river crossings, of the Uso, the Fiumicino, the Pisciatello, the Solo Rigosca Canal, the Savio, the Bevano, and the Ronco. By 25th October most of the divisions in the line had their forward units up to the Ronco, and that night two battalions from 4 Division managed to get across the river, in pouring rain that was visibly raising the water level and the force of the current. Beyond lay still more rivers, the Montone, the Lamone, the Senio, all fed by the same autumn rains furiously cascading out of the mountains. Any hope of sweeping through to the Po before winter set in had now almost completely evaporated.

In the mountains themselves XIII Corps was too dispersed along separate axes of advance to deliver any kind of telling blow. On II U.S. Corps' front an attempt was made; from 22nd October, to effect a concentrated breakthrough by 85 and 88 U.S. Infantry Divisions across Mt Castelazzo and Ribano Hill, the very last ridge line overlooking the Po valley. The attack was supported by two regiments from 91 U.S. Infantry Division, brought across to soak up German counter-attacks and to exploit any breakthroughs by the lead divisions. In the event, they were never called upon and the attack broke down around the village of Vedriano. On the night of the 23rd/24th Vedriano had become the focus of Fifth Army's desperate but waning efforts. A single company from 88 Division did manage to infiltrate the village but the rest of its battalion was unable to follow and the company was surrounded and captured. Renewal of the attack the following night brought almost no gains. "Dark clouds clinging to the mountains made it difficult for troops to call for accurate artillery support; cold rain and mud added to the misery of infantrymen already approaching the point of exhaustion. After dark on the 25th the 351st Infantry [Regiment] made one last effort to take Vedriano, but the attacking force, made up largely of fresh replacements, disintegrated in the rain and fog. A German counterattack then wiped out two companies."[5]

By the 25th, as Clark himself wrote, the offensive had all but "died out slowly and painfully, and only one long stride from success, like a runner who collapses reaching for, but not quite touching, the tape at the finishing-line."[6] It is possible to identify several underlying causes of the incipient Allied paralysis, all of which were largely beyond the control of both the Allied commanders and their front-line troops. The continued German possession of the Via Emiliana was one, for just as that road was sought by the Allies as a springboard for mobile operations in the Po valley, so did it provide the Germans with a lateral axis along which they could quickly redeploy divisions from one threatened sector to another. As Eighth Army bogged down in the Romagna, their attacks were too weak to pin German reserves in front of them and when Clark's offensive got fully under way, the Germans were able to switch divisions back to the mountains. During October, 29 and 90 Panzer-Grenadier Divisions were moved west in this way, and on the 25th itself 1 Parachute Division was on the move to help stem Clark's last desperate push around Vedriano.

Another source of German manpower was their eastern flank, where XIV Panzer Corps faced very weak American forces deployed from near Vergato to the Ligurian coast. By the 25th, increasingly convinced of Allied inability to mount significant attacks in this sector, the Germans shifted four divisions and much of the corps artillery to help in the defence of Bologna. Indeed, in a situation almost unique on any German front, II U.S. Corps now estimated that "the enemy had as many, and possibly more, infantry troops with which to hold the line as we had available for the attack."[7] American intelligence officers could certainly demonstrate that whereas in early September, at the beginning of its offensive, Fifth Army had faced only seven German divisions along its front, by 25th October this number had risen to thirteen, with a fourteenth on the way, all but four of which were ranged against II U.S. and XIII British Corps. These were not the ratios recommended for infantry assaults against fortified enemy positions.

Shortage of infantry doomed the Allies to a vicious spiral of disappointment. The element of surprise, an adequate basic plan, and considerable tactical skill and resolution had carried the Allies through the Gothic Line, but the victory, creditable though it was, incurred heavy casualties, and when these same divisions, in the absence of any appreciable reserves, had to attack again the Gothic hinter-lines, they simply could not gather the momentum to 'bounce' these unexpected extra defences. Instead, more heavy casualties were incurred, and each attempt thereafter to mount that 'one last push' was carried out with fewer and fewer men and with less and less effectiveness. Nothing reveals this dissipation of hitting power better than the casualty returns for a typical American infantry division, the 88th. In the drive towards Imola, after the Gothic Line had been breached, this division suffered 2,100 battle casualties in just under a fortnight, "which came close to equalling the total casualties of II Corps during the . . . period of the breaching of the Gothic Line."[8]

Yet all the American divisions were hard hit during October. In the first two weeks the four divisions of II U.S. Corps suffered 5,700 battle casualties, and by the end of the month they had lost a total of 15,700 men killed and wounded in combat since the beginning of the Gothic Line offensive. Of these, 5,026 had been in the spearhead 88 Division, which at the time of the Vedriano attacks was understrength by 1,243 officers and men. The shortage of junior officers and experienced noncoms was especially acute and made getting platoons and companies to push forward increasingly problematic. These deficiencies were accentuated by the fact that large numbers of the ordinary riflemen were now inexperienced replacements pitched into some of the most savage fighting of the war. What is truly remarkable is that these troops managed to claw their way as far forward as they did while just about 'running on empty'.

Another constraint on Allied offensive capabilities was the serious shortage of artillery ammunition. In mid-October it had been found that if expenditure of shells went on at its present rate, the Army Group would be compelled to go on to the defensive with only very meagre allocations per gun. It was partly this realisation that provoked the decision to renew the push on Bologna with exhausted troops. In the Eighth Army, for example, ammunition allotment for October was progressively reduced from an average of 75 rounds per day for field guns and 55 rounds for medium artillery to 25 and 15 rounds per day respectively. The problem was just as acute in Fifth Army. During the last week of October the divisional allowance was 7,000 rounds of high-explosive and 700 of white phosphorus, giving its organic artillery battalions an average of a little over 360 rounds each per day. "This was a derisory allowance compared with the scale of fire support previously given; indeed, the entire firing for the last week of October did not equal the amount fired during one eight-hour period on October 2nd . . . in front of Loiano."[9]

The terrain and the climate also remained intractable right up to the advance to the Ronco on 25th October. An official historian felt that the dreadful weather was "a defensive factor of the utmost value to the enemy . . . The rain and the floods were as useful to Kesselring as a couple of fresh divisions."[10] Conditions were equally grim for Fifth Army's two main corps in the mountains. The history of 34 U.S. Infantry Division referred to the reappearance of the autumn "men, mud and mules phase" of Italian campaigning, while 88 U.S. Infantry Division noted that all the roads in its sector were "in poor condition as a result of the October rains, and quickly became seas of rich, deep mud. Sprinkled generously throughout the area were rough cart roads and goat trails which, in the slick, slimy mud, were impossible to negotiate with anything less sure-footed than an Arabian or Missouri mule . . . The rains swelled the mountainous streams, and where before there had been a dry river bed or a small brook, there were now rushing rivers made from the rain which drained swiftly from these barren hills." The division was advancing on either side of the River Idice but whereas in September soldiers had merely waded across the river, before the end of October it was impossible to cross even by the known fords. "Toward the end of October the . . . Engineer Battalion had to construct an overhead tramway in order to get supplies and equipment across to the . . . Medical Battalion on the east bank."[11]

Along XIII Corps' front the individual peaks were "linked together by a narrow ridge, not much wider than the mule track it carried. Frequently the sides of these hills dropped away precipitously into deep winding ravines." An Indian Army historian described 8 Indian Division's axis along the River Lamone, north of Marradi, where the road ahead was just a long succession "of mountains, hills, ridges, knife-edge spurs and more mountains, with appalling weather conditions which taxed the endurance of the men to the utmost." So constricted was the route forward, and so exposed were they to German shelling, that the division's reserve brigade and its supply column had to remain well behind, in the valley of the River Sieve, north of Florence. This meant that all food, ammunition, stores and equipment had to be brought 25 miles over a 3,000-foot pass, along a narrow mountain road often enveloped in thick mist. The same road was a major corps axis, also carrying the traffic of 1 Infantry Division, yet many stretches were wide enough only for a single column of vehicles and had to be patrolled constantly by military policemen. "With the coming of the bad weather the surface of the road soon broke up under the constant stream of heavy lorries. Frequently it was closed for several hours to allow the sappers to effect vital repairs."[12]

Artillery units also found it extremely difficult getting their guns in position. 51 Medium Regiment R.A., after advancing its guns across the Savio, near Highway 9, "had a terrible time getting the guns into action; the roads were narrow with a deep ditch on either side and most of the fields were soft and boggy because of the recent heavy rains. The problem was to get the guns off the road without getting them hopelessly bogged down. The only way was to put them in the farmyards, and even before that could be done, the bridges over the ditches had often to be strengthened. The farmers naturally took a dim view of all the proceedings . . . The bang of a medium gun is enough to shake the tiles from the roof of any Italian farmhouse."[13]

One result of the appalling going was the virtual abandonment of motor transport in forward areas and the widespread adoption of the mule. Some stretches of Fifth Army's line were as much as 80 miles from the nearest railhead or advanced supply base and sometimes the last 30 miles were only suitable for jeeps and then mules. By the end of October the British had a fully-fledged Mule Corps in operation, with plans to expand the number of muleteers, originally Basuto and Indian military personnel, with a further 3,000 Italians. Many Italian volunteers had already been used, but most had proved unsuitable, and now arrangements were being made to set up a school at Orvieto for weeding-out and training.

The Corps contained something like 30,000 animals, many coming from Sicily and Cyprus and some from as far afield as South America. To lift one day's supplies for a brigade in the line required three-and-a-quarter mule companies, a total of about 1,000 animals. Central mule camps were established in a division's rear areas and these contained extensive veterinary facilities. The mule companies themselves were divided into sections, comprising a lieutenant and two other ranks as formation headquarters, and three sergeants, each in charge of a section containing one corporal and nine other ranks, an officer's charger and 33 mules. As one historian has noted: "To those looking out across the mud where thousands of animals were penned, and where columns of mules arrived and departed beside the lines of tents, the scene seemed to have gone back in time to the Crimea of almost a century before."[14] One of the main loads carried was food and this was held in huge Royal Army Service Corps supply depots near the camp. Typically, these "covered about twenty acres and consisted of several great food dumps. The food was in tins or wooden boxes, each heap lying in the open and segregated by a muddy path or a line of duckboards. The whole area was a hive of industry; carrying parties from different units arrived and departed; black African Basutos, carrying enormous weights, moved through the depot. The mules were led along the path and loaded."[15]

Mules were also used to carry ammunition and equipment. One Field/Mountain Regiment R.A., fighting with 10 Indian Division around Monte Cavallo, between the rivers Savio and Ronco, experienced a gruelling spasmodic advance during the last two weeks of October. For one of its gunners, "this was the climax of [our] battle against the mud. The guns had to be dismantled and loaded on to mules and unloaded and assembled, mostly caked with mud, every day for eight days, with long awkward marches between shoots. Often the moves were through unmarked minefields or across flooded rivers, in which case ammunition had to be ferried across by the mules with animals sinking or falling continually. Each time a mule fell in the water men had to sort out the load it carried as well as the animal itself. The worst thing was when an animal fell off a ledge while carrying a load along a mountain track. When the men reached a position which they were to occupy the first job was to dig in. The sticky earth had to be shovelled on to and off the spades. Men and mules were near exhaustion."[16] Even when a gun had been in place for several days, life did not necessarily become any easier for the supply echelon. In 76 Medium Regiment R.A., supporting 8 Indian Division around Monte Pianoereno, a daily round trip of 52 miles had to be undertaken as no supply or ordnance dumps could be established any nearer. Even though a fair proportion of this journey was made in motor vehicles – mules could only be expected to cover about 16 miles in a day – it was still a taxing ordeal negotiating the narrow, crowded, steep and tortuous roads, where visibility was often very limited.

Major Byrne Foxwell, an officer with 1 Kensington Regiment at the other end of XIII Corps' front, has written his own tribute to the "noble work" done by the mule trains which plied back and forth between the mule point at Appolinare and the front lines. "Night after night through the Spaduro battles . . . they groped their way along, climbing the steep, muddy ascent out of Appolinare – avoiding the swamp where a dozen mules had sunk by Gesso cemetery – passing the bogged-down tanks on the way to Gesso – picking their way through the minefield – quickening the pace through the ruins of Gesso to avoid the almost inevitable 'stonking' – floundering along the nightmare track of interminable length to Hill 387 – arriving after a four-hour journey at Sergeant Ganley's section at the very end of the world, only to find that some vital sandbag had dropped off a mule. Then the same procedure going back – getting very hungry – perspiring with the effort of squelching along in the mud – flopping into it to avoid a shell screaming down – stumbling into a shell-hole that wasn't there on the way up. At last, back in Appolinare, the muleteer got his well-earned one-twentieth bottle of rum and fell into some straw to sleep."[17]

Spare a thought also for the mules. The individuals who actually handled and cajoled the animals did become attached to them and often sympathised with their plight. In a novel based upon experience, Norman Douglas spoke for most of the muleteers plodding through the mud and pitch darkness on the 25th when he wrote that the mules "did not seem to mind noise, blast or violence of any description; they would take falls or wounds that would kill a man ... Sometimes the men would stick in the mud and the animals would pull them free. Sometimes the mules would be bogged down and a crowd of sweating soldiers would heave and urge the complaining beasts on to firmer ground. Sometimes the four-legged concentrations of dynamite would break free and bolt into the night, followed by a string of profanities and a furious, stumbling muleteer. Sometimes they would kick their keepers or each other over the edge of a mountain – and given no encouragement whatsoever, they would bite, buck and refuse to co-operate in any way with the bewildered troops. Yet the soldiers adored them, and were proud of them."[18]

The feelings of muleteers, however, had little part in the 'big picture' and the military authorities were prepared to drive the mules to the last extremity of suffering to ensure that the supplies got through. Doubtless they were justified, and this is certainly no place to debate animal rights, but it would take a stony heart not to be moved by the fate of the thousands of mules that pitched off the sides of mountain roads, drowned in mud, died of exhaustion, or were sliced, maimed and eviscerated by shells. In 88 U.S. Infantry Division's sector, in late October, the roads were "almost impassable, even for mules. Some of the mules broke their legs in frantic efforts to pull themselves out of the deep, sticky mud, and had to be destroyed." In 78 Infantry Division's sector, "some idea of the mud can be gauged from the fact that along one mule track could be seen the heads of many dead mules standing up in the mud where they had stuck, sunk, and been shot."[19]

Men, too, had to bend to the demands of the 'big picture' and it would be difficult to think of any military campaign in which front-line soldiers endured greater degradation than that inflicted in the Apennines and the Romagna in October 1944. By the 25th the rain had turned a 1 Kensington Regiment mortar platoon position into a water course. "Their once dry gulley was now a raging torrent ... The slit trenches had filled in; the men's kit was swamped; and soil was falling down the side of the gulley ... The whole mortar position was being swamped by water and landslides ... There was only one mortar above the water level ... [and] one had only one inch of muzzle showing ..."[20] Another battalion with 78 Division was 2 Lancashire Fusiliers, and for them "the rain and the enemy guns made 25th October a miserable sort of day. Rivulets ran coldly down the mountainside [and] freshly dug positions filled with muddy water ... The men sat and shivered in the cold and wet. Old hands agreed that at no time had they ever lived in greater discomfort."[21]

An inexcusable burden was added to the suffering of British troops in Italy by 'great socks scandal'. Though this does not seem to have been the result of flagrant profiteering, along the lines of the American cigarette scandal, it meant that for some weeks soldiers found it difficult to take the basic precautions against trench foot – the regular changing and drying of socks. One of the most eloquent descriptions of life at the 'sharp end' in the Apennines came from a soldier in 3 Welsh Guards, part of 6 Armoured Division whose infantry was holding positions around Monte Battaglia, in the centre of XIII Corps' front. According to an anonymous account quoted in the regimental history: "The rain filled the slit-trenches, and a slit-trench was the only place where a man could find shelter from the shell fire. He was permanently soaked to the skin, and permanently in danger. He spent his day in the bleak surroundings of stunted, decapitated trees, hundreds of waterlogged shell-holes, unburied corpses of American and German soldiers, sopping blankets and discarded ration tins. Night brought him little rest, no relief from rain or shell fire, and the added threat of an enemy raid on either side of our open flanks."[22] Take away the reference to American corpses in a British sector and this could have been the same regiment's description of a tour of duty on the Western Front at Ypres or on the Somme in the First World War.

About the only way out of this purgatory was to be wounded, but it was a high price to pay, and not just in terms of the pain and shock of the wound itself. The passage from the front line back to the aid station was potentially agonising. In 3 Welsh Guards at this time, "small relays of stretcher-bearers lived in positions dug in the side of the hill at 400 yard intervals along the track leading back to the road and by this means the 'carry' from the head of the causeway was reduced to three and a half hours; but on the steep and slippery track it was a horrible journey for a wounded man to take."[23] In 1 British Division, again part of XIII Corps, a wounded man might first have to be reached by his mates, climbing and scrabbling with hands and toes, before he was lowered down to a small piece of relatively open ground. Here he would be loaded on to a mule which might lurch down the mountain trails for six hours and more before it reached the aid post. There he received only emergency treatment before undergoing another eight-hour descent to his first motor transport, which bumped and skidded along the disintegrating road before finally putting the wounded man in the hands of a surgeon. Assuming, of course, that he had survived the journey, for many men died of shock or loss of blood long before reaching the operating theatre. One of the battalions in this division was 11 Lancashire Fusiliers, which often tried to use stretcher-bearers on foot rather than mules. But it is doubtful if they could have been any more sure-footed. In their sector "the mud was so thick and glutinous that a man's boots would become wider than a foot with clinging wet earth; it was difficult and heavy to take steps. Carrying a wounded man on a stretcher with mud coming above the ankle meant an awkward, clumsy descent with the casualty frequently sliding off, helpless, bleeding and in pain, or unconscious. Sandbags placed over the boot helped and although they didn't last long at least they could be peeled off together with the accumulated mud before entering a slit trench, which thus remained comparatively dry and mud-free."[24]

Walter Robson was a stretcher-bearer with 1 Royal West Kents, part of 4 Division which was slogging through the Romagna with Eighth Army. On 25th October he and his colleagues, together with five wounded men, were trapped in their makeshift aid post and unable to evacuate casualties back across the Ronco because the bridges were under constant fire. "So [as] they lay there in their wet clothes . . . I managed something of which I am inordinately proud. I brewed up on a candle. Wrapped it round with bandages and boiled half a mess-tin, just enough to make tea for the casualties. It is a tramp's job . . . known as 'dollying-up'. Another wrinkle: I dried wet matches in my hair. They are O.K. after a minute or two."[25]

If a soldier did manage to reach one of the points further down the chain, his chances of survival, in the hands of dedicated and expert medical teams, improved immeasurably. Every effort was made to bring surgical staff as far forward as possible and it was common practice to place such teams in the Advanced Dressing Stations where, in theory, only transfusions and other emergency treatment should be given. In 1 British Infantry Division, for example, mobile operating theatres, each transported by twenty mules and forty volunteer porters, were brought forward as far as brigade headquarters. Even so, the relief such facilities provided for the wounded was not always immediately apparent to an observer. John Blythe was a radio operator with 2 New Zealand Division, attached to the Advanced Dressing Station, and there, too, an operating theatre had been grafted on "close up to the battle scene". On the 25th Blythe was in a radio van just outside the front door of their requisitioned station. That morning he and his companions had watched two orderlies digging a deep pit just in front of the entrance. "Perhaps it was a rubbish hole? In a way it was. As the attack mounted and the night wore on casualties arrived in jeeps and carriers. Some even walked. From time to time there would be a flash of light, a door banged, and an orderly came out and dropped something into the pit . . . The surgeons were obviously engaged in amputations." For anybody actually going into the building the sight in the wards could be even more unsettling. In one of them there were some twenty men "and all were unconscious. Many of the beds were steeply tilted, some bodies were suspended on wires in strange positions, and connected to tubes. They were all enclosed in white mosquito nets stretching to the ceiling, seemingly caught in a ghastly cobweb. It was weird. I had heard wounded screaming or moaning more than once, but nothing like the scream from this sedated silence."[26]

By late October the cumulative effects of all the strain and suffering in the Apennines and the Romagna were beginning seriously to threaten combat efficiency. A regimental commander in 88 U.S. Infantry Division, Colonel James Fry, spoke eloquently of these last days in October. By the 25th his unit had spent an unbroken five weeks in the line. "To rifle company survivors this meant a continuous existence in the open, in foxholes or under any shelter available, such as rocks or trees for [36] days of hell." According to Fry, it was hard to see any semblance of co-ordinated action and a visit to the front lines was an unforgettable experience. "The trail was marked with German dead, but we had neither the time nor the inclination to evacuate the bodies. Their clothing, saturated with rain, and their faces sunken from decaying flesh, were worthy only of an impersonal glance as one went by. Life is cheap under such circumstances."[27]

American sources are especially candid about the deterioration of health and morale. In 85 U.S. Infantry Division in late October, large numbers of troops "were hospitalised for a combination of high fever and severe and prolonged attacks of diarrhea. The men were out in the mud and the rain most of the time, lying in dirty, water-filled foxholes. They considered themselves fortunate when they had the damp, stone floor of a dirty, three-walled, bombed-out barn in which to sleep. Practically every company was severely hit by these non-battle casualties."[28] In one company 38 of the usual 150 men were in hospital with fever and diarrhoea. The burden on the survivors was proportionately higher, especially on junior and non-commissioned officers who had to lead patrols two or three times more frequently than usual. In 34 U.S. Infantry Division morale sank to dangerous levels. General Clark remarked in his diary on 16th October that the division had become "diseased", and General Geoffrey Keyes, commanding

II U.S. Corps, was to write in November that "the division has maintained a consistently high AWOL [absence without leave] and Courts Martial rate for some time. An inordinately large proportion of Courts Martial cases have been for misbehavior before the enemy, disobedience of orders, aggravated AWOL, and related offenses."[29]

A doctor attached to 3/349 Battalion with 88 U.S. Division had just moved into the town of Fassineto on the 25th, directly behind the front lines on Monte Grande. Most of the companies in the regiment were down to half-strength and one had only forty men left. No replacements seemed to appear and according to the doctor, Karl Huebner, his battalion was fully 500 men short.

> The men are all weary, their morale is low, their tempers razor sharp, and their nerves exhausted . . . The casualties . . . are a sorry and pitiful lot. They have had a dog's life. They look thin and haggard, unshaven and unkempt, soaked to the skin and covered with grime. All their physical ailments are magnified since they are tired and exhausted dogfaces. Any unintentional unsympathetic word often sends a man into a rage of temper. The few replacements that drift in are of absolutely no help. They are forty-year-old men with flat feet and aching backs that have spent the last two years in rear areas serving as cooks, orderlies, or messengers and have been sent up to us in desperation. None of these last longer than a week at the most before they are ill with either bronchitis or pneumonia. I take one look at these fever-racked, coughing, and shaking miserable creatures and tag them for evacuation.[30]

British accounts tend to be more reticent about such matters but it is clear that many units had been grievously hurt. One such was 1 Royal Irish Fusiliers, part of 78 Division's famous Irish Brigade, which had fought a vicious battle on 19th October to try to take Points 416 and 387 on Monte Spaduro. By the 25th it was known that the battalion had lost 146 men, including five officers killed. "D Company had thirty left at the end of the battle, A and B a handful apiece, and C with most of the support company alone remained."[31] One officer, Colin Gunner, recalled: "After the shipwreck, the salvage began to restore the battalion as a fighting unit . . . I think it was then that that change came over me that came to all who started to count their close ones in the past, and to look to tomorrow with clouded eyes, and it was then that I wrote that letter home 'to be posted in the event of my death'." Yet Gunner was adamant that in an old regular battalion such as the 'Faughs' even this rump of survivors was an adequate cadre for rebuilding the battalion and inculcating once again the core traditions of battle honours, cap-badge and the Colours. "We were a regular battalion and from time to time those often-criticised, so easily and cheaply lampooned regulars had taken their hidings, picked themselves up, buried their dead and soldiered on. 'Close in on the Colours', that Ark of the Infantry's Covenant, was as real to those Old Faughs as it had been to the drunken, often flogged toughs who shuffled closer to their riddled ensigns on that bloody ridge at Albuhera while the dying Inglis screamed: 'Die hard, 57th, die hard!' Let those who see only their faults and irritating mannerisms never forget that."[32]

While many other units must have begun to wonder just how much longer the ties of loyalty and discipline could hold, British accounts also make it clear that even periods of rest and relaxation offered scarcely perceptible improvements in living conditions. The artillery suffered much the same privations as the infantry, and 3 Medium Regiment R.A. in the Romagna was hard-pressed to find anything that remotely resembled a rest area. On the 25th the Regiment moved to Cesenatica, on the coast below Cervio, reaching it in the late afternoon. The town was "generally voted to be a dump of the worst type. The Regiment was in two huge buildings without [glass in the] windows . . . It rained the entire time and water poured through the window-frames . . . The two days at Cesenatica were happily spent in clearing the billet, drying wet bedding, boarding up windows, winching vehicles out of the artillery parking place of soft deep sand, and staring disconsolately at the grey sea twenty-five yards away."[33]

For the infantry, who could usually only be spared in small groups while the battalion as a whole remained in the line, the opportunities for enjoying even the most basic amenities were equally limited. When, on the 25th, a platoon of 1 Kensington Regiment was ordered back off Monte Spaduro for two days' rest in Appolinare, it arrived there at dusk, all the men "soaked to the skin and thoroughly worn out after six days and nights under heavy fire. Two of them were sick, but they could not be evacuated as the Division's maintenance road to the rear had fallen away in a landslide." The little village, comprising only about ten houses in all, was already choked with two brigade HQs and so "half the platoon were squeezed into a stable already filled with other soldiers. An inch of water stood on the floor. There was no question of dry clothes. The best that could be done was to light fires inside the stable; huddle closely together; and hopefully hang socks over the fires on sticks."[34]

There were in Italy, however, at least half-a-dozen men who

actually blessed the ubiquitous and remorseless rain. These formed part of a scouting platoon under the command of Charles Frost, an officer in Princess Patricia's Canadian Light Infantry. On the 25th Frost was told to take a section and reconnoitre one of the battalion's flanks as it pressed towards the River Bevano. That night Frost and half the section approached a tiny village, climbed the stone wall at the side of the road and advanced through the back yards of the nearest houses. Frost was in the lead, and after a few minutes he felt the ground slowly give way and first one foot then the other began sinking into some unidentified mire. At shoulder height, just as he was about to take his chances and yell, his feet hit solid ground. "A pleasant warmth embraced my body; an overpowering stench hit my nostrils; sulphur fumes ate my eyes. I was up to my armpits in a farmyard cesspool. Involuntarily I raised my tommy gun over my head and moved forward as I was taught at Vernon Battle School. I looked back and saw my section, one by one, silently follow me into that stinking sumphole. We ploughed through the sewage in single file and climbed out at the far side of the pool, saturated with excrement and gasping for air."[35] In Italy, on 25th October 1944, that's about as funny as it got.

23

Reduced to Minus Zero

LIFE IN OCCUPIED ITALY

BENITO MUSSOLINI, the *Duce* or leader of Fascist Italy, was overthrown by his Cabinet and King on 25th July 1943, just a fortnight after the invasion of Sicily by British and American armies. For a few weeks the new government, headed by Marshal Pietro Badoglio, paid lip service to the alliance with Germany but it soon began extending peace feelers to the Allies, who insisted that nothing less than unconditional surrender would do. So, on 3rd September, such an agreement was signed, to come into effect on the 8th, one day before the Allies landed in mainland Italy. Immediately upon making the armistice public, Badoglio and King Victor Emmanuel III fled Rome for Brindisi to be near the British landings at Taranto. This was a wise move because the Germans reacted furiously to what they perceived as Italian betrayal. Mussolini was arrested and the Germans rushed seven divisions into Italy. Once Badoglio had surrendered, these troops set about disarming the considerable Italian forces on the mainland and in the Balkans.

The Italians had received no orders to turn against the Germans or to resist them, and by 14th September the OKW could report to Hitler that 56 Italian divisions had been completely disarmed and another 29 partially. Prisoners-of-war numbered almost 700,000 and roughly eighty per cent of Italy was now under German military control. Mussolini, who had been held prisoner at a ski resort in the Abruzzi, was released in a flamboyant but quite unnecessary 'rescue' operation by German airborne troops and taken to Germany. On 5th October he was back in Italy, installed at Salo on the banks of Lake Garda as head of the Fascist Social Republic in central and northern Italy.

The Salo Republic, as it is generally known, typified what was to be the most humiliating period of Italian history since unification in 1871. Its leader, discredited even before he took power, was clearly nothing more than a German puppet, with most decisions taken or vetted by their ambassador, Dr Rudolph Rahn. Equally demeaning was the fact that the Republic was continually shrinking as the German front, which marked its southern frontier, slowly pulled back. In the year or so between Mussolini's installation and 25th October 1944, he saw no less than two-thirds of his country swallowed up as the Allies advanced right up to the northern outposts of the Gothic Line. How long this latest frontier would hold good was entirely out of his hands.

Immediately upon being reinstalled Mussolini was keen to assemble his own Italian army to fight the Allies but the Germans only slowly and grudgingly permitted the formation of four infantry divisions. By October 1944, when two of these had finished their training in Germany, one was sent to the quiet western end of the Gothic Line and the other was employed on security duties in the rear. Both divisions had an allotment of much-resented German 'advisers' who were unable to prevent a wave of desertions as soon as the men reached Italy. Mussolini chose to ignore this depressing omen. On 25th October he inquired for the second time that month of Kesselring, the German supreme commander in Italy, "Where are the Italian divisions which returned from Germany? . . . What are they doing? Why are they not used? Why are the enemy armies using the peoples of five continents to attack Italy while the Italians, the best Italians, are not allowed to contribute to their defence? Inaction rapidly leads to the demoralisation of troops."[1]

Mussolini was also greatly exercised by the fact that the Germans would permit the creation of only four divisions, given that they had captured an enormous amount of military materiel in the September 1943 clampdown and that 600,000 of the Italian prisoners-of-war were still being held in Germany. According to the Papal Nuncio in Berlin, these men had been "transported, many without kitbags, in summer uniforms, without food, closed in cattle wagons, with no hygienic arrangements. Thus shut up, they travelled slowly to the north with unexplained stops and no food." It was a mode of transport the Germans had spent four years perfecting, and many of these men became virtual slave labourers, forced to work long hours in appalling conditions in German factories and mines and on roadworks and rubble-clearing. In many camps there were no washing facilities. Prisoners were beaten regularly, rations were barely above starvation levels, and up to a third of the inmates were in the so-called hospital, most suffering from T.B., pneumonia or malaria. In the more remote camps, where even the Germans could find little work to be done, the imprisoned *Badogliotruppen* simply rotted. According to the Nuncio, such men "spent the day in complete idleness, sitting on a few square yards of miserable ground under a perpetually grey sky in a cold northern climate, with nothing to eat but boiled cabbage and potatoes, under the eyes of a German soldier always ready to shoot or punish."[2] Living quarters were grossly overcrowded, with 250 men and more sleeping in dormitories for 100. Many had to place their thin straw pallets on the floor and there was a serious shortage of blankets. Bronchitis, pleurisy and T.B. were rife. Mussolini protested several times to Hitler, asking that these men be released to serve in the new Italian divisions, or at least be given more generous rations and accommodation. A few T.B. cases were released back to Italy but for the mass of the prisoners, many of them citizens of the co-belligerent Salo Republic, durance remained as vile as ever.

It was not only the Germans who seemed to be going out of their way to humiliate the Italians. The Allies, too, remained disdainful of their erstwhile enemies, and once again prisoners-of-war became a central issue. Thus, although the Badoglio government had declared war on Germany on 10th October 1943, one year later there were still 450,000 Italians held in Allied camps in North Africa, the Middle East, the United Kingdom, Australia and the United States. Their continued incarceration was not necessarily meant as a slight to the Italians or their armed forces but, as explained by the official historian, stemmed from the fact that freeing them "might have entailed the obligation to ship them back to their own country – a commitment which could not have been undertaken without grave prejudice to the Allied war effort." Nevertheless, the historian also acknowledges that this was never properly explained to the Italians themselves. He finds it "difficult to believe that the knowledge that nearly half a million of their countrymen were detained overseas, even when they were assisting to fight the German enemy, can have stimulated the war effort of the Italian people."[3] The Allies tried to make partial amends by permitting thousands of prisoners to serve as 'Co-operators', wearing Italian uniforms and serving under their own officers, performing a range of military duties short of actual combat. The Allies felt unable, however, to amend the Co-operators' legal status as prisoners-of-war, and so neither the Badoglio government nor its successor, headed from July 1944 by Ivan Bonomi, were prepared to sign an agreement formally recognising their existence.

All the same, the Allies approached the problem of soldiers captured in Italy with considerably better grace than the Germans. Few of those who had surrendered were interned by the Allies, who showed themselves increasingly ready to employ Italian units in combat and along the lines of communication. By April 1944 there were 17,300 Italian soldiers along Fifth U.S. Army's front and 23,000 around its rear areas, while the figures for Eighth Army were 4,000 and 30,000 respectively. Most of the combat troops were part of the *Corpo Italiano di Liberazione*, an expanded motorised group, comprising a scratch infantry division and the Nembo parachute division, under the command of General Umberto Utile. Some units served alongside Americans at Cassino and with Polish and Indian divisions up to the Gothic Line, but by 25th October the Corps had been taken out of the line to provide cadres for six new *Gruppi di Combattimento*, division-sized units based on original infantry divisions that had surrendered in Italy, Sardinia and Corsica. These units were being equipped to come into the line early in 1945. They were a wholly British responsibility (Roosevelt having refused to release any American weapons or equipment) and altogether comprised 2,600 officers and more than 50,000 men. When anti-aircraft and rear-echelon units were included, there were upwards of half-a-million men wearing the King of Italy's uniform, or at least his badge, in October 1944.[4] They were of tremendous assistance to the Allies who were desperately thin on the ground in Italy after losing seven divisions for the landings in southern France.

Italian units had provided invaluable support as combat soldiers at the front, and promised to do so again in 1945. They were also useful as security, logistics and administration personnel in the rear, where they were controlled either directly by the two Allied armies or by Allied Military Government (AMG) officials who administered activity well behind the front. The men of the Royal Italian Army were also a vital boost to Italian morale, both as symbols of a renascent, non-Fascist state and as a buttress to the authority of that state. Ever since the King had arrived in Brindisi he and his government had been permitted by the Allies to take over the administration of the more rearward liberated areas. In August, Rome was handed back, one month after the Italian government had returned, and by late October its authority extended to the southern boundaries of Tuscany, Umbria and the Marches, about one hundred miles behind the front. In a country still suffering from the collapse of the Fascist administration, the passage of Allied and German armies, the effects of systematic bombing, shelling and demolition, the floods of refugees, and the dislocation of food production and distribution, the presence of native troops, armed and uniformed, was a vital adjunct to the re-imposition of democratic civil authority.

The Royal Army was also fulfilling a vital role simply by providing half-a-million young Italian males with adequate rations, clothing, accommodation and a little pay. With these basics of life came a modicum of self-respect, to help these men cope with the traumas of invasion and occupation. Indeed, one of the most troubling effects of the war in Italy was the presence of thousands of relatively well-paid Allied soldiers whose purchasing power was completely beyond the means of most Italians at the time, so reducing them to a state of humiliating economic impotence. An English officer with the Field Security Police in southern Italy noted in his diary on 8th October that Allied soldiers "were in immediate collision with the local boys who had no work, no prestige, no money, absolutely nothing to offer the girls. A British private, wretchedly paid as he is, earns more than a foreman . . . while an American private – who can shower cigarettes, sweets, and even silk stockings in all directions – has a higher income than any Italian employee . . ." This economic power proved irresistible to many Italian girls and traditionally long, ritualised Italian courtships were fast being "replaced by a brutal, wordless approach, and a crude act of purchase. One wonders how long it will take the young . . . after we have gone, to recover from the bitterness of this experience."[5] It also seems legitimate to wonder just what would have happened if the millions of young men not in uniform and without a job had been joined by released prisoners-of-war. Almost all those the Allies might have released – not to mention the Germans – would have congregated within AMG and Italian government zones, adding a fearsome burden of some three-quarters of a million idle men on to already rickety social and economic structures.

Yet Italy's problems involved much more than the bruised egos of its young males. Men and women, young and old, from almost every social class, were all suffering the effects of an acute economic crisis that threatened even the bare subsistence level at which they lived. At the heart of it was the food shortage. The Italian diet was essentially farinaceous, with flour used to make the twin staples pasta and bread. The 1944 wheat crop was a good one but converting it into food on the table was fraught with difficulties. Just bringing in the harvest could be a perilous activity because many of the fields were sown with mines. The British official history speaks of "very heavy" civilian casualties during the autumn and also notes that the Allies had declared mine-clearance in the rear to be an Italian responsibility, even though there was an acute shortage of mine-detectors.

Hoarding was another problem. The relative wealth of Allied servicemen was made more damaging by the refusal of the American authorities to ban their servicemen from Italian restaurants and cafés. Throughout 1944 they continued to dine with gusto, forcing up prices while at the same time diverting more and more food into this sector of the market. An American serviceman wrote: "I remember watching the American acquisitive sense in action. We didn't realise, or we didn't want to realise, that we were in a poor country, now reduced to minus zero by war ... Everywhere we Americans went, the prices of everything sky-rocketed until the lira was valueless. And the Italians couldn't afford to pay these prices, especially for things they needed just to live on."[6] The Italian authorities endeavoured to buy wheat at official prices but the farmers were naturally keen to sell directly to private middlemen whose own prices better reflected the relentless demand from the occupying forces. At one stage the royal government reduced the rural bread ration to barely above starvation level until the farmers had handed in the harvest to the state granaries.

Even where this measure was successful, the authorities still faced enormous difficulties in getting the crop from these granaries to the big cities, where the clamour for flour was greatest, due to a terrible shortage of motor vehicles throughout Italy. Most of those in private hands that were still running had far more profitable options than transporting grain for the government. Some requisitioning was done but in the Rome motor pool, for example, only 1,500 of the 2,300 assorted vehicles were serviceable.

By late 1944, only 50 per cent of normal imports of flour were getting through to Rome, the shortfall made yet more serious by the presence of more than 200,000 refugees. Many of these were being held in special camps set up in the Cine Città area, the Roman equivalent of Hollywood. At the end of October, with help from the Vatican, food kitchens were doling out over 250,000 meals per day. It was not lost on most people that a government bread ration of 200 grams was less than the ration under German occupation, when a whole range of family and occupational supplements had been available. Food became the central preoccupation of every Italian and was a key item on the black market, where the price of such staples as flour and potatoes had risen 500 per cent and more since the liberation. Worse, the black market was increasingly dominating trade as a whole, so that by October 1944 it handled 80 per cent of all foodstuffs while only 3 per cent passed through the rationed market. The situation led to serious unrest in several cities, with mass demonstrations in Florence, Pisa and Pistoia. In Palermo on 19th October, Italian troops fired on a large crowd, killing 26 people and wounding 150 others.

Allied generals and politicians began to grow alarmed. Churchill wrote to Roosevelt on the 24th to tell him that "the situation in Italy is not good and might sharply deteriorate. There was a serious riot in Sicily and there has been trouble in Pisa . . . There may be trouble for all of us."[7] General Clark, commanding Fifth U.S. Army, was driven in mid-October to send a personal message of protest to Field Marshal Alexander, pointing out that the "civilian food situation throughout Fifth Army area is critical and will become increasingly so as we advance. The 100 grammes of bread distributed daily are inadequate. Widespread unrest is manifest . . . [and] unofficial sources indicate that more serious incidents may develop. If such occur combat troops may have to be diverted to maintain law and order."[8] The British official historian adds that pasta was in even shorter supply than bread, with only a small fortnightly distribution. Sugar was completely absent, salt and soap were now scarce luxuries, and for several months there had been no distribution of olive oil. He also points out that Clark might have taken some crumb of comfort from the halt order Clark had had to issue only a few days later, for this did at least mean that some military transport could now be spared to help the distribution of such civilian supplies as were available.

Lesser players on the Allied side provided more intimate impressions of the food crisis. In the slums of Naples, according to a British observer, people were crammed in at over 3,000 per acre and most lived "on the indescribable residue of offal bought in the slaughterhouses, or fishes' heads and tails, roots dug up in the fields, and, in the last resort . . . even the occasional cat."[9] But there were worse tortures than having to eat such swill, or even than gnawing hunger alone. In a novel based upon his experiences in the Mediterranean theatre, the American John Horne Burns highlighted the enormous gulf between G.I. affluence and the abject poverty of the *scugnizzi*, or urchins of Naples.

> I remember how the children of Naples pointed my dim conception of American waste. They'd stand about mess halls quiet or noisy, watching the glutted riches from our mess kits being dumped into the garbage cans. I remember the surprise and terror in their faces. We were forbidden to feed them . . . When I watched the bitten

steaks, the nibbled lettuce, the half-eaten bread go sliding into the
swill cans in a spectrum of waste and bad planning, I realised at last
the problem of the modern world, simple yet huge . . . After a while
many of us couldn't stand it any longer. We'd brush past the guard
with our mess kit full of supper and share it with Adalgisa and
Sergio and Pasqualino . . . I remember the wild hungry faces of
these kids diving into cold Spam. But our orders were that since
America was in no position to feed all the Italians, we must not feed
any. Just dump your waste in the GI cans, men.[10]

Another G.I. novelist, Winston Brebner, remarked on similar
occurrences in Florence, though without mentioning any actual ban
on sharing leftovers with civilians. Each day children, mothers and
old men "in desperation crossed the river from the poor section to
flock around the company mess halls, carrying buckets made out of
number ten cans and baling wire. They flocked around the garbage
cans between the mess halls and competed for food that remained in
the mess kits of the soldiers who came out . . . to wash their equipment.
The number of supplicants increased from meal to meal and with it
attendant anxiety and confusion."[11]

Malnutrition, overcrowding, and a general breakdown of medical
facilities inevitably brought disease. There were serious outbreaks of
typhoid in September and October 1944 in Naples, Benevento, San
Marino, Rimini and Prato – as well as a small-pox epidemic in the
Naples area. Norman Lewis, at that time stationed in Benevento as
the representative of the Field Security Police, was forced to realise
that he was to all intents and purposes "living in the Middle Ages . . .
Epidemics, robbers, funerals followed by shrieking women, legless
cripples dragging themselves about on wheeled platforms – even raving
lunatics they'd no room for in the asylum. People walked the streets
with handkerchiefs pressed over their noses as they probably did in the
days of the plagues of old. This morning I actually found myself in a
little square tucked away among the ruins where women were dancing
to drive the sickness away."[12]

The physical toll of war had fallen just as heavily on the fabric of the
country as on its inhabitants. Norman Lewis was again an eloquently
appalled witness to the devastation wrought by Allied bombs in
Benevento during the build-up to the Salerno landings. Well over a
year later the town of 50,000 inhabitants was still in ruins. Only one
house in five had been left standing, the 11th-century cathedral was a
shell, and the water supply was turned on for only a few minutes each
day. "One was warned to leave the tap on to collect what drips come

through. Eventually a small yellow pool collects in a bowl over the dark sediment it precipitates." Lewis's office was in the Hotel Vesuvio, once an imposing ten-bedroom building but now with only one corner room still standing, into which had been crowded "twenty or thirty hat stands, as many spitoons, and a small grove of potted palms." This room served as café, then restaurant and then "punctually at midnight Japanese screens are produced, and four iron beds normally standing on end against the walls are lifted into position. I sleep in one of these, much troubled by the mosquitoes and the heat."[13] In the local hospital the phones still did not work, the ambulance had been wrecked, and only one nurse remained to look after a hundred or so patients, most of whom slept on the floor between the extant beds.

Most damaging of all, perhaps, was the assault on the moral fabric of Italy as its increasingly desperate citizens had to resort to the most sordid expedients to acquire money for food. Exorbitant over-pricing was one way, even though this cut most of their compatriots out of the economic loop. Another possibility was collusion with corrupt Allied personnel to bring military supplies on to the black market. The young and the very poor usually had to fall back on street crime and mugging, while Italian officials at all levels could increase their meagre salaries by the hallowed method of not actually doing their job until they received a supplementary bribe or 'gift'. In the rural areas and smaller towns such transactions were still carried off with a sort of fly-blown civility and weary regret that men of honour should be reduced to such straits. Many in the cities, too, tried to cling to their self-respect. John Horne Burns was moved by the stoicism he saw all around him in Naples. "We Americans were still thinking in terms of nylons and chromium and that raise from fifty to sixty dollars a week. The Neapolitans weren't always sure they'd be eating that evening. But instead of inducing a squalor and envy in them, in most cases this bleak reality brought forth in them a helpless gaiety, a simplicity and a resignation that touched me and many other Americans."[14]

Burns was stationed in Naples at this time and his judgements are doubtless more considered than those of the thousands of Allied personnel who simply visited the city in transit or on leave, many of whom were struck only by the squalor of the city and its ambiance of vice and depravity. An English A.T.S. officer remembered the city as "a den of vice, a most dangerous place for women. Murder, mugging, drug-peddling and prostitution were rife . . . Even in those squalid slum areas not 'off limits' it was dangerous to walk alone . . . Children ran about with naked bodies caked with filth. Fat-bellied flies clustered over refuse, excrement and food alike; and out of doorways ran ragged children importuning any soldier within earshot: 'Hi, Johnnie, jig a jig, *mia sorella, molto bella!*' Others begged for cigarettes, chocolate, petrol, meat, even mosquito nets (from which they made underpants) . . . In those narrow slum streets gangs of Allied deserters, as well as Italian crooks had their hideouts with girlfriends. They could exist only by theft and dealing in stolen military goods, and they had no qualms about using their weapons if necessary."[15]

Prostitution was one of the most pervasive aspects of this moral decay as thousands of women could see no other way of feeding themselves and their families. Some at least struck up long-term relationships with soldiers stationed in a particular town or city, but in the big leave centres, Rome and Naples, any liaison was usually a brusque transaction, conducted in some back-street brothel, or in the street itself, or in some slum bedroom. In the Vicaria district in Naples, where overcrowding was especially intense, "most street-walkers bring back their customers. The chances are, when they arrive, that there will be tenants in the room – such as bed-ridden old people lying in wall bunks – who have to stay. They simply turn their faces to the wall."[16]

The Allied authorities did not trouble themselves much with the moral impact on Italian society, or indeed on the outlook of their own soldiers. But they did begin to get extremely anxious about the associated problem of venereal disease and the number of soldiers incapacitated in this way. All streets containing known brothels were soon placed out of bounds, but this only served to alert soldiers on leave to their exact location. In Naples and Rome, according to the official historian, "the infection rate among troops reached an appallingly high figure." Over 2,000 hospital beds had to be set aside for V.D. patients in Eighth Army alone, "of which 1,800 were in continual use, the turnover being about 3,500 patients a month."[17] Eighth Army statistics show that V.D. cases in 1944 represented 10 per cent of all diseased soldiers, and in a list of thirty diseases, for October of that year, V.D. ranked third behind meningitis and digestive disorders. In that same month V.D. cases were half as high as men wounded in combat.

The military treated V.D. cases harshly, concerned only to get the men back with their units when cured and to deter other possible offenders or re-offenders. Efforts to clap down on the disease also fell heavily on the Italians themselves. Any young woman came to be regarded as a potential prostitute and a source of infection. Periodic round-ups for compulsory medical screening put thousands of them through a shaming ordeal, undermining yet further the concepts of

propriety and honour to which families still tried to cling. John Horne
Burns recalled one girl, Aida, who was "arrested on the street where she
was walking and not bothering anybody. They jailed her in the
questura till her blood test turned out negative . . . I saw her in her pink
cotton dress and sandals, rolling up her sleeve for the needle. Her tears
fell on her brown chest. We Americans stood around laughing and
asking Aida how much she charged."[18]

Burns goes on to place this one vignette in a gallery of weeping
Italians whose portraits combine into an angry panorama of the
desolation of war and of the indifference of the triumphant Allies. He
recalled also Neapolitan women "who wept because they couldn't get
food at black market prices . . . I remember faces out Caserta way
standing in their fields and crying over the drought . . . I remember a
scugnizz' on Via Roma crying . . . because the American major
confiscated his can of shoe polish, saying that he stole it from the
americani." He remembered the family Russo "looking at the place
where they and their blood had lived for two hundred years." Now it
was nothing more than "a pile of chalk. I remember how the mother put
her face on the father's shoulder, how both of them rocked together,
how [the sons] simply sat down on the dust of the place where they had
been born." He remembered others who "wept sometimes out of fury
and a refusal to accept their own destiny", whose tears taught him that
"the individual is never so responsible as the moralists hold" and that
by late 1944 the whole "Italian personality had been stymied by a
collective hell."[19]

*

Conditions were also hard in the ever-shrinking Salo Republic, though
the concentration of much of Italian industry in the north made life
there somewhat easier than in the Allied zones. A notable difference
in mood could be felt among Italians in the north. Many behind
the German lines saw their way much more clearly and strove to
drive out the invaders and to shake off the indigenous Fascist regime.
The reappearance of Mussolini and his convocation of a grand Fascist
congress in November 1943 had marked what many Italians saw as the
start of a civil war, with a whole array of quisling police, paramilitary
and combat units assisting the Germans against anti-Fascist partisan
bands which had proliferated throughout the more remote hills and
valleys. These partisans fought under the banner of the National
Liberation Committee for Northern Italy (CLNAI), which had been
formed in Milan in January 1944. The following June, in response

to the rapid expansion of this guerrilla war, the CLNAI set up its own military headquarters, the General Command of the Corps of Volunteers for Freedom (CG/CVL), headed by Ferruccio Parri and Luigi Longo.With Parri a leading member of the centre-left Action Party and Longo of the Communist Party, the CLNAI established itself as an explicitly broad-based political organisation that was as much interested in the shape of postwar Italian society as it was in helping the Allies to drive out the Germans.

The Allies, however, were suspicious of the 40 per cent of almost 100,000 partisans who were members of the Communist Party's 'Garibaldi Brigades' and would not recognise the CNLAI as the official pro-Allied resistance movement in the country. To try to obtain some leverage over the Committee, they parachuted in General Raffaele Cadorna, the best of the Italian generals who rallied to the Allies in September 1943, to head the CG/CVL, a task at which he was not entirely successful. In a report in early October he suggested that the Allies were doomed to disappointment if they ever hoped to harness "the partisans as a normal military campaign, refusing to recognise its predominantly political character. It must be stated very clearly that the resistance movement could not have existed without the political organisation and that in the partisan warfare the Communist Party is predominant . . . [It] does not try in the least to hide its intention of seizing the reins and setting up a regime similar to the Russian . . . They declare openly that they wish to lean upon Russia and Tito and will rebel rather than submit to the orders of the Western Allies."[20]

It is far from clear whether this would have been to Stalin's taste at this time, but the western Allies continued to fear that the more radical partisans might attempt to seize power for themselves. Throughout their advance northwards, the British and Americans sedulously disarmed any partisan who found themselves on the Allied side of the front line. Although this was rarely done at the point of a gun, it was made plain to the partisans that they had little option but to hand in their arms and submit to a debriefing and demobilisation procedure in one of the special camps set up in Florence and Pescia, by AMG and the Italian government. Each partisan was vetted to determine whether he was an authentic 'patriot' or just a bogus free-loader, or even a spy. Patriots were defined as "persons in the ranks of the genuine bands who have carried arms against the enemy, engaged in sabotage, or secured important military information for the benefit of the Allied war effort."[21] An added incentive to handing in weapons was that afterwards one would be fed for a month at the camp, provided with new clothes, and receive whatever medical attention might be needed.

On the other side of the front the partisans fought on, although the month of October 1944 found their military fortunes at rather a low ebb. During the first half of that year they had achieved an impressive aggregate of guerrilla victories – ambushing German and Fascist patrols, attacking guard posts and road convoys, cutting the railways, sabotaging power installations, and sending back captured documents and intelligence reports – and the Germans had been forced to pay more and more attention to this menace. Their response was typically draconian. In June Kesselring had ordered: "The fight against the partisans must be carried on with all means at our disposal and with utmost severity. I will protect any commander who exceeds our usual restraint in the choice and severity of the methods he adopts against partisans." Two weeks later he specified that "every act of violence committed by partisans must be punished immediately . . . Wherever there is evidence of considerable numbers of partisan groups a proportion of the male population will be shot . . . Should troops be fired on from any village, the village will be burnt down."[22]

This particularly savage style of counter-insurgency was soon in full swing. Kesselring's orders coincided with a period of rapid German retreat between Rome and the Gothic Line, a retreat which emboldened the partisans and persuaded General Alexander to ask them to step up their operations in the enemy rear. The partisans saw political opportunities, too, and the chance to emulate Yugoslav successes in setting up permanent liberated zones where political and social reconstruction could begin to take place alongside military operations. According to one authority, "on the basis of the Yugoslav Partisans' experience, the CVL recommended that there be parallel forces wherever feasible – one mobile and available for attack; the other an administrative presidio unit." In a number of liberated regions, some of the larger ones dubbed Republics in their own right, civil administrations were set up and shared between popular delegates and political officers from the partisan bands. But the tactic turned out to be premature. Not only were the Germans and Fascists now in a more vicious mood, arms drops to the partisans fell away due to a shortage of suitable aircraft, the Allied advance stalled just as it emerged from the Gothic Line, and the partisans found the terrain in many of the liberated areas unsuitable for sustained guerrilla defensive operations. The valleys and clusters of valleys chosen, though always remote, were also fairly bare, covered at best with scrub *macchia* and much less of an obstacle than Yugoslavia's heavily forested mountains. This "denuded terrain" was altogether "unsuitable for fighting a mechanised foe".[23]

All in all some fifteen liberated zones came into existence in Piedmont and Emilia, in Lombardy, in two regions of Liguria, and in Carnia and Friuli in the Veneto. Among the larger zones were the Montefiorino Republic, covering territory in Modena and Emilano provinces, just to the south of the cities of Modena and Parma; the Domodossola Republic between Lake Maggiore and the Swiss frontier, embracing over 1,600 square kilometres and 80,000 inhabitants; and the Carnia Republic, north-west of Udine in Friuli province and stretching up the Austrian border near Villach. This latter was the largest of all the liberated zones, covering 2,600 square kilometres and containing 90,000 inhabitants. In each of these zones the Fascist and German authorities were ejected and local CNLAI committees took charge. Attempts were made to convene locally elected assemblies, most taxes continued to be collected, the various political parties sloganised and squabbled, and in the Domodossola Republic the new regime went so far as to issue its own bank coupons and postage stamps. But all were very short-lived. To Mussolini and his German masters, such uprisings, albeit localised, represented an intolerable provocation and sizable military forces were swiftly dispatched against them. The Montefiorino Republic lasted only from 18th June to the end of July, the Domodossola from July to late October, and Carnia from September to late October.

On 25th October these last two republics were just on the point of being snuffed out, as Italian and SS police and army units continued to scour the area with their so-called *rastrellamenti*, raking or dragnet operations undertaken by the counter-insurgents. Sometimes they "employed an entire division for the combings and blocked off whole valleys with the goal of either destroying or dispersing the partisans. Several motorised columns would advance from the valley floor in an encircling fashion toward a cul-de-sac." The same basic tactic was used on each individual village, as a British officer with the partisans noted. "A group of armoured vehicles with infantry would drive up to a mountain village. The infantry would be marched to a point a kilometre or so from the village and then fan out and beat round towards the village with their armoured cars covering all possible exits. It was rather like putting a crowd of terriers into a patch of rough ground with the guns waiting for the rabbits to bolt."[24]

A few villages and remote hill-tops continued to hold out, some of these in lesser enclaves outside the liberated republics. But most communities had now been thoroughly raked over. Thousands fled the

Salo Republic altogether, making their way south to join the Allies, eastwards to link up with Tito's partisans, or north-west into Switzerland. The Swiss had recognised the neighbouring Domodossola Republic shortly after its proclamation, and once the partisans were forced to scatter, civilians and guerrillas alike continued to stream across the frontier throughout the second half of October. The Swiss laid on three special trains and then sent all refugees to Basel, "where they were sorted out and 'disinfected' in a large empty show-ground pavilion before being sent to camps in central Switzerland." The local Fascist prefect reckoned that up to three-quarters of the inhabitants of the Republic had fled but claimed that many soon began to return "as it became known that he was carrying out no reprisals . . . With pride . . . [he] informed the Duce that by 26th October all the frontier posts on the Swiss border were again in Fascist hands."[25]

Fascist clemency was less apparent to the people of Domodossola themselves. According to an American news report some weeks later, twenty members of a partisan rearguard were "captured and hung up on meat hooks. I talked to their comrade who had to make his way to the town at night and shoot them as they hung, still writhing. Their screams, which continued for hours, carried up to the mountains, and were crazing to the rest of them." Equally ruthless measures were employed in Carnia and, according to one Italian resistance leader, by late October it was not unusual to find at the roadside "boys in the strange attitudes of the hanged dangling from little trees, their feet just touching the ground. For the mass executions 30 or 40 were loaded on a truck that went around the villages, each of which had to provide a quota to be hanged corresponding to the degree of partisan valour attributed to it. The rope was tied around the neck of the condemned while he was still on the truck, which then moved off."[26] This sort of testimony was emphatically confirmed by a U.S. engineer officer serving with the O.S.S. in Italy. Captain Steven Hall had been dropped over the mountainous north-west of Carnia in early August 1944 and had been caught up in the *rastrellimento*. Hiding out in an isolated mountain village throughout October, he whiled away some of the time writing letters to his wife, to be posted he knew not when. In one he wrote: "The atrocities are true; I've seen them; and they're universal. Villages burned, children hanged, men tortured, old people turned out into the snow, civilians shot for sport – I've seen these things with my own eyes."[27]

The inhabitants of Carnia, and indeed much of the whole Veneto region, also had to face a threat that must have seemed nightmarishly bizarre even in the context of a vicious guerrilla war. A major component of the forces deployed against the partisans were five regiments of Cossacks, under their own leader General V. Naumenko. From the Don, Terek and the Kuban, they had volunteered to fight against Stalin and had for a time been established in a new homeland in Novogrudok in White Russia. Driven from there, they had finally been promised a new *stan* in north-east Italy, around Tolmezzo. These strange allies began arriving in Italy in July, bringing their families and household possessions with them. They came by train, but once disembarked they presented an almost medieval picture. "Transport was drawn by horses, mules, bullocks and camels ... There was a pungent stench of animal dung, and the air was full of neighing and the braying of camels and donkeys."[28]

Delighted by their first sight of Friuli and Carnia, and the great fertile plain of Udine, already named Kossackenland by the Germans, the Cossacks threw themselves into the task of disposing of the existing population. According to a local archbishop who reported back to Mussolini, by early October "thousands and thousands of people [had been] forced out of their homes without shelter or rations of any sort; the majority had to leave with the clothes they had on their back at the moment of forced eviction." Some were arrested, beaten and thrown into prison while others, especially "women, old men, and the sick [were] thrown on to the roads, their suffering unheeded." The prefect of Trieste confirmed that throughout October the Cossacks gave proof of their "detailed intentions of colonisation which have surprised even the local commanders of the SS." They usually advanced in two columns, one the nominal fighting troops "who instead of fighting made violent assaults on unarmed people that disgusted both the Germans and the Italians", and a second column of non-combatants "consisting of both women and men [who] have taken possession of houses, evidently intending to stay permanently. It is terrible to think that Friuli will be governed by these illiterate savages, and for the population it is a punishment which transcends every shame."[29]

The newly destitute inhabitants of Kossackenland would have been the first to assure their compatriots to the south that there were, after all, worse things than being liberated by the Americans and the British.

24

The Commando and Alphabetical Type

III BRITISH CORPS IN GREECE

DESPITE the presence of two full Allied armies in Italy, operations there were severely hampered by a shortage of infantry, and so when events in Greece suddenly called for the deployment of British troops in October 1944, only a scratch force could be assembled.

For much of the war Greece and the Aegean islands had been occupied by various Axis divisions, latterly German forces grouped under the theatre headquarters OB Süd-Ost. With the collapse of German defences in the Balkans it was decided to withdraw these forces northwards, through Yugoslavia, before they were cut off completely by the advancing Red Army and Tito's Partisan divisions. The withdrawal had begun on 14th September and soon opened up a power vacuum in Greece. Collaborationist officials were massacred wholesale as soon as the last German soldier left a town and local guerrilla groups took over much of the day-to-day administration. But these groups, notably the leftist EAM and the more conservative EDES and EKKA, were at loggerheads. The EAM, and its armed wing ELAS, were ultimately under the control of the Greek Communist Party, the KKE, and except in the EDES heartland, in Epirus, they set about killing their political rivals with the same zeal that they had butchered Nazi and Fascist sympathisers. A Greek government-in-exile had been formed in Alexandria but it was uncertain how much authority these politicians would wield when they returned to Athens, especially if they advocated the return of the monarchy in the form of King Georgios II, an institution widely reviled on the left.

In the light of this unstable situation, and despite having thrashed out an agreement between the guerrillas and the provisional government at Caserta in September, the British decided to dispatch a miniature expedition force to Greece to keep up some nominal pressure on the retreating Germans and, more important, to prevent a possible Communist *coup d'état* in Athens. In a minute to Foreign Secretary Anthony Eden, on 6th August, Churchill had grumbled about the "absolutely intolerable" behaviour of EAM and the necessity to stand up to the "snarlings of the miserable Greek (communist) banditi".[1] In a letter to President Roosevelt on the 17th, he wrote: "The War Cabinet and Foreign Secretary are much concerned about what will happen in Athens when the Germans crack . . . If there is a long hiatus after the German authorities have gone it seems very likely that EAM . . . will attempt to seize the city . . . I do not expect you will relish any more than I do the prospect of chaos and street fighting or of a tyrannical Communist government being set up."[2]

All this is not to deny a genuine humanitarian impulse behind British intervention. Incompetence, corruption and Axis rapaciousness had reduced the whole of Greece to penury, with little food to be had outside the black market and inflation so rampant that by October, according to one British journalist, a loaf of bread cost 40 million drachmas. Such an amount could only be carried about in a small sack, and in practice most everyday transactions were done by barter.

The commander of the British forces in Greece, all nominally under the umbrella of III Corps, was General Ronald Scobie, who described in his diary a meeting on 25th October with various senior politicians and military men. The financial discussions "lasted over two hours. A great deal of useless theory discussed . . . Found it most difficult to keep them down to the most vital point, which is currency stabilisation in the next few weeks."[3] After this same meeting Eden telegraphed to Churchill: "E.A.M. is active and we should be unwise to under-estimate its strength . . . Most immediately urgent question, however, is runaway inflation which is so serious as to resemble the situation of Germany after the last war . . . Unless we can deal with it the Government will be swept away and anarchy will take its place."[4]

Military planning for the Greek operation, eventually to be dubbed Operation MANNA, had begun in late August when the independent 23 Armoured Brigade in Egypt had been reorganised as an Infantry Brigade Group, with an expanded staff, to be known as Force 140. Two of its tank battalions, 40 and 50 Royal Tank Regiment, were reorganised as infantry, as were two squadrons of 46 RTR, the third being equipped with armoured cars. On 2nd September Force 140 became Arkforce, and then on 19th October reverted to 23 Armoured Brigade once more. Still without tanks, the Brigade sailed from

Alexandria on 12th October, bound for Athens. Another smaller convoy sailed from Taranto, in Italy, on the 14th, carrying Scobie and his staff, as well as Harold Macmillan, the British political representative, and the Greek provisional government, headed by Prime Minister Giorgios Papandreou. These latter were to transfer to a venerable Greek battleship, the *Overoff*, just before actually arriving off the mainland.

However, Scobie and 23 Armoured Brigade were not the first British troops to arrive in Greece, as two other forces had already been put ashore to expedite the official arrival in Athens. One of these made up the other major component of III Corps, comprising 4, 5 and 6 Battalions of the Parachute Regiment, which had flown from Italy to drop over Megara, 40 miles west of Athens, between 12th and 14th October. Once assembled the Brigade had immediately made its way to the capital. Yet another force, about 450 men belonging variously to a Special Boat Service squadron, two companies of the Highland Light Infantry, a section of 40 (Royal Marine) Commando, a Long Range Desert Group squadron and a squadron from the RAF Regiment – and known for no apparent reason as Bucketforce – had landed on 23rd and 24th September, most of them going ashore at Katakolon, but with an advance party of paratroopers seizing the airfield at Araxos. This force, commanded by Major Lord Jellicoe of the SBS, then sent patrols into various towns in the Peloponnese and pressed on with the main force to Athens. No wonder that a staff officer with 23 Armoured Brigade, which was temporarily to command all the units converging on Athens, described them as "a conglomeration of almost uncontrollable smaller units of the Commando and Alphabetical type."[5]

By 18th October all these units were on Greek soil and, for the most part, had assembled in Athens. Scobie himself had landed on the 17th, and the government was officially installed the following day. Despite immediate and monotonously frequent EAM and KKE marches and rallies, the British troops were generally rapturously welcomed everywhere they went in Greece. A British journalist, Marsland Gander, wrote of Bucketforce's triumphant procession: "At every village we were bombarded with rose petals, fruit, flowers, grapes and rice in such quantities that at some convenient stop we had to halt the car to empty it all out on the roadside again . . . In their ecstasy of joy, people in some places flung down carpets on the road for our car to run over . . . Oleander and olive branches were strewn in our path."[6] The politicians, too, were well satisfied. On the 18th, Macmillan concluded: "Had there been any longer delay between the departure of

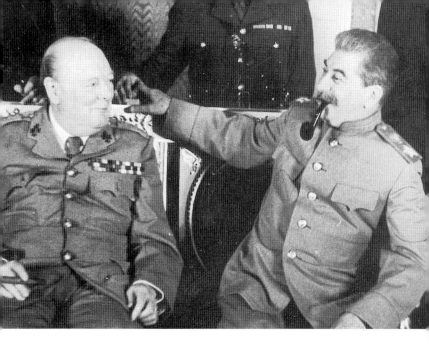

1. Prime Minister Winston Churchill and Soviet Premier Joseph Stalin in Moscow, October 1944
2. Rival Allied commanders General Dwight Eisenhower and Field Marshal Bernard Montgomery

3. American troops enter the Hürtgen Forest (*left*)

4. French infantry clear out a village in the Vosges (*below*)

5. Yugoslav partisans march into Belgrade (*right*)

6. Soviet armour in Poland (*below right*)

7. An RAF Halifax bomber over the Ruhr (*far left*)

8. A V2 rocket being prepared for launch (*left*)

9. Hitler enters the command bunker at his 'Wolf's Lair' in East Prussia (*below left*)

10. A group of nuns and elderly people await evacuation in Holland (*right*)

11. New arrivals at the Auschwitz death camp (*below*)

12. Chinese troops march up Burma Road to fight off Japanese attempts to cross the Salween River

13. American troops and equipment coming ashore on Leyte Island in the Philippines

14. U.S. B-29 bomber over Japan (*above*)

15. Chinese Nationalist leader Chiang Kai-shek and the U.S. commander in China and Burma, General Joseph Stilwell (*left*)

16. The Japanese battleship *Yamato* under aerial attack in Leyte Gulf, 25th October 1944 (*below*)

17. The long day closes on Pelelieu in the Central Pacific

the Germans and the arrival of the Greek government; or had the government arrived without the disembarkation of substantial numbers of British troops and Air Force at the same time, I think EAM would have seized power."[7]

On 19th October Scobie felt secure enough to disperse his forces once more. The armoured brigade remained in Athens but the parachute battalions went hither and thither, with one, and all the commandos, preparing to embark for a landing in Salonika, in early November; another undertaking security operations in the Thebes area; and the third carrying on through Thebes to pursue the retreating Germans to the Yugoslav border. In fact, this battalion, the 4th, also halted awhile in Thebes to allow supplies of petrol, oil and food to catch up with them. Finally they got going again in "the most amazing assortment" of scrounged and requisitioned vehicles, "ancient trucks, battered buses, even an ambulance or two and several taxis."[8] Happily there were also a few jeeps that had been put ashore at Athens.

The 4 Parachute Battalion was only one part, albeit the major one, of the pursuit force. The whole, some 950 men identified as Pompforce and under the command of newly-promoted Lieutenant-Colonel Lord Jellicoe, also contained SBS and RAF regiment personnel from Bucketforce, though it could never be described as a compact formation. One member wrote that the Germans "were blowing all the bridges and roads as they went, so it was not easy to follow and we didn't always have a lot of petrol." Even the paratroopers themselves were widely dispersed and "at one stage it was rather like having a company each at Bristol, Southampton and Plymouth."[9] By the 25th Pompforce had caught up with the German rearguards, near Korzani, almost 200 miles north of Athens, where, according to one paratrooper, "the Germans surprised us by making a stand." Another recalled: "We tried to persuade the Germans to surrender at Korzani. I sent in Geoffrey Morrison, who was fluent in German, with Lord Jellicoe, to try and persuade the retreating Germans to surrender but they were convinced we were brigands."[10] Plans were laid for an attack on the 26th, by C Company, up an almost vertical rocky slope below the German positions.

Also in contact with the Germans was a 40-strong SBS patrol that slipped into Salonika on 22nd October to reconnoitre for the November landing. For the next few days until the German withdrawal on the 27th, this small band, commanded by a Dane, Captain Anders Larsen, constantly harassed the German rearguard, at one stage tearing into the centre of town in four captured fire engines. One squad had been "befriended by some Greeks who hid them in a cellar. There they received periodic visits from a Swiss Red Cross representative who kept saying 'They haven't gone yet', and apologising because he could bring no food. However, with almost every visit he brought them a bottle of brandy, so that they remained in a state of cheerful inebriation."[11]

By the end of October, then, the story of the 'Alphabeticals' in Greece was hardly one of a major British Army commitment and is not without its faintly comic side. Yet the political rationale behind the whole endeavour was important and was there from the start. Already 4 Indian Division and 3 Greek Mountain Brigade had also been alerted for transfer to Greece early the next month, and on 21st October a staff officer from 7 Indian Brigade arrived to make a preliminary reconnaissance. Even as it became clear that the Germans would be out of the country by the end of the month, these orders were not rescinded. The presence of German forces had provided a very useful excuse for landing British troops but it was EAM and KKE which were consistently seen as the main enemy, at least by Churchill and Roosevelt. Just days before, at a conference with Stalin in Moscow, he and Churchill had come to a tacit agreement on the postwar balance of power in Europe, the terms hastily scribbled out on a piece of paper that the Prime Minister had passed to the Soviet leader and watched him tick. Their respective postwar influence in this country or that was defined in percentage terms. Greece was to be 90 per cent British. 'Buckets', 'Alphabeticals' and other flummery aside, and MANNA from heaven notwithstanding, Scobie's III Corps was being deployed for the next war, the Cold War, even before it had a name.

PART FIVE

The War Against the Kriegsmarine

25

Schnorchelling

U-BOATS AT BAY

OVER THE ten years to 1944 the German Navy, or *Kriegsmarine*, had commissioned almost exactly one thousand U-boats. At the end of October 1944, 394 of these remained in commission, of which 130 were operational, the so-called *Frontboote*, and 260 or so were either new boats working up with their crews before becoming operational or old boats used for training replacement crewmen and specialists.

Of the operational boats, 58 were at sea, 25 of them on patrol in European waters and the Atlantic, 11 in the Indian Ocean, and the remaining 22 in transit, sailing to and from patrol areas or from one port to another. The boats on patrol comprised 19 in the Arctic, 3 in the North Atlantic and 3 in inshore areas round the British Isles.[1] In other words, in the main Allied sea lanes – the North and English Channels, the American eastern seaboard, the Caribbean, and the North Atlantic – which had constituted the merchant shipping killing grounds in the first years of the war, only six U-boats were on active patrol on 25th October. This figure represented 10 per cent of the U-boats at sea and a dismal 4.6 per cent of the total number of *Frontboote*. Yet more dismal is the percentage of the whole commissioned fleet thus engaged, with a mere 1.5 per cent of these boats actively prowling the Allied convoy routes to find merchant shipping and escort vessels to sink.

In many ways Admiral Karl Dönitz, Commander U-boats, was grappling with a problem similar to that faced by Generals Arnold and LeMay with their B-29 bombers, which in October were still dropping only paltry bomb tonnages that were depressingly disproportionate to the number of planes built and the vast expense. Considerable power existed on paper, both in U.S. Army Air Force inventories and

German submarine pens, yet the projection of that power was proving intractably difficult.

Some 'leakage' of commissioned U-boats was, of course, inevitable. Boats (and crews) returning from patrol required extensive overhauls and trials; newly commissioned boats needed yet more exhaustive trials; and new crews could only be trained in sea-worthy submarines. Moreover, U-boats were very much the sea-slugs of naval operations, taking an inordinate time to travel from port to their designated hunting-grounds. As one expert has tellingly reminded us: "These craft were certainly not capable of dashing through the depths at great speed. Supposing one would superimpose a map of Europe over the Atlantic. Then a U-boat on Berlin, Warsaw, Prague or Vienna might be ordered to attack a mobile object in London. The U-boat would travel there on the surface at the speed of a pedal cyclist. Once submerged its speed would be cut down to walking pace."[2] No wonder that U-boats were at sea for three or four months at a time, with the longest recorded German patrol lasting all of 203 days.

Dönitz's problems went deeper than the innate constraints of this 'slow-motion' mode of warfare. For these constraints by themselves should not have been enough to stop him mounting an effective submarine campaign. The weapon itself was not lacking. Despite an abysmal shortage of U-boats at the beginning of the war, Dönitz had managed to step up production considerably, with the number of boats in commission rising steadily. Totals for the final month of the years 1939–43 were 53, 73, 236, 381 and 424, where a plateau was reached.

Yet the weapon was now lacking where it was most needed, and figures for *Frontboote* did not keep pace with this increase in the number of commissioned boats. For the first years operational availability did remain fairly constant. In 1940, the average daily number of U-boats at sea represented roughly 25 per cent of the average number in commission. The equivalent figure for 1941 was 17 per cent and for the next two years 25 and 21 per cent . In 1944, however, availability at sea began to decline markedly, reaching a low of 8 per cent in July and for the year to October, averaging out at 12.5 per cent, or not much more than half of the average for the preceding years.

Another way of highlighting this decline in 1944 is offered by the detailed charts of individual U-boat operations compiled by interned U-boat staff officers after the war. These indicate when U-boats actually reached and left their patrol areas and so present a 'snapshot' of U-boat deployment on any given day. The table below shows the number of boats on patrol, in the North Sea and Atlantic, at certain peak dates between 1939 and 1943, and also at random dates in 1944. The precipitous decline in U-boat effectiveness is clear.[3]

1939		1943	
15 September	29	30 January	54
		5 July	51
1940		6 November	38
19 June	19		
28 November	12	1944	
		25 February	19
1941		30 May	7
21 February	18	7 June	34
21 June	34	29 August	12
31 August	45	28 September	9
11 November	43	25 October	6
1942			
16 January	22		
9 May	29		
5 December	51		

U-boats actually on station on selected dates 1939–44

Given that Dönitz saw his fleet essentially as commerce raiders, an even more direct indicator of efficiency was the amount of Allied merchant shipping U-boats succeeded in sending to the bottom. The available figures show that U-boat potency began to wane before 1944, and the decline is evident in two ways. The gross tonnage sunk increased steadily to March 1943, exceeding 500,000 tons per month in May, June, August and November 1942 and in March 1943; then it fell away rapidly, only four times exceeding even 50,000 tons for the rest of the war. Even more depressing for Dönitz, the effectiveness of individual U-boats consistently declined almost from the very beginning. Again taking the average daily number of U-boats at sea per month and setting it against the monthly tonnages of ships sunk, we find that the annual averages of this ratio were as follows:

1939	10,200 tons	1942	6,900 tons
1940	16,300 tons	1943	1,500 tons
1941	9,500 tons	1944	500 tons (to October)

This second set of figures shows that the decline in sinkings was due not just to fewer U-boats on station but also to the reduced efficiency of the weapon itself. Of course the mounting numbers and expertise deployed by Allied anti-submarine forces played their part. Despite having taken part in one close-fought Battle of the Atlantic between 1914 and 1918, the British began the next war with a cavalier disregard for the potential of the U-boat. The submarine, it was felt, had been subdued once and for all by advances in underwater sound detection (asdic/sonar), and so all the painfully learnt lessons about convoying and convoy escort were soon blithely forgotten. When the Americans entered the war in 1942, they too resolutely refused to draw any lessons from the destruction then being wreaked, and allowed their own unregulated coastal shipping to serve as U-boat target practice. Eventually, however, hard lessons were learnt and Allied air forces, navies and merchant marines, gradually, and sometimes grudgingly, combined in a systematic, day-in, day-out effort to make life almost impossible for the U-boats.

The essence of their tactics was to find the U-boat before it found the convoys, for the convoy was not of itself adequate protection against submarines. Even though U-boats usually chose to attack on the surface in so-called wolf-packs, they offered a very small target to enemy observers. In daylight they were almost impossible to spot unless framed against the horizon, and usually they elected to attack at night. Though a pack of ocean-going boats in the midst of a convoy might sound like a substantial target for accompanying destroyers, frigates, sloops and corvettes, it was in fact surprisingly dispersed, elusive and almost invisible.

In the first years of the war, then, there could be no question of deliberately drawing U-boats to the convoy, the better to destroy them – as Allied bombers were to do to Luftwaffe fighters in 1944. Three options remained. First, to route and re-route convoys to avoid the wolf-packs, which formed long patrol lines in front of the anticipated course of a convoy and then concentrated for the kill once one U-boat had established contact. Secondly, to hunt down U-boats along these patrol lines or while they were sailing to and from them. Just forcing these U-boats to take evasive action would reduce their effectiveness but it would be better still if, as a third option, anti-submarine warfare (ASW) possessed the wherewithal to destroy U-boats on the surface or submerged. Such weapons would clearly also be of great value on those occasions when U-boats did still manage to penetrate a convoy.

Simply avoiding U-boats was a frequent tactic, especially early in the war. This was made possible by good intelligence, which derived partly from Dönitz's own preferred wolf-pack tactics. To assemble U-boats on patrol lines and for the concerted kill required that they communicate by radio in coded messages with one another and with U-boat headquarters in France. However, the Enigma cypher machines that transmitted these messages were familiar to the Allies, and from an early date decoding produced vital details about U-boat positions. Radio could also be intercepted in another way, and one that did not require the ability to read the messages. Pinpointing the position from which a transmission was made itself fulfilled the main requirement of Allied naval intelligence – knowing where to put the flag on the plot chart. From early 1941 these positions could be accurately determined using ship-borne and land-based High Frequency Direction Finding Equipment (HFDF or 'Huff Duff'). This was quite invaluable in those periods when Enigma was unreadable or when decoding lagged badly behind real time.

Hunting down U-boats did not begin to make any real mark until mid-1942. Up till then only 87 U-boats (22 per cent of the total commissioned to that date) had been lost, whereas in the following eight months that figure was equalled and by the end of October 1944 a further 357 U-boats had been destroyed. The basic tactic was to use a combination of aircraft and naval vessels and is succinctly described by the naval historian Stephen Roskill. By late 1943, "four years of continuous struggle had taught us that by far the most effective counter-measure to the U-boats was to employ radar – and Leigh Light-fitted aircraft in conjunction with radar – and asdic-fitted surface escorts – the aircraft to carry out widespread searches, and the ships to hold contact and attack until the enemy was destroyed."[4] The Leigh Light was an 80 million candlepower searchlight. With a range of 5,000 yards, it was switched on in half-minute bursts, and was employed in night-flying Wellington and Liberator aircraft of Coastal Command. Roskill perhaps underestimates the role of these aircraft, especially the Very Long Range Liberators which scored quite a few kills of their own on U-boats they hunted down.

The efficiency of the escort vessels was gradually improved by a whole range of technological measures so that by late 1944, they had at their disposal reliable asdic/sonar to detect submerged submarines, ASV X 3cm radar to seek them out on the surface, towed acoustic decoys to deceive the German torpedoes, range recorders to tell operators exactly when to launch conventional depth-charges, and forward-firing Hedgehog and Squid depth charges which allowed a much more precise timing of an attack as well as last-minute setting (in the Squid) of the detonation depth.

Long before then Dönitz felt the struggle had turned too much against him and in May 1943 ordered his U-boats to withdraw from the

North Atlantic. At this stage he was laying much of the blame for his defeat on Allied aircraft, especially the Leigh Light planes that criss-crossed his transit routes through the Bay of Biscay. Consequently he set much store by equipping the U-boats with quadruple AA mounts instead of their small naval guns. Once sufficient boats had been re-armed, he renewed the Atlantic battle in September 1943. Less than three months later he again conceded defeat, the new Flak boats being hardly more successful than their predecessors in getting through to their patrol billets.[5] Wolf-pack tactics were now simply unsustainable and those few boats that were sent to the Atlantic sailed singly, and remained so, with orders to seek out their own targets of opportunity.[6]

Finding such targets demanded that U-boats operate mainly on the surface, both to cover an adequate search area and to execute radar or binocular searches. It was just these methods that made them most vulnerable to Allied counter-measures, and even when the U-boats were not actually destroyed, they were relentlessly harried and forced to remain submerged, creeping along at a snail's pace and with a snail's eye view of a few thousand square yards of Atlantic swell. To Dönitz, it was fast becoming apparent that "the existing types of U-boat, which had been designed largely to operate on the surface, were handicapped by blindness, slow speed and poor endurance now that Allied A/S measures were forcing them to spend much of their time submerged."[7] Essentially these boats were based on First World War designs and by 1944 ASW developments had rendered them obsolete.

Dönitz's problems did not end there. Until June 1943 his opera-tions had been immeasurably helped by his own crypto-analysts, the Kriegsmarine's B-Dienst, which had achieved considerable success against British Naval Cypher No.3, known to the Germans as the 'convoy cypher'. Enhanced British security had made it briefly unreadable by the end of 1942 but within two months B-Dienst had mastered it once more and were soon reading most days' signals. In June 1943, however, Cypher No.3 was replaced by the much more elaborate No.5 and this remained impenetrable to the Germans. Any hope of making up for the crypto-analytical black-out with aeriel reconnaissance came to nothing.

The last straw was the loss of the French U-boat bases following the invasions of France in June and August 1944. The main bases were in Brittany, at Brest, Lorient and Saint-Nazaire, and the 31 sea-worthy boats there began pulling out on 6th August. By the 16th 15 of them had left for La Pallice and Bordeaux, to the south. Only 7 of these boats got through but even before these had all arrived Hitler ordered the evacuation of U-boats from all French ports. The 30 U-boats scattered among the five Biscay bases were then told by Dönitz to proceed to bases in Norway, some directly and some via patrol billets in the North Channel. Of the 26 that got away, 4 were sunk and the rest arrived at Bergen and Trondheim between mid-September and late October.

Though safe from the advancing Allies, the U-boats were now at an even worse operational disadvantage. For the transit routes from the Norwegian bases were perhaps the most rigorously patrolled sea lanes of all and even more hazardous to U-boats than the Bay of Biscay. Moreover, these bases had never been designed to support major U-boat operations. Repair and refit facilities were adequate for only thirty boats and the rest were obliged to spend days sailing back and forth between German ports and Norwegian bases. "For these reasons the *Frontboote* were inactive for more than double the time it had previously taken to refit them in the Biscay bases. Allied bombing raids on Bergen, Trondheim, Kiel and Hamburg, and increased mine-laying off the Norwegian bases and in the Baltic Belts, compounded the problem."[8] Especially serious was a raid on 4th October which wrecked the Bergen repair yards and knocked out the electrical wiring in the submarine pens. Four U-boats were either destroyed or written off.

*

The German U-boat force was in a sorry state in October 1944 – harried out of its bases of choice by Allied land forces, heavily bombed in those that remained, and comprehensively outfought in the Battle of the Atlantic. Yet Admiral Karl Dönitz did not feel himself to be down and out. If the Allies had won the last few rounds through technological superiority, he had reason to hope that it was now his turn to alter the balance. For he was now fitting his submarines as fast as he could with a new device, the schnorchel, which was supposed to solve the problem of U-boat vulnerability on the surface. The schnorchel was an air-intake which projected just above the surface from a submerged submarine and provided a continually habitable atmosphere below decks, removing the need to surface in order to dispel accumulations of carbon dioxide. The air taken in also allowed a U-boat's diesel engines to function underwater, by expelling the poisonous fumes they generated through an exhaust outlet that was built into the main schnorchel tube. Diesels running underwater enabled U-boats to travel much faster submerged than was possible with electric motors. Just as important, the diesels could be used to recharge the U-boat's batteries underwater, so eliminating the other main reason for conventional submarines having to run regularly on the surface. With the schnorchel, U-boats could drastically reduce the risks in getting to their patrol billets as well as take much more effective evasive action once there.

Those U-boats that had been re-equipped in 1944 were in many ways living up to expectations, with most of them getting to and from their Norwegian bases without being detected by either aircraft or surface vessels. In the month as a whole, British naval intelligence estimated that of the 49 U-boats known to have left these bases, 42 passed through the search zones undetected. Almost all of these had been fitted with schnorchels. Yet the benefits of this new freedom of movement remained somewhat elusive and it was soon found that while permanently submerged boats had a greatly enhanced survivability, their efficacy as a weapons system was diminished.

Schnorchelling U-boats were very slow, for even when running on diesels, speed underwater had to be kept to 6 knots because if it were any higher the periscope stem would snap. Partly due to this constraint, "the official procedure was to use one shaft for recharging the battery and the other for going ahead at half speed on the electric motors. This method, we found, took almost as much out of the batteries as it put in and as a result . . . [we] spent most of our time paddling like lame ducks . . . while our batteries were on trickle charge."[9] As a result, an inordinate amount of time was spent going to and from the patrol areas. A U-boat staff officer pointed out that "whereas in August 1942, during a 100-day period, the average U-boat spent 40 days in harbour and 60 at sea, of which 40 were spent in the operational area, during the last three months of 1944 a U-boat spent 63 days in harbour and 37 days at sea, of which only nine days were spent in the operational area."[10]

Slow speeds also had serious implications for U-boat range. When Allied convoys were re-routed to the south of Ireland, Dönitz wished to send U-boats to operate in the English Channel but was forced to acknowledge in a report that "as a rule we shall be unable to use the Type VIIC boats in the Channel since the passage takes so long that they would be unlikely to arrive in a fit state to operate under such difficult conditions."[11] In other words, the ocean-going U-boat that was available in the greatest numbers was now not capable of sailing the length of the North Sea.

Even when U-boats arrived on station, so long as they were forced to remain submerged they could not hope to do much hunting or killing. Their slow speed made it difficult to pursue convoys, or indeed spot them in the first place as the lookouts were restricted to the peri-scope's small field of vision in daytime. At night, of course, the U-boats were completely blind. The schnorchel also made them deaf. "When U-boats had recharged their batteries on the surface, at least there had been look-outs with binoculars on the bridge, but now, recharging at periscope depth, the only means of keeping in touch with the out-side world were the hydrophones, and these were rendered useless by the roar of the diesels."[12] By October it had become standard procedure to stop schnorchelling once every twenty minutes for an all-round hydrophone search, during which the boat usually dived to twenty metres.

Remaining submerged also had serious navigational implications, especially in the English Channel. If the periscope were used for terrestrial navigation, it was necessary to approach very close to shore to get a sighting and this invited detection by ASW assets or running into a minefield. Taking a fix from radio beacons along the French coast was even more hazardous as raising the radio aerial meant putting the whole conning-tower above the surface. The only alternative was dead reckoning but this was complicated by the lack of known depth lines in the Channel and the strong tidal flows. Even when a U-boat was sure of its position relative to a possible convoy interception, it often proved impossible to hold that position while lying in wait. "The situation was compounded by the boat's gyro-compasses and echo-sounders having to be switched off to reduce noise every time A/S vessels approached. After some hours of manoeuvring, to dodge or shake off enemy patrols, commanders and navigators were frequently left with no idea of their position."[13]

Finally, even if a schnorchel-boat did actually spot a target, its chances of actually sinking it were slim. The essence of submarine tactics in the 'happy' hunting grounds of 1940–42 had been to run on the surface to gain advantageous position, either singly or in packs, before firing the torpedoes. Submerged boats did not have the speed to improve their position and unless they were on a fortuitously converging course, had no option but immediately to fire off their torpedoes in the general direction of the enemy. It is hardly surprising to learn that not only did U-boats claim no kills on 25th October, they sank not one single merchant ship or naval vessel in the Atlantic, Channel, North Sea or Arctic, throughout the whole month.

This lack of success only compounded the miseries of the U-boat crews themselves. For life on board any of the schnorchel-boats at sea was, if anything, even more unpleasant than on conventional submarines. By this stage of the war 50 per cent and more of the U-boat crews at sea were on their first voyage and the intense strain of claustrophobia, cheek-by-jowl living conditions, and day and night harassment by ASW forces was only intensified by never having the opportunity to even poke one's head out of the conning-tower. That said, many of the youngsters were so racked by seasickness that all other aspects of their predicament were but dimly perceived. "The poor lads were gripped by an agony of the soul. If only they could get out – simply climb overboard and jump into the sea – instead of being shut in, battened down, in this deafening, reeking, reeling tube of steel."[14]

Even old sweats could gradually succumb to the nerve-racking ordeal of a schnorchel patrol. Most commanders felt that a target as small as a schnorchel head was too dangerous to expose in daylight and these hours were normally spent at a depth of about 60 metres, chugging along on the electric motors. Schnorchelling was limited to about three hours each night, when the boat was 'hung up' at periscope depth, the batteries were recharged and the air in the boat was refreshed. But each period had its problems. In daylight hours the key constraint was that the oxygen obtained during schnorchelling, or the 'snort', had to be conserved over twenty hours before the next one. So almost all activity had to be restricted to the snorting interlude. "Cooking, eating, drinking, moving about, even sitting instead of lying down, consumed too much oxygen. 'All hands to the bunks' was a routine order with us for as long as we were at sea. We spent so much time on our backs, that our leg muscles became soft and we all began to suffer from pains in the back. I have never seen men do voluntary exercises (knee bends, deep breathing etc.) with such enthusiasm as . . . during the few hours when we were snorting and fresh air was free."[15]

To some submariners this might have seemed rather foolhardy behaviour. A schnorchelling boat with its diesels running would be even more voracious for air then the men. Not only was the boat damp and freezingly cold because of the continual gale blowing through during a 'snort' but eardrums would be strained by incessant variations in pressure caused by the float-valve in the schnorchel head, an essential precaution against water being drawn into the intake in a choppy sea. Seas around the British Isles and beyond were almost always choppy, and worse, and so the schnorchel head was for ever being continually swamped. The valve always did its work but the diesels then immediately sucked out all the air left in the boat. The near vacuum brought intense pain to the eardrums and more than a few men had to be invalided out. Even in a relatively calm sea, a U-boat on trim at periscope depth was in a very delicate state of balance. Just one man "walking from one part to another would upset the trim. When schnorchelling, however, excessive movement could easily cause the . . . valve . . . to close and create an unpleasant vacuum. For essential movement through the boat, the men had first to obtain permission so that the . . . operators could prepare for a new trim."[16] The callisthenics described above, then, do seem to have been a rash indulgence.

Disposal of rubbish was another problem faced when submerged through most of a patrol. Previously it had simply been thrown over-board when the boat surfaced but now it had to be stored, usually in the torpedo room, filling the empty covers which had protected the torpedoes during loading. "Forty to fifty men produced a vast quantity of rubbish. Potato peel and vegetable waste alone made huge heaps. The dampness of the interior usually made other products such as bread go mouldy, which then had to be added to the waste pile. Normally the atmosphere inside a U-boat was foul enough but the additional garbage stench made life even more difficult for the crew."[17] The ordinary seamen suffered the most as their mess was in the torpedo stowage compartment. This only exacerbated yet another problem associated with schnorchelling. At the beginning of a patrol the seamen had to share their mess with the spare torpedoes and these were stored at deck level. Until some torpedoes had been fired and the tubes reloaded, the spares were covered with a temporary wooden plank deck whose height made it impossible for the occupants to stand erect or even sit in the usual way. As the schnorchel-boats of October 1944 found precious few targets and must be assumed to have fired commensurately few torpedoes, seamen were obliged to spend yet longer periods on their backs in their hammocks.

The mental condition of men after weeks of this sort of existence can scarcely be imagined. Boredom was always a preoccupation of U-boat commanders and methods of combating it featured prominently in a widely disseminated lecture to new commanders.[18] But the word seems barely adequate to describe the strains of life constantly underwater, in such sparse surroundings and against such a ubiquitous and implacable opponent. Many men developed a neurotic condition not dissimilar to the front-line infantryman's 'combat fatigue'. Characterised variously by utter lassitude, helpless despair or hypersensitive reactions and reflexes it was known to the Germans as *Blechkrankheit*, or *Blechkoller*, which could be translated as 'tin-can-itis', a hysterical aversion to being cooped up in a tin can, living out of tins. The word *Blech* can also mean 'rubbish' or 'balderdash', which might accurately describe many of the new hands' reflections on the glowing recruiting posters that had tempted them to the U-boat arm in the first place.

Perhaps the most telling depiction of the U-boat crews' state of mind in the last months of the war, and one particularly relevant to the foetid, furtive life on board a schnorchel-boat, is that of a German officer of the time: "From 1943 onward the U-boat men began to feel not only isolated but excluded from the normal world. Whenever they appeared on the surface of the seven seas they would be harried and hunted to death. It gave them a currish mentality – Dachshund conscience they called it – cringing, [yet] at the same time waiting only for the chance to snap back at their pursuers."[19]

*

Not all U-boat commanders were cringing in October 1944. On the 25th Kapitän-Leutnant Peter Cremer, with his new crew, had just taken charge of submarine U-2519. The boat had been launched only a week before and was still being completed by the builders. But Cremer and his officers took a keen interest in this work and from the 19th divided their time between the U-boat and the depot-ship *Veendam* on which they ate and slept. The U-boat was one of the new Type XXI class and it "won the crew's total approval, particularly as its larger dimensions gave them greater freedom of movement than the former 'greater German diving tubes' as . . . [one U-boat veteran] had called them. There were two living and sleeping spaces with a bunk for everyone and a washroom with showers. And, most important, there were three toilets instead of the former primitive lavatory which frequently had to serve as food store as well."[20]

Test runs did not begin until after the 25th and the boat was commissioned, but other commanders and senior U-boat staff were already aware that a powerful weapon was now beginning to come off the slipways. For the boats' improved accommodation was really only an afterthought and what was really impressive about the Type XXIs was their significantly improved all-round performance as an underwater weapons system.[21]

The key feature was that the maximum speed underwater was faster than the surface speed. Although this was only possible for an hour or so before the batteries would need charging again, it was more than enough to allow U-boat commanders to glide in unobserved for an attack and then make a speedy exit. It was still not as fast as the more modern escorts, but the difference was small and would only tell if an escort was able to stay on the track of the U-boat from the moment of an attack. As soon as contact was lost the high silent-running submerged speed of 5 knots, which could be maintained for two days or more, virtually guaranteed a safe escape. The much improved underwater performance was made possible by using new, super-light, high-capacity batteries. The number of batteries was also increased in the more capacious hulls, originally designed for the revolutionary Walter turbine submarines. Despite the Walter's promise of greatly enhanced submerged performance which generated its own oxygen, the turbine depended on Perhydrol for fuel and that was extremely expensive, explosively sensitive to impurities, and was in much demand for the V-2 rocket programme.

The Electro-boats, as the Type XXIs were often known, seemed a more the than adequate compromise between the traditional boats and the Walter design, which was put on the experimental back burner. Promising much more than just high underwater performance and endurance, the Type XXIs were also equipped with sonar on the conning-tower and hydrophones in the bows, a sophisticated passive echo chamber which could track, identify and range multiple targets up to 50 miles away while the boat was completely submerged. "Attack was carried out in a very different manner from that in conventional boats. Once the target had been sighted or revealed by radar or hydrophones, the manoeuvre consisted of running at high speed on a collision course at depth, until the target area was reached. Without recourse to the periscope, target distance and bearing could be determined with a high degree of accuracy by sonar and hydrophone and computed in a fire control centre."[22] These computations were automatically set in the new Lut torpedoes which were then fired, from depths of up to 160 feet, in spreads of six at five- and fifteen-second intervals. The torpedoes spread out fan-wise until they covered the entire length of a convoy and then began running in loops, zig-zagging across the convoy's mean course at a speed calculated to guarantee a hit on one ship or another. Other refinements in the Type XXIs were a schnorchel head coated in radar-absorbent 'stealth' synthetic rubber and hydraulically loaded torpedoes. Six bow torpedo tubes could be loaded in twelve minutes, as compared to the ten to twenty minutes it took to load just one tube in a Type VIIC. Once enough boats were available, Admiral Dönitz hoped to resume pack tactics in the Atlantic, and to this end he began elaborating procedures for employing Luftwaffe reconnaissance aircraft.

On a purely technological level, therefore, Dönitz was perfectly justified in placing great faith in these boats. As he himself wrote: "The advent of these new types put an end to the supremacy which the enemy's defence had enjoyed over the U-boat since 1943 and which had been due to the introduction of the ultra short-wave surface radar. The U-boat would remain undetectable by radar under water, it could now operate at a depth at which it was safe and deliver its attack from the same depth. New possibilities had been opened up for the boats, new successes were within our grasp."[23]

Such optimism had been virtually unalloyed in June 1943, when Dönitz had seen the first blueprints of the new boats, and had percolated through to Hitler and his Minister for Munitions, Albert Speer. When Speer took over responsibility for building the new boats from the Naval Construction Branch he delegated it to the Central Shipbuilding Commission, under Otto Merker, which insisted that only mass-production techniques, using prefabricated parts built at various inland sites and then assembled in three proper dockyards, could meet the urgent demand for the new boats. Merker proved his case emphatically. Whereas the Kriegsmarine had been able to promise only two prototypes by December 1944, the ex-industrialist guaranteed mass-production versions by late spring. A monthly production of 40 Type XXIs and XXIIIs was planned and approved by Hitler but the programme got off to a bad start, and just how optimistic Dönitz remained in October 1944 is open to question. Certainly, he still had no Type XXIs at sea by the 25th.[24] Difficulties in obtaining lead and rubber for the batteries and other electrical fittings, poor workmanship in the prefabrication plants, labour shortages, and the increasing tempo of Allied bombing of the dockyards, prefabrication sites and electrical firms, and most crucially of all of the canals by which the huge prefabricated sections were taken to the ports, all meant that the Electro-boat programme fell further and further behind schedule. By the end of October, there should have been some 160 Type XXIs and XXIIIs in commission but the actual number was only 50. Worse, familiarising the crews with the mass of sophisticated equipment and the new tactical doctrine it must engender was proving remarkably time-consuming and no Type XXI seemed anywhere near ready to go out on patrol.

Nevertheless, the Allied ASW organisation was most definitely worried about the possibility of a renewed U-boat offensive. Not only did it have wind of a new revolutionary type of enemy submarine, it was also painfully aware that even the old types, when equipped with the schnorchel, were proving extremely difficult to detect. At first the

Allies thought the schnorchel was exclusively for the new Walter boats, and then learned that it was being fitted to existing U-boats. When, at the end of April, photo–reconnaissance flights picked out Type XXIs being assembled, it was clear that these were a quite different type of boat. The photos also prompted the disquieting deduction that they were being completed in six weeks rather than the normal five months associated with the naval dockyards. ULTRA decrypts of reports sent by the head of the Japanese Naval Mission in Berlin gave details of the general nature of these new Electro-boats. In October the Royal Navy's Intelligence Division drew up a report summarising the Japanese conclusions that "the Type XXI is an epoch-making U-boat, to the construction of which the Germans have devoted every possible effort and made use of practical fighting experience as well as the cream of scientific knowledge. Though the boat will no doubt need certain improvements the Naval Attaché felt that its tactical value could be very great."[25]

Many RN officers were as alarmed as the Japanese Naval Attaché was hopeful. One of the most anxious was Captain Roger Winn, in charge of the Submarine Tracking Room at the Navy's Operational Intelligence Centre. He "began, from October onwards, to emphasise more and more strongly in his verbal and written reports the dangers which might still lie ahead and the folly of prematurely lowering our guard."[26] One Tracking Room report was passed on by the First Sea Lord, Admiral of the Fleet Sir Andrew Cunningham, to Winston Churchill and his covering note of 23rd October suggested that "the introduction of the SNORT . . . and the new type of U-boat . . . may provide us with a tough proposition.[27] Winn himself was predicting 25 operational Type XXIs and XXIIIs by the end of November and 73 by February 1945.

Equally concerned were the instructors at the Liverpool Tactical School who taught the theory and practice of ASW to officers in the convoy Escort and Support Groups. The submerged speed of the new U-boats was what worried them most, as this might force pursuers to sail at speeds at which their asdic and sonar were ineffective. Also worrying was the suggestion that by the time any escort armed with conventional depth charges had got itself into the standard position ahead of the U-boat, for a stern-launched salvo, a Type XXI would already have fled the danger area. Forward-throwing Hedgehog and Squid launchers offered better prospects but these had only been installed on some of the newer escort ships.

A further worry, for intelligence staff and tacticians alike, was that a new, concerted U-boat offensive in the Atlantic might dangerously overstretch Allied resources. Having seemingly won the Battle of the Atlantic, the Americans were now directing more and more naval resources to the Pacific, leaving the British and Canadians to look after North Atlantic convoys. The Royal Navy was also finding that it could spare fewer and fewer ships for Atlantic escort and patrol as numerous escort vessels had to be deployed in British coastal waters where the schnorchel-boats were mostly lurking.

In October 1944 the Allies were also concerned that U-boats had virtually disappeared from the intelligence picture and that enormous naval and air force resources were swallowed up in chasing will-o'-the-wisps. Although the schnorchel may have been a mixed blessing to a U-boat commander, it represented a fearsome threat to Allied intelligence. By running submerged most of the time, U-boats could not use their radios and so offered no transmissions for Huff Duff to pinpoint or for ULTRA to monitor or decrypt. Even when routine signals traffic revealed the date a U-boat had left base, it was proving increasingly difficult to predict later positions as the average speed of submerged boats varied considerably.

Radar, too, was largely neutralised. The U-boat crews, still fearful of aircraft after their experiences in the North Atlantic and the Bay of Biscay, were acutely sensitive to the possibility of the schnorchel head being detected. In fact, only 3cm radar had any real chance of picking up such a small target, and only then in a fairly calm sea. An official RAF staff history of operations at this time concluded that "the aircraft had descended from its exalted position of 'U-boat Killer No.1' to the humble yet useful role of scarecrow to ensure the continual submergence of U-boats while at sea and consequent lack of mobility."[28] Surface craft were equally handicapped and found that asdic was much less effective in coastal waters, especially in the shallows where rocks and wrecks produced false echoes and tide-rips and density layers deflected the beam. The First Sea Lord was moved to write at about this time: "We are having a difficult time with U-boats . . . The air [force] are about 90 per cent out of business. The asdic is failing us."[29] The Submarine Tracking Room was similarly discouraged, having to admit that its plot for much of October "did not succeed at all closely in reproducing the reality".[30]

This new technological myopia greatly increased the tempo of ASW operations. As air and surface radar operators became aware what a small target a schnorchel head was, they began to see them everywhere. The trouble was that genuine schnorchel head "contacts were indistinguishable from those coming from flotsam such as casks, crates, oil drums etc. and the more momentary echoes off prominent wave-tops, whales spouting or even porpoises leaping. Many of the echoes disappeared off the ASV screen, due to some of the above natural reasons, as the aircraft homed towards them, but could give rise to a suspicion that a U-boat had detected the ASV impulse and dived."[31] Such false contacts were often passed as genuine and would generate a flurry of extra patrol activity by supporting aircraft or surface vessels. And all this occasioned by that same fleet of old Type VIIs and IXs once thought to be moribund.

In fact, far from being a spent force, these U-boats, with the simple addition of a schnorchel, were tying up an increasing proportion of Allied ASW assets at the very time they feared a renewed oceanic offensive by brand-new schnorchel-boats, with a virtually fire-and-forget torpedo system and able to do that forgetting at a considerable rate of knots. These new boats would probably also remain immune to signals interception. Some might not communicate with base at all. Others might do so only occasionally, to receive cryptic elaborations or confirmations of written orders received when leaving base, and which would thus mean nothing to any eavesdropper. Yet others might communicate via a *Sonderschlüssel* cypher machine, using key settings unique to an individual U-boat and therefore impervious to the generalised 'number crunching' methods of the ULTRA bombes. Equalling worrying was the existence of *Kurier*, a prototype off-frequency, high-speed transmission apparatus which was known to have transmitted from a U-boat in August and been picked up in Germany, but had not been intercepted at the time by any British stations.

October, then, was a distinctly sombre month for all those concerned with organising U-boat countermeasures. Yet at least one of the U-boats at sea on the 25th must have given those privy to ULTRA some grim satisfaction and reassurance that Enigma machines had not gone completely silent. When this boat, U-1227, came on station off Gibraltar, its presence only became known to the Allies through the decrypt of a signal assuring the captain that its surprise appearance should offer a good chance for success.

26

The Lonely Queen

TIRPITZ AND THE GERMAN SURFACE FLEET

WHILE Dönitz's U-boat fleet was haplessly doggy-paddling around the coastal waters of Britain, his men seeing little through their periscopes and sinking precisely nothing, the individual captains could at least buoy themselves up with the hope of better days to come. Commanders and crews in the surface fleet had no such consolation. They were part of a force in manifest and irreversible decline and one which the Führer held in little short of contempt. Before the war he had seemed to display a traditional Wilhelmine concern for building up a powerful High Seas Fleet and had endorsed a naval expansion plan, Plan Z, that envisaged building by 1947 a fleet of 23 battleships and battle-cruisers, 4 aircraft carriers, 27 cruisers and 136 destroyers and torpedo ships. Yet Hitler chose to go to war before this construction was properly under way and this soon called for a major diversion of the necessary plant, raw materials and workers.

As early as 1941, Plan Z was nothing but a faint memory for the Kriegsmarine and by the following year just the mention of German surface ships could spoil Hitler's day. In December 1942, two German heavy cruisers and some destroyers had sailed out of Altenfjord, in Norway, to attack one of the Allies' Arctic convoys to Murmansk, a sortie for which Hitler had come to entertain high hopes. In the event, at the Battle of the Barents Sea, very little was achieved and Hitler was so enraged that he demanded the decommissioning and possible scrapping of the entire surface fleet. The naval commander-in-chief, Admiral Erich Raeder, managed to placate Hitler a little, but only at the cost of his resignation and it fell to his successor, Dönitz, to wheedle a six-month stay of execution, pending more stirring naval exploits.

The six months passed without the High Seas Fleet doing much to restore its reputation, but by then Hitler seemed to have forgotten, or chose to forget, the original deadline. Although the Fleet survived, it was as a moribund force, a mere shadow of what it had been in 1940, let alone of the Z Plan projections. The table below highlights this decline, in terms both of ships extant on 25th October 1944 and of the firepower these individual units represented:[1]

Type of Ship	Commis- sioned*	Sunk	Immob- ilised	Operat- ional†
BB	4	2	2	–
PBB	3	1	–	2
CA	3	1	1	1
CL	6	2	2	2
DD	40	21	3	16
TDD	47	26	5	16

Size of Gun	Number of guns on ships that were:				
	Commis- sioned*	Sunk	Immob- ilised	Operat- ional†	% Oper- ational
15″	16	8	8	–	–
11″	36	15	9	12	33.3
8″	24	8	8	8	33.3
5.9″	195	79	41	75	38.5
5″	128	81	8	39	30.5
4.1″‡	97	53	11	33	34.0
4″	18	18	–	–	–

*To October 1944. German-built only.
†Includes ships on training duties.
‡Not A.A.

In short, none of the big-gun battleships and battle-cruisers were still operational in October, or likely to be again, and of the other ships commissioned, roughly two-thirds of their firepower had been lost at sea or was tied up in port and dry-dock.

The fate of the larger ships, including heavy cruisers, was the bitterest blow to Dönitz and the commander-in-chief of the High Seas Fleet, Admiral Meendsen-Bohlken. One battleship, *Bismarck*, had been sunk and her sister ship, *Tirpitz*, had been so heavily mined and bombed that she was being shored up in a Norwegian fjord to serve more or less as a 'floating battery'. One of the battle-cruisers, *Scharnhorst*, had also been sunk and the other, *Gneisenau*, was in dock at Gotenhafen after being bombed in February 1942, with plans for a refit now abandoned. Of the pocket-battleships, *Graf Spee* had been scuttled, though *Lützow* (ex-*Deutschland*) and *Admiral Scheer* were both available for operations in the Baltic. Of the heavy cruisers, *Blücher* had been sunk, *Admiral Hipper* was training U-boat crews, and *Prinz Eugen* was undergoing repairs at Gotenhafen (Gydnia). It is hardly surprising that what made dismal reading for Dönitz and Meendsen-Bohlken proved terminal for Admiral Rudolf Peters. Appointed as Commander-in-Chief *Kampfgruppe* in June 1944, a post originally known as C.-in-C. Battleships and later C.-in-C. Cruisers, his job was abolished on 25th October.

A prime reason for the abolition of a separate battleship command was the fate of the *Tirpitz*. This impressive ship was armed with eight 15-inch and twelve 5.9-inch guns, had a main belt of 12.6-inch armour above the lower deck, yet was capable of a top speed of 30 knots. Since January 1942 the ship had been stationed in Norway, where she represented a potent threat to Allied convoy routes both in the Atlantic and the Arctic. In December 1941, indeed, Hitler had asserted that "every ship that is not in Norway is in the wrong place", but in fact his rationale was largely defensive. Ever since the commando raids on the Lofoten Islands and Vaasgö, in the spring and summer of that year, he had been obsessed with the possibility of an invasion of Norway, and it was to guard against this that *Tirpitz* had been dispatched.

Commerce raiding, then, was to receive only a low priority and whenever such operations were mooted, Hitler imposed so many constraints about guaranteeing non-intervention by British battleships and aircraft carriers that *Tirpitz* was hardly ever able to leave port, and its record in Norwegian waters made sorry reading. From January to July 1942 she was moored in Foettenfjord, near Trondheim, sallying forth only once, from 6th to 9th March, to attack Arctic convoy PQ12. The great warship's only achievement on this occasion was to evade a torpedo attack by the Fleet Air Arm. On 2nd July, *Tirpitz* left Trondheim for Altenfjord from where she moved against convoy PQ17 on the 5th, but remained at sea for only 4½ hours and never closed with the convoy. She returned to Altenfjord and stayed there until late October, when she returned to Trondheim for a refit, which took until March 1943, before moving back to Altenfjord. From then until 15th October 1944, except for brief sea-trials, the battleship ventured forth offensively only once, for an attack on a small British and Norwegian meteorological station at Spitzbergen on 6th September 1943. A few wooden buildings were destroyed and some prisoners taken, and the station was rebuilt within a few weeks. This proved to be the only time

Tirpitz fired its main armament against a surface target, and from January 1942 to October 1944 it never fired at another warship, nor a vessel of any description. Various destroyers were also stationed with *Tirpitz*, as well as at other Norwegian ports, and their routine was equally circumscribed by Hitler's extreme caution. This "in practice meant months of inactivity, swinging to buoys or moored to piers in remote, inaccessible fjords far in the north of Norway ... Morale suffered through boredom and the level of junior officers' and ratings' training deteriorated badly. Time at sea averaged only two days per month."[2]

Chafe, blush even, as the sailors might at their dismal combat record, those on *Tirpitz* were entitled to feel some satisfaction with their achievements. For though their ship rarely poked its bows out of the narrow fjords, its mere presence in Norwegian waters posed such a threat to Allied shipping that large numbers of capital ships, cruisers and destroyers were tied up off the northern coast of Britain, either to provide protection for the Arctic convoys or to stage a repeat performance (though less panic-stricken) of the hunt for *Bismarck* in May 1941. For by 1944 the Germans were beginning to make a virtue out of necessity and were touting *Tirpitz*'s enforced idleness as the Kriegsmarine's version of a 'cunning plan'. In April, Dönitz reported to Hitler at his Berghof headquarters that *Tirpitz* was "to be repaired and to remain stationed in Norway ... Regardless of how much work and manpower is involved, the repairs must be made. After all, the presence of the *Tirpitz* ties up enemy forces. The ship will hardly have any further opportunity for action ... [as] air attacks have shown that a ship is helpless without fighter escort ... The Führer voices his wholehearted approval."[3] But just because these pronouncements were largely an *ex post facto* rationalisation does not mean that they were invalid. Even in October 1944, when the critical Battle of the Atlantic seemed to have been won by the Allies at least temporarily, and at a time when Churchill and the Royal Navy were brazenly trying to gatecrash a substantial British fleet presence into the Pacific War, not only were considerable forces stationed in northern and east coast naval bases but just one Arctic convoy, JW61, which sailed from Loch Ewe on 20th October, was thought to require a force of three escort carriers, one cruiser, seven destroyers, twelve escort destroyers, two sloops and three corvettes.

Yet the British had not been content to maintain a purely defensive posture. Always keen to free ships for Atlantic duties and later for deployment to the Pacific, the Royal Navy made continual efforts to rid

itself of the menace of the *Tirpitz*. To the Norwegians, she had become
known as the *Ensom Donning*, or 'The Lonely Queen', but to Churchill
and the Admiralty she was more a malevolent Queen of Spades, to be
trumped at the earliest opportunity. To this end, a whole series of raids
had been staged after the failure of the *Victorious* strikes during
Tirpitz's sortie against convoy PQ12. Bomber Command was the first
to try and made repeated raids on Trondheim during January, March
and April 1942. None inflicted any damage and eleven bombers were
lost. In October of that year the Royal Navy took charge and mounted
a courageous attack by two human torpedos, or 'chariots', into
Frettenfjord. Unfortunately, they were never actually launched as both
broke the connections securing them to the trawler mother-ship and
were lost. Undismayed, the Navy tried again the following September,
once more calling upon so-called 'volunteers for hazardous operations'.
This time they tried to sneak up on *Tirpitz* in X-boats, 4-man
miniature submarines each carrying two 2-ton Amatex side-charges.
Two of these craft did manage to release their charges near the battleship and the subsequent time-delayed explosions caused considerable
damage. Two 15-inch turrets were lifted off their turntables, electrical
equipment, propellers and rudder were smashed and buckled, and
many tons of water flooded into the lower compartments.

   Without a dry-dock, repairs proved tricky, involving many
ingenious extemporised techniques, and the ship was not battle-worthy
again until early March 1944. The Royal Navy almost immediately
took up the challenge once more, this time with the Fleet Air Arm.
Between April and August six carrier strikes were mounted (and four
others aborted due to bad weather), but only the first of these did any
real damage to *Tirpitz*. Fourteen 1,600-lb and 500-lb bombs hit the
target and damage to the ship's superstructure, especially in the
wardroom, gunroom and mess decks, as well as to the complex fire-
control system, was considerable. Some keel plates had also been
buckled, and this again caused underwater flooding. Almost 450
officers and men were killed or wounded.

   Even so, the damage was still far from terminal, mainly because
none of the bombs had penetrated the 8 inches of armour on the lower
deck, that protected the engine and boiler rooms and the underwater
portion of the hull. Because of the fast-approaching deadline for the
transfer of Royal Navy ships to the Pacific, the Allied Joint Planning
Staff began to take an increasing interest in *Tirpitz*'s fate and in August
it was suggested that the 'contract' be handed back to Bomber
Command. Air Chief Marshal Harris described his response to this

request with his inimitable curmudgeonly superciliousness: "During all this period the Admiralty continued to worry about the German Navy and . . . our battleships, with their usual large complement of ancillary craft, were kept hanging about at home in case the Germans should decide to send the poor old lone *Tirpitz* to sea . . . I was accordingly asked to intervene in this fantastic 'war' between these dinosaurs which both sides had just managed . . . to preserve from their long overdue extinction. I was quite willing to do so, but only if this did not seriously interfere with more important operations; I gave an undertaking that we would sink the *Tirpitz* in our spare time."[4]

After the failure of the earlier bombing attacks on *Tirpitz*, it was realised that Bomber Command could not really afford to be as casual as Harris implied. Far from assigning the task to any squadron with nothing better to do, the authorities chose 617 Squadron which had a reputation second to none for precision bombing. The squadron, uniquely, had been formed to carry out one specific mission, the destruction of the four Ruhr Dams, and, under the leadership of Squadron-Leader Guy Gibson, two of these had been breached in May 1943. Subsequently, however, it was realised that the squadron's collective expertise and specialised equipment, such as the SABS bombsight, made the crews too valuable simply to be dispersed back to their original units. So the squadron survived and was used for whatever precision missions Harris was prepared to sanction. These included raids on Italian power stations in July 1943, on the Dortmund–Ems Canal in September, on various French armaments factories in May 1944, and on the Saumur railway tunnel just after D-Day.

In this latter raid the 'Tallboy' bomb had been used for the first time. This 12,000-lb bomb had been specially designed by Professor Barnes-Wallis to penetrate great thicknesses of earth, rock, concrete, armour-plate or whatever before it exploded. Containing 5,100lb of Torpex, its optimal dropping height was 18,000 feet, at an air speed of 170 m.p.h., in which event it should plummet to earth in just under forty seconds, impacting on the target at roughly 750 m.p.h. The depth at which it actually exploded could be accurately pre-set with three time-fuses in the tail. The 'Dambusters' were clearly the ideal team to try to bring Tallboy and *Tirpitz* together, though for this mission they were joined by 9 Squadron, generally regarded as the most accurate of the normal bomber squadrons.

The first raid was made on 15th September 1944, while *Tirpitz* was at the Altenfjord anchorage. This was too far from British airfields to permit a continuous round trip and so the bombers staged from a Russian air base at Yagodnik, near Archangel. Twenty-seven Lancasters took part, of which 21 carried a single Tallboy, the others being loaded with 'Johnny Walker' buoyancy mines. Vital to *Tirpitz*'s protection in Altenfjord was an elaborate early-warning radar system and a whole array of smoke generators in adjacent trawlers and on the surrounding high ground. Smoke could be belching out within 7 to 8 minutes of a radar alert and so it was on the 15th. In fact, only the lead Lancaster even saw *Tirpitz*, and then only her mastheads, but this proved sufficient for the master-bomber who sent a Tallboy smashing through the battleship's bow. A few other planes registered near misses, which with bombs of that size were enough to weaken and buckle plates and fittings.

It was the actual hit that did the real damage. The bomb had passed through the bow and the side and then exploded beneath the keel. This explosion "and the huge mass of water which it raised rolled back the deck of the ship as one rolls back the cover of a tin of sardines. More serious . . . was the fact that the explosion had damaged the forward frames, already strained by the charges from the X-craft, so badly that the ship could no longer steam more than six knots."[5] The explosion also ripped open a huge hole in *Tirpitz*'s side, fully 32 feet wide and 48 feet long, into which gushed more than 1,000 tons of sea-water. This caused the bows to settle eight feet deeper than usual and even when counter-flooding once more put the ship on an even keel, it was three feet lower in the water. Once again 617 Squadron had proved the aptness of its motto, '*Après moi le déluge*'.

German engineers soon concluded that *Tirpitz* was effectively finished. Repairs would take at least nine months and could only be done properly in a German dockyard. As it was extremely unlikely that *Tirpitz* would survive such a long and dangerous passage, Dönitz decided to designate her officially as a *schwimmende Batterie*, floating battery, that would help to repulse any attempted Allied landings in Normandy, a contingency still much feared by Hitler. But Altenfjord was now perilously close to the battle front, as the Russians pushed forward in the wake of retreating 20 Mountain Army. So *Tirpitz* was moved one last time on 15th October when she left Altenfjord for Tromsö, 200 miles to the south. She was to be moored off Haakoy Island, three miles west of the town, where the ship would form part of a new defensive line being cobbled together in the Lyngenfjord area. "The entire damaged bow section was 'hinged' on the port side, and temporary stringers were welded across the gaping hole in the starboard side, stiffening the structure sufficiently to allow the ship to proceed at a maximum speed of 8 knots."[6] In this way *Tirpitz* reached Tromsö safely on the 16th.

The Haakoy anchorage had been chosen because the water there was sufficiently shallow that were *Tirpitz* to be attacked and holed again she would not capsize, and even if she sank her guns would remain above water. Unfortunately, once the battleship was moored it was found that the original soundings were incorrect and that there was more than enough water beneath her keel for the ship to overturn completely. As further air attacks were deemed almost inevitable, it was decided to revise the soundings the hard way, by dredging and dumping one million cubic feet of rubble under and around the ship to reduce the depth of the water.[7]

Not privy to such details, the British were only interested in establishing just what damage had been done to *Tirpitz*, for clearly the vessel had not sunk. A photo-reconnaissance flight on 20th September obtained some pictures but the battleship itself was in shadow. Enigma decrypts of messages sent by Dönitz on 16th and 25th September provided more encouraging news. The first admitted that the ship had been hit and that this had had "serious consequences", while the second, sent to all naval attachés, stated that in public the Germans would withhold details of the extensive damage inflicted. A further decrypt on the 29th, of a message to all U-boats, confirmed the new status of *Tirpitz* as a floating battery, affirming that she "has now sustained a bomb hit but by holding out in the operational area the ship will continue to tie down enemy forces and by her presence confound the enemy's intentions."[8]

The British were presumably somewhat non-plussed, therefore, when *Tirpitz* contrived to sail to Tromsö, albeit in a very gingerly manner, and it was this more than anything that prompted the Admiralty to ask Harris to attack the battleship once again. In further Enigma decrypts, received after the move to Tromsö, a Norwegian agent confirmed her arrival, and two sets of photographs were obtained by Fleet Air Arm Fireflies and a PR Mosquito, but none of this seems to have convinced the Admiralty that *Tirpitz* was now virtually *hors de combat*. One writer on this topic has criticised the decision to launch another bombing raid, suggesting that "it may be wondered why so many lives should have been risked and so much effort expended in attacking a target that had now ceased to threaten them."[9] All the same, it was not entirely clear to the authorities just how permanent was the damage to *Tirpitz*, and it would have ill-behoved the British to stop attacking her and so give a clear signal that they had no intention of attempting the landings in Norway that the Germans so much feared. If two squadrons of bombers could help persuade the Germans to keep troops in Norway – and on 25th October there were three mountain, one weak panzer and thirteen infantry divisions in the northern theatre – then even heavy aircraft losses were still a very good bargain for the Allies.[10]

If *Tirpitz*'s move to Tromsö persuaded the British to undertake another bombing mission, again by 617 and 9 Squadrons, it also considerably simplified the task. For Tromsö was within range of the most northerly British air bases and so there would be no need to stage at the bleak, albeit hospitable Russian Arctic base. Nevertheless, with the huge Tallboys on board, the planes would still be at the extreme limit of their reach. When final plans were issued for a raid on 24th October, provision was made for emergency landings at two Russian bases or at a specially equipped airfield at Skatsta on the north mainland of the Shetlands. But these were last resorts and the RAF devoted most of its effort to reducing the Lancasters' normal weight to allow them to accommodate both the Tallboys and extra fuel. Planes and ground crews moved from their home bases at Woodhall Spa and Bardney in Lincolnshire up to Lossiemouth in Scotland, and there the fitters worked night and day to get the planes ready for take-off on the 28th. Mid-upper turrets were removed, as well as the requirement for this crew member; front guns and ammunition went too, as well as much of the rear turret ammunition, the pilot's armour plate, numerous oxygen and nitrogen bottles, and the Tri-cell flare chute. Overall weight of each plane was cut by some 68,000lbs. Most of the flight was to be carried out at 2,000 feet to conserve the meagre supplies of oxygen. To maximise range, the Merlin engines were all replaced with the more powerful Mark XXIVs scavenged from aircraft throughout Bomber Command. Finally, each aircraft was fitted with extra fuel tanks to provide an extra 252 gallons of gasoline that should just about get them there and back.

On the 25th, as the groundcrews began to strip and re-equip the bombers, the flight personnel went over the details of Operation OBVIATE, as the raid had been dubbed. Due to the distance to the target, no fighter escort could be provided. It was vital not to alert German radar defences and so stir up the *Gruppe* of Messerschmitts from 5 *Geschwader* that had recently arrived at the nearby air base at Bardufoss. RAF radar reconnaissance aircraft had already plotted German radar in this area and had found that there was a gap in the cover provided, as long as the intruders flew at 1,500 feet or below. To ensure surprise, RAF planners decided to keep the bombers beneath this height once within radar range, but when through the gap on the central Norwegian coast, "they were to continue almost due eastwards over the mountain range and into Sweden; then, keeping the mountain barrier as a screen between themselves and the prying German radar beams, the bombers were to approach *Tirpitz* from the landward side where they were least expected."[11] The climb to the correct height for dropping the Tallboys was to be delayed to the last possible moment.

As Bomber Command plotted the final destruction of the 'Lonely Queen', the battleship and its few accompanying vessels tried to make the best of this last berth.[12] *Tirpitz* had just taken a new captain on board, Kapitän Robert Weber, who immediately busied himself with establishing an adequate defensive screen. With *Tirpitz* had come the AA guns from Altenfjord, sixty in all, as well as the smoke generators. The guns were already in place but installing the smoke equipment was proving extremely difficult and was unlikely to be finished before December. On the ship itself only a skeleton crew remained, with 500 men, mainly from the engine-room, having been billeted on shore. But Kapitän Weber's main concern was to compensate for the sounding error and lay his hands on the one million cubic feet of rubble as well as to round up the requisite hoppers and dredgers. By 25th October, the work had still not begun. All in all it was a sorry situation for every member of the Kriegsmarine when their only surviving battleship was incapable of ever going to sea again and was largely concerned with just how and where she was going to sink.

*

Other than *Tirpitz* and her escorts, the rest of the German surface fleet in late October was stationed in the Baltic. Essentially this was due to there being few other ports open to German shipping, but there were also valid military reasons, for what had once been a German lake was now becoming a battle zone, with large stretches of the coastline falling to the enemy. On 10th October Russian forces had driven through to the Lithuanian coast, around Memel, and bottled up Army Group North in the Courland peninsula and Memel itself. Most worrying of all was the loss of the Finns as an ally after their armistice with the Russians in September. Previously the Germans had been able to contain the Soviet Baltic Fleet in the Gulf of Finland, with a combination of barrages, natural ice and their naval presence. Now, however, the Soviets could make use of ports on Finland's western coast and, indeed, plans were already afoot to base Allied submarines there. The Finnish defection had also alarmed the Swedes who, although neutral, on 26th September had halted iron ore shipments to Germany. Yet the Germans were still running numerous convoys from Norway, and it was to protect those, in the North Sea and the Skaggerak, that the Kriegsmarine had stationed the light cruiser *Köln*, five destroyers and six torpedo boats back at Horten, 30 miles south of Oslo.

It was in the eastern Baltic that the threat seemed most imminent, especially to the U-boat training areas where the first Type XXI and XXIII boats were working up. To provide protection, several of the ships that Hitler had written off as so much scrap metal in late 1941 were rescued from idleness or lowly training duties and attached to a new *Kampfgruppe* Number Two, under the command of Admiral August Thiele. The pocket-battleships *Lützow* and *Admiral Scheer*, heavy cruisers *Prinz Eugen* and *Admiral Hipper*, and light cruisers *Emden*, *Leipzig* and *Nürnberg* were all made available for operations with Thiele, along with fourteen destroyers and torpedo boats.

By late October, when the Soviet naval threat had still not materialised and with no opponents afloat, the *Kampfgruppe* found itself drawn into the land battles along the coastline, particularly those raging in Courland and Memel. As early as August, *Prinz Eugen* had steamed into the Gulf of Riga to support a German armoured counter-attack around Tukkums with its 8-inch guns, and since then numerous sorties had been made by variously constituted task forces to provide gunfire support and escort, run in supplies, and take off casualties and evacuees. In October the two focuses of this activity were Memel (Klaipeda) and the island of Ösel (Saaremaa). The latter formed part of the Moonsund Archipelago, a group of four islands covering the mouth of the Gulf of Riga. By taking them the Soviets would be able to deny access to German ships, and infantry and marines detached from the Leningrad Front had landed there on 27th September. Three of the islands – Vormsi, Muhu and Hiiumaa – were only lightly garrisoned and had all been cleared by 5th October. On Ösel, however, was a divisional-sized force sent there immediately after Finland's capitulation, and though these troops had been forced to give up most of the island by the 10th, they were able to make a resolute stand on the Sworpe peninsula in the island's drooping southern 'tail'. Despite being reinforced to six divisions, by the 25th repeated Soviet attacks had been unable to break through the heavily-wooded defence lines.

It was the destroyers and torpedo boats that ran most of the missions to Ösel and Memel but bigger ships were involved from time to time. *Prinz Eugen* and *Lützow* added their guns to the support of the Memel garrison while *Admiral Hipper* and *Lützow* performed similar service off Sworbe on the 24th. They were also planning to return on the 28th should the Luftwaffe be able to provide adequate air cover. The rest of the big ships had by then suffered a catalogue of disasters and only *Admiral Scheer* and *Nürnberg* were still available. *Emden* was refitting at Königsberg, while *Prinz Eugen* and *Leipzig* both went into dock at Gotenhafen for repairs. While returning from the latest Memel mission, *Prinz Eugen* was in collision with a light cruiser. Both ships remained locked together for 14 hours, and on separation it was found that the cruiser *Leipzig* was effectively written off. The damage to '*der Prinz*' was much less serious. After examining her, the dockyard chief vowed that she would be ready for sea again in only two weeks. When Thiele and the ship's officers seemed sceptical, they were told that the chief's son had been killed aboard her when she was bombed in Brest in 1941 and that the dockyard chief regarded its repair as a sacred trust. By 25th October the repairs were, indeed, almost completed though there could have been few among her crew who really believed that her 8-inch guns could ever count for much in the awesomely one-sided balance of firepower in Lithuania and East Prussia. Grand Admiral Alfred von Tirpitz had himself once stated: "A warship's best characteristic is that provided it can stay afloat and horizontal it is a gun platform." By late October 1944, both the ship named after him and those deployed in *Kampfgruppe* Number Two were pretty clear evidence of the impotence of such mere '*schwimmende Batterien*'.

PART SIX

Slave Labour and Genocide

27

A Vision of Hell

HITLER'S 'Vengeance Weapons' fell rather short of inducing the civilian terror he sought but they nevertheless remain intimately connected with the very extremes of human suffering. Despite being part of the world's first aerospace industry, V1 and V2 production had little in common with modern perceptions of industrious, white-coated technocrats, gleaming production lines or even government largesse. V2 production was largely undertaken at the Mittelwerk, in the Harz Mountains, a grim labyrinth of dank tunnels and galleries, some up to 90 feet high, and the whole enterprise under the control of Heinrich Himmler's SS. Like most government departments, the SS was perennially short of money and was constantly looking for profit-making businesses of its own. By late 1944, under the aegis of the WVHA, the Main Office for Economics and Administration, Himmler had built up a ramshackle 'conglomerate' of quarries, brickworks, furniture shops, fish processing and mineral water plants, and even a fine porcelain factory. The day-to-day running of these concerns was the responsibility of SS-Gruppenführer Richard Glücks whose Amtsgruppe D was also in charge of running the huge network of German concentration camps. Most of these were slave labour camps and the use of such labour was inseparable from the SS version of capitalist endeavour.

Even such an urgent and precision project as the V2 was no exception. Not only had the Mittelwerk been built by forced labour but in October 1944, when production was rising to a peak, the 2,000 German technicians employed on the V2 project were outnumbered by 32,000 slave labourers – mainly Frenchmen, Belgians and Russians – although the production lines themselves employed a higher

305

proportion of Germans. Allied bombing had forced the Germans to move manufacture of parts and sub-assemblies to the Mittelwerk as well, and so the proportion of German technicians rose from 40 to 55 per cent. Because the overall ratio had serious security implications, 3,000 SS guards of a typically vicious disposition policed the factory and the nearby 'Dora' barracks where the prisoners lived and soon died. Dora was a satellite of the Buchenwald concentration camp and was run according to the same sadistic regime. In charge of transferring prisoners from the main camp to Dora was SS-Gruppenführer Hans Kammler, who had been closely involved in the design of the gas chambers in use at the extermination camps, such as Auschwitz. Although there were no such extermination facilities at Dora, well over 50 per cent of those brought to Mittelwerk died of hunger, disease or physical abuse.

Every slave labourer's day in the Mittelwerk was a living nightmare. When they arrived at the entrance to the main tunnel to start their shift they found two rows of SS guards "shrieking so loudly and lashing out with such ferocity that they were like demons. It really was the gates of hell." During 1944 something like 10,000 workers died, and those still alive worked 12- to 18-hour shifts "at the end of which their reward was three potatoes. Those who became too ill to work were loaded into rail trucks and were never seen again. Those who worked too slowly were killed on the crane, which served both as gallows and execution block."[1] Assembly line workers were treated just as harshly as the others but they at least expended less energy for their three potatoes, and neither did they have to choke on the ammonia dust that rose in clouds with each blow of a pick-axe or hammer. The dust alone could kill but most ordinary labourers succumbed long before that to exhaustion and to pneumonia, dysentery, T.B. and typhus, all of which were rife among the prisoners. Probably the worst job of all was on the actual assembly line in the galvanising and paint shop in Gallery 39, where the fumes were so toxic that no worker was expected to last for more than four weeks.

Mittelwerk was not some sort of experiment, not a hellish anomaly buried under the mountain for fear and shame. This was part and parcel of SS economics, just one of hundreds of enterprises run by WVHA bureaucrats who had contrived to turn the 'dismal science' into an infernal one. For slave labourers were not confined just to the Mittelwerk and other specifically SS sites; they also manned hundreds of enterprises throughout Germany, many of them major armaments works. They were usually quartered in camps and barracks built alongside as satellites to one or other of the big 'feeder' camps. Many of the big camps, which had been in existence for some years, were designed originally to house political prisoners and unregenerate criminal elements. Dachau was the first such, set up in 1933, and even before the outbreak of war it had been joined by Sachsenhausen, Buchenwald, Flossenburg, Mauthausen and Ravensbrück. To cope with the flood of prisoners from Poland and western Europe, other camps were opened, in 1939 and 1940, including Stutthof (near Danzig), Bogusze, Szebnie, Czeszanow and Auschwitz (in German-occupied Poland), Natzweiler (in Alsace), and Neuengamme and Gross Rosen in Germany itself. Of the hundreds of other camps and sub-camps opened up over the following four years, many were evacuated in the face of the Soviet advance into the Ukraine, Poland and the Baltic States, yet still around 20 official camps, 150 or more main labour camps, and literally hundreds of satellites still operated in October 1944. Dachau alone had almost 170 such sub-camps and Buchenwald more than 130. Some sources speak of as many as five million slave labourers toiling on Germany's behalf, including almost two million Soviet prisoners-of-war and countless other civilians rounded up in the aftermath of the Polish and Russian campaigns.

Despite the retreat in the East, slave labourers were still being drafted in their thousands, as for example in the aftermath of the Slovak Uprising, and sent first to one of the bigger camps. To arrive at such a place was to pass in an instant beyond the reach of humanity itself. Prisoners at Ravensbrück, a women's camp, sometimes arrived in proper passenger trains. Upon alighting with hastily-packed suitcases and bags, "we were greeted by cudgels, angry shouts and police dogs. Pushed and slapped, we were lined up in ranks of five and hurried on our way by more blows." The women were marched at the double into an immense hall which had just two doors set into one wall. Pushed and kicked into line, they were propelled through a door one by one, to reappear a few minutes later through the other one. By then they were

naked, empty-handed ... head shaved. Things happened fast behind those doors: a moment to set the bags down, to undress quickly, hastened on by hands that reached out to tear the clothing off; a moment to lie on the table, where one woman held us down while another passed an exploring finger into all our natural orifices; a moment to sit on a stool to have our hair cut off ... [before being given] a scrap of soap, a towel no bigger than a handkerchief, a shower, and then we filed naked and at top speed past women who, with devilish yells, tossed grey drawers fastened with a string, grey shirt, striped dress and mismatched clogs at our heads. We slipped into these things. '*Schnell, schnell.*' Slaps were landing right and left and abusive language exploding all around us. Once again in columns, we were herded outside . . . *schnell, schnell* . . . we scurried . . . *schnell* . . . dragging the clogs over the black sand.[2]

This physical and psychological onslaught was absolutely standard procedure. At Flossenburg new arrivals were met by SS men screaming out orders to do everything at the double, with countless buffets to the head and whip lashes, frenzied dogs barking and snarling and, if at night, under piercing searchlights. "An SS-man asked our group if any of us were boxers, and almost without waiting for a reply he hit some of us with clenched fists. Then we were forced to run up the hill to the camp . . . We were forced to strip naked for disinfection. At the same time we had to give up wedding rings, our watches, everything else of value that we had . . . As we showered – one scalding, one freezing – an SS-man accompanied us mockingly on an accordion. It was pure madness from the word go. People died within the first two hours of arrival – from pure shock, I am sure."[3]

At Mauthausen, an Austrian camp near the Danube, new arrivals were driven into a vast reception area hemmed in on all sides by thick stone ramparts with wooden catwalks attached. On either side of the main entrance were two guard towers and directly opposite it a small building with a granite balcony affording a good view of the camp's surroundings and the desolate approach road. On this balcony was wont to appear the camp commandant, SS-Standartenführer Frank Ziereis, who would scowl down "from his lofty perch and make threatening gestures, pointing to the tall crematorium chimney which endlessly belched black, acrid smoke." The prisoners passed beneath his gaze into the showers where they might begin to rouse from their appalled stupor to find themselves "squatting naked on a wet concrete floor under a communal showerhead and in a wallow of slime, froth and diarrhoea." As one prisoner recounted: "The hair on my bruised [head and] body had been shorn to the skin by a quack 'friseur' plying electric clippers and a cut-throat razor. Hosed free of filth, the next stage of my initiation into the camp was the disinfection room, where a stinging solution of black liquid was daubed over my head and applied to my private parts. Still naked, I was moved to a glory hole densely packed with youths and older men similarly plucked and suffering from skin lesions and bleeding ulcers . . . We crossed, twenty at a time to the clothing store in the main street . . . Strips of rag were issued to cover the feet and I received a pair of 'claquettes', manufactured from wood and canvas. The life of these open-toed sandals was short, yet invariably they outlived the wearers."[4]

Many were still utterly overwhelmed by this fast-track dehumanisation, bereft of rational thought and of any ability to shape responses, feelings, actions that were remotely applicable to this moral anarchy. One spoke of a feeling that was essentially indescribable, of "total despair . . . a terrible, terrible desperate feeling . . . I felt lost and beyond hope."[5] But the corralling, the stripping, the shearing and the spraying were not the end of the matter. Prisoners were now to find out just where they would live and sleep. Their quarters were usually filthy brick-built barrack rooms, or 'Blocks', where washing facilities were long overhead pipes with holes punched in them, latrines were holes cut in cement platforms or wooden planks over holes in the ground, and where beds were wooden or cast-iron bunks, with a thin covering of straw or rags and accommodating three, four, even five sleepers at once. In Buchenwald one prisoner shared a wide wooden bunk with nine others, sleeping on the bare boards and provided with a single blanket of very thin material but "weighed down with fleas and lice, vomit and blood. We slept sardine-like, overwhelmed by the smell of human excreta and diseased bodies, with crawling things constantly gorging on the flesh of skulls, legs, arms and testicles. Throughout the long nights, voices cried out in hunger, in fear, in pain, or from a blow of an unneighbourly fist. Some men still had the strength for strife and scraps." At a satellite camp of Natzweiler the prisoners slept on a three-tiered structure of rough boards covered with straw. "Blankets were very rare and continuously stolen or grabbed in the dark of night, as were clothes and shoes. We slept fully dressed with our muddy shoes or wooden sandals as pillows. There was only enough room to sleep on your side."[6]

Long before dawn the prisoners were brutally roused from their bunks. This was the responsibility of "pugnacious room helps, motivated by extra rations, [who] would roughly waken those fortunate enough to be sleeping, 'encouraging' them with a hail of blows from a stick to the buttocks or a brutal attack in the ribs with any weapon that came to hand." Once awake, prisoners were immediately herded outside under a continuing hail of blows and kicks and were made to form punctiliously dressed lines to answer roll-call, no matter what the weather. By October it was a nightmare experience. At the best of times the prisoners were always hungry, stupid with exhaustion and probably very ill. Come autumn, at a camp like Buchenwald, they also had to contend with parade grounds that were muddy "quagmires, slimy with body filth, blood and phlegm from diseased throats and lungs. Icy winds assailed our body frames as they howled down the bare alleys of the camp ... Each roll-call claimed its victims ... [Many] silently expired where they stood." The procedure at Auschwitz was identical, and on many mornings there were also the bodies of a few prisoners who had died in the night. These had been counted in during evening roll-call the previous day and therefore had to be properly accounted for one last time. "For in this world of 'law and order' the rules are followed meticulously: the dead are laid out on the ground in neat rows, next to the living, for the final count. Across the length of the camp, thousands of gaunt and cringing shapes ... waver in ranks like the dried-up sweepings of subhumanity. The roll call is an elaborate ritual, a macabre mass. The smallest mistake in the checkoff and the count starts anew. Twice a day, I stand immobile, sometimes for hours, in the icy winds."[7]

Roll-call was policed by the same 'room helps' who rousted the prisoners out in the morning. They played a vital role in the hierarchy of oppression in the camps though they were themselves prisoners. Mainly hardened criminals, these people had been among the first to be sent to the camps and, given their complete lack of scruple, proved useful to the authorities in terrorising the mass of political and racial prisoners. Most served as block orderlies and block leaders, *kapos* and *Blockälteste* respectively. The kapos were the NCOs of the system who buffeted, kicked and whipped the prisoners through their daily calvary. According to a prisoner at Sachsenhausen, kapos were "nearly all dishonourable people ... They were really the creatures of the SS ... I never knew any kapos personally, though, and I don't know anyone who did. Most of them only communicated through the bludgeon, the whip and the knife. With my own eyes I saw one kill a prisoner by driving a pick-axe into his stomach. People would run on to the wire and electrocute themselves rather than submit to the sadistic punishments of the kapos."[8]

The only way to minimise their savage attentions was to become utterly non-assertive, a sort of human wraith that hardly ever impinged upon their consciousness. A prisoner who experienced several camps soon realised that one of the essential rules of survival was "absolute submission". Any sense of humiliation or anger had to be completely suppressed until submission "became second nature. For the slightest murmur or pause, look, or gesture that could be interpreted as lack of humility was seized on by the SS and the kapos as sufficient reason for condemning a person on the spot . . . We pressed ourselves against the wall when an SS or a kapo walked into our barrack; we froze and snatched off our caps when we met a German crossing the yard; we tried to be behind the guard or kapo when he turned this way or that, to avoid his glance if it wandered in our direction. We did everything possible, in short, to make ourselves invisible."

Such an intense psychological ordeal relentlessly eroded the will to survive as any sense of self-worth dissolved amid all the cringing and kowtowing. Furthermore, the absolute arbitrariness of camp rule and one's own utter helplessness inevitably left one in a state of constant, acute anxiety. A young prisoner in one of the remaining Polish camps, Plaszow, recalled: "We would go to bed hoping to be able to rest, but in our dreams we relived the things that had happened during that day. We would go to bed with fear and wake up in the morning with it, because each day marked a new, different and often more deadly set of horrors . . . I aged quickly because of the burden of worry and sorrow that I carried around the whole time and the uncertainty of what the next minute might bring. All this preyed on our minds and nerves."[9]

Part and parcel of the systematic dehumanisation of the prisoners was their diet, which was only distinguishable from pig swill by its lower food content. Calorifically it could maintain life for only a few months and, given the vicious work regimen, more usually only for a few weeks. At Ravensbrück, work details breakfasted at 4 a.m. before marching for several miles to a factory in the chill October winds. To sustain them prisoners were given "an unsweetened infusion that was called coffee, nothing else." They got nothing to eat until the morning shift ended, when lunch was "a soup made of cabbage or turnips. Nothing else. No meat and no fat; just water and grit. For dinner, a slice of bread . . . With the bread merely the liquid part of the cabbage or turnip soup. That was all. We were toiling twelve to fourteen hours a day, not counting the roll calls, the *Strafstehen* [punishment roll calls] and the extra details." At one of Natzweiler's satellite camps, where the prisoners were engaged in heavy construction work, the daily meals consisted of: "In the morning one slice of bread with something on it, in the afternoon at work a slice of bread without anything on it, in the evening 1 litre of soup with potatoes in their skin or a lot of unwashed vegetables." A new arrival at Buchenwald, already in a state of shock, was nauseated when he sat down to his first meal. "They gave us stinking soup – it really smelt like sewage; and there was no salt; although we were very hungry, we simply couldn't eat this soup."[10] At Neuengamme, in October 1944, the prisoners were surprised to find bits of meat in their soup, albeit remarkably unpalatable. This in fact was an economy measure as an internal market had been established by which the kitchen kapo and the crematorium kapo sold off any edible soup ingredients to privileged prisoners and fed the others on corpses.[11]

Quite soon, in fact, prisoners would eat almost anything. New arrivals rarely turned up their noses for long, as a newcomer to Buchenwald soon discovered. Most of his block had only just arrived and so a whole pan of soup was being spurned. "The prisoners who were already there got wind of this, and they came over to us. They were skeletons, teeming with lice . . . And they fought each other for the soup. One of the cauldrons was overturned and they fell on the ground, licking the liquid from the dirty floor." Others received a slightly gentler introduction to the realities of camp life. A 15-year-old Polish boy gagged at his first bowl of rotting soup but was told by an older prisoner opposite him that eating anything and everything put in front of him was his only slight hope of survival. Within a few weeks he too was waiting only for mealtimes "when a helping of lukewarm liquid in a rusty container makes the emaciated body tremble in anticipation. You cradle your bowl lovingly, looking for a quiet place where you can eat undisturbed. With closed eyes you sip mouthful by mouthful the ambrosia inside . . . You lick the bowl clean, then your lips and your teeth, and like a Pavlovian dog you begin thinking of that distant hour when the whistle will sound again."[12]

This whole question of the prisoners' diet is a fundamental insight into the nature of the Nazi camp system. Those who ran it remained incapable of repressing their psychopathic instincts so that the slave labourers could at least perform a useful day's work. Instead, those in charge of the camps were permitted to turn the feeding of the prisoners into just one more torture, and one that must inevitably lead to death. Neither was that torture just a question of ever-present, agonising, demented pangs of hunger, to which "all other sensations, even the feeling of pain or the fear of death, become secondary."[13] It was also a means of completing the prisoners' utter degradation. For the vegetables in the soup, usually cabbage, almost always unwashed, would inevitably bring on acute diarrhoea. Not the slightest effort was ever made to prevent this and "excremental assault has been correctly defined as one of the central lines of attack by the SS on the inmates. Diarrhoea was universal and unavoidable; but privies were small and primitive, and could be used only at certain times of the day, or with permission." "Otherwise," in the words of one prisoner, "you just had to go where you stood and let it run down your legs."[14]

A prisoner in one slave labour camp remembered the nights when he extricated himself from his crowded bunk, clambered to the floor and then stumbled 250 yards through the mud to a "small draughty shed with a beam for sitting on when the weakness of your knees proved to be greater than your abhorrence of the shit that dripped from the beam. Paper was not available. Anyone in desperate need who tried to relieve himself just outside was certain to be beaten unconscious by the night guards." At Auschwitz even bodily functions were tightly regimented. Prisoners were allowed to go to the latrine, without paper and for ten seconds each, only once a day. Some went the rest of the time "whenever the need overtook them", so that everywhere in the camp they "were living in the stink of human excrement."[15]

A typical refinement to this daily humiliation was the *Abort-kommando*, or latrine cleaning detail. The procedure at Buchenwald was fairly typical. There the 'good job' was carrying large wooden boxes of slopping excrement to the cesspools. Much worse was to be "forced to climb down into the latrines – deep pits dug in the ground, a stout pole serving as a seat, another for a back rest – to lift out bodies that had toppled over, submerged and eventually drowned in the muck – which dyed our hands, legs and feet." At Dachau, SS pranksters liked to man the latrine detail with professional men and the intelligentsia. "We had to empty the latrine ditches into a soil-wagon, but they didn't give us buckets to do the job, just flat wooden spades. Of course that was on purpose, so that the mess would spill on us and on to our clothes as we worked, and we smelt of excreta day and night." Even so, such men were not more tainted than all the other inmates. At Dautmergen, in Alsace, the barracks contained only a few buckets "for four hundred men to relieve themselves, so the floor was flooded with shit and urine . . . [For] two months not only did I not wash but never, not for one minute, did I undress. Underwear and pyjamas became inseparably attached to my skin by a thick layer of grime and faeces."[16]

On top of all this ceaseless, implacable abuse most prisoners were expected to work, either in the SS's own enterprises or in ordinary German factories, mainly those involved in the manufacture of munitions. Products as diverse as synthetic fuel and bazookas, aircraft engines and uniforms were all turned out with the help of slave labour. The firm of I.G. Farben alone employed at least 20,000 such workers, and thousands of others worked for Junkers, Krupp, Siemens, Telefunken and Porsche. Such firms either had camps erected near their plants or built new ones adjacent to the large concentration camps. A major addition at Auschwitz, for example, was the Auschwitz

III complex at Monowitz, where I.G. Farben had set up a facility to produce synthetic rubber.

Life in a 'civilian' factory was no easier than in one run by the SS. In a synthetic fuel plant belonging to the Steinoel company, the workers came mostly from the nearby Neuengamme camp. Despite the vital importance of the work, the factory and sub-camp were devoid of all amenities. To protect themselves from the plummeting temperatures the prisoners tried to insulate their pyjamas with paper from cement bags lying around the site. The punishment for this 'offence' was twenty-five lashes administered in public. Starvation and disease were routine yet the camp had no medical officer apart from a single orderly who was a bricklayer by trade. Sometimes he was assisted by even less competent inmates, one of whom stated: "Personally I admired the manner in which he set to work, but as he was operating in a haphazard fashion on persons who were already three-quarters dead, it is not surprising that they all died . . . [He] had a scalpel with which he did all his operations. He disinfected it with petrol he stole from the garage. He also had some small pincers and a pair of scissors. There were no anaesthetics . . . The patient was either held down by me or bound to the table."[17]

In autumn 1944 the Germans were frenziedly trying to disperse their most vital war industries away from the cities and usually chose sites close to concentration camps. So it was at Kaufering III, a Dachau satellite, where underground aircraft factories were being quarried out. The treatment of the labourers by the kapos and supervising engineers, from the *Organisation Todt* was so brutal that there were "occasions when the SS stepped in to put a stop to it. The new arrivals . . . were lodged in 60 and 70 round tents, made of papery material, sleeping in trenches which they dug themselves, which were covered in corrugated cardboard for protection against the elements . . . [The] medical facility . . . provided a white powder, based on coal, against diarrhoea (the most common ailment), and iodine as a panacea. However, as in most camps, very few people who dared to complain of illness were given any treatment other than blows to the head." More feverish building was going on at Mühldorf, another Dachau satellite, where assignment to the cement *Kommando* was regarded as an especially sure sentence of death. One man who worked on it saw his companions "falling like flies from the cement; it settled in their lungs. Nobody lasted more than two, three weeks in that commando. They just dried up, visibly dried up as it settled on their lungs. Whether they contracted tuberculosis, or it had the effect of tuberculosis, in any case their noses started running, they developed gangrene in their feet, infection set in. Literally, there were people falling off the gangplank with their bag of cement, and falling dead. There was a death wagon especially to haul away people who died at work."[18]

Again and again one comes up against the lunatic contradiction within the Nazi war machine that demanded, on the one hand, huge increases in war production yet, on the other, was incapable of putting an end to the systematic incapacitation, torture and murder of the very workforce that was supposed to bring these increases about. Some of the ways in which certain officials tried to resolve this contradiction truly reflect the logic of the madhouse. At Porta Westphalia slave labourers were building yet more underground factories, this time to house the Philips electrical plant when it was evacuated from Holland. They were tunnelling through granite and almost fifty per cent of the original prisoners were dead within six months. The workforce was kept topped up with drafts from Neuengamme, mainly Danes. The first wave had been resistance fighters who "knew why they were there; but later the Germans brought in criminal elements they had arrested in Denmark – they simply arrested anyone with a criminal record in order to keep crime down after they had deported 25 per cent of our police."

At a Stutthof sub-camp the prisoners were employed to level sand dunes for an airfield. They were provided with shovels, with which they flung the sand into open trucks as they moved forward. The pace was relentless, both to keep up with the lorries and to keep ahead of the heavy concrete-laying machines which pressed hard on their heels. "It was back-breaking . . . [but] none of the 800 men and women at Kochstadt died at work because every second counted. Prisoners who couldn't make it were loaded on to lorries and taken back to the gas chambers at Stutthof. The lorries brought fresh people back as replacements the same day . . . We were always kept topped up to 800."[19]

Occasionally a very senior Nazi not attached to the SS would attempt to emphasise productivity over sheer sadism. Albert Speer had issued several orders in 1944 about safeguarding workers in aircraft factories, including the slave labourers. At one factory near Stuttgart the orders were given some heed. This factory, too, was built under a mountain and the prisoners lived in a camp outside. During the frequent raids by Allied bombers one of the factory shifts was always sleeping in the camp and the Germans were assiduous in hustling them out of bed and back underground until the raid was over. "Sometimes we'd be shunted back and forth between mountain and barracks several times a day or night." But German solicitude proved as deadly as their more usual malevolence. "More effectively than hunger, more than illness or mistreatment, the systematic denial of sleep over a protracted period of time drained us of our last reserves. We would have given anything, even have risked death by Allied bombardment, for a few hours of uninterrupted sleep. The constant state of exhaustion decimated the population of the camp. Men, eyes glazed, would for no apparent reason suddenly go raving mad. They would be taken outside and shot."[20]

Not all prisoners could be assigned to war work and a few had almost tolerable tasks, physically at least, helping to run the camps themselves, perhaps working in the medical block, sorting the clothing of newly arrived prisoners, working in the kitchens or doing basic maintenance work. Usually, however, the prisoners were allotted far more arduous tasks, no matter how nonsensical. At Dachau anyone not working for the Reich was required to spend several hours a day practising an elaborate drill, responding en masse to a series of orders that had to be carried out to the exact split second. Anyone who missed the beat or flagged was beaten on the spot. The drill was simply an endlessly repeated sequence of five movements, as the prisoners went from 'At ease' to 'Attention', then at the order 'Caps off' swept their caps down to their sides, holding them precisely between thumb and forefinger. Next came the order 'Caps on' and then 'Rectify', when the cap was exactly centred on one's crown. Finally it was back to 'At ease'.

One of the most horrific exercises in organised futility was the granite quarry at Mauthausen where slabs of the rock were hewn out for no discernible reason and then carried by hand up a 150-step ascent to the top. Almost passing out from malnutrition and fever, thin rags on their backs, their sandals ripped and shredded on the hard rock, men were loaded with blocks of granite weighing over 100lb. These were carried on hods strapped to their backs or on their bare shoulders. The ascent was the final penance of the day's shift and all the 2,000 prisoners were assembled at the bottom in a column of ten abreast. The first men to receive their burdens often had to stand for an hour or more waiting to move off. When they finally began the climb, each rank was tightly crammed shoulder-to-shoulder for even at its widest point the stairway was only twelve feet across. "Each of the crumbling steps was aligned to the average size 'clip clop' [so] men with large feet had to climb splay-footed. Sometimes men, overcome by exhaustion, fits, strokes and madness, let go their granite blocks; as a result many of those bringing up the rear suffered crushed bones. The flashpoint having been reached at the summit, the front ranks waited for the battered ranks to be rebuilt. This was the most dangerous, unpredictable stage, hinging on the breed and moods of the guards standing by up front. Foul play, a regular practice, was to gun-butt the front rank; in the debacle that followed an avalanche of men and blocks skittled to the bottom of the steps." Here was one hell where the ascent was more terrible than the fall. According to a Polish prisoner, if a man ended up with what the guards regarded as too small a stone "they would beat him to death ... Prisoners would kill themselves by jumping from the top of the quarry on to the broken stones below ... Others were propelled over the chasm by force, singly, in pairs and in a chain of linked hands. The guards had a fancy for nicknaming the sites where some of the worst casualties were recorded ... such as Parachutist's Leap ... And the Commandant, Ziereis, used to let his little son, who was about 11, shoot at prisoners for sport."[21]

The concentration camps, then, were not an environment in which there was any opportunity for resistance, individual or collective. Physical debilitation and spiritual degradation soon conspired to rob prisoners of any hope or confidence in their ability to withstand the implacable dehumanisation. Many simply gave way to total despair and became what were known as 'Musselmans', glassy-eyed zombies in whom the spark of life had been extinguished even before the body's physical defences had collapsed. Yet it would be seriously misleading to imply that the camps were populated simply by sadists and their cowering or utterly passive victims. Although submission to the camp authorities was an absolute prerequisite of survival there were thousands of prisoners who had determined to take cover at the very edge of the abyss and wage their personal, internal, surreptitious struggle for survival.

The struggle had its physical and psychological dimensions. Finding a close friend was tremendously important to mental stability but it could at the same time have other practical implications. One pair of slave labourers managed to find "ways to swap our clothes when we alternated between day shift and night shift, so that the one who was out in the cold would not freeze." It also paid to remain alert to the smallest details of camp routine. At evening meals these same two prisoners "realised that at the very beginning or the very end of the servings, the gruel was often thicker, and depending how deeply the trusty manipulated the ladle we would be either first or last in line." It was also vital to remember that the SS and the kapos were only too ready to liquidate prisoners who seemed unfit for work. Next to submission "the second rule of survival burned into my mind [was] never admit the least sign of infirmity ... Don't improvise anything that the guards can spot as a makeshift bandage. Hide any mark of illness, no matter how serious or how slight." In some respects camp life was like an extreme form of infantry combat, as in the muddy slit-trenches of Holland, the Hürtgen Forest or the Vosges. A Dutch prisoner at Auschwitz III stressed the importance of looking after one's feet. "Fortunately, I knew how to keep my feet warm in clogs by wrapping them ... I looked about me constantly on the work-site and in the camp for scraps of paper or rags with which to keep my feet warm and dry. The protection of my feet was the key to my survival ... I saw wet and frozen toes of some my fellow-prisoners rot from gangrene."[22]

A key psychological feature of surviving in the camps was that one's attitude to fellow-prisoners had to be the complete opposite of the total submission to one's overseers. Aside from possibly one or two close companions, one had to be "hard" and keep oneself "rigorously apart", to put aside "all sensitivity, all modesty." Only then could one hope to keep going in the merciless world of the camps, "a world whose reality one cannot grasp if one depends on such abstract concepts as honour, dignity or human rights." Another prisoner was more specific about the ceaseless scrounging and scavenging that was involved. "The most important word in the Auschwitz language: 'organisation' was the key to survival. It meant to steal, buy, exchange, get hold of. Whatever you wanted, you had to have something to barter for it. Some people spent every waking moment 'organising': stealing from their fellow prisoners, bribing others, swapping a crust of bread for a can of water, a crumpled sheet of notepaper for a more comfortable corner of a bunk."[23]

Yet survival was not a complete moral abnegation, and as desperately as they clung on to life, many also resolutely refused to lose all sight of what they had once taken for granted as the hallmarks of human civilisation. On the Dachau *Abortkommando*, even as the filth slopped around on their shovels and they paddled ankle-deep in the cess-pits, the doctors, teachers, lawyers, musicians "invented diversions: the members of the team would take turns in whistling melodies, and the others would then guess where they were from – from what opera or from what symphony. Or we would recite poetry to each other – Goethe, Schiller, Heine, Lessing – or quiz each other about Greek mythology ... They could make our bodies shovel shit, but they couldn't make our minds do it."[24]

*

Whatever the transcendent powers of the human spirit, or the possibility of individual resistance against the SS, it was still the case that for the Nazis all those in the camps were already as good as dead, and the slightest flicker of individuality was likely to result in immediate execution. These prisoners were not there to be changed or reformed; they were simply to be liquidated sooner or later, and anything they did to buck or deny that fact would only hasten it. This willingness of the Nazis, determination even, to round people up for mass elimination had become apparent in 1939 and 1940 when they organised 'selective' killings of Polish officers, politicians and intellectuals as well as Jewish leaders. It was the Jews who were especially anathematised, though for a while the Nazis contented themselves with deporting the mass of German and Polish Jewry into special ghettos and labour camps in the east. This campaign, organised by such SS luminaries as Reinhard Heydrich and Adolf Eichmann, continued after the conquest of the Low Countries and France. With the invasion of the Soviet Union, however, when the SS were needed at the front and railway space was at a premium, it was felt that more drastic measures were required. With more than two million Soviet Jews to be cleared out of the Baltic States and the new German *Lebensraum*, the Nazis resorted to systematic mass murder, sending in an *Einsatzgruppe*, a 1,000-man 'action group', with each of the three invading army groups. Their task was simply to round up and kill all Jews within their zone of operations. The same fate was also decreed for all Red Army commissars and suspected 'Bolsheviks', while the rank-and-file of the Red Army that were taken prisoner were to receive a level of care so minimal that it too amounted to mass murder. The *Einsatzgruppen* alone are estimated to have disposed of 1.5 million people.

Such methods seemed by far the most efficient, and by 1942 the ghettos had come to be regarded as an untidy and only temporary solution to the Jewish problem. In January, at the Wannsee Conference, senior Nazis and SS leaders thrashed out a Final Solution, involving nothing less than the extermination of the whole race. In fact, the ghetto programme would have accomplished this eventually through starvation and terrible overcrowding but, for whatever reason, the Nazis decided to hasten the process and established in Poland a small network of *Vernichtungslager*, extermination camps, with their own dedicated railway network to speed transfer from mass round-ups in the Soviet Union, the Baltic States, Poland, the Balkans and the West, and with the facilities – usually carbon-monoxide gas chambers or gas vans – to dispose of prisoners on arrival. At Auschwitz, the process was to be streamlined by installing high-temperature ovens to dispose of the bodies. The other camps had to burn the corpses stacked in pits, a much more laborious and time-consuming task.

Most slave labour camps also had crematoria but these were only for the disposal of the natural wastage from disease, starvation and over-work. Due in large part to the zealous commitment of Adolf Eichmann to this key SS mission, the extermination camps achieved horrific levels of production-line slaughter, almost all of it by the end of October 1944. The figures for the extermination camps were:[25]

Camp	Date Operative	Date Closed	Months Operative	Number Killed	Deaths per Week	Main Ghetto
Chelmo	Dec 1941	April 1943	16	300,000	4,700	Lodz
Belzec	March 1942	Nov. 1942	8	570,000	17,800	–
Treblinka	July 1942	Sept. 1943	14	900,000	16,100	Warsaw
Sobidor	May 1942	Dec. 1943	19	250,000	3,300	–
Auschwitz	May 1942	Nov. 1944	30	1,800,000	15,000	–
Majdanek	June 1942	March 1944	22	130,000	1,500	Lublin

Except at Auschwitz, the great orgy of killing was over by the end of 1943, with most of the main ghettos having been liquidated. Yet there were still opportunities for the truly dedicated SS man. Eichmann, arriving in Budapest in the immediate aftermath of the Nazi putsch, was able the throw his boundless energies into the extermination of the relatively unscathed Hungarian Jews. Between 15th May and 7th July 1944, in an unprecedented spasm of manic butchery, 437,000 Jews were deported to Auschwitz and marched off the trains straight into the gas chambers. Eichmann's Amt-IV-B and the Auschwitz personnel under SS-Hauptsturmführer Rudolf Höss were now working at peak efficiency when, to their chagrin, they learnt that their well-oiled killing machine was soon to shut down. There were still plenty of potential victims, even after killing 90 per cent of the Polish and Baltic Jews, 75 per cent of Greek and Hungarian, and 65 per cent of those in occupied Soviet territories, but the military situation had placed most of them, especially in Rumania, France, Bulgaria and Finland, back behind Allied lines.[26]

Worse still, the Soviet advance into Poland had necessitated the closing down of most of the extermination camps and now, in October, even Auschwitz (Oswiecim, to the Poles) was under threat. But there is no evidence that Eichmann regarded this as anything more than an inconvenient, temporary loss of capacity. On the 25th, from his suite at Budapest's Hotel Majestic, he was still sending out urgent orders to round up the 160,000 Jews still living in the city. Already, 35,000 had been taken since his arrival on the 17th and, despite the military's claims to all available rolling stock, he was determined to resume the deportations. To one intermediary on the Jews' behalf he said: "I am back. You probably imagined that the Rumanian and Bulgarian story would be repeated here. Now mark my words, this government does what we tell it to do. I'm in touch with the Minister for Internal Affairs. The Budapest Jews will be transported, and this time they'll have to go on foot. We need our trains for other purposes. We are going to act promptly and efficiently. Understand?"[27]

However, Heinrich Himmler, the head of the SS, was not now so rigidly committed to the Final Solution. This new equivocation had nothing to do with moral unease but stemmed rather from a variety of typically sordid considerations. One was the question of war guilt should Germany be forced to surrender unconditionally as the Allies demanded. It was this, and the relentless Soviet advance in Eastern Europe, that had prompted Himmler to close down most of the extermination camps and to try to obliterate all trace of their existence. A special Unit 1005 was also set up to disinter bodies from SS and *Einsatzgruppen* mass murder sites. The bodies were then burnt, along with those of the exhumation parties who were also shot. Incriminating evidence also existed at the Anatomical Institute at the University of Strasbourg, consisting of a large collection of 'Jewish-Bolshevik' skulls belonging to specially executed prisoners and intended for 'scientific' comparison. Following a worried letter from Himmler on 15th October, Professor Hirt and his researchers were busily destroying the exhibits but, without specific orders relating to the mass of accompanying documentation, had not thought to burn that also, or even to remove it.

Another reason for caution was Himmler's grotesque vanity. Subtly played upon by his personal physician and by Walter Schellenberg, effectively Himmler's deputy, both of whom were becoming increasingly anxious about their implication in war crimes, he was persuaded to see himself as a more 'reasonable', alternative Führer who might even now rescue Germany by using the surviving Jews as bargaining chips in negotiations with the western Allies. Some talks had already taken place with neutral and with Jewish representatives, and the latter had been pressing for the release of at least one train-load of Jews to Switzerland or Sweden, as a sign of Nazi good faith. Himmler declined to do this without a reciprocal commitment to supply financial or material aid to prosecute the war in the East. Figures of $1,000 per Jew released or a one-off payment of so many thousand military trucks were bandied about. At the end of September, Himmler was persuaded to read enormous significance into President Roosevelt's sending his personal representative, the Quaker leader Roswell D. MacClellan, to Switzerland to take part in these negotiations. On 30th September, Himmler informed the Jewish Rescue Committee that he had suspended mass deportations to Auschwitz, while in mid-October he authorised the departure of a train-load of Jews for Switzerland and later that month met up near Vienna with Dr Jean-Marie Mury, a prominent Swiss Jew, to discuss further concessions. According to Schellenberg, who was also at this meeting: "Just before Mury left for Switzerland I persuaded Himmler to prove his sincerity by conceding one of Mury's special requests: that a number of prominent Jews and Frenchmen should be released. Himmler reluctantly agreed and asked me to be responsible for seeing that the arrangement was carried out."[28]

By 25th October, however, the killings had still not stopped, especially at Auschwitz. Certainly the tempo of the slaughter had lessened with the halt in the mass Hungarian deportations, and the two great Auschwitz slave labour camps were being wound down in the face of the approaching Red Army. Not that this did their inmates much good. Two hitherto relatively favoured groups, the gypsies (who fascinated Himmler) and the so-called Family Camp, had been gassed and thousands of other prisoners were sent on forced marches westward to less vulnerable camps, notably Stutthof and Mauthausen, during which large numbers perished en route. Most SS functionaries did not share even Himmler's vague unease about continuing to strive for the Final Solution and throughout October, despite his assurances to the Rescue Committee, the machinery of extermination continued to work as train-loads of north Italian and Slovakian Jews, as well as those from the now redundant 'show camp' at Theresienstadt, trundled into Auschwitz for *Sonderbehandlung*, or special treatment.

The trains were usually made up of cattle trucks supplied by the German *Ostbahn* company which "offered a special reduced price for groups of four hundred or more. Children under ten went half-fare. Those under four went free. These were one-way fares. The guards on the trains were charged round-trip fares. The fare was for passengers, but the Jews travelled in freight cars."[29] These were designed to hold around eight horses or, at a pinch, forty soldiers. The deportees were packed in – men, women and children – until there were up to 150 people in each truck. The doors were locked and nailed shut during the whole journey, with at best only one tiny barred window to let in air and light. The journey sometimes lasted several days but no food, water, heating or ventilation was provided. At the embarkation points "women were publicly stripped and subjected to an examination by a midwife . . . Sick people who had recently undergone operations, mothers in childbirth, those in pain and those who were mad were all, in the literal sense of the word, crammed into the trucks . . . Normally such a large number of people would not have been able to stand in the trucks, so it was necessary for the police to pack them in, using clubs and bayonets. Often they did it by simply firing their rifles at the front row."[30] The single bucket that might be provided for sanitary purposes was, of course, absolutely useless in such a press of bodies. "The filth and the stench were indescribable. Some prayed, some screamed, some were silent, some went mad. A train carrying a thousand Jews would arrive – on time, as scheduled – with as many as two hundred already dead."[31]

By the time the train arrived at the camp most prisoners were too stupefied or traumatised to take much notice of their surroundings, but nothing that followed was likely to reassure them that they had not passed into another dimension of palpable evil. Arrival usually took place at night, and the wagon doors were opened to reveal a "scene from Gogol: it was just like, actually like, you imagine an arrival at the gates of hell. The flames from the chimneys rose five metres above them." According to another: "The wagon doors were torn ajar. The shouts were deafening. SS men with whips and half wild Alsatian dogs swarmed all over the place. Uncontrolled fear brought panic as families were torn apart. Parents screamed for lost children and mothers shrieked their names over the voices of the bawling guards." The dogs were especially terrifying. One young prisoner watched in horror as "several of the great beasts leaped into our car. In the space of seconds, two or three of the half-conscious prisoners were torn to pieces."[32]

Once the survivors were assembled the men were separated from the women and children. Most of the latter were already doomed, having little value as slave labourers. Nevertheless, both columns edged forward to the selection point where they were assigned either to the slave pool or to the gas chambers. In charge of selection was SS-Hauptsturmführer Dr Josef Mengele, immaculately uniformed with gleaming riding boots and white gloves, usually whistling an operatic aria, who told off the shuffling newcomers to right and left – right to a few weeks of hellish limbo in the slave compounds, left to immediate and agonising death. Literally hundreds of thousands of people had already passed before this insane popinjay, "this automaton . . . at his macabre game of doling out life and death with his forefinger. Like a metronome this finger swayed from side to side as each victim appeared before him, with a face moulded in ice, without a flicker of an eyelash."[33] For those ordained to die immediately less than an hour of life still remained. When Auschwitz was first in operation the trains had stopped over a thousand yards from the gas chambers but in April 1944, to increase through-put of the Hungary trains, a spur had been built that went almost to the gates of two of the chambers.

Even now, when word of the death camps had reached most surviving Jewish communities and when the threat of dispatching someone '*durch den Kamin*', up the chimney, was the new German version of the bogeyman, the SS guards and their assistants seem to have tried to maintain the fiction that the gas chambers were shower rooms, where prisoners would be disinfected before being sent to work. The ploy had not the slightest humanitarian intent and was aimed solely at minimising panic among the victims which might delay their orderly elimination. Some, mercifully, believed the lie, unable to accept that fellow human beings could countenance the alternative. Their self-delusion provided but a speck of comfort on a mountain of pain, and lasted only the few minutes allowed to the victims to undress themselves and their children before being chivvied into the showers by the *Sonderkommando*, Jewish prisoners granted a few extra weeks of life, and some of the perquisites of the condemned man, in exchange for operating the gas chambers and crematoria.[34]

The truth of what was about to happen must have become apparent to all as more and more people were crammed into the shower room, sometimes with small children being pushed in over the heads of the adults, and foreboding became certainty as the double doors were sealed shut and the Zyklon-B crystals (hydrogen cyanide) were dropped through vents in the roof. Twenty minutes later the electric air conditioners were switched on and after a further few minutes the *Sonderkommando* entered the chamber.

> The bodies were not lying here and there throughout the room but piled in a mass to the ceiling. The reason for this was that the gas first inundated the lower layers of air and rose but slowly toward the ceiling. This forced the victims to trample one another in a frantic effort to escape the gas . . . I noticed that the bodies of the women, the children and the aged were at the bottom of the pile; at the top, the strongest. Their bodies, which were covered with scratches and bruises from the struggle . . . were often interlaced. Blood oozed from their noses and mouths; their faces, bloated and blue, were so deformed as to be almost unrecognisable . . . The

Sonderkommando squad, outfitted with large rubber boots, lined up around the hill of bodies and flooded it with powerful jets of water. This was necessary because the final act of those who die by drowning or by gas is an involuntary defecation. Each body was befouled and had to be washed. Once the 'bathing' of the dead was finished . . . they knotted thongs around the wrists . . . and with these thongs they dragged the slippery bodies to the elevators in the next room.[35]

There were five crematoria all told, each of which had four large elevators that could accommodate some 25 corpses. Once an elevator was full a bell was rung and it climbed to one of the incineration rooms, each with five giant three-retort ovens which between them could burn 15 bodies every 20 minutes. Other members of the *Sonderkommando* dragged the bodies back out of the elevators and on to a conveyor belt that took them towards the furnaces. On the way, all the victims' hair was shaved off and stored, and an eight-man Tooth Commando prised open the jaws with hooks. They were looking for gold teeth and prised or knocked out any they found with pliers and hammers. The hair went for stuffing mattresses and the like and it has even been alleged that longer women's hair was cleaned and woven into glove and sock liners for U-boat crews. The gold teeth were melted down into bullion, which formed a significant part of the $300 million worth of stolen gold transferred by the Nazis to Switzerland.

In Auschwitz there was also a handful of prisoners who had still barely grown any teeth. Almost all children under fourteen went straight to the gas chambers, but Mengele had a particular fascination for twins, who occupied some niche in his lunatic construct of biological theories. Any who arrived at Auschwitz, therefore, were housed in a special barracks. One of the older ones recalled: "The first word the little children who could not yet speak learned was '*Nachtwache*'. This was because in the night they had to go to the toilet, and if they couldn't call for the *Nachtwache* or say 'I need to go to the toilet', they lived no more. If they urinated in their bed they would be sent to the crematorium. That is why children one year old, one-and-a-half years old, would say, '*Nachtwache*, I need to make pee-pee.'"[36]

PART SEVEN

The Philippines

28
Approach to Leyte Gulf

THE JAPANESE went to war in 1941 to secure for themselves the Dutch East Indies and their rich deposits of raw materials so vital to Japanese industry and, in the case of oil, to the armed forces. In December they dispatched their fleet to launch a pre-emptive strike against the U.S. Pacific Fleet in the hope of putting it out of action for good. Although achieving spectacular results on the day, this attack on Pearl Harbor in Hawaii proved to be a short-term success. Not only did the Japanese fail to sink the American aircraft carriers, which were at sea, but most of the battleships that did go down in their shallow anchorages were later recovered. Moreover, the Japanese had completely misjudged their opponents' reactions and, far from being 'shamed' or demoralised by their defeat, the Americans immediately inaugurated a massive naval building programme, established last-ditch defensive positions in New Guinea and Guadalcanal, and dispatched the carriers on bold, albeit relatively minor missions against enemy island bases. The fierce resolve of the Americans was greatly strengthened by their ability to decipher Japanese signals traffic, which enabled them, on occasion, to anticipate enemy movements. This MAGIC intelligence, as it was known, was especially valuable in June 1942, when the Americans learnt of a Japanese naval task force heading towards their base on Midway Island and decided to position their own carriers, although seriously outnumbered, to intercept the enemy's ships. In the ensuing battle – perhaps more than any other in history – fortune favoured the brave, and in a matter of minutes three large Japanese carriers were fatally damaged by carrier aircraft, with a fourth added to the list some hours later. All sank that same day.

With the enemy's naval aviation so dramatically weakened, the

Americans felt able to take the offensive themselves. In July 1942 the Joint Chiefs of Staff issued a directive which set Army and Marine divisions on the long road towards the East Indies where they could cut off the flow of raw materials to Japan. Their route was to be by way of the Solomon Islands, the Bismark Archipelago and New Guinea, and they were to be under the command of General Douglas MacArthur. Although an Army general, in charge of the South-West Pacific Area, MacArthur also had under his command the U.S. Seventh Fleet to protect his amphibious bounds from one island stepping-stone to the next. Yet the Navy had no intention of acting merely as subordinates to the Army. While expecting to receive over the coming months a stream of new ships, from aircraft carriers to destroyers, far in excess of anything needed to support MacArthur's advance, naval commanders demanded their own separate axis, and in October 1943 the Joint Chiefs allocated the major portion of the Pacific Fleet (still based at Pearl Harbor) its own route across the Pacific. Under the overall command of Admiral Chester Nimitz, it was to keep up the carrier strikes against Japanese bases but at the same time was to seize certain of them in its own island-hopping advance through the Marshalls, the Carolines and the Marianas.[1] The islands taken would also accommodate airfields for American ground-based aircraft as well as advanced anchorages for the fleet and its immense logistical back-up. The airfields in the Marianas were to be used by the big B-29 bombers which would then be in range of the Japanese mainland.

By 1944, MacArthur's ultimate objective had changed somewhat, after it was agreed that enemy supply routes could be cut just as easily from the Philippines. Taking back these islands from the Japanese would also enable MacArthur to honour his pledge, given when he had fled in March 1942, to return as a liberator. At the same time, Nimitz's own axis, in what was known as the Central Pacific Area, drew him towards the Philippines as well, and in October 1944 the two converged, with the whole Pacific Fleet now providing cover for the General's amphibious assault on Leyte, the first of the Philippine islands to be retaken. Close cover for the landings, which took place on 20th October, was still mainly the responsibility of MacArthur's 'private navy', while the rest of the Pacific Fleet stood further out to sea to guard against any sortie by the Japanese fleet from its bases in Japan and Singapore. These American ships from the Central Pacific axis were grouped together in Admiral William Halsey's Third Fleet, at the heart of which were the fleet carriers and fast battleships of Task Force 38 under Admiral Marc Mitscher.[2]

The decision to allocate most of the Pacific Fleet to protecting the Leyte landings was to prove a shrewd one. Despite assiduous MAGIC eavesdropping, the Americans knew nothing of a Japanese decision to send out most of their fleet to stage a major spoiling attack against the Leyte landings. This fleet was not, however, the balanced carrier strike force they would have wished. Japanese naval aviation, painfully rebuilt after the disaster at Midway, had been destroyed once more in the Battle of the Philippine Sea in June 1944, and in air battles off Formosa, in early October, when the best surviving carrier pilots were deployed on land. In any battle off Leyte, the Japanese would now have no counter to American fleet carriers and so they purposely decided to use the ill-equipped, ill-trained carrier force that they were able to scrape together as a sacrificial bait. By trailing its coat well to the north of Leyte Gulf and luring away Halsey's carriers, the Japanese navy hoped its battleships and cruisers would be free to wreak havoc among the American landing force.

This diversionary sortie was just one element in an extremely complex Japanese plan, involving four different approach routes to Leyte from Japan, the Ryukyu Islands and the Lingga Roads anchorage off Singapore. The decoy force would sail around the northern end of Luzon and straight away try to attract Halsey's attention. The remaining routes approached Leyte from the west, with one force sailing around the northern end of Samar, through the San Bernadino Strait, and the other two converging in the Sulu Sea to pass through the Suriago Strait around the southern end of Leyte itself. These approaches from the west were to form the twin arms of a pincer attack on Leyte Gulf, where MacArthur's invasion fleet was assembled. The plan was known as SHO-ICHI-GO, Operation Victory, and the four main groups set sail between 18th and 22nd October. Altogether the Japanese had assembled 6 battleships, 6 carriers, 15 heavy and light cruisers and 29 destroyers.[3]

Admiral Soemu Toyoda, the Navy's commander-in-chief, had ordered that the rendezvous in Leyte Gulf should take place on 25th October, but several ships from the northern arm of the pincers, commanded by Admiral Takeo Kurita, never even got within sight of the San Bernadino Strait. For although MAGIC had revealed little about Japanese movements, other snoopers had been more successful. From the 22nd two American submarines, *Darter* and *Dace*, were in constant attendance with Kurita's ships, sending in vital reports of the presence of at least eleven large vessels. Finally they closed in on Kurita, whose ships were steaming in two columns, and succeeded in sinking one from each, the heavy cruisers *Atago* and *Maya*, at around 7 a.m. on the 23rd. Yet another hit was recorded by *Darter* torpedoes on the heavy cruiser *Takao*, which blew off the ship's rudder and two propellers. The cruiser had no choice but to quit the column and limp back to Brunei. Two destroyers, the *Naganami* and the *Asashimo*, were also detached to escort the cruiser. In one of the most successful submarine attacks of the war, Captains McLintock and Claggett had already deprived Kurita of three heavy cruisers and two destroyers, not to mention giving Kurita a forceful reminder of the rigours of war at sea. The *Atago* had been his flagship and in the twenty minutes or so before she went down, Kurita, still recovering from a bout of dengue fever, was hastily transferred to the destroyer *Kishinami*. On the afternoon of the 24th he transferred again to the battleship *Yamato*, but by that time he had lost about half of his communications personnel, just when there would be no further need to maintain strict radio silence.

In fact, his own position was now being closely monitored. Although *Darter* and *Dace* lost contact after the sinkings, it was re-established by the submarine *Angler* at 9.30 that evening. This ship was unable to attack but it followed the Japanese on a north-easterly course which seemed to indicate an intended passage through the Mindoro Strait. When yet another submarine, the *Guitarro*, followed Kurita's south-west turn through the Strait, it confirmed that the destination was San Bernadino Strait and Leyte Gulf.

Kurita next fell victim to planes from Halsey's carriers which, alerted by the submarines, sighted the Japanese at dawn on the 24th. Six carrier strikes in all were launched and further serious damage was inflicted during what became known as the Battle of the Sibuyan Sea. One of Kurita's battleships, the *Musashi*, was hit repeatedly by bombs and torpedoes during the morning and the afternoon. An internal explosion wrecked the steering gear and blew off the first bridge, and the ship finally sank at 7.35 p.m. Also hit were the heavy cruisers *Myosho* and *Haguro*, and a torpedo so damaged two of the former's propeller shafts that the ship turned back for Brunei. By late evening the destroyers *Kiyoshimo* and *Hamakaze* were also Brunei-bound, having picked up about 1,400 survivors from the *Musashi*. A further 1,000 perished. Since first being detected, Kurita's force had now been deprived of one out of five battleships, three out of ten heavy cruisers and four out of fifteen destroyers.

Badly shaken by his ordeal, Kurita at one point reversed course away from San Bernadino Strait and his rendezvous in Leyte Gulf.

Only two hours later, however, his sense of duty had again prevailed and he headed east once more. At almost exactly midnight on 24th/25th October, Kurita's ships pounded into the narrow channels of the Strait, braving the numerous shoals at an awesome 20 knots.

The Americans meanwhile had made sightings on the 24th of the two forces converging in the Sulu Sea, en route for Suriago Strait to form the southern arm of the Japanese pincers. More carrier strikes were launched by Halsey's ships but these inflicted little damage. The decoy force, commanded by Admiral Jisaburo Ozawa, was also spotted on the 24th, but only after four days' ever more frantic coat-trailing. At 11.15 a.m. American carrier planes finally stumbled across Ozawa's ships, upon which Ozawa immediately flew off his callow pilots towards the Americans to convince them that his was indeed a bait worth taking. One group of his planes simply disappeared over the ocean while the other was shot out of the sky by one of Halsey's carrier task groups. But they had achieved their purpose.

By 3.40 p.m. reports began filtering through to Halsey's flagship of a Japanese carrier force to the north, and at 8.20 p.m., after a brief consultation, to which several key planning and intelligence officers were not invited, Halsey stabbed his finger on the plotted position of Ozawa's carriers and, rather in the manner of a cattle boss to his top hand, told his chief-of-staff, "Here's where we're going, Mick. Start them north." Orders then went out to his task group commanders to rendezvous one hour before midnight ready to hunt down the enemy. Having made his decision, Halsey turned in.

Others in Third Fleet were less relaxed, feeling that Halsey might be setting off on a wild goose chase, and that he was abandoning the invasion fleet, still his main responsibility. With two of his task groups at present almost directly west of the exit from San Bernadino Strait, Halsey was ideally placed both to counter any Japanese carrier force sailing south and to fend off Kurita's ships when they emerged from the Strait. For although the Japanese were thought to have lost ships in the Sibuyan Sea attacks, there was no reason to believe that it was not still a formidable force of heavy gunships steaming towards Seventh Fleet. But Halsey's order stood. In the spate of signals that followed was one that completely misled the commander of Seventh Fleet, Admiral Thomas Kinkaid, into thinking that his northern flank was still protected. He soon learnt that Halsey was departing with his carriers but an unfortunately ambiguous signal intercepted by his staff lulled him into believing that Halsey had left his fast battleships, Task Force 34 under Admiral Willis Lee, behind to guard the Strait. In the early hours of the 25th, then, wishful thinking seemed to be the order of the day for the Americans, with Admiral Kinkaid putting his trust in a non-existent flank-guard and Admiral Halsey snapping at Ozawa's bait while at the same time convincing himself that Kurita's force had already largely been written off.

Thus, with the southern arm of their pincers about to enter Suriago Strait, the Japanese seemed poised for a triumphant culmination of all their elaborate planning. Ironically, however, Japanese commanders were the least optimistic, and do not seem to have believed it would be possible to lure away all of Halseys task groups or that they could be kept at arm's length. While they might well penetrate into Leyte Gulf, most of the Japanese seemed to believe that they would perish there. A typically Japanese sense of self-sacrificial foreboding hung over the whole enterprise. On 18th October, when Army commanders at a Tokyo conference urged the Navy to reconsider the whole SHO-ICHI-GO operation, the chief of the naval operations section pleaded that the fleet be allowed a "fitting place to die" and "the chance to bloom as flowers of death. This is the Navy's earnest request." Kurita, too, remained grimly fatalistic. Before quitting the Lingga Roads, he had told his staff that "the war situation is far more critical than any of you can possibly know", and because of this, "I am willing to accept even this ultimate assignment to storm into Leyte Gulf. You must all remember that there are such things as miracles." A week later, as he headed into San Bernadino Strait, he signalled naval headquarters in Tokyo: "Braving any loss or damage we may suffer, the First Striking Force will break into Leyte Gulf and fight to the last man."[4]

29

Crossing the T

THE BATTLE OF SURIAGO STRAIT

WITH THE FIRST surface contacts between American vessels and Admiral Nishimura's Southern Force late on the 24th October, the most westerly American patrol line, made up of PT boats, moved in to make torpedo attacks, none of which registered a hit. Many naval officers felt that PT boat attacks were a waste of time and that these craft should be limited to reconnaissance duties only. But the PT force was not under Kinkaid's direct command and so he was forced to wait until honour had been satisfied before the boats found time to report the sightings at around half past midnight on the 25th.

In fact, the long delay since the last sightings the previous morning had not handicapped Kinkaid particularly. Even at that early stage Nishimura's objective had been fairly clear and from 9.15 on the 24th Kinkaid and his staff were working on the assumption that the Japanese would attempt to force the Suriago Strait at around two o'clock the following morning. It was 2.23 a.m. when he instructed Admiral Jesse Oldendorf, commanding the old battleships and heavy cruisers that provided Seventh Fleet's fire support during amphibious landings, to deploy these ships across the northern exit from Suriago Strait.[1] Despite convening a planning conference for late in the afternoon, Oldendorf had already drawn up a plan for defending this approach to Leyte Gulf. His intention was to form three parallel lines of ships across the exit, with the battleships forming the most northerly line and in front of them the cruisers and then the destroyers divided into left and right flank groups. Battleships and cruisers were to steam back and forth across the Strait while destroyers provided a forward patrol line.

Once the enemy fleet appeared, the destroyers were to harass it with torpedoes, their classic function, and then withdraw, leaving heavier gunships a clear field of fire. Because of the narrowness of the Strait – only 12 miles wide in the south, opening out to 25 miles at the northern end – the Japanese would probably be sailing in line, one ship in front of the other, which would make it difficult to deploy many of their guns against a target directly in front of them. The Americans, steaming laterally to-and-fro at right-angles to the enemy, would be able to deliver a continuous enfilading fire down the whole length of the Japanese column. Such an unequal juxtaposition of firepower had long been the naval tactician's dream, or nightmare, and was generally known as 'capping' or 'crossing the T'. Rather surprisingly, Admiral Kinkaid later rejected the notion that his ships had succeeded in doing it, as for him the manoeuvre in its pure form demanded that two forces sail parallel to one another before one managed to gain speed and sail across the enemy's bows. "Actually, we did nothing of the sort. We put the cross up there and the Japs walked into it in confined waters and completed the T. It was just a trap and they walked right into it. All of our ships could bear on their leading ships. We didn't cross the T in conventional style, but that's all right. It makes a good story."[2]

The distinction seems a trifle pedantic. Whether or not the Americans put the cross of the 'T' in place before the Japanese supplied the tail, it was certainly their intention all along to engineer just such a favourable alignment of forces. Admiral Oldendorf was clearly not at all bothered by such naval casuistry. His only concern was to deploy the maximum firepower at his disposal against the enemy, and how much better if that enemy had an inferior force. After the war he explained: "My theory was that of the old-time gambler: 'Never give a sucker a chance.' If my opponent is foolish enough to come at me with an inferior force, I'm certainly not going to give him an even break."[3]

Nishimura did his best to oblige, providing probably the Imperial Japanese Navy's best ever approximation of a sucker. Despite knowing now that co-ordinating his arrival in Leyte Gulf with Kurita's was impossible, Nishimura made no effort to slow his own approach, even though this offered the only real chance of confusing the Americans, and at the same time allowing Shima to catch up. In fact, of his own accord, Shima had twice increased his speed to try to catch up with Nishimura and enter Leyte Gulf together. At 4 p.m. on the 25th, Nishimura deployed his fleet in approach formation and two hours later, just before entering the Strait itself, took up the line ahead battle formation that Kinkaid and Oldendorf were banking on. Leading were the four destroyers, *Michishio*, *Asagumo*, *Yamagumo* and *Shigure*, and

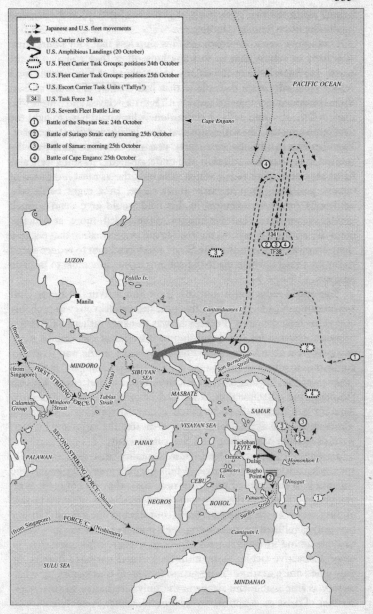

The Battle of Leyte Gulf 24th/25th October 1944

behind them the two battleships, *Yamashiro* (flagship) and *Fuso*, and finally the heavy cruiser *Mogami*.

Nishimura was to go down with his ship less that four hours later. It is hard to believe that he was anything other than resigned to the worst. He knew little of the enemy forces ahead of him, except for a report from *Mogami*'s float-plane that had spoken of forces at least three times stronger than his own. With Kurita delayed and Shima who knew where, it would be Nishimura alone who would have to fight the first punishing rounds, with ships that were hardly a major strike force. Even his two battleships were thirty-year-old dreadnoughts, partially refitted to be sure, but still slow and undergunned. His ships were also handicapped by poor radar, which gave only the vaguest indication of enemy positions, even at fairly short range. In a night battle, the enormous American advances in this field would give them a much greater advantage. Had Nishimura commanded more and better ships, he would still have been forced to sail in a formation that negated their firepower. Negotiating the Strait also forced him to reduce speed to thirteen knots, which made the column more vulnerable to torpedo attack.

The speed reduction would still leave him arriving in Leyte Gulf well ahead of Kurita, though by this time that rendezvous was probably one of his least concerns. Perhaps he was thinking rather of a meeting of spirits because his son Tenji, top of his class at the Etajima naval academy, had been killed in the Philippines early in the war. The only commanding officer to survive the coming battle, Commander Shigeru Nishino of the *Shigure*, told American interrogators after the war that "in preparing for this action, Admiral Nishimura had emphasised the need for spiritual readiness as much as combat readiness. Nishimura was reconciled to death. His attitude permeated the ranks and his men went along with him willingly on this suicidal duty."[4]

In fact, Nishimura's death-ride mentality was not universally applauded by his subordinates. While the Japanese fully accept the obligation to die for the Emperor if necessary, they do not see it as an end in itself. For them the paramount consideration in life must be that of duty, or *on*, to the Emperor, one's country and one's family. In war that duty is fulfilled by maximising one's military usefulness and where possible acting in concert with others to execute some stratagem or other. Collective victory is the ultimate aim and one has a duty to die only when one's death is the best contribution to that victory, or when victory is impossible and death is the only alternative to surrender. Neither of these cases applied to Nishimura, whose overriding duty on the morning of the 25th should still have been to work with Kurita to wring at least some modest success out of Operation Victory. As it was, he seems to have succumbed to a personal death-wish and, even at "the Brunei Bay meetings, prior to the Leyte jump-off [according to one of his captains] . . . 'Nishimura's tactical conceptions were quite different from those of the other ships under his command' . . . Responsible commanders expressed their disgust at the lack of co-ordinated command, and Admiral Nishimura's apparent indifference at not attending the briefings."[5]

So Nishimura steamed serenely into Suriago Strait where, until 3 a.m., he faced only persistent but ultimately harmless attacks by more of the PT boat sections that had buzzed around his flanks all the way from the south-eastern tip of Bohol. The boats' patrol lines extended all the way up the Strait as far as Bugho Point on Leyte itself, but their last significant attack was made at about 2.15 near the southern end of Panaon Island. All these sorties were uniformly unsuccessful, only one out of 34 torpedoes fired finding a target. As each boat carried only a puny 37mm gun, was totally unprotected against shellfire, had almost no training in delivering torpedo attacks, and offered an extremely unstable weapons platform, it seems reckless to have employed them for anything but reconnaissance duties. But at least they had speed and manoeuvrability. In the four main attacks on Nishimura, mainly on the cruiser *Mogami* and the four destroyers, only three boats were hit, killing one man and wounding eight. Only one boat, PT 493, was lost, and then not until after it had been beached and the crew evacuated.

Once Nishimura had entered the Strait, it became feasible to involve Oldendorf's next line of defence, the destroyers, the ships best suited to delivering harassing torpedo attacks. These were in three squadrons, one on each flank off Leyte and Hibuson Island, and one serving as an anti-submarine picket commanded by Captain Jesse Coward, in front of the main battle line. Coward had simply informed Oldendorf that in the event of a surface contact to the south, "I plan to make an immediate torpedo attack and then retire to clear you." Oldendorf quickly approved this bold announcement and Coward submitted his plan. Shortly after 2 a.m. the next morning he called his ships to General Quarters and at 02.25, a quarter of an hour later, received at PT boat report that put Nishimura to the east of Panaon. Coward immediately ordered the PT boats to clear the area and radioed Oldendorf, "I'm going to start in a few minutes."

The American ships were formed in two groups, *Monssen* and

McDermut sailing fairly close to the western side of the Strait and Coward's group – *Remey*, *McGowan* and *Melvin* – heading almost due south to form just west of Hibuson Island. Both groups demonstrated that a fierce sense of duty was not a Japanese prerogative. Commander C. K. Bergin of the *Monssen* told his crew: "We are going into battle. I know each of you will do his duty. I promise you that I will do my duty to you and for our country." Commander R. P. Fiala of the *Remey* calmly stated: "Tonight our ship has been designated to make the first torpedo run on the Jap task force that is on its way to stop our landings in Leyte Gulf. It is our job to stop the Japs. May God be with us tonight."[6]

Coward ordered the destroyers to close with the enemy at 30 knots, relying on torpedoes only as he knew that their 5-inch guns were ineffective against battleships and that in a night battle their flashes would give away the ship's position, unlike the virtually imperceptible launching of torpedoes. "The Naval War College in Newport had been preaching this doctrine for years, but it had seldom been practiced in World War II and had never quite 'clicked'."[7] Target detection was done by radar and a pair of torpedo directors, which generated a constantly changing 'firing solution' as new data on the target's and their own ship's course and speed were fed. in. As the five destroyers charge forward, closing with the Japanese at a relative speed of some 50 knots, the two groups headed to each side of the enemy column, Coward designating targets for each ship. After the *Remey* bore to the left, *Melvin* confirmed visual contact and at fractionally after 3 a.m. the whole eastern group fired 27 torpedoes at the enemy 10,000 yards to the south-west and then swung sharp north-east to race away from the torpedo tracks in the opposite direction, making smoke and zigzagging independently. During the firing, which took only about 75 seconds, and the subsequent turn, *Remey* got caught in a bright searchlight beam and all three ships came under fire from *Yamashiro* and the Japanese destroyers. Soon shells were splashing all around but the searchlight was lost and, despite numerous starshells bursting nearby, the ships pulled out of enemy range. A few minutes later, several explosions were heard, and looking back the Americans saw the largest ship in the enemy column slow down and veer to starboard. The battleship *Fuso* had been hit by a torpedo. But Nishimura did not see any of this and apparently no one cared to give him the unwelcome news, for he continued sending orders to the stricken battleship as if she were still in column.

The two other destroyers, with the western group commanded by

Captain Richard Phillips in *McDermut*, were seven or eight miles west of Coward's ships and about six miles to the rear when he was informed that Coward's ships had all fired and were retiring. He maintained course, his ships passing almost at right-angles to the Japanese, and then swung fifty degrees towards his target to reach the planned firing point. Coming under fire, he swung due south once more to allow *McDermut* and *Monssen* each to dispatch their 'spread' of ten torpedoes from almost the optimum 90-degree angle. Nishimura took evasive action, turning east and then north, but it served only to bring him back into the track of the torpedoes. Like Coward, Phillips immediately reversed his course after firing and, turning back due north, was close to the Leyte shoreline when a series of explosions was heard. *Monssen* managed one hit, on the battleship *Yamashiro*, but it failed to inflict significant damage. *McDermut*, however, hit three of the four Japanese destroyers in what was probably the most successful single torpedo attack of the whole war. *Yamagumo* blew up almost immediately, a thunderous incandescence that could be seen from the battle line twenty miles away. The battleship "sank with a loud sizzling sound, like a 'huge red-hot iron plunged into water'."[8] *Michishio* was presumably hit in the engine-room for she sheered away from the column and slowed until the vessel was simply drifting uncontrollably. *Asagumo* was also blown out of the column, with the bow torn off, and after puttering around forlornly she began slowly to withdraw.

Even before either of Coward's groups had fired their torpedoes, the six destroyers of the right-flank squadron, under Captain K. M. McManes in *Hutchins*, had been alerted to attack down the western side of the strait. At two minutes past three they had received the order to proceed in two groups, *Hutchins*, *Daly* and *Bache* steering due south, close to the shore, while *Killen* and *Beale* were led by HMAS *Arunta* on a more south-easterly course further out into the strait. The *Arunta* group fired first, at the head of the Japanese column. The wakes of 14 torpedoes fanned out towards the target but only one registered a hit, on the battleship *Yamashiro*, which slowed temporarily. The destroyers then turned sharply towards the shore and raced back to their original patrol line. The *Hutchins* group fired 15 torpedoes, then turned sharp north before looping back to attempt another run at the enemy column from closer range. As they were completing this loop, *Fuso*, which had been limping away southwards after the strike by Coward's ships, was convulsed by a series of huge explosions ripping through her magazines. The ship was literally blown apart and the two halves, blazing furiously, continued to drift south for three quarters of an hour until the bow sank, to be followed by the stern about an hour later. McManes pressed on, heading north-eastwards and firing his guns at the nearest targets, thought to have been the damaged Japanese destroyers *Michishio* and *Asagumo*. *Hutchins* managed to loose off another five torpedoes at the bowless *Asagumo* just as she was beginning a clumsy turn but the torpedoes fizzed harmlessly by. But this turn was the death of the wallowing *Michishio* which drifted helplessly into the torpedoes' path, collided with at least one of them and immediately blew up and sank.

Nishimura, in his flagship *Yamashiro*, pressed on regardless, firing his main batteries at the Battle Line and taking the *Hutchins* group under fire with his secondary. His gunners seemed unaffected by the death and destruction that marked their course. Commander R. G. Visser of *Daly*, in the shoreline group, reported that one of these salvos "was so accurate in deflection that its tracer gave him the sensation of a center fielder on a baseball diamond waiting for a fly ball to land right in his glove. Fortunately the salvo was an over – and Visser did not jump for the ball."[9] The heavy cruiser *Mogami* had begun to retire southwards some time before four o'clock, exchanging gunfire with *Hutchins*, *Daly* and *Bache* as they passed. All four ships emerged fairly unscathed, and McManes' group ceased firing at 4.05 a.m. as the *Hutchins* group returned to its original patrol positions.

Meanwhile, Oldendorf had called in a third squadron, serving as his left-flank screen under Captain Roland Smoot. At 3.35, as McManes was stealing back towards the enemy for his second torpedo attack, Smoot was ordered to join the fray with the words, "Launch attack – get the big boys!" Five minutes later, one of the big boys, *Fuso*, was already gone but Smoot pressed on with his squadron divided into three 3-ship sections – one to the east, passing by the western shore of Hibuson Island, was Captain T. F. Conley's group; one to the west, roughly halfway between Hibuson and Leyte, was Commander J. W. Bouleware's group; and between these two groups was Smoot's own trio of ships, which included the *Albert W. Grant*.[10]

The flank sections attacked first, with Captain T. F. Conley's shore-line ships loosing off 15 torpedoes from long range before turning back towards Hibuson Island. All these torpedoes missed, as did those from Captain Bouleware's central group which then veered away back towards the Battle Line with shells from both *Yamashiro* and *Shigure* chasing behind them. All these torpedoes had been launched in ten minutes before 4 a.m. By the time the last one was released, however, the Battle Line and the cruisers began to make their presence felt. The six battleships and eight cruisers split between the left and right flank forces, registered the Japanese formation on their radar screens and at 3.33 the battleships were alerted to open fire from 26,000 yards away. In fact, the cruisers began firing first, to be followed two minutes later by the Battle Line, and for the next seven minutes Nishimura grimly steered straight into this hail of fire, supported only by two other Japanese survivors, the cruiser *Mogami* astern of him and the destroyer *Shigure* to starboard. The American fire continued for almost twenty minutes, forcing the Japanese to turn away, *Mogami* and *Yamashiro* to port and *Shigure* to starboard.

A horrendous volume of fire descended on the three ships. Captain McManes spoke of a "wall of gunfire" and the gunnery officer of HMAS *Shropshire*, one of the right-flank cruisers, wrote that "the enemy must have been simply appalled by the drenching fire which was being most accurately poured on to them."[11] The bald figures are remarkable enough, given the brevity of the bombardment. The five left-flank cruisers fired off 3,100 rounds, no less than 1,147 of which came from one ship, the *Columbia*, and the three on the right flank chipped in with 1,181 rounds. The six battleships, some of whose shells weighed more than a ton each, loosed off 141 16-inch and 141 14-inch shells, most of them zeroed in on their targets by the most modern fire-control radar.[12] Even so, not all the shells found a target. *Shigure* was hit just once, by an 8-inch shell that passed through her without exploding, though even near-misses had a powerful concussive effect, putting the gyro compass and radio temporarily out of action, as well as damaging the rudder and making her hard to steer. *Yamashiro* and *Mogami* retaliated with gunfire but only one near miss was recorded by the Americans. The two Japanese ships, however, were being hit continually and they and *Shigure* eventually turned away and retreated down the strait. Nishimura was the last to turn, at almost the same moment as Admiral Oldendorf ordered his guns to cease firing, not out of compassion for the shattered Japanese remnants but because American ships were also coming under this devastating fire.

While this phase of the battle had been raging, the last group of American destroyers had appeared on the scene, the three ships in Smoot's own centre group. These, with *Newcomb* leading, headed straight for Nishimura's now meagre formation and, shortly after four o'clock, fired off 13 torpedoes at a range of 6,000 yards. Two of these slammed into *Yamashiro* at approximately 4.11, as recorded with chilling detachment in the log of the battleship *West Virginia*: "0411: [Radar] pip reported to 'bloom' and then fade. 0412: Target disappeared. Can see ships burning. One is a big fire."[13] The battle-ship was soon just a mass of flames. After drifting south for a few minutes *Yamashiro* sank at 04.19 with the loss of all but a handful of the crew. Admiral Nishimura was among the missing. *Mogami* and *Shigure* continued to withdraw, the latter in reasonably good order after temporary repairs had been made to the rudder. *Mogami* had been hit by a shattering salvo, probably from the cruiser *Portland*, which destroyed the bridge, killing the captain, executive officer and all others present, as well as scoring telling hits in the engine- and fire-rooms, slowing her to a crawl. Yet even in these extremities both *Mogami* and *Yamashiro* had observed Smoot's approach and managed to get off several salvos of their own just as the destroyers were turning away.

The very last American destroyer to quit the 'field', the *Albert W. Grant*, was hit by several 4.7-inch shells after the battle had already been decided. As *Grant* and the other destroyers continued to steer what they hoped would be out of 'harm's way', they found that American gunnery was proving to be a more serious threat than anything Nishimura's cripples could manage. After the battle Smoot wrote almost poetically of the cruisers and battleships: "The deva-stating accuracy of this gunfire was the most beautiful sight I have even witnessed. The arched line of tracers in the darkness looked like a continual stream of railroad cars going over a hill. No target could be observed at first; then shortly there would be fires and explosions and another ship would be accounted for." On another occasion he varied his imagery slightly: "It was quite a sight. It honestly looked like the Brooklyn Bridge at night – the tail-lights of automobiles going over."[14]

At the time, however, few of Smoot's crews could have been so appreciative, especially aboard *Grant* as she absorbed several more hits, eleven of them 6-inch shells fired by a 'friendly' ship, probably the cruiser *Denver* in the left-flank line. By 4.20 she was dead in the water. *Grant*'s captain, Commander Terill Nieswaner, described the moments just before the Japanese shells struck home. The very first shots landed directly ahead, "and, believe me, it was slightly uncanny and terrifying. One could pick up a slight flash of the Japanese ships and then this pinpoint of light would get bigger and bigger until suddenly with a roar like a freight train, it would pass close ahead and splash on the opposite side of the ship. Some of the misses must have been 200 yards away but one felt as if they could almost reach out and touch them. I remember only too well my own mental gyrations of thinking, 'This is like a tennis game when one keeps turning one's head from side to side to follow the ball'."[15]

There was little time for mental gyrations once shells began hitting, especially when American rounds replaced Japanese. *Grant*'s After Action Report gave a matter-of-fact but compelling account of the avalanche of fire that engulfed the hapless destroyer: "Additional shell hits began to riddle the ship. Hit forward at waterline flooded forward storeroom and forward crew's berthing compartment. Hit in 40mm No. 1 exploded 40mm ammunition and started fire. Hit through starboard boat davit exploded, killing ship's doctor . . . five radiomen, and almost entire amidships radio party. Other hits in forward stack, one hit on port motor whaleboat, one hit and low-order explosion in galley. One hit in scullery room, one hit in after crew's berthing compartment, and one additional hit in forward engine-room. All light, telephone communications, radars and radios out of commission. Steering control shifted aft."[16]

Commander Nieswaner found the ship's blinker-gun and flashed out a message: "We are dead in the water. Tow needed." Down below his surviving crew laboured heroically. The unscathed and lightly wounded concentrated upon keeping the ship afloat, pumping and bailing water, fighting fires, plugging shell-holes with bedding and mattresses, jamming tables and other furniture against damaged and weakened bulkheads, and groping round in the engine-room while trying to repair damaged machinery. The ship continued to drift helplessly but these repair parties did manage to keep her afloat. Other repairs were equally urgent. In all 34 men had been killed and 94 wounded. With the ship's doctor and a Pharmacist's Mate dead, it was left to the remaining one, W. M. Swaim Jr., to cope, supervising the sick-bay amidships, the forward dressing station and an improvised dressing station in the aft 'head', tending sailors who had lost an arm or a leg. One such was Radioman First Class W. M. Selleck, who typified this epic day in the history of U.S. destroyers when heroism that would seem almost embarrassing in a movie was in fact the order of the day. The ship's executive officer wrote Selleck's obituary: "Both legs blown off, and near death from loss of blood, Selleck went out a hero. His last words as he lay on the wardroom table . . . were, 'There's nothing you can do for me, fellows. Go ahead and do something for the others'."[17]

Oldendorf ordered his ships to cease fire as soon as he got word of *Grant*'s predicament at ten past four, but it was not until 5.15 that *Newcomb* and *Leary* were able to get back to the crippled destroyer to rig a tow and put extra medical corpsmen aboard. By 6.30 *Grant*, under tow by *Newcomb* according to one account and lashed alongside according to another, was finally extricated from Suriago Strait, a most unwilling participant in this last but nonetheless awesome demonstration of optimally deployed naval gunfire.

By now the tail of the 'T' had all but melted away. Having alerted his ships to *Grant*'s exact position, Oldendorf had been ready to resume fire at 4.19 but by then *Yamashiro* had sunk and *Mogami* and *Shigure* were out of radar range. However, even as Nishimura's fleet was being destroyed, Admiral Shima himself had been steaming up Suriago Strait. Of his fellow admiral's fate he knew little, the last direct communication having been at midnight when Nishimura reported the active presence of the PT boats. For Shima himself, the next two hours were uneventful until, at 3.15, almost directly south of Panaon, he was attacked by PT boats, and again ten minutes later. In this second attack the PT boats finally took a 'scalp'. PT-137 had been firing at a destroyer moving out of Shima's column to take up a position in the rear and, not unusually, the American boat had missed. But the torpedo ploughed on and a minute or so later struck the light cruiser *Abukuma* on her port side. Thirty of the crew were killed and, slowing to barely ten knots, she pulled out of the formation.

Meanwhile, Shima pressed on, raising his speed to 28 knots, and by four o'clock, during the height of the gunfire phase, was almost due east of the narrow strait dividing Panaon and Leyte. At this juncture his column "sighted broad on the starboard bow what appeared to be two big ships on fire. Passing west of them, Shima concluded that they were *Fuso* and *Yamashiro*, which was not very encouraging. Actually they were the two halves of *Fuso*."[18] Equally discouraging were the next ships to loom out of the darkness, the slightly damaged *Shigure* steaming away from the battle and then the blazing *Mogami*, seemingly dead in the water. Shima's flagship, *Nachi*, challenged the destroyer with her blinker-light, flashing the message: "I am the *Nachi*" and received the unhelpfully terse reply: "I am the *Shigure*. I have rudder difficulties." If it is possible for a whole ship to go into shock, then this would seem the only explanation for such a monumentally inadequate summary of the fate of Nishimura's fleet, as well as a pathetic caption to what otherwise, as ghostly ships passed in the night, illuminated by another burning furiously, would have been a scene worthy of the best samurai legend.

Nevertheless, with his two heavy cruisers and four destroyers, Shima continued north and at 4.24 picked up on his radar what were thought to be two enemy ships. The cruisers bore right a little and each fired eight torpedoes. S. E. Morison claimed that so bad was Japanese radar that the target selected was in fact Hibuson Island, where two beached torpedoes were found the next day. More recent commentators, who found this somewhat patronising, have suggested that Shima did at least have vague representations of the cruisers *Louisville* and *Portland* on his screen. Be that as it may, all sixteen torpedoes failed to find a target, at least one that was afloat, and this salvo proved to be Shima's only contribution to the battle.

It was a fateful one for his own ship, for in concentrating on the torpedo launch those aboard *Nachi* had failed to realise that *Mogami* was not in fact dead in the water but was under way, be it ever so slowly. At 4.30 the two ships collided, badly damaging *Nachi*'s stern and reducing her speed to 18 knots. Immediately after the collision, as *Nachi*'s crew was recovering from the shock and the damage control parties were being assembled, a ghostly voice boomed out from a megaphone on *Mogami*'s bridge: "This is *Mogami*. Captain and executive officer killed. Gunnery officer in charge. Steering destroyed. Sorry."[19] Even before this Shima had decided the situation in Suriago Strait was so confused that he radioed his immediate superior, Admiral Gunichi Mikawa, in Manila, to report his force "had concluded its attack and is retiring from the battle area to plan subsequent action."[20] At about 4.35, with *Mogami* just managing to tag along, Shima turned south. Some twenty minutes later he reversed course again in a surge of defiance, but common sense soon prevailed and on the hour he turned south for the last time.

Shima's first withdrawal had already been picked by Kinkaid's ships and the left-flank cruisers, including Oldendorf in his flagship *Louisville*, and a reserve destroyer screening group, Division X-Ray, set off down the Strait in pursuit. Right-flank cruisers were also ordered south a few minutes later, but although Shima's brief 'turn again' registered on the radar screens, he still managed to keep out of range of his pursuers. When the cruisers discerned three Japanese ships, two of them on fire, they shifted course to the right to attack and engaged what turned out to be *Mogami*. After several hits she was seen to be "burning like a city block", but still she stayed afloat. At 5.37 the Americans reversed course. Oldendorf had still not got much beyond the northern tip of Dinagat but he decided to withdraw his cruisers, "probably because . . . [he] was unwilling to place them in Japanese torpedo water".[21]

The X-Ray destroyers, however, were still in the chase and there was still the PT boat gauntlet to be run again. As the Japanese column reached the southern exit to Suriago Strait, these latter fired torpedoes, though none found their target. The Japanese fought back. *Mogami*, remarkably, was still under way and still capable of laying down 20 minutes of heavy fire against PT-491. Some shells landed only 25 yards away but the boat was able to make good its escape. *Mogami*, now having worked up to 12 to 14 knots, repeated this show of defiance against PT-137.

By this time Oldendorf had turned south once more, feeling that the coming of dawn at 6.30 would minimise the risk of any Japanese counter-attacks. At 6.32 he detached two light cruisers and three destroyers from X-Ray division "to polish off enemy cripples". It was gone seven when the force caught up with damaged destroyer *Asagumo*, and the renewed shelling soon started her sinking. As she went down her crew more than matched the fierce dedication shown by the *Grant* at the other end of the Strait. As the bows began to slip underwater, the stern turret continued firing its last salvo until it too disappeared beneath the waves. At about the same time, with the flotsam of the day's battle littering the Strait and numerous survivors now clearly visible in the water, the Americans witnessed another side of the Japanese sense of duty, as most of the survivors resolutely refused to be picked up. When the destroyer *Halford* came alongside one small boat every man aboard rose together and jumped over the side. Of the hundreds of men sighted in the water that morning only a handful could be persuaded to accept rescue.

This was the end of the surface encounter in Suriago Strait. At 7.23 the detached force was recalled by Oldendorf. Quite why remains unclear, but it proved to be a prescient decision, for only ten minutes later Oldendorf received startling news from the north, where Admiral Kurita's main portion of the First Striking Force had just joined battle with the Escort Carrier Task Group attached to Seventh Fleet. Any thought of pursuit would have to give way to improvised planning for a second battle. Ironically, however, planes from these same escort carriers were still in the hunt, searching for whatever ships had survived the storm of shells in Suriago Strait. Shortly before 9 o'clock they found Shima's column and concentrated their attack on the already battered *Mogami*. She was soon dead in the water but resolutely refused to sink, allowing the accompanying destroyer time to take off survivors before that ship itself, *Akebono*, finally dispatched *Mogami* with one of its own torpedoes. In all, 196 of the crew of 850 were lost. *Akebono* was allowed to proceed with its mission of mercy because the carrier planes had returned to refuel at the rudimentary Tacloban air base, on Leyte, and there had learnt of the plight of their mother ships.

A message from *Shigure*, at 10.15, to Kurita and Toyoda bluntly stated the facts about Nishimura's force: "All ships except *Shigure* went down under gunfire and torpedo attack."[22] News of Shima's withdrawal had already been received and so it was now clear that the southern pincer had disintegrated and the Japanese navy was short of two battleships, one heavy cruiser and three destroyers. What Toyoda and his staff mercifully did not know at this stage was that the sacrifice had been largely in vain. Nishimura's ships had landed only seven shells on a lone American target, the destroyer *Albert W. Grant*, which remained afloat, while Shima's ships only ever fired seven projectiles in total towards their main target, none of which hit anything of the slightest military significance.

30

No Higher Honour
THE BATTLE OF SAMAR

WHEN Admiral Kurita emerged from the San Bernadino Strait just after midnight on the 25th, he was expecting to be confronted by the American Third Fleet. Halsey's aircraft had already pounded him in the Sibuyan Sea and the Japanese commander had no reason to believe that they would not once more be lying in wait, along with the surface firepower of the American fast battleships and heavy cruisers. In the event, Kurita's arrival went largely unnoticed, Halsey having been lured away, albeit belatedly, by Ozawa's decoy carrier force, and Kinkaid preoccupied with events in Suriago Strait, as well as secure in his own mind that Halsey had left a powerful Task Force behind to guard the San Bernadino exit. In reality, all there was between Kurita and Leyte Gulf was Admiral T. L. Sprague's Escort Carrier Group, Task Group 77.4, stationed off the east coast of Samar and made up of three Task Units, known for convenience by their radio call signs Taffy-1, -2 and -3. Each of the Taffys was made up of six aircraft carriers and a screen of three destroyers and four or five destroyer escorts. Escort carriers were essentially logistical protection vessels, at their most effective when providing ocean convoys, in the Pacific or the Atlantic, with anti-submarine aircraft to reconnoitre, deter or attack any enemy submarines that appeared on the surface. This remained one of their main duties during static amphibious operations, although the 500 or so planes on Sprague's carriers were also a potent asset for providing air cover and ground support to the troops ashore. Each carrier had aboard an average squadron of 16 fighters and 12 torpedo-bombers. As part of Kinkaid's Seventh Fleet, and so as relaxed as he was about the supposed protection left behind by Third Fleet, Sprague felt no need on the 25th to look beyond the invasion beaches.

For several hours in the very early morning of the 25th Kurita was able to round the north-east corner of Samar completely undetected and speed south towards Leyte Gulf. The first contact made with American forces was with Taffy-3, the northernmost of Sprague's Task Units. Commanded by Admiral C. A. F. Sprague, it had the usual complement of ships, comprising the escort carriers *St Lo*, *Kalinin Bay*, *Gambier Bay*, *Kitkun Bay*, *White Plains* and *Fanshaw Bay*, protected by the destroyers *Hoel*, *Heermann* and *Johnston*, and the destroyer escorts *Dennis*, *John C. Butler*, *Raymond* and *Samuel B. Roberts*. The ships were arranged in their normal formation, an inner ring of escort carriers some 5,000 yards in diameter, and an outer ring of destroyers, each another 3,500 yards further out. The carriers were to retain their formation, at least approximately, throughout most of the battle, though the circle did become somewhat stretched because of inevitable speed differentials. The destroyers, too, continued to defend the carriers, displaying exemplary dedication, but they tended to become committed at the most threatened points of the compass rather than maintaining a 360° degree perimeter.

The encounter began at 6.45 a.m. when one carrier picked up an unidentified contact on the radar screen and what might have been Japanese voices were heard on the fighter direction net. Two minutes later an American anti-submarine pilot reported the sighting of a large body of ships, including four battleships. Sprague assumed that this must be part of Task Force 38 until, within seconds, his own lookouts excitedly pointed out the unmistakable bridge-cum-mast structures found on Japanese battleships and cruisers, looming over the northern horizon like so many paddling pagodas. On the destroyer *Roberts*, one of the nearest ships, the executive officer remained remarkably calm, announcing to the ship's company over the tannoy, "Now hear this. All hands desiring to see the fleeing remnants of the Japanese fleet, lay up topside."[1] This was undoubtedly one of the day's more glaring misinterpretations of events, but few others got the chance to share it. At a few minutes before seven the first Japanese shells landed, throwing up huge geysers just astern of Taffy-3. Sprague now had two immediate priorities: to distance himself from the enemy and to launch his aircraft. Unfortunately, the two were not entirely compatible. Aircraft carriers still had one thing in common with old 18th-century ships-of-the-line, having always to pay close attention to the wind direction. Planes had to be launched into the wind to gain the additional lift to get airborne during their short take-off. That morning the wind was blowing from the north-east, and if Sprague turned tail to the

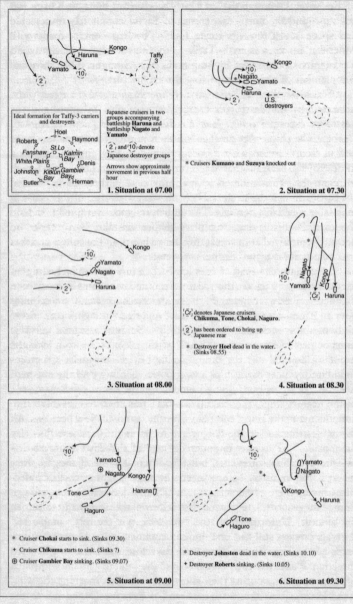

1. Situation at 07.00

Ideal formation for Taffy-3 carriers and destroyers

Hoel
Roberts   Raymond
Fanshaw   St Lo   Kalinin
White Plains   Bay   Denis
Johnston   Kitkun   Gambier
Bay   Bay   Herman
Butler

Japanese cruisers in two groups accompanying battleship **Haruna** and battleship **Nagato** and **Yamato**

(2) and (10) denote Japanese destroyer groups

Arrows show approximate movement in previous half hour

2. Situation at 07.30

* Cruisers **Kumano** and **Suzuya** knocked out

3. Situation at 08.00

4. Situation at 08.30

(Cr) denotes Japanese cruisers **Chikuma, Tone, Chokai, Naguro.**

(2) has been ordered to bring up Japanese rear

* Destroyer **Hoel** dead in the water. (Sinks 08.55)

5. Situation at 09.00

* Cruiser **Chokai** starts to sink. (Sinks 09.30)
+ Cruiser **Chikuma** starts to sink. (Sinks ?)
⊕ Cruiser **Gambier Bay** sinking. (Sinks 09.07)

6. Situation at 09.30

* Destroyer **Johnston** dead in the water. (Sinks 10.10)
+ Destroyer **Roberts** sinking. (Sinks 10.05)

Leyte Gulf: the Battle of Samar 25th October 1944

south, his most obvious escape route, he would need to turn back and sail towards the enemy if he were ever to launch his planes. He therefore adopted a compromise, turning east on a course that would both take him away from the enemy and give his pilots sufficient wind starting across the decks to boost them off. As he turned he gave the order for his planes to prepare for take-off.*

Admiral Kurita had spotted the Americans at almost exactly the same moment that he was discovered. He reacted to the sighting just as quickly as Sprague and gave immediate orders for 'General Attack'. Unfortunately the order came only a few minutes after an earlier one to deploy from a five-column cruising formation to a circular one on a more easterly heading. 'General Attack' was very much a free-for-all manoeuvre, leaving direction and choice of targets to individual captains, and coming in the middle of another change of formation it caused considerable confusion. Even before battle was joined, in fact, Kurita had already made his most serious mistake, attributable, no doubt, to the fact that he had now gone 72 hours without sleep and was still not recovered from his bout of dengue fever. No historian of the battle has seriously quarrelled with S. E. Morison's judgement that the order was "a fatal error. Kurita should have formed battle-line with his . . . battleships and . . . heavy cruisers, which would have allowed his superior firepower to count, and he should have committed [destroyers] immediately for torpedo attack. But complete surprise seems to have deprived the Admiral of all power of decision, and the result was a helter-skelter battle. His ships . . . were committed piece-meal and so defeated."[2] Kurita's Chief-of-Staff, Admiral Toniji Koyanagi, while admitting that "little heed was paid to co-ordination", loyally asserted that 'General Attack' was ordered because the American carriers had already been seen to turn away and "in a pursuit the only essential is to close the gap as rapidly as possible and concentrate fire upon the enemy."[3] But as a British historian has pointed out, the Japanese never seemed to make closing the gap their main priority. Rather, they seemed to try to keep to the north of Taffy-3 to prevent the carriers heading into the wind and launching planes. As Kurita remained convinced that he was facing the fleet carriers of Task Force 38 his caution is understandable. Yet the fact remains that his ships clearly did not attempt to close as quickly as possible, but persistently sought to box Sprague in from windward, tracking his turn

---

* Sprague's overall track on the 25th is shown in the map on page 335. His movements during the actual battle, from 6.45 to 9.20 a.m., are shown in the charts on page 350.

south and then south-west from the 'outside lane' rather than cutting the corner with at least some of the powerful array of gunships.[4]

Admiral Sprague was in no position to know that Kurita had already forsaken a precious advantage. All he knew was that his less than imposing collection of 'jeep carriers' and destroyers was being pursued by approximately ten Japanese 'battlewagons' and heavy cruisers that completely outgunned him.[5] By 7 a.m. he had increased speed, his planes were taking off, his ships were all beginning to belch out smoke, as ordered, to mask their positions, and he had sent out an urgent SOS to any who could hear. The call for help was quickly answered and Admiral Kinkaid granted immediate permission for the other escort carrier groups, Taffy-1 and Taffy-2, respectively 130 miles and 35 miles to the south, to launch support strikes of their own. The commander of Taffy-2, Admiral Felix Stump, captured the panicky mood of the moment even as he tried to reassure 'Ziggy' Sprague over the radio: "Don't be alarmed, Ziggy – remember, we're back of you – don't get excited – don't do anything rash!", but with each phrase his own voice was rising to a high-pitched crescendo.[6] To launch his own planes Stump had to sail directly towards Kurita and Sprague, and as he did so he debated with one of his officers the advice he attributed to John Paul Jones (in fact it was Nelson) that no naval commander could go very far wrong if he placed his ship alongside those of the enemy. But once his launch was completed he made up his mind: "John Paul Jones to the contrary notwithstanding, the time has come to get the hell out of here."[7]

By now Japanese salvoes were landing in profusion just to the rear of the carriers and getting nearer every time, especially to the carriers *Fanshaw Bay* and *White Plains*. In less than five minutes *White Plains* was assailed three times by salvoes of 14-inch shells, the final one slewing the ship, throwing men to the deck, and momentarily cutting off some of the electric power. The experience was reminiscent of some hellish firework display as the Japanese battleships, to assist range-finding, distinguished their shell splashes with different coloured dyes. *Yamato*'s were pink and *Kongo*'s yellow, while other ships favoured red, green, blue and purple, or in one case no colouring at all. Some of these paint-box eruptions rose 150 feet in the air. Admiral Sprague wrote: "Wicked salvos straddled the *White Plains* and their coloured geysers began to sprout among all the other carriers . . . The splashes had a horrid kind of beauty." A seaman on board *White Plains* is supposed to have called out at one point: "Look, they're shooting at us in Technicolor!"[8]

Sprague realised that it could not be long before the splashes included chunks of his own ships. He later recalled that "the enemy was closing with disconcerting rapidity and the volume and accuracy of fire was increasing. At this point it did not appear that any of our ships could survive another five minutes of the heavy-caliber fire being received."[9] He remained pessimistic even after all his planes were airborne for he had been unable to arm many of them with torpedoes, the only weapon that gave any realistic hope of success against heavily armoured battleships and heavy cruisers. Preparing torpedoes was a very time-consuming and finicky business and by the time extra torpedoes had been mounted, some of the carriers might already have been sunk. Even those still afloat would have been forced to turn south to avoid being driven away from the rest of Seventh Fleet – and south was downwind, denying the heavily-laden torpedo bombers the additional lift they needed from sailing into the wind. Consequently planes had taken off pretty much 'come as you are', with many Avenger torpedo planes carrying no effective payload. *Gambier Bay* put up nine Avengers, of which two had no bombs at all and two were armed with inappropriately fused depth-bombs. Of the two which did carry torpedoes, one had only enough gasoline for a few minutes' flying time, after which it had to pancake into the sea. Nor could Sprague realistically expect much from his destroyers and destroyer-escorts, the former armed only with five 5-inch guns and ten torpedoes, the latter with two 5-inch and a mere three torpedoes. Worse, the crews aboard destroyer-escorts had never trained in mounting torpedo attacks, having spent most of their time on anti-submarine missions, fire support, and as anti-aircraft vessels on radar watch.

At six minutes past seven, however, Sprague's fortunes improved slightly. The smoke laid by all ships was already beginning to provide some sort of cover when the Task Unit ran into one of the sheeting rain-squalls that scud across the Philippine Sea at this time of year. These micro-fronts rendered ships almost invisible to anyone more than a few hundred yards away and provided retreating Taffy-3 with what one historian has memorably described as "seagoing foxholes".[10] As his ships ducked into this providential cover, Sprague took the opportunity to turn south and south-west. The squall and the change of course probably saved Taffy-3, for the turn was missed by Kurita as he ploughed on eastwards, allowing the range between him and Taffy-3 to open up beyond the reach of inadequate Japanese search radar. The gunfire that had been steadily zeroing in on Sprague's carriers quickly became wild and scattered. The toothless carrier planes were able to play their part. Showing remarkable courage, all his pilots pressed their attacks vigorously, even unarmed planes buzzing battleships and cruisers with seemingly deadly intent. As Kurita's commanders still assumed that they were facing a doughty fast carrier Task Group rather than just a startled Taffy, they took evasive action that held most of Kurita's ships to their easterly course until about 07.50. And because each ship took this evasive action individually, the Japanese never had the chance to recover formation after the dislocation caused by the original order for 'General Attack'.

Though Sprague must have realised that Japanese gunfire was, for the moment at least, receding, he felt that he had no option but to call upon his destroyers to make their own hazardous, even suicidal sortie. The order was given at 7.16 to *Hoel*, *Heermann* and *Johnston*, although the latter had already on its own initiative started towards the nearest enemy ship, the heavy cruiser *Kumano*. *Johnston*, whose captain, Commander Ernest Evans, was a full-blooded Cherokee, was already delivering rapid salvo fire from 5-inch guns when the formal order to attack came, and at about 7.20, from a range of only 10,000 yards, loosed off all ten torpedoes. As the destroyer jerked round and sought the cover of its own smoke again, those on board claimed to have heard two or three underwater explosions. After the battle Admiral Kurita admitted to only one torpedo hit from destroyers during the entire day, but it was a deadly one, slamming into *Kumano* shortly before seven-thirty and leaving the ship burning furiously as it began to drift out of the ragged Japanese line. The commander of 7th Cruiser Division shifted his flag to the accompanying heavy cruiser *Suzuya*, only to discover that she too had been hit, several bombs reducing the vessel's speed to 20 knots. Neither ship was to play any further part in the battle. *Suzuya* was hit by another bomb at about 8.45, and she sank almost five hours later.

Several other Japanese ships were now beginning to concentrate their fire on the single destroyer, and at about 7.30 *Johnston* "got it. Three 14-inch shells from a battleship, followed thirty seconds later by three 6-inch shells from a light cruiser, hit us. It was like a puppy being smacked by a truck."[11] The ship was devastated. Fire- and engine-rooms were knocked out, all power to the steering engine and the after 5-inch guns was gone, the gyro compass was useless, and many men had been killed below as well as three officers on the bridge, one of whom had been decapitated. Commander Evans had lost two fingers from his left hand and had all clothing above the waist blown off.

Ignoring other wounds to his neck and chest, Evans shrugged off offers of medical aid and told the ship's doctor, "Don't bother me now. Help some of the guys who are hurt."[12] Evans made do with a handkerchief wrapped around his bleeding hand and proceeded to restore his ship to fighting trim, giving thanks as it slipped into the same rain squall that had shrouded the escort carriers at their moment of crisis. All gun stations were found to answer to test calls and partial power was restored to all but one of the after guns. Steering was shifted to the after steering compartment, where sailors laboured to operate the hydraulic rudder system by hand in response to orders telephoned down from the bridge.

Meanwhile, *Johnston* had not been the only terrier nipping at Kurita's southern flank. *Hoel* and *Heermann* had also responded swiftly to Sprague's command and *Hoel* began an approach on the nearest battleship, *Kongo*, in Kurita's starboard quarter, coolly trading gunfire with this giant until hit in the bridge at 7.25. Two minutes later *Hoel* managed to launch five torpedoes, all of which missed, but was immediately hit again by several shells which knocked out the port engine, three guns, and jammed the rudder hard right. *Hoel* was now headed straight for *Kongo*, until an even nearer target loomed into view, the heavy cruiser *Haguro*, at which *Hoel* fired her last five torpedoes. These exploded in the vicinity of the Japanese cruiser and were recorded as hits in *Hoel*'s log, though as Japanese records state that *Haguro* received only one bomb hit, at around 8 a.m., it seems likely that the torpedoes exploded prematurely, perhaps when they hit the cruiser's wake.

Hoel's attack on *Haguro*, in fact, became part of a second general destroyer attack, ordered by Sprague at 7.42 and actually executed at 7.50. The third destroyer, *Heermann*, which had been furthest away from the Japanese, had missed the first attack completely but joined in the next, having steamed right through the Taffy formation and formed a column behind *Hoel*. This second order of Sprague's really only applied to these two ships. It was addressed to the 'Wolves', codename for the destroyers as distinct from the destroyer-escorts, and could not be expected to include *Johnston* which had already expended all her torpedoes. But this was not Commander Evans' reading of the situation and he, too, joined the column, believing it to be his duty to 'provide fire support', although only two of his guns could maintain a normal rate of properly aimed fire. Even as *Johnston* tagged along, the column acquired another unbidden guest, the destroyer-escort *Samuel B. Roberts* which, after querying whether 'Wolves' also included 'Little

Wolves' and being quickly brushed off, joined up with the destroyers anyway, following some 3,000 yards behind them.

Hoel led off this second attack with its failed torpedo attack on *Haguro*. Shortly after that *Heermann* came plunging up behind her, narrowly missing a collision with the crippled ship whose speed she misjudged. At just before 8.00 a.m. *Heermann*'s captain, Commander Amos Hathaway, launched seven torpedoes of his own at *Haguro*. All missed, as did the fifteen gunfire salvos from the Japanese in reply. Even as they fired, Hathaway and his gunnery officer picked out the rest of the scattered Japanese battle line and promptly turned towards it. While 14-inch shells began splashing all around him, Hathaway calmly selected a target, the battleship *Haruna*, launched his remaining torpedoes and directed his gunfire against the towering bridge superstructure. He then turned away and resumed laying smoke. "Everything looked rosy," Hathaway commented later, "but only because the splashes were coloured red by the dye-loads."[13] This may even have helped Hathaway a little because he was now 'chasing the salvos', or alternating his course to head for the splashes made by the last Japanese salvo in the hope that the enemy would correct his fire solution so as not to hit the same spot twice.

If neither *Hoel* nor *Heermann* had made any physical impression upon the Japanese battle line, they had certainly compounded Kurita's ongoing problem of creating a compact formation in close touch with the enemy. While firing at one of the destroyers, Kurita's flagship, *Yamato*, noticed torpedo tracks bearing 100 degrees starboard and turned to port, eventually bearing almost due north, to evade them. The turn put the battleship between two spreads, one on each side of the ship, chasing her from astern. Not daring to reverse, the huge ship continued on the same bearing for almost ten minutes until the torpedoes' motors ran down and the tracks disappeared. The battleship *Nagato* remained close behind *Yamato* throughout the battle and she too followed this manoeuvre which had added ten miles and more to the ships' track by the time they turned back. With these torpedoes, probably fired by *Hoel* at *Haguro*, the American destroyers effectively took two battleships out of the pursuit, and the commander of the Japanese fleet with them.

Both *Johnston* and the destroyer-escort *Roberts* had also formed up for this second attack and each played their part in keeping up the pressure on Kurita's heavy ships, forcing them to take continual evasive action. The *Roberts* went into battle in a spirit which would have been applauded on any of their opponents' vessels. The captain,

Commodore Robert Copeland, spoke over the tannoy to his crew – mostly reservists with less than twelve months' service – telling them that they were heading towards "a fight against overwhelming odds from which survival could not be expected, during which time we would do what damage we could."[14] Probably because he had such a small supply of torpedoes, Copeland held his fire as he raced towards the Japanese and under cover of the drifting smoke approached to within 4,000 yards (point blank range in naval terms) before loosing his three 'fish' at the heavy cruiser *Chokai*, at about 8.00. One of these may have scored a hit but does not seem to have caused any appreciable damage. Copeland then retired, but with the Japanese themselves beginning to turn south and the remaining Japanese cruisers coming together in the van (see map on page 350), his ship came under continuous gunfire from just after eight o'clock. As for *Johnston*, with all torpedoes expended, the partially crippled destroyer unflinchingly took the battleship *Kongo* under fire with a 5-inch gun. According to one survivor, "As far as accomplishing anything decisive, it was like bouncing paper wads off a steel helmet, but we did kill some Japs and knock out a few small guns. Then we ran back into our smoke. The battleship belched a few 14-inchers at us but, thank God, registered only clean misses."[15]

Though the actions of the three destroyers and *Roberts* can be seen as the most concerted attack of the battle, it should never be thought that the remaining destroyer-escorts were avoiding the fight. Though unable to link up with the other ships, both *Dennis* and *Raymond* responded to Sprague's second order and, quite independently, engaged the heavy cruisers. *Raymond* charged towards *Haguro* and, under fire, launched its torpedoes, all three of which missed. *Dennis* also came under attack from *Haguro* but managed to fire torpedoes at either *Chokai* or *Tone*. Again no hits were recorded and at 8.09, her guns pounding away at the cruisers, *Dennis* turned south-west and soon fell in with the ships retiring from the main destroyer attack.

These now comprised only two destroyers and a destroyer-escort, for *Hoel* had been the first to pay the price for the screen's extraordinary dedication. The one remaining engine was not enough to permit *Hoel* to pull clear of the Japanese and the destroyer became boxed in, with *Kongo* slamming in shells from the port beam and the cruisers firing from the starboard quarter, all from a range of 7–8,000 yards. *Hoel* took some forty hits from 5-, 8-, and 16-inch shells, mostly armour-piercing. These simply punched a hole right through the ship, though enough of them passed out below the waterline to slow her down more and more. At 8.30, after firing 500 rounds from two forward guns, *Hoel* was hit by a shell that smashed into the engine-room and the ship left dead in the water. She was now listing heavily to port and settling by the stern, and five minutes later the order was given to abandon ship. As the Japanese passed around to the north-east all ships continued to pump fire into the crippled vessel until, at 8.55, she rolled over and sank. Of the crew of 300, 19 were wounded and 253 killed and missing. The captain, Commodore L. S. Kintberger, spoke no more than the simple truth when he wrote: "Fully cognisant of the inevitable result of engaging such vastly superior forces, these men performed their assigned duties coolly and efficiently until their ship was shot from under them."[16]

Meanwhile the four surviving Japanese cruisers – *Tone*, *Chikuma*, *Haguro* and *Chokai* – began to forge ahead of the rest of the still disorganised formation and to edge the Taffy eastwards into the fire of the following battleships. The menace from these cruisers was now clear to all and at 8.26 Sprague ordered his third attack of the day, just as the survivors of his screen were bustling southwards to retake their stations. *Heermann*, *Johnston* and *Roberts* were already involved in something of a running battle with these cruisers, even as they withdrew. Trading shots with the Japanese was clearly an uneven battle, especially as those destroyer-escorts with torpedoes still aboard never found an opportunity to fire them. *Dennis* received three serious hits and was forced to retire behind the smokescreen. *Heermann* was also hit by a shell from *Chikuma* and shortly afterwards came under fire from *Tone*. The destroyer's Action Report records that one of these shells "hit a storage locker full of dried Navy beans and reduced the beans to a paste. Another hit the uptake from the forward boiler. The bean paste was sucked up by the hot blast of the uptake and thrown in the air. Lieutenant Bob Rutter was nearly buried in the stuff."[17] Rutter was the ship's supply officer.

Whether the irony was much appreciated at the time is doubtful. Certainly there was no cause for one scintilla of amusement aboard *Roberts*. She was hit at about 8.50 and at 9.00 experienced a tremendous explosion that tore a jagged hole, thirty to forty feet long, in the port side. Number 2 engine was destroyed, fuel tanks were ruptured and a fire raged astern. All power was lost and most of the stern half of the ship had the appearance of a jumble of scrap iron. But still Number 2 gun fired, the gun crew getting off six shells entirely by hand, knowing that the gas injection system was not working and the terrible risks this entailed. While firing the seventh shell, the gun exploded, killing or fatally wounding all but one member of the gun crew. According to the ship's Action Report, "the first man to enter the [gun-]mount after the explosion found the gun-captain, [Gunner's Third Mate Paul Henry] Carr, on the deck of the mount, holding in his hands the last projectile available to the gun. He was completely torn open and his intestines were splattered throughout the inside of the mount. Nevertheless, he held in his hands the 54-pound projectile, held it above his head and begged the petty-officer who had entered the mount to help him get that last round out."[18] Carr died within the next five minutes. Horror and heroism went hand-in-hand on *Roberts* that day. The third round to strike the ship had severed its main steam line, directing scalding steam into the forward fire-room rather than the turbines. Three men were poached alive and another died later. The fifth, Jackson McKaskill, terribly burnt also, made his way through the scorching darkness to shut off the affected boiler and then took a portable phone from a dead shipmate and made his damage report. "By the time he had completed these level-headed actions, all the flesh had been scorched from the bottoms of both feet."[19] At ten minutes past nine Commander Copeland had no alternative but to order 'Abandon Ship'. Every wounded man was given first aid before being placed in the life-rafts. Finally the ship slowly sank by the stern just after ten o'clock.

However, one American ship, *Johnston*, had already broken off the action. Noticing the Japanese light cruiser, *Yahagi*, and four destroyers rapidly closing with the American carriers from their port quarter, Captain Evans, his ship in a pitiable condition, immediately turned towards this new threat. At 8.50 Admiral Kimura, the commander of 10 Destroyer Squadron, noted in his log that an "enemy destroyer plunged out of the smokescreen on our port bow and opened gunfire and torpedo on us."[20] The crew of *Roberts* also had a sight of *Johnston* as she passed in the opposite direction, again emerging suddenly from a bank of smoke. The whole scene is remarkably reminiscent of the ghostly meeting of *Shigure* and *Nachi* in Suriago Strait, just five hours earlier. As the terribly "mangled destroyer passed close by *Roberts*, Copeland could see her Cherokee skipper on the fantail, shouting conning orders down through the hatch leading to the after steering compartment. Evans was stripped to the waist and covered with blood. As *Johnston* steamed by, Evans looked up at Copeland and casually waved. Copeland returned the wave . . . *Johnston* disappeared into the veils of smoke as hauntingly as she had appeared."[21]

The carriers were now at possibly the most critical moment of the whole pursuit, with torpedo-laden destroyers to starboard, heavily-gunned cruisers to port and battleships bearing down astern to mop up survivors. The commander of the carrier *Kitkun Bay* wrote that at this moment "there appeared only one possible outcome of the encounter – complete annihilation."[22] The destroyer screen had obviously done all they could, and more, but even they were not able to prevent some Japanese shells from finding a target. *Kalinin Bay* was hit by an 8-inch shell from one of the cruisers and by about 8.30 had taken twelve more 8-inch hits and possibly one from a battleship's main armament. *Fanshaw Bay* took four 8-inch hits, at 8.50, and *White Plains* part of a 6-inch salvo at about the same time. But on the whole Japanese fire was poor. *Gambier Bay* and *Kalinin Bay* were the ships nearest the enemy and because they were sailing with the wind behind them got little cover from their own smoke and none from anybody else's. As the commander of the *Gambier Bay*, Captain Walter Vieweg, wrote in his Action Report, the Japanese cruisers were getting into "excellent position to pour in a rather heavy fire . . . which they proceeded to do without delay. However, this fire was somewhat inaccurate, not very fast, salvos were about a minute and a half apart, and not particularly large. Their spotting was rather methodical and enabled us to dodge."[23] For fully half-an-hour, in fact, Vieweg successfully avoided or chased the salvos. The Japanese were using mainly armour-piercing shot which simply punched straight through the carriers without exploding and detonating the copious quantities of gasoline, bombs and torpedoes aboard each frail carrier. But even armour-piercing shells could leave their mark, as the crew of *Kalinin Bay* could vigorously testify. Only by the most strenuous efforts did they manage to keep their ship in formation. "Boatswain's crews worked in as much as five feet of water to plug holes below the water-line; engineers and firemen risked death by scalding steam, working knee-deep in oil, choked by the stench of burning rubber, to repair ruptures in the power plant. Main steering control was knocked out and quartermasters steered the ship by hand from down in her bowels, like helmsmen on the ancient Spanish galleons."[24]

Not all these shells failed to explode. *Gambier Bay* also came under cruiser fire and of the subsequent fifteen hits for which details were recorded, ten shells exploded within the ship or on impact, two failed to explode and the results of the other three are not recorded. Many of these hits were serious. One of the ship's photographers saw several shells bounce across the flight deck without even detonating but when one internal hit did explode he was appalled to see the flight deck undulate like a wave approaching the shore. Fires were soon started in the hangar and then on the flight deck, and one of the next shells holed the forward port engine-room below the water-line. Within minutes the engine-room had to be abandoned as the ship slowed to eleven knots and dropped astern of the formation. By 8.30. she was listing 20 degrees and was now under fire from heavy cruisers *Chikuma*, *Chokai* and *Haguro*, light cruiser *Noshiro* and a destroyer.[25] A few minutes later all steering controls had been shot away and the after engine-room was hit. Water gushed in at something like 19,000 gallons a minute, though the pumps could handle only a maximum of 1,200 gallons. Within a minute or two the ship was dead in the water and beginning to sink. When Captain Vieweg gave the order to abandon ship, 750 of the crew of 854 were got over the side but several were killed in the water by shell fragments as the Japanese continued to pound the carrier until she sank at 9.07. The survivors assembled in seven or eight groups, lashing life-rafts and assorted wreckage together to create ramshackle floating sanctuaries. They hoped for a fairly speedy rescue as the waters in this part of the world were shark-infested, and it was found that by some grotesque series of mischances every water breaker on the life-rafts had been drained of the last drop of drinkable water.

Despite this somewhat ignominious flight by the escort carriers, it should not be thought that they were entirely incapable of fending for themselves. One of Sprague's first actions had been to get some of his planes aloft and these, imperfectly armed though many of them were, persisted with their attacks even when they had nothing left but bullets. Sprague described how the air group commander from *Gambier Bay* was obliged to "glide his Avenger through flak to make dry runs on enemy capital ships, once flying down a line of cruisers to divert them from their course and and throw off their gunfire for a few precious minutes."[26] Their efforts were handsomely assisted by Taffy-2 to the south-east, which managed to get off four separate strikes which pitted a further 44 fighters and 59 torpedo-bombers against Kurita's fleet. Their contribution was especially welcome as the Avengers had been rigged for torpedoes the night before and were able to attack with this most effective of weapons. Even when a torpedo missed, its target became involved in much more elaborate evasive manoeuvring than for bombs, with an increased likelihood of losing distance and formation. According to Kurita's operations officer, the American attacks "were almost incessant ... The bombers and torpedo planes were very aggressive and skilful and the coordination was impressive; even in comparison with the many experiences of American attacks we had already had, this was the most skilful work of your planes."[27]

Eventually they were rewarded with a kill, when shortly before 9 a.m., an Avenger from *Natoma Bay* launched at least one torpedo into the heavy cruiser *Chikuma* which soon began to slowly sink.

Nevertheless, it was Taffy-3 itself that was responsible for most of the Japanese losses. Cruisers *Kumano* and *Suzuya* were already hit, one by gunfire and a torpedo from *Johnston*, the other by a bomb from an unknown aircraft and left sinking. Another cruiser, *Chokazi*, got closer to the carriers but at about 8.50 was repeatedly hit by gunfire from *White Plains*' solitary 5-inch gun. A sailor manning one of the ship's quadruple anti-aircraft mountings became so excited watching these shells hit home that he yelled out, "Hold on a little longer, boys, we're sucking them into 40 millimetre range!"[28] The shells caused unexpectedly severe damage, smashing a forward turret and putting the cruiser's engines out of commission. They were also a serious distraction. Some of *Kitkun Bay*'s planes had been out on routine patrol when, hearing of Taffy-3's plight, they flew to an airfield to refuel and rearm before returning to lend their ship a hand. They arrived over *Chokai* just after nine o'clock and dived into the attack. Since leaving Leyte most of the planes had become separated and it was just four Avengers that, according to their leader's Action Report, "completed all dives in about 35 seconds, scoring five hits midships on the stack, one hit and two near-misses on the stern and three hits on the bow. The third plane hitting the stern sent the heavy cruiser into a sharp right turn. After pulling out of the dive, I observed the heavy cruiser go about 500 yards, blow up and sink within five minutes."[29] Kurita had now lost four of his six heavy cruisers.

Over on the starboard side of Taffy-3 *Johnston*, which had sailed forth to give battle against a Japanese light cruiser and four destroyers, was beginning to fire at the light cruiser, *Yahagi*. As the range closed from 10,000 to 7,000 yards, upwards of a dozen hits were observed on *Yahagi* after which the cruiser was seen to turn 90 degrees to port and break off the action. This, in fact, was standard procedure to allow the Japanese destroyers to launch torpedoes, which they began to do at 9.15. However, *Johnston* had so unsettled the Japanese squadron that it was firing at the Taffy from extreme range (about 10,500 yards) and while the escort carriers were steaming away at 18 knots or so. The torpedoes were going to have a very long run to their targets. On seeing this, and knowing that he had provoked them to fire prematurely, Evans, according to one of his officers, "was so elated that he could hardly talk. He strutted across his bridge and chortled, 'Now I've seen everything!' [But] we had more fighting to do, and GQ Johnny's number was about up."[30] For the Japanese destroyers now began to concentrate their fire on *Johnston*, and were soon joined by the cruisers as Evans turned to port and closed range on them. According to the officer just quoted, Lieutenant Hagen, for the next half-hour *Johnston* engaged first the cruisers and then the destroyers, "alternating between the two groups in a somewhat desperate attempt to keep all of them from closing with the carrier formation. The ship was getting hit with disconcerting frequency throughout this period. At 0910 we had taken a hit which knocked out one forward gun and damaged the other. Fires had broken out. One of our 40-mm ready-lockers was hit and exploding shells were causing as much damage as the Japs."[31]

Eventually a whole salvo hit home, knocking out the remaining engine-room. All communications in the ship were severed and just one 5-inch gun was still firing, manually. At 9.40 *Johnston* went dead in the water and five minutes later the captain gave the order 'Abandon Ship'. The Japanese destroyers closed in and started circling the ship while still firing, reminding Hagen of "Indians attacking a prairie schooner". At 10.10 *Johnston* rolled over and began to sink. One Japanese destroyer continued to fire at her but as she went down it is said that the captain came to attention on his bridge and saluted. Of *Johnston*'s crew of 327, 50 were killed in action, 45 died of wounds while in the water or on life-rafts, and 92, including Commander Evans, went missing in the water.

These men had performed a remarkable service, perhaps saving the very best until last by thwarting a concerted torpedo attack that should have wreaked havoc among the carriers. Admiral Kimura, displaying the same manic optimism that had infected commanders during the air battles off Formosa, claimed in his battle report that three enemy carriers and one cruiser were observed to sink in quick succession, though he also included the somewhat contradictory detail that all were enveloped in black smoke at the time. In fact, the destroyers hit nothing and such torpedoes as might have posed a threat were running so slowly by the time they reached the carriers that one was strafed and detonated by an American pilot and a second was deflected away from *St Lo* by that ship's 5-inch gun. As S. E. Morison concludes: "One of the most threatening episodes in the entire action proved a complete fiasco."[32]

Japanese accounts remain unclear as to how much of these events was known to Admiral Kurita, still well astern of his cruisers and destroyers. One assumes not very much, because at 9.10, while destroyers were steaming in to launch torpedoes and two of his cruisers, *Haguro* and *Tone*, were charging ever nearer to the fleeing carriers and their battered screen, Kurita gave the order to suspend the pursuit and for all his units to close. By 9.20 both cruisers had turned away, prompting one of the signalmen on Sprague's flagship, *Fanshaw Bay*, to yell, "Goddammit, boys, they're getting away!" Sprague himself recounted that, "I could not believe my eyes . . . It took a whole series of reports from circling planes to convince me. And still I could not get the fact into my battle-numbed brain. At best, I had expected to be swimming by this time."[33]

Kurita's immediate reasons for this about-turn were that he wished to regroup his scattered formation and was also worried about the amount of fuel being consumed by the destroyers. But the underlying reason was that Kurita, his brain befogged by recent illness, immersion in the Sibuyan Sea and lack of sleep, was not fighting the real battle. Throughout the action he and his staff were convinced that they had stumbled across the southern task group of TF 38 and that the ships running before them comprised five or six fleet carriers, two battleships and at least ten cruisers and destroyers. Most of what happened in the battle itself served only to confirm Kurita in this misapprehension. Visual identification of the American ships remained difficult. As Kurita's Chief-of-Staff wrote, "Because of the enemy's efficient use of squalls and smokescreens for cover, his ships were visible to us in the *Yamato* only at short intervals." Moreover, because of the incessant zig-zagging and evasive action prompted by the continuous attacks from American destroyers and carrier aircraft, Kurita's ships, even running at full speed, were not making very fast progress as the crow flies. Koyanagi, again, stated that their fleet pursued the Americans "at top speed for over two hours but we could not close the gap; in fact it actually appeared to be lengthening. We estimated that the enemy's speed was nearly thirty knots, that his carriers were of the regular, large type [*Essex*-class], that pursuit would be an endless see-saw, and that we would be unable to strike a decisive blow."[34]

Though Kurita sailed his fleet due north until 10.55, it seems that it was his intention eventually to turn back south in tighter formation and fulfil his original mission to enter Leyte Gulf and attack the American transports. From 10.55 he turned west, south-west and west again, and until 12.15 seemed to be heading directly for the Gulf. But this manoeuvring was less purposeful than it appeared and was done partly to avoid air attack while Kurita finally decided upon his next move. The more he thought about it, the less tempting did Leyte Gulf seem. Admiral Shima had already given word that he was retiring from Suriago Strait and a message from *Shigure* indicated that it was the only survivor from Nishimura's force, making a mockery of the pincers stratagem. Moreover, the route to Leyte Gulf was still blocked by the retreating carrier force and, retreating or not, Kurita continued to believe that it was one of Halsey's task groups. Other messages were picked up by the Japanese communications centre in Formosa and relayed to Kurita. Several of these reinforced his fears about American air-power, whether from other task groups in Task Force 38 or from the airfield on Leyte, which he seems to have thought would be crammed with land-based and staging carrier aircraft. If such a force were to descend upon him after he entered Leyte Gulf, it would almost certainly result in another Sibuyan Sea debacle. And for even less purpose, for it seemed reasonable to suppose that the Americans would have quickly guessed the Japanese objective and pulled most of the transports out of the Gulf.

As his weary mind turned over this murky kaleidoscope of half-truth, inference and guesswork, Kurita gradually convinced himself that "the prospects in Leyte Gulf were both thin and grim, and that he had better save the rest of his fleet, possibly to fight another day." At 12.36 p.m. he informed Toyoda in Tokyo: "First Striking Force has abandoned penetration of Leyte anchorage. It is proceeding north searching for enemy task force. Will engage decisively, then pass through San Bernadino Strait."[35] In fact, he had already turned away from Leyte Gulf at 12.15, setting a south-westerly course which he worked round to due north when he transmitted his message. Its last sentence indicates that Kurita's mind was still not properly made up. For he seems to be saying that he intended to be the victor in a fleet-to-fleet encounter and then to retreat, a most unusual way of conducting naval operations. Perhaps he realised that his actual options were those that had faced the southern pincers in Suriago Strait, to court annihilation as Nishimura had done, or to decide with Shima that discretion was the better part of valour and simply withdraw.

At the same time, it should never be forgotten that a prime cause of Kurita's indecision was the extraordinary valour shown by some elements of the American surface fleet. He and his staff mistook a weak task unit for a fast carrier task group not only due to the poor visibility, but also because in this battle destroyers did behave as if they were heavy cruisers, authentic blue-water gun-ships rather than a humble anti-submarine picket line. After the war Admiral Sprague wrote that Taffy-3's survival could be attributed to the smokescreen, the destroyer counter-attack, continuous harassment from the air, timely manoeuvring, "and the definite partiality of Almighty God".

I prefer to leave the last word with Commander Copeland, whose tribute to his own crew on *Samuel B. Roberts* is a fitting memorial to all seven ships of the Taffy screen and to their decisive contribution to the battle. His men, as we saw earlier, had been informed from the beginning that the odds were overwhelming and survival was not to be expected. "In face of this knowledge the men zealously manned their stations wherever they might be, and fought and worked with such calmness, courage and efficiency that no higher honour could be conceived than to command such a group of men."[36]

31

Attacking Strength Nil

THE BATTLE OF CAPE ENGANO

DURING MOST of the Suriago Strait encounter Admiral Kinkaid had been able to comfort himself with the belief that at least his rear was secure, with Halsey's carriers covering the approaches from the northern Philippines and his battleships guarding the exit from San Bernadino Strait. The position of the battleships was, in fact, merely an inference by Kinkaid from an ambiguous message sent out by Third Fleet. One of Kinkaid's staff officers did try to seek confirmation at around 4 a.m. on the 25th, but before Halsey's reply was received Kinkaid was urgently appraised by an extremely anxious Admiral Sprague that not only was the stable door at San Bernadino open but the horse had indeed bolted and was getting ready to stomp on Taffy-3.[1]

After the bad tidings reached Kinkaid's flagship a stream of ever more vociferous messages went out from Seventh Fleet appealing for assistance. The first was sent at 7.07 and the last at 8.29. They began by simply explaining the situation, noting the attack on Taffy-3, the composition of the enemy force, and the fact that Kinkaid's own Battle Line was now low on ammunition. Later messages requested immediate aid and forcefully suggested what form it should take. "Request Lee proceed top speed to cover Leyte; request immediate strike by fast carriers"; "Help needed from heavy ships immediately"; "Situation critical, battleships and fast carrier strike wanted to prevent enemy penetrating Leyte Gulf."[2]

Among the commanders who overheard these exchanges, Admiral Nimitz in Hawaii became so concerned over the plight of Taffy-3 that he decided to make a rare intervention in the tactical handling of his ships. At 9.45, Philippine time, he sent a message to Halsey asking,

"Where is Task Force 34?" By the time the message was in Halsey's hands, at just after ten, it was an altogether more complicated and controversial document. At the beginning and end were a few words of nonsense, appended to confuse Japanese SIGINT personnel, and the yeoman sending the message, detecting some urgency in his chief's voice, had also inserted a 'Repeat' after the first two words. Halsey flew his flag in the battleship *New Jersey*, and when the message reached the communications centre, it now read: "Turkey trots to water RR From Cincpac Action Com Third Fleet Info Cominch CTF Seventy-Seven X Where Is Rpt Where Is Task Force Thirty-Four RR The World Wonders." The padding at the beginning of the message was clearly meaningless but the phrase at the end, echoing a line from Tennyson's 'The Charge of the Light Brigade', could well be taken to be part of the main message, albeit couched in rather offensive terms. (Did the yeoman know, one wonders, that 25th October 1944 was the ninetieth anniversary of the Charge of the Light Brigade?) The receiving yeoman decided he had better leave these words in, despite the regulation use of the letters 'RR' to bracket the actual message. So what was handed to Halsey now read: "Where is, Repeat, Where is Task Force 34 RR The World Wonders."[3]

The tone of the message infuriated him. By Halsey's own admission, he was "as stunned as if I had been struck in the face. The paper rattled in my hands. I snatched off my cap, threw it on the deck, and shouted something I am ashamed to remember. Mick Carney rushed over and grabbed my arm: 'Stop it! What the hell's the matter with you? Pull yourself together.' . . . I was so mad I couldn't talk. It was utterly impossible for me to believe that Chester Nimitz would send me such an insult."[4] But he had to swallow it for even without the unfortunate last phrase the message was a clear attempt to prod Halsey to do something to assist Taffy-3. In fact, he had already begun to realise that his headlong dash north might not have been the soundest of decisions.[5] When the first of Kinkaid's appeals had arrived, according to one who was actually in the flag-plot, Halsey, "who had never expected to hear of a carrier force overtaken by surface ships in this man's war, was pretty dashed . . . His face was ashen." Within minutes of receiving the message Halsey directed Admiral John McCain's TG 38.1, now racing northward to join in the hunt for Ozawa's carriers, to change direction and get in position to launch the earliest possible strike against Kurita's fleet. But the battleships were not diverted and they, including Halsey's flagship, continued steering towards Ozawa's carriers. According to the same flag-plot eye-witness, after Halsey had recalled McCain he made it clear that this would be Third Fleet's only contribution to the Samar battle and then "sat silent on his transom. Suddenly, to no-one in particular, but as if talking to himself, he muttered, 'When I get my teeth into something, I hate to let go.' Then he lapsed into silence, his jaw set like a bulldog's."[6]

Halsey's grudging response to Kinkaid's early appeals – McCain's task group was actually the one furthest away from the Samar fighting and its planes could not possibly be on the scene before midday – is at least partly understandable. The order to McCain went out at 8.48, after Halsey had begun hearing reports of successful strikes by his other carrier planes indicating, in other words, that his battleships would find plenty of easy targets once they arrived on the scene, Despite Halsey's headlong pursuit of Ozawa's carriers, actual contact with them was very sporadic and only at 7.10 a.m. on the 25th did Third Fleet get a 'locked on' sighting. By this time, keen to be able to react immediately to any contact within range, Mitscher had ordered his first carrier squadrons to scramble at 5.40 a.m. and these orbited well ahead of Task Force 38, waiting for word from the reconnaissance aircraft. By 7.10 the two carrier fleets were still some 150 miles apart, but Mitscher's planes were only half that distance away, just waiting to pounce. The battleships of Task Force 34 had also formed up by then and taken station ten miles north of the carriers. One group of officers on *New Jersey* "watched the great ships surging forward in line abreast. *South Dakota* had broken out its battle flag – an enormous Stars and Stripes that stood gloriously straight as Task Force 34 rushed ahead."[7]

The Battle of Cape Engano, against a motley collection of empty aircraft carriers, was hardly one of the U.S. Navy's more notable victories. Nevertheless, as the only confrontation between fleet carriers on 25th October, it does offer a chance to see them in action. Fleet carriers were impressive beasts, the *Essex*-class vessels 872 feet long, displacing just over 27,000 tons and having a maximum speed of 33 knots. They could carry up to 100 aircraft – Hellcat or Corsair fighters, Helldriver dive-bombers and trusty Avenger torpedo-bombers.[8] The *Independence*-class light carriers were also far from negligible weapons platforms. Though less than half the displacement of the *Essex*-class, at 11,000 tons, they were still 622 feet long, had a maximum speed of almost 32 knots and carried 45 aircraft. On these ships there were usually no dive-bombers and fewer fighters and torpedo-bombers. As the famous war correspondent Ernie Pyle found, even a light carrier "was a very large ship . . . She had all the facilities of a small city, and all the gossip and small talk too . . . All she lacked was a hitching rack and a town pump with a handle. She had five barbers, a laundry, a general store . . . She had a daily newspaper. She carried fire-fighting equipment that a city of 50,000 back in America would be proud of. She had a preacher, she had three doctors and two dentists, she had two libraries and movies every night, except when in battle."[9] The fire-fighting equipment was absolutely essential as carriers were floating incendiaries. Those of the *Essex*-class carried not just their own fuel but also 230,000 gallons of aviation gasoline, as well as 1,500 bombs ranging from 100-lbs to 1-ton. Nor did this lethal load get appreciably smaller during a long period at sea. Carriers were known to spend up to 70 days continuously at sea and a remarkable logistical system was instituted to keep the task groups regularly replenished.

If a carrier was akin to a small town, it would be misleading to see its captain as the mayor. While at sea, and most especially when surging forward to close with the enemy, as TF 38 was now doing, carrier captains, all of them naval aviators in their own right, were exclusively concerned with what happened on the flight deck and with maintaining position in the circular task group formation. During most of his time at sea the captain lived on the narrow bridge, occasionally grabbing a few hours of fitful sleep in his adjoining emergency cabin. Responsibility for life below decks was largely delegated to the executive officer, he himself relying heavily on his heads of navigation, air gunnery, communication, engineering, supply, medicine, and damage control. The latter had been of prime concern during the last 48 hours, and for most of the 25th the carriers were at General Quarters, or Material Condition Affirm, which came into effect two minutes after the GQ bugle was blown, when "every hatch and scuttle is bolted down, every door jogged tight. That's to keep fire, flooding and other damage confined to the smallest possible space . . . Once it's set you can't get from one deck to another, can't even get through into the next compartment . . . Damage-control parties [are] posted to handle fire-hoses, shut-off valves, and plug busted pipes – and see all doors dogged."[10]

At 5.15 a.m. the pilots sat around in the squadron ready-rooms, on the galley-deck immediately below the flight-deck. They had just received their mission briefings and though each pilot still sprawled in his big leather armchair he was ready to spring to his plane and take off within fifteen minutes. At about 5.30 the scramble came, the loud-speakers blaring out the order, 'Pilots man your planes'. The flyers, mostly very young ensigns, or lieutenants (j.g.) from Navy flying schools, leapt to their feet, some looking nervous but all jostling to be first on to the flight deck, loaded down with Mae West, parachute harness, goggles and helmet with oxygen mask, pistol and survival knife, and sometimes jabbing one another accidentally with their sharp-cornered plotting-boards. Arriving on deck the pilots dashed to their planes, each recognising his own only by the fact that the plane captain, the mechanic assigned to a particular pilot, was standing by it. It was a peculiarity of the Navy that a pilot did not have his own plane but had to clamber into whichever one was assigned for the sortie.[11]

Once in the cockpit, the pilot was strapped in by the plane captain. Shortly afterwards the assistant air officer picked up his bull-horn and shouted, 'Prepare to start your engines' and then, when the deck crew had got out of the way of the propellers, 'Start Engines'. Sometimes the hissing and fizzing starter cartridges did their job, but on a wet early morning like this many engines had to be wound up, the deck crew moving in again and heaving at the propellers to crank up the compression in the cylinders. Eventually all were started, including occasional replacements for recalcitrant planes which had been whistled up from the hangar deck via one of the big elevators. Pale blue flames now flickered from the exhausts and the propellers soon vapourised any moisture still left on the flight deck. The noise was stupendous. "The incomparable sound of perhaps 60 radial engines turning over, forming the bass chorus for the high-pitched whine of inertia starters, and the punctuation of shot-gun type cartridges kicking over pistons in Pratt and Whitneys or Wrights was deafening. Three-bladed Hamilton-Standard propellers on blunt-nosed Hellcats and big-bellied Avengers and four-bladed Curtis Electrics on Helldivers jerked into motion by fits and starts and then blurred into invisibility. The clouds of light blue smoke which seemed to hang over the flight decks never stayed long, for they were swept away in the relative wind and ever-increasing prop wash."[12]

The deck crew in their colour-coded tunics, red for ordnancemen, green for catapult crews, yellow for plane directors who gave orders to the blue-shirts actually manhandling the planes, had cleared the flight deck, leaving only 'Fly One', the launch officer, to see each plane into the air.[13] First the carrier heeled into the wind and the yardarm displayed the red and white Fox flag at the dip and then, as the ship steadied on its new course and the wind began to howl down the flight deck, the order 'Two-block Fox' went to the signalmen and the flag soared up the yard. This was the signal to begin launching. The first planes, with less deck to play with, were sometimes catapulted off but the rest relied on the wind, as the ship headed 'handsomely', the optimum angle for take-off with the wind slightly on the port bow. Fly One stood abreast of the carrier's island structure, holding aloft a black-and-white chequered flag. One by one the planes taxied into position guided by the launch officer's assistants, the flight deck chief and the taxi signalmen, who gestured to the pilots, nodding, shaking their heads, pointing and beckoning, to bring the planes to 'the spot'. Then Fly One, standing at the starboard wingtip, "thrusts his left arm upward and twirls his hand rapidly; the pilot pushes his throttle far forward, racing the engine to a piercing crescendo. The plane quivers and strains at its braked wheels. Suddenly the . . . [launch] officer points at the pilot, who curtly nods, indicating his readiness to be off. The officer glances quickly up the deck, sees all clear, and abruptly brings his flag down."[14] This signal was given just as the ship's bow was coming up in the swell and as the flag slashed down and forward "the pilot – with engine run up to maximum RPM, prop in flat pitch, and flaps lowered for more lift – kicked in right rudder to offset the powerful port torque, released his brakes and was lunging down the deck."[15]

A whole deckload of planes could be cleared in as little as fifteen minutes, the fighters going first, then the dive-bombers and finally the torpedo-planes which, heavily-laden, needed to start their runs from much further aft. Once aloft the planes circled in an appointed sector, until all had taken off, and formed into three- and four-plane divisions which then combined into squadrons and air groups. Before six o'clock the first of these groups was on its way, and at 8.03 the leaders sighted Ozawa's Main Force and immediately went into the attack. Ozawa had already seen most of his planes depart to fulfil the deception mission, and of those remaining most were away on reconnaissance flights. His carrier fleet, therefore, could put up only 18 planes to meet the Americans and most of these, with their callow pilots, were shot down in short order. As if to rub in the overwhelming American superiority, this first strike by 175 aircraft included 27 'aces', pilots who had already shot down five or more enemy aircraft.[16]

Deprived almost immediately of their meagre air cover, the Japanese still did their best to counter the American onslaught. All their ships made drastic manoeuvres, zig-zagging during the bombers' and torpedo-planes' approach and saving their sharpest turn until last, just before the planes released their loads. The cruisers and hybrid battleships sometimes swung a full 180 degrees and could be seen firing their main armament at the low-flying Avengers. For dense anti-aircraft fire was the other Japanese defensive ploy. *Ise* and *Hyuga*, in particular, virtually doubled as AA ships with 16 5-inch guns and no less than 108 25mm AA guns. As at Samar, different ships fired different coloured dyes, and the battleships were also equipped with 180 5-inch rocket launchers. One pilot from *Lexington* wrote: "They were using new AA guns with wires and burning phosphorus – all different colored smoke and fire in the bursts around our planes. It looked like the Fourth of July laid on by the Chamber of Commerce at Virginia Beach."[17] In terms of planes destroyed, even this volume of fire was remarkably ineffective, with only ten TF 38 aircraft being lost to AA during the entire day. But it did grant Ozawa's ships at least temporary reprieve by forcing pilots to take evasive action, so that the percentage of hits they obtained was very small.

Ozawa's Chief-of-Staff, Captain Ohmae, told interrogators after the war: "I was witnessing the bombing. I thought that the bombing . . . wasn't so efficient."[18] This enforced evasive action also meant that pilots were climbing away from their target before their bombs or torpedoes hit. Some pilots were honest about it. Ensign Bruce West, from *San Jacinto*, wrote later: "I released the torpedo at about 600 feet above the water, about 12,000 yards from the target, at a speed of 200 knots. I wish I could say that I saw it hit the target but I can't, I was too busy. Once you release, your whole attention is taken up trying to get the hell away."[19] Other pilots were not so scrupulous, and often wishful thinking was the order of the day. In the first strike, for example, the pilots from just one of the carriers involved claimed 13 direct hits on one of the battleships. At the end of the day, after five more strikes and something like 600 sorties in all, intelligence officers whittled total claims down to 22 hits on one of the battleships and 15 on the other. Eventually, "from the best Japanese sources available after the war it [was] learned that only one direct hit was made on the *Hyuza* [sic] and none on her sister ship. Near misses damaged the blister of the *Ise*, but no direct hits were made on her."[20]

Nevertheless, some of the hits had grave consequences for the Japanese. The carrier *Zuiho*, which had immediately pulled out of the formation as the Americans roared in, managed to get away with just one bomb hit which failed to slow her down. *Chitose*, her sister ship, was less fortunate and took several hits, including three which holed her below the water-line. Together these proved fatal and she sank at 9.07 with the loss of 900 lives. The mighty *Zuikaku* was also hit, this time by a solitary torpedo aft which knocked out her communications and left her listing by six degrees. The steering controls were also damaged and she slowed to 18 knots, barely manoeuvrable and that only by hand. With his flagship so vulnerable, Ozawa's staff begged him to move from *Zuikaku* to another ship, but he was most reluctant. 'What is the good?' he asked bitterly. 'All my vessels are destined to be sunk. Our task is accomplished. I wish to die in the *Zuikaku*.'[21] Finally, his staff managed to prevail upon him and at about eleven o'clock he transferred in a small boat to the light cruiser *Oyodo*.

Before this took place, however, a second strike arrived shortly after 9.45, much smaller than the first, with only 6 bombers and 16 torpedo-planes supported by 14 fighters. A target co-ordinator from the first strike remained at the scene, there being no Japanese air cover, and other pilots radioed advice to the incoming planes as they passed on their way to refuel and rearm. The new pilots soon scored several bomb hits on the only unscathed carrier, *Chiyoda*, which was set fiercely ablaze before heeling over sharply from serious flooding. One bomb had also hit the ship's engines and soon brought her to a halt. Hits were also claimed on Ozawa's three light cruisers, and one bomb does seem to have struck *Tama* which, while not dead in the water as some pilots claimed, was slowed to ten knots, trailing considerable oil.

Ozawa resolved to proceed northwards with most of his surviving ships, but delegated *Hyuga*, the light cruiser *Isuzu* and destroyers *Shimotsuki* and *Maki* to take *Chiyoda* in tow and rescue survivors. These ships were quite likely to become mere target practice for any subsequent American carrier strikes, but Ozawa was now more convinced than ever that none of his ships had any realistic chance of survival. He himself was only sailing north because in that way he could best prolong his decoy mission and draw Halsey after him, away from the major battle he hoped was now taking place in Leyte Gulf. Ozawa has left an account of his reasons for doggedly courting "total sacrifice, total destruction of my carriers. Considerations which influenced the decision to draw the enemy further north . . . were based on my knowledge that there were no aircraft available for our use; reconnaissance strength, attacking strength was nil, and the enemy's actual attacking strength was unknown."[22]

It was towards the end of the second American strike that Halsey heard from Nimitz and finally had to recognise that sending McCain's single task group to Sprague's aid, when McCain would be unable to launch a strike for another half-hour, was just not an adequate response. Even now Halsey did not back down graciously. For the next hour he remained closeted with 'Mick' Carney, who has ever since declined to give any clue as to what was said between them. Yet the very length of the meeting, at such a critical juncture, would seem to indicate that there was no harmonious meeting of minds. Still, a decision, however grudging, was made to dissolve the battleship group TF 34. At 11.15 most of its ships were ordered to reverse course along with Admiral Bogan's carrier task group TG 38.2, to take on Kurita once again. Halsey's flagship was to sail with this force, denying him the chance to be present at the destruction of Japan's only operational carrier force.[23]

In fact, Halsey was now too late to share even in the destruction of Kurita's battleships and cruisers. His nickname among his fellow admirals was 'Bill' but the press and many ordinary sailors found this too bland and usually preferred 'Bull' Halsey. The admiral had never taken to the sobriquet but he was to like it even less when his pursuit first of Ozawa's fleet and then of Kurita's, both equally unsuccessful, became known as 'The Battle of Bull's Run'. His last hope of personally taking Kurita under fire disappeared at 1.45 in the afternoon when the Battle Line had to slow down to refuel, which took more than two and a half hours. A detached group was then sent ahead, consisting of two battleships, three cruisers and eight destroyers (known as TG 34.5, under Admiral O. C. Badger) but this never managed to catch up with Kurita. He had re-entered the San Bernadino Strait at around 9.40 that evening, and Badger's force did not arrive there until an hour after midnight on the 26th. The only ship they encountered was the destroyer *Nowaki*, delayed while picking up survivors from *Chikuma*, and she was promptly sunk by gunfire. An officer aboard *New Jersey* described this thumping anti-climax: "Radars scanned, and *Iowa* signalled a skunk hugging the shore. Not a fit target for fast battleships, so cruisers went forward to take care of it. From the flag bridge we saw the arcing shells, then the bright explosion. Scratch one Japanese warship. On *New Jersey* unrelieved dejection. Not one gun fired in the whole Battle Line. End of 'Bull's Run'."[24] The only other reward for Halsey after his bootless chasing hither and thither were six survivors from the heavy cruiser *Suzuyu* who allowed themselves to be picked up.

Neither were Halsey's carriers able to contribute much to these attempts to block Kurita's retreat. McCain's task group had been given almost as difficult a chase as that of the Battle Line, and his planes needed to be launched at the earliest possible moment to have any chance of overtaking the Japanese. Indeed they would have to carry extra fuel tanks in order to get back to the carriers. The weight of these tanks precluded carrying any torpedoes and so bombs were loaded, though these were invariably ineffective against battleships and heavy cruisers. The strike was launched at 10.30 a.m. with exactly 100 aircraft, but when it finally reached Centre Force, nearly three hours later, only one bomb actually hit its target, the heavy cruiser *Tone*, and that turned out to be a dud. Bogan's TG 38.2, which had sailed south with the Battle Line, was unable to launch any strikes at all until the next morning. Even the escort carriers were unable to take advantage of Kurita's decision to withdraw, made some time after noon on the 25th. Although Taffy-2 planes had played a crucial role in persuading Kurita to break off his pursuit of Sprague, their sixth and last strike of the day, launched shortly after 3 p.m. with 50 planes, failed to accomplish anything.

The gunships of Seventh Fleet also were unable to harry Kurita's withdrawal. On first hearing Sprague's appeals, Kinkaid immediately considered taking his own Battle Line out of Leyte Gulf to square up to Kurita. Indeed, orders to that effect were issued and extra destroyers were delegated to beef up Oldendorf's screen. Meanwhile, Oldendorf was ordered to stand by a few miles north of Hibuson Island, but then a further message directed him to take half his force north to assist Taffy-3. By the time this message was received, Kinkaid had heard about Kurita's withdrawal and Oldendorf's move north was quickly cancelled. At 11.27, when it seemed that Kurita's withdrawal was only temporary, Oldendorf was ordered north once more but this, too, was countermanded some ninety minutes later and though Oldendorf had by now steamed beyond the eastern entrance to Leyte Gulf, the putative mission was scrapped once and for all.

Kurita, then, after his notably lack-lustre performance off the coast of Samar, got off fairly lightly, losing no more ships on the 25th than had already succumbed to the escort carriers and destroyers. Admiral Ozawa, on the other hand, was not about to escape so easily. Two of Mitscher's carrier task groups were still involved in the chase and planes that rearmed and refuelled after the first strike were employed in four subsequent strikes, launched by Third Fleet Task Groups 38.3 and TG 38.4 between midday and five-fifteen in the afternoon. A little under 400 sorties were got off, and these arrived over Ozawa's ships between one and six o'clock. Ozawa's carriers, of course, were still the main target, and a pilot with the first strike of the afternoon has left a vivid description of this attack. *Zuiho* and *Zuikaku* were the prey, both running north at 20 knots even though *Zuikaku* was trailing a long, oily wake. The American planes appeared suddenly at 6,000 feet out of broken, hazy cloud, leaving the Japanese only a few seconds to try to register their AA guns. "The *Zuiho* limped on, burning, but the *Zuikaku* stopped and started to die on one side. She needed no more, but was very slow to sink, and her AA battery was very nasty." As strike co-ordinator, this pilot, Captain Hugh Winters, remained on the scene while the other planes left to rearm and refuel. When each strike departed the Japanese guns would cease firing and Winters would slowly drop down to 4,000 feet to take a closer look at the damage caused. "They would get excited then and open up on us; then I would pull out and climb back up to do it all over again. It got to be an almost friendly maneuver."

More American planes soon arrived and they concentrated first on pounding *Zuiho*, which was brought to a virtual standstill by 1.30 p.m. "Our *Zuikaku* still had her head above water but I kept strikes on her till a destroyer went alongside to take off survivors and got the destroyer as well. It was then time for another circuit to keep tabs on the battleships and cruisers in the area. Upon our return, the *Zuikaku* rolled the rest of the way and sank without steam, smoke or fire. It was nice of her to wait for our return. I was afraid she wouldn't." Throughout the battle Winters had perfect radio contact with the carriers of TF 38 but its commanders remained dubious about his reports of Japanese losses. He mostly communicated with one of Mitscher's staff officers, Commander James Flately, and "finally, all concern was removed when I was able to say, 'Jim, they are not burning or exploding, or sinking, they are *under water.*' We were running out of gas and had to turn the remnants over to the leader of the next incoming strikes."[25]

None of these last strikes succeeded in doing any further real damage to Ozawa's remaining ships and it was left to surface gunnery to notch up the other victories of the day. When Halsey had finally decided to turn south with his Battle Line, four cruisers and ten destroyers from TF 34 remained with Mitscher and were soon formed into a mini-battle line to run ahead of Sherman's carrier task group. Admiral Laurence du Bose was in command but before he could join up with Sherman he received new orders to form up for a night torpedo attack on Ozawa's stragglers. Du Bose set off in pursuit but only managed to overhaul the wallowing carrier *Chiyoda*, which was sent to the bottom just before 5 p.m.

Admiral du Bose continued northward, taking his course from carrier night-fighters that soon picked up three Japanese destroyers. Within a quarter-hour of this sighting, at 6.53 p.m., the light cruiser *Mobile* opened up at almost 14 miles range, upon which the heaviest of the Japanese ships, *Hatsuzuki*, took it upon herself to cover the retreat of her companions, *Wakatsuki* and *Kuwa*. These two were soon out of range and the American cruisers then concentrated their fire upon *Hatsuzuki*. Twice, she too seemed to be making a run for it but twice she turned back towards the cruisers to attempt a torpedo attack. Du Bose was under strict orders from Mitscher not to allow any of his ships to be immobilised by battle damage and his cruisers on both occasions took drastic evasive action. Just after seven-thirty the cruisers pulled back a little and, though they kept up long-range fire, the main task was handed to the destroyers which closed in to make a torpedo attack from directly astern. Whether they scored any hits is unclear but something soon caused the Japanese destroyer to slow. After 8.40 it was possible to keep the target constantly illuminated by star-shells, and with the range down to less than 4,500 yards, du Bose ordered all guns to cease fire and a destroyer to finish her off with a torpedo. Before this could be done, however, *Hatsuzuki*, burning furiously, sank to the accompaniment of six very heavy underwater explosions. She had been literally punched to pieces, with the two American light cruisers alone expending over 1,700 6-inch and almost 1,000 5-inch shells. It is said that the destroyer captain sent to deliver the *coup de grâce* complained in a signal, "He has gone down, we were cheated!" – to which du Bose replied, "It breaks our hearts!" A more gracious response to the extremely gallant conduct of the Japanese destroyer was provided by the always even-handed S. E. Morison. At the end of his description of this encounter he notes: "One of the American destroyer captains insisted that she must have been a heavy cruiser – the same compliment that Kurita's officers accorded to Admiral Sprague's destroyers."[26]

One last fleet encounter around Leyte Gulf was briefly considered. At 8.41 p.m., on first hearing of *Hatsuzuki*'s plight, Ozawa resolved to go to her aid, doubtless to compensate for his hitherto inglorious role in the whole venture. He gathered the two hybrid battleships and one destroyer, and his new flagship *Oyodo*, and turned south. Even after deciding that *Hatsuzuki* must have been sunk, he maintained his course in the hope of running into some or other American ships. Shortly before midnight, however, for whatever reason, he gave up and turned away from the Philippine Sea for the last time. His diversion south had never been spotted by the Americans, and when his remnants were picked up again by American night-fighters, it was too late for du Bose, who had himself already retired southward.

Although Ozawa had been unable to save or even avenge *Hatsuzuki*, he should have derived some satisfaction from successfully carrying out his mission to lure away Halsey's carriers. Certainly, he had lost all of his own, including his flagship, but this was an inevitable and accepted consequence of his decoy role. Even as his ships were dodging Mitscher's last strike, Ozawa could comfort himself that these planes were not over Leyte Gulf nor attacking such forces with which Kurita and Nishimura were engaging MacArthur's invasion shipping. For as soon as Mitscher's first strike had appeared overhead in the morning, Ozawa had reported it to Tokyo and to Kurita's Striking Force, emphasising that he was being attacked by carrier aircraft.

At that stage Ozawa was still flying his flag in *Zuikaku* and, unknown to anyone on board, there was a fault in the transmitter. Part of the message was picked up by a Japanese wireless station on Formosa, but neither Tokyo not Kurita were privy to this. The first Kurita heard of the carrier strikes was after Ozawa had transferred his flag, by which time he had already decided to withdraw. Thus, even though the Japanese plan to lure away Halsey's fleet carriers had succeeded almost beyond expectations, no advantage could be derived from this tactic because no one else knew that the Americans had risen to the bait. Kurita, already somewhat 'shell-shocked', continued to imagine Halsey's fleet arrayed against him, with task groups both barring the way into Leyte Gulf and ready to interpose themselves should he attempt to join up with Ozawa. But it was misconception about approaches to the Gulf that was so crucial. As far as Kurita was concerned, Taffy-3 continued to be a Third Fleet task group, and therefore any attempt to penetrate the Gulf could only result in an even more merciless pounding than he had received in the Sibuyan Sea.

Kurita's withdrawal left the Imperial Navy with a sorry balance sheet at midnight on the 25th. For the loss of one fleet carrier, three light carriers, three battleships, six heavy cruisers, one light cruiser and five destroyers, a total of 285,000 tons of irreplaceable naval shipping, the Japanese had accounted for three escort carriers, two destroyers, one destroyer-escort and one PT boat, totalling just 29,000 tons. Moreover, the invasion timetable was hardly put back at all. All in all, the Battle of Leyte Gulf must be considered one of the Imperial Japanese Navy's most dismal performances, where a combination of communications failures, both accidental and wilful, unyielding fatalism, tactical ineptitude and an overly nervous suggestibility reduced a major naval operation to a series of disconnected and inglorious encounters, one involving their own toothless carriers, the others against antiquated battleships, cut-price carriers and outgunned destroyers.

32

Radiant in the Morning Sun

KAMIKAZE PILOTS AT LEYTE GULF

A N ESSENTIAL PART of the SHO-GO plan was the use of airpower to cripple the American invasion fleet even before it arrived in Leyte Gulf. This mission was entrusted to the Navy's First Air Fleet and the Army's Fourth Air Army, both based in the Philippines, and to the Second Air Fleet based on Formosa. Despite the failure of Second Air Fleet in the battle of early October against Halsey's carriers, it did nothing to diminish Japanese optimism that their air forces could still play a decisive part in the forthcoming naval confrontation. Even as the various elements of the Combined Fleet were approaching the Philippines, they fondly believed that "land-based naval air forces were to meet the enemy invading forces at a distance of 700 miles from the islands; to reduce his strength by means of aerial attack with bombs and torpedoes; and in co-operation with the Army Air Force to annihilate the remainder of the enemy force at the invasion point."[1]

Just how much faith the Japanese admirals really had in their much diminished air forces is uncertain, but they certainly found them a useful scapegoat after the battle. Admiral Ugaki's last entry in his diary on 25th October read: "The damages of today's decisive battle were not proportionate to the results achieved . . . Its failure was attributed, though in some respects to its planning, mostly to the extreme inactivity of the base air forces, probably hindered by bad weather." Kurita's Chief-of-Staff, Koyanagi, was even less charitable, particularly to the Navy's own air fleets: "As it turned out, these two air fleets achieved practically nothing during the battle, whereas in planning the *Sho* Operation we had counted heavily on them. They should have conducted all-out attacks on the enemy fleet to support our surface forces in this battle."[2]

An attempt had been made to boost the number of aircraft in the Philippines by flying in Admiral Fukudome's Second Air Fleet, some 300 to 400 aircraft, followed by a further 800 planes garnered from China and the home islands themselves. Fukodome's planes flew in on 22nd and 23rd October, most of them to Clark airfield on Luzon, and by the 24th total remaining naval air strength in the Philippines was some 350 aircraft. Also available were about 250 Army planes, 80 of these recent reinforcements. On the 24th and 25th all these planes made several attacks. About 300 planes got airborne on each day but failed to make much of an impression on the Americans. The attacks on the 24th were mainly directed against Admiral Sherman's TG 38.3, and they cost the Japanese upwards of 190 planes as opposed to the loss of only 10 American carrier aircraft. The fleet tug *Sonoma* was sunk when an Army plane dived straight into it.

Ugaki was probably right to lay some blame on the weather. Other Japanese sources claimed: "That morning the weather was particularly bad, giving our scout and fighter pilots no end of trouble."[3] For Sherman the weather was a boon and, like Sprague and his captains off Samar, he was able to dodge many attacks by manoeuvring his carriers into rain squalls while their planes were airborne. The Japanese attacks on the 25th were, if anything, even less effective than those of the day before. One Japanese naval source glumly states that they succeeded in "inflicting no damage on the enemy", but the record does show that a Japanese plane of unknown provenance did at least manage to strafe the destroyer-escort *Richard M. Rowell*, part of Taffy-1.[4] If this was an Army Air Force success, it had been achieved at the cost of 90 other planes shot down.

This lamentable record in conventional air attacks was not lost on some Japanese commanders, especially in the Navy, for they were well aware that Japanese military aviation was beset by technical and manpower problems that almost vitiated its usefulness. For one thing, the training of the pilots was now lamentably poor, with an acute shortage of trainer aircraft and of competent instructors, most of the latter having already been drafted to the front. Poor training generated its own vicious circle, with the neophytes being lost in combat almost immediately and thus increasing the demand for yet more pilots.

The problem was equally acute for the Army. At the beginning of the war their flyers had attended a three-and-a-half year course between enlistment and graduation but from mid-1943 this was cut to eighteen months, only the last two of which involved any actual flight training. Deficiencies were supposed to be sorted out at the front, where pilots would undergo several months of 'limited' exposure to combat conditions under the eyes of experienced flyers – who by 1944 were so few and far between that they could do little more than act as extremely remiss mother hens, leading their chicks off to meet a whole host of predators. "In September . . . a number of American pilots observed that many of the planes they destroyed were single-engined biplanes – training planes. Particularly on Negros Island the airmen of the *Essex* found the pickings easy, especially among the army planes they met. The answer was simply that they were meeting young pilots who in America would not yet have qualified for combat training."[5]

Losses of planes and pilots spiralled. The Japanese Navy between 1st January and 10th October (before Formosa) lost 5,209 pilots, 42 per cent of its total aircrew. These losses were not simply a function of inadequate training. Another cause was the inability of the overstretched Japanese munitions industry properly to match their weapons to their weapons platforms or to the tactical task they were supposed to perform. The standard carrier dive-bomber, for example, was the Aichi 99 which was a pre-war design and terribly vulnerable to the latest American fighters. Even so, it was too fast and heavy for any but the biggest Japanese carriers and could not be flown from the much smaller ones that made up most of new production. The more modern Aichi D4Y3 was equally unsuitable, and so the Navy had to turn to the trusty Zero, attaching a special 500-lb bomb release mechanism and calling it a dive-bomber. Unfortunately, the bolt-on mechanism was poorly-engineered and frequently failed to let go of the bomb. Some pilots were at the last minute unable to release their payload, and as they attempted to return to the carrier were pulled down into the sea, out of fuel because of the unanticipated extra weight. At one stage losses from such accidents were thought to exceed losses in combat.

Land-based planes were proving no more effective against the American task groups. Whatever type of bomber or torpedo plane was used, they usually found themselves overwhelmed by the swarms of U.S. fighters: expertly flown, well-armoured and surprisingly nimble Hellcats and Corsairs as well as the older but still very serviceable Wildcats operating from the escort carriers. The Japanese rarely got the chance even to begin a bomb or torpedo run at an enemy ship, and morale plummeted. In the Philippines and surrounding Japanese bases "the morale of bomber and torpedo plane pilots . . . had been dropping so alarmingly that Tokyo had considered taking disciplinary action against them . . . Bombing and torpedo raids had become almost useless. Enemy defences were so powerful that many pilots simply turned back when they encountered them, without even trying to get through."[6] The morale of the fighter pilots assigned to escort these futile missions also slumped, as they proved unable to protect the bombers or to inflict any significant damage of their own on the Americans. So alarmed were senior commanders in Tokyo that, most unusually, they ceased handing down detailed instructions on tactics and mission timetabling and left it to commanders on the spot to find some solution to the problem.

Their response, as devised by the commander of the First Air Fleet, Admiral Kimpei Teraoka, and by the senior officers of 201 Air Group serving under him, was to abandon bombing and torpedo missions against Third/Fifth Fleet and to bolster the fighter pilots' sense of purpose by letting them take over the offensive role. This was to be done through 'skip-bombing', using Zero fighters carrying 550-lb bombs that would be released close to an enemy ship and very near the surface of the water, so that they would skim or bounce to their targets, rather in the manner of the RAF's 'Dambuster' raids in the previous year. The Japanese technique was probably even more hazardous. Planes had to execute their attack runs below the level of the target's deck, no more than 35 feet, and at such low level even the best pilots found it difficult to estimate their height correctly. This was especially true when the sea was very calm, yet that was the only weather condition that would permit successful skip-bombing. Training accidents were common, and invariably fatal.

Another problem was that the approach had to be made at a speed of around 280 m.p.h., with the bomb being released only 250 yards from the ship. A Japanese airman recalled that the "difficulty in this method of attack is to get the plane safely clear after dropping the bomb. If the fighter continues in a straight line towards the target after release, the bomb may bounce up and strike the plane, or the plane may be damaged when the bomb explodes at the target. The pilot must therefore change his course by a rapid acrobatic manoeuvre as soon as he drops the bomb. A second's error may mean the loss of plane and pilot." It was reckoned that pilots had at most two seconds to escape after release. No wonder, as an historian of 201 Air Group recorded, the consensus of those involved was that "this was a very dangerous method of attack [and] little hope was entertained for the safe return of personnel." [7]

In mid-October, Admiral Teraoka was replaced by Admiral Takijiro Onishi, but the problem of giving Japanese air power any kind of cutting edge remained. Onishi, who had spent some time attached to the Ministry of Munitions, was keenly aware that production difficulties at home and the acute shortage of raw materials would make it impossible to replace aircraft losses incurred at the present profligate rates. He arrived in Manila on 17th October with one possible solution to air force effectiveness which he discussed with the outgoing Teraoka on the 18th. Teraoka summarised their conversation in his diary and their agreement that "we can no longer win the war by adhering to conventional methods of warfare . . . Instead we must steel ourselves against weakness . . . If fighter pilots set an example by volunteering for special attack missions, other units will follow suit."[8]

Presumably Onishi had been briefed by Teraoka on the skip-bombing experiment for he seems to have combined this method with that of the dive-bombers to have each fighter, with bomb still aboard, deliberately fly into a ship. It was estimated that a pilot resolutely determined to ignore all anti-aircraft fire should have an 80 per cent chance of flying through to hit his target, which also opened the possibility of specifically directing planes against the most valuable targets of all, the American fleet carriers.

On 19th October Onishi made a surprise appearance at the headquarters of 201 Air Group, at Mabalacat, and ordered all staff officers to a meeting. As they hurried in and settled Onishi addressed them, first outlining the nature of Nishimura and Kurita's mission to "penetrate Leyte Gulf and there annihilate enemy surface units. The First Air Fleet had been designated to support that mission by rendering enemy carriers ineffective for at least one week. In my opinion this can only be accomplished by crash-diving on the carrier flight decks with Zero fighters carrying 250-kilogram bombs."[9]

As soon as Onishi had finished the Group's executive officer, Commander Asa-ichi Tamai, asked permission to withdraw to confer with the squadron commanders. He returned within the hour, assuring Onishi that all pilots would be eager to co-operate and asking only that the Group itself be allowed to take charge of organising the 'special attack missions'. On the morning of the 20th, Onishi met the 24 pilots who were to form the new corps in the small garden adjoining his headquarters. With tears in his eyes he told them: "Japan now faces a terrible crisis. The salvation of our country is beyond the power of ministers, the general staff, and lowly unit commanders like myself. It is now up to spirited young men such as you."[10] At this stage, Onishi still saw the mission of these pilots as softening up the American carrier force, and on his return to Manila asked the fleets to delay their sailing to allow 201 Group time to prepare and conduct the first attacks.

But by then the Japanese ships had already set forth. Onishi pressed on with his preparations, unable to think of any other tactics that might usefully contribute to the forthcoming battle. Efforts were also made to recruit pilots at other bases, and on the 20th twenty pilots at the Cebu base unhesitatingly came forward. Onishi also tried to enlist pilots from Fukodome's Second Air Fleet. At a meeting on the 23rd, he explained that his own air groups had only fifty operational planes between them and that "with so few planes it is impossible for us to continue fighting by conventional tactics . . . I am not in a position to deny the value of mass-formation attacks such as you have trained for, but their effectiveness in this situation is very doubtful. We firmly believe that [our] special attacks will bring about the desired results, but we need more planes. We wish you to share some of your fighters with us."[11]

For the moment, however, Fukodome remained committed to conventional attacks, which he intended to launch on the 24th and 25th to coincide with the appearance of the naval contingents. Disappointed, Onishi pressed on with the conversion of his own air fleet to suicide bombing. The new corps was called the *Shinfu Tokketai Ei*, or Divine Wind Special Attack Force, the Divine Wind being typhoons that had twice wrecked Mongol fleets attacking Japan in 1274 and 1281.[12] It was divided into four sub-groups, code-named *Shikishima*, *Yamato*, *Asahi* and *Yamazakura*, after the key words in a *waka*, or short poem, by the 17th-century scholar and fervent nationalist, Norinaga Motoori.[13] All these units incorporated pilots from the Mabalacat air base, but the four-plane *Yamato* unit soon flew to Cebu as a cadre for the kamikaze group being formed there.

Western sources tend to highlight suicide bombing as a peculiarly irrational and callous squandering of human life, but it does the pilots of these planes an injustice to write them off as deluded fanatics. To them kamikaze missions were a most rational deployment of fast-dwindling resources. Another speech by Admiral Onishi to his assembled pilots made this point clear when he told them: "On behalf of your hundred million countrymen, I ask of you this sacrifice, and pray for your success. You are already gods, without earthly desires. But one thing you want to know is that your own crash-dive is not in vain. Regrettably we will not be able to tell you the results. But I shall watch your efforts to the end and report your deeds to the Throne."[14]

The crucial point in Onishi's address is that of the pilots' deaths not being 'in vain'. In other words, the point of kamikaze attacks was not mere self-immolation but rather maximising the possibility of getting a 500-lb bomb, not to mention quite a few gallons of burning aviation gasoline, into the innards of an American carrier. Even so, it is still not entirely convincing to present kamikaze tactics simply as especially rigorous military utilitarianism. To those from the West, Japanese culture and ethics seem morbidly introspective and display a strange fascination with the style of death. One book on Japanese naval aviation noted that the Japanese had five different words for death in action that was "caused by an act of will by the person who died", and that these highlighted "distinctions [that] are important to surviving members of the family and to Japanese culture in general."[15] Neither could the attitudes of Japanese commanders be regarded simply as a cool appraisal of resource allocation. Shortly after the formation of the Special Attack Force Admiral Onishi felt inspired to pen a *haiku*:

Kiyo sakite, asu chiru	In blossom today, then scattered;
Hana no wagami ka na;	Life is so like a delicate flower.
Ikade sono ka wo kiyoku	How can one expect the
todomen?	fragrance to last forever?

For the first few days after the formation of the Special Force, Onishi and his pilots had to endure similar frustrations to those of Admiral Ozawa, as he had vainly tried to find the American task groups for which he was supposed to be the bait. The first attempted suicide mission was from Cebu, on the afternoon of the 21st, when six planes were readied after hearing of a sighting of some of Halsey's carriers. Not all of the planes were suicide-bent. In any group roughly half were there to serve as conventional fighter escorts and also to report back on their compatriots' success. However, no sooner had the planes been hauled on to the airstrip from their camouflaged entrenchments, than a group of Hellcats roared down, strafed the strip from end to end, and set every plane on fire. As soon as the Americans had left three more planes were manhandled out of their shelters and these did manage to get airborne. Two of them were forced to return after they failed to sight any American shipping whatever, being hampered by bad weather, but the third insisted on continuing the search. It is presumed to have crashed into the sea after running out of fuel because no American ship ever reported even a failed attack. Six planes also took off from Mabalacat that day but they too made no sightings at all in the poor conditions. The bad weather persisted right through until the 25th, and though some Special Attack units took off each day, they did so "in vain; and when they returned to the field they never expected to see again [they] would tearfully apologise to the commander for [their] failure to find [an] opportunity to die. Surprisingly, these pilots did not become nervous or desperate but were as composed as if they had just returned from a routine mission."[16]

Equally frustrating was the fact that no reports of American carriers had come in from their reconnaissance planes. By the 25th the commander of the *Shikishima* unit, Lieutenant Yukio Seki, was beginning to despair. For today, he knew, was to see the climactic naval rendezvous and several reports already seemed to indicate that large numbers of enemy carrier aircraft were operating close to Leyte Gulf. Finally, tired of waiting to hear news from other planes, he once again prepared to lead his unit in their own search for suitable targets. Prior to take-off the volunteers once again went through the mixture of routine and ritual that had preceded each of the last few days' missions. Waiting for the call to man their planes, the pilots lounged around, seemingly unaware that their sortie was to be anything out of the ordinary. "Some read magazines long out of date. Others stretched out on the floor, lazily listening to popular Japanese melodies scratched out by a battered old gramophone in the corner – anything mechanical deteriorates rapidly in the tropics. Another small group, more professionally minded, studied air navigation charts. Boxed lunches and flight gear were close at hand. Nowhere was there any outward sign that these men were awaiting a call for their one-way mission."[17]

Clearly all these men were well aware that almost certain death lay only a few hours away, but even here it is important to realise that this prospect was not all that different from their likely fate in any combat mission at this stage of the war. For months past they had all been engaged in virtual suicide operations and had arranged their affairs as though each mission would probably be their last. Personal belongings were kept to a minimum – a change of underwear, a couple of towels, some aerial charts, pencils and a few personal mementoes – all of which could fit into a small bag or box, neatly inscribed with the pilot's name, that could be returned to the next-of-kin with the least inconvenience. Some had already forsworn this life, such as Lieutenant Kanno who, long before kamikaze tactics were adopted, had written on his label: "Personal effects of the late Lieutenant-Commander Naoshi Kanno", for it was the custom in the Navy and the Army to promote posthumously by one rank all those killed in action.

Finally, at around 7.15, the pilots were called to their planes and, fully accoutred, they jogged down the narrow lane to the command post. There they lined up in front of the other flyers and base personnel, all assembled to see them off. On a small table was a container of water left by Admiral Onishi personally and each pilot in

turn took a sip from a canteen cup filled from the container. After they
drank they stood to attention, each with his forehead covered with a
white *hachimaki*, the samurai declaration that he expected to fight to the
death, and now also decorated with poetic calligraphy and a rising sun
symbol. As they stood their comrades sang the sombre, ancient
warrior's song, *Umi Yukaba*:[18]

Umi yukaba	If I go away to sea,
Mizutsuku kabane	I shall return a corpse awash.
Yama yukaba	If duty calls me to the mountain,
Kusu musu kabane	A verdant sward will be my pall.
Ogimi no he mi koso shiname	Thus for the sake of the Emperor
Nodo hiwa shinaji.	I will not die peacefully, at home.

By now the pilots' planes were armed and ready, the fuel checked
and topped off, and the engines warming up. As the song died away the
pilots walked towards their planes, giving a farewell wave before
closing the cockpit canopy. At 7.25 they took off, climbing eastward to
begin their search. Altitude would be their main protection against
enemy interceptors and soon all nine pilots, five kamikaze and four
escort, had donned their oxygen masks. Finally, at 10.50, they spotted
a group of American carriers and, probably assuming them to be part
of Halsey's Third Fleet, prepared to attack. The "kamikaze pilots ready
their bombs by removing the fuse safety-pin . . . The lead plane banks
slightly and signals, 'All planes attack!' The raised arm of the leader is
plainly visible and one can almost make out his broad smile. Each pilot
selects his target, preferably an aircraft carrier, and plunges towards its
most vulnerable spot – the flight deck elevator."[19]

In fact, the ships were only escort carriers belonging to Admiral
Sprague's already sorely tried Taffy-3. Having seen off Kurita,
Sprague's task unit was now to be one of the first to witness the new and
terrifying tactics of the naval air arm. This particular attack, moreover,
was extremely well orchestrated and, even granting that Sprague and
his captains had other things on their mind that morning, the jeep
carriers were taken completely by surprise. The carriers were getting
into position to recover their own aircraft and the Japanese never
showed on the radar screens. They approached from very low altitude
and then climbed rapidly once inside radar range before starting their
dive from about 5,000 feet. So sudden was their appearance that
patrolling American aircraft were unable to intercept.

The first plane to dive flew towards the carrier *Kitkun Bay*. It
crossed the bow and then executed a climbing roll that took it straight

towards the bridge. Happily, the pilot was not quite low enough and he passed over the bridge and the entire 'island' superstructure before smashing into the catwalk on the other side of the ship and bouncing off into the sea 25 yards to port. The bomb he was carrying exploded on impact, causing considerable damage and starting several fires. The remaining four planes paired up to attack the carriers *Fanshaw Bay* and *White Plains*. The first pair were both shot down and the other two were forced to pull out of their dive at about 500 feet. They then split up, doubtless burning with shame, and as one circled the Taffy the other renewed its run on *White Plains*. The carrier's rudder was heaved hard to port and it threw up another hail of fire, the tracers of which could be seen ripping into the plane's fuselage and wing roots. When only a few yards astern the plane rolled over and dived, this time missing the port catwalk but exploding just before it hit the water. Eleven sailors were injured and the flight deck was showered with fragments of plane and pilot. The captain, in his Action Report, was moved to refer to kamikaze pilots as 'devil divers'.

The final *Shikishima* plane, deflected from *White Plains*, turned towards the carrier *St Lo*, which also opened fire immediately, but the pilot kept his head, riding his luck to the bitter end to make his first and only carrier landing. His bomb exploded on impact, ripping a huge hole in the flight deck while the remains of the plane skidded along it and over the bow, scattering red-hot fragments in their wake. The explosion started fires on the hangar deck below and very soon the ordnance there began erupting in a quick succession of tremendous explosions, almost tearing the ship apart. Whole planes and great chunks of the flight deck rose hundreds of feet into the air. The flight deck elevator was blown right out of its mounting and deposited upside down on the deck. Some 25 feet of the flight deck was peeled back like the top of a huge sardine can. The ship was soon ablaze from stem to stern. At 11.25, not long after the order to abandon ship, the carrier sank and 112 officers and men lost their lives.

While *St Lo* was in her death throes, Taffy-3 endured the last of its ordeals that day. A force of fifteen planes, generally identified as 'Judy' dive-bombers, appeared overhead and began another suicide attack. *Kitkun Bay* had another narrow escape, shooting its attacker's wings off and dislodging his bomb only 25 yards off the starboard bow. *Kalinin Bay* was not so lucky, with one plane crashing into the flight deck, though without penetrating it, and another into the after stack.[20] Some fires were started but these were quickly extinguished and, with the destroyer screen remaining behind to pick up survivors, the four remaining Taffy-3 escort carriers steamed away unmolested. They rendezvoused with Taffy-1 late that afternoon and, after organising a new screen, sailed off to Manus for refit.

In fact, this was not the first kamikaze attack of the day, but the origin of that attack remains somewhat mysterious. There is broad agreement that it took off from Davao in south-east Mindanao, and that it comprised six planes. Several sources say that these planes were Zeros, a Navy plane, and one claims that this was the *Asahi* unit. A Japanese source, however, says that all except the *Yamato* unit on Cebu were based at Mabalacat airfield. A recent book says that the attackers were Army planes belonging to 1 Air Group attached to the Fourth Air Army. Claims that it was the *Yamato* unit that carried out this attack have been contradicted by a Japanese observer who says that the Cebu planes did not take off until the 26th. It is certainly evident that some authors have confused this strike with the one on the day before because both had the same target, Taffy-1.[21]

What does seem clear is that four planes attacked Admiral T. L. Sprague's Taffy-1 at 7.35, just as he was recovering and rearming planes from other missions, before sending them to the aid of his namesake. (The two Spragues, 'Ziggy' and 'Tommy', were not related. The latter was also the overall commander of all three Taffys, which comprised Task Group 77.4.) The two planes that did not attack were probably there as escorts/observers and were seen to fly off after the attack. Of the actual suicide aircraft, three started their dive almost simultaneously while the other circled overhead, perhaps summoning up his resolve, perhaps waiting to see what targets would remain. One plane roared in towards the carrier *Santee*, coming out of very low cloud cover and not allowing the ship's gunners one single shot at it. Gunner's Mate Third Class John Mitchell "stared at the oncoming plane in disbelief. It was obvious the plane was not pulling out of its dive. He knew it was not because the pilot had been killed or wounded since none of the *Santee*'s guns were firing at him. Mitchell screamed, 'Pull out, you bastard, pull out!' But to no avail. The plane flew into the flight deck just a few feet forward of the after elevator . . . [Mitchell was] tossed into the air by the crash . . . He came down in his gun tub, which had filled with water when *Santee* heeled over from the impact. He thought he had been tossed into the sea and began trying to swim before he realised he was still on board."[22] The plane bored right through into the hangar deck where its bomb exploded, blowing a hole 15 feet by 30 feet, starting fires very close to a clutch of eight 1,000-lb bombs, and disembowelling several depth-charges that spilled their explosive innards over the deck. The fires were fed by gasoline gushing out from the wrecked suicide plane, and some American planes on the flight deck were also set ablaze. The *Santee* was now a floating bomb, waiting to go off. But heroic work by the damage-control parties, abetted by sheer good luck, prevented any fatal detonation while the most vulnerable ordnance was being jettisoned overboard. Just eleven minutes after the kamikaze pilot struck, the fires were under control, the casualties numbering 16 American sailors killed and another 27 wounded.

The remaining two planes in this attack bore in together. Then one pulled out of its dive, perhaps to select another target, and while it was circling the carrier *Suwannee* astern, it was hit by her AA guns. The plane spiralled down, still under control, rolled over into a dive and headed towards the carrier *Sangamon*. But *Suwannee* still had the plane in its sights and one 5-inch shell fired from its main gun blasted the plane into the sea, still some 500 yards from its target. The bomb exploded as the plane hit the water and one unlucky sailor was killed by shrapnel. The other plane had taken the carrier *Petrof Bay* for its target but it flew into the concentrated AA fire from at least three carriers and was brought down short of any of them, though close enough to *Petrof Bay* to shower the flight deck with sea-water.

The fourth pilot was still circling above, at 8,000 feet when all guns turned on him and he too was hit. Trailing smoke, he put his plane into a steep dive towards *Suwannee*, which had already accounted for one of his fellows. This time its marksmanship failed and the plane hit the flight deck on the starboard side, opening up a ten-foot hole. Again the bomb exploded between the flight and hangar decks, with much of the blast being directed downwards, causing numerous casualties on hangar and main decks. Several sailors were blown overboard. The ship's steering was temporarily disabled and the aft elevator put out of commission but, remarkably, overall physical damage was slight. Fire-control and repair procedures were once more impeccably adhered to and within only two hours the carrier was flying off aircraft once more.

The kamikaze pilots had given commanders on both sides pause for thought. For the loss of nine pilots and planes the Japanese had sunk one escort carrier, badly damaged another and left others needing extensive repairs. Compared to the surface navy's grotesque outlay of battleships and cruisers just to sink one escort carrier and three destroyers and escorts, this was a remarkably economical tally and one that must force a drastic reappraisal of navy priorities. Onishi was sufficiently cheered to send a message to Toyoda reporting the success and within a few hours this was passed on to the Emperor. It prompted a swift Imperial reply, which Onishi read out to his pilots. "When told of the special attack, His Majesty said, 'Was it necessary to go to this extreme? They certainly did a magnificent job.' His Majesty's words suggest that His Majesty is greatly concerned. We must redouble our efforts to relieve His Majesty of that concern. I have pledged every effort toward that end." Indeed, Onishi straightaway renewed his efforts to win Admiral Fukodome over to the new tactics. Conferring with him for a third time, late on the 25th, Onishi insisted: "The evidence is quite conclusive that special attacks are our only chance. In this critical situation we must not lose precious time. It is imperative that the Second Air Fleet agree to special attacks."[23] At two in the morning on the 26th, Fukodome finally gave way and agreed to allow his pilots to volunteer for suicide attacks.

33

Mud and Muddle

LEYTE ISLAND

O<small>N</small> 25th October 1944, General Douglas MacArthur, commander-in-chief of the South-West Pacific Area, or in the 'Pacific-speak' of the time, CINCSOWESPAC, was moving house. Up to nine days before, his advance general headquarters had been at Hollandia, in New Guinea, in a large prefabricated building overlooking Lake Sentai. Rumours abounded concerning the opulence of these quarters, yet everything was pretty much government-issue, consisting mainly of wallboard and whitewashed canvas. Its reputation probably rested on the magnificent setting, overlooking the deep-blue waters of the lake and itself overlooked by Lake Cyclops, from the centre of which sprang a towering, powerfully gushing waterfall. All around lay a complex of tents, Quonset huts and shanty-town warehouses, linked by bulldozer-scraped roads and muddy tracks, that did little to complement the natural vista. The great advantage of the site was that for the first time MacArthur had been able to bring together most of the subsidiary headquarters, army, air force and navy, which put his plans into action. Until a few months previously he had spent far too much of his time flying between one far-flung jungle or off-shore command post and another.

When the Leyte invasion began, most of these staff personnel were still at Hollandia. MacArthur himself had left more than a week before, having embarked with a skeleton staff on the light cruiser *Nashville*, which formed part of the vast invasion armada destined for Leyte in the Philippines. He had arrived off that island late on the 19th, and had gone ashore the next day, shortly after the main assault forces, to be photographed striding purposefully from landing-craft to beach through the knee-high waters of Leyte Gulf. The striking

393

pictures that soon appeared in the world's press prompted some cynics to suggest that they were posed. This was not the case, though a staged arrival on another beach the next day produced only very ordinary photographs.

No one can say, however, that MacArthur was not acutely sensitive to the value of good publicity, and oversensitive about the not-so-good. In the early days on Leyte, as throughout most of the Pacific campaign, MacArthur took great pains with his appearance, striving for a 'warrior of the people' look that would endear him to both the fighting soldier and the potential voter. Just a few garments and accessories defined the look: immaculately pressed army shirt and trousers, an A-2 leather flying jacket, a pair of Ray-bann aviator sun-glasses, a braided but battered officer's cap and an enormous corn-cob pipe. The pipe, which resembled a small wicker basket on the end of a piece of half-inch dowel, was virtually unsmokable. The cap dated from his days as commander-in-chief of the Philippine armed forces in the late 1930s, when he had assumed the rank of Field Marshal, a rank not normally used in the U.S. Army. With the rank went a distinctive uniform and the whole "outfit was crowned with a cap that sported a large American eagle. The design principle on which the cap was based was glittering; MacArthur was going to set a new American record for the amount of gold braid stitched on to a single piece of headgear . . . He loved it. He treasured the field marshal's cap for the rest of his life."[1]

The cap was also prominent along the Leyte beaches in the days immediately after the invasion. MacArthur slept and retained his headquarters aboard the *Nashville* until 24th October, while going ashore each day to visit a different beachhead. On at least one occasion he was to be found in the very front line, showing a studied disdain for any danger this might entail. There were also political duties to be performed. On the 23rd he installed Sergio Osmena, who had travelled with him on the *Nashville*, as President of the Philippine Commonwealth and then saw Osmena swear in local guerrilla leader Colonel Ruperto Kangleon as Governor of Leyte. The ceremony took place on the steps of the provincial capitol building in Tacloban, shortly after which MacArthur left to inspect a suggested new headquarters.

The large, cream-coloured house, which had belonged to an American plantation-owner, Walter Price, until he was killed early in the war, was imposingly built of brick and concrete around a cool courtyard. It had been used as a Japanese officers' club only a few days before. MacArthur arrived and agreed with his staff that this was far superior to the accommodation at Lake Sentani. At the same time, he was uneasy about a large and well-appointed air-raid shelter cut into the front lawn. When the Japanese invaded the Philippines in December 1941, MacArthur had remained behind with his troops until the following March and was one of the few officers to be evacuated at the last chance. The grim fate of those that stayed to endure the Bataan 'death march' provoked a wave of malicious gossip, most tellingly that MacArthur had been afraid to expose himself above ground, so leading to the widespread nick-name 'Dug-out Doug'. He hastily ordered the Tacloban shelter to be filled in and the lawn re-turfed.

On 24th October MacArthur does not seem to have ventured ashore at all, preoccupied as he was with the land battle and the disappointingly slow progress of most of the divisions. He remained aboard the *Nashville* the next day too, fascinated by what he was able to learn about the epic naval battle going on to the south and to the east of Samar. Because MacArthur refused to go ashore, the *Nashville* remained out of the fire-fight in Suriago Strait, though the general is said to have been keen to take part in his first naval battle. Later in the day, as the Navy was mustering ships to pursue Japanese remnants fleeing this battle, MacArthur was finally persuaded to leave the ship though only to board the Amphibious Force Flagship *Wasatch*, where General Walter Kreuger, commander of U.S. Sixth Army troops on Leyte, was also present with his small staff.[2]

Sharing with subordinates, however, was not to MacArthur's taste and he soon disembarked for good, making his way once more to the Price house. In the evening, while junior personnel installed furniture, telegraph equipment and maps, and engineers started demolishing the shelter, MacArthur sat down to dinner with his staff. According to his air chief, General George Kenney, commanding U.S. Far East Air Forces, discussion not unnaturally still centred on naval events. The Army's attitude to the Navy, and *vice versa*, rarely rose above disdain and there was much hostile speculation on the to-ing and fro-ing of Admiral William Halsey's Third Fleet which was said to have steamed off into the blue, leaving the amphibious force unprotected. As the whiskey passed round some cursed 'that bastard Halsey' and others called him 'a stupid son of a bitch'. MacArthur became visibly annoyed. He "brought his clenched fist down on the table. 'That's enough,' he barked. 'Leave the Bull alone. He's still a fighting admiral in my book."[3]

*

Leyte Gulf on 25th October was the focus of the whole Pacific War, with U.S. naval power concentrated there to a quite unprecedented degree. In the event, both Third and Seventh Fleets had had to take part in a major series of battles with the Japanese, though the Seventh Fleet's participation was completely unforeseen. It had been intended that Halsey's fast carriers would put up the main defence, and such classic ploys as crossing the 'T' in Suriago Strait or the heroic destroyer skirmishing off Samar, were the last type of action Admiral Kinkaid's commanders could have expected. Their ships were there primarily to provide close fire support and logistic back-up for the four infantry divisions put ashore on the 20th, while Third Fleet's task was to ensure additional air cover until the strips on Leyte were back in commission for MacArthur's Fifth Air Force planes. These were supposed to be operating by the 25th and in theory, had the Japanese not intervened, Halsey's carriers and battleships might soon have been steaming off to launch strikes against more remote targets. Yet this would still have left an enormously impressive array of ships in Leyte Gulf to support an amphibious assault against an island only 115 miles long and 45 miles wide.

At certain points along the axes of advance, territory had to be staked out, mainly to insert land-based air-power and neutralise that of the enemy. To do this troops had to be transported to the particular atoll, island or beachhead, put ashore in landing craft, and provided with the necessary supplies and equipment to overcome the enemy and construct the specified airfields, anchorages, military bases, storage depots or repair facilities. The job was not the stuff of headlines and the ships to do it were the ugly ducklings of the navy – escort carriers, superannuated battleships, attack cargos, tankers and landing ships. But these vessels were just as important a component of amphibious oceanic warfare as the fabled Task Force 38/58, and it is important to realise the scale of the naval effort off Leyte, with or without the attentions of Admiral Kurita and other Japanese commanders.[4]

The primary task of Seventh Fleet was to transport the four divisions to two designated beachheads on the east coast of Leyte, near Tacloban and Dulag. Two of these divisions had left Hawaii on 13th September and sailed to Manus which they reached on 3rd October. On 11th October they sailed once more, and by the 17th made ocean rendezvous with ships carrying the other two divisions, some of which had come from Hollandia and some from Manus. Once all the ships had come together they formed the largest convoy yet seen in the Pacific. Three Task Forces were present: the 183 vessels of TF 77 were mainly warships, while most of the 518 ocean-going vessels in TFs 78 and 79 were transports, cargo ships and landing ships. In all, there were

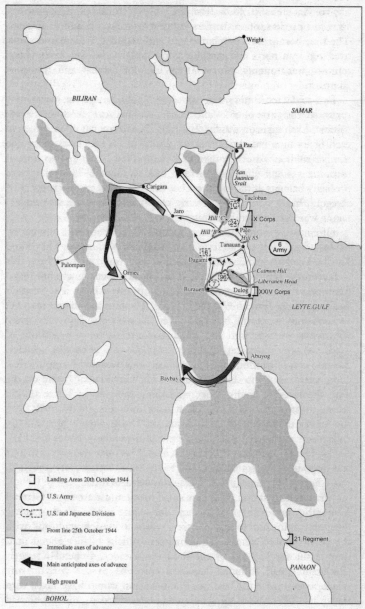

Leyte Island 25th October 1944

157 combat ships: 6 old battleships, 5 heavy cruisers, 6 light cruisers, 18 escort carriers, 86 destroyers, 25 destroyer-escorts and 11 frigates. The transport vessels numbered 420 and included 5 command ships, over 200 transports and landing ships, and 100 landing craft. Total tonnage was roughly 660,000 tons each of combat and transport shipping.

By 25th October all four divisions were ashore on Leyte, though one regiment, the 381st of 96 Infantry Division, was yet to be committed to combat. Each division was fielding roughly 750 combat infantrymen in each of its nine battalions making a total of 36 battalions or 27,000 combat soldiers ashore, individually supported by almost 50 tons of shipping – which does not include cargoes carried. The calculation probably belongs at the lower end of the 'not many people know that' category, but it does indicate fairly clearly what an expensive undertaking was Pacific island-hopping.

Of course, Seventh Fleet was hampered in its support mission by having to fight off the attentions of Admirals Nishimura, Shima and Kurita. Yet even without this distraction they would not have been able to hasten the build-up as much as had been hoped. It was not just a question of getting the supplies and equipment ashore. The weather had been fairly calm and on the first day the ships had managed to get 107,000 tons on to the beaches. Over the next few days they made substantial inroads into the total requirement for the landing of 1,500,000 tons of general equipment, 235,000 tons of combat vehicles, 200,000 tons of ammunition, and 200,000 tons of medical supplies. But even when calm, the skies had been somewhat lowering, and on the 25th the weather finally broke, signalling the start of Leyte's rainy season. Almost an inch of rain fell in just a few hours and the roads from the American beachheads at Tacloban and Dulag, already breaking up, collapsed completely under the weight of the endless lorries and half-tracks. In the Tacloban beachhead contact between the two divisions was impossible except on foot, and to the south lorries were unable to move beyond the outskirts of Dulag towards Burauen.

Many felt then and later that some blame must attach to General MacArthur and his immediate staff for failing to take account of the inevitable rain and to make every effort to find beachheads with the most durable terrain. The American official history stated that, despite the forebodings of the local commander, General Kreuger, Macarthur "had assigned logistical missions to the Sixth Army which, even under the best of circumstances, would have taxed it to the limit . . . Because of the shortage of engineer troops, the lack of road metal, and the continuous traffic, the construction and maintenance of roads presented a critical and continuing problem." Kreuger himself was particularly resentful of the failure to allow for the fact that "bivouac areas, depots and dumps cannot be established in swamps and rice paddies."[5]

Terrain and weather were also making a mockery of MacArthur's over-optimistic projections for establishing his own air cover on the island. By the 25th, just five days after the initial landings, he was expecting there to be facilities for seven fighter squadrons (including one night), one photo-reconnaissance squadron, four or five medium bomber squadrons, three patrol bomber squadrons, and one Marine reconnaissance squadron, a total of something like 450 aircraft. MacArthur's engineers had vigorously protested at this timetable from the outset. Colonel W. J. Ely of Sixth Army stated that previous experience with the sort of soil and inadequate drainage on Leyte, as well as the shortage of engineer troops, made it virtually impossible to keep to the short lead time. "Perhaps we can mud and muddle through again on a shoestring but the shoestring must be frayed by this time and if it broke we may lose our shirt as well as our shoe."[6] MacArthur's General Headquarters was apprised of these objections but decided to stick to the original timetable. Once on Leyte, however, it became clear that Ely's fears were well-founded. By 22nd October, engineer reconnaissance parties declared that of the six proposed airfields, only the one at Cataisan Point, across the bay from Tacloban, was usable, and that only with difficulty.

Far from being completed by the 25th, the whole project was degenerating almost into chaos. The collapsing roads were causing increasing delays, especially to the heavily-laden trucks carrying gravel, coral and sand to prepare the surface on which to lay the steel-matting runways. Assisting with the work were men from 7 and 8 Squadrons of 49 Fighter Group and they reported that the whole of the Cataisan Peninsula was an "unadulterated bog" and that the "confusion was awe-inspiring".[7] Much of the proposed runway, as well as approach roads to the airfield, were littered with Army supplies that had been dumped there when several landing ships were redirected to the peninsula after being shelled in their original anchorage. To get planes flying as quickly as possible, hundreds of Air Force service troops had come ashore in the first few days. The engineers who were now so desperately needed had been given a lower landing priority and still languished offshore while the service troops had little to do except dash to and from their slit-trenches around the airfield to dodge the successive Japanese air raids. To make matters worse, U.S. aircraft from both Seventh and Third Fleet carriers began using Tacloban as an emergency air strip. Almost 100 planes attempted to land on the 25th, a quarter of which crashed. One of these sparked off a huge explosion in one of the fuel dumps that was heard for miles around.

The basic tasks of the Leyte forces were first to seize the Tacloban and Dulag airfields, then to push up the Leyte Valley northward to Carigan Bay and south to Abuyog, and finally to drive across Leyte's central highlands west to Baybay and south to Ormoc, where the Japanese would most likely attempt to land any reinforcements. The American landings had been only lightly opposed, largely due to the Japanese decision not to stake everything on their beach defences but to retreat inland when the American bombardment began. By the time their troops started to return to their bunkers and dug-outs the Americans were already firmly established ashore. The fighting over the next few days took on a somewhat desultory aspect, with the bulk of the Japanese slowly pulling back to more defensible positions overlooking Leyte Valley and the two main roads that linked each side of the island.

To the north U.S. X Corps met very little resistance and 1 Cavalry Division was able to push up to the ferry crossing in San Juanico Strait to frustrate any Japanese trying to infiltrate from Samar. The division's casualties were a modest 40 killed and 199 wounded. In XXIV Corps' southern beachhead the going was somewhat tougher, although even here 96 Division lost only 96 men killed and 433 wounded after the first five days, remarkably light losses in the beachhead phase of a Pacific island assault. But just moving forward could be trial enough. When two battalions of 96 Division moved out they encountered "a deep swamp . . . few supplies had been brought forward because the vehicles of the battalions had advanced only 200 yards when they bogged down. The troops hand-carried their weapons and communications equipment while civilians with about eight carabaos [domesticated water buffalos] helped carry the supplies . . . Ammunition was given priority over rations and water, even though the supply of the latter items was nearly exhausted. The men made free use of coconuts for food and drink."[8]

Although Leyte Valley contained very few naturally defensible positions, the Japanese made best use of whatever favourable ground there was and fought numerous small delaying actions. Often these involved individual snipers who found perfect cover in the shoulder-high cogon grass that covered those parts of the valley not given over to rice paddies or swamp. The Japanese tied clumps of grass to their helmets, to hide tell-tale gaps in the swaying surface, and waited for the Americans to pass before firing on them from behind. "They usually shot from ground level and most of our sniper casualties were hit from the hips down. Some of them also used pointed bullets made of wood and paper [which they] fired over a G.I.'s head, the paper bullet would explode with a loud pop, causing [him] to turn in that direction. This gave the sniper more time to aim a more deadly shot with the real bullet."[9]

By the 25th each of the four American divisions was engaged in slow, methodical advances against their allotted objectives. In the southern beachhead, 96 Division was attempting to pinch out and clear Catmon Hill, while 7 Division sought to seize the Burin airfield and the Burauen–Dagami road just beyond. To the north, in the Tacloban beachhead, 1 Cavalry Division was still making the most of its largely unopposed push up the coast, but 27 Division was having an altogether more wearisome day advancing west along the Palo–Cangara road. The hills flanking the eastern end of the road were still held by the Japanese who were fighting fierce delaying actions that required the Americans to organise two set-piece regimental attacks.

One of these involved a battalion from 19 Regiment and enjoyed some comic aspects, though these were probably not apparent to the men taking part. The feature they were attacking was known as Hill 'B' and 2/19 Battalion's first assault on 22nd October had been repulsed. A renewed attack the next day made better progress, and it was assumed that the crest of the hill had now been reached. On the 24th, the battalion struck once more, to consolidate its hold on the whole feature, only to discover that the ridge already taken was not the actual crest. The advance faltered in the face of fire from the true crest and the battalion commander decided to wait until the following day, the 25th, to renew the assault from a jump-off point further to the east. This approach also turned out to be well-covered by Japanese emplacements, some of them six feet deep and five feet wide. Enemy fire was continuous and heavy and one of the two attacking companies had to fall back. The commander decided to move the second company that night to yet another ridge which might give a dominating jump-off point, and then to move the rest of the battalion up to it. Company 'G' moved off as ordered and, once in position, the other companies set off to join it. However, "starting in the dark, the battalion lost its way. At midnight the troops came to the true crest of the ridge where the enemy had an observation post surrounded by prepared positions. All were empty. The Japanese had formed the habit of going to the villages for the night and returning in the morning to man their posts. The night movement of the battalion [as the division later reported] 'literally caught them napping away from their defences' . . . The hills guarding Leyte Valley were now in American hands."[10]

Slinking off for a comfortable night's sleep was hardly standard operating procedure for the Japanese Army and a much more obdurate attitude was taking hold at more senior levels. The chain of command in the Philippines devolved from Southern Army (Field Marshal Terauchi), through Fourteenth Area Army (General Yamashita), to Thirty-fifth Army (General Suzuki), with Leyte itself being held by 16 Infantry Division (General Makino). Yamashita was a recent arrival, from Manchuria via Tokyo, and he replaced General Kuroda who had been dismissive of Japanese plans to smash a Philippines invasion largely through air-power. Just before being replaced, on 9th October, he had bluntly stated: "That concept is good, but you cannot fight with concept alone. Words alone will not sink American ships and that becomes clear when you compare our airplanes with theirs. That is why the major battles have been occurring on land. We can say that the power of our air force is negligible at this time."[11] Yamashita, on the other hand, had no time for pussy-footing around with concepts and as soon as he was sure that Leyte was the first American destination in the Philippines he instructed Makino and his men: "The Army has received the following order from His Majesty, the Emperor: Enemy ground forces will be destroyed."[12]

This spirit was also evident in Thirty-fifth Army headquarters. On 23rd October its personnel moved from the island of Cebu to Leyte and at about the same time, according to Suzuki's chief-of-staff, they "determined to take offensive after offensive and clean up American forces on Leyte. We seriously discussed demanding the surrender of the entire American Army after seizing General MacArthur."[13] Various commanders, notably Terauchi, Suzuki and Admiral Mikawa, in charge of South-West Area Fleet, were all resolved to make a serious stand on Leyte, rather than withdraw to Luzon for the decisive battle, and plans were soon afoot for the dispatch of individual battalions and later whole divisions to Leyte. These were all to arrive at the small port of Ormoc, though by the 25th the TA Operation, as it became known, had put ashore only 450 troops, while other Japanese units were already ear-marked to sail.[14]

Just where these units would be positioned was still uncertain, though General Makino set up his command post in Dagami, dividing his division into a Southern Defence Force to hold the area from north of Burauen to just west of Catman Hill, and a Northern Defence Force to occupy the hill itself as well as the high ground south of Tanauan. The two battalions which the Americans had driven off the various hills in XX Corps sector would have to shift for themselves. None of this was known to the Americans and ULTRA intelligence sources had as yet produced no evidence of the Japanese decision to reinforce Leyte. Indeed, right up to early November both MacArthur and Kreuger's headquarters continued to believe that the Japanese were about to evacuate the island.

Yet it was Filipino evacuees who for the moment presented one of the main problems for the American authorities. Considerable efforts had been made to inform the civilian population in the proposed beachheads that there was to be a big bombardment and they should make every effort to evacuate the area. The word was successfully spread by an American liaison officer working with the Filipino guerrillas, such that all the affected villages were evacuated except Tacloban "where the Japanese garrison refused to let the people depart. As a result (since Tacloban was spared), not one Filipino lost his life in the pre-landing bombardment."[15] Even so, a large number of civilians did lose their houses, most of their possessions and, for a while at least, their livelihood. These people naturally kept as far away from the Japanese as possible and instead accumulated around the American lines where units attached to Sixth Army Service Command head-quarters had to make the refugees their first priority. By 21st October these numbered 2,000 in the northern beachhead and some 7,000 in the southern. In both sectors the refugees were moved off the beaches into towns (Palo and Dulag) but as more continued to flood in, numbering 30,000 in Dulag by 23rd October, it was decided to move them back to the beaches. The refugees went with great reluctance to an area that measured about 1,000 by 600 yards and consisted of a coconut grove and a beach. By the 25th, the two main refugee areas contained some 45,000 Filipinos, being fed with American 'C' and 'K' rations supple-mented with rice, fish and a little meat captured from the Japanese. Fortunately, the bulk of the refugees came from villages now under American control, and from the 24th it was possible to make a start on dispersing them back to the *barrios*.

34

The Fleet Train

U.S. NAVAL LOGISTICS IN THE PACIFIC

IN A VAST oceanic theatre such as the Pacific a navy is, almost by definition, much more mobile than an army. Soldiers are largely rooted to their various island garrisons, only able to put relatively small numbers of men to sea at any one time and only able to convey them from one island to the next with extreme circumspection. A navy, however, especially one built around the long-range thirty-knot carriers and battleships of the U.S. Pacific Fleet, could range much more freely, steaming enormous distances before launching devastating air raids at almost any point on the enemy's defensive perimeter. Nevertheless, ships were as dependent as any other weapons platform on fuel, ammunition, spare parts, maintenance facilities, and sustenance for the crews. After a certain time, the ships had to return to base to be resupplied with these items or for refit and repair.

When the war started, the Americans already possessed developed bases at Pearl Harbor, Dutch Harbor in the Aleutians, and Pago Pago in Samoa. In the next months frantic efforts were made to extend the Pacific Fleet's logistical infrastructure, and so new bases were leased and constructed at Bora Bora (Society Islands), Nandi and Suva (Fiji), Noumea (New Caledonia), Efate and Espiritu Santo (New Hebrides), Tulagi (Solomon Islands), Wellington (New Zealand), Brisbane and Sydney. Once reliable lines of communication were in place, linking the United States, Pearl Harbor and Australasia, the advance against the Japanese could begin, and over the next months the U.S. Navy marked its remorseless progress westwards with the construction of enormous fleet anchorages at Majuro, Eniwetok and Ulithi, and complex repair facilities at Manus and Guam, both of which boasted dry docks capable of handling vessels as large as a battleship. Indeed

Guam's naval installations were reckoned to be worth more than $30 million. All of them were small cities in their own right, and by late 1944 Eniwetok, for example, was served by more than 11,000 naval personnel and Guam by 78,000. Among overseas naval personnel as a whole, in October 1944, there were more men ashore than afloat – 1,800,000 as opposed to 1,400,000. In the Central Pacific Area, however, the ratio was 240,000 to 280,000.

Even this network of bases was not enough to allow Admirals Nimitz and Halsey to maintain an optimum tempo of operations. Between 6th October 1944 and the end of the following January, Halsey's Third Fleet was at sea for thirteen out of the sixteen weeks, and this was only made possible by its not having to return to one base or another every time fuel or munitions ran low. Such independence of fixed installations was achieved by creating a mobile fleet base, the Service Force Pacific Fleet under Admiral William Calhoun. The Service Force was sub-divided into various squadrons, of which probably the most important were Service Squadron 10 (Servron 10) and Servron 8. The former, also referred to as the Mobile Service Base, was responsible for supporting naval units during an amphibious operation and for bringing stores and installations forward from one advanced base to the next. It comprised all manner of vessels, including provision ships, barracks ships, tankers, hospital ships, a survey ship, new tenders, pontoon assembly ships, buoy boats, harbour and salvage tugs, a floating dry-dock, a degaussing vessel and a floating crane. There were also several enormous steel or concrete barges which were used for the offshore storage of oil as well as of fresh and dry provisions, clothing and small stores. The real workhorses of the Squadron were the provisions ships, or Stores Issue Ships (AKSs). "These floating general stores carried some 5,000 items in 90 classes, from steel plates for battle damage to toilet paper. Since today's Navy is a floating cross-section of contemporary civilisation, about 40,000 different items are required to take care of ships at sea; the 5,000 carried by the AKSs were merely the most urgent."[1]

On 25th October Servron 10 was busily engaged in setting up its new headquarters in Ulithi, having moved there from Eniwetok in the first two weeks of the month. One of its high-priority tasks was the installation of a floating 'tank farm', comprising half-a-dozen obsolete oil tankers, each holding between sixty and a hundred thousand barrels of fuel. This ad hoc arrangement was preferred to the permanent built-in tank farms found at Pearl Harbor, Guam and Saipan as offering more flexibility in day-to-day operations.

The other vital component of the Service Force, Servron 8, was also referred to as the At Sea Logistics Service Group. These were the ships that served Third/Fifth Fleet at sea during a series of carrier strikes or after a naval battle, and they were primarily concerned with the supply of oil, ammunition and replacement aircraft. The configuration of the Group on the 25th makes these priorities clear for, as well as the protective 18 destroyers and 26 destroyer-escorts, it comprised 33 fleet-oilers, 10 escort carriers with replacement planes, 10 fleet tugs, and 13 ammunition ships, one of which went by the ominous name of USS *Nitro*.[2] The tankers, which also carried certain basic provisions and essential aircraft spares, were divided into three groups of 9 to 12 ships to work with the individual carrier task groups. The three supply groups were in turn subdivided into task units of three tankers or so, with one unit of empty ships being replaced every three or four days by replenished ships from Ulithi. Each of these task units was also accompanied by an escort carrier and its complement of replacement aircraft. It is unclear whether these aircraft could have offered any protection to the tankers for such assistance was never called upon. Of the dozens of rendezvous between carrier groups and Servron 8 ships, all set at very short notice by Halsey and Spruance, not one was ever discovered by the Japanese.

It was at just such a refuelling rendezvous, in the Kossol Passage at the northern end of the Palau Islands, that Admiral McCain's TG 38.1 received Halsey's urgent summons on the morning of the 25th to return to Leyte and assist Sprague's beleaguered escort carriers. How much oil McCain had managed to take aboard seems not to be on record, but it is worth noting that in the two months up to the end of October, Servron 8 delivered to Third Fleet 4.5 million barrels of fuel oil and 7.25 million barrels of aviation gasoline. Clearly, without these floating cornucopias U.S. naval aviation would have been a much less fearsome asset, the strikes against the Okinawa and Formosa airfields in October would have been much diminished and the Japanese, in consequence, might have been able to transfer enough aircraft to the Philippines to embarrass Kinkaid, Halsey and MacArthur seriously. Without Servrons, barrelage, AKSs and AEs it is unlikely that the American advance across the Central Pacific would have got much beyond the Marianas by August 1945.[3]

In war hardly anything goes without a hitch, and replenishment of the task groups before the Leyte operation was not able to alleviate every shortage. Task Force 38 had left Ulithi on 6th October after spending the last three days there on the fringe of a slow-moving typhoon, which caused such heavy seas in the lagoon that lighters and provisions vessels were unable to come alongside and the warships were forced to sail with only half the requisite food on board. Much of this shortfall could, of course, be made good later by the At Sea Logistics ships, though not of certain items normally carried in the refrigeration vessels, or 'reefers'. The Service Force suffered from a chronic shortage of these vessels and its impact was felt especially on the fleet carriers whose aircrew, especially the officers, had become accustomed to cuisine rather than mere 'chow'. Thick steaks, fried eggs, fried potatoes, buttered toast, even ice-cream were all standard items on even the breakfast menu. By 25th October, however, shortages were making themselves felt. "Nobody in the fleet went hungry; but owing to [the typhoon] and the insufficient number of reefer . . . ships . . . fresh and frozen provisions could not be delivered in the quantities to which sailors, especially the naval aviators, were accustomed. Menus became somewhat supercharged with spam and beans."[4] It can be assumed that the riflemen on Leyte, poking around in the tin-cans and waxed boxes from their 'C' and 'K' rations, would have been less than moved by the sailors' plight.

PART EIGHT

The Submarine War Against Japan

35

Death of the Marus

THE JAPANESE MERCHANT FLEET

WHILE THE Americans worried about getting enough ice-cream to their aircraft carriers, the Japanese were finding it increasingly difficult to get any kind of supplies or reinforcements to their island garrisons, or to bring back the precious oil and strategic raw materials from the East Indies to Japan. Indeed, by October 1944 it was becoming clear that Japan's attempt to hold permanent sway over much of East Asia and the Pacific was one of history's more striking acts of strategic hubris. Not the least of their overweening miscalculations were those concerning logistics. When the Japanese declared war on America in December 1941, they transformed the already demanding China campaign into an enormous imperial enterprise. In the modern jargon, they sought to project their power along an extremely wide radius, through eastern China, Burma, the Dutch East Indies and the Philippines, with the particular aim of securing the raw materials of the East Indies to support military operations in China, a powerful, mobile navy in the Pacific and increased military production at home.

The need for an overseas transfusion was certainly pressing. According to criteria formulated by the Royal Institute of International Affairs, Japan in the late 1930s was not self-sufficient – even for peacetime industry – in coal, iron or molybdenum (used in steel alloys), and was largely or entirely deficient in oil, copper, lead, tin, zinc, bauxite, manganese, tungsten, phosphates, potash and rubber.[1] Given long-standing American hostility to Japanese ambitions in China and the Pacific and a readiness to resort to economic embargo, it is at least possible to understand why Japan felt it had to guarantee access to vital raw materials by physically seizing the deposits. What still seems remarkable, however, is the failure of the Japanese to see that such seizure did not guarantee that they would be able to get what they extracted back to the home islands. To do so required an adequate merchant marine, and one moreover that could be consistently replenished to make up for the inevitable war losses.

The Japanese were keen students of naval affairs and, despite a disdain for ships without guns, their naval planners must have been aware of the deadly menace posed by the U-boat assault on Allied merchant shipping in the First World War. Yet the military as a whole chose resolutely to ignore the fact that the Japanese merchant fleet was far weaker than that of other great maritime powers. Of the 62 million tons of merchant shipping that entered Japanese ports in 1938, only 37 million tons, roughly 60 per cent, was under the Japanese flag. An even higher proportion of the most valuable raw material, oil, was carried in foreign tankers. Even worse, the Japanese had no effective contingency plans for increasing merchant ship production in the event of war, and this was likely to be especially serious in a protracted struggle. Unless enough raw materials were earmarked for merchant shipbuilding from the very start, inevitably there would be an increasing shortage of ships to bring in the very iron and steel with which any new ships were supposed to be built.

The Americans were not slow to see that Japan's sea lanes offered a promising military target. From early in 1942 both aircraft and submarines were employed to seek out the scattered and usually unescorted Japanese merchant ships, or *marus*. Even at that time, when the American war effort was still somewhat diffuse, Japan's blasé attitude to her merchant fleet cost her dear. The U.S. Strategic Bombing Survey, compiled after the war, noted: "In this period [to August 1942] it is astonishing that the Japanese should have prepared so inadequately for an ocean war that, in spite of the windfall of captured ships, an [American] attack as weak and sporadic as that directed against them in the first nine months of the war should have been able to accomplish the signal success of starting Japanese net merchant tonnage on the downward trend as early as April 1942."[2]

Later in the war the Japanese did manage to make some amends for their original cavalier attitude to their merchant fleet and the 260,000 tons of merchant shipping (77 ships) built in 1942 increased to 1,415,000 (581) in the first ten months of 1944. Tanker production was better still, the comparable figures being 20,316 tons (7 ships) and 515,300 (166). Unfortunately, these efforts were nowhere near enough to offset losses to American planes, submarines and surface ships. From an average of just under 90,000 tons of Japanese merchant shipping lost per month in 1942, the losses rose to 152,000 in 1943 and 273,500 tons in 1944. The peak month in 1944 was October when more than 512,000 tons of shipping went down. Tanker losses rose from a meagre 800 tons per month in 1942 to 69,000 in 1944. Again the peak month was October.

The effects of all this were calamitous. At the end of December 1941 the Japanese merchant marine comprised 5.5 million tons of shipping. By the end of 1942 the initial decline had been reversed and total tonnage had crept up to 5.6 million. Throughout 1943, however, this accelerated ship-building was still not enough to offset losses and the total tonnage on 31st December was only 5.1 million. During 1944 the race was well and truly lost and the combination of ever more powerful American attacks and dwindling Japanese imports reduced the fleet at the end of September to only 2.6 million tons. In the month of October the fleet was reduced by a further 13 per cent, to less than 2.3 million tons.

The only consolation for the Japanese was that tanker tonnage available had actually risen from 591,000 tons at the end of 1941 to 840,000 tons by the end of October 1944. But it was poor consolation because, on the one hand, industry could not live by oil alone, and, on the other, even this increased supply was inadequate to meet the demands of industry and the Army's and Navy's aircraft and warships. Moreover, certain Japanese were probably becoming aware that throughout 1944 the Americans were attempting to target tankers specifically. Thus, as the percentage of tankers among total merchant shipping increased, as it had done from one-tenth to one-third, the more vulnerable these ships would become. The point was brought home forcibly in October when altogether 132,500 tons of tankers went to the bottom, almost one-third of the total tonnage sunk that month. In the third quarter of 1944, in fact, oil imports had been 1.1 million barrels, a dramatic fall from the 3.4 million barrels in the same quarter in 1943.[3]

Indeed, imports generally were grievously hit by the tightening American blockade. The figures in the table below, showing total and percentage fall in imports of selected raw materials between 1943 and 1944, in thousands of metric tons, make this abundantly clear.[4] These shortfalls made it very difficult for the Japanese war economy to produce any high quality munitions at all, let alone to keep up with the prodigious output from the ever-burgeoning American arsenal. No wonder that an official at the Japanese Bureau of Total Mobilisation wrote of events to autumn 1944: "Shipping lost and damaged [since

the beginning of the war] amounts to two and one half times newly
constructed shipping, and forms the chief cause of the constant
impoverishment of national strength."[5]

Raw Material	1943	1944	Percentage decrease
Coal	5,180	2,615	50
Coking Coal	2,940	1,435	51
Iron Ore	4,300	2,155	50
Finished iron and steel	980	1,100	+12
Bauxite	910	375	69
Lead	25	17	32
Tin	27	23	15
Zinc	10	6	40
Phosphorite and phosphate	240	90	63
Dolomite and magnesite	435	295	32

The chief cause, in reality was the American submarine force in the
Pacific, but Japanese efforts at convoy protection and anti-submarine
warfare proved, on the whole, to be shambolic. Even before the war
began the relevant, albeit minor, section of the naval general staff had
concluded that Japan's imperial ambitions, and their logistical sustenance, would require a dedicated escort fleet of at least 360 destroyers. Each year thereafter the Japanese staff officer responsible for
shipping protection submitted his escort plan and reiterated the
estimate of the number of ships required. Each year the high command
refused to divert any but the most dilapidated vessels to such duties.
Finally, in September 1943, a Grand Escort Fleet was established and
in March of the following year an organised convoy system was
introduced with regular shipping routes and groupings of roughly
twenty ships.

It was too little, too late. At most only 150 vessels were assigned, and
the five escort carriers among them were soon sunk by the Americans.
Four had gone down by the end of October 1944 and none had escorted
more than two convoys. Worse still, though 901 Air Flotilla was
dedicated to convoy protection, its best planes and pilots were quickly
absorbed by the Combined Fleet to help rebuild the shattered carrier
squadrons, and most of these were squandered in the October air
battles over Formosa. According to a staff officer with the Grand
Escort Fleet, during these battles, "aircraft suitable for scouting and
anti-submarine work were practically eliminated."[6] Not that the
Flotilla had ever operated at maximum efficiency. Aircraft radar was
not available until late 1944, and then was so crude that visual search

was always preferred during daylight. Moreover, communications between aircraft that did find American submarines and the Japanese escorts were extremely slow and unreliable, often having to be routed via the aircraft's base. This same totally inadequate equipment was also installed on the escorts, and a postwar technical report by the Americans concluded that throughout the war the Japanese had had to make do with equipment and components that, "while well made, closely resembled those available to amateur radio enthusiasts in the United States in the early 1930s."[7]

The full list of Japanese shortcomings in the war against the submarine becomes almost poignant, and by October 1944 they were still only playing at convoys. So unreliable was the radar that in September the new commander of the Grand Escort Fleet, Admiral Nomura, had to order that convoys on many routes should sail only in the daytime as American radar dominance at night was almost total. Even in daylight convoys had to take increasingly circuitous routes, hugging the coastline wherever possible. The average journey from Singapore to Japan took three weeks, twice as long as it had in early 1942. The U.S. Strategic Bombing Survey reckoned that in these last months of the war "convoying and rerouting decreased the freight moved per ship by a factor amounting to 43 per cent."[8]

Statistics also reveal a particular absurdity in Japanese maritime transport. For most of the war merchant shipping was separately assigned to the army, the navy and the civilian wartime shipping ministry. In October 1944 the share-out of ships between these three was, respectively, 18, 22 and 60 per cent.[9] But the 40 per cent of shipping assigned to the armed forces usually took supplies from Japan to the islands and then sailed back empty, while the civilian shipping left Japan in ballast and only loaded up when they arrived at south-east Asian and Indies ports. "Thus developed the paradox of a maritime nation, desperately short of ships, waging a far-flung war across the seas, but still permitting a condition to exist where empty ships might frequently pass each other going in opposite directions."[10] Whether that actually happened on 25th October is unverifiable, but it is certainly true that there would have been dozens of *marus* at sea, putting themselves squarely in harm's way without even the consolation of trying to deliver vital strategic materials.

36

Tang, Dace, Halibut and *Jallao*

U.S. SUBMARINES IN THE PACIFIC

IT WAS American submarines that spearheaded the onslaught against the Japanese sea lanes. Even though their share of *maru* sinkings had fallen from 76 per cent in 1943 to 64 per cent in 1944, the latter was still the peak year, and October the peak month with 329,000 tons going to the bottom of the sea. The submarine arm was shared between the two main commands in the Pacific, with both Nimitz's Pacific Fleet and MacArthur's Seventh Fleet having its own allocation. By October 1944, there were around 100 submarines under the command of Admiral Charles Lockwood with Pacific Fleet and 40 with Admiral Ralph Christie in the South-West Pacific. Not all the vessels were at sea at the same time, of course, and on 25th October there were 38 Pacific Fleet submarines west of the Bonins-Marianas and north of Luzon, with 17 of Christie's boats east of the Philippines–East Indies and two more in the Java Sea.[2]

In essence these boats were operating as maritime guerrillas, behind enemy lines as represented by the supposedly impregnable island barrier running from Sumatra, via Luzon and Formosa, to Okinawa and the main islands. Beyond this barrier, in the South China and East China Seas, ran what were left of Japan's sea lanes and here the submarines preyed on ships carrying raw materials back to Japan and munitions and reinforcements from China and the home islands.

In addition, submarines were often directed to form patrol lines and act as lifeguards for downed carrier- or land-based pilots, and during the great amphibious strides to a new island group some would be directed towards Japanese fleet anchorages to report any sorties by the Imperial Navy. On 20th October, Lockwood had three submarines on just such a mission to the east of Kyushu, while Christie had deployed a dozen boats to intercept and report on fleet movements from the Lingga Roads.

During a naval battle, however, most submarines remained well outside the fighting and kept up their hunt for merchant shipping. They operated in groups of two or three, referred to as wolf-packs, each co-ordinated by a pack leader who would bring patrolling boats together against a promising target. Wolfish or not, the submariners certainly adopted a buccaneering pose and packs usually adopted brash nicknames, such as Wogan's Wolves, Blakeley's Behemoths, and Coye's Coyotes – though the names of the submarines could seem a little bathetic. They were all named after fish, and the swashbuckling Roach's Raiders actually comprised the *Haddock*, *Tuna* and *Halibut*. Still, there are a lot of fish in the sea and Benson's Dogs united the suitably voracious *Razorback*, *Cavalla* and *Piranha*. American submariners also displayed a vengeful attitude to Japanese shipping areas. These were given code-names by the operations officer at Pearl Harbor, Commander Richard Voge, and some of the most fruitful in October 1944 were Convoy College, named after a simulation training course at Pearl, Hit Parade, and Marus' Morgue.

In the early months of the war American submarine efforts had been seriously undermined by a marked lack of aggression by commanders who had been trained according to extremely pessimistic assumptions about submarine survivability, and by an unpardonable official intransigence about obvious defects in the torpedoes. By the autumn of 1943 both matters had been properly addressed, and from then on the innate superiority of American technology became manifest.

The submarines were now extremely effective and cost-effective weapons platforms. A typical 'fleet' submarine displaced around 1,500 tons, was just over 300 feet long, had surface/underwater speeds of 20/9 knots, and carried 24 torpedoes which could be fired from six bow and four stern tubes. Firing torpedoes accurately was a fiendishly difficult business as it was neither possible to fire along the line of sight, because the target would have moved a considerable distance in the minute or so it took the torpedo to reach it, nor to 'spot' misses and make quick visual corrections. The torpedo thus had to be fired ahead of the target, to hit a predicted future position, and working out that position required mathematical juggling with the speed and bearing of target, submarine and torpedo.

Captain and executive officer at the periscope, rapping out the ritual commands of 'Bearing – mark!' and 'Range – mark!' remain the enduring Hollywood image of the firing procedure, with the captain usually presented as some sharp-shooting Dead-Eye Dick. Indeed, the captain's coolness and concentration were always vital ingredients of successful patrols, but by October 1944 a lot of the mental gymnastics and reliance on simple instinct had become redundant due to a combination of early computers and radar. The Torpedo Data Computer, or TDC, was an electro-mechanical device that had been available since the beginning of the war in new submarines, and that subsequently went through three 'Marks'. It was located in the conning tower and, constantly updated as ranges and bearings were fed to the control room, provided the captain with a continuous display on dials of the relative positions of target and submarine, together with an up-to-the-second running solution to the problem of what angle to fire the torpedoes. Best of all, it kept the gyro compasses in the individual torpedoes set to the constantly shifting course, which allowed the captain to fire at any time from whatever bearing he happened to be following. The main drawback was the possibility of severe 'garbage in, garbage out' distortions, with even minor errors in data input continually magnified in the subsequent sequence of 'solutions'.

From 1943 the TDC was supplemented by accurate radar, the high-definition centimetric SJ surface radar, similar to that developed for anti-submarine warfare in the Atlantic. This could detect targets up to 15 miles away and provided commanders with visual information of targets below the horizon, at night, or in adverse weather conditions. From late 1943 this radar 'picture' was presented as blips of light on a plan position indicator (PPI), showing the submarine in the centre with all other contacts in their correct relative positions. "Their range and bearing could be read off rapidly for use in plotting course, speed, pattern of zig-zag without recourse to approximations of 'angle on the bow' and estimated speed from visual observations."[3] As the blips were of different sizes, it was also possible to tell which, if any, represented escorts, and this allowed a submarine to take up firing positions that gave the best chance of avoiding detection, or at least of evading pursuit.

Another major problem was the vulnerability of submarines when on the surface. Again just like guerrillas, submarines cannot afford to face many types of warships in a conventional surface engagement. Closing with the enemy or simply avoiding detection, especially from the air, necessitates running underwater. But while mechanically very well adapted to this environment, a Second World War submarine could offer precious little human comfort once it had dived. Few were able to replace depleted oxygen and so debilitating levels of carbon monoxide soon built up. Within hours almost all the crew would be affected by lassitude, nausea and headaches, symptoms made worse by the rising heat (soon over 100°F in the Pacific), the foetid, cramped living and fighting quarters, and the 100 per cent humidity. Even so, American submarines had a marked technical advantage here, as from the beginning of the war new boats were equipped with air-conditioning. There seems some doubt whether this was installed from humanitarian motives or mainly to reduce the exposure of the boat's electrical systems to extreme condensation, but the fact remains that in the Pacific it was a tremendous boon to the crews. Yet even air-conditioning would not solve the carbon monoxide problem, while a submarine detected from the surface usually had to order 'silent running' which required shutting off the air-conditioning completely.

By late October 1944, then, American submarines in the Pacific represented a potent threat to the survival of the Japanese empire. They were available in large numbers and could be stationed directly across Japanese sea lanes. ULTRA intelligence, derived from merchant shipping codes broken early in 1943, was transmitted to submarine commanders on a daily basis and revealed convoy routes, dates and composition, while radar enabled them to pinpoint precise locations and close in for the kill. The month as a whole represented a peak for Japanese merchant shipping losses, with U.S. submarines accounting for 329,000 tons, as compared to monthly averages of 213,000 in 1944 as a whole, 114,000 in 1943 and 47,000 in 1942.[4]

Submarine operations were in fact a war-winning arm of the service operating at close to peak efficiency. The case of USS *Tang* is typical.

*

The *Tang* left Pearl Harbor to conduct a lone patrol and between 23rd and 26th October was operating in the same area in the Formosa Strait as two wolf-packs, 'Blakeley's Behemoths' and 'Bannister's Beagles'.[5] In these 72 hours the two packs and the loner sank seventeen Japanese merchantmen, a total of around 90,000 tons, many of them transporting reinforcements to the Philippines. None of the submarines, however, seems to have sunk a ship on the 25th.

This is not to say that the day was uneventful. The *Tang*'s captain, Commander Richard O'Kane, was one of the greatest of all Second World War submariners, and his mission once the Japanese fleet had set forth for the Philippines was to track Admiral Shima's small force. Having failed to find him early on the 23rd, O'Kane decided instead to hunt for *marus*. He found a small convoy that very day and with nine torpedoes accounted for three small freighters. On the 24th, he was able to loose off another ten torpedoes, sinking two more freighters for a total tonnage of almost 20,000 in the two days. The second attack provoked a tenacious reaction from the Japanese escort vessels and O'Kane decided to haul off to take a breather and load his last two torpedoes.

He pulled away some five miles and, having shaken off the pursuing escorts, checked the remaining torpedoes and loaded them into two of the forward tubes. The *Tang*, still on the surface, then returned to the fray. Slipping silently among the convoy vessels once more, O'Kane identified a freighter dead in the water and fired off the torpedoes, the last one leaving number four tube at about 2 a.m. on the 25th. As it left, giving the submarine the customary sharp recoil, the crew let out a cheer, knowing that no more torpedoes meant an immediate return to base.

As O'Kane and the eight men with him on the bridge watched the phosphorescent trails of the two torpedoes, they were alarmed to see the second swerve sharply to the left, porpoise and then execute a hairpin turn. Whether this was caused by a jammed rudder or a faulty gyro or steering engine can never be known, but the torpedo was now following a tight, circular course that must bring it back to the firing point. O'Kane shouted for emergency speed and for the rudder to be thrown full over, first to the right and then to the left. After the war he wrote of completing "part of the fishtail maneuver in a futile attempt to clear the [torpedo's] turning circle . . . It struck abreast of the torpedo room with a violent explosion about 20 seconds after firing. The tops were blown off the only ballast tanks aft and the three compartments flooded instantly. The *Tang* sank by the stern much as you would drop a pendulum suspended in a horizontal position."[6]

Even as the boat fell away beneath him, O'Kane shouted to the telephone operator in the conning tower to close the hatch above his head. But there was no time, and sea-water flooded into the tower and control room. As the boat plummeted to the perpendicular, most of it under water, the group on the bridge were left floating in the sea nearby. They formed a circle and were joined after about five minutes by an officer from the conning tower. With the water flooding in he had managed to find a tiny air-pocket and, after a few breaths, had moved to the still open hatch and found another pocket. He then moved to yet another one under the bridge overhang, which sustained him long enough to duck out and swim to the surface.

As O'Kane listened to a gasping account of this remarkable escape, the bow of the *Tang* suddenly let out a gurgling stream of bubbles and sank beneath the water. O'Kane was actually cheered by this as it seemed to indicate that those still inside the submarine were attempting to level her off by counter-flooding. Even sunk to the bottom of these coastal waters, escape would be much more feasible from a boat on an even keel. O'Kane was certainly right in thinking that there were men still alive on the *Tang*, doing their best to stay that way. Of the 78 men that remained on board only 30 had managed to survive the initial explosion and inundation. These had battled their way forward and by prompt action had sealed off the after part of the submarine to confine the flooding. They had also managed to close the hatch between the conning tower and the control room, thus limiting the amount of water that poured in from the bridge. "Then they had opened the vent valve to number two main ballast tank, using the hand-operating gear, since hydraulic power had also been lost, and by this means lowered the bow of the ship to the bottom. They were thus in an excellent position for escape . . . in 180 feet of water, not too far from the coast of China."[7]

Now events were conspiring to thwart the survivors cruelly. The approximate spot where the *Tang* went down was located by Japanese escorts which proceeded to pummel the area with numerous depth-charges. This went on until approximately 6 a.m., and as well as intensifying the trapped men's ordeal, it started a fire in the forward battery compartment, which proved impossible to bring under control and necessitated the sealing off of this compartment. Most of the rest of the boat also had to be sealed off because of progressive flooding from a sprung hatch in the control room. The survivors crowded into the forward torpedo room, which gradually turned into a death trap as heat from the fire blistered the paint off the after bulkhead. The smoke mingled with that from an earlier attempt to burn the submarine's papers and seeped into the horribly cramped torpedo room. And all this time, of course, the depletion of oxygen was sapping the crew's strength yet further.

Most wearisome of all was the crew's supposed lifeline. Every submarine carried a number of Momsen Lungs which were a type of oxygen rebreathers. By flooding the torpedo room, equalising sea pressure and the pressure in that room, men wearing the Lungs could leave the submarine, from depths of up to 100 feet and more, via a specially located hatch. At 180 feet, however, the pressure was considerable and the effort required to use the apparatus successfully was too much for many of the already debilitated sailors. In the end, only thirteen of them got away in four parties. The rest were asphyxiated when the rubber gasket on the door between the torpedo room and the battery compartment burned or was blown out by the mounting water pressure.

Of the thirteen men who got out of the torpedo room only eight reached the surface. They joined O'Kane's original group but by ten o'clock, when the survivors were picked up by a Japanese escort, only O'Kane and seven others were still afloat. They were taken to the port of Takao, on Formosa, but on the way there, bound hand and foot, they were brutally worked over by Japanese sailors. Some of these tormentors, blackened and dishevelled, had been picked up after O'Kane's successful attacks and he remained splendidly philosophical about their subsequent conduct. "When we realised that our clubbings and kickings were being administered by the burned and mutilated survivors of our own handiwork, we found we could take it with less prejudice."[8]

*

Compared to the grim tale of the *Tang*, the exploits of submarine USS *Dace* on 25th October strike an almost light-hearted note. Under Commander David McClintock, the *Dace* and the *Darter* (Commander Bladen Claggett) left Mios Woendi on 1st October for a patrol of the Palawan Passage. The whole trip thus far had been tediously unproductive with only one sighting, resulting in two *marus* sunk, in more than three weeks. On the 23rd, however, the patrol suddenly became one of the most important of the Pacific War, transmitting a definite report on the position of Admiral Kurita's Force 'A' and then sinking two Japanese heavy cruisers, crippling another, and obliging Kurita to detach two further destroyers to escort the cruiser back to Brunei.

The sinkings had been accomplished between 06.35 and 07.00 and for the rest of the day the two submarines concentrated on trying to finish off the damaged *Takao*. The destroyers made a surface attack impossible, however, and the two commanders decided to use the *Darter* as a decoy, to draw off the escorts by making a very wide sweep around the cruiser. In attempting this, steering according to a 24-hour old and slightly inaccurate dead reckoning, the *Darter* ran aground on a reef in the Bombay Shoal. Impact was at a brisk 17 knots and the submarine found itself completely wedged in the coral, with much of the boat out of the water. The *Dace* came to assist and it was decided, at 03.45 on the 24th, to abandon the stranded submarine. The *Darter*'s crew transferred to the *Dace* in two small rubber boats, which took a good three hours of to-ing and fro-ing, and then the *Dace* attempted to scuttle her sister. Demolition charges proved totally inadequate. Four torpedoes all hit the reef and 21 4-inch shells along the water-line holed but did not dislodge the *Darter*. Curious Japanese vessels arrived during the day and forced the *Dace* to stand off and submerge. Late that night she finally got permission from headquarters to return to Fremantle.

The 25th was the first day of the eleven-day run back to base, and as such it was probably the least trying. Even so, it did not take many hours for the novelty of the situation to wear off. Submarines are notoriously cramped at the best of times, with the demand for living space always losing out to the requirements of the engine-room, battery compartments, ballast tanks and torpedo storage. The *Darter* had sustained no casualties and a full complement of 81 officers and men were added to the *Dace*'s crew of 74. "In such close quarters Claggett could only tell *Darter*'s men to pick one place and stay there – except when they had to go to the head. Meals were brought to them at their places. *Dace* men shared the available bunks with them, and others made do on empty torpedo skids and the like."[9] By the last days of the voyage all hands were subsisting on a diet of mushroom soup and peanut butter sandwiches.

Boredom especially afflicted the *Darter*'s officers who could not be allowed to take over any actual duties. Almost as soon as the boat set sail, they sat down to a game of poker which lasted almost without a break for the rest of the voyage. The consistent winner was a lieutenant who had taken care to salvage the little notebook in which he kept tally of his already substantial winnings. Most of the others, including the captain, were steady losers. One persistently unlucky player was also a persistent moaner about his losses. Eventually another player curtly asked him why, in that case, did he continue playing? The officer replied: "The only way I can get a seat in this damned boat is to buy it; and I intend to sit on a cushion from here to Australia no matter how much it hurts my pocketbook."[10]

*

Although American submarines had started the Battle of Leyte Gulf in bravura style, they were unable to offer a comparable finale. Even though these boats were still referred to as 'fleet' submarines, except for preliminary reconnaissance their operations were not closely co-ordinated with those of Third Fleet. The first request for submarine back-up was not sent out by Mitscher to Lockwood until the afternoon of the 25th, and the message took some ten hours to get through. In fact, already knowing of the battle in progress, Lockwood had found that two of his wolf-packs, which had recently left Saipan for Luzon Strait, were well-placed to intercept any of Ozawa's stragglers. At 08.15 these boats, *Halibut*, *Haddock* and *Tuna* as 'Roach's Raiders' and *Pintado*, *Jallao* and *Atule* as 'Clarey's Crushers', were directed to appropriate scouting lines, taking up position by 18.30.

The *Halibut* (Lieutenant-Commander Ignatius Galantin) could actually see the pagoda-like superstructure of *Ise* or *Hyuga* from around 17.40, but was not within realistic torpedo range. But he could hear the chatter of Navy pilots still buzzing around overhead. One pilot identified a battleship, two cruisers. Another exclaimed, "Let's get going and get this over with", and shortly afterwards he claimed to have done just that, yelling out, "Yippee, I got a battleship!" and then, "Forget the battleship, get the cruiser."[11] Throughout something very like a battleship remained squarely in Galantin's sights and finally came within range at 18.44 when he fired all his six forward tubes. Galantin uttered his own silent "Yippee" when loud explosions were heard and he authorised the breaking out of the two bottles of beer per man that submarines now carried. What he actually hit remains a matter of debate. Official sources at first credited him with nothing, and one eminent historian, in 1958, felt it was "still a mystery. Looks like a whale to me."[12] More recently Galantin was officially credited with a destroyer, probably the *Akitsuki*, although other sources attribute this sinking to air attacks in the morning.

There followed a period of some confusion, further evidence of the difficulty submarines had in correctly identifying their targets. Immediately after sinking the 'battleship', the *Halibut* surfaced and deduced that the ships' lights which were still visible must be those of the accompanying Japanese destroyers. Shortly after this, contact was established with the *Tuna*, which reported that she had more battleships in view and was moving off to attack. Thinking these new targets more attractive than destroyers, the *Halibut*'s captain decided to tag along. In fact, the two targets were the same group of ships, the *Tuna* having correctly identified the *Ise* and the *Hyuga* as still afloat. These ships and their escorts were steaming away at 19 knots, and though the two submarines took up the chase, they were unable to haul ahead and take up a firing position. At six on the morning of the 26th, they finally turned away and let Ozawa's battered Main Body head back to Japan. The *Haddock* had also joined in the pursuit, and according to her captain, Commander John Roach, "Disappointment was a foot thick on this ship."[13]

All the same, the submarines did manage to finish off one straggler on the 25th. The second of the redirected wolf-packs took up station about 60 miles north-east of the *Halibut*, and at 20.04 the *Jallao* picked up a radar contact, correctly identified as the damaged light cruiser *Tama*, hit by Mitscher's aircraft earlier in the day. The other two submarines were informed, and as the *Pintado* also picked up the cruiser and got a periscope sighting, the *Jallao* (Commander Joseph Icenhower) fired three torpedoes from its bow tubes at a range of 1,200 yards. They both missed, and the *Jallao* turned to fire four more from the stern tubes at 700 yards. In the misty moonlight and surface refraction the cruiser now seemed to Icenhower "as big as the Pentagon Building". Three of the torpedoes hit, the first about amidships, the second near the after mast and the third between the bow and the bridge. Icenhower observed these hits shortly after 11 p.m., only the second salvo he had fired in anger, and immediately dived to reload in case a *coup de grâce* was required. When he resurfaced thirty minutes later, there was no ship to be seen, for the *Tama* had sunk in plain sight of the *Pintado* almost as soon as she was hit. 'Clarey's Crushers' carried on the chase after Ozawa until 11.10 the next day when they were redirected to their original patrol line.

*

The scheduled duration of an American submarine patrol was sixty days, though few lasted this long before a boat ran out of torpedoes or received damage that required repair back at base. Submarines that left Central and South-West Pacific Areas in October 1944 were at sea for an average of 51 days.[14] Sometimes submarines had to return to an American port, notably Mare Island in California, but more normally they used advanced bases, such as Guam, Midway and Manus (Admiralty Islands) or fleet bases at Pearl Harbor, Fremantle and Perth.

Almost any patrol was an extremely arduous and nerve-racking experience. Returning crews were often at the limits of mental and physical exhaustion. It became the practice to make the arrival of a submarine something of an event, with a reception party and sometimes a band at the quayside which was also piled high with crates of fresh fruit and vegetables, an ice-cream freezer and a sack of mail. The executive officer of one submarine wrote: "The business of welcoming a submarine back from war patrol had been started as a sort of morale booster, and to say that it hit the mark is putting it mildly. After having been deprived of those things for about two months we were almost as avid for fresh fruit and leafy vegetables (lettuce and celery especially) as we were for the mail – and it was not at all uncommon to see a bearded sailor, pockets stuffed with apples and oranges, reading letter after letter in quick succession and munching on a celery stalk at the same time."[15]

At the advance bases, however, the initial euphoria and vitamin high soon gave way to profound anti-climax. Rest and refit usually took about a fortnight and on Midway, for example, "where the only things of interest were gooney birds and whiskey" served at the Gooneyville Tavern, things could quickly become boring. A particular frustration was the lack of women at the advance bases. Even on Hawaii, where all American females had a plethora of senior or socially well-connected younger officers to choose from, enlisted men's liaisons were usually brusque commercial transactions.

Perth, in western Australia, was altogether different. When USS *Hawksbill* docked there on 18th October 1944 after her first patrol, the executive officer, Lieutenant George Grider, found "there was no city in the world like Perth for submarine men". It was the headquarters for Admiral South-West Pacific Submarines "and if ever an admiral saw to the welfare of his men, Admiral Christie did . . . [His] theory was that the way to make submarine men efficient was to give them a luxurious life when they were recuperating, and he spared no pains to see that we had it." Each submarine was assigned two automobiles on arrival, one for the officers and one for the men, both driven by attractive female chauffeurs. "The men had an hotel that was all theirs, the junior officers had another, and the captains had a couple of bungalows in a beautiful residential area known as Birdwood." But the real hallmark of earthly paradise was that Perth was almost entirely bereft of young males. It housed no other important military installation and, so Grider assumed, most Australian males of military age were either overseas or with training formations up in northern Queensland. And so "the girls were everywhere . . . and no able-bodied men except the submariners . . . There were beautiful girls at the clubs, in the stores, on the streets and romance was everywhere. I don't know how many submariners under Admiral Christie's command married Aussie girls, but the number must have been impressive."[16]

In fact, the situation in Perth was becoming something of a national scandal and was increasingly elaborated upon in the press. The most lurid rumours reached Australians in uniform and provoked deep animosity towards Americans – American sailors and submariners in particular. Even after the war, when Grider was on a train in the United States and unwittingly revealed himself as a submariner to four soldiers from Perth, he soon realised that it would be most politic to deny flatly ever having enjoyed R. and R. there.

37

I-56 and the Japanese Submarine Fleet

IN MID-OCTOBER 1944 the Japanese Navy could deploy just 57 submarines against the American 228. Only 32 of the Japanese vessels were operational: two were being used for supply missions to beleaguered garrisons, four were in the Indian Ocean, and thirteen were newly commissioned boats on shakedown cruises.[1] That left 13 submarines available to support the Leyte Gulf operation and these had been on alert since 17th October. In the event, they left Japan after the surface units and so did not arrive on station, to the east of Samar, until early on the 25th. The delay made it impossible to fulfil either of their main missions in support of the fleet – providing intelligence on the enemy's approach and inflicting damage prior to the surface action.

The Japanese submarine fleet was a far cry at this time from what had been envisaged at the beginning of the war when submarine crews were an elite, expected to make a major contribution to any fleet encounter and, rather like American sharpshooters of old, range around the battle lines, picking off ships with unerring accuracy. While official doctrine conceded that a full salvo of eight torpedoes might be required against aircraft carriers or battleships, commanders were forbidden to use more than one against destroyers or merchant ships. In fact, the chances of gaining a hit from any single shot, except at very short range, were slight, especially as Japanese fire-control equipment never offered the captain a constantly updated solution to the correct angle of attack. Marksmanship was also badly affected by a chronic lack of practice. After April 1942 Japanese submarines rarely worked with the surface fleet and were eventually reassigned mainly to attacks on merchant shipping or to running supply and evacuation (*mogura* or 'mule') missions to by-passed Japanese islands. Yet even the campaign against merchant shipping was never more than a token effort.

The shortage of submarines and their non-aggressive posture was further hampered by the same technological inadequacy that plagued the anti-submarine effort. Weak and unreliable radar offered scant protection against American destroyers and aircraft whenever the vessels were forced to come up to the surface to recharge their batteries. It is therefore hardly surprising to discover that by October 1944 "U.S. anti-submarine technology had rendered Japanese submarines practically powerless . . . [and] they found themselves harried mercilessly. It had become a question of survival rather than attack or even reconnaissance."[2]

Such powerlessness and relegation to the despised *mogura* missions badly affected the submariners' morale, leading to a distinctly un-Japanese distaste for aggressive tactics, even when the opportunity offered. An American report drawn up after the war stated that the authors' "unbiased opinion of the attack audacity of Japanese submariners" could only be that "the percentage of overly discreet [commanders] was large . . . Even the Japanese commanding officers [interrogated] could not disguise their embarrassment."[3] In his appended conclusion to a Japanese popular history of submarine operations, the former Chief-of-Staff of the Combined Fleet, Admiral Fukudome, stated bluntly: "They considered themselves superior in technique in the field of submarine warfare to any in other navies. But when it came to the test of actual warfare, the results were deplorable."[4]

Basic air-conditioning was installed in submarines built after 1941 but it was never as efficient as that in American boats. After long periods at sea, the sanitation on Japanese submarines became especially noxious. An American writing just after the surrender noted: "Any American who boarded or passed to the leeward of a surrendered Japanese submarine before the Japanese were forced to clean it up will agree that it is a wonder that they were able to do even as well as they did."[5] But Americans have always been well-scrubbed mariners. In autumn 1944, the South-West Pacific submarine commander, Admiral Christie, noted in his diary that a recent British arrival, HMS *Clyde*, was "the dirtiest submarine that ever made a dive" and would "have to be generally refitted and *blasted* out of port."[6]

We have no way of knowing how boldly the thirteen submarines sent out to the Philippines in October approached their mission, but even before the 25th three of them had been sunk by U.S. destroyers. The survivors took up positions off Samar and remained submerged, among them *I-56*, commanded by Lieutenant-Commander Masahiko

Morinaga. By 8 a.m. his boat had been submerged for some time and many of the crew were stripped to their loin-cloths, or *fundoshi*, in the oppressive heat. They had already breakfasted on *miso-shiro*, a kind of vegetable soup. The diet, at least, was still perfectly acceptable as they were not long out of port and supplies of fresh meat and vegetables could still be used to supplement the usual rice, pickles and dried seaweed.

Suddenly Morinaga made visual contact through his periscope. He had got among Taffy-1, to the south of the main escort carrier battle with Kurita's force. The American carriers in Sprague's force were fending off kamikaze attacks when Morinaga locked on to the carrier *Santee*. He fired five torpedoes almost immediately, from a depth of thirty feet, and claimed to have heard the sound of five hits. A destroyer, the USS *Trathen*, spotted at least one of the torpedo tracks and immediately turned to run it down, throwing out depth-charges over the estimated firing position. The *I-56* dived, but other destroyers joined the fray and the submarine was pelted with depth-charges for several hours. All the lights went out and the engine-room was partially flooded. This caused panic at first, but Morinaga nipped it in the bud by identifying the cause as just a single valve that had been shaken loose. He remained submerged for several hours, only to discover when finally surfacing that one depth-charge had failed to go off and was wedged on the after part of the upper deck. According to a Japanese source, "it was shaped like a 30-kg bomb and was carefully taken back to Kure dockyard", though this seems a somewhat fool-hardy venture.[7]

Morinaga had surely been somewhat unlucky. His five hits were in fact only one, and this was on the *Santee*, which minutes before had also been hit by a kamikaze plane that had smashed through the flight-deck and started a fire near bomb-racks in the hangar below. Remarkably, none of the bombs detonated, while the torpedo strike, minutes later, was merely a glancing blow. There was some flooding in starboard and centre compartments and a consequent six-degree list, but within a very short time the carrier was back on station and making a healthy 16.5 knots. She was even able to resume flight operations after a few hours. Throughout this ordeal the efforts of the *Santee*'s crew were exemplary, but it has been rightly pointed out by Samuel Eliot Morison that things might have gone much worse had the *Santee* not been one of the *Sangamon*-class CVEs. Unlike the scratch-built, extremely basic Kaiser yard carriers, those of the *Sangamon* class were converted tanker hulls and retained those ships' more thorough compartmentalisation and other damage-limitation features. In the final analysis, the submarines of the Japanese Combined Fleet fared just as poorly at Leyte Gulf as had Kurita's battleships and Ozawa's carriers. One escort-carrier slightly damaged remained their total tally, the only other observed submarine activity taking place little more than an hour before midnight on the 25th when another Taffy-1 destroyer escort, the *Coolbaugh*, spotted a periscope. Admiral Sprague ordered all ships to execute a 90-degree emergency turn, and two torpedo tracks shimmered along each side of the carrier *Petrof Bay* and passed harmlessly into the night.

PART NINE

Pacific Outposts

———

38

In the Boondocks

MOPPING UP ON PELELIEU AND GUAM

———

I F ONE OF the principles of war is concentration at the decisive point, nothing illustrates the difficulty of achieving this better than the struggle in the Pacific. With or without the attendant naval battle, MacArthur's assault on Leyte as the prelude to driving the Japanese out of all the Philippine Islands, was the most significant American amphibious effort in the second half of 1944. Yet on 25th October the landings were being contested by only one Japanese and four American divisions out of a total of 35 and 27 respectively stationed throughout the various island systems. There were also three Australian and one New Zealand division stationed outside their mainlands.[1]

The reasons for this dispersion are various. For the Japanese, it was largely a reflection of their overweening ambition in the first months of the war, especially the decision to push forces into New Guinea and the Solomon Islands. But they were also handicapped by a lack of knowledge about Allied strategic intentions and had to guard against possible offensives across the Central Pacific, through New Guinea and the Molucca (Spice) Islands, or from the Indian Ocean against Sumatra and Java. Even when the Japanese were able temporarily to discount one axis or another, or when they wished to reinforce an island under immediate threat, they increasingly lacked the merchant shipping to make any meaningful redeployments. For the Americans, with their war production in top gear by late 1944, shipping also remained a serious constraint on their own ability to move large bodies of men to any one target island or atoll. Advance along a particular axis was made much less logistically demanding if it could be done by fairly small amphibious forces leapfrogging from one island chain to another or, in the case of New Guinea, one beachhead to another. This methodical leapfrogging, and the garrisoning of islands and bases left behind, was also a function of the need to build, maintain and protect airfields which would provide air cover for subsequent amphibious bounds. In some cases islands were also earmarked as fleet anchorages to prevent the great armadas from having to spend more and more of their time making round trips to Pearl Harbor or Espiritu Santo.

There was another important reason for the scattering of U.S. forces around the Pacific – the necessity to engage in lengthy mopping-up operations on many of the conquered islands. Usually islands were declared secure after only a few days', or at most weeks' fighting. That status was defined by the ability to start largely unhindered base and airfield construction, despite there being perhaps hundreds, even thousands of Japanese still alive in the vicinity. Thus the continued security of any air, naval or supply base depended on regular harassment of enemy bands or at least the maintenance of a firm military perimeter. Though the battles on Leyte Island may have represented America's strategic front line in the Pacific in late 1944, for many hundreds of her riflemen and marines the front line was far to the rear, on some God-forsaken lump of coral or in a dank hot-house where the enemy had lost much, certainly, but not their unwavering readiness to die for the Emperor.

The most bitterly contested mopping-up operations in the Pacific were on Admiral Nimitz's Central Pacific axis. On Peleliu in the Palau Islands, and on Guam in the Marianas, Army and Marine units were still struggling to snuff out the last Japanese resistance. Both these island chains had been selected as sites for air bases, the Palaus to provide cover for MacArthur's northern flank during the approach to Leyte and the Marianas as a complex of bases for B-29 bombers – huge, very long-range aircraft that would bring the Japanese mainland within range. Both operations had been the responsibility of the Marines' III Amphibious Corps, commanded by General Roy Geiger, though by October his headquarters had handed over responsibility for mopping up to local commanders, and was itself engaged in planning for future operations in the Ryukyu Islands, most especially Okinawa.[2]

Two of the Palau Islands had been selected as air bases, Peleliu and Angaur. Each had been occupied by resistant Japanese forces. On Angaur, 81 U.S. Infantry Division was pitted against roughly 1,600 Japanese, and though organised resistance was broken within four days of the first landings on 16th September, mopping up of stragglers who had retreated into the caves of Ramuldo Hill in the island's north-east corner was not completed until 23rd October. By that time two 6,000-

foot runways had been completed and thirteen B-24 bombers were already operating.

The hardest task of all was the taking of Pelelieu. When 1 U.S. Marine Division went ashore on 15th September, the island was garrisoned by 10,000 Japanese, about half of whom belonged to two regiments of 14 Infantry Division and an Independent Mixed Brigade. From the start the enemy's resilience was badly underestimated. Marine commander General William Rupertus predicted that the campaign would be "a quickie, rough but fast", and his planners remained remarkably blasé about the steep, rocky terrain near the assault beaches, insisting against all the evidence that the island was everywhere low and flat. For the most recent historian of the campaign "there lingers the unpalatable conclusion that some persons on all levels who were responsible for intelligence evaluation and planning did not do as thorough a job as could and should have been done."[3] Even the Navy got caught up in the air of blithe optimism and the pre-landing bombardment was halted early because Admiral Oldendorf claimed that his battleships had run out of targets.

Nothing could have been further from the truth. Progress at each end of the island was quite good in the first days, with two Marine regiments able to move along the captured coastal road and around the worst of the central mountain barrier. Mopping up in the north was completed by 2nd October, while in the south four Marine fighter and one torpedo-bomber squadron began using the airfield from the end of September. By 8th October a 6,000-foot bomber strip had also been completed. Yet, despite the assault stage being declared over on 12th October, and the American flag already flying over the island, Japanese resistance was far from exhausted. By the middle of that month up to 90 per cent of the Japanese defenders had been killed or, very occasionally, captured, but the survivors, the remnants of three infantry battalions, remained holed up in the Umurbrogol mountains that dominated the longer western stem of Pelelieu's rough V-shape. After gaining a foothold in these mountains on 17th September, progress thereafter by 1 Marine Regiment was agonisingly slow. By the 21st it had suffered 56 per cent casualties, and one sergeant observed: "This ain't a regiment. We're just survivors."

They were replaced by 321 Regiment (brought over from 81 Division on Angaur) which pushed up the coastal road skirting Umurbrogol, leaving 7 Marine Regiment to keep up the pressure on the mountain. The 7th Marines fared no better than the 1st, and though they captured two important ridges, they had to be withdrawn on 5th October. Some battalions had been reduced to one quarter of their effective combat strength. Now it was the turn of the 5th Marines who by dint of methodical, yard-by-yard set-piece attacks succeeded in taking most of the high ground on the northern side of Umurbrogol. But they, too, were progressively ground down, and on 15th October they were relieved by 321 Regiment which now had to tackle the feature head-on. Five days later 81 Division took over the whole responsibility for 'mopping-up' on Pelelieu.

By this stage there were roughly one thousand Japanese left on the Umurbrogol, in a pocket no more than 850 by 400 yards, and the terrain remained as grimly intractable as ever. Umurbrogol was not a single ridge but a corraline-limestone honeycomb, riddled with intersecting valleys, steep walls and deep cavities along the numerous fault-lines. Erosion by wind and water had produced sponge-like rock formations and jagged crags, and a detailed survey of this region after Pelelieu had been captured counted more than 500 caves, of which 200 had been created by the Japanese while the rest were naturally formed. All vegetation had been stripped away by continuous American shelling and bombing, and attacking troops could rarely find much cover or shade in which to seek relief from temperatures that rose as high as 115°F. One marine described the ridge as "the face of the moon defended by Jap troglodytes". Another remembered the terrain as "abominable ... the worst I've ever encountered. It was as though several submerged reefs had been forced up out of the water with their jagged edges making several ridges that were up to two or three hundred feet high. The sharp coral cut the shoes and clothing of the Marines."[4]

Such terrain would have been difficult enough when fighting against surface emplacements, but the American task was further complicated by the remarkable defensive system underground. Some of the caves on Umurbrogol were big enough to contain a battalion of infantry or artillery pieces and 150mm mortars, and most of them had been 'customised' for twelve months before the landings. Japanese 214 Naval Construction Battalion had been assiduous in turning formidable natural defences into an almost impregnable bastion. Their engineers worked to several basic designs, with 'Y' and 'I' shapes used for smaller caves, for storage and local defence, and larger caves being quarried and blasted into 'E' shapes in the side of a ridge, while 'H' types were in a flatter area close to a road at the bottom of a ridge. "One of the most complicated caves [was] a series of intersecting H's over 300 feet in length and [comprising] five laterals, three of which were over 150 feet long."[5] Others were five and six storeys high, with living quarters for whole companies. Extensive use was made of coral sand and concrete to further protect entrances, embrasures and inter-connecting tunnels, and in some of these sliding armoured doors had been installed. The Japanese Army also fashioned caves in 'W', 'I', 'L', 'T' and 'U' shapes, used mainly to protect troops from small-arms fire. "Many of the caves sloped sharply downward from the mouths or had a sharp turn close to the entrance, and most had niches cut into the walls for the defending infantry to use. Combat caves . . . were generally clustered together at lower elevations, each located so that it could give support to the other caves or strong-points. Many of the smaller caves were obviously suicide caves designed to allow the occupant to bring his automatic weapon to bear on the advancing enemy, but having no secondary exit."[6]

The features still to be cleared on Umurbrogol enjoyed such names as the China Wall, the Five Brothers, Walt Ridge and the Horseshoe. A main approach route was known, almost inevitably, as Death Valley. 321 Regiment continued to chip away at the Japanese defences until 26th October. An over-ambitious, three-battalion assault on the 22nd stalled as the regiment was being progressively relieved by 323 Regiment. On the 25th, there was something of a lull in the fighting, partly attributable to a marked worsening in the already squally weather, with rain beginning to lash down in earnest and winds approaching typhoon-force. Soldiers from both regiments contented themselves with clinging to their forward positions.

Two tactical points were emphasised by commanders to relieving forces. One was the use of flammables, sometimes in flamethrowing Sherman tanks which could shoot out flames 40 to 50 feet and send them flicking round corners, sometimes from an improvised 300-yard pipeline attached to a tanker truck parked on the coastal road. Booster pumps maintained a constant pressure and at the other end a nozzle sprayed oil into areas inaccessible to tanks. The oil could be set alight by infantry or artillery fire. Napalm bombs were also dropped by Marine planes, though by October it was common to use unfused napalm tanks which were ignited at the chosen moment by phos-phoros shells called down by the attacking infantry. The infantry flamethrowers consumed so much fuel that the supporting air group had to fly in 4,500lb of hydrogen to replenish the supply.

The second tactical method employed by 321 Regiment was a consequence of the reliance on napalm and flamethrowers which, together with the rain of artillery or mortar shells, as well as explosive bombs, blasted and burnt all vegetation from the coral ridges and robbed advancing infantry of cover. Even when they did seize a particular feature, soldiers found it impossible to dig into the coral to consolidate. The solution to the problem was the humble sandbag, which became a key component of the regiment's tactics, making it possible to take and hold exposed positions. As the only sand available was along the beaches, a large proportion of the division's rear-echelon personnel spent their time filling those bags which were then carried by trucks or tracked vehicles into the forward area, before being passed hand-to-hand right up to the front. "Once an attack was successful in a given locale, the sandbags were brought up and the new positions fortified, enabling the infantry to withstand heavy Japanese fire from neighboring ridges. In many cases infantrymen advanced pushing the sandbags ahead of them with long poles."[7] The Army's official historian has described an attack at this time and the use of "the now omnipresent sandbags. The battalion's men, prone on the ground, inched their sandbags forward with rifle butts or sticks, laboriously expanding a hold and almost realising the infantryman's dream of portable foxholes."[8] Such tactics would have been entirely familiar to Vauban and other 17th-century siege experts who would have recognised the technique of 'sapping', or creeping forward under cover created by oneself to approach the enemy's works.

This, then, was 'mopping-up' on Pelelieu, a full fortnight after the main fighting was deemed to be over, with three battalions of U.S. infantry inching forward like olive-drab dung beetles, pushing their loads before them over the razor-like coral, alternately scorched in the blazing sun or lashed by torrential rain, while others were calmly "going about their business on the airfield and in the south of the island." The boundary was a ridge known as Bloody Nose and the "post office was less than 300 yards south. A movie was set up not very much farther away, and the sound was constantly out-voiced by the rumble of heavy artillery . . . One night, because of the interruptions . . . the feature did not finish until 02.00 . . . Some of the men who lived in the workaday world could not quite avoid the feeling that things were not so bad up in the ridges as they were made to seem. A few men went north looking for souvenirs – and were promptly shanghaied into the lines, this by order."[9] They soon found just how bad things really were.

*

Ghastly though conditions were on Pelelieu, the whole campaign had only been going for forty days. On Guam mopping-up had become almost a way of life for some units. The island was invaded on 21st July 1944 and declared secure with the raising of the Stars and Stripes on the 28th. On 10th August, after the seizure of Mount Santa Rosa a couple of days earlier, General Geiger announced that all organised resistance was at an end, and on the 15th Guam was handed over to the local commander, General H. L. Larsen USMC. Its sister islands Saipan and Tinian were earmarked as fleet and air bases, the latter mainly for the B-29 Superfortress bomber, and construction work began almost as soon as the troops started moving inland. By 25th October there were on Guam, in addition to the 21,800 resident Chamorros, 65,000 U.S. Army soldiers, 78,000 Navy personnel and 59,000 Marines – a total population of 224,000 on an island only 30 miles long by 8 miles wide. For all those not actually at the front, Guam had one most endearing feature: the Japanese seemed to have used it as their main liquor supply dump for the whole central Pacific. As one historian wrote: "Nowhere else did troops on our side ever come on such prodigious stores as were captured there: Scotch and American whiskies, and Japanese imitations thereof, sake galore and beer in quantities . . . Before the occupation was far along, men who would have given their all for a snort of [locally distilled] jungle juice . . . were becoming choosy as to brands and accepting no substitutes."[10]

Such luxuries were rarely available at the front, which remained fairly active right through to late October. Even after the suicide of the local Japanese commander, General Obata, on 12th August, some 9,000 Japanese remained at large, mostly retreating in small groups to the thick jungle in the north of the island. The Americans retained one of the original assault divisions, 3 Marine, on the island, and while one regiment trained for the forthcoming Iwo Jima landings, two others went about the tedious business of combing the jungle and mopping up. Japanese survivors were mainly concentrated in an area of about 50 square miles which was staked out with fortified Marine base camps from which platoon-size patrols were regularly sent out. Alvin M. Josephy of 21 Marine Regiment has given an excellent description of what was essentially a counter-insurgency campaign carried out by three battalions scattered miles apart in the jungle:

It was the rainy season and the boondocks were a miserable place in which to live. Each outfit had its own camp, consisting of a few fly and pyramidal tents for officers and mess-halls, and an area of foxholes covered by ponchos and shelter-halves. The ground was always muddy and the holes full of water . . . Out in the boondocks we were still living in holes, still washing with rain water caught in helmets from the flies of our tents, still eating a hundred-per-cent canned food diet . . . The camps were circled by barbed wire . . . and maintained listening outposts, connected by telephones. All day long, and during the night, for weeks, men went out on patrols . . . looking for enemy bands. When they weren't patrolling they worked on the camp and stood guard in shifts. This was no rest period. We snatched sleep the way we snatched it in combat – in brief periods here and there. Most of the time we were wet and muddy; our bones ached; and we were lonely, cut off from civilisation . . . The folks back home thought the battle of Guam was over. And no-one could tell them differently; censorship was on, and we couldn't send word home that the Japs hadn't given up.[11]

Of course, life was very much worse for the Japanese. After a few weeks in the jungle they began to run out of food. Whatever rations they had had were soon gone and though the jungle at first provided an adequate diet of coconuts, breadfruit, papayas, bananas and the odd chicken or pig, the depredations of so many scavengers in a small area soon picked it clean. By October only coconuts and breadfruit remained, which on their own had very limited nutritional value. Increasingly desperate, the Japanese tried to raid the Marines' camps and supply dumps to pilfer rations and many were caught and mown down in ambushes set up near such sites. Other Japanese were too far gone even to skulk around American camps. According to one marine, "we were beginning to bring in sick and starving men who could hardly stand up without our help. Our patrols were finding them lying in cave entrances or in the jungle. Sometimes they were asleep . . . as in the case of . . . a young . . . war correspondent we found in a coma in a native hut."[12] All the prisoners taken were in appalling physical condition. Their bones clearly showed beneath their sagging skin and their stomachs were terribly distended. Many had untreated open wounds, sometimes riddled with maggots, and all were filthy. Their hair was matted and crawling with lice and their legs and feet were a mass of infected scratches and running sores.

Remarkably for the Japanese, not all the prisoners had been caught napping. An increasing number began to give themselves up voluntarily, in response to a vigorous 'public relations' campaign by the Marines to induce stragglers to surrender. They adopted several ploys. One was a large-scale leaflet campaign, with messages dropped from aircraft or pinned to trees by the patrols. "Do not be afraid," they read. "You will not be harmed. Advance alone and unarmed to where

American troops are located with your hands up, stripped above the waist, carrying this leaflet and walking down the center of the road. Those who do so will receive food, water and medical treatment."[13] These leaflets had only limited success. Some of the many Japanese civilians who had fled with the soldiers and sailors did come forward but almost all of the latter remained faithful to the Emperor, or else were convinced that the Americans would kill all prisoners out of hand.

To counter this firm belief, hammered home by Japanese instructors and officers, the Americans opted for a more direct approach and sent out some sound trucks, regular army vehicles rigged with a loudspeaker system which blared out entreaties from Japanese who had already given themselves up and had volunteered to go along and try to persuade their comrades. They repeated again and again that the Americans lived up to their promises and that they themselves were testimony to the fact that all prisoners would be fed and given medical treatment. Marine veterans were at best sceptical, referring to the vehicles as 'vote-getting trucks', but were duly astonished when quite a few soldiers and sailors did give themselves up, usually frantically brandishing the leaflets whose promises they still clearly did not entirely believe. Some of the prisoners told of a large group of survivors holed up in dense coconut groves and rugged terrain below the cliffs along the northern shore. There were no roads into this area so it was decided to replace one of the sound trucks with what came to be known as the 'Peace Ship', a small green landing craft that had been used as a rocket launcher during the main battle. Loudspeakers were installed, all the lines were hung with signal flags and pennants, and volunteer prisoners repeated over and over again their reassuring message. The American crew also included three men from the assault signal company, who liaised with Marine patrols on the clifftops. They were to guide the patrols down to any suspicious locations where it was thought recalcitrant Japanese might be lurking. The loudspeakers then warned that the alternative to surrender would be a Marine patrol that was not concerned with taking prisoners. Again, some Japanese did respond to these efforts but, on the whole, they chose to remain in the jungle, ragged and starving, and almost helpless if cornered by a patrol. Between 11th August and the end of October a further 5,000 Japanese are known to have died.

Alvin Josephy came out of the line before 25th October, and his account of life among the rear echelons is equally valuable for the picture it presents of the *anomie* of 'rest periods' on almost all of the conquered Pacific islands. According to Rodgers and Hammerstein, the essential problem was that 'we ain't got dames', but Josephy paints a much bleaker picture of almost a spiritual vacuum, a gnawing introspection that separated the combat soldier, first from everyone outside his own outfit, and then progressively even from his buddies. For the first day or so, the sheer physical relief of not being on patrol or wallowing in a muddy foxhole was solace enough. "It was a strange sensation, lying down on something soft again. All through the camp, we could hear men sighing contentedly, as they climbed beneath their mosquito nets and stretched out on their cots." But once the men had slept off the worst effects of fatigue and anxiety, they soon became prey to lassitude and boredom, especially at night. "I was in a tent with three other[s] . . . We had no lights. Night after night we lay on our sacks in the darkness, trying to fall asleep, but kept awake by the warm and merry noise coming from the officers' wine mess on the hill where our officers had music, weekly liquor rations, and the companionship of nurses to help dispel the loneliness." In these long hours men had time to think. Their thoughts inevitably turned to home and to a widespread fear that girls, buddies, employers, parents even would have forgotten about them. "Such brooding was to have its effect: to make us feel as if we were living in a vacuum, unattached to social units in the outside world. Few of us ever discussed what we were fighting for . . . Each man's life was a little world in itself, and personal happiness was the common goal . . . [and] the satisfying of needs . . . To most men home was where these needs were satisfied. Home was where the family was, where the girl friend lived, where the food was good, where the bed was soft and the toilet was private. That was what we were fighting for."[14]

39

Continued Neutralisation

FIRST AUSTRALIAN ARMY IN THE PACIFIC MANDATES

WHEN AUSTRALIA swiftly declared itself an ally of Britain in the war against Hitler, its politicians and generals had their eyes firmly fixed on Europe and the Middle East. Australian pilots and bomber crews trained to fight against the Luftwaffe and the first army divisions to go overseas all went to North Africa and Syria. The entry of Japan into the war, however, made the Australian task rather more complex. An untrammelled Japanese advance could threaten Australia's own vital strategic interests, notably communications through the Indian and Pacific Oceans, as well as the territories mandated to her by the League of Nations, the islands of Bougainville and New Britain and part of eastern New Guinea. If all these fell, it was not impossible that the Australian mainland itself would come under threat. For a while the Australians attempted to fight a two-front war, but after they had lost a whole division in the Singapore debacle it became clear that this would be beyond their means. By December 1942 all overseas divisions had been recalled and were now based at home or in the New Guinea mandate. The government ditched grandiose plans for an army of 12 divisions and an air force of 73 squadrons, and by October 1944 the number of divisions was down to eight, with two more scheduled to disappear early the following year. The New Guinea commitment had also been run down. Up to late summer 1944 the Australians had maintained three divisions there, on the Huon peninsula between Lae and Saidor, but once this area was secure and the Americans further west had leapfrogged along the coast right to Sansapor (via Aitape, Hollandia and Wakde Island), these divisions were withdrawn back home. The responsibility for garrisoning the conquered beachheads fell to the Americans, who in October 1944 had six infantry and one airborne division in New Guinea.

The need to garrison the various air and naval bases in New Guinea, including MacArthur's South-West Pacific General Headquarters at Hollandia, was inescapable; MacArthur's leapfrogging up the coast had simply by-passed the main Japanese forces, leaving their Second and Eighteenth Armies loosely concentrated in the areas Aitape–Wewak, Wakde–Sarmi and the Vogelkop. These forces still contained substantial elements from five infantry divisions. Altogether there were something like 80,000 Japanese still at large throughout New Guinea, who above all had to be prevented from interfering with air and supply operations to and from the various Pacific bases. With his eye on Leyte, Manila and beyond, MacArthur was not especially enamoured of tying up troops in static defence, and as early as March 1944 he had suggested to General Sir Thomas Blamey, the Australian Commander-in-Chief, that his troops might return to garrison the mandates. As a sop to Australian pride, MacArthur also hinted at the possibility of two Australian divisions taking part in the Leyte landings. With or without this offer, however, the Australian government was keen both to re-establish their presence in their overseas possessions as well as to earn themselves a place at any table debating the postwar settlement in the Pacific. Though discussions between MacArthur's and Blamey's staffs were protracted, and the prospect of Australian troops on Philippines beachheads became ever more chimerical, there was never any real doubt that they would replace American troops in the mandates.[1]

There were, however, considerable disagreements about the exact implementation of the changeover. One of the more surprising was MacArthur's insistence that the Australians employ more troops than they thought were necessary. Blamey and his planners reckoned seven brigades of infantry would be more than adequate to hold all three mandated territories but MacArthur insisted that nothing less than twelve brigades would do, and this was eventually written into an order he issued in August. The Australian official historian is extremely suspicious of MacArthur's motives, suggesting that the decision to insist on more troops "was a puzzling one in view of American staff doctrine that when a commander has been allotted a task he himself should decide how to carry it out, and the question arises whether considerations of *amour-propre* were involved: whether G.H.Q. did not wish it to be recorded that six American divisions had been relieved by [only] six Australian brigades."[2]

One consequence of the insistence on deploying larger forces was that Blamey felt he now had the manpower to abandon the normal American policy of simply containing the Japanese in by-passed islands and hoping that they would 'wither on the vine'. In fact, according to Blamey, on American-held islands the surviving Japanese were "left in comparative peace and developed a large measure of 'self-sufficiency' by cultivating gardens and employing natives to do so, importing seeds, and supplying critical items such as medical supplies and signal stores by submarine and aircraft."[3] Blamey's view that Australian prestige demanded much more aggressive action prompted him to draw up a three-stage plan to be followed once the Americans had been relieved.

At first the troops would concentrate on "aggressive patrolling to gain information of enemy strengths and dispositions, about which little was known by American formations." Once the enemy had been pin-pointed, large-scale operations could be mounted, with the pre-liminary aim of "systematically driving him from his garden areas and supply bases" and later harrying him continuously, "forcing him into starvation and destroying him where found. Eventually to bring about his total destruction." The patrolling stage was to be broken down into two "overlapping phases", first "pushing forward of native troops into the wild to ascertain the location and strength of the enemy", and then, when a particular Japanese band had been pin-pointed, sending out Australian "light forces to localities which can be dealt with piecemeal." These forces would also "form the nuclei from which patrols would contact and destroy the enemy by normal methods of bush warfare."[4] Even though Blamey was not suggesting that American methods were inadequate to the primary task of defending their base areas – for, after all, the Japanese had shown little disposition to mount any significant attacks since the late summer – it is nevertheless interesting to see reference to 'bush warfare' and the age-old dispute over whether counter-insurgency should rely on static containment or on aggressive search-and-destroy missions.

Blamey told General Vernon Sturdee, the commander of Australian First Army which was to oversee this new deployment, that operations should be conducted "without committing major forces". Sturdee, unclear as to whether this allowed anything more than patrol activity, queried how Japanese forces were actually going to be destroyed. He even wondered, hypothetically, whether any sort of aggressive policy was advisable. "Jap garrisons," he noted, "are at present virtually in POW camps but feed themselves, so why incur a large number of Australian casualties . . . eliminating them?" A little later, however, he did concede that there might be telling non-military reasons for an aggressive posture in at least one of the mandates. "I realise that there may be some question of prestige that makes the cleaning up of Bougainville an urgent necessity, or alternatively the elimination of the Japs in that area to reduce inter-breeding to a minimum and so avoid the potential trouble of having a half native-Jap population to deal with in the future."[5]

MacArthur's original timetable had called for Australian troops to take over responsibility for the "continued neutralisation" of the mandates by 1st October in Bougainville, and 1st November in New Britain and New Guinea. In the event, by 25th October the Australians had taken charge in none of these territories, and even on Bougainville the Americans were still sending out patrols. An advance party from II Australian Corps had arrived on 6th October but had not yet sent out its first patrol.[6]

New Britain was garrisoned by American 40 Infantry Division, mainly around Cape Gloucester on the western extremity of the island. The Japanese were concentrated at the other end, some 300 miles away at Rabaul on the Gazelle peninsula. Allied estimates of Japanese strengths varied between 30,000 and 40,000 men, although in reality there were 92,000 troops there. Rabaul had once been their major forward air and naval base, but by October 1944 only a few ships or planes remained. As a springboard for power projection, Rabaul had truly withered on the vine. The base had become progressively ringed around with American airfields and anchorages, the building of which the Japanese had not been able to prevent or even significantly delay. As S. E. Morison wrote, the campaign to neutralise Rabaul "pointed out in unmistakable terms the folly of building up a great overseas base and garrison without a navy capable of controlling the surrounding waters and air."[7] An Australian guerrilla group had been operating on the island's southern coast since June 1944, and in the first week of September an advance party from 5 Infantry Division arrived on the island. Troops from the division's 6 Brigade did not begin landing in force in Jaquinot Bay to the south-west of the island until 4th November, although one battalion was landed at Cape Hoskins on 8th October and put under command of 185 U.S. Regiment.

On New Guinea, the takeover of the Aitape beachhead, to the west of Japanese Eighteenth Army headquarters at Wewak, began on 15th September with the arrival of an advance party from 3 Base Sub-Area, the logistical support for 6 Infantry Division. The Japanese made no attempt to interfere. Over the next weeks the Australian rear echelons found themselves in the vanguard as a Works Company, a Field Security Detachment, a General Transport Company, a General Hospital, a Docks Operating Company and a Mobile Laundry all went ashore. A shortage of shipping delayed the first combat units that followed, ships arriving in ones and twos at three- or four-day intervals up to 23rd October.

By the 25th the only significant combat unit ashore was 2/6 Cavalry (Commando) Regiment, which took over from a company of 172 U.S. Infantry Regiment, part of 43 Infantry Division. Unfortunately, according to one Australian officer, "little information was available . . . from American sources" as they had had no real contact with the enemy since the end of July 1944. It was considered that "the enemy had moved a large portion of his forces inland in order to gain control of the valuable food producing areas there."[8] Such information as there was came from Australian-led guerrillas who had been operating around Aitape and Sepik since April. A later report by 6 Division stated: "Long-range patrols operated without troop support and, for their own protection, inaugurated a type of guerrilla warfare. Selected village natives called 'sentries' were taught to use grenades and Japanese rifles. The sentries, besides furnishing Intelligence . . . accounted for large numbers of the enemy."[9] By the end of October two of the three American divisions had already left Aitape, one bound for Morotai and the other for the Philippines. But the Australians had still not sent out patrols of their own and there seemed little chance that it would be feasible to relieve the third American division by 10th November as planned.

Some American troops were still stationed in all the mandated territories on 25th October, but it was on Bougainville that they were most heavily committed. The beachhead there was defended by the Americal Division and it was as miserable a spot as any in the Pacific.[10] The original landings by U.S. Marines in November 1943 had been made on the western coast, around Torokina at the northern end of Empress Augusta Bay, avoiding Japanese strongpoints to the south but dumping the Marines in an area the Japanese thought too horrible to be worth defending. One newcomer observed that "it rained at four o'clock every day on that goddamned island. It was almost impossible to keep dry." Another soldier also noted that the rain only came in the late afternoon, after several hours of enervating heat and humidity, to be "followed by the chill. It was miserable. There you would be lying in a hole with a wet poncho. You'd be soaked and you'd get so goddamned cold you thought you were going to die."[11]

The damp was all-pervasive even when it was not raining. Much of the western coast was dissected by numerous rivers which carried the rainfall into the sea. These carried silt which over time had built a sort of dam all down the coast, leaving large swamps and unsavoury lagoons only a hundred yards inland. An American war correspondent reported that "the wetness made clothes moldy, swelled pencils, decomposed cartridge belts, turned food into slop. Every day you had to check the grenade pins for rust, and the only way you could keep matches dry was to seal them inside a contraceptive."[12] Men went mouldy, too. Said one sergeant. "Your feet began to rot, your clothes were stinking, you would get skin ulcers between your legs to the point where you ran around with Kolex on and were just downright miserable." A regimental commander recalled that "Jungle rot was the major problem. We had very little change of clothes. The sand rubbing against your skin and the heat and the wet combined to make it easy to get jungle rot which is a form of fungus. Got it primarily on scalp, under arms, and in genital areas. I had it all above my knees. And it was miserable – no other word for it. No real cure for it . . . The kids were miserable."[13] At least the Allied troops were spared one of the normal effects of swampy terrain – malaria. By clearing obstructions in some creeks and hand-digging numerous new channels, which drained approximately four million square yards of swamp, and by regularly oiling the areas that remained, the incidence of this disease was dramatically reduced.

By October there had also been other improvements. Although the Americans in the front line were still living in holes in the ground, they were at least living in 'better 'oles' than those hastily scooped out by the Marine landing parties. An American infantryman described how, as the perimeter gradually congealed, these first crude excavations were converted into veritable "pillboxes. We dug the holes and built them with trees we cut down. These were 12 to 15 feet square and they were not more than eight feet deep . . . We would reinforce them with other trees . . . Some of the pillboxes were connected by trenches and some by a tunnel you could crawl through . . . These normally had four to six men to a pillbox and we made little cots from the strong vines."[14]

Despite Australian suspicions to the contrary, the Americans were not content simply to man these defences and wait for the Japanese to attack. Right up to their relief by the Australians, their policy was to keep the Japanese off-balance by sending out regular patrols and maintaining strongpoints far in front of the main fortified perimeter.

These patrols varied considerably in size and purpose, from occasional and very compact ambush and sniper patrols to squad or platoon reconnaissance missions or full company-size combat patrols. Large patrols were kept covert and mobile and, "if aggressively handled, can raise havoc with an enemy battalion and vanish into the jungle before strong resistance can be organised."[15] On 25th October most of this patrolling was being done by 132 Regiment, which had just relieved the 182nd and was attempting to dominate no-man's-land between the villages of Piaterpaia and Sisivie, roughly twelve miles inland and seven miles beyond the main perimeter.

By late October the battle for domination seemed to have been almost won because contact with Japanese patrols had virtually ceased. The Americans took this to mean that Japanese fighting efficiency had slumped due to lack of food and poor morale, but the Australian intelligence staffs largely rejected these conclusions, stressing the fact that supplies were still being brought in by submarine, that a planned agricultural programme, using forced native labour, was well under way, and that several units had been disbanded to maintain the combat efficiency of the rest. But they did agree that upwards of 3,000 Japanese had died between July and September, mainly from malnutrition. It is difficult now to choose between these different assessments. The most authoritative American historian paints a bleak picture of the Japanese situation. Their normal daily rice ration of 750 grammes had been cut to 250 grammes in April and disappeared completely in September. Numerous fruit and vegetable plots had been established but "Allied pilots took delight in dropping napalm on these garden plots wherever possible. The native workers ... there were the first to defect, but soon many soldiers also just walked away from their units, taking the chance of surviving in the jungle on what could be gathered."[16]

Stories about such stragglers were a regular feature of Bougainville scuttlebutt, and two that remained current for some weeks concerned certain Japanese who had infiltrated right into the rear echelons. One was supposed to have become an avid spectator at divisional baseball games, hiding out in the shadows of the jungle off right field but occasionally getting sufficiently carried away to clap and grunt approvingly. Yet more incautious was a Japanese soldier who found a seat in the tangled branches of a banyan tree to watch the Hollywood movie being shown at the divisional 'drive-in'. Also being shown was some captured Japanese film of the sinking of the carrier *Lexington* in May 1942, and seeing this, the gatecrasher could contain himself no longer and gave vent to several cries of 'Banzai!', before being grabbed and led away to the prisoner-of-war compound.

Personally, I do not believe a word of it, but it is intriguing to discover that 'urban myths' were alive and well more than fifty years ago, in one of the least urban settings it would be possible to imagine.[17]

40

Pacific Stepping-Stones

FOR THE MAJORITY of the 850,000 American soldiers, 520,000 sailors and 200,000 Marines serving in the Pacific in October 1944, neither combat nor mopping-up and patrolling had any part in the daily routine. Mid-twentieth-century warfare had become more a matter of deploying, supplying and servicing ever more powerful and voracious weaponry, and the logistical implications of this were nowhere more evident than in the vast expanse of the Pacific. Here the quartermaster's map looked like some starkly minimalist painting-by-numbers exercise as supply routes traced the enormous distances between one tiny island group and the next. By the 25th much of this 'painting' had already been done and behind the front lines on Leyte, Pelelieu and Guam there stretched an intricate tracery of naval, air and cargo bases, all manned by large numbers of communication personnel and a few garrison troops. Air bases were established on almost every island that was invaded – and indeed were usually the main reason for landing at all.

In early 1944 the main fields for land-based air strikes in the Central Pacific had been in the Marshall Islands, Eniwetok and the Kwajalein atoll (which also included Roi and Namur), though most squadrons in the Pacific were with General Kenney's Fifth and Thirteenth Air Forces, based on or off the coast of New Guinea, with rear and depot facilities at Port Moresby, Milne Bay and Dobodura, main bases at Nadzab and Finschhafen, and airfields at Saidor and Cape Gloucester (New Britain). The dual Pacific advance really got under way in the next few months, and by October both Nimitz and MacArthur were converging on the Philippines, with new bases and airfields in the Marianas and on Morotai.

An enormous logistical price had to be paid to maintain this scattered network of air bases, for which almost every conceivable item had to be shipped or flown in over immense distances. Airfield and aircraft maintenance, as well as the fuelling and arming, clearly had to be given priority and this meant that aircrew and groundcrew alike found living conditions at the lower end of a scale basic to primitive. To Marine pilot Captain John Foster, the Green Islands atoll looked from the air "like an emerald circlet containing a center stone of blue sapphire." Yet even though the base had been operational for eight months in October 1944, "on the ground we had a rude awakening. Not enough mattresses and blankets were available, so each of us had the choice of one or the other, but not both. A long tent contained canvas cots for our use. The mess hall and tents were immersed in a gooey mass of mud and the whole was overshadowed by the trees of the jungle and serviced by a solitary road. Near the landing strip the constant coral dust and human sweat created a hard exterior for all of the Marines and New Zealanders [of the garrison force]. There were no shower baths. Water was precious."[1]

Such conditions, aggravated by the complete lack of leisure facilities, did little to lift morale which had already been seriously eroded by a chronic shortage of replacements for increasingly weary pilots and groundcrew. Most had already gone up to two years without rest or rotation and some flyers had clocked up as many as 700 combat hours in the air. One wing commander "observed that many of his flyers regarded surgeons' certificates of combat fatigue as the only way to get home alive."[2] In some medium bomber squadrons only one third of their crews were deemed fit for combat, with almost all the rest grounded due to mental exhaustion.

Though these flyers might have been somewhat sceptical, the fact was that combatants and non-combatants alike all found life in the Pacific a considerable ordeal. For almost any island west of Hawaii turned out to be equally inimical to providing even a memory of life's little pleasures. Midway was supposed to be a haven for returning submariners but, after the initial euphoria, life quickly became just as monotonous as it always was for the base personnel and the garrison. One visitor recalled the time he " 'did Midway', as they said, or perhaps it was the other way round. As an enlisted man going about his job and incidentally wondering if his chit for transfer had ever been seen, much less honored, there were occasional forays to the beer parlor for warm, green beer, occasional baseball games, occasional boxing matches, and less than occasional mail from home."[3]

Navy bases were usually much better appointed than Army rear areas, probably because they were used for an ongoing cycle of major refits and revictualling while Army bases were just staging areas, temporary accommodation for troops being funnelled up to the front-line islands. On New Caledonia, an important transit camp ever since 1942, there was a dual standard of living. "Soldiers living in thatched huts with dirty floors enviously eyed the sturdy, dry, wooden barracks of their navy counterparts. When bases had electricity, or refrigeration, the navy usually had it first. Navy mess halls appeared better built and served better food – and the sailors always seemed to have more beer."[4]

A few hundred miles to the north was the island of Espiritu Santo, an important anchorage for Navy Task Forces since mid-1942. The Navy had rather flippantly code-named it 'Button', but for 27 Infantry Division, resting there after the fighting on Saipan in the Marianas, such levity seemed totally inappropriate. The last units had quit Saipan on 4th October, destined for a 'rehabilitation period'. However,

> whatever Espiritu Santo may have been to others, to the 27th Division it was a hell-hole, ill-suited for rehabilitation and poorly chosen as a home for troops fresh out of great battle . . . The Division's stay there was the worst single memory of the war . . . Santo is a tropical island whose climate is hot and humid. Early in the war it had been one of the most important of all American bases in the Pacific, but even the intense activity of that earlier period had not served to transform the area from a malarial clearing on the edge of a vast and impenetrable jungle, populated by head-hunters and pythons. The Division was not even furnished with any housing facilities. As they arrived in the island troops built their own camps in the great coconut plantations ten miles from the naval base. There was no place to go even if the men got a pass. The main base at Santo had a big Red Cross recreation center, an ice-cream parlor, and a beer garden but it was inadequate even for the personnel on the island prior to the arrival of the Division. Twelve open-air theaters were constructed by the Division where second-rate movies were shown. No first-class theatrical troupes ever visited the area. A recreational hall was built, and this was served by two or three girls twice a week. On these occasions it served coffee and doughnuts.[5]

Home leave was granted to the division at the niggardly rate of fifty men per month. They were chosen by regimental lotteries. Even after the commander's most vociferous complaints the number was only raised to 250 per month. This guaranteed a man home leave within five years, by which time a combat infantryman was much more likely to have been killed or wounded. A final discouragement "caused an almost complete breakdown of morale within the Division." This concerned an article in *Time* magazine about the dismissal of the divisional commander, General Ralph Smith, during the Saipan battle and which accused virtually the whole division of cowardice. The men had written hundreds of letters "of vehement denial to *Time* or to their own families. Because these letters contained classified information, they were virtually all returned to the senders by the censors."[6] General George Griner, the new commander, had written his own letter of complaint to *Time* but even this was consigned to the slow grind through official channels. By 25th October it had just reached Admiral Nimitz, who was minded to approve forwarding the letter to the magazine's editor.

At least it gave the men of 27 Division something to occupy their minds. Despite their historian's misgivings about morale, the *Time* incident probably did a lot to harden the division's *esprit de corps* as they prepared to commence training for landings in Okinawa, notification of which had come through in mid-October. For most troops out of the line, however, the worst problem was having nothing to do and nothing to distract one from mindlessly trivial introspection. Lieutenant K. Stewart, with a rifle company in 43 Infantry Division at Aitape in New Guinea, had been a couple of weeks out of the line when he wrote home to his parents: "You will note that I am still sitting, safely and monotonously, here in New Guinea . . . I censor a pile of letters every day and it's an . . . interesting job (however boring) in that you learn that you are not the only person in the world who has troubles. Staying here, isolated this way, and comparatively inactive, is very depressing to everyone's morale. You can sense it in the letters. Worries about home affairs become magnified, lack of feminine companionship becomes unbearable, petty annoyances assume large proportions, the specter of a coming campaign becomes terrifying. In our small company alone in the past 3 weeks two boys have been evacuated as psycho–neurotics. That's a polite name for going batty."[7]

On Peleliu, several Marine units were awaiting shipment to their rehabilitation areas, and even though they had not been long out of the line, the relief of quitting the savage battle was already beginning to give way to a sense of utter lassitude, almost hopelessness, in the face of hour after hour, day after day of nothing to do but make small talk, play cards or sleep. Even the prospect of drill or some other military routine offered some sort of relief from absolute vacuity. In a letter home, Lieutenant David Brown wrote: "If for a day we disengage ourselves from the endless round of military rituals and routine, the whole structure might collapse into nothingness. For out here it is nothingness, emptiness that men fear. The military treadmill, the mission in the offing, is our one tangible proof of reality. The conquest of desolation, of sheer ennui, is a matter of genuine heroism, as much as battle itself."[8]

The ultimate Pacific hell-hole for the Marines was Pavuvu, in the Russell Islands, just to the north-west of Guadalcanal. Like the Green Islands, the Russells had looked from the air like a verdant mini-paradise and no reports on the grim reality were ever enough to persuade the powers-that-be to look for a new staging or rest area. But to those in the know the islands were "only famous for mud, rain and coconut plantations." For one Marine regimental commander the accommodation on Pavuvu was "more like a hog lot than a rest camp."[9] A Marine historian conceded the "lyric sensuality" of the name and its evocation of hulas and swaying palms, but then bemoaned the total irrelevance of such a vision to Pavuvu where "there were no hulas, and where the swaying palms had all rotted . . . Pavuvu was literally one in a million: mud, rain, rotted coconuts, jungle fever, depression. There were no lights on the island, not even in the Division command post."[10]

The island had once been the site of a large Unilever coconut plantation but after it was abandoned the coconuts and trees rotted in the pouring rain and the tropical humidity. The jungle growth was rampant and large Pavuvu rats, ugly bristled blue-black crabs, mosquitoes and other pestiferous insects were everywhere. As another Marine recalled: "On Pavuvu, simple living was difficult . . . Most of the work parties . . . were pick-and-shovel details to improve drainage or pave walkways with crushed coral, just to get us out of the water. Regulations called for wooden decks in all tents, but I never saw one on Pavuvu. Of all the work parties the one we hated most was collecting rotten coconuts. We loaded them into trucks to be dumped into a swamp. If we were lucky, the coconut sprout served as a handle. But more often, the thing fell apart, spilling rotten coconut milk over us. The stench of rotting coconuts permeated the air. We could even taste it in the drinking water."[11]

Worse, there was virtually nothing to do on the island except brood upon its unrelieved ghastliness. Some Marines managed to shove a few books into their knapsacks and these would be seized upon and read avidly by men who hitherto had hardly ever bothered to even open a newspaper. One marine who lent from his own small stock recalled that meetings were convened to discuss what they had read: "I don't know whether some of these Marines have ever discussed a book since, but they did on Pavuvu. Sometimes we got angry enough . . . to go out and fight in the company street." But often the heat was too much even for reading and the men would simply doze under their mosquito nets. "Afterwards we went for another shower and then made some more coffee. There were days when we took six or seven showers and drank ten or twelve cups of coffee. It helped pass the time."[12]

Indeed, as long as one was not clearing rotting coconuts, there was a lot to be said for being worked hard in these Pacific bywaters, for the labour got one through the day and the fatigue helped one sleep at night. Speaking of his overall experiences in the Pacific with 495 Port Battalion, part of the U.S. Army Transportation Corps, Sy Kahn remembered "a general malaise and aching sense of isolation and loneliness . . . During our service in the South Pacific, only two men from our company were sent to Australia for rest and recreation . . . An overnight pass or weekend leave was meaningless, there was simply no place to go in New Guinea or on a tropical island . . . Some men did eventually run amok, attacking others and wounding themselves, and as time went on these psychotic episodes and emotional breakdowns, though always alarming, were never surprising. All of us had felt the pressures."[13]

Yet on 25th October, on the island of Biak, Kahn's diary entry bespoke a reasonably contented man. His unit was engaged in loading freighters taking supplies and equipment to Leyte. The work was hard but Kahn himself had been promoted to corporal just the previous day and was enjoying the responsibility. He was beginning to master handling the electric winch and was looking forward to grappling with the somewhat more intractable steam winch. Many of the men under him were negroes and "they are really funny sometimes, and I like to work with them, and sometimes prefer it . . . They have a great sense of humor and are most always bright-spirited. They are combat troops out of the 93rd [Infantry Division (Colored)] who have been converted to service troops." But what really pleased him was that he would be assuming "quite a responsibility because I will be in charge of a hatch by myself. Also I have some difficult men to deal with, and I am the youngest man in the section. Nevertheless, I welcome it. For one thing, no more KP and guard duty . . . But this is what I need to build up confidence, poise, and get used to giving orders instead of continually carrying them out."[14]

Rear echelon personnel like Kahn and his battalion were the constant butt of front-line soldiers' jibes. Still, the job was no sinecure and the hours worked were probably much more onerous than those of many longshoremen back home. In October, the battalion had gone into "a 6-on, 12-off schedule. It's a killing routine. It slowly wears one down. Twelve hours in 24 is a lot doing something you don't like. It's difficult to sleep well during the day."[15] Nevertheless, to no combat soldier's great surprise, he did have one of the longshoremen's great perks – the opportunity to pilfer from the enormous throughput of supplies. According to his diary, the amounts taken were fairly modest, aimed more at supplementing the regular rations than at black-market profiteering. On the 25th, he and his buddies were still availing themselves of five gallons of coke syrup stolen on the 17th, listening to V-discs on a 'victrola', all taken on the 13th, and tucking into Milky Ways and chocolate mints stolen that very day. Kahn's diary entry for the day concluded: "First real candy I've had in many months, and with the first piece I found I've completely lost my taste for sweets. Damn, but I'm tired."[16]

PART TEN

China and Burma

41

Driving Sheep to Feed Tigers
THE WAR IN CHINA

IF WAR in the Pacific absorbed the greater part of Japanese naval, air and logistical resources, it was there, too, that the Japanese lost the war strategically, proving incapable of defending the ocean empire they had seized. Nevertheless it should not be thought that the Japanese fought only on the high seas or in fanatical defence of coral outcrops and island jungles, nor that the Americans were their only adversary. Ever since the turn of the century the Far East had been a cockpit for aggressive Japanese imperialism. Sakhalin, Formosa, Kwantung and Korea were all seized between 1895 and 1910 and then the whole of Manchuria (Manchukuo) in 1932.* Five years later the Japanese invaded the remaining provinces of China, pushing down from Manchuria to take Peking and putting troops ashore at Shanghai to 'protect' Japanese nationals there. When the Chinese responded aggressively to this last provocation, the Japanese quickly poured in reinforcements of their own, and in the ensuing battles China's elite divisions were all but destroyed. The Chinese government, under Chiang Kai-shek, was evacuated to Chungking and the remnants of Chinese core forces withdrew to the mountainous strongholds of Szechwan and Yunnan.

The Japanese found it impossible to concentrate sufficient men and materiel for a knock-out blow, or even to extend their writ much beyond the main towns, roads and railways. By October 1944, something like 1.5 million Japanese soldiers had been sent to China and at no time were less than 850,000 men stationed there. Year after year

---

* The former Chinese provinces of Liaoning, Kirin, Heilungkiang and Jehol. I have retained transliterations of Chinese place names that were current at the time. The same applies to Chinese personal names.

they assembled large armies and embarked on concerted campaigns to extend their hold along the main communications routes and to consolidate their occupation of peripheral regions. Advances from Peking across the Yellow River to Hankow (Wuhan) and from Shanghai to Nanking and further south to Nanchang were brought to a halt by obdurate Chinese resistance that kept the Japanese out of Changsha, repulsing three separate offensives between 1939 and 1942. After that, with their attention centred on other theatres, the Japanese allowed the China front to congeal, their only real success being to the north, in the Taihang mountains, a base for Communist guerrillas along the Shansi–Hopei border. However, a subsequent offensive in northern Hupei in summer 1943 was balked, as was yet another drive in Hunan, in November.

This whole period was succinctly summed up by an American observer who noted that from 1937 to 1943, despite the vastness of the theatre and the distances covered during many advances, "the campaigns the Japanese fought were foraging expeditions rather than battles. They had no greater strategic objective than to keep the countryside in terror, to sack the fields and towns, to keep the Chinese troops at the front off balance, and to train their own green recruits under fire."[1] The war, he noted, was waged almost entirely along the north–south rail and road links that ran through central China. The Chinese made repeated efforts to cut these routes and the Japanese fought hard to keep them open, both sides helping to create a devastated no-man's-land between 50 and 100 miles wide in which towns were repeatedly shelled, besieged and stormed, villages were burnt to the ground, and the peasants starved. For six years almost all the fighting took place within this narrow zone, and even in 1944, when the Japanese were determined to undertake a major push southwards, the axes of advance remained relatively narrow, along the main railway lines connecting Peking with Liuchow and Canton.

Nevertheless, this renewed offensive had more ambitious aims than just foraging, pillaging or striking terror. By the beginning of that year the Japanese High Command had been forced to acknowledge that China was becoming important in the war overall as the Americans made increasing efforts to utilise Chinese manpower and territory to back up their own operations. The U.S. Fourteenth Air Force had secured bases south and south-east of Chungking and, aided by Tenth Air Force units based in India and Burma, were providing Chinese troops with effective tactical air support. Japanese anxieties were heightened by reliable intelligence that the Americans intended to base their new very long range B-29 bombers in China, which would almost certainly be used to attack Japan itself.

Burgeoning American air power was not the only worry. Roosevelt and Marshall, who had long been anxious to make China a useful ally against Japan, had arranged for Lend Lease supplies to begin arriving as early as March 1941, nine months before Pearl Harbor. In December General Joseph Stilwell was posted to China as a senior adviser to Chiang Kai-shek, and in 1942 he commanded Chinese forces involved in the retreat from Burma. Soon American interests in eastern Asia were combined into a new overall command, the China-Burma-India (CBI) Theater, with Stilwell in charge. By October 1944 he was wearing several commanders' hats at once, not only as commander-in-chief of the CBI, but as chief-of-staff to Chiang Kai-shek, deputy Supreme Commander at South-East Asia Command (SEAC), the inter-Allied headquarters in this theatre, and controller of the allocation of Lend Lease supplies to China.[2] Stilwell also had day-to-day command of a new Chinese expeditionary force in Burma, though Chiang retained the ultimate authority over its deployment and commitment to battle. By 1944 there were 21 American-equipped and trained divisions, five of them in northern Burma, advancing towards Myitkyina, and the rest in Yunnan, poised to cross the River Salween. The ultimate objective of both these forces was Lashio, where they could join up Burma's two main northern supply routes, the Ledo Road and the Burma Road, somewhere near Nankham.

Fearful of this increasing integration of China into the Allied war effort, the Japanese opened up their own ICHI GO offensive, first to secure the main north–south Peking–Canton railway and the feeder line from Hengyang to Kweilin and Liuchow, and second to eliminate the easterly group of U.S. air bases that straddled this line between Hengyang and Liuchow. As Japanese forces pushed southward they were to link up with other divisions pushing north out of Indo-China, somewhere around Nanning. Such a junction would pose a long-term threat to the rear of the Chinese divisions in Yunnan, either forcing Chiang to redeploy them or at the very least making him think twice about pressing forward across the River Salween. Even more important, it was claimed, would be the forging of a new route along which raw materials might be funnelled overland to the starving industries in Manchuria and mainland Japan. Given the lack of "rolling stock or automobiles to utilise such a route", it is difficult to understand how the Japanese "could have been so stupid as to think of the drive as an opening to the South Seas". The fact remained that during the

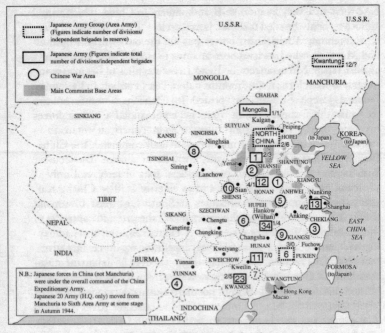

The War in China 25th October 1944

second half of 1944 their "propagandists were trumpeting loud and long about their impregnable corridor to the south."[3]

In other words, misguided or not, the Japanese High Command still attached great importance to the Chinese theatre. This also becomes strikingly apparent from a glance at the Japanese order of battle for 25th October 1944. Of their 35 divisions deployed in the Pacific, 19 were cut off behind the American advance and 16 were still to be overcome. There were also 9 Japanese divisions in South-East Asia and 15 in Japan itself. In China and Manchuria, 38 divisions were stationed, allocated thus:

KWANTUNG ARMY (Manchuria)   12 divisions
CHINA EXPEDITIONARY ARMY
   North China Area Army   9 divisions
   6th Area Army   13 divisions
   13 Army   4 divisions
                        Total: 37 divisions

This comparison in no way plays down the task confronting American, British and Australian soldiers in the Far East and the Pacific. Japanese units fought everywhere implacably, even when reduced to so-called remnants and stragglers. On the whole the Japanese stationed their better divisions in the Pacific and Burma while the Kwantung Army and the China Expeditionary Army had been bled of some of their best divisions, no less than 17 of them transferred to the Pacific by October 1944.[4] These veteran Japanese formations, almost all formed before 1942, were replaced, if at all, by newly-raised, poorly equipped divisions from Manchuria and the homeland. Despite all this, the Japanese continued to maintain almost as many divisions in China as they did in the remaining parts of their empire in Burma, Indo–China and the Pacific. In a country as poor as China, and with occupiers as savagely ethnocentric as the Japanese, these divisions represented a terrible threat to the livelihoods and often the very lives of the great mass of poor peasants. Perhaps the least known and most important of all the campaigns in the Far East is the seven-year struggle against the Japanese in China, in which millions of civilians and ill-equipped foot soldiers endured the very worst excesses of total war to make their own significant contribution to the progressive collapse of the Japanese war machine.

The most obvious Chinese contribution to the Allied war effort were the divisions assigned to General Stilwell in northern Burma and Yunnan. These troops formed the main component of Stilwell's Northern Combat Area Command (NCAC) and were in two main groups: X Force, with 5 divisions in northern Burma, and Y Force, with 16 divisions in two 'army groups' in Yunnan. Chiang Kai-shek had agreed to an offensive in Burma as early as July 1943 but then prevaricated until the following January when the drive to extend the Ledo Road began. This advance on Myitkyina was supported by U.S. Galahad Force, better known as 'Merrill's Marauders', and by General Orde Wingate's Long Range Penetration Brigades, the 'Chindits'. All troops suffered badly during this campaign, and with the taking of Myitkyina on 3rd August 1944 both the Marauders and the Chindits were disbanded. The Chinese were allowed time to rest and refit, and then, in mid-October, Stilwell issued orders for a renewed three-pronged push across the Irrawaddy river. By 25th October three divisions had reached a line running from just south of Mohnyin, via Broadway, to a couple of miles north of Myothit, and they were confidently expecting to be over the Irrawaddy and the Taping by the beginning of November.

Based as it was in China, Y Force was more immediately available for parrying any threat to Chiang's Szechwan heartland. Consequently he was doubly cautious about committing it to Burmese operations, and it was not until May 1944 that a westward advance was allowed to begin. On the 17th, forces under General Wei-Li-Huang crossed the River Salween in strength and advanced on two main axes towards Lungling on the Burma Road and Tengchung to the north. The campaign soon took on a positively medieval aspect, with Tengchung laid siege to early in July and the whole city finally cleared on 15th September. To the south, Sungshan and Lungling had come under siege in early June, with the former eventually succumbing on 9th September. Lungling changed hands several times until the Chinese finally repulsed the Japanese towards the end of August, recapturing part of the Burma Road. In the end, fearful of the threat to their rear, Chinese forces pulled back into Lungling and another ring of siege lines. By 25th October Chinese generals were confidently predicting the imminent fall of the city. In the meantime the two axes had converged, and while the Chinese prepared for a concerted drive towards Mangshih and Wanting, Y Force patrols made contact with other Chinese troops probing across the Irrawaddy.

Remarkably, a British official publication, giving an admirable short account of the war in Burma, offers a much more evocative description of the fighting in western Yunnan than does the Chinese Nationalists' own account of the war. According to Frank Owen:

> It is not easy to describe the Salween front, except to say that it was probably the hardest in the world. On the 11,000-foot Kaolikung Mountains, which are a spur of the Himalayas, there raged a battle for many months in sleet, snow and fog, in which strategic points were mountain peaks bare of every kind of vegetation. In khaki shorts and straw sandals, with no raincapes and less than a blanket per man, the Chinese infantry and gunners fought their struggle. The planes of the U.S. 10th and 14th Air Forces gave them determined but, in the nature of things, inevitably intermittent air support. In this desolate rock land large bodies of troops could not be manoeuvred, and the fate of territories depended not upon divisions but battalions. The front was fluid, with harbours of resistance, and war was largely a battle between individual soldiers. 'Kuli' these mountains are named. It means 'Bitter Strength', and no words so well define the quality of the Chinese infantryman who fought and died there.[5]

On the whole, Chiang Kai-shek's reluctance to commit his best, American-equipped divisions was perfectly understandable. Important as their contribution to the Allied war effort was in the latter half of 1944, tying down three of the ten Japanese divisions in Burma, they were actually marching directly away from China's own most threatened front, in Kwangsi province. The ICHI-GO offensive had finally got under way in April 1944 and was divided into two stages. The first consisted of a converging thrust, north and south along the railway linking Chengchow and Hankow, in Honan and Hupei provinces, combined with another westward push along the line to Sian, just south of the Yellow River. By mid-June the entire Peking–Hankow railway was in Japanese hands, although necessary repairs meant that the first through train from Peking did not run until 10th October. The westward drive pushed to within 100 miles of Sian, and the whole campaign revealed terrible weaknesses in the Chinese army. Upwards of forty of their divisions had simply melted away before the Japanese advance, with vital features being given up without a shot fired and local commanders requisitioning all available motor transport to get their personal possessions and booty to safety. When other officers began to help themselves to peasant oxen to bolster the army supply system, their owners, who depended on these animals to plough their wheat fields, turned on the soldiers and disarmed them in large numbers. All in all, an army of 60,000 Japanese soldiers had provoked the complete collapse of a 300,000-strong Chinese force.

The next phase of the Japanese offensive continued the drive southward from Hankow, towards Changsha, which fell in mid-June, and Hengyang, which held out until 8th August. After its capture, the Japanese began a pincers attack to encircle the rest of Hunan and northern Kwangsi provinces. The Japanese Eleventh Army resumed its march southward down the railway as far as Kweilin, where it was to link up with 23rd Army moving westward from Canton along the Hsi and Hsungshui rivers. The third phase of this operation would continue the drive south to meet Japanese troops advancing from Hanoi in the vicinity of Nanning. The offensive began on 26th August under the command of a new headquarters, 6th Area Army, which had been specially set up.[6] Both axes made considerable progress during September but at the end of that month, as seemingly in almost every other theatre of war across the world, heavy rains set in and movement became extremely difficult. Even so, by 25th October, Eleventh Army had advanced as far as Kweilin, and clearly it was only a matter of days before the city would fall.

Twenty-third Army was still short of its main objective at Liuchow, having been held at Kweiping and Pingnan, some 90 miles to the south-east, on the River Hungshui.

The Chinese had done better in southern Hunan and Kwangsi than in Honan. They forced the Japanese to take half as long again covering the 220 miles from Hengyang as they had the previous 600 miles. But it was simply not to be expected that the Japanese could be halted for good, let alone forced to pull back. By now the Chinese no longer had the advantage of raw numerical strength and, according to their official history, the two Chinese divisions in Kweilin were confronted by five Japanese.[7] These troops, like all those not equipped by the Americans, which made up the bulk of their forces, had to labour under every possible military disadvantage. They were very badly supplied, partly as a result of inadequate logistic support. General Arnold, the U.S. Air Force commander-in-chief, always felt that "the Generalissimo [Chiang] was not realistic. He brushed too many important things aside. He cast aside logistics and factual matters as mere trifles. Apparently he believed in man's 'will to do'; that will power could force the impossible."[8] The chronic supply shortages were also a function of Chiang's fear – in a country bedevilled by squabbling regional warlords, jealous of each other and of central authority – that any one of them should become too powerful a rival. Such suspicions were especially apparent in Chiang's relations with Hsueh Yueh, who commanded the Fourth War Area in Hunan and Kwangsi. It has even been claimed that from June 1944 Chiang refused to allow any supplies to be sent to him.

Such paranoia also had deleterious effects on the chain-of-command which Chiang increasingly disregarded, intervening to countermand local decisions taken at the lowliest level. According to one of his generals, Li Tsung-jen, commanding the Fifth War Area in Hupei province, one of the greatest obstacles to effective military operations was "Chiang's practice of bypassing his subordinates to direct the fighting personally. He was expert neither in commanding soldiers nor in directing generals and preferred to sit in his headquarters and use the telephone to direct operations . . . Unfortunately, Chiang's judgements were not accurate and his decisions were not decisive . . . He merely sat in his headquarters and, on the spur of the moment, acted on conjecture. The entire operational system would thus be thrown into confusion."[9]

It might be thought that this daily, sometimes hourly resort to the telephone at least implied an adequate communications network within the Nationalist army. Unfortunately, Chiang was one of the few commanders with free access to a field telephone and only 20,000 of them were ever distributed throughout the whole war. Thus, jump as a commander might at Chiang's behest, he was often hard-pressed to pass that behest on to his own subordinates. Neither was it necessarily much help to avoid being pestered by Chiang in person. Generals were never allowed to act on their own initiative and were also constantly bombarded with written directives. Worse, this paper barrage was rarely abreast of the actual situation on the ground. "Responsibility was ill-defined, communication slow, and co-ordination tedious. An order had to pass through six separate offices between the general staff and the operational division which was to execute it."[10]

One is bound to wonder just how effective the Chinese army could have been even with better logistic and command arrangements, for the ordinary soldiers, on whom all operations ultimately depended, received appalling treatment. Often they were not properly paid, the requisite funds being delivered direct to senior commanders whose hefty cut, together with that of others lower down the chain of command, rarely left anything for the great mass of ordinary riflemen. The food also was terrible, consisting mainly of rice and salt, with vegetables and meat only to be had by stealing them from the peasants whose villages they passed through or garrisoned. General Stilwell had spent eighteen months trying to get authorisation for an increase of just one pound of meat and a few pounds of beans per month for his Yunnan divisions. The troops were poor physical specimens even when they were first conscripted. At the base at Ramargh, in Assam, where new X Force intakes were processed, 68 per cent of recruits were rejected by American doctors as being unfit for military service. There were no such niceties in the Chinese system and hardly anyone who could stand on two feet was likely to be rejected. Indeed, Chinese medics played very little part in the life of their soldiers generally. Between 1940 and 1944 only a pitiful 791 doctors were called up to cater for an army with some 2.5 million men at the front. There again, what use would even triple the number of medics have been when one learns that during the whole war with Japan up to 1944, the army received only 10,500 tons of medical supplies of all kinds? This to tend to an army with 211,000 battle casualties in 1944 alone, even by the Chinese own parsimonious estimate. Moreover, the general health of the soldiers was very poor. The chronic shortage of food weakened their constitutions drastically and they were vulnerable to all sorts of infection. Probably one in ten was tubercular and their habit of eating communally, each dipping his chopsticks into a single bowl, made it almost impossible to prevent the spread of disease. Little wonder, then, that as one Nationalist general reports, "the wounded or sick faced conditions that defy description."

This same general was also critical of the whole conscription and training system, which produced little more than a poorly disciplined horde of bemused and frightened levies. The "authorities of the central government simply grabbed men from all over the country for military service. The new recruit was ill-trained and sent to the front hurriedly. This was like driving sheep to feed tigers."[11] The troops were so prone to desertion, flight or becoming casualties that at one stage the annual replacement rate reached 120 per cent, and it was never less than 60 per cent throughout the war. One source points out that by late 1944 the army had drafted in all twelve million men but had only four million on the rosters. "What had happened to the other eight million? No one knew for sure." Perhaps one million had become casualties, but the rest "had simply vanished. They were missing because they had died of sickness or hunger or because they had deserted individually to their homes or en masse to the enemy."[12] Such massive haemorrhaging of men created an insatiable demand for new recruits that resulted in wholesale and quite arbitrary press-ganging. One observer felt that "abuses in the selection and care of the selectees . . . is the darkest aspect of the whole China war. The draft system completely breaks down in the hands of the village heads . . . They have arrested villagers at night without notice and hold it as a weapon over people who offend or deny them . . . They have often accepted bribes for substitutes and connived at returning deserters; they have turned in required numbers of selectees with false names and without regard to the health and age limitations."[13]

The grimmest aspect of the whole recruitment system was the endless marches that new draftees were subjected to before they even got to their training camp or front-line unit. The idea was to get the men as far away from their homes as possible and so reduce the temptation to desert. One American observer was adamant that the recruits were "literally marched into thin skeletons over hundreds of miles". Theodore White, on the other hand, while convinced that military service "was usually a death sentence", believed that "more men died on their way to the army . . . than after getting into it." A British volunteer was told by a Chinese doctor: "Speaking from a strictly medical point of view, these men are beaten to death more than anything else. It doesn't matter if they're sick or tired – they're just forced to keep on walking, and if they don't walk they're beaten till they drop." A government official then chipped in to point out that a conscription officer with, say, a thousand conscripts would be expected eventually to hand over 850 men out every thousand (150 allowance for dead and runaways) or pay a fine of so much per head. "That's why, when they get near the end of their journey, they flog even the half deads along, so as to fill the quota. If they're too far below numbers they begin to impress [from the villages en route]."[14] Brutal and sometimes horrific events took place on 25th October 1944 but few were more utterly grotesque than the picture of a regime conducting death marches for its own troops.

It was not just conscripts who were on the march. Throughout China, on any given day, thousands of soldiers from some of the 180 infantry divisions would also be trekking hither and thither, whether responding to one of Chiang Kai-shek's whims, retreating before the Japanese advance, or simply seeking a new billeting area to pick clean. Theodore White observed such a column of troops in Hsueh Yueh's war zone. Wherever he looked there were thin columns of soldiers on the march. "They crawled on foot over every footpath through the rice paddies; they snaked along over every ditch and broken bridge." Their uniforms were threadbare. Most had a couple of grenades thrust in their belt but only a third of them had rifles, the rest being weighed down with boxes and sacks of supplies, ammunition, telephone wire and occasional machine-gun and mortar parts. There were only a few pack animals, no motor vehicles of any kind, and no artillery. The company kitchen was usually a single blackened cook-pot dangling on a pole held by two soldiers. Every soldier carried his rice ration, strung around his neck in a long blue-mesh stocking. White, who accompanied one such column for some distance, noticed a knot of peasants huddled under guard at a way-station. "The unit commanders stopped at these stations to pick up baggage bearers, just as a truck in any other army would stop to pick up gasoline at a filling station. The peasants marched with the troops until they were exhausted, then fell out, were fed rice, and were sent back to the service station again . . . On wet days the march was a column of agony, the soldiers soaked through and through, their feet encased in balls of mud and clay."[15]

How many such troops, if indeed any, were marching towards beleaguered Kweilin on the 25th remains uncertain. What is known is that the American airmen based there had already given up the ghost and evacuated after destroying the air base. The bombers and fighters departed first, followed by the cargo planes of Air Transport Command flying out as much equipment as possible. All the runways had been extensively cratered with 1,000-lb bombs which had had their fuses replaced with plastic explosive attached to detonators. The various air strips were cluttered with over 500 assorted huts and barracks, and each of these was methodically destroyed by standing a can of gasoline on a packing case and firing a bullet into it from the doorway. With their thatched roofs and wooden walls these buildings exploded rather than burned, and all that could be seen afterwards were hundreds of little black squares and rectangles, looking from the air like the smudged charcoal plan of some childish architect. The city itself had also been evacuated, most civilians leaving by road or by crowding into the last trains. There remained the soldiers, some positioned in the old red-light district where the Americans had been wont to take their boozy relaxation. All these establishments were now deserted. "The Central Cafe . . . [had] boarded its doors. The Ledo, the Paramount, the Red Plum, the Lakeside, the Lockchun, all the other happy establishments were closed too; on the boards the departing civilians had pasted patriotic strips in red and black calling for resistance." In the streets soldiers were preparing barricades and machine-gun emplacements, and as they waited for the Japanese to begin their assault, they raided the empty shops and restaurants, stockpiling food and wine inside their positions.

As for coherent resistance, these "last days at Kweilin were sheer fantasy." An attempt was made to call up the Kwangsi militia, disbanded by Chiang in 1939 for fear of an armed uprising, but this soon foundered on an almost total lack of arms or competent officers. Nor was the 'regular' army in much better shape. In the immediate Kweilin region it had all but collapsed. According to White, one division of 14,000 soldiers possessed only 2,000 rifles. When reserves were rushed in from other fronts, they were scattered over 500 square miles of surrounding territory, with no one seeming to possess the authority or the initiative to concentrate them at key points. Many were virtually untrained and few units boasted many competent officers. Ammunition was desperately short, provision having to be made for an amazing variety of antiquated Chinese, Japanese, Russian and German rifles and artillery pieces. "The fifth column was everywhere, and the unsettling gossip and fear of it were worse than the column itself. Behind every soldier was the shadow of a traitor."[16]

In Nationalist China in late 1944, however, the word 'patriotism' had become somewhat otiose. The only rallying-cry the government could offer was simple xenophobia, and it could point to no policies, actual or proposed, that might induce any significant level of popular support. Just as in the army, the state as a whole was plagued by the triple evils of incompetence, elitism and corruption. By 1944, according to Theodore White, most Americans viewed the Chinese with contempt. Most of their contacts were with corrupt government officials and black marketeers and thus they immediately assumed that the whole Chinese people must be similarly venal and grasping. Particularly blatant was the diversion of Lend Lease aid. Pilots became furious and demoralised by knowing that many of their loads were made up of non-essential items such as flashy office equipment and that much else would be diverted immediately into some Chinese official's private *godown* or warehouse. According to another observer, a "large proportion of medical stores were sold straight into the black market . . . [In late 1944] a chemist's shop in Kumming advertised every sulpha drug in the Pharmacopoeia. Each tablet was being sold for ten shillings . . . When I complained to a Government spokesman that I could buy as many sulpha drugs as I could afford at the black market rate, while Chinese soldiers were dying for lack of them, he said that if I could point out the offending shopkeeper he would have him shot. He would indeed. 'Face' would have been saved by his execution, and four or five hundred others would have continued to do a flourishing business."[17]

Indeed corruption was endemic throughout the whole government machine. Inflation was allowed to go unchecked. Workers on the American bases received wages of $25 a day at a time when the Chinese dollar was worth just 0.27 U.S. cents. The bases were built on land bought from its original owners for a mere pittance even though Chiang had already received the money to reimburse them at realistic rates. In the country as a whole inflation increased enormously in the war years. By the end of 1944 the price index of 100 at the beginning of the war in 1937 had risen to a ludicrous 125,000. Exquisite banknotes, specially printed in Brooklyn, were hauled over the Hump, the air supply route from India across the Himalayas, sometimes taking up more than 10 per cent of total tonnage. They were then pumped into the economy at a water torture rate of $5 billion Chinese per month. Even forgetting the terrible blight on general living standards, this inflation greatly impeded the war effort as price rises outstripped budgetary increases by fifteen-fold and more. The ordnance department of the Chinese army found it less expensive to order American copper, brought in over the Hump, than to purchase it from the government's own factories situated only a hundred miles or so from the munitions plants.

Government steel production fell by 80 per cent because army arsenals could not afford to buy the finished steel. Non-government factories were spared this particular problem as one of the Nationalists' anti-inflation measures was to make forced purchases at barely one-third the cost of production. Moreover, "little effort had been made to organise workable transportation, to carry out rationing, or to regulate tax-collecting which through corruption and inefficiency now delivered no more than one third of its revenues to the Central Government."[18]

The Americans seethed impotently as they observed the arrant incompetence and silky avarice all around them. Stilwell, never the most even-tempered of men, who referred to Chiang Kai-shek as the 'Peanut' and to Chungking as the 'Manure Pile', raged in his diary about the "Chinese cesspool. A gang of thugs with the one idea of per-petuating themselves and their machine . . . Cowardice rampant, squeeze paramount, smuggling above duty, colossal ignorance and stupidity of staff, total inability to control factions and cliques, continued oppression of masses." An American captain, after six months in China, wrote home: "I'd like to get a year's leave of absence from the Army to organise a really efficient revolution in this country."[19]

This last remark is interesting. On the one hand, despite its obvious sympathy for the ordinary Chinese, it reveals the racism implicit in much of such criticism and the belief that anything non-American was by definition inefficient, lazy and probably corrupt. Cultural relativism was never an American strong point throughout the Second World War. The remark was especially wide of the mark in suggesting that only outsiders could organise a decent revolution in China. In fact, ever since the 1920s an organised, highly motivated revolutionary movement had existed in the country. This was based around the Chinese Communist Party which, after years of sponsoring failed uprisings in the cities in pursuit of an orthodox Marxist 'proletarian' revolutionary strategy, finally recognised that only the peasantry, comprising more than 90 per cent of the population, could ever be the engine for lasting and far-reaching social and political change.

Certainly they had the grievances to fuel that engine. Even before the Japanese invasion and their manifold depredations, the rural masses were being progressively pauperised. Land *per capita* was steadily declining, and this shortage was relentlessly pushing up prices and rents. Few peasants could afford to keep themselves in the period between sowing and harvesting without borrowing money at penally high rates of interest to tide them over. As prices rose, rent contracts became increasingly short-term, adding to the peasants' sense of chronic insecurity. The small landowner was usually little better off than the tenant. His holding would rarely be more than five acres and in the more densely populated south and west might be as little as one acre. Often these meagre holdings would be divided into scattered strips which the peasant had to walk between to tend each in turn. And for landed and landless alike there was a bewildering variety of local and central taxes that added up to a crushing annual burden. The army requisitioned food, animals and household goods with impunity, and for much of the year the peasants had to live on credit, at savage rates of interest that eventually forced those who owned their land to surrender it to their creditors. "A loan – for seeds, tools, family emergencies – enmeshes the farmer in the web of usury . . . Credit still remains in the hands of the village pawnbrokers and loan sharks – often the same men who are the large landlords. Interest rates run from 30 to 60 per cent a year and higher. Once caught in the grip of the usurers, a man has little chance of getting out."[20]

To feed themselves and scrape together some sort of surplus to fend off these endless extortions, the Chinese peasants literally worked themselves to death. All work was done by hand, using sickles, crude ploughs, flails and stone rollers that had not changed for centuries. Few could afford to maintain draught animals and families spent from dawn till dusk weeding their fragmented plots, fertilising them with their own conserved excreta, sowing, harvesting, and threshing. In the brief twilight the women would cook whatever bare minimum they dare spare for the family's own subsistence, while the men gathered and twisted every wisp of grass to use as fuel or wove together rice straw to make baskets, hats and sandals. All this labour and heartbreak was endured so as to give almost everything one produced to loan-sharks, landlords, merchants and bureaucrats, retaining for oneself only the privilege of having to do it all again next year.

The indefatigable Theodore White visited many such villages in the second half of 1944 and saw for himself the sordid reality of life at humanity's margin. "A poor village – and most of them are poor – is a mass of crumbling yellows and browns. The homes have no ceilings but the raftered roofs; they have no floors but the beaten earth. Their windows are made of greased paper, admitting so little light that the inner recesses are always dim. In his house the peasant stores his grain; in it he keeps his animals at night; in it is the ancestral shrine that he venerates . . . The villages are covered with a blue haze of smoke that curls from each homestead as the evening meals are cooked . . . In the larger villages yellow light may gleam for a few hours from the doorways of the more comfortable, who can afford oil for illumination; but in the smaller villages the smoke fades away into the dark, and when night is come, the village sleeps, with no point of light to break its shadows."[21] In those shadows some peasants succumbed to utter exhaustion while others were denied even sleep as they fretted about taxes and loans due, unmarried daughters, having one's only son and helper pressganged by the army, having to divide a tiny holding among several sons, and the possibility of drought and flood, illness and injury.

All this could only be made worse by the privations of enemy occupation, for no one could ever accuse the Japanese of displaying even a glimmer of enlightenment to those they had conquered. At best they were rapacious, picking clean whole areas in which they were billeted or through which they marched. A Chinese pun on the Japanese word for their army, *kogun*, involved the use of the character for *hungjung*, also meaning an 'army of locusts'. Nevertheless, there were worse things than locusts. When on pacification missions, the Japanese adopted a policy they dubbed the 'Three Alls' – 'Kill All, Burn All, Destroy All'. These 'Alls' meant what they said. In October 1944 a British observer with the Chinese Communists visited a unit of peasant militia stationed in a ruined village on the Shensi–Suiyuan border. Many of the militia had lived in the village until the previous winter when the Japanese had appeared. "So thorough had the Japs been in their destruction of this village that they spent three days there methodically levelling every building . . . Grim-faced survivors told incredible stories of the Japs' bestiality. Women stripped and raped, then tied to trees and used for bayonet practice. Babies were tossed into the air and spitted on bayonets. Boys were drowned slowly by having their heads ducked in and out of the ice-holes in the river."[22] No wonder that another Chinese term for the Japanese was *dongyang kuizi*, or 'fearsome foreign devils'.

Only in the Communist Party, under the leadership of Party Chairman Mao Tse-tung, did the peasantry find a champion to help them fight against the whole host of devils, foreign and home-grown, who plagued their daily lives.[23] Once Mao had finally discredited the urban-fixated, insurrectionary line advocated by an earlier party leader, Li Li-san, he was able to concentrate on his own favoured strategy of gradually building up a secure revolutionary base area in a fairly remote part of the country where party cadres and military leaders could create a guerrilla army. Such an army would at first, perforce, be made up of small poorly-armed peasant units tied to the defence of their own villages. But it was central to Mao's long-term strategy that a small proportion of these self-defence militias would become proficient enough, and capture sufficient arms, to transform themselves into semi-regular units, capable of coming together for pitched battles with enemy forces and preventing them from venturing too far into the base area.

The Communists' struggle had begun long before the Japanese invasion and their first campaigns had been fought against the Chinese Nationalists who acted on the whole as upholders of landlord power. The first experiment with the Maoist line was in the Kiangsi-Fukien Soviet, but this eventually fell to successive Nationalist 'Encirclement Campaigns', and only after retreating from the last of these in the epic Long March of 1934-5 was Mao able to establish a base area sufficiently remote from Nationalist forces. The new base was centred around Yenan, in northern Shensi, and was the headquarters for the so-called Eighth Route Army. It was subdivided into five military regions, centred in the more inaccessible, and feebly administered, border regions of seven northern provinces, from Liaoning (in Manchuria) in the east to Suiyuan in the west, and as far south as Shansi and Shantung. A Chinese Communist report of the time claimed that 50 million people lived in these military regions, of whom 16 million were 'organised' and 1.5 million were members of the local militias. There was also a base area in central China, home of the Communists' New Fourth Army and comprising eight military regions in Anwhei and the provinces that form a ring around it. Here 30 million were said to be under Communist administration but only 5 million were organised with half a million in the militia. This whole area had been weakened by the Japanese offensive in Hunan and Hupei, and elsewhere it contained substantial numbers of pro-Nationalist troops and guerrilla units. In October 1944 the Communists were no stronger here than they had been five years earlier and "the eight military regions . . . were weak in all respects compared to those of North China."[24] What had increased in both bases was the number of regulars, the militiamen who had graduated from part-time local defence – about 20 per cent of their week on average – to full-time uniformed military service. One set of figures suggests that, by the end of 1944, Eighth Route Army and New Fourth Army between them had grown from 470,000 regulars in June to 780,000, while the militia numbers had fallen from 2.1 to 1.7 million. Exactly how much of that increase had taken place by the end of October is unclear but it seems reasonable to assume that regularisation in place of the decline was already afoot.

In October 1944 Communist forces were deployed more to combat possible Japanese incursions than against the Nationalists. During the war years the Communists and Nationalists reached an uneasy accommodation, partly because both wished to see the Japanese driven out but also because neither was really capable of fighting effectively against two completely different enemies. Although clashes between rival Chinese forces were numerous, on the whole they were the result of local antagonisms and the fighting remained parochial and short-lived. Nevertheless, both sides knew that a showdown was inevitable and that it could only be an armed confrontation. Whether it is explained in terms of Mao and Chiang's craving for power, an international communist conspiracy, or the stirrings of a brutally oppressed peasantry, China was in the throes of a civil war that could only have a military resolution. It is this, more than the threat from the Japanese, that explains why the Communists were in the throes of expanding their regular forces, which were to be used to overwhelm the Nationalist armies once the Japanese had finally been defeated.

Mao fully understood that this latter defeat would only take place in the context of the world war, and would be achieved mainly by the American navy and air force. His own military operations against the Japanese remained on a fairly small scale, limited on the whole to local guerrilla operations. The war against Japan he saw as essentially an interim holding operation, and it is surely significant, as one historian has pointed out, that such a keen theoretician of revolutionary warfare and the transition to regular mobile operations as Mao, "wrote no important military articles between 1941 and 1945".[25] His commander-in-chief, Chu Teh, had taken up his pen in 1944, to write a *History of the Red Army's First Army Group*, but he too was at pains to downplay the role of regular forces at this stage of the struggle. At one point he castigated "comrades . . . [who] during the present anti-Japanese war. . . . have not learned conscientiously from past experience . . . some people still try to fight large battles. They do not realise that we should engage in guerrilla warfare and should boldly spread our forces out to win over the masses and increase our strength . . . During the anti-Japanese war, our troops have grown enormously. This is because Chairman Mao has a firm grasp of the relevant matters."[26]

A senior Comintern agent attached to the Yenan headquarters was equally convinced about Mao's firm grasp of the essentials but he was scathing in his assessment of what these actually were. In his diary for 14th October he wrote: "The country's split is the main reason behind Japanese success . . . In the enemy's success Mao Tse-tung sees a factor which undermines the power of Chiang Kai-shek . . . Chiang Kai-shek must be weakened by any means. This is the essence of the policy of the CCP leadership. And let the Japanese seize Chinese land and burn towns!"[27]

Some contemporary accounts emphasise the small-scale guerrilla nature of Communist tactics in 1944. According to Theodore White, the regulars were sometimes employed but they only "operated in bands of three to four hundred men" and "could not challenge any important Japanese garrison post or Japanese control of the railways system defended by earthworks and heavy armament. Though they could blunt a Japanese spearhead or turn it aside, they could not stop it . . . [Usually] the Communists fought when they had the opportunity to surprise a very small group of the enemy and to capture more than enough rifles and ammunition to make up what they spent in the fray." A U.S. War Department analysis, describing the Communist guerrilla movement as it existed in October 1944, noted that as soon as they came under pressure "the Communist troops usually retreated before the Japanese [and] few actual battles were fought . . . It was not the Communist armies that suffered so much as the people who were left prey to Japanese vengeance."[28]

According to a British observer, the lowliest type of operation made up what was known as 'sparrow warfare'. "Like sparrows they were everywhere, picking off a Jap here and a puppet there. A straggler behind a column of Japs on the march would be quickly dispatched by a knife in the hand of an innocent-looking [passer-by] . . . A handful of shots fired from ambush would kill two and wound three, the ambushers then scattering so as to afford no target for revenge."[29] A refinement of this was 'segmented worm' warfare where the retreating ambush party dropped off a few of its members at each of the villages it passed through, with the Japanese told helpfully by the peasants that the whole party had just sped through. Eventually the Japanese would realise that they were now pursuing no guerrillas at all and wearily retrace their steps, only to be ambushed once again by the reconstituted 'worm'.

Even so, it is important to realise that such guerrilla actions, as well as others on a somewhat larger scale, were happening all the time and it did not take too long to establish a respectable cumulative balance-sheet of victories. An American journalist who operated with the guerrillas in 1944, in the eighth sub-region of the north-west Shansi liberated area, described this mountainous base as roughly circular, with a radius of about 40 miles and a population of some 200,000. Of these, 20,000 in all bore arms and about 5,000 were uniformed regulars. Opposed to them were "6,000 Japanese and over 3,000 puppets, stationed in two fair-sized towns and over 100 blockhouse forts on its periphery. This is a typical situation. Throughout North China the Japanese are trying to cut the Communist-led pockets into ever smaller pockets, and finally to eliminate them, by driving lines of small forts – two or three miles apart – through them." In the three weeks this reporter was with the guerrillas he calculated that they had destroyed three blockhouses, attacked a small town, killed 70 or 80 Japanese and captured two alive, and seized sufficient arms to equip two companies. The Communists, he reckoned, were three-quarters equipped with "captured Japanese rifles, machine-guns, mortars, blankets, ammunition belts and other kit." Obviously these tallies required more than just 'segmented worms' and our reporter described how these were combined with a few larger, set-piece attacks into a strategy of 'offensive blockade-smashing', in which the Communists sought to immobilise most of the blockading units and isolate and destroy a selected few. Whenever any Japanese did issue forth from one of the towns or larger blockhouses, the regulars would disperse to the periphery of the area attacked, leaving the Japanese no identifiable military objective. The non-regulars, "by evacuating villages of all food and by constant harassment [would] reverse their . . . role of keeping the enemy tied down, and instead try to keep him constantly on the move. When the Japanese begin to withdraw to the periphery, the regular Eighth Route forces concentrate again and try to isolate and destroy at least one of their columns."[30]

The other main targets for larger attacks were the more vulnerable of the blockhouses which had become the favoured Japanese counter-insurgency measure. They had, in fact, always used them for guarding railway lines and bridges and to form an outer defence line around larger cities, but by the autumn of 1944 they had become a basic element of a strategy that allowed slow leap-frogging from one defensive line to the next. At the same time they chopped base areas into ever smaller segments, too small to hide the guerrillas and each corner of which could mutually support the others. A typical block-house was a circular building about 20 feet in diameter and 25 feet high, built of stone, mud and bricks, and bristling with loopholes for rifles and machine guns. Attached were the garrison's quarters, usually built underground. The whole structure would be erected on commanding ground and ringed by rifle-trenches and, beyond them, deep ditches up to 15 feet wide crossed by drawbridges. Sweeps from these block-houses were divided into two types, known as 'shaving hair' and 'combing hair'. The former, known to the Chinese as 'village purging', involved the arrest and relocation of villagers, with butchery a common extra option, and the destruction of the village itself. This was especially popular at harvest time, to deny future supplies to the enemy. 'Combing hair' involved broad front advances by groups of about twenty Japanese, with the groups spaced so that they could quickly converge and encircle any guerrillas they flushed out.

The blockhouse system only worked efficiently if the Japanese could move outside them from time to time to patrol the intervening areas and to extend the system out further. The Chinese, of course, were keen to deny such opportunities and to keep the garrisons locked up in their own little prisons. In this they were extremely successful, partly through sniping and noisy diversionary activity at night to keep the defenders on edge, but mainly through laying minefields all round these miniature fortresses. The mines – also used to defend Chinese villages – were a basic weapon at this stage of the war and were manufactured mostly by the Chinese themselves. One observer "saw men, women and children at work making black powder, casting mine-moulds, and piling up loaded mines in neat heaps. Because of a shortage of metal . . . some . . . were hollowing out big rocks to make stone mines; others were filling bottles, jugs, even teapots."[31] Another stated that the Chinese had first become interested in mines in 1942, and by late 1944 "had lifted mine warfare almost to the level of an indigenous national sport." Peasants were encouraged to bring in whatever scrap metal they could and in return received the equivalent weight in empty shells to fill with home-made black powder. They made the fuses themselves and, he confirmed, "if metal was lacking, they made mines out of porcelain, logs or rock." Around the villages the mines were laid each night and removed in the morning. A single pathway would be left clear, which changed each night and was known only to a few village elders. "The Communist newspapers . . . encouraged the villagers' ingenuity with every propaganda trick conceivable, even to publicising local 'mine heroes' the way American sports writers nominate home-run kings."[32]

Here, then, was a quite remarkable type of army. Comparable in many ways to Tito's Yugoslav Partisans, it had been built from nothing and was now holding down an appreciable number of enemy divisions. Not their best perhaps, but by October 1944 the Japanese were obliged to deploy ten divisions from three separate armies to contain and to harass the Communist-liberated areas. Whatever the ultimate ambitions of the Party leadership in building up their guerrilla bands and uniformed regiments, it is difficult not to feel a great deal of admiration for the rank-and-file who fought so long and so hard against a barbarous enemy. And they did not have the Yugoslavs' consolation of seeing the enemy in full retreat from their country. Their own villages were still at the mercy of the Japanese, and if they knew anything of events elsewhere in the country it would be only that to the south the Japanese were freely advancing through province after province. Yet they fought on. One American observer provided two vignettes that perfectly encapsulated their mood of determined self-sacrifice and patient stoicism. One featured a grizzled Eighth Route Army regular who made clear that even their most sophisticated operations were fought with none of the materiel and firepower that were *de rigueur* on battlefields elsewhere. "We . . . feel like wrestlers in a never-ending contest. Because we have no rear base to supply us with the wherewithal to fight, we must always be on the initiative to search out the enemy's weak spots so as to attack these for weapons and supplies. Moreover, offence is the best defence. But when the enemy concentrates and we find ourselves hard-pressed, we merely melt away. In battle we fight mostly at night, using bayonets and grenades, since our weapons are inferior and ammunition extremely scarce." The soldier, part of Mao Tse-tung's elite forces, went on, "We fight the enemy, too, with propaganda, hand-bills [and] shouting campaigns . . ."

A little later this journalist visited a Chinese village where a small group of regulars were helping to train about a thousand militia from other villages round about. They were "an unforgettable sight, with their very mixed assortment of arms, including red-tasselled spears and broadswords, shotguns, blunderbusses, flintlocks, landmines, battered old rifles, and Chinese-made Tommy-guns [with] no more than a handful of bullets for each . . . The quaintest of the weapons was the wooden artillery. I saw a whole company . . . heaving their home-made cannons on their shoulders. The cannon of three-inch bore were made of elm logs about three feet long and twelve inches in diameter. In action they were loaded with scrap iron, stones, or anything at hand, and fired by a matchlock mechanism tripped by a long string."[33]

Revolution, Mao had written, grew out of the barrel of a gun. One can quite see why, in October 1944, he was prepared to bide his time.

*

Discussion of the war in China so far has necessarily been in very general terms, attempting to assess the progress of a major military offensive in the south and a burgeoning war of national liberation in the north. Yet individuals, too, had their part to play in October 1944. General Stilwell openly despised Chiang Kai-shek, his government and the Chinese ruling elite. Chiang, in his turn, had long resented Stilwell's insistence on deploying the best Chinese divisions outside the country, his effort to minimise unnecessary luxuries carried over the 'Hump', and above all his lack of proper deference to Chiang's authority, such as it was. Whenever possible he had voiced his criticisms of Stilwell to visiting Americans, the latest being General Patrick Hurley, Roosevelt's personal representative, who had arrived in Chungking in September. When the visit began, Roosevelt was still a keen supporter of Stilwell, strongly advocating that he be made commander-in-chief of all Chinese forces, including the Communists. In mid-September he sent Chiang a stern telegram, of which Stilwell was the delighted bearer, lambasting Chiang's latest threat to withdraw his divisions behind the Salween. The rebuke was a terrible slap in the face for Chiang, especially as he knew other Americans would also have seen it. Stilwell was certainly exultant and in a letter to his wife was moved to verse:

> The little bastard shivered
> And lost the power of speech.
> His face turned green and quivered
> As he struggled not to screech.

However, while Chiang could not afford to flout Roosevelt's wishes entirely, he was determined to save face by standing up to the Americans. Especially irritating was the lofty counsel that he should reinforce and press on with "your Salween armies . . . while at once placing General Stilwell in unrestricted command of all your forces".[34] Instead he determined that Stilwell must go and hammered away at this point during his talks with Hurley. By 5th October, Roosevelt was weakening, asking only that Stilwell be allowed to retain command of the Burma divisions. But Chiang was not to be gainsaid, and on 19th October Roosevelt pulled the plug, offering no further objections to Stilwell being removed not just from his Chungking post but also from those with the CBI and with SEAC. These various hats were to be distributed among different commanders but even before they arrived to take up their posts Stilwell had already left China.

Referring to himself as "a fugitive from a Chiang gang", Stilwell was flown first to Kumming, then to Paoshan (the Y Force headquarters), Myitkyina and Remargh to make brief farewells. On the 25th he was in Delhi, awaiting transport back to the United States. In some undated notes thought to have been written that day, Stilwell accepted that his relief was ordered "for good and sufficient reasons", given that he was now "persona non grata" with the Chinese government. He regretted, however, both the failure of his government to back him in his arguments with Chiang and its refusal to face military realities in China. He especially deplored the decision to "give the bulk of the [Hump] tonnage to the Fourteenth Air Force and to depend on the Chinese ground forces to protect our bases. I argued that as soon as the Japs felt the effect of an [air] attack from bases in China, they would stage an attack to take the bases from us, and that the Chinese troops available were not competent to prevent it. This opinion was not accepted by the Combined Chiefs of Staff. We have now lost all our bases east of Kumming and have nothing to show for all the effort and expense involved."

On the lack of effective support from his masters back home, Stilwell simply wrote: "The trouble was largely one of posture. I tried to stand on my feet instead of my knees. I did not think the knee position was a suitable one for Americans."[35]

42

The Chindwin and the Burma Road

FOURTEENTH ARMY IN BURMA

WHEN the Japanese declared war in December 1941 their first concern was to destroy American naval power in the Pacific, both the Fleet itself at Pearl Harbor and the various other naval bases in the Central Pacific and the Philippines from which any surviving battleships and aircraft carriers might operate. They were also determined to make a clean sweep of western imperialism in Asia, and by early May 1942 they had driven the Dutch out of the East Indies and the British from Malaya and Burma. In Indo-China the pro-Vichy mainly French regime had already been prevailed upon, after a 48-hour war in September 1940, to accept the presence of 40,000 Japanese 'guests'. Despite their peremptory eviction, however, the western Allies remained keenly interested in South-East Asia, though their motives differed significantly. The British were interested above all in regaining their imperial prestige, along with possession of the lost rubber plantations, oil wells and the like. The Americans, on the other hand, were extremely hostile to old-fashioned European colonialism. Although they supported a renewed British invasion of Burma, that was only because the country offered the most obvious route for pushing through supplies to China.

These differing perspectives on the war in Burma involved British and American planners in numerous arguments, and relations between them were hardly ameliorated by the local American commander, General Joseph Stilwell, who had a deep loathing for the 'Limeys' and all their works. Nevertheless, even though American eyes were usually turned northwards to the 'Hump' and the 'Burma Road' and British ones south towards the Yenangyaung oilfields and Rangoon, both countries were agreed on the necessity of supporting a significant

military presence in Burma, a presence that would have to be supplied
via the British Raj in India.

Because of its logistical significance, not to mention its imperial
lustre, India became the object of Japanese attentions. They eventually
determined upon military conquest, and in March 1944, only a month
or so before the monsoon season began, they set forth on the
grotesquely overweening U GO offensive, or 'March on Delhi', in the
course of which it was confidently expected that three divisions,
crossing the Chindwin with supplies for only 14 days, would seize the
Imphal–Dinapur road, clear Assam, and then swiftly prise out the jewel
in Britain's imperial crown. Savage battles were fought at Imphal and
Kohima and General William Slim's Fourteenth Army was often hard-
pressed to find and funnel in reserve units. Nevertheless, British and
Indian troops resolutely refused to cave in as the Japanese had clearly
expected, and by the end of June the invaders had conceded defeat,
finally receiving the Emperor's permission to withdraw on 2nd July.
This retreat soon became the Japanese Army's own Death March, in
which two of the divisions involved, 15 and 31 Infantry, were reduced
to a starving, disease-ridden, traumatised rabble, and only the third, 33
Infantry, often travelling by road instead of barely perceptible jungle
tracks, was able to maintain any sort of cohesion or offer any significant
rearguard resistance.[1]

Slim, with his troops now convinced of their superiority over the
Japanese and of their ability to master jungle warfare, decided to press
the pursuit of the retreating Japanese right through the monsoon,
which ran from April to October, and to push them back across the
River Chindwin. The pursuit was to employ only a minimum of troops
so that in the meantime Slim could rest and train his other divisions
to be ready for the main offensive across the Chindwin. This assault,
known as Operation CAPITAL, would begin after the monsoon and
was intended to clear the central plain between the Chindwin and
the Irrawaddy. It had the full backing of Slim's immediate superior,
General Sir George Giffard, commanding 11th Army Group in
Delhi, and Vice-Admiral Louis Mountbatten, at the head of the inter-
Allied South-East Asia Command (SEAC) in Ceylon.

The Americans were less enamoured of such a drive southwards,
which clearly looked beyond the Chindwin-Irrawaddy confluence to
Mekteila, Yenangyaung and Rangoon. Nevertheless, at the OCTAGON
Conference in Quebec, in September, they approved the development
of CAPITAL and even a proposed amphibious assault on Rangoon
(Operation DRACULA) in January 1945. In October, because of the

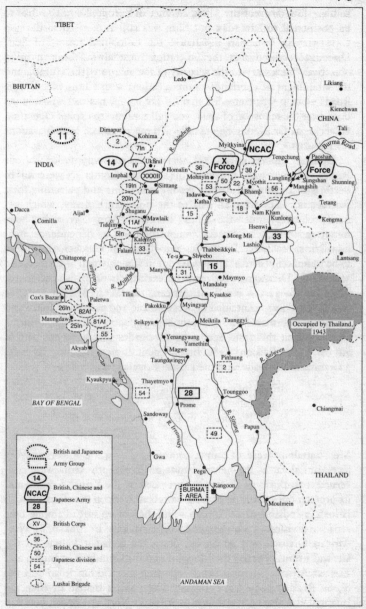

The War in Burma 25th October 1944

sudden slow-down of the Allied advance in Europe, DRACULA had to be postponed to late 1945 but Slim was still authorised to develop CAPITAL. At American insistence, the Combined Chiefs of Staff Directive required that the Operation must always bear in mind objectives "necessary to the security of the air route [the Hump], and the attainment of overland communications with China [the Burma Road]", but it was conceded that "if DRACULA has to be postponed until after the monsoon of 1945, you will continue to exploit Operation CAPITAL as far as may be possible without prejudice to preparations for DRACULA."[2]

By late October, however, CAPITAL was still only notional. Four British divisions were already in the field but another six were still in north-west Burma and Assam, resting, retraining and patrolling their perimeters. They were all part of the Fourteenth Army, which felt itself to be very much the Allies' 'Forgotten Army'. What has been forgotten, in fact, is its racial composition and its dependence upon non-British soldiery. In Burma and Assam in October 1944 were to be found ten 'British' Divisions, but in fact only two of these, 2 and 36 Infantry Divisions, were made up exclusively of British battalions, while all the rest – one East African, two West African and five Indian divisions – contained between 70 and 100 per cent African and Indian infantrymen.[3] The total number of infantry battalions in Burma and Assam at this time, including 3 brigades that were not part of any of these divisions (286 Independent Indian Infantry Brigade, 3 Commando Brigade, and the Lushai Brigade), is as follows:

British infantry battalions	39
Indian infantry battalions	56
E. and W. African infantry battalions	28
TOTAL	123

Most battalions were, of course, commanded by white officers at every level, but as far as the fighting units of Fourteenth Army were concerned, two-thirds of them were provided by the British Empire and its protectorates. Only 35 of these battalions were on the offensive – 10 British, 7 Indian and 18 African – and these were spread among four separate divisions, each pursuing a different axis. In Arakan, 81 West African Division was advancing down the Kaladan Valley; on the Central Front, between the Manipur and the Chindwin, 5 Indian and 11 East African Divisions were following the Tiddim Road and the Tamu Road (Kabaw Valley) respectively; and a British division, 36 Infantry, had also been attached to Stilwell's Northern Front, between the upper Irrawaddy and the Chinese border, and was pressing down from Mohnyin, along the 'Railway Corridor'.

The prime aim of Stilwell's front, the Northern Combat Area Command, was to push Japanese forces, comprising their Thirty-third Army, southward so that work could go ahead on opening up the final stretch of the Burma Road between the Irrawaddy and the Salween rivers via Bhamo and Namkhan. Slim was also interested in harrying the Japanese southwards, in his case Fifteenth Army, but he had more ambitious ulterior motives. Whereas the Americans wanted only to keep the Japanese away from the supply route into China, the British, especially Slim, were looking to clear the west banks of the Chindwin and the Myittha so as to form the start line for their concerted offensive to sweep the Japanese right out of Burma. Operations in Arakan were also governed by this master plan. Just as on the Central Front, 81 W. African Division's push into the Kaladan Valley was meant as a preparatory move, intended to secure the north-eastern flank of a later, much bigger offensive against Akyab, itself intended to seize base areas for supplying the main drive on Rangoon, once this outran its lines of communication through Assam. Though Slim's autumn operations in Burma may look fairly penny-packet on the map, and are indeed often overlooked in many histories, they nevertheless constituted an essential preparatory phase of a clear and carefully considered offensive strategy. For uppermost in Slim's mind ever since the humiliating retreat from Burma in 1942 was the firm conviction that all roads, valleys and corridors led back, eventually, to Rangoon.

It was for this reason that Slim always regarded the Central Front as the most important, and had now commited two of his four divisions to it. Their mission was to clear the mountainous corridor between the Manipur and the Chindwin, with 5 Indian Division following the road through Tiddim to Kalemyo and 11 E. African Division the trail through the Kabaw Valley, just inside Burma, towards Kalewa. The East Africans were also expected to clear potential bridgehead sites on the west bank of the Chindwin at Sittaung and Mawlaik. This twin drive began in earnest in early August and both divisions pressed slowly forward, averaging about two miles per day along flooded jungle and mountain trails in the drenching monsoon. There were no significant battles as such, rather a series of small Japanese rearguard actions and ambushes. Much of the story is summed up in this account of a firefight by a signals officer with 5 Indian Division:

> The Japanese . . . fought a delaying action all the way, holding up
> our advance at various points and then withdrawing. He waited

concealed in trenches commanding the road, fired upon our leading patrol to kill or wound several good men, whereupon, if the remainder of the company could not drive back this enemy party, artillery would batter the spot with what restricted ammunition the parachute supply detail allowed us to expend. When opposition was very stiff, Hurricanes would be summoned to bomb and strafe in their excellent and triumphant manner; as a result, more often than not, our probing infantry section, at morrow's first light, would find the block empty, the enemy having departed in darkness to take up fresh places from which to halt our progress and inflict as many casualties as he could.[4]

In late August, 5 Indian Division crossed over into Burma itself and between 16th and 20th September, its leading troops crossed the Manipur river. In early October the notorious 'Chocolate Staircase' was outflanked and on the 17th Indian troops moved into Tiddim, already evacuated by the Japanese. The 'Chocolate Staircase', with Tiddim at its summit, climbed 3,000 feet in seven miles, around 38 precipitous hairpin bends. It was called 'Chocolate' because in the monsoon the golden-coloured dust turned into dark brown mud.

From Tiddim the road zig-zagged sharply on its way to Kalewa, with two almost right-angle bends north of Kennedy Peak and east of Fort White. The first of these had been dubbed 'Vital Corner', and it was here that the division's leading troops were held up by fierce Japanese rearguards on the 25th. A strong attack was put in that day, but even after a sustained preliminary artillery bombardment and Hurricane attacks, the battalions involved were unable to make much headway. Of the division's other brigades, the 9th was still some way behind down the Tiddim road, while 161 Brigade continued pushing southwards off the main road, attempting to outflank Kennedy Peak by rejoining the road just to the south of Fort White.

As for 11 E. African Division, advancing from Tamu to Kalewa, its lead units pushed through the Kabaw Valley whilst one brigade veered off towards the bridgehead sites at Sittaung and Mawlaik. The first was taken without a fight but not Mawlaik which, after a failed attack by 21 E. African Brigade, on 20th October, was still holding out in most determined fashion five days later. The rest of the division had fared somewhat better. The only significant stand along the main Kabaw Valley axis had been at Yazagyo and on the whole the division made slow but steady progress so that by 25th October it was only twenty miles or so from Kalemyo.

However, the enemy was not the only problem facing Allied troops in Burma. Just as in almost every other theatre, climate and terrain were equally implacable foes. In Assam and Burma the troops had to grapple with the jungle, the monsoon and the intense heat. The jungle greatly inhibited mobility, confining troops to the few roads and narrow tracks, yet denying them the ability to concentrate forces for a full-scale attack. Although the monsoon was almost at an end by mid-October, its effects were still very evident. The relentless rain that had fallen for weeks and months on end, turned all the roads and tracks to little rivers of mud. In the thickest parts of the jungle they took months to dry out, and in more open stretches the 110°F temperatures only served to dry out the surface while preserving all the deep ruts and holes created in the molten phase.

An officer with 11 E. African Division described the still muddy sections of the trail into which men "plunged their squelching boots, got stuck, gripped trees and pulled, and floundered on after the column. To march in deep mud while carrying a heavy pack is to find out just how strong you are. It cannot be called marching; it is more a form of wading, or hopping from one firm point to another until you slip, or hop quicker than your eye, when you flounder. The askaris [African troops] cut bamboo sticks and used them as a sort of crutch, and laboriously the column moved forward." Even where the trail was drying out, the easier going underfoot was more than counterbalanced by the blazing sun overhead. "Salt tablets are an issue to the men and these are taken with plenty of water. Without replacement of lost salts and fluid comes heat exhaustion accompanied by high temperature and quite often death. The exhaustion that comes to marching infantry who have ... [endured such] sharp, eye-searing heat, is something that troops do not talk much about ... As they march they tighten this strap, loosen that belt, shift that weight just a little and stare with a dulled fascination at the glistening neck of the man in front."[5]

Most wheeled traffic soon found the going almost impossible, with roads only kept open by dint of the ceaseless labours of engineer and pioneer units, though these were in short supply in the Far East. During the advance down the Tiddim and Tamu roads it was found that there were only sufficient engineer resources to keep one of these routes open. On the Tiddim Road 5 Indian Division could only allow the surface to collapse behind it, under the ravages of the monsoon, and had to rely for supply, reinforcement and evacuation almost entirely on air transport. Usually supply drops had to be parachuted into small jungle clearings, but occasionally a whole landing strip was carved out, on which light aircraft and gliders could come down. The gliders were also used to evacuate casualties, who were hooked up off the ground by Dakotas flying very low overhead.

In 11 E. African Division each brigade had its own composite platoon from the Service Corps. A typical drop for a brigade would be done by 15 to 20 Dakotas over a period of days. "An air-dropping zone that has been in operation for a few days looks like a laundryman's nightmare. Hundreds of snow-white parachutes festoon the trees and litter the ground. The white canvas containers for the supplies lie everywhere . . . The collected mass of stores is an amazing sight . . . [including] petrol, Jeep engines, hand grenades, Penicillin, Mepacrine, blankets, rum rations, and twenty-five pounder shells . . . [which] come down with loaves of bread, marrows and onions."[6] Stacking and loading this mass of materiel was not the only chore. If a parachute had snagged in a tree it was often necessary to cut the whole tree down as climbing up after the loads invited the attentions of Japanese snipers. The supply platoon often had cause to curse the airmen, some of whom scattered their drops over wide areas, but then they had problems of their own. The unloading was carried out by men who stood in the doorway of the plane and kicked the containers out. Finding enough men to do this was a perennial problem and "volunteers, British and Indian, were called for to augment the numbers. It was not an easy task . . . Extreme care had to be taken that the loaders did not accompany the article which they pushed out of the aircraft, and tragedies sometimes occurred with inexperienced men."[7]

Nevertheless, the Tiddim Road was not entirely closed to traffic. Due almost entirely to the already legendary jeep, which seemed able to perform the vehicular equivalent of walking on water, limited amounts of essential supplies and equipment were carried and towed forward. Artillery received a high priority and on the 25th, 129 Mountain Regiment was being hauled into position to support the attack towards Vital Corner and Kennedy Peak. The journey proved to be a 'nerve-wracking test . . . negotiating about ten miles of what must have been one of the most treacherous tracks in the world. The narrow ledge, not much more than a footpath, was in places hardly wide enough for a jeep, but by building up a little at these parts the necessary clearance was obtained. Falls of rock, too, added to the ordeal and a wrong step or a side-slip meant a drop of many hundreds of feet . . . The gun, mounted on a 'jury axle' . . . was pulled by a jeep, the No. 1 walking in front and the remainder of the detachment in rear, their job being to steady the carriage by means of the muzzle."[8]

What most singled out Burma from all the other battlefronts of the Second World War was the threat of disease. Indeed, the country was probably one of the most unwholesome spots on earth in which to fight a war. One brigade of 5 Indian division lost just 9 men killed and 85 wounded but in 26 days suffered a further 507 casualties from sickness. Figures for the theatre as a whole for October 1944 are even more dramatic, with a total of 49,195 hospital admissions for disease (excluding venereal) as opposed to only 602 for battle wounds. On the Tiddim and Tamu roads two diseases predominated, malaria and scrub typhus. Just what caused malaria was at that time still somewhat unclear, though it had been established that the disease was transmitted from sufferer to potential victim by the mosquito. These thrived in Burma, and "in the Kabaw Valley . . . we noticed that the large and voracious mosquitoes started to search for blood at five o'clock in the evening when it was still quite light. They were so hungry they could not wait for night, as most mosquitoes usually do, but came humming about with a persistence that was quite surprising." Various solutions were tried. To avoid being bitten men applied repellent creams and were required to sleep under mosquito nets, and on occasion even perform sentry duty draped in them. At night, sleeves had to be rolled down, shirts tucked in, and long trousers and puttees worn. To suppress the symptoms of the disease, if one was bitten, all soldiers were required to take one tablet of mepacrine each night. These yellow tablets were a substitute for quinine, unobtainable since the Japanese occupied Java, and had the unfortunate side-effect of also turning the face yellow. This wore off after a few days and was a fairly small price to pay given that, as an officer with 11 E. African Division commented, "it is possible that mepacrine kept the advance going down the Kabaw Valley."[9]

Another tactic employed against the mosquito was to kill them, which became feasible with the appearance of DDT, first used on a large scale in Naples in 1943. Just how much of it was available in the Far East in October 1944 is not clear, and neither is the frequency with which it was sprayed, whether by the troops themselves or by the light aircraft that eventually became a common sight. DDT was also an excellent weapon (at least, in theory) against the other main carrier of disease, the rat-borne mite that caused scrub typhus. This disease, also known as Japanese river fever, incapacitated men for up to three weeks, either in a high fever or a low-temperature torpor, and was sometimes fatal. The mite and its host thrived in the uplands between the Imphal and the Central Burmese, or Shwebo, Plains and they wreaked havoc right through October 1944. One British battalion, in 5 Indian Brigade, saw no less than 18 per cent of its strength go down with the disease in two months, while in 11 E. African Division 900 cases were recorded during the passage of the Kabaw Valley.

Another disgusting hazard were the leeches that abounded throughout the jungle and pertinaciously "crept up nostrils, into ears, and even entered the penis . . . They squeezed through the lace holes of boots, and their presence only became known when blood squelched out. They battened on to their victims until they were four or five inches long. As many as one hundred had to be removed each day . . . [and they] injected a liquid into the wound which prevented clotting and the diamond-shaped marks quickly turned into maggot-infested sores."[10]

In the Railway Corridor, 36 Division had taken over from a Chindit brigade, just south of Mohaung, in the second half of July and had slowly pressed forward to Pingshaw and Mohnyin. They then picked up the pace considerably and by the 25th were on the outskirts of Mawlu, where the Japanese had elected to stage one of their periodic delaying actions. The going was as tough as elsewhere, and their path "lay through tall teak forests, swamp and flooded rivers . . . Every village liberated by the Allies was found desolate. Many had long since been abandoned by their inhabitants and were overgrown with weeds and 10-foot elephant grass." The monsoon was just about over by then but this region was "one of the most heavily drenched on earth [and still] oxen were lost in mud-holes, and mules fell asleep from exhaustion as they walked."[11] The deserted villages proved to be perfect breeding-grounds for the mites and rats that spread scrub typhus and the whole region was endemically malarial. In October a remarkable 541 cases of the disease were evacuated from the division to the nearest Forward Treatment Unit. Scrub typhus, dysentery and infective hepatitis also reached near peak levels during this month, with a sharp rise towards the last ten days or so.

Like the troops on the Tiddim and Tamu roads, 36 Division was largely supplied by air, though its supply echelon was also able to derive some advantage from the eponymous railway that ran along its axis of advance. As soon as they had hit the northern end of the corridor, some American engineers attached to the division "fitted flanged wheels on a couple of jeeps and set them at either end of a line of trucks to pull and push a 'jeep train'. One of the sights on this railway was to see [the divisional commander, General Frank] Festing, a six-foot-four-and-a-half giant, acting as engine-driver of his own headquarters train by driving the fore jeep."[12] Both troops and equipment were moved forward on this railway and British engineer units were already busy cobbling together two locomotives, 'Windsor Castle' and 'Lancaster Castle', from salvaged Burma Railway wagons, British engines and Japanese gearboxes. Festing was a remarkable character, in or out of a train, and was usually to be found driving a jeep at breakneck speed "or tramping through the jungle aided by a stick almost as tall as himself. He always carried an American carbine. He wore enormous American Ranger boots, an Australian bush hat, a fur-lined Air Force leather jacket when it was cold, and anything when it was hot . . . He hates books on war or by women, but reads *The Scottish Minstrel Over the Border* every night. Nearly always, a prodigious pipe, in keeping with the man, dangles out of his mouth."[13]

In Arakan, on the western coast of Burma, there were four Indian and African divisions, but only one of them, 81 W. African, was on the move in October. Its task was to advance down the Kaladan Valley and clear XV Corps' flank for a subsequent offensive that would open up logistical bases for an alternative supply route to Slim's main advance in 1945.[14] By late October the division was advancing along three separate axes, having just crossed the Indian frontier on the 18th, and with a preliminary objective of Paletwa. Only two of the division's three brigades were involved. The other, 3 W. African Brigade, was the Chindit formation that had been relieved by 36 Division and it was now enjoying a well-deserved rest.

A typical day's advance along the Kaladan, given by one of 81 Division's officers, highlights the extreme caution with which all units in Burma inched forward and the absolute importance of vigorous patrol activity. He himself was in command of a patrol sent out from one of the advanced platoon areas and with his men "advanced cautiously along the tracks by the river; here again was the curse of jungle-fighting: there was only one track beside the river, the jungle being so thick it was impossible to move apart from along the track. As a result, ambushes were to be expected at any turn of the path. No noise was made – this indeed was the secret of patrol work in the deep jungle country. After a three hours march in the heat of the morning sun, the patrol, soaked with perspiration, approached . . . [a village]. The door of each hut was kicked open and the huts were found to be empty. The village was unoccupied . . . [We] withdrew from the village and decided it was time to have lunch, which consisted of tea and bully. A fire was lit in a small opening so that no smoke would be shown, and a pot of 'char' was brewed. Villages in Burma were places to be avoided at all costs, owing to the fact that a force in a village is easily surprised, thus the reason for getting out as quickly as possible."[15]

If 81 Division's progress down the Kaladan Valley was not much different from that of any of the other divisions on the move in Burma in late October, its composition and customs set it clearly apart from other British, Indian and even E. African formations, and emphasise how conventional depictions of the 'British' Army in the Second World War fail to portray just what an enormously variegated institution it was. For a start, almost all the soldiers were black, with individual battalions recruited exclusively in the Gold Coast, Nigeria, the Gambia and Sierra Leone. Indeed, on 25th October, most of the officers were also black because in the field the British officers would smear their faces with a greasy black compound they carried in a compact tin box. According to one officer: "White faces were rather over-conspicuous among Africans. Much better targets than the whites of eyes."[16]

Another striking feature of the division was the way officers and men communicated with each other. Because of the proliferation of languages and dialects, the *lingua franca* was English, but of a pidgin variety that would have remained largely impenetrable to most British battalions. The same officer, in the novel *Three Rivers to Glory*, based upon his experiences along the Kaladan, provides us with a snatch of pidgin in a section of interior monologue during a gruelling march. The Africans involved had just drunk deep of the river-water without first adding their water-purification tablets. "The first of the . . . Africans had dropped out half-way up the crest of the preceding hill. He had had belly palaver for quite an hour now. It was hum-bugging him too-much. Then others got it. Belly belongem no good. One by one . . . they fell out of the column. Their legs no agree for walk. Their bellies done hurtem plenty. They no savvy why they shiver, they no savvy this fever. Captains gone too far. Amadu, Sedeku, Fode, all you men go tell captain we no fit for march, we sick."[17]

Obviously race was the crucial dividing line in the division, with all authority residing with the white officers. Still, the Africans themselves were hardly a homogeneous whole and along with their various clan and tribal loyalties there was a fundamental schism between the 'bush men' and the 'savvy men'. The latter were the "products of the missionaries and the Government schools, and their smug, glossy conceit when it came to a comparison of themselves with the up-country bushmen" was most distasteful to many of the officers.[18] The division was not above exploiting the schism, letting the bush men work as porters in the so-called 'Aux. Group'. Essentially these were the native bearers beloved of many an exotic Rider Haggard or Rice Burroughs movie, and were a priceless asset for a division with no motor transport and almost entirely dependent on air drops. For 81 Division, these drops were computed in 'head loads'. Once again, Sidney Butterworth's novel gives us a splendid picture of these men on the march, beginning with the musings of a Corps press officer who has just suggested that the West Africans have cut their trail through to the Kaladan

> like charging bulls, with their heads down . . . [He] then corrected himself. Not like charging bulls. Because their heads were up. All their stores were head-loaded by a freak part of the Division called the Aux. Group. He saw hundreds of them setting out, in single file, with food, ammo, office stores, medical supplies, all carried on their heads. What was comical was their hats on top of the pile. It made them look like the 8-ft. giants you saw in carnival processions, with huge wobbly heads. They walked as gracefully as ballroom professionals and erect as kings. Yet somehow, too, they moved like sleep-walkers, for although their heads were high their eyelids seemed closed as they watched where they put their feet.[19]

One other force should be mentioned in this account of 11th Army Group's fragmented advance in Burma in October 1944. The independent Lushai Brigade was operating on the western side of the River Manipur, and by 25th October it had penetrated somewhat further south than the adjoining 5 Indian Division, and had lead units near the villages of Falam and Haka. These settlements belonged to the Chins, a small but warlike people who provided the Brigade with its most mobile contingent. Its total complement was three regular Indian battalions and part of another, as well as the Chin Hills Battalion, also known as the Chin Levies. In theory the whole formation was supposed to be a guerrilla-type force for, according to Slim, "as an orthodox infantry brigade it left something to be desired. There had been very little indeed in the way of equipment or transport to give it; its signals were improvised, it had neither engineers nor artillery."[20] But this very lack of equipment, it was felt, should make the brigade that much more mobile. Indeed stories were told of these units moving up to twelve and fifteen miles in a day.

According to the British commander of the Chin battalion, however, it was his men alone who provided real hit-and-run mobility and his memoirs are positively indignant about the sluggishness of the Indian battalions, and of brigade headquarters which remained ensconced in Aijal even after the Chins had set up their own HQ south of Falam. Lieutenant-Colonel Oatts claims that the Brigadier's two staff officers were especially hide-bound types who, instead of keeping the brigade concentrated, so as to combine mobility with hitting power, only allowed the Indian troops "to enter the Chin Hills in 'penny packets' and wander ineffectively behind the Levies." Oatts's most remarkable claims, however, concern his men's motives for fighting. On the whole they do seem to have preferred British colonial rule and were eager to speed the Japanese retreat out of their home-land. Their most hated enemy, however, were the Indians fighting with Subhas Chandra Bose's Indian National Army, a scratch division of which had taken part in Operation U Go, along with other groups of roughly 200 irregulars each, attached to every Japanese division. By 25th October the National Army was probably in even greater disarray than the retreating Japanese and its own division had simply ceased to function.[21] It was these remnants that the Chins confronted in late October, along the Daung Va river.

> They did not die easily and the Levies' casualties were heavy. The Chins hated the Indians with a kind of dark ferocity which they did not show towards the Japs. The Japs committed atrocities; they gave the women a thin time; and they had an extraordinary habit of slapping people's faces – yet when they were in a good temper they could be quite pleasant fellows. The Indians were never pleasant nor in a good temper, but knocked everyone about continually and practised such revolting habits as sodomy and bestiality in public. The Chins thought they had come straight out of hell, and had every intention of sending them all back at the first opportunity.[22]

Yet at least one officer, with 9 Brigade's signals section, found reassurance that even the brutal passage of armies up and down the Tiddim Road could not completely snuff out the flickerings of humanity at large in the scattered villages of the Chin Hills. Although many of these villages were still deserted, especially those that had become charnel houses for the Japanese dead and wounded abandoned during their retreat, others, like the village of Sezang, only a few miles behind the front, were already shrugging off the vicissitudes of war. Normal day-to-day life in the Chin Hills might not have seemed much to millions of people in the developed world, yet on 25th October there were many thousands of others, in rocket-shattered streets in southern England, demolished towns and villages in France and Belgium, scavenging for food and fuel in Holland, fleeing the retreating Germans and the Soviet 'liberators' from the Baltic states to the Balkans, who would have envied these Burmese the relative ease with which their enemy passed and was forgotten.

On that day Captain Brett-James and a companion clambered down to a village, nestling in a bend in the winding road, some 800 feet below. There were about forty houses all told, built on terraces cut out of the hillside, most of them made of wooden planks and roofed over with red corrugated iron. Each had a garden hedged around with cactus, bamboo or blackberry, and the flat area was usually extended out over the hillside by a platform supported on scaffolding. "On these platforms women and children picked grains of Indian corn which they threw into baskets, and they dried beans and little cakes of what appeared to be a mixture of dung and bean stalks." Warmly welcomed into the first garden they entered, they asked to buy eggs. Three were produced and the seller showed great delight at the crisp rupee note offered in exchange. Moving from garden to garden they noticed that the villagers had taken advantage of an earlier British withdrawal through this area and collected all kinds "of military equipment, steel helmets, pullovers, khaki shorts, mule saddles, canvas shoes and cable drums, which served them as stools . . . Whereas most of the women remained out of sight in the back rooms, afraid to come forward in our presence, those few whom we did see wore gay necklaces and heavy bracelets which they had purchased months before in the bazaar in Tiddim . . . In two houses we found faded yellow photographs pinned to the massive beams of the verandahs . . . Even a crudely coloured picture of the King and Queen adorned the walls, in company with the household rows of jaw bones, bows and darts and bamboo brushes." After they had purchased more eggs and various vegetables, two of the villagers accompanied them up the steep pathway out of the village. As they rested briefly during the climb they looked out over the valley to the "sunbathed ridge . . . through Vital Corner to Kennedy Peak, and wondered how our troops would capture these lofty ridges. Deep below us other villages appeared on the sides of the valley, smoke gently curling above the huts, the barking of dogs rising clear in the hot atmosphere."[23]

43

Operation Matterhorn

B-29 BOMBERS IN CHINA

O<small>N</small> 25th October 1944 some eighty B-29 Boeing Superfortresses took off from bases in southern China, west and south-west of Chungking, to bomb a Japanese aircraft production complex at Omura in Kyushu, the most southerly of the main Japanese islands. At that time there were over 200 B-29s in China but shortages of fuel limited the number that could fly. Fuel considerations also defined the choice of target. At this stage of the war, American analysts had picked the Japanese aircraft industry as being the most 'cost-effective' target for sustained bombing but almost three-quarters of this industry was located within a thirty-five-mile radius of the three big cities of Tokyo, Nagoya and Osaka. The maximum safe range of the B-29, about 1,600 miles, would only extend to the very fringes of the main islands in eastern Kyushu.

On this bright morning, at each of the nine bases around the Kwangchan–Likiang–Kumming triangle, some fearsome aircraft were taxiing forward for take-off. They were carrying 500-lb M-64 general-purpose bombs and M-67 incendiary bombs, at a ratio of two to one, and fully loaded each aircraft weighed 65 tons. The four engines revved up to their maximum 8,800 horsepower and then, at fifty-second intervals, the planes slowly started off down the mile-and-a-half runways. Though the thunderous pounding of piston engines was heard instead of the whine of jets, the Superfortresses were very much the 'Jumbos' of their day, dwarfing other bomber types and with extremely slender wings whose slight swaying seemed altogether inappropriate to the task of getting even the four massive engines airborne let alone the rest of the enormously long plane.

As they gathered speed down the runway it began to seem possible

496

that the increasing acceleration might actually create enough lift to get the monster off the ground. To the crew looking out of the plexiglass nose and canopy, the runway seemed to be disappearing frighteningly fast and the co-pilot began to sing out the ground speed in ten-miles-per-hour increments. At last, at 160 m.p.h., the enormous flaps depressed at the back of each wing redistributed the air-flow sufficiently to provide the necessary lift. The pilot firmly but slowly pulled back the stick, signalled to the co-pilot with his thumb to retract the landing-gear, and the plane took off. But the lift generated still felt as if it might be snatched away at any moment and the pilot concentrated on raising his speed. With the landing-gear fully retracted and enclosed, the pilot pushed the control column slightly forward, dropping the nose to level the plane out and so build up more speed. The dip had to be gentle for if the plane jerked down too much it would simply smash belly-down into the Chinese countryside. As the pilot held the plane steady he slowly straightened the flaps out again, reconfiguring the enormous wing area to make the most of its low-drag, high-speed characteristics, and then he began the long, slow climb to cruising altitude. Many of the crew felt as enervated by the tension of take-off as if they had already flown the whole mission, but in fact less than one minute of the thirteen-hour flight had elapsed.

Being safely airborne did not entirely dispel the crew's fears for their safety, though their continued worries owed little to the scattered fighter opposition over China. For most of them the problem was a lack of confidence in their own aircraft. The Superfortress had turned out to be an enormously expensive machine. The first B-29 to be built cost more than $3.3 million, not to mention another $3 million spent on 10,000 pre-production drawings, but all this outlay was still no guarantee of reliability, especially during these early months of service. It had been ordered straight from the drawing-board, only the second American aircraft to be so procured, and by the time the first production model appeared, in July 1943, firm orders had already been placed with Boeing for 1,600 planes.

Inevitably design corners had been cut and matters came to a head as the Air Force began to organise overseas deployment early in 1944. Many faults had been diagnosed by then but there was no civil or military structure in place that could apprise sub-contractors of the various modifications or conduct quality control of their work. It seemed there was no way to get planes overseas by the specified deadline until Air Force Chief-of-Staff General H. H. Arnold, whose promise to President Roosevelt had defined the deadline, appointed a special Project Co-ordinator to sort things out. "There followed a period of frenzied activity known in Air Force history as the 'Battle of Kansas' or the 'Kansas Blitz', an effort to complete and deploy the 150 bombers to the C.B.I. [China–Burma–India Theater] by mid-April."[1]

Mechanics in gloves and fully-lined flying suits worked outdoors through the freezing nights at the Wichita plant and, by the end of March, they had the first B-29 verified for overseas service. Not all the design problems had been properly sorted out, most especially in the Wright supercharged, 18-cylinder radial R-3350 engines. The main difficulty was overheating. The engines were so compacted, with rows of cylinders front and rear, that there was simply not enough air flowing around and cooling them, especially the exhaust valves on the rear row of cylinders. The effects were most noticeable at 30,000 feet and above and often resulted in the magnesium accessory housing igniting and burning at that metal's extremely high temperature. The extinguishers in the engine could rarely cope and such a fire usually burnt through the engine firewall into the wing, which caused it to shear away. "Once that housing caught fire the crew had one and a half minutes to bale out. The few survivors of such crashes said that the gyrational forces of the spinning plane pinned them to a given spot . . . They were unable to move and escaped only if the airplane broke apart at their station and they were hurled out."[2]

Of course every effort had been made to remedy this deadly fault, including new engine baffles to direct cooling air on to the exhaust valves, improving the flow of oil to the valves, and adjustable cowl flaps on top of the engine. But the problem was far from solved in October 1944. In April, when the first planes were deployed overseas, the average life expectancy of an engine was only 15 hours. In one week in late April, as B-29s began arriving at stop-over bases in western India, near Karachi, five of them crashed, all due to overheated engines. All planes were grounded for two weeks and more, but failures continued and by October there had been at least 20 accidents attributable to faulty engines. In October itself, no fewer than 16 planes were lost for 'operational', or non-combat, reasons though probably not all to do with overheated engines. Nevertheless, as one pilot recalled: "The engine fire stories were not overdone and if anything they were underplayed. I had more two- and three-engine time on the B-29 than I had with all four engines running. It got so I'd tell my flight engineer to keep his mouth shut about how hot they were running. I said I didn't want to know."[3] Flight engineers were prominent among those who dubbed the R-3350s 'flying flamethrowers'.

Even so, as long as the crews could manage to put the fear of fire to the back of their minds, there was much to admire in the Superfortress as an optimised weapons system. The rationale of the plane was to carry large bomb loads for long distances and this it could most certainly do. Practical range was about 1,600 miles and bomb load around 20,000lbs, often in the form of forty 500-lb bombs. Comparable figures for the B-17G Flying Fortress were 950 miles and 2,600lbs (normal). The new plane carried an 11-man crew, comprising the commander, co-pilot, bombardier, navigator, flight engineer (all officers), and a radio operator, a radar operator and four gunners. Because the Superfortress was required to fly at heights of up to 30,000 feet parts of the plane were pressurised, to maintain a constant atmosphere equivalent to about 8,000 feet. Three areas were so protected: the cabin, containing the seven men operating the various instruments, a central section housing the gunners, and an isolated tail-gunner's position. Cabin and centre section were connected by a 3 foot diameter tube, allowing hands and knees access between the two. Beneath this crawl-way was the bomb-bay which obviously could not be pressurised because of the need to open the bomb-bay doors.

In the original design the doors were opened electrically and very slowly. The consequent drag could cause air speed to drop as much as 15 m.p.h. which would make it impossible for the bombardier to maintain accurate bomb-sight synchronisation. In production models, therefore, the doors snapped open pneumatically, in less than a second. But electrics were the rule throughout most of the rest of the plane. Existing generator equipment could not provide the required total capacity and each production plane contained almost 130 specially designed electric motors, which added substantially to the overall weight.

One big user of power was the unique gun-control system. The B-29 specifications had always required streamlining, and the original intention was to make the usual plexiglass turrets retractable, so as to ensure a sleek fuselage for most of the flight to and from the target. But Boeing were already experimenting with a new computerised control system that would provide optimum firing solutions for the guns, much as the Torpedo Data Computer did in American submarines. The gun turrets were remotely controlled by one dorsal and two waist gunner/observers and by the bombardier. Because the guns were not being targeted along the line of sight there was no need for a gunner to be in the turret, which could be kept small and streamlined. The gun's bearing on the target was worked out by the computer, which could correct automatically for range, altitude, differential air speed and temperature. Even better, the computer could handle all the guns simultaneously, and so it was possible for any gunner without a visual target to relinquish control of his gun to one of the others. Combining additional turrets required only the flicking of a switch by the dorsal Central Fire Control Gunner who controlled the master gunnery panel.

The Air Force had embraced the new system with enthusiasm, as it allowed them to extend pressurisation to turret areas and crew, which was not possible in conventional manned turrets. The system also reduced gunner fatigue on such long missions. Being physically separated from the guns meant that they were less exposed to the deafening racket associated with .50 calibre machine guns or the jar and vibration of recoil – though there was a down-side. The first specifications proposed that both crew compartments should be fully sound-proofed against outside noise, but the perennial problem of excess weight meant that this had to be abandoned. Worse still from the crew's point of view, so too was the requirement for two or three bunks where they could snatch a nap and redistribute their body-weight. 'B-29 backside' was not the least of the travails of these long missions. One man who did get to move about a bit was the radar operator, whose seat was also the chemical toilet. Explained one operator: "Radar countermeasures equipment had been installed at the last minute . . . So it had been necessary to make certain compromises. Naturally, the RCM observers were forced to endure numerous wise-cracks about the appropriateness of their position."[4]

A major consideration on the 25th October mission, as on any long-range sortie, was fuel efficiency. After take-off the planes levelled out at about 5,000 feet and the pilots eased back the throttles and settled down to a 'lean burn' cruising speed of around 200 m.p.h. Greater speed could have been achieved at 20,000 feet, in the more rarefied atmosphere, but the climb would consume lots of fuel as the aircraft was still very heavy with well over 6,000 gallons of aviation gasoline in the tanks. So wherever possible the climb was delayed until they neared the target area and the enemy defences, by which time climb would consume probably 20 per cent less fuel. The planes remained at high altitude over the target itself and each man donned his flight suit and oxygen mask as the planes were depressurised to prevent explosive decompression if the hull should be punctured by enemy fighters or flak.

As the bombers steadied themselves over Omura, 14 of them were hit, two by flak and the others by enemy fighters. One of these later crashed in China where its crew, except for the flight engineer, baled out successfully. B-29 gunners claimed a modest ten enemy aircraft destroyed, although the actual number was probably fewer. In all, 59 of the bombers successfully dropped their loads on Omura, with 156 tons landing on the target at about 10 a.m. Visibility was unlimited and reconnaissance photographs later showed destruction of a number of the aircraft plant buildings, including a foundry, storage structures, and a large assembly plant. Unfortunately, damage to the main engine manufacturing works appeared to be only slight.

As soon as the bombs were dropped the planes headed for home, flying at maximum speed until the mandatory 60 miles from the target, when they reduced power and began a very gradual descent. At 15,000 feet the planes levelled out for the main leg of the return journey, some five or six hours of quite tedious flying. Final descent began about 250 miles from base, by which time the planes, minus their bomb loads and most of their gasoline, had reduced fuel consumption from 23lbs per mile during the preliminary climb after take-off and 11lbs per mile during the high-level approach to the target, to less than 7lbs per mile during the last descent.

*

Whatever satisfaction crew and base commanders felt about hitting the target and getting all but one of the planes back safely was not shared by higher command. For General Curtis LeMay, heading XX Bomber Command in China itself, and General Arnold, in command of the overall B-29 headquarters, belonging to the Twentieth Air Force in Washington, the plane was becoming something of a white elephant, with the vast sums spent on its development realising only slight strategic benefits. The U.S. Air Force, more than most in the late 1930s, had made a whole-hearted commitment to the doctrine of 'strategic bombing' and the potential of a sustained aerial offensive against the enemy's industrial capacity. To this end the potential of the B-29 had been touted even more vociferously than that of the B-17s and B-24 Mitchells that were soon flying such missions over Europe. The very fact that the new planes had been grouped into their own Air Force, commanded by the Chief-of-Staff himself, and thus directly answerable to the Joint Chiefs, was a telling indication of the status of the weapon.

From the very beginning the problem had been where to deploy it. When first conceived in 1938, the very long range bomber had been seen as a weapon for hemispheric defence should any foreign power establish bases in Latin America. Once that danger evaporated it proved consistently difficult to find a new role for it. Churchill and Roosevelt had told the Combined Chiefs of Staff that the defeat of Germany had priority over the Pacific, but it was difficult to see how the B-29 could significantly affect that campaign. The European theatre was too far away for them to be based in America, while the delay before it would be available in large numbers meant that a bombing campaign against Germany would have to be based around the aircraft available, notably the Flying Fortresses and the Mitchells. By the time B-29s were available in any quantity, it was thought, Germany would be almost defeated, making it difficult to justify the enormous logistical and administrative upheaval of deploying a radically different type of aircraft. This reluctance only increased when it was realised that few if any B-29s would be available even to support the invasion of France in June 1944.

For many senior airmen, therefore, the second enemy on the itinerary, Japan, seemed the more logical target for the B-29s, with some planners reckoning on no deployment before 1947. Almost by default, then, the B-29 came to be seen as a weapon for the Pacific theatre, and at the Casablanca Conference in January 1943, General Marshall, U.S. Army Chief-of-Staff, backed Air Force suggestions that Japanese industry would be especially vulnerable to sustained bombing. Throughout 1943 the Joint War Plans Committee and the Committee of Operations Analysts thought through this suggestion, drawing up lists of vital raw materials, armaments plants and general industrial choke points, as well as attempting to prioritise these various targets. The Omura raid was one result of a significant shift in this prioritisation, as aircraft manufacturing had only recently been given precedence over the original 'hot tip', coking ovens for the steel industry.

Much of this analysis and planning had a rather unreal feel to it as many of the prime targets in Japan were not within range of any American bombers, including the much-vaunted B-29. A few seconds with a map and a pair of dividers showed that the nearest possible base that brought the whole of Japan within reach was the Marianas, a group of islands that were not scheduled for invasion until June 1944. Even after they were secured it would take several months more to complete the renovation and extension work on existing airfields there. The only other possible base was China, long an object of American sympathy and support, but exasperatingly incapable of maintaining a firm defensive front. The tendency of the Chinese army to buckle under any concerted military pressure by the Japanese made it very risky to consider basing planes and support personnel anywhere except in the remote south-western provinces of Szechuan, Kweichow and Yunnan. Not that these could be deemed entirely safe even though they only allowed the B-29s to nibble at the very edges of mainland Japan.

Arnold and the Joint Chiefs' response to this dilemma was, not for the first time, to compromise. On the one hand, they bowed to the inevitable and accepted that the Marianas offered the best base for a sustained offensive against the whole Japanese war economy. As U.S. Army Air Force official historians have pointed out: "The one point of agreement among most people concerned was that the Marianas, when available, would provide the best base area. It was the interim use of B-29s which they debated."[5] This debate, and the acceptance that there should be interim bases, was the other hand of the compromise. The most favoured options were China, the Aleutians, Australia and India (with planes staging in Ceylon). What nobody seems to have suggested was that *any* interim solution would not be worth the enormous investment of materiel and money and that it might be better to concentrate on training and familiarisation in the United States, and perhaps a temporary Pacific landing strip, and simply wait until the Marianas airfields were secured and brought up to standard.

One reason for this, of course, was that the planes were going to be bought and paid for long before they could land at Saipan, Guam or Tinian and the media, politicians and public opinion alike would make the most of any suggestion that such expensive weapons were being mothballed. Another reason was that the Air Force had long been a fervent lobbyist for a 'new' type of warfare, strategic bombing, and simply could not contain its eagerness to expose Japan to the same sort of punishment that was being unleashed over Germany – especially as Air Force commanders felt the particular weapon to be used in the Pacific was far superior to anything available to the Eighth Air Force in England, or to RAF Bomber Command. But perhaps the most telling reason of all was that the whole debate was more or less hijacked by one of the interest groups.

Propping up Chiang Kai-shek's Kuomintang regime had long been a central feature of American policy in the Pacific. Given that in 1944 the Chinese were holding down almost 40 divisions there and in Manchuria, it is hardly surprising that the commitment to China remained a major war aim. In February 1942, convinced that

American air support and military advisers were vital to buttress the chronically faltering Chinese war effort, the Americans established an area headquarters, the China–Burma–India Theater (CBI), to channel this support. Ground operations centred around American-trained Kuomintang divisions in the Northern Area Combat Command (NCAC) while the Fourteenth U.S. Air Force provided the air effort. Overall CBI commander was General Joseph Stilwell and Fourteenth Air Force was under General Claire Chennault. The two men rarely agreed on anything but both were keen to build up American air power in China. In early 1944, Chennault shot off peremptory demands to Roosevelt and Arnold that all B-29s be stationed in China and placed under his immediate command. Shortly before this Stilwell had proposed his own plan, code-named TWILIGHT, which recommended advance B-29 bases along the Kweilin–Changsha railway, with staging bases near Calcutta from which the bombers would fly their own fuel into China for use in subsequent missions. Stilwell also suggested that as many as fifty U.S.-trained and equipped divisions would be required to protect these bases.

Neither Chennault's arrogance nor Stilwell's airy proposal for a brand-new Chinese army found much favour in Washington, although they did tally with a suggestion by Arnold's own staff that operations from China were one option for getting the B-29s into combat as soon as possible. They, too, foresaw logistical problems and recommended that special B-29 tankers be used to carry fuel from India into China. Airfield defence would be provided by Chennault's fighters. This plan was known as SETTING SUN. Chennault, Stilwell and Arnold made up a vociferous trio and, given Roosevelt's own sympathy for the Chinese, these various proposals came to the attention of the Combined Chiefs. Though ill-received at the QUADRANT Conference in August 1943, they were approved at SEXTANT in December. By this time Air Force staff had refined earlier plans into a new one dubbed MATTERHORN, with a target date of March 1944 for the first B-29 mission from China. According to the new plan, all B-29s were to be based in the Calcutta area, staging through to advanced fields around Chengtu for actual missions. Supply would be by the Superfortresses themselves until Fourteenth Air Force was able to build up reserves sufficient for itself and XX Bomber Command. By October 1944, the B-29s, comprising two wings of four combat groups each, should be able to mount some 300 sorties per month – though even by this date each combat sortie would require three B-29 transport sorties from Calcutta to Chengtu.

Even at the SEXTANT Conference few would accept MATTERHORN

on its own merits, while some Air Force planners had actually had second thoughts about the whole China option. But SEXTANT was interrupted by a 'Big Three' meeting in Teheran, where, at Stalin's insistence, it had been decided to mount a supplementary amphibious landing in France, around Marseille, to divert German reinforcements from the Normandy breakout. This operation, code-named ANVIL, would need its own allotment of landing craft and these could only come from South East Asia Command, in the Bay of Bengal. Parting with these craft would seriously undermine SEAC's hopes of staging an amphibious diversion to draw the Japanese away from the projected land invasion on northern Burma. This invasion was dear to Chiang Kai-shek's heart as it would open up a highway for bringing American supplies into China. But Stalin's insistence on ANVIL caused the cancellation of the amphibious diversion and this in turn delayed any major commitment in northern Burma. Chiang's prestige at home was badly tarnished and so his enthusiasm for future ground operations in support of Stilwell and Fourteenth Army waned. Some Chinese face could still be saved if there were to be some tangible recognition of China's important place among the Allies, and what better than the Superfortress, a monster weapon at the cutting edge of military technology and one whose presence would necessitate a greatly increased flow of dollars and materiel into China? So it was, then, for the sake of Chiang Kai-shek's domestic prestige as much as any other reason, that the Americans committed the B-29 to the far-flung vastness of south-east China.

Thus MATTERHORN, as it existed in October 1944, represented power-projection at its most attenuated. For one thing, it had required an enormous preparatory investment of money and engineering expertise. Between December 1943 and September 1944, when the last Chinese base was completed, two complexes of airbases were built on either side of the Himalayas, at the end of a supply line that extended all the way back to the United States. Discounting the enormous effort in getting supplies to the Calcutta bases, just their transfer on to China was an enormously wasteful effort, with three B-29 flights out of every four made for non-combat purposes.

Even this effort was not enough, and by October it was becoming apparent to those in the know that the B-29s simply could not be made self-sufficient. Especially disheartening was the question of gasoline. Converted B-29 tankers could lift "seven tons of octane fuel at a time, but it was not particularly cost-effective. On a good day it took two gallons of fuel burned by the delivery aircraft to transport one gallon to

Chengtu. On a bad day, with head winds and diversions to avoid bad weather over the Himalayas, this could rise to twelve gallons for every one delivered."[6] A B-29 pilot was caustic in his own appraisal of MATTERHORN self-sufficiency: "For every combat mission we flew, we had to make six round-trip flights over the Hump. We were wearing out those B-29s. It was a hell of a way to run a railroad."[7]

Particularly affected by the endless shuttling back and forth were the B-29 tankers, and by late October General Arnold was considering their complete removal from such missions. Attempts to supplement the deliveries of fuel and other supplies by using C-46 squadrons from Air Transport Command were only partially successful as General Stilwell was in charge of allocating Hump tonnage and he was never sympathetic to any command that was not subordinate to him. Only the Joint Chiefs could alter these allocations and they consistently refused to overrule Stilwell in favour of XX Bomber Command. But self-sufficiency was pretty much a sham anyway, and of the total 42,000 tons of supplies delivered to XX Bomber Command in China only 14,500 tons, one-third, were delivered by the Command's own planes.

By October the situation was becoming faintly ludicrous as the Air Force's most vaunted strike weapon wore itself out flying arduous supply missions that permitted only infrequent, often weak and ineffective, raids against the enemy's outermost ramparts. Between 5th June and 25th October, only ten raids were mounted from China, with an average of some 70 planes actually releasing their bombs, not always over the target. All in all, to 2nd October, 438 tons were dropped, a monthly average of only 110 tons. Equivalent figures for Eighth Air Force over Germany were 176,718 tons of bombs dropped at a monthly average of 44,180 tons. Figures for October 1944 were just over 1,000 tons for XX Bomber Command and almost 40,000 tons by Eighth Air Force. Obviously the Eighth Air Force figures involved a much greater number of aircraft, but that the China effort should be delivering a punch roughly 150 times less effective than that from the United Kingdom was a very poor return on the immense investment already made in MATTERHORN. Neither were casualty figures particularly reassuring. Few B-29s were being lost to Japanese aircraft but other combat and non-combat losses were taking their toll of the $750,000 planes. Between April and October 88 were lost, 21 of these in the latter month. Eighth Air losses were a horrendous 1,825 but this represented a ratio of one bomber lost per 117 tons of bombs dropped compared to one B-29 for every 28 tons. The Superfortresses were also two to three times more expensive, and development and production costs already totalled upwards of two billion dollars. The official history came out particularly strongly against MATTERHORN, both its absurd supply situation and the relative ineffectiveness of the China bombing missions. The supply situation, it claimed, "was fantastically uneconomic and barely workable", while the whole "record of XX Bomber Command was not a successful one. The [original] title for the MATTERHORN plan was 'Early Sustained Bombing of Japan'. The bombing was neither early nor sustained. It achieved no significant results of a tangible sort and . . . [any] intangible effects were obtained at a clear price."[8]

No wonder, then, that by late October 1944 many senior figures were contemplating pulling the B-29s out of China altogether. Both Chennault and Chiang Kai-shek felt that the planes were absorbing too much of the Hump supply allocations and wanted them redeployed, a request supported by the U.S. Ambassador to China, Patrick Hurley, in a message to Washington. By this time, General Arnold was thinking of removing XX Bomber Command to the Marianas and had largely given up hope of its planes ever being self-sufficient. On the 17th, he signalled General LeMay that "it would be desirable to get out of the transport business."[9] LeMay needed little urging in this respect and even declined an offer of more planes for combat duties. "He was frank in telling Arnold that operations out of the CBI could be justified only until bases in other theaters became available."[10]

For the 'bomber barons', then, 25th October 1944 was hardly a high-water mark in their fortunes. No matter what their claims of success in the war over Germany, the real apple of their eye, the B-29 Superfortress, was struggling to make even a limited tactical impact on Pacific operations, let alone deliver the strategic knock-out blow that had been predicted.

Morale at the bases was poor, with a rising incidence of venereal disease as airmen increasingly made "furtive departures to the rice paddies around the perimeter of their bases. There, while young 'Rice Paddie Hatties' relieved some of the tension of eager airmen, their mothers picked G.I. pockets while they were otherwise engaged."[11] Even the airfields themselves were beginning to deteriorate considerably. They had been constructed using local workers in a brutally labour-intensive fashion more reminiscent of the *corvée* than of modern military engineering. The mud and crushed rock that made up the runways was no substitute for concrete and the frequent landings and take-offs by planes laden with bombs or gasoline were breaking up the runways badly, while the Joint Chiefs were wary of paying Chiang's extortionate rates for repair work.

For General LeMay, who had learnt his trade in massed daylight raids over Germany and who would one day relish the prospect of bombing a whole nation "back to the Stone Age", it must have been especially galling. MATTERHORN, far from offering a clarion-call for full-scale strategic bombing, had thus far produced nothing more than a strangled peep.

*

Despite the immense disappointments in China, the picture was not entirely black. If that theatre was looking increasingly inappropriate as a base for strategic bombers, an alternative was now becoming available. From the beginning the MATTERHORN plan had always envisaged the Marianas as probably the optimum base, these islands being much closer than Calcutta to the United States for supply purposes, and Saipan 800 miles closer to Japan than was Chengtu for bombing missions. Potential air bases on the islands had been secured militarily by mid-August 1944 and two Naval Construction Brigades, the legendary Sea Bees, and several Army Engineer Aviation Battalions were immediately set to work. This mainly involved extending and improving existing Japanese airfields and two each on Guam, Tinian and Saipan were upgraded, the last pair by the Army battalions. Like the Chinese bases these too were under the command of Twentieth Air Force and General 'Hap' Arnold in Washington, although the particular formation based in the Marianas was part of XXI Bomber Command led by General Mansell S. Hansell. He had been Arnold's original chief-of-staff in Twentieth Air Force but took over in the Marianas in September 1944. On 12th October the first B-29 landed on Saipan in the Marianas, with Hansell on board. A second plane came in on the 18th and by the 25th some twenty planes had been assembled. A small shake-down mission to Truk was already being planned for the 27th.

The need to integrate Twentieth Air Force with Admiral Nimitz' Central Pacific Area had been confronted well in advance. In April 1944, Arnold sent General Walter H. Frank to work with Nimitz's staff on air force requirements in the Marianas and in August General Millard Harmon was put in charge of a new Air Force headquarters, Army Air Forces in the Pacific Ocean Area. The two services did not always work in harmony. Though the required runways were being given a high priority and much work had already been done, there were not many air force personnel who felt that Navy logisticians had given much thought to even their basic amenities. General Curtis LeMay "somehow acquired a copy of ... [the Navy's] priority list and discovered that his needs were on page five ... They built tennis courts, they built residences for their senior commanders, they built recreation and rehabilitation centers, they built docks for inter-island service craft, 'and every other damn thing in the world,' wrote LeMay, 'except subscribing to their original purpose in the occupation of these islands.'"[12] Even the runways were far from finished when Hansell arrived. The situation overall, he wrote, "was pretty bad. We thought we had two bases with four paved runways ... Well, one of the bases couldn't handle B-29s at all ... The other was half-finished with only one runway and it was paved for only 6,000 feet ... Instead of a hundred hardstands for each base, we had about forty all told, and no facilities: no shops, no warehouses, nothing but gasoline storage and a bomb dump."[13]

By 25th October only one field was suitable for operations, and that barely so. Elsewhere on the three islands the engineers and Sea Bees were working all hours, literally blasting hills out of the way and filling in gullies and ravines with the pulverised coral from these hills. On Saipan 200 miles of connecting roads were built and a mile-long airfield completed in just twelve days. Asphalt for the roads and runways was made in a makeshift plant constructed from Japanese salvage. Senior air force engineers had said that no black-top would be available as it could not be shipped in liquid form. The engineers on the spot asked for drums of hard asphalt to be shipped, and this they melted in a boiler from a former Japanese sugar plant. They were soon producing 700 tons a day as 'icing' for the 2,000 tons of coral that was also quarried. As well as the gruelling labour in this sort of climate, the engineers faced various more esoteric hazards – such as the rampant rats, huge beasts that scuttled over food and supine Americans with equal impunity.

Another hazard was the Japanese stragglers, many of whom penetrated well within the Marine picket line and lurked around the airfields. There were hundreds still at large on all three islands and they spent most of the day hiding out in the thick foliage, behind rocks and in caves. Some holed up in abandoned tanks or the ruins of a pill-box or dug tunnels in the jungle floor. At night, however, they emerged to scavenge supplies, prey on American nerves or perform their last suicidal mission for the Emperor. One of the air-service groups, which had pitched its camp on the edge of the jungle, "was so unnerved by the

sights and sounds of the prowling Japanese that at night they arranged
their vehicles in a big semi-circle and directed all their headlights into
the wilderness. The Japanese laughed at them and threw stones at the
headlights."[14]

Even though the geographical position of the Marianas promised
the possibility of massed bombing of the whole Japanese mainland,
sustained strategic operations were, at best, still some weeks in the
future. On the 25th itself, such planes as were available were armed
with 2,000-lb bombs and held ready to lend their assistance at Leyte
Gulf should Nimitz so request. He never did. For the moment the
Superfortresses in the Marianas were condemned to strategic and even
tactical impotence.

Arnold, Harmon and Hansell were not to be discouraged. Despite
their continuing frustrations, all three were confident that an adequate
scale of operations could eventually be achieved. They were also
beginning to shape the doctrine that would guide these operations. At
that time many Air Force planners were committed to the 'precision
bombing' of carefully selected military-industrial or logistic targets,
with coking ovens for the Japanese steel industry having just
surrendered pride of place to aircraft factories and their suppliers.
Other analysts were beginning to wonder if a much more indiscriminate targeting would not be equally effective. Their premise was
that Japanese industry was remarkably concentrated, with more than
40 per cent of the workforce concentrated in only fourteen urban areas.
Nagoya alone produced some 40 per cent of all aircraft engines, four
cities accounted for more than half of all machine-tool production,
three for fully 90 per cent of electronic manufacturing, and just two for
almost a third of all aircraft assembly. Take out these areas as a whole,
bombing simply by the acre, and one could not fail to cut a huge
swathe through key industries, destroying both plant and labour
force. This tactic was already known to the British as 'area bombing'
and had been enthusiastically adopted by Air Marshal 'Butch' Harris
of RAF Bomber Command. Unfortunately the greater, and increasing,
dispersal of German industry, and their ability to get damaged factories quickly back into production, had seriously blunted the night
bombers' cutting edge.

Yet Japanese cities, built mainly of wood, remained vulnerable, and
for several years American officers had been drawing attention to the
appalling devastation caused by fires started in the aftermath of
the 1923 Tokyo Earthquake. Less than a year later General Claire
Chennault, commanding USAAF units in China, insisted that from

these bases he could "burn up Japan's two main industrial areas."[15] In America itself early repugnance over the use of incendiaries soon dissipated. Even in 1941, the Chemical Warfare Service had established an incendiary laboratory at the Massachusetts Institute of Technology, while the National Defence Research Committee set up its own incendiary weapons section. One such weapon, Standard Oil's M-69 napalm bomb, appeared at about the same time.

Some of the most enthusiastic advocates of fire-bombing were insurance men from the National Fire Protection Association. Their chief spokesman urged the need to pool their expertise to "keep a constant pressure on the air force and their scientific advisers to get on with the business of exploiting fire attack to bring about the end of the war."[16] From spring to November 1943, the Committee of Operations Analysts worked on their own evaluation of incendiary attacks and their final report fully endorsed the potential impact of fire-raids. In June 1944 they set up a Joint Incendiary Committee which went to work on ear-marking six prime urban area targets in Japan and assessing the most effective way to raze them to the ground. Another C.O.A. Report, on 12th October 1944, sent to Vannevar Bush, head of the Office of Scientific Research and Development, asserted that "incendiary attack of Japanese cities may be at least five times as effective, ton for ton, as precision bombing of selected strategic targets."[17] On the following day Bush forwarded these conclusions to Arnold. Though he endorsed the military and economic conclusions, he noted that "the decision on the humanitarian aspects will have to be made at a high level if it has not been done already."[18]

PART ELEVEN

The Manhattan Project

44

Inventing the Secrets

THE WAR IN the air between 1939 and 1945, especially the see-saw struggle over bomber penetration and survivability, was fought at the cutting edge of contemporary technology and thus under very tight security. In late 1944, the most 'hush-hush' unit of all was not actually engaged in combat operations but was based at Wendover Field, Utah, a remote airbase that had been used originally for training P-47 fighter pilots. Its new occupants were a squadron of massive B-29 bombers, brand-new, very long range, four-engined aircraft which were at present staged mostly in China and the Marianas island group in the Pacific. However, 393 Squadron, part of 504 Bombardment Group which had been training with B-29s at Harvard Field, Nebraska, was suddenly detached from the parent group and on 11th September moved to Utah. There the men learnt that they were to form the backbone of a new elite bomber unit in which 15 B-29s were to be backed up by almost 2,000 ground personnel manning the organic engineering, maintenance, technical and military police units, as well as its own ordnance and troop transport squadrons. These were to be constituted as a new Composite Air Group although by late October it still had no official unit designation.

The reason for making such a small unit as self-contained as possible was purely security, to keep contact with other air force units to an absolute minimum. Security was also tight at Wendover itself, way out in the desert, 125 miles east of Salt Lake City. "Top officers were enjoined to secrecy ... without being told what it was they weren't supposed to reveal. Enlisted men on three-day passes were warned to keep quiet. Security agents prowled the streets of Salt Lake City and reported men who talked too much ... Civilians on important business arrived continually at the base ... [and] questioners were told they were sanitary engineers ... Technical shops were off-limits except to a few men with special badges." The aircrews with 393 Squadron spent most of their time training but the experience was very different from anything they had done previously. Bombing runs were always carried out at 30,000 feet, with the bombardiers squinting through the standard Norden bomb-sight to try to hit a 500-foot circle marked out in the sand. Single bombs only were dropped and "relentless emphasis was placed on visual bombing. This puzzled some of the bombardiers who were veterans of the air war over Europe, since a clear day for visual bombing had been rare there and was even rarer over Japan."[1] The only half-credible rumour to explain this monotonous routine was that the crews were practising to drop land-mines over Formosa.

Among the few at Wendover who knew the real reason were Colonel Roscoe Wilson, the air project officer attached to the so-called Manhattan Project, and Colonel Paul Tibbets, the commander of the putative air group. Both were under the strictest instructions to divulge nothing to anyone else, and while this did not really affect Wilson, who remained a shadowy figure, it did little to help Tibbets form a good relationship with his men. Much of his time was spent in top-secret discussions with extremely important-looking sanitary engineers or else away from the base entirely. In fact, "Tibbets, with the greatest knowledge of the unit's role, was 'gone about 90 per cent of the time', according to ... [393 Squadron's commander]. Tibbets seemed to be in a world apart and would sit at table for hours without saying a word to anyone."[2] Nor was it helping morale that Tibbets had filled many of the key posts in the group, and in 393 Squadron itself, with strangers from his original bombardment group in Europe.

Concentrating largely on 'marksmanship' at this stage of their training, the bomber crews used ordinary practice bombs in their endless passes over the Utah bombing range. Others, however, were working on the configurations of the actual bombs to be dropped on the first combat missions, whenever they might be. Two types of atomic bomb were involved, weapons of supposedly unparalleled destructiveness and whose production was the exclusive task of the Manhattan Project. Much still needed to be clarified about the exact mechanism and explosive effect of these weapons, but it had now been confirmed that they could be contained within a plane-portable munition and dropped in the conventional manner. In fact, convention was of the essence. Due to their exorbitant expense, only two bombs were likely to be produced in the near future, and the Project director, General Leslie Groves, decided that such high priced ordnance would have to be dropped visually, on a clear day, to minimise the uncertainty associated with radar and bad weather bombing.

The B-29 had always been the delivery system of choice and preliminary tests with early bomb designs had been made at Muroc Dry Lake from March 1944. One type of bomb, short and bulbous in appearance, was called Fat Man and another, more svelte but over 17 feet long, was known as Thin Man. The latter would involve extensive conversion work on the B-29 bomb-bays and eventually a way was found of shortening this device to more conventional dimensions. Renamed Little Boy, it and its rotund cousin underwent a further series of tests until in late August 1944 the configurations of both had been frozen and passed on to the Martin aircraft company in Omaha, which was to modify the 15 combat B-29s. By 25th October the first of these planes was ready to be flown to Wendover and plans were also well advanced to provide mock-up bombs, known as 'pumpkins', of the right size and shape.[3]

Uppermost in Tibbets' mind as he planned the new training programme with the modified aircraft was the question of evasive action after dropping such a shatteringly powerful bomb. The scientists he had talked to remained unsure just what TNT equivalents were involved but thought that a plane would need to be at least eight miles away from the detonation point to avoid potentially fatal structural damage from the blast. Six of these miles were accounted for in the plane's altitude. Tibbets, with his experience of test-flying B-29s, was of the opinion that the other two miles might soonest be gained by making an immediate, sharp 160-degree turn and nosing the plane down to gain speed. In the 43 seconds between dropping the bomb and it exploding there should be just enough time to roll out of the steep turn and claw back the extra couple of miles.

This element of uncertainty about the predicted blast from the explosion was symptomatic of the whole Manhattan Project in October 1944. Its origins could be traced back to a small band of European and American scientists who had had a hunch that an atomic bomb might be a practical spin-off from recent discoveries in nuclear physics. Many of these advances had been made in Germany and from 1939 the hunch had grown into dread that the Nazis might be well on the way to developing such a weapon. Albert Einstein became the spokesman for this anxiety and eventually he got the ear of President Roosevelt and his advisers. Despite the unsubstantiated nature of the scientists' fears and

the enormous research and industrial effort that would be involve
in developing an atomic weapon of their own, Roosevelt took seriou
heed of these warnings. The British government also added its voic
of alarm in a memorandum from the Maud Committee in 1941. I
members grimly declared: "We have now reached the conclusion tha
it will be possible to make an effective uranium bomb which, containin
some 25 pounds of active material, would be equivalent as regard
destructive effect to 1,800 tons of TNT and would also release larg
quantities of radioactive substances, which could make places near
where the bomb exploded dangerous to human life for a long period."
Once the Pearl Harbor attack had dragged America into a war on tw
fronts, Roosevelt felt he had no option but to order top-priorit
research. If the enemy got atomic weapons first, it would leave th
Allies totally vulnerable to widespread devastation, or the threat of it

Roosevelt was no stranger to 'big government' but it is doubtfu
whether even he realised just what a mammoth project he ha
sanctioned. The federal cheques were soon flying like confetti, and b
October 1944 something in the region of $1.7 billion had been spen
creating an industrial infrastructure that was actually bigger than th
entire U.S. automobile industry – all to produce just a few pounds
fissile material. Just as the Curies had once crushed, boiled and distille
their way through 10 tons of pitchblende to produce a faintly glowin
speck of radium in the corner of their makeshift laboratory, so too di
American physicists, chemists and engineers, civilian and militar
have to perform a like task on an epic scale, designing and buildi
huge industrial plant of unprecedented complexity.

All manner of precise and intricate pioneering processes wer
needed to turn tens of thousands of tons of uranium ore into melon
sized lumps of its most potent fissile derivatives – the uranium isotop
U-235 and the associated element plutonium. 'Fissile' meant that whe
either of these materials was bombarded with an external neutro
source, the nuclei of any of their atoms that were hit would split in
new nuclei of different isotopes or elements, made up between them
most of the original nuclei protons and neutrons, but also releasin
'spare' neutrons that would continue and amplify the bombardment.
a mass of U-235 or plutonium of sufficient size and of an appropria
shape this fission would become so pervasive, in such an infinitesimal
short space of time, that the sudden build-up of energy would manife
itself as an enormous explosion.

When the Americans set to work, the physics of the thing had alrea
been predicted, based largely on observations in British laboratorie

Yet, for the chemists and engineers endeavouring to manufacture the components of a workable bomb, these predictions were on a par with the proverbial suggestion, "If we had some bacon we could have bacon and eggs, if we had some eggs." Even the fissile materials themselves were known to exist only as embedded, proportionally fractional parts of a lump of the more common isotope, U-238. The desirable U-235 existed within it naturally but formed a mere 0.7 per cent of the main element, while plutonium was only created when U-238 was itself subjected to controlled neutron bombardment.[5] To make the bomb it would be necessary to extract one or the other of them, in one case 'raw', in the other enriched, and this presented enormous difficulties. The extraction of the plutonium was in many respects a straight-forward chemical engineering task, using familiar separation tech-niques, but these were enormously complicated by the lethal radio-activity of the material to be processed. There was also considerable uncertainty about how much plutonium would be produced, and how reliable the enriching process would be. The problems with U-235 were more daunting still, where a Curie-type distillation would have to be performed but on a mega-industrial scale and with very little known about the actual techniques to be employed. In normal times, of course, the Americans would have concentrated upon one type of bomb or the other, U-235 or plutonium, knowing they had an alternative line of research to pursue if necessary. But this was war-time, with its ever-present anxiety about progress being made by the enemy, and a commensurate dread of following one's own research down a blind alley. So the Americans had boldly opted to pursue both bombs, 'panning' for the two precious isotopes simultaneously in the fervent hope that at least one could be obtained quickly in usable quantities.

There were of course, in theory at least, alternative methods of producing each type of fissile material. With plutonium the choices hinged upon the original enrichment process and which type of reactor was to be used, particularly the moderator which slowed down the bombarding neutrons to maximise their potential for making hits. Graphite and heavy water were both extremely effective but here, at least, the Americans really had little choice as the former, a crystalline carbon, was readily available in the United States while the latter was produced only in Norway, which had been occupied by the Germans since April 1940. All that was known about U-235 separation, however, was that there seemed to be three possible methods, all equally daunting. Uranium contained three isotopes, U-238, 235 and 234, all of which were chemically identical and thus not amenable to conventional separation techniques. The only remaining possibilities were to exploit the minute differences in weight and size of their respective atoms. The weight differences might be exploited in two ways, by the so-called centrifuge and gaseous-diffusion processes, and size by the electro-magnetic process. Centrifuge separation introduced vaporised uranium into a large, rapidly spinning machine and drove off the heavier isotopes from the slightly lighter U-235, rather like separating cream from milk. In the first months of the war this method had seemed the most promising, but General Groves remained unimpressed, and by the spring of 1943 it had faded from the picture. Yet even when it had still had priority, the two other processes were also being carefully investigated.

Chronic uncertainty over an ultimate pay-off constantly forced the Americans to hedge their bets. This was especially the case with gaseous-diffusion and electro-magnetic separation. Both of these were accorded an equally high priority right through 1944 in experimental work at universities, commercial laboratories and military sites (notably Berkeley, Columbia and 'Project Y' at Los Alamos), leading to the design and construction of huge production sites for each type of process. This latter point applied equally to plutonium, and by October, at Oak Ridge, Tennessee, and Hanford, Washington State, corporations such as Eastman Kodak, M. W. Kellogg and Du Pont had already created the largest publicly-funded engineering project in the history of the world – all without knowing whether any of the processes involved would actually produce a working bomb. The Manhattan Project, then, was the biggest roulette game in town, in which the players had to bet heavily on every number while having to accept that none of them might come up. In Manhattan roulette you risked everything without even knowing what the odds were.

Oak Ridge, in the Clinch River valley, was the centre for U-235 extraction and contained twin sites for both the gaseous-diffusion and electro-magnetic methods. Officially known as the Clinton Engineer Works, the two sites were about 17 miles apart. The first to start construction, in February 1943, was the electro-magnetic plant, code-named Y-12, an industrial enlargement of Professor Ernest Lawrence's cyclotron, at Berkeley, in which electrically charged vaporised uranium was passed through an intense magnetic field. The uranium atom moved through the field, in a circle whose radius differed slightly according to the weight of the isotopes. The lighter U-235 atom moved in a tighter arc than the U-238, and when their respective trajectories were confined within a semi-circular vacuum tank it should be possible to collect separated atoms in their respective small hoppers, placed just 0.3 inches apart at the bottom of the semi-circle. When the atoms struck the bottom of the steel and graphite hoppers they gave up their electrical charge and were deposited as minute flakes of metal.

However, as the U-235 isotope was present in uranium in only minute quantities, and it was estimated that around 90lbs of the metal would be required to initiate an explosive chain-reaction, it was clear that these calutrons, as they were called, would have to be deployed on a lavish scale. There was no question of using a single magnet, even the 200-ton monster that Professor Lawrence had assembled in his laboratory, so it was decided to install them in clusters, thick sausage-shaped arrangements of 96 twenty feet by two feet magnets encased in steel jackets. Every pair of magnets was interspersed by twin D-shaped vacuum tanks, and the whole array, 250 feet long, soon became known as a 'racetrack'. They were certainly something of an attraction. Until they were fitted with strengthened floor fittings the D-tanks were regularly dragged several inches towards the magnets while those who worked near them had "hammers and screwdrivers jerked out of their hands when they came too close; men even felt the pull on the nails in their shoes."[6]

There were two racetracks in each of the enormous Y-12 buildings and they were operated by a small army of about 15,000 young women, mostly high school graduates, housewives and farm girls from the local area, none of whom had any prior technical knowledge or had even heard of nuclear physics. They were no wiser after several months on the job, the first racetrack having been switched on in late October 1943. All they knew was that each day they had to stand in their individual cubicles, a long double row of tall control boards facing each other, with every girl in charge of four such boards. Each board comprised about twenty different dials and a dozen knobs, and it was the girls' job to monitor the needles on these dials and, if they moved beyond certain limits, to try to correct the reading by moving the appropriate knobs, sometimes singly, sometimes in combination.

Sometimes the meters did not respond and the needle refused to come back to normal position. In such a case, the operator would call the supervisor, or would use the telephone which hung on each board. Technicians would appear immediately, try to correct the oscillation, and phone some incomprehensible messages to somebody in another place. Then everything would work again and

. . . [the girl] would never know who repaired what or where. They never knew why they were turning those knobs, or what the meters controlled . . . They had no idea what sort of plant this was, or what it produced. The supervisors, although they had some technical training, did not know either, and nobody asked questions. They were all told in no vague terms that their work should never be discussed with anyone. Not with their families, not with any other Oak Ridge employees. Everything they saw and did had to remain an absolute secret.[7]

It is as well they did remain ignorant about the electro-magnetic process as a whole, otherwise they might have become extremely downhearted. For Y-12 was simply not doing the job. Despite a financial outlay not far short of half a billion dollars, despite a complex of over 250 buildings covering an area larger than twenty football fields, despite TVA-supplied generators that supplied more electricity than needed by a small city, despite electro-magnets coiled round with $300 million of silver borrowed from the Treasury, despite pumps that maintained more cubic feet of vacuum than the total pumped down everywhere else on earth at that time, and despite a total workforce of 22,000, the calutrons were not filling their hoppers. In December 1943, less than three months after the first racetrack began operation, it was closed down completely and extensive modifications were made to the magnets which had been shorting because of a heavy build-up of rust and other dirt-particles in the lubricating oil. A modified racetrack finally came on line in January 1944, but even when provided with the requisite magnetic field, the uranium atoms could not be induced to follow their theoretical trajectories. In fact, 90 per cent of the uranium fed into the calutrons resolutely refused to describe an orderly semi-circle and scattered to deposit itself on the walls of the apparatus. As even unseparated uranium was a valuable commodity, all this lost material "had to be recovered from the walls of the containing vessels and from parts of the moving parts, for atoms tended to combine, physically or chemically, with the metals comprising the separating equipment. All parts of the operating mechanisms, therefore, had to be removed periodically, then cleaned and washed by steam and electrical stripping." The uranium thus recovered was tainted with all kinds of impurities such as iron, copper, nickel and other metals and needed extensive chemical treatment before being reusable. Even the ventilating air in these chemical areas was treated so as the extract any uranium dust that otherwise would be carried out into the open

Tennessee air. Finally the recovered uranium "was run back through the calutron, which would again waste 90 per cent of it. Thus many of the atoms were being reprocessed hundreds of times before they followed the right beam into the right receiving basket."[8]

To add insult to injury, even those atoms that eventually found their way into the appropriate hopper did so with the same over-enthusiasm as the errant 90 per cent. Instead of depositing themselves as tiny flakes of U-235, the atoms usually hit the walls of the hopper with such energy that they buried themselves and remained embedded in the stainless steel. By October 1944 there were in fact two types of racetrack at Oak Ridge, the 96-magnet 'Alpha' layouts having been supplemented by improved 36-magnet 'Beta' versions which took the recoverable output from the former and reprocessed it to a higher purity. Even then the whole set-up was producing only 40 grams of U-235 per day, implying a totally unacceptable lead-time for amassing the 45 kilograms required to make a bomb. A recent historian of the Manhattan Project waxed almost poetical about the shortfall between the amounts of processed uranium that were needed for a working bomb and the actual quantity turning up in the hoppers. "The Alpha calutrons smeared uranium all over the insides of their vacuum tanks, catching no more than 4 per cent of the U-235; that valuable fraction, reprocessed and fed into the Beta calutrons, reached the Beta collectors in turn at only 5 per cent efficiency. Five per cent of 4 per cent is two thousandths. A speck of U-235 stuck to an operator's overalls was well worth searching out with a Geiger counter and retrieving delicately with tweezers. No essence was ever expressed more expensively from the substance of the world with the possible exception of the human soul."[9]

Still, at least the calutrons were producing something. The other large site at Oak Ridge, employing the gaseous-diffusion method of separation, had so far proved a complete bust. This method, too, depended upon distinguishing uranium atoms by weight in a vaporised sample, but here the gas was to be mixed with fluorine and forced progressively through a series of hundreds of fine filters, known as a 'cascade', to isolate the more precious isotope. As General Groves remarked: "This method was completely novel . . . The heart of the process was the barrier [or filter], a porous thin metal sheet or membrane with millions of submicroscopic openings per square inch. These sheets were formed into tubes which were enclosed in an airtight vessel, the diffuser. As the gas (uranium hexafluoride) was pumped through a long series, or cascade, of these tubes it tended to separate, the enriched gas moving up the cascade while the depleted moved down. However . . . it was impossible to gain much separation in a single diffusion step . . . [and] there had to be several thousand successive stages."[10]

Building the gas-diffusion plant, code-named K-25, had begun when the surveyors arrived in May 1943. The first concrete was laid in October and by April 1944 the main building was finished. This in itself was a remarkable structure, a giant U-shaped, four-storey building designed to accommodate the endless stages of the cascade, some of whose diffusion tanks had a 1,000-gallon capacity. It was fully half-a-mile long and its floor area was something like 43 acres. It had required 350,000 cubic yards of concrete, as well as 40,000 tons of structural steel, 15,000 tons of sheet steel and five million bricks. The specifications alone required 20,000 pages of drawings and instructions and the building itself was the world's largest construction under a single roof. The cost had been something like $100 million. Running costs included a steam-generating electricity station sufficient for the entire needs of the city of Boston.[11]

For Groves and his contractors this sort of overnight eighth wonder of the world was becoming almost routine. What his scientists and engineers could not get to grips with was the construction of the cascades themselves. They knew what was required in theory and had already mapped out the sequence of the cascade and the functions of its millions of components; the practical drawback was the extreme corrosiveness of uranium gas, and no one seemed able to produce either barrier material or piping valves and pumps that were sufficiently resistant. While in the calutrons the uranium gas whizzed around and then coyly buried itself in the equipment, in the cascade it simply ate the whole thing up. The contract for producing the barrier material for all the five million diffusion tubes had already been assigned to the Houdaille-Hershey Corporation in April 1943, and they were even now building a brand-new factory to produce it. Unfortunately, they were still unsure as to exactly what they were supposed to produce. Two experimental methods of manufacturing the barrier were being examined, both using nickel which was impervious to corrosion. One was based on an English immigrant's patent for a paint-sprayer mesh and the other on a technique for compressing nickel powder into sheets.[12] However, one of the resultant materials was strong but not suitable for mass-production, while the other was more amenable to industrial production but too brittle and not of uniform quality. Groves, not for the first time, had little option but to 'wing' it and order preparations for mass-production of the inferior material to begin anyway, hoping for adequate improvements along the way.

While research into both methods continued, largely to the utter frustration of those involved, Harold Urey, the scientist behind the whole idea of gaseous-diffusion, completely lost faith in it. Then a new type of barrier, a combination of the two methods, seemed to offer a breakthrough, and Groves was urged to switch manufacturing priority. In November 1943, after much soul-searching, he declined to take such a radical step in the hope that the completed factory would soon have something worth producing. By the end of the year Houdaille-Hershey had also lost faith in the mesh barrier they were supposed to manufacture, the so-called Norris-Adler version, and began to advocate a switch to the hybrid Johnson-Kellex barrier.

Groves finally decided in January 1944 to strip the whole Decatur plant, due to come on-line the following May, and re-equip it for Johnson-Kellex production. Before long some progress had been made in quality control of the compressed nickel powder through simplified test procedures, but not until the end of April was the powder itself available in sufficiently pure form. The quality of finished barrier material jumped from 5 to 38 per cent in May but the switch from one process to the other meant that almost half of the manufacturing plant had to be re-equipped. In June, "barrier production started at the . . . plant. By then the total cost of K-25 and its components had reached $281 million and was still climbing. But barrier quality was still so poor that Professor Taylor [from Columbia] declared most of it unacceptable."[13] Only in late August was the barrier material deemed adequate for production of the tubes, and by then Groves had already decided that gaseous-diffusion was going to be so delayed that the upper section of the cascade, where the later stages of separation took place, should not be fitted out. Instead, once the uranium had been purified to 50 per cent U-235, the residue would be transferred to the calutrons for final enrichment. By 25th October, then, though Groves could rest considerably easier in the knowledge that gaseous-diffusion problems should now be limited to the fitting out of his concrete horseshoe at Oak Ridge, he was still far from sure that industrial-scale diffusion would work, that the Beta calutrons could handle their new part in the process, or that he was much nearer getting his 40 to 45 kilograms of U-235.[14]

Of course U-235 was not the only material that could be used to induce explosive fission. The other was plutonium, a non-natural element created when uranium was subjected to controlled neutron bombardment. But the method embodied a typically Manhattan Project level of profligacy, with only one in 4,000 uranium atoms actually transmuted into plutonium, an amount equal to the volume of a U.S. dime coin from every two tons of uranium and fission products. Such ratios were now par for the course for Groves and he had steadfastly backed yet another huge investment of money, men and resources into plutonium production. Once the experimental reactor, or pile, at the University of Chicago had gone critical in December 1942, full-scale production, by the Du Pont chemical company, was approved and a 5,000-acre site purchased at Hanford, in Washington State, on the west bank of the Columbia River. Though extremely remote, among vistas of uncultivated sagebrush, it was close to such crucial power sources as the Bonneville and Gran Coulee dam systems. Although many of the original 1,500 inhabitants had to be evicted, a few scattered fruit orchards around the periphery were allowed to continue growing their cherries, plums and apricots.

The core site was cleared completely, however, and in August 1943 building work began on the two enormous chemical separation plants that would extract the plutonium from the enriched uranium. Each of these was 800 feet long, 65 feet wide, and 80 feet tall, the proportions of enormous concrete pencil-boxes. Those working on them dubbed them the 'Queen Marys', and it was in fact the case that the real ship of that name was only 20 per cent longer. The interiors were largely taken up with sunken cells for the actual processing and these were surrounded by concrete walls seven feet thick and sealed by six-foot thick covers. Each of these weighed 35 tons and could only be moved by a 60-foot bridge-crane that trundled up and down the whole length of the building. The cells occupied the first storey of the plants, flanked by three observation galleries running alongside behind the thick concrete walls. The entire area above the cells, rising to a height of 60 feet, was known as the 'canyon' – a permanent, intensely radioactive 'no go' area. The crane was designed accordingly and "the operator stood in a cab shielded with lead from where he could maneuver the crane and the two [submarine] periscopes, one mounted on each side of the cab, so that he could get a stereoscopic view of the . . . canyon."[15]

Into the containing cells were to go irradiated uranium slugs from the reactors. There were three of these planned, sited 10 miles to the north-east, and work on the first of them had begun in October 1943. The graphite pile itself was installed in February 1944, but it was not until September that the last construction workers left. On the 26th the pile was ready to go critical. Housed in another enormous concrete box, it comprised a 28-foot by 36-foot graphite cylinder, on its side, penetrated from one end to the other by over a thousand aluminium tubes. These were loaded with 200 tons of uranium slugs, 'canned' in aluminium and about the size of a roll of quarters.[16] The pile was also pierced by a number of cadmium rods which inhibited the reaction by absorbing bombarding neutrons. These rods were progressively extracted to start the reaction and were available as a safety precaution should it seem to be getting out of control. Just before the reaction began, the powerful water-cooling system was also switched on and then, with only the sound of rushing water audible, the pile went critical. "Chain reacting with 1,200 tons of graphite, the uranium would generate 250,000 kilowatts of heat; cooling water pumped through the aluminium tubes around the uranium slugs at the rate of 75,000 gallons per minute would disperse the heat . . . When they had burned long enough, 100 days . . . the irradiated slugs could be pushed out the back of the pile simply by loading fresh slugs at the front. The hot slugs would fall into a deep pool of pure water that would safely confine their intense but short-lived fission-product radioactivity. After 60 days they could be fished out and carted off for chemical separation."[17]

Such at least was the theory, and on 25th October Groves and the Hanford team should have been looking with some confidence to just another seventy days cooking in the 'Water Boiler', as this first reactor was commonly known, before they could eject their first batch of enriched uranium. Adding the required cooling and separation time would have meant there were still some months before there was actually any Hanford plutonium to look at, but at least there would have been a definite schedule to work to. Unfortunately, come the end of October, Groves was in an even greater state of uncertainty about plutonium production than he was about U-235. For, after an initially reassuring purring, humming and swishing, the reactor had faltered almost immediately. For the next 18 hours or so the pile barely puttered along, even with all the cadmium rods removed, and thereafter it began to run in 12-hour cycles of desultory activity and complete shut-down.

The problem turned out to be the result of the pile 'poisoning' itself by producing neutron-gobbling xenon which decayed after several hours but was reborn once the pile kick-started itself back into life. The diagnosis was confirmed in one of the several experimental piles now available at the University of Chicago and the solution was thought to be the use of several hundred spare aluminium tubes already drilled into the graphite. Incorporating these tubes into the active pile involved considerable work, which included attaching them to the cooling system. By late October there were still no piles in operation.

The whole affair had done little to enhance Groves' opinion of 'long-haired' scientists. With some asperity, he drew their embarrassed attention to the fact that they had never test-run the Chicago pile at full power, round the clock, as he had explicitly ordered. This test would have thrown up the xenon effect months earlier. On top of this, it was only by pure luck that the extra pipes existed in the Hanford piles at all, for they were the work of du Pont engineers who had taken heed of their own worries about reactor poisoning and with "stubborn insistence . . . had allowed large margins and left extra space in the pile [504 additional tubes], despite the disagreement of scientists who thought such precautions were completely unnecessary and served only to slow the completion of construction."[18] The most obdurate of the engineers had been one George Graves, and as the vital importance of his safety margin became apparent – for without the extra tubes all three reactors would have required rebuilding which would have thrown the plutonium programme back months – an anonymous ballad went the rounds that October:

> We'd call up a tight design
> Hewn strictly to the longhairs' line.
> To us it looked almighty fine –
> A honey, we'd insist.
>
> But Old Marse George, with baleful glare,
> And with a roar that shook the air,
> Cried, "Dammit, give it stuff to spare –
> The longhairs may have missed."[19]

All this, of course, left the separation plants with nothing to process. The intense secrecy meant that none of the operatives there knew much about the reasons for the delay, how long it would last, or even what it was they did not have, but they must have welcomed the opportunity for extra training and dry runs. Given the intense radioactivity in the canyon, all work in the separation plants was to be carried out entirely by remote control. Every task in the plants was to be performed using techniques for remote guidance and optical surveillance, including plastic lenses to avoid radioactivity blackening glass, various types of periscope, primitive television units, modified 'fly-eye' bombsight lenses, underwater microscopes, and 'jumpers', remote-controlled wrenches for connecting pipes and wires, of which there was mile upon mile in each plant. With the 'jumpers', "by watching through special optical instruments and correcting their connection maneuvers by the sounds coming over a microphone (the mechanics' experienced ears could even distinguish among various noises made by screw threads entering the grooves), the operators worked something after the fashion of an expert safecracker, listening to the tumblers falling in a combination lock."[20]

The first teams of operatives already had hands-on experience of many of these techniques, and by the 25th most of the equipment – some of it extremely delicate – was in place. Ready, too, were the water tanks in which the irradiated slugs would first be cooled, the square, heavily shielded casks in which they would be moved from the reactor site for further cooling, the rail flatcars that would transport these casks to the canyon, and the chemicals to fill the dissolving cells. The first 'Queen Mary', indeed, was almost ready to sail. All that was missing was her precious cargo.

The problem of the missing plutonium was also keenly felt at the third major Manhattan Project site at Los Alamos, New Mexico, where the race was on to produce a bomb of this type suitable for testing. Los Alamos, or Project Y, had originally been a school, run according to a 'good clean air and plenty of exercise' regimen and aimed mainly at sickly pupils. Situated 35 miles north-east of Santa Fe, it was taken over by the government in April 1943 and, perched on top of a high mesa dubbed 'the Hill', became the centre of a 45,000-acre site devoted to working out just how to maximise the explosive potential of these new fissile materials. At the other Project sites much of the work was being done by industrial chemists and engineers who were employed to turn theory into mass-production. At Los Alamos, however, deadlines were so pressing that almost the first bombs produced would have to be the ones actually dropped. In consequence the theoretical physicists there discovered that they were also their own ordnance engineers, give or take a little help from the Army and Navy. What they experiment-ally assembled in the laboratory would be pretty much what ended up in the bomb-bay of the designated B-29. This was literally the case with the 'Little Boy' bomb, for it had long been realised that there was no chance of producing enough U-235 for an extra test device. The theory of detonating such a bomb, by bringing two lumps of U-235 together to form a critical mass, with one lump being fired cannon-like into the other in a so-called 'gun-bomb', had been worked on throughout 1943 and 1944. In October 1944, James Bryant Conant, one of the leading scientific overseers of the Project, "had travelled out to Los Alamos to ascertain . . . [the bomb's] prospects. To Vannevar Bush [head of the Office of Scientific Research and Development] he reported that the gun methods of detonation seemed 'as nearly certain as any untried new procedure can be'. The availability of a uranium gun bomb, which Los Alamos expected would explode with a force equivalent to about 10,000 tons of TNT, now depended only on the separation of sufficient U-235."[21]

There was no such confidence over the future of the plutonium bomb. Right through the first half of 1944 it had been assumed that such a bomb could also be triggered in a gun-type arrangement, but in July of that year it was discovered that this could not be done. Yet another experimental reactor had been set up at Oak Ridge and in November 1943 it discharged its first five tons of irradiated uranium. Chemical separation had begun in late December and by the following summer very small quantities of plutonium were arriving at Los Alamos. The desirable plutonium isotope, similar in its essential fissile characteristics to U-235, was numbered Pu-239. But when plutonium was formed it also contained another isotope, Pu-240, an alpha emitter that exhibited a much higher rate of spontaneous fission. "This meant that, with neutrons being constantly released by the isotope, a gun-type assembly [muzzle velocity 3,000 feet per second] would be much too slow to block a possible reaction." At this speed the plutonium bullet and target would melt down and fizzle before the two parts had time to join. If this happened with Oak Ridge plutonium, then supplies from the Hanford reactor, the only possible source of adequate amounts of the metal, would have an even higher rate of spontaneous fission because of denser initial neutron bombardment. "The plutonium bomb was therefore an impossibility – unless some fantastically fast way of assembly could be discovered. Morale at Los Alamos sank to its lowest point."[22]

So serious was the crisis that J. Robert Oppenheimer, the director and research co-ordinator at Los Alamos, considered resigning. Cooler heads insisted that one potential avenue of research still remained. From the outset one scientist, Seth Nedermeyer, had urged that the quickest way to bring a bomb's fissile core to critical mass was implosion, in which a non-critical spherical core, hollow, fragmented or compressible, would be squashed together by simultaneous, exactly equivalent explosions all around its outer surface. Nedermeyer was allowed to pursue experiments along these lines despite a prevailing scepticism about the ability to predict and control explosions so as to produce an exactly symmetrical spherical shock wave. His first experiments were with cylindrical shapes, simply to assemble some preliminary data. The charges were kept small to ensure that enough of the shapes actually survived. One fellow scientist, however, was downright derisive and questioned Nedermeyer's seriousness. "To my mind he is gradually working up to what I shall refer to as the Beer-Can Experiment. As soon as he gets his explosives properly organised, we will see this done. The point to watch for is whether he can blow up a beer-can without splatting the beer."[23]

By October 1944 Groves and Oppenheimer would have gladly toasted Nedermeyer in his weight in beer. As Groves guardedly remarked, once the Pu-240 problem was confirmed, "making it extremely difficult to employ . . . [plutonium] in a gun-type bomb . . . we were very thankful for Nedermeyer's persistent belief in the feasibility of an implosion bomb and the advance work in which this had resulted."[24] Throughout autumn 1944, indeed, implosion research was at the very heart of the Los Alamos effort.

Once over his initial intense disappointment, Oppenheimer resolved, in the words of the Project's official history, "to throw the book at it." He decided to carve two new establishments out of the existing Ordnance Division – G, for 'Gadget', the unofficial code-name for the bomb, to grapple with the physics of implosion, and X, for explosives, to perfect implosive lenses. When it was suggested that this work should no longer be overseen by the head of Ordnance, he was suitably outraged. But "Oppenheimer prevailed . . . In the months ahead the laboratory, which had swollen to 1,207 full-time employees by the previous May, would once again double and redouble in size."[25]

Much of their work involved long and tedious sequences of calculations about varying explosive clusters and effects. They were allowed almost exclusive use of several IBM mechanical computers, machines that automatically made complex calculations from data punched on to cards. It was whilst watching these machines that John von Neumann, a member of G Division, began to develop his first ideas about the possibility of electronic computers. Another field of intense activity was the development of diagnostic techniques. Rather like the V2 scientists, the implosion experts were dealing with events hidden from the human eye, in this case because they happened too fast, and leaving no evidential residue. To observe the shaping of detonation waves as they passed through solid blocks of high explosive, or their impact on a completely enclosed metal sphere, the physicists of G Division had to develop all kinds of innovatory methods involving high-current X-ray tubes, high-speed photography, stereoscopic cameras and betatron accelerators. One of the cameras devised, with a revolutionary flashlight, could take a picture in one ten-millionth of a second; another was able to take 100,000 pictures per second.

Ultimately it was the implosion lens, the speciality of X Division, that offered the real hope of eventual success. Months of experimentation with encasing a spherical core in conventional explosive, studded with point detonators, never achieved symmetrical results, mainly because the shock waves from such point detonations "spread out into the surrounding explosive just like the waves set off by a pebble hitting water. Thus it is always a curved wave front that hits the surface of the core, not the flat even one which could produce the necessary symmetry. Furthermore, when several detonations are fired, their diverging shock waves meet and interfere with one another, causing all manner of eruptions in the explosive and destroying any possibility of symmetry."[26] A member of the newly-arrived mission, James L. Tuck, suggested that the explosions be managed in the same way as in the latest shaped-charge, armour-piercing shells, using an explosive lens to focus the whole force of the warhead directly towards and thus right through the thick armour plate of the latest enemy tanks. The ability to focus each detonation and shape the resultant shock waves would permit the creation of a single exactly converging wave tailored to the shape it needed to compress. It was the millions of calculations required to turn this theory into practice that, throughout the autumn of 1944, kept the IBM calculators busy 24 hours a day, seven late days a week. Despite all this work, by late October the project had not moved much beyond the calculation stage with its endless combinations of variables and grindingly slow narrowing down of options – though there was evidence of some practical work. Each day roughly a ton of explosives went off in a series of experimental detonations, mostly concerned with the lens problem. But this effort, too, still had thousands of variables to shuffle with and "tests throughout October and November gave no indication that the explosive lens approach would easily produce the necessary symmetry."[27]

Nevertheless, if these problems could be surmounted in time, not to mention those in the Hanford reactor, it was still hoped that it might be possible to test fire a plutonium device. The site for such a test had already been chosen, at Alamogordo, as had its code-name, Trinity. Yet in his October letter to Vannevar Bush, James Conant was still so dubious about implosion that he estimated the yield of such a bomb as equivalent to only 1,000 tons of TNT. "That was so relatively modest a result that he invited Bush to consider the gun bomb strategic and the implosion bomb tactical."[28]

For the tens of thousands of people involved, living on the Oak Ridge, Hanford and Los Alamos sites was a somewhat bizarre experience, rather like attending summer camp in the middle of a construction site – but all on an epic scale. Hanford, for example, was served by 386 miles of road, some of it eight-lane highway, and 158 miles of railway. Construction of the whole site was reckoned to be the equivalent of building the housing for a city of 400,000 people. The town was only two-thirds complete by October 1944, and some families were still living in trailer parks. Oak Ridge, too, contained over 300 miles of paved roads and streets and it was estimated that the eventual population would be in the region of 75,000, occupying a small city 6½ miles long and 1½ miles wide. In it there were – or were being built – nine schools, a 300-bed hospital, two supermarkets, 22 tennis courts, two roller-skating rinks, seven theatres, a big library and a swimming pool. According to one mass spectrometer operator, Oak Ridge "was really a hellhole of a place. It was all wooden sidewalks, and the town was swarming with rats. There were more rats than people. It was a walled city. There was a big fence all around. They'd bulldozed this town in the mountains. There was no proper housing for a long time for married GIs . . . We lived out in a room in a motel."[29] And there were worse things than wooden sidewalks. One of the dominant motifs at Oak Ridge was mud – red, sticky Tennessee mud churned up by the thousands of pairs of feet and the hundreds of construction vehicles. Another anonymous balladeer had the following comments:

> In order not to check in late,
> I've had to lose a lot of weight
> From swimming through a fair-sized flood
> And wading through the goddam mud.

> I've lost my rubbers and my shoes,
> Perpetually I have the blues.
> My spirits tumble with a thud
> Because of all this goddam mud.

At Hanford the main problem was the frequent sandstorms that, according to one resident physicist, "were caused by tearing up the desert floor for roads and construction sites. [They] were suffocating. Wind-blown sand covered faces, hair and hands and got into eyes and teeth . . . Buses and other traffic came to a stop until the roads were visible [again] through the grey-black clouds of dust."[30]

In the extremes of climate experienced at Los Alamos, the roads were either dustbowls or quagmires. There were never any sidewalks, some said because of the cost, and neither was there any street lighting. The available housing always lagged behind the number of would-be occupants, while the water system soon fell short of both. The standard of accommodation varied considerably. Senior scientists and administrators were housed in commodious properties belonging to the original school, and situated on what was enviously known as 'Bathtub Row', while less privileged employees with families were given duplex and four-plex apartments and the singles roughed it in single-room dormitories. All agreed that the central heating was the biggest problem, and was invariably either stiflingly hot or, especially in winter, hardly working at all. The wood-burning stoves could be pressed into service to compensate for the cold weather, but the residents never ceased to marvel how, hot as they became, they never seemed able to cook anything properly. Temperature fluctuations also affected the water supply, such as it was. It was carried in overland pipes, laid on trestles, and often froze up at night.

At the same time, there were compensations. Some employees derived a real sense of adventure, mission even, from the lack of amenities. The wife of one scientist wrote: "I felt akin to the pioneer women accompanying their husbands across uncharted plains westward, alert to dangers, resigned to the fact that they journeyed, for weal or woe, into the Unknown." For a few of the more privileged the work was its own reward, not least because its ultimate aim was the defeat of two odious political regimes. One physicist recalled: "Los Alamos was a community of great single-mindedness and intensity. We thought of ourselves as being in the front line. The only way we could lose the war was if we failed our jobs . . . We never had such a sense of fraternity in a little community before . . . You knew all that was going on. Within the community there was a complete openness. Fermi, Bethé, Neumann, Kistiakowsky, Teller were all there. There were no secrets to which we were not privy. We were inventing the secrets. We were writing the book."[31]

Although everyone worked tremendously hard, putting in long hours six days a week, young people – the average age of the scientists was 27, hardly any were over 40 – do not live by physics alone and their weekly compensation was to unwind at boozy Saturday night parties and square dances, with restorative walking and riding trips on Sundays. Those suffering from mid-week ennui on Wednesday 25th October would be looking forward to playing hard at the weekend. This was especially the case with "single men and women [who] sponsored dorm parties fuelled with tanks of punch made potent with mixed liquors and pure Tech Area grain alcohol and invited wall-to-wall crowds. The singles removed all the furniture from their dormitory common rooms to make areas for dancing and by unwritten rule kept their upstairs doors open through the night."[32]

Others left their doors open for more sordid reasons. Some of the more poorly paid, or merely avaricious, female employees floated their sexual favours on the market, and found it resiliently bullish. The lowlier military ranks in general had a poor time of it at Los Alamos, even those working in the labs. Life in their separate barracks was very tightly regimented, the Army's usual instincts heightened by their acute fears over security. Worse, many of the scientists instinctively looked down on the military, even soldiers with a creditable engineering background. One scientist recalled: "I don't think the military personnel we had out there was particularly adequate, that was part of the problem. The military were just not going to put guys on this project who, as they described it, could be out winning the war." At Oak Ridge and Hanford military personnel were rarely assigned to anything but the most mundane tasks. One GI mass spectrometer operator commented on his uninspiring work: "I got a job that was crazy . . . I tested the product out of the stream to be sure impurities weren't getting into it. We had to handle it with asbestos gloves. I never knew how it worked. It was a deadly dull job. Nobody could adjust the machine, except some guy in Washington."[33]

Another group almost totally separated from the scientists and process operatives were the construction workers, several hundred of whom were still at work on the three Project sites. At Hanford they were quartered in barracks straggling round the outskirts of the small town of Richland. At its peak the construction camp contained almost 1,200 buildings and the trailer park, reckoned to be the largest in the world, numbered over 600 such vehicles. With a fifteen to one ratio of men to women, the town resembled something straight out of the Old West. The inhabitants were described by one law enforcement official as "very rough hombres, with no respect for the law, themselves or God Almighty." A scientist at Hanford spoke of "a tough town. There was nothing to do after work, with the result that occasionally bodies were found in the garbage cans the next morning."[34] These were the detritus of fights that usually followed copious drinking in the many saloons, which had been built with windows that hinged downwards to make it easier to lob in tear-gas grenades. Contractors and military authorities did their best to keep the men occupied and provided a 4,000-capacity dance-hall, movie theatres, baseball diamonds and visiting swing bands. Yet they remained distrustful of labour, organised or not. So concerned was Groves about the possibilities of large-scale unrest, sabotage or treason that many of the bar-keeps in the saloons were in fact secret-service agents.

Security, of course, was a major concern for the whole Manhattan Project, and nowhere more so than at Los Alamos where they were trying to build the bomb itself. Just as in the Hanford saloons, several of the waiters in nearby Santa Fe hotels were reputed to be secret service agents. The site itself was very tightly guarded. A high barbed-wire fence surrounded the whole area, patrolled by armed Military Police, and another ringed the sensitive laboratories in the 'Tech Area'. Passes had to be carried and shown regularly and the wives of some key personnel even had to display them to the military guarding their own front doors. Drivers' licences had numbers instead of names and were not signed. All had 'Engineer' in the 'Occupation' box, and an identical address, P.O. Box 1663, Santa Fe. This was the only address allowed to any of the thousands of Los Alamos residents and all their mail had to be so addressed. Letters and telephone calls were censored on a spot-check basis and the outgoing mail of the more prominent scientists was vetted 100 per cent. This "provoked great emotion among the scientists and after many protests and even threats of leaving, some rules were drawn up in common agreement. [By autumn 1944] families were notified that letters were being read and the civilians agreed to avoid any mention of the words 'Los Alamos', 'uranium', 'atom', and 'fission', as well as the names of distinguished scientists."[35]

Nevertheless, the residents were still not going to be allowed to vote in the November presidential election, which would involve giving name and address, and neither could they appear in court. Although this had its advantages, notably a blind eye cast on speeding offences, it also denied certain basic rights such as divorce. Even speeding was something of a novelty in October 1944. Up until a few weeks before travel away from the immediate vicinity of the site had been forbidden except on laboratory business or in minutely scrutinised cases of emergency. According to Groves, "the removal of these limitations was a cause of general rejoicing, and resulted from my feeling that the improvement in morale would outweigh the increased security risks." Even so, Groves was leaving little to chance. Visits to Santa Fe were still limited to just one a month and, according to one wife, "the town was full of men from G2 [Army Intelligence]; you could always spot them because they wore snap brimmed hats – straw in summer, felt in winter. G2 followed Hill people around town to see that they didn't speak to anyone in the street. People from Los Alamos were supposed to cut their own parents if they met them on the street. G2 saw to it that they didn't mail any letters surreptitiously and tailed them into La Cantina."[36]

A common joke on the Hill was that they were living in the Nobel Prize Winners' Concentration Camp, which showed how little they understood the difference between G2 and the *Allgemeine-SS*. But this is not to decry the psychological rigours of life at Los Alamos, or indeed any of the Manhattan Project sites. For Groves was not merely molly-coddling his 'longhairs' when he worried about the state of their morale. Admittedly, he began with a low opinion of what he once – to their faces – called "the largest collection of crackpots ever seen", but even he could see that life behind barbed-wire, nameless in the middle of nowhere, could be a considerable strain. Another scientist's wife remembered feeling for army doctors at Los Alamos, men who had prepared for battlefield surgery and ended up delivering babies or faced "with a high-strung bunch of men, women and children – high-strung because the altitude affected us, because our men worked long hours under unrelenting pressure, high-strung because we were too many of a kind, too close to one another, too unavoidable during relaxation hours; high-strung because we felt powerless under strange circumstances, irked by minor annoyances that we blamed on the Army and that drove us to unreasonable and pointless rebellion."[37]

One suspects, however, that even as phlegmatic a character as General Groves must have felt like kicking several billion atoms to hell and back by the end of October 1944, for the game of Manhattan roulette was not going at all well. He had already laid out millions upon millions of dollars in attempting to cover all possible bets, but the wheel was simply not spinning properly. Centrifuge separation had been effectively written off; electro-magnetic separation was proving to be unacceptably erratic, gumming up the works in the most dramatic fashion; gaseous-diffusion had the gas but nothing through which it could be reliably diffused. The only on-line industrial reactor had been closed down after displaying acute suicidal tendencies; and even if plutonium was now being produced, the chemical separation plants were not yet complete or the majority of operatives fully trained. Perhaps Groves derived some bitter consolation from knowing that, even if one of these numbers had come up, the task of actually getting his winnings to the bank was also extremely problematical. For it was already clear that U-235, if available at all in sufficient quantities, would have to be dropped in an untested bomb, while plutonium was now only likely to work in a pseudo-optical device of awesome complexity and precision, the first partial mock-ups of which were almost risibly inadequate.

Still there were some optimists to be heard, chiefly among scientists who remained largely oblivious to the bomb's military *raison d'être* – to end the European and Pacific wars within the next year or so. Such a one was James Conant who, in his October letter surveying progress to date, wrote: "By various methods that seem quite possible of development within six months after the first bomb is perfected, it should be possible to increase the efficiency . . . [so that] the same amount of material would yield something like 24,000 Tons TNT equivalent. Further developments [might] run this figure up to several hundred thousand tons . . . or perhaps a million . . ."[38]

Here was a man who always looked on the bright side. Brighter, even, than a thousand suns.

Notes and References

The publishers of source books are in London unless otherwise stated. A selected bibliography of the key works used in research for this book is given at the end of the notes.

Prologue: *The Big Three*

1 Churchill's speech recorded in *Hansard* and quoted in Martin Gilbert's *Winston Churchill*, Heinemann, 1986, vol. 7, p. 1040.
2 Quoted in R. E. Sherwood, *The White House Papers of Harry L. Hopkins*, Eyre & Spottiswoode, 1949, vol. 2, p. 828.
3 J. M. Blum, *Years of War 1941–45: From the Morgenthau Diaries*, Houghton Miflin, Boston, 1967, pp. 314–15.
4 Churchill's letter to Lord Cranborne, dated 24th October 1944, in the Churchill Papers 20/138. (Gilbert, p. 1037.) See also Sherwood, *loc. cit.*
5 W. A. Harriman and E. Abel, *Special Envoy to Churchill and Stalin 1941–46*, Hutchinson, 1967, pp. 366 and 367.
6 W. D. Leahy, *I Was There*, Gollancz, 1950, p. 122.
7 W. F. Kimball (ed.), *Churchill and Roosevelt: the Complete Correspondence*, Collins, 1984, vol. 3, pp. 356–7.
8 *Ibid.*, p. 359.
9 *Ibid.*, p. 371. The telegram is quoted in Roosevelt's telegram to Churchill on the same day.
10 Quoted in H. L. Stimson and M. Bundy, *On Active Service in Peace and War*, Harper, New York, 1948, p. 577.
11 Quoted in Harriman and Abel, *op. cit.*, pp. 364–5 and 361–2.
12 Kimball, *op. cit.*, p. 364.
13 I. Deutscher, *Stalin: a Political Biography*, Penguin, Harmondsworth, 1990 (rev. ed.), pp. 456–7.
14 S. M. Shtemenko, *The Soviet General Staff At War 1941–45*, Progress Publishers Moscow, 1970, p. 121.

15 *Ibid.*, pp. 137 and 119.
16 *Ibid.*, p. 267 and S. M. Shtemenko, *The Last Six Months: Russia's Final Battles with Hitler's Armies in World War II, Kimber,* 1978, p. 37.

Chapter 1: *Eisenhower and Montgomery*

1 Quoted in F. H. Hinsley *et al., British Intelligence in the Second World War: Its Influence on Strategy and Operations,* HMSO, 1988, vol. 3 part 2, p. 367 and H. Essame, *The Battle for Germany,* Bonanza Books, New York, 1969, p. 13.
2 R. Bennett, *Ultra in the West: the Normandy Campaign of 1944–45,* Hutchinson, 1979, p. 145.
3 A. D. Chandler *et al.* (eds.), *The Papers of Dwight David Eisenhower: the War Years,* John Hopkins Press, Baltimore (Md.), 1970, vol. 4, p. 2235.
4 Quoted in R. Lamb, *Montgomery in Europe 1943–45,* Buchan and Enright, 1983, p. 294.
5 A. Chalfont, *Montgomery of Alamein,* Weidenfeld and Nicolson, 1976, p. 255.
6 Montgomery of Alamein, *The Memoirs,* Collins, 1958, pp. 267-8.
7 *Ibid.*, pp. 271-2 and 274.
8 Chandler *et al., op. cit.,* p. 275.
9 Montgomery, *op. cit.,* p. 275.
10 Quoted in Lamb, *op. cit.,* p. 282.
11 Chandler *et al., op. cit.,* p. 2215.
12 Quoted in Montgomery of Alamein, *The Memoirs,* Collins, 1958, p. 317.

Chapter 2: *The Scheldt*

1 Quoted in J. L. Moulton, *Battle for Antwerp,* Ian Allan, Shepperton, 1978, p. 118.
2 Quoted in W. D. and S. Whitaker, *The Battle of the Scheldt,* Souvenir Press, 1985, pp. 109–10.
3 R. W. Thompson, *The 85 Days,* Four Square, 1960, pp. 95 and 103–4.
4 G. Rawling, *Cinderella Operation: the Battle for Walcheren 1944,* Cassell, 1980, p. 39.
5 Whitaker, *op. cit.,* p. 250.
6 Thompson, *op. cit.,* pp. 105–6.
7 C. P. Stacey, *The Victory Campaign (Official History of the Canadian Army in the Second World War),* Queen's Printers, Ottawa, 1960, p. 369; and Thompson, *op. cit.,* p. 61.
8 Thompson, *op. cit.,* p. 96.
9 Quoted in Rawling, *op. cit.,* pp. 54–5.
10 Whitaker, *op. cit.,* p. 298.
11 Thompson, *op. cit.,* p. 72; and quoted in Whitaker, *op. cit.,* pp. 276–7.
12 Thompson, *op. cit.,* p. 73.
13 Quoted in Whitaker, *op. cit.,* p. 298.
14 See J. Williams, *The Long Left Flank,* Leo Cooper, 1988, p. 164.
15 Quoted in Whitaker, *op. cit.,* pp. 224 and 225.
16 Quoted in Stacey, *op. cit.,* p. 385 and Williams, *op. cit.,* p. 110.

17 Quoted in Whitaker, *op. cit.*, pp. 223 and 224.
18 Quoted in T. Copp and B. McAndrew, *Battle Exhaustion: Soldiers and Psychiatrists in the Canadian Army 1939–45*, McGill-Queen's University Press, London, 1990, pp. 143–4.

Chapter 3: *Advance to the Maas*

 1 H. Essame, *The Battle for Germany*, Bonanza, New York, 1969, pp. 51–2.
 2 J. D'Arcy Dawson, *European Victory*, MacDonald, n.d., pp. 226–7.
 3 B. Fergusson, *The Black Watch and the King's Enemies*, Collins, 1950, p. 282.
 4 Dawson, *op cit.*, p. 227.
 5 R. W. Thompson, *The 85 Days*, Four Square, 1960, pp. 65 and 84.
 6 R. Woollcombe, *Lion Rampant*, Chatto & Windus, 1955, pp. 174–5.
 7 M. Lindsay, *So Few Got Through*, Collins, 1946, p. 106.
 8 Quoted in P. Delaforce, *Churchill's Desert Rats: From Normandy to Berlin With the 7th Armoured Division*, Alan Sutton, Stroud, 1994, p. 115.
 9 K. Tout, *Tanks Advance: Normandy to the Netherlands 1944*, Robert Hale, 1987, pp. 194–5.
10 Quoted in C. Blacker and H. G. Woods, *Change and Challenge: the Story of the 5th Royal Inniskilling Dragoon Guards 1922–78*, Clowes, 1978, p. 65.
11 *Ibid.*, p. 64 and quoted in C. J. Boardman, *Tracks in Europe: the 5th Royal*, in *Inniskilling Dragoon Guards 1939–46*, City Press Services, Salford, 1990, p. 197.
12 A. Wilson, *Flamethrower*, Corgi, 1973 (orig. 1956), pp. 112–13. This book is a memoir but is written in the third person.
13 *Ibid.*, p. 115.
14 P. Ryder, *Guns Have Eyes: One Man's Story of the Normandy Landings*, Robert Hale, 1984, p. 107.
15 Tout, *op. cit.*, p. 197. See also the first chapter of Tout's *To Hell With Tanks!*, Robert Hale, 1992, for more details on his part in Operation ALAN.
16 Lindsay, *op. cit.*, pp. 106–7.
17 P. J. Lewis and I. R. English, *Into Battle with the Durhams: 8 D.L.I. in World War II*, London Stamp Exchange, 1990 (orig. 1949), p. 294.
18 Quoted in P. Delaforce, *The Fighting Wessex Wyverns: from Normandy to Bremerhaven with the 43rd Wessex Division*, Alan Sutton, Stroud, 1994, pp. 172–3 and K. Ford, *Assault on Germany: the Battle of Geilenkirchen*, David & Charles, Newton Abbot, 1980, p. 32.
19 Quoted in D. Hawkins and D. Boyd (eds.), *War Report: a Record of Dispatches . . . by the BBC's War Correspondents . . . 6 June 1944–5 May 1945*, Oxford University Press, 1946, pp. 266–7. This report was broadcast on 23rd November after the Canadians had taken over the Nijmegen salient. Nevertheless, I can think of no reason why it is not an accurate description of British front-line positions there in late October, or, indeed, of any slit-trench or foxhole along much of the Allied front.
20 Quoted in G. P. B. Roberts, *From the Desert to the Baltic*, Kimber, 1987, p. 218.
21 Paraphrased and quoted in J. North, *North-West Europe 1944–45: the Achievement of 21st Army Group*, HMSO, 1977 (orig. 1953), p. 151.
22 Quoted in A. K. Altes and N. K. C. A. In't Veld, *The Forgotten Battle: Overloon*

and the Maas Salient 1944–45, Spellmount, Staplehurst, 1995, pp. 81–2.

23 Quoted in P. Delaforce, *The Black Bull: From Normandy to the Baltic with the 11th Armoured Division*, Alan Sutton, Stroud, 1993, p. 168.

24 Quoted in Altes and Veld, *op. cit.*, p. 103; and J. Pereira, *A Distant Drum: War Memories of the Intelligence Officer of the 5th Battalion Coldstream Guards 1944–45*, Gale & Polden, 1950, pp. 121–2. Again, the Coldstream Guards did not take over these positions until 3rd November but it seems legitimate to assume that they had not changed much since the departure of their previous occupants, 8 Rifle Brigade.

25 S. Jary, *18 Platoon*, Sydney Jary Ltd., Carshalton Beeches, 1987, p. 70.

26 Pereira, *op. cit.*, pp. 109 and 111.

27 Jary, *op. cit.*, p. 71.

28 *Ibid.*, p. 68.

29 Lewis and English, *op. cit.*, p. 295.

30 Quoted in P. Delaforce, *Monty's Ironsides: from the Normandy Beaches to Bremen with the 3rd Division*, Alan Sutton, Stroud, 1995, p. 139.

31 G. Picot, *Accidental Warrior: in the Front Line from Normandy Till Victory*, Penguin, Harmondsworth, 1994, p. 258.

32 A. Borthwick, *Battalion: a British Infantry Unit's Actions from El Alamein to the Elbe 1942–45*, Bâton Wicks, 1994 (orig. 1946 as *Sans Peur*), pp. 170–1. 5 Seaforths in fact served with 51 Highland Division south of s'Hertogenbosch but their snipers' exploits can be taken as typical of battalions in all British sectors.

33 Quoted in Delaforce, *Wyverns, op. cit.*, p. 175; and Pereira, *op. cit.*, p. 110.

Chapter 4: *Siege at Dunkirk*

1 L. M. White (ed.), *On All Fronts*, First European Monographs, Boulder (Col.), 1991, pp. 195–6.

2 *Ibid.*, pp. 197–8.

Chapter 5: *Liberation – in Holland and Belgium*

1 W. D. and S. Whitaker, *The Battle of the Scheldt*, Souvenir Press, 1985, pp. 13–14.

2 *The Diary of Anne Frank*, Pan, 1954, p. 165. Anne Frank was already at Auschwitz on 25th October, but as this entry in her diary, written in April 1944, refers to all the previous 21 months it seems reasonable to assume that things had certainly not improved by October.

3 R. Gill and J. Groves, *Club Route in Europe: the Story of 30 Corps in the European Campaign*, Hanover, 1946, p. 95.

4 W. D. and S. Whitaker, *op. cit.*, p. 246. My whole account of the destruction wrought at Woensdrecht is drawn from pp. 239 and 245–6 of this invaluable book.

5 Quoted in K. Tout, *To Hell With Tanks!*, Robert Hale, 1992, p. 51.

6 J. Jones, *Me and Mine*, Hamish Hamilton, 1946, p. 366; G. Martin, *The History of the 15th Scottish Division*, Blackwood, Edinburgh, 1948, p. 312; and A. K. Altes and N. K. C. A. In't Veld, *The Forgotten Battle: Overloon and the Maas Salient 1944–45*, Spellmount, Staplehurst, 1995, p. 168.

7 C. MacInnes, *To the Victor the Spoils*, Penguin, Harmondsworth, 1966 (orig. 1950), pp. 35, 34 and 38.

8 J. Prebble, *The Edge of Darkness*, Penguin, Harmondsworth, 1976 (orig. 1948), pp. 67–8.

9 J. Pereira, *A Distant Drum: War Memoirs of the Intelligence Officer of the 5th Battalion Coldstream Guards 1944–45*, Gale & Polden, Aldershot, 1950, pp. 117–18.

10 H. Essame, *The Battle for Germany*, Bonanza, New York, 1969, pp. 134–5; and M. Henniker, *An Image of War*, Leo Cooper, 1987, p. 205.

11 MacInnes, *op. cit.*, pp. 79 and 31.

12 N. Smith, *Tank Soldier: the Fight to Liberate Europe*, Book Guild, Lewes, 1989, p. 135.

13 Altes and Veld, *op. cit.*, p. 159.

14 Quoted in *ibid.*, pp. 160 and 161.

15 *Diary of Anne Frank, op. cit.*, p. 163. See Note 2 above.

16 D. Dilks (ed.), *The Diaries of Sir Alexander Cadogan 1938–45*, Cassell, 1971, p. 674.

17 R. McMillan, *Miracle Before Berlin*, Jarrolds, 1946, p. 91.

18 J. D'Arcy Dawson, *European Victory*, Macdonald, n.d., p. 237.

19 McMillan, *op. cit.*, p. 90; B. McBryde, *A Nurse's War*, Chatto & Windus, 1979, p. 141; and Dawson, *loc. cit.*

20 D. Belchem, *All In the Day's March*, Collins, 1978, p. 222.

21 Quoted in J. Thompson, *Imperial War Museum Book of Victory in Europe*, Sidgewick & Jackson, 1994, p. 203, and P. Delaforce, *The Black Bull: From Normandy to the Baltic with the 11th Armoured Division*, Alan Sutton, Stroud, 1993, p. 174.

22 P. Bright, *Life in Our Hands*, MacGibbon & Kee, 1955, pp. 143–4. All punctuation as in the original.

23 Prebble, *op. cit.*, pp. 119–20.

24 G. Brel, *The Normandy Nobodies*, Blandford, 1988, p. 95.

25 *Ibid.*, pp. 106–7.

26 *Ibid.*, p. 94.

27 A. Wilson, *Flamethrower*, Corgi, 1973 (orig. 1956), p. 145.

28 Smith, *op. cit.*, p. 173 and Brel, *op. cit.*, p. 95.

29 G. Stewart, *These Men My Friends*, Caxton Printers, Caldwell (Idaho), 1954, p. 283.

30 M. Lindsay, *So Few Got Through*, Collins, 1946, p. 258; and S. F. Crozier, *The History of the Corps of Military Police*, Gale & Polden, Aldershot, 1951, p. 121.

Chapter 6: *First U.S. Army and the Hürtgen Forest*

1 Quoted in R. F. Weighley, *Eisenhower's Lieutenants: the Campaigns in France and Germany 1944–45*, Sidgewick & Jackson, 1981, p. 366.

2 C. B. MacDonald, *The Siegfried Line Campaign (US Army in World War II)*, GPO, Washington, 1990 (orig. 1963), p. 90.

3 Weighley, *op. cit.*, p. 326.

4 Quoted in MacDonald, *op. cit.*, p. 320.

5 C. B. MacDonald, *Company Commander*, Bantam, New York, 1978 (orig. 1947), p. 91. The same author as the official historian cited above.

6 *Ibid.*, pp. 27–8 and 36–7. The incidents described here took place in the first half of October, but as MacDonald's company took the pill-box over from one rifle company and handed it on to their successors, it seems reasonable to assume that his description of life in this little piece of the line is generally applicable throughout the month.

7 *Ibid.*, pp. 95, 86 and 97.

8 W. S. Tsuchids, *Wear It Proudly*, University of California Press, Berkeley, 1947, p. 5.

9 C. Whiting, *Bloody Aachen*, Leo Cooper, 1976, p. 61 and quoted in R. G. Martin, *The GI War 1941–45*, Little Brown, Boston, 1967, p. 192.

10 Quoted in K. Ford, *Assault on Germany: the Battle for Geilenkirchen*, David & Charles, Newton Abbot, 1989, p. 32.

11 MacDonald, *Siegfried*, *op. cit.*, p. 323; and C. B. MacDonald, *The Battle of the Hürtgen Forest*, Jove, New York, 1993 (orig. 1963), p. 5.

12 C. B. Currey, *Follow Me and Die: the Destruction of an American Division in World War II*, Military Heritage Press, New York, 1984, p. 87.

13 *loc. cit.*

14 R. Ingersoll, *Top Secret*, Partridge, 1946, pp. 184–5.

15 Quoted in D. Congdon (ed.), *Combat: European Theater*, Dell, New York, 1958, p. 247. Again I have taken slight liberties in that this soldier, writing in *Yank* magazine, was from 4 Infantry Division which did not advance into the Forest until November. However, there is no reason to believe that Sergeant Mack Morris was not describing defences much the same as those encountered by 9 Division.

16 MacDonald, *Hürtgen*, *op. cit.*, p. 80.

Chapter 7: *Third U.S. Army Before Metz*

1 H. H. Semmes, *Portrait of Patton*, Paperback Library, New York, 1970 (orig. 1955), p. 215.

2 Quoted in A. Kemp, *Metz: the Unknown Battle*, Warne/Leo Cooper, 1981, p. 99.

3 G. S. Patton, *War As I Knew It*, W. H. Allen, n.d., pp. 145 and 135.

4 Quoted in R. F. Weighley, *Eisenhower's Lieutenants: the Campaigns in France and Germany 1944–45*, Sidgewick & Jackson, 1981, p. 386.

5 R. S. Allen, *Lucky Forward: the History of General George S. Patton's Third US Army*, Macfadden, New York, 1965 (orig. 1947), p. 123.

6 Patton, *op. cit.*, p. 154.

7 Quoted in H. M. Cole, *The Lorraine Campaign*, *(U.S. Army in World War II)*, GPO, Washington, 1997 (orig. 1950), p. 259.

8 Patton, *op. cit.*, p. 136.

9 J. Wellard, *The Man in a Helmet: the Life of General Patton*, Eyre & Spottiswoode, 1947, pp. 173 and 174.

10 Cole, *op. cit.*, pp. 277–8.

11 *Ibid.*, p. 278.

12 Quoted in G. Forty, *Patton's Third Army at War*, Ian Allan, Shepperton, 1978, pp. 94–5.

13 Cole, *op. cit.*, p. 295.

14 Patton, *op. cit.*, p. 156.

15 Kemp, *op. cit.*, p. 128.

16 Cole, *op. cit.*, p. 597.

17 D. D. Eisenhower, *Crusade in Europe*, Heinemann, 1948, p. 346.

Chapter 8: *The Vosges*

1 J. J. Clarke and R. R. Smith, *Riviera to the Rhine (U.S. Army in World War II)*, GPO, Washington, 1993, p. 251.

2 *Ibid.*, p. 290.

3 M. U. Duus, *Unlikely Liberators: the Men of the 100th and the 442nd*, University of Hawaii Press, Honolulu, 1987, pp. 176–7.

4 Quoted in F. Steidl, *Lost Battalions: Going for Broke in the Vosges Autumn 1944*, Presidio, Novato (Calif.), 1997, p. 80.

5 Quoted in *ibid.*, pp. 21–2; See also L. K. Truscott Jr., *Command Decisions*, Presidio, Novato (Calif.), 1990 (orig. 1954), p. 445; and Clarke and Smith, *op. cit.*, p. 240.

6 Quoted in Duus, *op. cit.*, p. 164.

7 Quoted in Clarke and Smith, *op. cit.*, p. 295.

8 K. E. Bonn, *When the Odds Were Even: the Vosges Mountain Campaign October 1944–January 1945*, Presidio, Novato (Calif.) 1994, p. 95; and M. D. Doubler, *Closing With the Enemy: How GIs Fought the War in Europe 1944–45*, University Press of Kansas, Lawrence, 1994, p. 102.

9 W. S. Tsuchida, *Wear It Proudly*, University of California Press, Berkeley, 1947, p. 14.

10 F. K. Franklin, *Road Inland*, Panther, 1959, p. 149.

11 Tsuchida, *op. cit.*, pp. 3, 15 and 17.

12 Clarke and Smith, *op. cit.*, p. 313.; and quoted in Steidl, *op. cit.*, p. 91.

Chapter 9: *Troopships*

1 All the above quotations are from B. C. Zorns, *I Walk through the Valley: a World War II Infantryman's Memoir of War, Imprisonment and Love*, McFarland, Jefferson (N.C.), 1991, pp. 61–3.

2 Quoted in A. Tapert (ed.), *Lines of Battle: Letters from American Servicemen 1941–45*, Times Books, New York, 1987, p. 181. Pfc. Winton belonged to 100 Infantry Division which had crossed the Atlantic between 6th and 10th October, but it seems reasonable to assume that his experiences were no different from those of men in the 14 Armored Division convoy.

3 M. van Creveld, *Fighting Power: German and US Army Performance 1939–45*, Arms & Armour Press, 1983, p. 77.

4 Quoted in M. D. Doubler, *Closing with the Enemy: How GIs Fought the War in Europe 1944–45*, University Press of Kansas, Lawrence, 1994, p. 247.

5 Quoted in S. Terkel, *The Good War: an Oral History of World War Two*, Penguin, Harmondsworth, 1986, p. 304.

6 I. Shaw, *The Young Lions*, Jonathan Cape, 1949, p. 593.

7 R. Granat, *The Important Thing*, Corgi, 1962, p. 78.

Chapter 10: *First French Army*

1 J. J. Clarke and R. R. Smith, *Riviera to the Rhine (US Army in World War II)*, GPO, Washington, 1993, p. 307.

2 Quoted in R. Aron, *De Gaulle Triumphant: the Liberation of France August 1944, May 1945*, Putnam, 1964, p. 315.

3 Marshal de Lattre de Tassigny, *The History of the First French Army*, Allen & Unwin, 1952, p. 219.

4 General de Gaulle, *War Memoirs: Salvation 1944–46 (Documents)*, Weidenfeld & Nicolson, 1960, pp. 50–1.

5 Aron, *op. cit.*, pp. 299–300.

6 *Ibid.*, p. 325.

7 De Gaulle, *op. cit.*, pp. 28–9.

8 *Ibid.*, pp. 60–1.

9 De Lattre de Tassigny, *op. cit.*, pp. 172 and 177.

10 *Ibid.*, p. 170.

11 Quoted in Aron, *op. cit.*, p. 295.

Chapter 11: *The Riviera*

1 G. M. Devlin, *Paratrooper: the Saga of Parachute and Glider Combat Troops during World War II*, Robson, 1979, p. 439.

2 R. H. Adleman and G. Walton, *The Champagne Campaign*, Leslie Frewin, 1973, p. 259.

3 Quoted in *ibid.*, pp. 253–4.

4 All the preceding quotes from *ibid.*, pp. 228–31 and 233–5. Clearly, this chapter relies heavily on Adleman and Walton's spirited account for its 'human interest'.

Chapter 12: *Sledgehammers and Nuts*

1 P. H. Vigor, *Soviet Blitzkrieg Theory*, Macmillan, 1984, pp. 88–9.

Chapter 13: *The German Army in the North*

1 A. Upton, 'End of the Arctic War', in *History of the Second World War*, Purnells, 1968, vol. 5, no. 16, p. 2232.

2 S. Jagerskiold, *Mannerheim: Marshal of Finland*, Hurst, 1986, p. 185.

3 *The Memoirs of Marshal Mannerheim*, Cassell, 1953, p. 503.

4 J. Lucas, *Alpine Elite: German Mountain Troops of World War II*, Janes, 1980, p. 139.

5 M. Kräutler and K. Springenschmid, *Es war ein Edelweis: Schicksal und Weg der zweiten Gebirgsdivision*, Stocker, Graz, 1962, p. 431.

6 Upton, *loc. cit.*

7 S. M. Shtemenko, *The Last Six Months: Russia's Final Battle with Hitler's Armies in World War II*, Kimber, 1978, pp. 375–6.

8 H. Guderian, *Panzer Leader*, Michael Joseph, 1952, p. 355.

9 J. Lucas, *Germany's Elite Panzer Force: Grossdeutschland*, Macdonald & Janes, 1978, p. 88; and quoted in A. J. Barker, *Panzers at War*, Ian Allan, Shepperton, 1978, pp. 131–3.

Chapter 14: *The Red Army in East Prussia and Poland*

1 W. E. D. Allen and P. Muratoff, *The Russian Campaigns of 1944–45*, Penguin, Harmondsworth, 1946, pp. 215–16.

2 H. Guderian, *Panzer Battles*, Michael Joseph, 1952, p. 361; and 'Strategicus' [H. C. O'Neill] *The Victory Campaign (May 1944–August 1945)*, Faber & Faber, 1947, p. 126.

3 J. Thorwald, *Flight in the Winter*, Hutchinson, 1953, p. 15.

4 Quoted in E. F. Ziemke, *The Soviet Juggernaut*, Time-Life, U.S.A., 1980, p. 188.

5 J. J. Baritz and G. Jukes, 'War on the Eastern Front: the Russian View', in *History of the Second World War*, Purnells, 1968, vol. 5, no. 8, pp. 2002–3.

6 H. Seton-Watson, *The East European Revolution*, Methuen, 1961, p. 117.

7 Quoted in Guderian, *op. cit.*, p. 358.

8 J. Garlinski, *Poland in the Second World War*, Macmillan, 1985, p. 306.

9 C. W. Snydor, *Soldiers of Destruction: the SS Deaths Head Division 1933–45*, Princeton University Press, 1977, p. 307.

10 J. Erickson, *The Road to Berlin: Stalin's War with Germany (vol. 2)*, Weidenfeld & Nicolson, 1983, p. 424.

11 S. M. Shtemenko, *The Soviet General Staff at War 1941–45*, Progress Publishers, Moscow, 1970, pp. 300 and 303.

12 V. I. Chuikov, *The End of the Third Reich*, Panther, 1969, pp. 64 and 65.

13 *Ibid.*, pp. 58–9 and 60.

14 Guderian, *op. cit.*; and G. Sajer, *The Forgotten Soldier*, Sphere, 1977, pp. 475–6.

Chapter 15: *Slovakia, Hungary and Rumania*

1 J. Erickson, *The Road to Berlin: Stalin's War with Germany (vol. 2)*, Weidenfeld & Nicolson, 1983, p. 295. My discussion of the Slovak Uprising relies heavily on Professor Erickson's account in pp. 290–307 of this book. See also the very useful maps in K. Kratsky and A. Snejdarek's 'The Slovak Uprising' in *History of the Second World War*, Purnells, 1968, vol. 6, no. 1, pp. 2241–51.

2 M. M. Minasyan *et al.*, *Great Patriotic War of the Soviet Union 1941–45: a General Outline*, Progress Publishers, Moscow, 1974, pp. 311–12. The deep breakthrough was nowhere more than 20 miles.

3 M. Windrow, *The Waffen–SS*, Osprey, 1995 (rev. ed.), p. 26.

4 Erickson, *op. cit.*, p. 304.

5 G. Reitlinger, *The SS: Alibi of a Nation*, Heinemann, 1956, p. 378, and H. Höhne,

The Order of the Death's Head: the Story of Hitler's SS, Pan, 1981 (orig. German ed. 1966), p. 503.

6 Erickson, *op. cit.*, p. 306.

7 *Ibid.*, p. 370.

8 Casualties against the Soviets, since June 1941, had totalled 381,000 killed and missing and 243,000 wounded.

9 M. Axworthy, *Third Axis, Fourth Ally: Rumanian Armed Forces in the European War 1941–45*, Arms & Armour Press, 1995, p. 202.

10 Erickson, *op. cit.*, pp. 393–4.

11 E. F. Ziemke, *Stalingrad to Berlin: The German Defeat in the East (Army Historical Series)*, GPO, Washington, 1968, p. 362.

12 *Ibid.*, p. 364 and E. Bauer, *The History of World War II*, Gallery Press, 1984, p. 545.

13 A. Seaton, *The Russo-German War 1941–45*, Arthur Barker, 1971, p. 495.

Chapter 16: *Bulgaria and Yugoslavia*

1 S. M. Shtemenko, *The Last Six Months: Russia's Final Battles with Hitler's Armies in World War II*, Kimber, 1978, p. 193.

2 Quoted in G. Lepre, *Himmler's Bosnian Division: the Waffen-SS Handschar Division 1943–45*, Schiffer, Atglen (Pa.), 1997, p. 268.

3 E. F. Ziemke, *Stalingrad to Berlin: the German Defeat in the East (Army Historical Series)*, GPO, Washington, 1968, p. 378; and W. Berthold, *Brandenburg Division*, Panther, 1962, p. 157.

4 J. Erickson, *The Road to Berlin: Stalin's War with Germany (vol. 2)*, Weidenfeld & Nicolson, 1983, p. 388; and A. S. Zheltov, 'The 3rd Ukrainian Front in the Balkans', in *The Great March of Liberation*, Progress Publishers, Moscow, 1972, p. 139.

5 F. Maclean, *Eastern Approaches*, Pan, 1956, p. 402.

Chapter 17: *Industry in the Soviet Union*

1 Self-propelled artillery mounted both field and anti-tank guns, these being non-traversable and simply bolted into the chassis of a conventional, often obsolete, tank. Non-traversability was a drawback, of course, but such guns were easier and cheaper to manufacture, could accommodate a bigger gun, and usually had a greater rate of fire.

2 S. J. Zaloga and J. Grandsen, *Soviet Tanks and Combat Vehicles of World War II*, Arms & Armour Press, 1984, p. 175.

3 W. L. White, *Report on the Russians*, World Publishing Company, New York, 1946, p. 49.

4 Quoted in H. Keyssner and V. Pozner, *Remembering War: a U.S.-Soviet Dialogue*, Oxford University Press, New York, 1990, p. 94.

5 H. C. Cassidy, *Moscow Dateline*, Cassell, 1943, p. 218.

6 White, *op. cit.*, p. 149.

7 *Ibid.*, p. 151.

8 A. Jacob, *A Window in Moscow*, Collins, 1946, p. 143.

9 White, *op. cit.*, p. 212. Also short quotes below.

10 Keyssner and Pozner, *loc. cit.*

11 W. Kerr, *The Russian Army*, Gollancz, 1944, p 100.

12 A. Werth, *Russia at War 1941–45*, Barrie & Rockliff, 1964, p. 762. The 'nasty' jam was presumably marmalade, which had been included amongst the 4 million tons of food the Americans sent over as part of their enormous Lend Lease shipments to the USSR.

13 White, *op. cit.*, pp. 229–30; and A. Solzhenitsyn, *One Day in the Life of Ivan Denisovich*, Penguin, Harmondsworth, 1964, p. 19. Solzhenitsyn was not arrested until February 1945.

14 R. Conquest, *The Great Terror: Stalin's Purge of the Thirties*, Macmillan, 1973 (rev. ed.), p. 463. This whole paragraph derives from Chapter 10 of this book.

15 Given that the prisoners would probably have died at a fairly steady rate through the year, unlike military casualties which peak and trough, it seems likely that on our chosen day 7,000 or so political prisoners were worked to death.

16 White, *op. cit.*, pp. 87 and 93–4.

17 By the end of September 1944, according to the most recent figures, Soviet armed forces had lost 10.13 million men killed, missing and died of disease, and 15.07 million wounded and sick.

18 Kerr, *op. cit.*, p. 103.

19 B. Pasternak, *Doctor Zhivago*, Collins and Harvill Press, 1958.

Chapter 18: *Hitler at The Wolf's Lair*

1 A. Speer, *Inside the Third Reich*, Avon, New York, 1971, p. 499.

2 Quoted in D. Irving, *Hitler's War*, Hodder & Stoughton, 1977, pp. 726–7.

3 G. Blumentritt, *von Runstedt: the Soldier and the Man*, Odhams, 1952, p. 268.

4 S. Westphal, *The German Army in the West*, Cassell, 1951, pp. 178–9. And short quote following.

5 W. Warlimont, *Inside Hitler's Headquarters 1939–45*, Weidenfeld & Nicolson, 1964, p. 481.

6 O. N. Bradley, *A Soldier's Story: the Allied Campaigns from Tunis to the Elbe*, Eyre & Spottiswoode, 1951, p. 437.

Chapter 19: *Bomber Command Over Essen*

1 W. S. Churchill, *The Second World War*, Cassell, 1948–54, vol. 2, pp. 567 and 405–6.

2 Quoted in A. Beaumont, 'The Bombing Offensive as a Second Front', in *Journal of Contemporary History*, no. 22, January 1987, p. 6.

3 J. Ellis, *World War II: a Statistical Survey*, Aurum Press, 1993, p. 234.

4 Quoted in C. Webster and N. Frankland, *The Strategic Air Offensive Against Germany (History of the Second World War: U.K. Military Series)*, HMSO, 1961, vol. 4, p. 172.

5 S. Zuckerman, *From Apes to Warlords 1904–46*, Hamish Hamilton, 1978, p. 243.

6 Quoted in Webster and Frankland, *op. cit.*, pp. 173 and 174–5.

7 A. Harris, *Bomber Offensive*, Collins, 1947, p. 237.

8 On 12th November Portal was to write: ". . . I have, I must confess, at times wondered whether the magnetism of the remaining German cities has not in the past tended as much to deflect our bombers from their primary objectives as the tactical and weather conditions which you so describe so fully . . . I would like you to reassure me that this is not so." (Quoted in R. C. Cooke and C. Nesbit, *Target: Hitler's Oil*, Kimber, 1985, p. 160.)

9 A more detailed breakdown of planes dispatched on 25th October is given below:

Air Force	Bombers Dispatched	Target	Type	Tonnage Dropped	Bombers Lost	Bombers Damaged	Aircrew Killed/Missing
8 U.S.	752	Hamburg	Oil	1,590	2	110	18
	225	Neumünster	Airfield	590	–	–	–
	142	Hamm	Railway	222	–	49	–
	131	Schloven	?	246	–	39	–
Total	1,250*			2,608	2	198	18
RAF Bomber Command	759	Essen	Area	?	4	?	28
	231	Homburg	Oil	?	–	?	?
	990			?	4	?	?
15 U.S.	4	Klagenfurt	Aircraft Factory/ Railway	?	–	–	–

(R. Freeman, *Mighty Eighth War Diary*, Janes, 1981, p. 370; M. Middlebrook and C. Everitt, *The Bomber Command War Diaries*, Viking, 1985, p. 607; and private communication with Mark Axworthy.)

As all raids on the 25th were daylight raids this chapter concentrates only on the Bomber Command effort, to avoid unnecessary overlap. Those interested in American bomber operations will find a detailed treatment of the B–29 campaign from China in a later chapter.

10 See S. Willis and B. Hollis, *Military Airfields in the British Isles 1939–45*, pvte. pub., Kettering, 1987, *passim*. No. 6 Group was wholly Canadian. No. 5 Group began conducting its own Pathfinder operations from March 1944. For the purposes of comparison, Eighth U.S. Air Force at this time comprised 3 Bombardment Divisions, 14 Bombardment Wings, and 39 Bombardment Groups, each of the latter containing 4 squadrons. This gave a total of 156 U.S. bomber squadrons as against 99 in Bomber Command. In theory an American squadron contained 18 aircraft as against 24 in a British or Commonwealth squadron. The U.S. Army Air Force in England took up only 68 airfields as opposed to Bomber Command's 92, but its Bombardment Groups managed to get four squadrons on each field.

11 Harris, *op. cit.*, pp. 238 and 239.

12 C. Olsson, 'Twenty Lancasters' in M. Garbett and B. Goulding, *The Lancaster at War*, Ian Allen, Shepperton, 1971, p. 36.

13 G. Musgrove, *Pathfinder Force: a History of 8 Group*, Macdonald & Janes, 1976, p. 275.

14 J. Wainwright, *Tail-End Charlie*, Macmillan, 1978, pp. 93 and 98–99. Other

stations seemed to have relied on simple caffeine tablets rather than benzedrine. And as has been pointed out, pure adrenaline was an extremely effective drug on most bombing missions. See also J. Currie, *Lancaster Target*, Goodall, 1981, pp. 101–2.

15 W. E. Jones, *Bomber Intelligence: 103, 150, 166, 170 Squadrons Operations and Techniques 1942–45*, Midland Counties, Leicester, 1983, p. 79.

16 Currie, *op. cit.*, p. 25.

17 J. Shelton, 'Prelude to Hell', in Garbett and Goulding, *op. cit.*, p. 45.

18 M. Tripp, *The Eighth Passenger*, Corgi, 1971, p. 41.

19 Garbett and Goulding, *op. cit.*, p. 58.

20 Currie, *op. cit.*, p. 26; and Shelton, *op. cit.*, p. 46.

21 M. R. Ford-Jones, *Bomber Squadron: Men Who Flew With XV*, Kimber, 1987, p. 207, and Wainwright, *op. cit.*, p. 102.

22 Currie, *op. cit.*, p. 168.

23 H. Archer and E. Pine, *To Perish Never*, Cassell, 1954, p. 79. Some pilots preferred to have both hands on the 'stick' just before take-off and then it was the flight engineer who actually pushed through the gate on command.

24 *Ibid.*, pp. 76–7.

25 Tripp, *op. cit.*, p. 44. Bomber Command's reluctance to fly in formation during daylight raids was the main distinguishing factor between their tactics and those of the American strategic bombers. The latter always flew in formation to maximise their bombers' firepower against enemy fighters – a legacy from the days when there were few if any fighter escorts. In such circumstances the bombers were supposed to form a sort of flying phalanx, rather like the 'pike and shot' infantry formations of the 17th century. But the Americans also bombed in formation, and in unison, on the instructions of a lead-bomber, in an attempt to maintain a tight pattern of hits around the target.

26 W. Clapham, *Night Be My Witness*, Corgi, 1965 (orig. 1948), pp. 207–8.

27 In October 1944 these consisted of 308 'Serrate' sorties to intercept German night-fighters by picking up transmissions from their Lichtenstein radar; 238 A1 Mk. 10 sorties to pick up night-fighters with own radar; 12 nights of Mandrel screen to noise jam German fighter controllers; 11 diversionary 'Window' operations, dropping aluminium foil to overwhelm German ground radar, but over decoy targets; 181 electronic intelligence (Elint) sorties, many of them in connection with the German V-2 rocket sites; 173 intruder sorties against German airfields; an unspecified number of escort missions using aircraft fitted with 'Monica' tail-mounted radar to pick up enemy fighters. During October also some squadrons were having their 'Monica' replaced by the far superior 'Perfectos' transmitter-receiver which activated Luftwaffe IFF sets and gave distance and direction of the enemy plane. (See M. Streetly, *Confound and Destroy: 100 Group and the Bomber Support Campaign*, Janes, 1985, p. 70.) Many of these sorties were concerned with disrupting the German night-fighter force and I have been unable to ascertain exactly what sort of effort was staged directly in support of the Essen mission.

28 Other methods of marking, with Target Indicators dropped to the ground, were 'Newhaven' and 'Paramatta', all three code-names deriving from the home towns of three of 8 Group's serving personnel.

29 Jones, *op. cit.*, p. 145. See also D. C. T. Bennett, *Pathfinder*, Sphere, 1972 (orig. 1958), pp. 173–4.

30 G. Jones, *Raider: the Halifax and Its Flyers*, Kimber, 1978, p. 153.

31 R. Ollis, *101 Nights*, Cassell, 1957, p. 248.

Chapter 20: *The Luftwaffe in Defence of Germany*

1 The Bf 109G, or 'Gustav', appeared in summer 1942, as a successor to the B, C, D, E ('Emil'), and F models. The E was produced in at least 13 variants and the F in 10. The G appeared as the G1, G1 (Trop), G2, G2/R1, G3/4, G5, G5/U2, G6, G6/R1, 2, 4 and 6, G6/U2, G6/U4, G6/U4N, G6/N, G6 (Trop), G7, G8, G10, G10/R1, 2, 4 and 6, G10/U2, G10/U4, G12, G14, G14/R1, G14/R6, G14/U4, and G16. N = *Nacht*. U = *Umrüst-Bausatz*, a modification to the airframe. R = *Rüstsatz*, a 'bolt-on' to the airframe, usually to accommodate extra armament.

2 Quoted in M. Caidin, *Flying Forts: the B-17 in World War II*, Ballantine, New York, 1969, pp. 468–9.

3 A *Jagdgeschwader* was the equivalent of an Allied fighter group. It was usually divided into three *Gruppen*, the equivalent of Allied wings, and these in turn comprised three or four *Staffeln*, or squadrons, each of *circa* ten planes.

4 G. Bloemertz, *Heaven Next Stop: Impressions of a German Fighter Pilot*, Kimber, 1953, pp. 148–9; and J. Steinhoff, *The Last Chance: the Pilots' Plot Against Göring*, Hutchinson, 1977, pp. 41–3.

5 Albert Speer, who as Minister of Munitions would have had to oversee such a massive production switch that he told Galland he had no intention of even attempting it.

6 H. Herrmann, *Eagle's Wings*, Airlife, Shrewsbury, 1991, p. 235.

7 Steinhoff, *op. cit.*, p. 42.

8 W. H. Tantum and E. J. Hoffschmidt.(eds.), *The Rise and Fall of the German Air Force 1943–45*, WE Inc., Old Greenwich (Conn.), 1969 (orig. Air Ministry, London, 1948), p. 316.

9 United States Strategic Bombing Survey (Military Analysis Division), *Defeat of the German Air Force*, GPO, Washington, January 1947, p. 6.

10 Herrmann, *op. cit.*, p. 238.

11 H. J. Nowarra, *The Messerschmitt 109: a Famous German Fighter*, Harleyford, Letchworth, 1966 (rev. ed.), p. 88.

12 W. Heilmann, *I Fought You From the Skies*, Award Books, New York, 1966 (orig. 1951), p. 83 and quoted in J. Scutts, *USAAF Heavy Bomber Units ETO and MTO 1942–45*, Osprey, 1977, p. 43.

13 Quoted in A. Lee, *Göring: Air Leader*, Duckworth, 1972, p. 192.

14 A. Speer, *Inside the Third Reich*, Avon, New York, 1971, p. 517.

15 United States Strategic Bombing Survey (Overall Economic Effects Division), *The Effects of Strategic Bombing on the German Economy*, GPO, Washington, October 1945, p. 159.

16 According to Günther Bloemertz, it was in autumn that "the first women engineers, mechanics, armourers, and radio technicians began to report for duty

... The squadron's chief mechanic started grousing about discipline. His female ground staff were a little too susceptible to the advances of their male colleagues. Particularly the pilots took quite a fancy to the attractive assistants in snugly fitting black overalls who leaned down into their cockpits to help them with their belts ..." (Bloemertz, *op. cit.*, p. 148.)

17 "But by this time even the test-firing of guns had been discontinued owing to the shortage of ammunition, and a label was inserted in the cockpits of all newly-delivered aircraft warning pilots to exercise caution when firing the guns for the first time!" (W. Green, *Warplanes of the Third Reich*, Macdonald and Janes, 1970, p. 13.)

18 USSBS, *Defeat of the German Air Force*, *op. cit.*, pp. 14–15.

19 J. R. Smith, *Messerschmitt: an Aircraft Album*, Ian Allan, Shepperton, 1971, p. 88.

20 A. Price, *World War II Fighter Conflict*, Macdonald & Janes, 1975, p. 74.

21 Heilmann, *op. cit.*, p. 86.

22 Because there were no Allied night raids either on the 24th/25th or the 25th/26th I have omitted any discussion of the German night-fighter force. It, too, was at a very low ebb, inflicting only 64 losses on 8,446 sorties in the month of October. For a succinct discussion of the reasons for this see R. V. Jones, *Most Secret War: British Scientific Intelligence 1939–45*, Hamish Hamilton, 1978, pp. 468–9.

Chapter 21: *The V1 and V2 Offensive*

1 F. I. Ordway III and M. R. Sharpe, *The Rocket Team*, Heinemann, 1977, pp. 39 and 80.

2 The tunnels were begun in 1917 to exploit ammonia, gypsum and anhydrite deposits. They closed in 1934 but were re-opened and expanded from 1937 as a petroleum and chemical storage plant. By 1944 the A-4 assembly plant occupied 1,200,000 square feet of floor space and comprised two main 25 foot high tunnels, extending for more than a mile and connected by almost fifty cross-tunnels, each of these roughly 30 feet wide and 25 feet high. Delivery from raw materials and feeder plants was done down one of the main tunnels, machining, welding and sub-assembly in the cross-tunnels, and final assembly down the other main tunnel. Standard-gauge railway tracks ran through the main tunnels to permit loading and unloading out of sight of Allied reconnaissance aircraft.

3 It was not, as might be expected, the ramp which inspired the name 'ski sites' but the three long, thin storage buildings which were curved at one end to contain blast if attacked by bombers. On aerial photographs these buildings closely resembled skis laid on their side.

4 See Ordway and Sharpe, *op. cit.*, p. 236.

5 Quoted in C. B. MacDonald, *The Siegfried Line Campaign*, (*U.S. Army in World War II*), GPO, Washington, 1963, p. 229; and Anon., *The Story of the 79th Armoured Division*, Hamburg, July 1945, p. 179. (See also the photograph in B. Ogley, *Doodlebugs and Rockets*, Froglets Publications, Westerham, 1992, p. 156.).

6 A. D. Chandler (ed.), *The Papers of Dwight D. Eisenhower: the War Years*, John Hopkins Press, Baltimore, 1970, vol. IV, p. 257. From early September Allied commanders had ben discussing how best to deal with the threat to Antwerp and

on 4th October had charged the chief SHAEF air defence officer with organising appropriate measures. To help him several AA regiments and radar units were transferred from England over the next four weeks. On the 24th, SHAEF was also given access to the most up-to-date intelligence on V1 and V2 development and launch sites, the so-called CROSSBOW intelligence, but it was likely to be several weeks before this could be properly disseminated and acted upon. Moreover, air attacks against such sites as had already been identified were limited by a shortage of suitable aircraft. The weather could also be a problem and at least one fighter squadron engaged in ground-attack operations from a base in Belgium did not fly at all between 21st and 28th October.

7 On 25th October there were 16 firing batteries of V1s under the command of General Wachtel's *Flakgruppe* Kreil, known until very recently as 155 (*Werfer*) Regiment. Batteries were based in the Eifel and the Westerwald, in Germany, and east of Apeldoorn in Holland. Although part of the Luftwaffe, they were under an Army command, XXX Corps, under General Erich Heinemann.

8 The descent was supposed to be powered but barely 4 per cent of V1s managed this as the dive angle invariably cut off the fuel supply, leaving the bomb to glide to the ground in an eerily disconcerting silence.

9 R. F. Pocock, *German Guided Missiles*, Ian Allan, Shepperton, 1967, p. 26.

10 R. A. Young, *The Flying Bomb*, Ian Allen, Shepperton, 1978, p. 143.

11 There were 8 batteries of V2s in all on 25th October, based in The Hague, Zwolle and Enschede in Holland, and north-west of Munster and near Merzig in Germany. All were targeted on London or Antwerp. They, too, were supposed to be under the command of XXX Corps (see Note 7) but in fact had been taken over by Himmler's SS. He had contrived to get himself appointed Special Commissioner for A-4 Development and Training and command of V2 units in the field had been entrusted to his Deputy Special Commissioner, *Gruppenführer* Kammler.

12 G. P. Kennedy, *Vengeance Weapon 2: the V2 Guided Missile*, Smithsonian Institution Press, Washington 1983, p. 40. The Zippelius quotation is from Ordway and Sharpe, *op. cit.*, p. 196.

13 Kennedy, *op. cit.*, p. 44.

14 *Ibid.*, p. 45.

15 Quoted in Ordway and Sharpe, *op. cit.*, p. 199.

16 F. Pile, *Ack-Ack: Britain's Defence Against Air Attack During the Second World War*, Harrap, 1959, pp. 368, 373 and 375..

17 Quoted in *ibid.*, p. 377. The site was manned by 409 Heavy AA Battery.

Chapter 22: *The Gothic Line in Italy*

1 In October 1944 this army group was actually known as Allied Armies in Italy but I have retained the original designation, readopted in December, to maintain consistency.

2 In June the Germans renamed this position the Green Line but as Allied intelligence of the time, and historiography since, ignored the change, I shall stick with 'Gothic Line'. Kesselring was also overall theatre commander, or *Oberbefehlshaber* (OB) Süd-West.

3 E. Linklater, *The Campaign in Italy*, HMSO, 1951, pp. 390–1.

4 C. G. Starr, *From Salerno to the Alps: a History of the Fifth Army 1943–45*, Battery Press, Nashville (TN), 1979 (orig. 1948), p. 331.

5 *Ibid.*, p. 359.

6 M. Clark, *Calculated Risk; His Personal Story of the War in North Africa and Italy*, Harrap, 1951, p. 378.

7 Starr, *op. cit.*, p. 361.

8 *Ibid.*, p. 338.

9 D. Orgill, *The Gothic Line*, Pan, 1969, p. 239.

10 Linklater, *op. cit.*, pp. 402–3.

11 P. L. Schultz, *The 85th Infantry Division in World War II*, Battery Press, Nashville (TN), 1979 (orig. 1949), p. 155.

12 D. Pal, *The Campaign in Italy 1943–45 (Official History of the Indian Armed Forces in the Second World War 1939–45)*, Combined Inter-Services Historical Section, New Delhi, 1960, pp. 512–13.

13 A. L. Brown, *Bulletins*, pvte. pub., Worcester, 1989, p. 218.

14 Orgill, *op. cit.*, p. 232.

15 N. Douglas, *And No Glory*, Corgi, 1958, p. 136.

16 W. Goldstein, *Farewell Screw Gun: the Tale of the 85th Field/Mountain Regiment R.A./T.A.*, The Book Guild, Lewes, 1986, p. 132.

17 Quoted in B. Harpur, *The Impossible Victory: a Personal Account of the Battle for the River Po*, Kimber, 1980, p. 89.

18 Douglas, *op. cit.*, pp. 136 and 140.

19 Schultz, *op. cit.*, p. 183 and Anon., *The London Irish at War: History of the London Irish Rifles in World War II*, London Irish Rifles Old Comrades Assoc., n.d., p. 187.

20 Quoted in Harpur, *op. cit.*, p. 87.

21 J. Hallam, *The History the Lancashire Fusiliers 1939–45*, Alan Sutton, Stroud, 1993, pp. 148–9.

22 Quoted in L. F. Ellis, *Welsh Guards at War*, London Stamp Exchange, 1990 (orig. 1946), p. 247.

23 *Ibid.*, p. 248.

24 Hallam, *op. cit.*, pp. 177–8.

25 W. Robson, *Letters From a Soldier*, Faber & Faber, 1960, p. 149.

26 J. Blythe, *Soldiering On: a Soldier's War in North Africa and Italy*, Hutchinson, 1989, pp. 168–9.

27 J. C. Fry, *Combat Soldier*, National Press, Washington D.C., 1968, pp. 212–16.

28 Schultz, *op. cit.*, p. 165.

29 E. J. Fisher, *Cassino to the Alps (United States Army in World War II)*, GPO, 1977, p. 379; and quoted in L. K. Truscott, *Command Missions*, Presidio, Novato (Calif.), 1990 (orig. 1954), p. 461.

30 K. H. Huebner, *Long Walk Through War: a Combat Doctor's Diary*, Texas and A.M. University Press, College Station, 1987, p. 152.

31 J. Horsfall, *Fling Our Banners to the Wind*, Roundwood Press, Kineton, 1978, p. 210.

32 C. Gunner, *Front of the Line: Adventures with the Irish Brigade*, Greystone, Antrim, 1991, p. 116.

33 Anon., *The History of the 3rd Medium Regiment Royal Artillery 1939–45*, pvte. pub., 1945, p. 230.

34 Quoted in Harpur, *op. cit.*, p. 87.

35 C. S. Frost, *Once a Patricia: Memoirs of a Junior Infantry Officer in World War II*, Vanwell, St Catherine's (Ontario), 1988, p. 340.

Chapter 23: *Life in Occupied Italy*

1 Quoted in R. Lamb, *War in Italy 1943–45*, Penguin, 1995, p. 118.

2 *Ibid.*, p. 108.

3 C. R. S. Harris, *Allied Military Administration in Italy 1943–45 (United Kingdom Military Series)*, HMSO, 1957, pp. 151–2 and 153.

4 King Victor Emmanuel III abdicated in January 1944, naming his son Umberto as Lieutenant of the Realm.

5 N. Lewis, *Naples '44*, Collins, 1978, p. 193.

6 J. H. Burns, *The Gallery*, Secker & Warburg, 1948, p. 260.

7 Churchill's telegram to Roosevelt of 24th October quoted in *Roosevelt and Churchill: the Secret Wartime Correspondence*, edited by F. L. Loewenheim *et al.*, Barrie & Jenkins, 1975, p. 596.

8 Quoted in Harris, *op. cit.*, p. 193.

9 Lewis, *op. cit.*, p. 158.

10 Burns, *op. cit.*, p. 264.

11 W. Brebner, *La Signora* (orig. *Two Lakes*), Ace Books, 1959 (orig. 1951), p. 129.

12 Lewis, *op. cit.*, p. 171.

13 *Ibid.*, pp. 161 and 165.

14 Burns, *op. cit.*, p. 308.

15 E. Taylor, *Women Who Went to War 1938–46*, Robert Hale, 1988, p. 204.

16 Lewis, *op. cit.*, p. 158.

17 Harris, *op. cit.*, p. 427.

18 Burns, op. cit., pp. 299–300.

19 *Loc. cit.*

20 Quoted in D. W. Elwood, *Italy 1943–45*, Leicester University Press, 1985, p. 158.

21 Quoted in C. F. Delzell, *Mussolini's Enemies: the Italian Anti-Fascist Resistance*, Princeton University Press, 1961, p. 410.

22 Quoted in Lamb, *op. cit.*, p. 64.

23 Delzell, *op. cit.*, pp. 416 and 417.

24 *ibid.*, p. 357 and V. Milroy, *Alpine Partisan*, Corgi, 1958, p. 128.

25 Lamb, *op. cit.*, p. 220.

26 Both quoted in B. B. Carter, *Italy Speaks*, Gollancz, 1947, pp. 121 and 122.

27 Quoted in A. Tapert (ed.), *Lines of Battle: Letters from American Servicemen 1941–45*, Times Books, New York, 1987, p. 209.

28 Quoted in Lamb, *op. cit.*, p. 242.

29 Quoted in *ibid.*, p. 243. According to Lamb, "Hitler had no intention of allowing White Russians to take over this attractive area," which was to become part of Austria after the war, and "the sophisticated White Russian generals must have known in their hearts that this was a delusion" (p. 241).

Chapter 24: *The British in Greece*

1 Quoted in Winston Churchill's *The Second World War*, vol. 6, Cassell, 1954, p. 97.
2 Telegram No. 755, 17th August 1944 (HMSO) quoted in F. L. Loewenstein *et al.*, *Roosevelt and Churchill: Their Secret Wartime Correspondence*, Barrie & Jenkins, 1975, p. 562.
3 Quoted in H. Maule, *Scobie, Hero of Greece: the British Campaign 1944–45*, Arthur Barker, 1975, p. 75.
4 Earl of Avon, *The Eden Memoirs: the Reckoning*, Cassell, 1965, p. 489.
5 Quoted in Maule, *op. cit.*, p. 9.
6 M. Gander, *After These Many Quests*, MacDonald, 1949, p. 262.
7 H. Macmillan, *War Diaries: the Mediterranean 1943–45*, Macmillan, 1984, p. 557.
8 N. Riley, *One Jump Ahead*, John Clare, 1984, p. 104.
9 Quoted in M. Arthur, *Men of the Red Beret*, Hutchinson, 1990, p. 226.
10 Riley, *op. cit.*, p. 110 and Arthur, *loc. cit.*
11 Maule, *op. cit.*, p. 67.

Chapter 25: *U–Boat Wolf Packs*

1 The full figures for the 58 U-boats are: *Inshore Patrols*: sailing to and from patrol 11 boats; on patrol 3 boats. *Remote Atlantic Stations*: to and from 7 boats; on patrol 3 boats. *Arctic*: on patrol 19 boats. *Sailing from France to Norway*: 2 boats. *Sailing from Norway to Saint-Nazaire*. (Transport): 2 boats. *Indian Ocean*. (At sea and in port): 11 boats. Derived from V. E. Tarrant, *The Last Year of the Kriegsmarine*, Arms and Armour Press, 1994, pp. 155–6, 171, 179; MOD (Navy), *The U-Boat War in the Atlantic*, HMSO, 1989 (orig. 1945/46?), vol. 3, pp. 109–18 and Diagrams 26–27; J. Rohwer and G. Hummelchen, *Chronology of the War at Sea 1939–45*, Ian Allen, Shepperton, 1974, vol. 2, p. 464.
2 J. P. Mallmann Showell, *U-Boats Under the Swastika*, Ian Allen, Shepperton, 1973, p. 151.
3 MOD (Navy), *op. cit.*, Diagrams 1–26. The high figure for 7th June reflects a concentration in the English Channel against D-Day assault and supply shipping.
4 S. Roskill, *The War at Sea*, HMSO, 1961, vol. 3 (part II), p. 68.
5 Allied activity over this part of the Atlantic had intensified yet further from October 1943 when the first Allied squadron arrived in the Azores, to operate from bases newly leased by the Portuguese.
6 Such opportunism might have seemed a better bet in the more compressed sea lanes of the Mediterranean, except that the relative compactness of the theatre had also allowed the Allies to concentrate their ASW forces in so-called 'Swamp' operations. The last U-boat in the Mediterranean was sunk in September 1944, although no Allied merchant shipping had been sunk since the previous May.
7 Tarrant, *op. cit.*, p. 15.
8 *Ibid.*, p. 157.
9 H. Busch, *U-Boats at War*, Ballantine, New York, 1962, p. 157.
10 MOD (Navy), *op. cit.*, p. 91.
11 Quoted in *ibid.*, p. 83.

12 Busch, *op. cit.*, pp. 125–6.

13 Tarrant, *op. cit.*, p. 87.

14 Busch, *op. cit.*, p. 132.

15 *Ibid.*, p. 154.

16 Showell, *op. cit.*, p. 110.

17 *Ibid.*, p. 111.

18 See the lecture by Kapitän W. Luth given as an appendix to V. E. Tarrant, *The U-Boat Offensive 1914–45*, Arms and Armour Press, 1989, pp. 177–85.

19 Busch, *op. cit.*, pp. 133–4.

20 P. Cremer, *U-333: the Story of a U-Boat Ace*, Grafton Books, 1986, p. 262.

21 The relevant figures compared with the standard Type IXC/40 were:

Type	Displacement (tons)	Max. Speed (knots)	Endurance (naut. miles at knots	Max. Depth (feet)	Torpedoes	Crew
IXC/40	1,144/1,257	18.8/7.3	16,800 at 10/63 at 4	330	19	48
XXI	1,621/1,829	15.6/17.2	15,500 at 10/365 at 5	376	20	57

Where two figures are given, the first refers to surface performance, the second to submerged.

22 E. Bagnasco, *Submarines of World War Two*, Arms and Armour Press, 1977, p. 76.

23 Admiral Doenitz, *Memoirs Ten Years and Twenty Days*, Weidenfeld & Nicolson, 1959, p. 427.

24 Of the 58 boats at sea on 25th October, 35 were Type VII variants, 22 Type IX variants and one a Type XB.

25 Quoted in F. H. Hinsley *et al.*, *British Intelligence in the Second World War*, HMSO, 1984, vol. 3 (part I), p. 526.

26 P. Beesly, *Very Special Intelligence: the Story of the Admiralty's Operational Intelligence Centre 1939–45*, Hamish Hamilton, 1977, p. 247.

27 Quoted in Hinsley, *op. cit.*, vol. 3 (part II), p. 479.

28 Quoted in Tarrant, *Last Year*, *op. cit.*, p. 162.

29 Quoted in J. Terraine, *Business in Great Waters: the U-Boat War 1916–45*, Mandarin, 1990, p. 657.

30 Quoted in Hinsley, *op. cit.*, vol. 3 (part II), p. 471.

31 Quoted in Tarrant, *Last Year*, *loc. cit.*

Chapter 26: *Tirpitz – The Lonely Queen*

1 Table is based on J. C. Taylor, *German Warships of World War II*, Ian Allan, Shepperton, 1966, *passim*; and M. J. Whitley, *Destroyer!: German Destroyers in World War II*, Arms and Armour Press, 1983, pp. 268–80.

2 Whitley, *op. cit.*, pp. 215 and 219.

3 Admiralty, *Führer Conferences on Naval Affairs 1939–45*, Greenhill, 1990 (orig. 1947), p. 389.

4 A. Harris, *Bomber Offensive*, Collins, 1947, p. 255.

5 D. Woodward, *Tirpitz*, New English Library, 1973 (orig. 1953), p. 152.

6 V. E. Tarrant, *The Last Year of the Kriegsmarine*, Arms and Armour Press, 1994, p. 138.

7 The original and corrected soundings were 40 and 56 feet. It was decided not to move the ship as the terrain overlooking all the other suitable anchorages would seriously limit her AA guns' arc of fire.

8 Quoted in J. Winton, *Ultra at Sea*, Leo Cooper, 1988, p. 92.

9 L. Kennedy, *Menace: the Life and Death of the Tirpitz*, Sidgewick & Jackson, 1979, p. 152.

10 There was also one mountain division and one infantry division preparing to transfer to other fronts.

11 A. Price, *Instruments of Darkness*, Panther, 1979, p. 285.

12 With *Tirpitz* were five destroyers and two light cruisers of First World War vintage converted into AA ships.

Chapter 27: *A Vision of Hell*

1 Quoted in the *Observer*, 11/5/97, p. 9; and R. A. Young, *The Flying Bomb*, Ian Allan, Shepperton, 1978, p. 129.

2 M. Maurel, *Ravensbrück*, Digit, 1958, pp. 12–13.

3 Quoted in A. Gill, *The Journey Back from Hell: Conversations with Concentration Camp Survivors*, Grafton, 1988, pp. 318–19.

4 A. Faramus, *Journey into Darkness*, Grafton, 1990, pp. 246–7.

5 Quoted in D. Dwork, *Children with a Star: Jewish Youth in Nazi Camps*, Yale University Press, 1991, p. 225.

6 Faramus, *op. cit.*, p. 188 and F. B. Bekels, *Nacht und Nebel/Night and Fog*, Lutterworth Press, Cambridge, 1993 (orig. 1977), p. 166. Clearly Faramus could not have been in two concentration camps at once on 25th October (see note 4) but I have taken both descriptions as being typical of life in that camp on most days in 1944. Similar considerations apply throughout this chapter, especially as most prisoners were often not able to distinguish one day or even one month from another.

7 Faramus, *loc. cit.*; and S. Pisar, *Of Blood and Hope*, Cassell, 1980, p. 69.

8 Quoted in Gill, *op. cit.*, p. 311.

9 Pisar, *op. cit.*, p. 70; and G. Turgel, *I Light a Candle*, Grafton, 1987, p. 55.

10 Maurel, *op. cit.*, pp. 108–9; Bekels, *op. cit.*, p. 166; and quoted in Gill, *op. cit.*, p. 37.

11 Gill, *op. cit.*, pp. 35–6. The Neuengamme deal came to light in November 1944 when a prisoner found a human jawbone in his soup.

12 Quoted in Gill, *loc. cit.*; and Pisar, *op. cit.*, pp. 58–9.

13 Pisar, *loc. cit.*

14 Quoted in Gill, *op. cit.*, p. 173.

15 Bekels, *op. cit.*, p. 166; and Pisar, *op. cit.*, p. 79.

16 Faramus, *op. cit.*, pp. 189–90; and quoted in Gill, *op. cit.*, pp. 227–8.

17 Lord Russell of Liverpool, *The Scourge of the Swastika*, Corgi, 1956, pp. 118–19.

18 Gill, *op. cit.*, p. 227; and quoted in Dwork, *op. cit.*, p. 237.

19 Quoted in Gill, *op. cit.*, pp. 120 and 142.

20 Pisar, *op. cit.*, p. 87.

21 Faramus, *op. cit.*, p. 253; and quoted in Gill, *op. cit.*, p. 335.

22 Pisar, *op. cit.*, pp. 63 and 71; and quoted in Gill, *op. cit.*, p. 301.

23 Pisar, *op. cit.*, p. 68 and B. Rogarsky, *Smoke and Ashes: the Story of the Holocaust*, Oxford University Press, 1988, p. 94.

24 Quoted in Gill, *op. cit.*, p. 228.

25 Auschwitz was in fact a combined concentration and extermination camp while Majdanek was never an official death camp.

26 The 8,000 Danish Jews who should still have been behind enemy lines had in fact been spirited away to Sweden with the help of the local population.

27 Quoted in A. Weissberg, *Advocate for the Dead*, Four Square, 1959, p. 174. The remark about Bulgaria and Rumania was an angry reference to these country's laudable prevarication over the deportation of their own Jewish populations.

28 W. Schellenberg, *The Schellenberg Memoirs*, Andre Deutsch, 1964, p. 167.

29 Rogarsky, *op. cit.*, p. 71.

30 Quoted in Russell, *op. cit.*, pp. 152–3.

31 Rogarsky, *op. cit.*, p. 70.

32 Quoted in Gill, *op. cit.*, p. 349; quoted in Rogarsky, *op. cit.*, p. 73, and Pisar, *op. cit.*, p. 55.

33 Quoted in Rogarsky, *op. cit.*, p. 74.

34 The men of the *Sonderkommando* "lived in special quarters in the crematoria buildings . . . 'The table awaiting us,' one of the few survivors later wrote, 'was covered with a heavy silk brocade tablecloth, fine initialled porcelain dishes, and place settings of silver . . . all sorts of preserves, bacon, jellies, several kinds of salami, cakes and chocolates.' They drank fine cognac until they could no longer stand up, and then they fell into bed on linen sheets. Some of the *Sonderkommando* went mad, and some committed suicide, but most of them struggled on for three months or so and then . . . their successors steered them, unprotesting, willing and perhaps even eager to die, into the gas chamber." (O. Friedrich, *The Kingdom of Auschwitz*, Penguin Books, 1994, p. 79.) Earlier in October, some of these men, knowing that Auschwitz was being run down and their stay of execution would be even shorter than usual, managed to blow up Crematorium IV. The men of Crematorium II tried to follow their example and in all 450 of the *Sonderkommando* were shot.

35 Quoted in Friedrich, *op. cit.*, p. 69.

36 Quoted in Dwork, *op. cit.*, p. 230.

Chapter 28: *Approach to Leyte Gulf*

1 In fact, Nimitz wore several hats. As commander-in-chief of the Pacific Fleet (CINCPAC), he commanded all naval units in the Pacific, although some were lent to MacArthur. As commander-in-chief of the Pacific Ocean Areas (CINCPOA) he was in charge of the three Ocean Areas not within MacArthur's South-West Pacific Area, i.e. South, Central and North. These areas also had their own commanders but Nimitz doubled as the commander of the most important of them, where he was commander Central Pacific Ocean Area (COMCENPAC).

2 By 1944 the U.S. Pacific Fleet concentrated most of its modern ships into its Central Pacific Force, later upgraded to Fifth Fleet in April of that year. The core of this fleet was Task Force (TF) 58, made up of four Task Groups (TGs) of,

typically, two big *Essex*-class fleet carriers, two or three light carriers, two or more battleships or heavy cruisers and an assortment of light cruisers and destroyers. From June 1944, Fifth Fleet was given alternating commanders: the incumbent Admiral Raymond Spruance and the newly unemployed Admiral William Halsey, whose South Pacific Area had become an operational backwater. When Halsey was in command – from September 1944 – Fifth Fleet was redesignated Third Fleet and TF 58 became TF 38, though the latter retained the same commander, Admiral Marc Mitscher.

3 Two of the carriers, *Ise* and *Hyuga*, were hybrids fashioned out of battleships with a short flight deck cobbled on to the stern. This deck was to accommodate 22 floatplanes.

4 Quoted in J. Toland, *The Rising Sun: the Decline and Fall of the Japanese Empire*, Bantam, New York, 1971, p. 610; and M. Ito, *The End of the Imperial Japanese Navy*, Jove Books, New York, 1986 (orig. 1962), p. 120.

Chapter 29: *The Battle of Suriago Strait*

1 These ships comprised the Bombardment and Support Group (TG 77.2) and the Close Covering Group (TG 77.3) which were amalgamated by this same order. Together they numbered 6 battleships, 4 heavy cruisers, 4 light cruisers and 28 destroyers.

2 T. C. Kinkaid, 'Communications Breakdown at the Battle for Leyte Gulf', in J. T. Mason Jr. (ed.), *The Pacific War Remembered*, Naval Institute Press, Annapolis (Md), 1986, p. 277.

3 Quoted in S. E. Morison, *Leyte* (*U.S. Naval Operations in World War II*, vol. XII), Oxford University Press, 1958, p. 202.

4 M. Ito, *The End of the Imperial Japanese Navy*, Jove Books, New York, 1986 (orig. 1962), p. 146.

5 S. Smith, *The Battle of Leyte Gulf*, Belmont, New York, 1961, p. 92.

6 Quoted in A. Stewart, *The Battle of Leyte Gulf*, Robert Hale, 1979, p. 103.

7 Morison, *op. cit.*, p. 213.

8 J. Toland, *The Rising Sun: the Decline and Fall of the Japanese Empire*, Bantam, New York, 1971, p. 634.

9 Morison, *op. cit.*, p. 220.

10 The other two ships in Smoot's group were *Richard P. Leary* and *Newcombe*. Conley's group comprised *Bryant*, *Halford* and *Robinson*, whilst Bouleware led *Bennion*, *Leutze* and *Heywood L. Edwards*.

11 Quoted in Stewart, *op. cit.*, p. 111.

12 Three ships were so equipped, *West Virginia*, *Tennessee* and *California*. They fired 225 of the 282 16-inch and 14-inch rounds expended. The other battleships were *Maryland*, *Mississippi* and *Pennsylvania*, though the latter never found a target. All but the *Mississippi* had either been sunk or badly damaged at Pearl Harbor. As fleet battleships they had been totally superseded by the new *Iowa* and *North Carolina* classes, but as the crosspiece on a 'T' they were as effective as anything afloat.

13 Quoted in T. J. Cutler, *The Battle of Leyte Gulf 25–26 October 1944*, HarperCollins, New York, 1994, p. 198.

14 Quoted in Morison, *op. cit.*, p. 228 and Cutler, *op. cit.*, p. 195.

15 Quoted in Smith, *op. cit.*, p. 101.

16 Quoted in T. Roscoe, *Tin Cans: the True Story of the Fighting Destroyers in World War II*, Bantam, New York, 1968 (abridged: orig. 1953), p. 357.

17 Quoted *ibid.*, *loc. cit.*

18 Morison, *op. cit.*, p. 232.

19 Quoted in Toland, *op. cit.*, p. 637.

20 Quoted in Morison, *op. cit.*, p. 233.

21 *Ibid.*, p. 236

22 Quoted in *ibid.*, p. 238.

Chapter 30: *The Battle of Samar*

1 Quoted in T. J. Cutler, *The Battle of Leyte Gulf 25–26 October 1944*, HarperCollins, New York, 1994, p. 225.

2 S. E. Morison, *Leyte Gulf* (*U.S. Naval Operations in World War II*, vol. XII), Oxford University Press, 1958, p. 250. Kurita still retained a powerful strike force. Despite his losses on the 23rd and 24th, his ships, by column, comprised: (1st Battleship Division) *Nagato*, *Yamato*; (3rd Battleship Division) *Kongo*, *Haruna*; (5th [Heavy] Cruiser Division) *Haguro*, *Chokai*; (7th [Heavy] Cruiser Division) *Kumano*, *Suzuya*, *Chikuma*, *Tone*; (2nd Destroyer Squadron) *Noshiro* (light cruiser) and 7 destroyers; (10th Squadron) *Yahagi* (light cruiser) and 4 destroyers.

3 T. Koyanagi, 'The Battle of Leyte Gulf' in D. C. Evans (ed.), *The Japanese Navy in World War II*, Naval Institute Press, Annapolis (Md.), 1986, pp. 368 and 367.

4 See A. Stewart, *The Battle of Leyte Gulf*, Robert Hale, 1979, p. 151.

5 The Japanese battleships and heavy cruisers mounted between them nine 18.1-inch guns, eight 16-inch, sixteen 14-inch, fifty-six 8-inch and forty 6.1- and 6-inch.

6 Quoted in Morison, *op. cit.*, p. 252.

7 Quoted in Cutler, *op. cit.*, p. 256.

8 Quoted in Morison, *op. cit.*, p. 253.

9 Quoted *loc. cit.*

10 Walter Karig quoted in Cutler, *op. cit.*, p. 236.

11 Quoted in Morison, *op. cit.*, p. 257.

12 Quoted in Cutler, *op. cit.*, p. 232.

13 Quoted in Stewart, *op cit.*, p. 168.

14 Quoted in *ibid.*, p. 161.

15 Quoted in Morison, *op. cit.*, pp. 267–8.

16 Quoted in *ibid.*, p. 262.

17 Quoted in S. Smith, *The Battle of Leyte Gulf*, Belmont, New York, 1961, p. 113.

18 Quoted in T. Roscoe, *Tin Cans: the True Story of the Fighting Destroyers in World War II*, (abridged ed.), Bantam, New York, 1968 (orig. 1953), p. 366.

19 Cutler, *op. cit.*, p. 243.

20 Quoted in Morison, *op. cit.*, p. 272.

21 Cutler, *op. cit.*, p. 244.

22 *Loc. cit.*

23 Quoted in Smith, *op. cit.*, p. 111.

24 Morison, *op. cit.*, p. 279.

25 The peerless *Johnston* attempted to draw one of these cruisers' fire at about 8.30 a.m. but the Japanese ignored this, allowing the destroyer to slip away shortly afterwards when it discerned the Japanese destroyer attack from the opposite direction.

26 Quoted in *ibid.*, p. 280.

27 Quoted *loc. cit.*

28 Quoted in *ibid.*, pp. 284–5.

29 Quoted in *ibid.*, p. 285.

30 Quoted in *ibid.*, p. 273. 'GQ Johnny' was *Johnston*'s nickname amongst her crew, as she was reputed to have spent most of her active career at General Quarters.

31 Quoted in *ibid.*, pp. 273–4.

32 *Ibid.*, p. 273.

33 Quoted in *ibid.*, p. 288. According to Morison, *Haguro* broke off the pursuit at 9.05 a.m. though no reason for this decision is given. Another source adds the detail that *Haguro* was low on ammunition, which perhaps had something to do with it. It should also be realised that most of Kurita's destroyers (2nd Squadron) were kept to the rear of his formation, for mopping up after the main gunfire phase.

34 Koyanagi, *op. cit.*, p. 368.

35 Morison, *op. cit.*, p. 300.

36 Quoted in *ibid.*, pp. 297 and 271.

Chapter 31: *The Battle of Cape Engano*

1 The main problem was the lack of a direct link between any of MacArthur's forces and any of Nimitz's and all communications had to be routed via the huge communications centre at Manus naval base. This centre was almost overwhelmed on the 25th and messages between the fleets were taking at least an hour to deliver. It comes as little surprise to find that MacArthur was one of the villains of the piece. Suspicious of the Navy and wary of allowing any of his subordinates too much freedom of action, he had vetoed a suggested direct link between Kinkaid and Halsey.

2 Quoted in S. E. Morison, *Leyte Gulf* (*History of U.S. Naval Operations in World War II*, vol. XII), Oxford University Press, 1958, p. 294.
In his memoirs Halsey presents the first message as containing the words, "Where is Lee? Send Lee" but this seems to be an attempt to portray Kinkaid's state of mind rather than what was actually recorded in the message files. (See Halsey, *infra.*, p. 220 and Morison, *op. cit.*, p. 294.)

3 Quoted in E. B. Potter and C. Nimitz, *The Great Sea War*, Prentice-Hall, Englewoods (N.J.), 1960, pp. 389–90 ftnte.

4 W. F. Halsey and J. Bryan III, *Admiral Halsey's Story*, Curtis, New York, 1947, pp. 220–1. According to Halsey, he did not discover the truth for weeks, though this seems rather odd. It was standard procedure on his flagship to hand him messages on paper-tape directly from the decoding machine, with any padding removed. Even in this case, when the padding was not removed, the prefix letters 'RR' also remained. It seems surprising that neither Halsey nor Carney chose to

query the last three words. As Halsey implies, it was quite out of character for Nimitz to send such a sarcastic message to a subordinate.

5 Another commander not best pleased with Halsey was Navy Commander-in-Chief Ernest King, in Washington. McCain's predecessor in command of TG 38.1, Admiral J. J. 'Jocko' Clark, was on leave in Washington on the 25th and went to visit King. "I saw at once he was under great stress. Like a tiger he was pacing up and down in a towering rage. As I entered . . . he began to vent his ire on Admiral Halsey, saying, 'He has left the strait of San Bernadino open for the Japanese to strike the transports at Leyte.' . . . King was angrier than I had ever seen him – to say he was irate was an understatement." (J. J. Clark and C. G. Reynolds, *Carrier Admiral*, McKay, New York, 1967, p. 201.)

6 C. Solberg, *Decision and Dissent: with Halsey at Leyte Gulf*, Naval Institute Press, Annapolis (Md.), 1995, pp. 152–3.

7 *Ibid.*, p. 150.

8 By October 1944, fourteen *Essex*-class carriers had been launched, though not necessarily yet commissioned, as well as all nine light carriers. Only the light carrier *Princeton* had been lost, on 24th October.

9 E. Pyle, *Last Chapter*, Henry Holt, New York, 1946, p. 59.

10 Solberg, *op. cit.*, p. 46.

11 This from *ibid.*, p. 46. Other sources seem to imply that pilots did have their own planes.

12 B. Tillman, *Hellcat: the F6F in World War II*, Patrick Stephens, Cambridge, 1979, p. 16.

13 The men who worked on deck with the planes were known as 'Airedales', or merely as 'plane pushers'. They represented a distinct group not found on most warships. Ernie Pyle reckoned that some conventional seamen resented them, claiming they got too much of the limelight. "But," Pyle wrote, "as far as I could see, the Airedales haven't had an awful lot of glory. And their job is often a miserable one. The hours are ungodly, and in a pinch they work like fiends. I think the Airedale deserves what little credit he gets." (E. Pyle, *op. cit.*, p. 70.)

14 J. C. Shaw, 'Fast Carrier Operations 1943–45', included as an introduction to S. E. Morison, *Aleutians, Gilberts and Marshalls* (*History of US Naval Operations in World War II*, vol. VII), Little Brown, Boston, 1951, p. xxxiv.

15 Tillmann, *loc cit.* For good detail on U.S. carrier operations in World War II see also Solberg, *op cit.*, pp. 43–50 and P. Kilduff, *US Carriers at War*, Ian Allan, Shepperton, 1981, *passim.*

16 Not all the fighters went on a strike. Others, which had taken off earlier, remained in the vicinity of the carriers flying Combat Air Patrol (CAP). These were directed from the ship's Combat Information Center, deep below, in which the Fighter Direction Officer interpreted incoming radar signals on his circular Position Plan Indicator screen and vectored his planes to investigate 'bogeys' and intercept 'bandits'. He identified his own planes by the distinctive blip emitted by their Identification Friend or Foe (IFF) transponder.

17 Quoted in S. Smith, *The Battle of Leyte Gulf*, Belmont, New York, 1961, p. 129.

18 Quoted in C. Vann Woodward, *The Battle for Leyte Gulf*, W. W. Norton, New York, 1965 (orig. 1947), p. 156.

19 Quoted in Smith, *op. cit.*, pp. 125–6.

20 Vann Woodward, *op. cit.*, p. 156.

21 Quoted in A. Stewart, *The Battle of Leyte Gulf*, Robert Hale, 1979, p. 130.

22 Quoted in Smith, *op. cit.*, p. 131.

23 One is entitled to wonder whether TF 34, or a part of it, would have been detached much earlier if Halsey had not placed his flag aboard one of its most powerful battleships, so obliging the whole force to go where he went. The slimmed-down TF 34 contained all the original six battleships, three of the seven cruisers, and eight of the eighteen destroyers.

24 Solberg, *op. cit.*, p. 197.

25 Quoted in Smith, *op. cit.*, pp. 129–30. *Zuikaku* was hit by three torpedoes shortly after 1 p.m. and sank at 2.14. *Zuiho* was set on fire by an unknown hit at about the same time but this was got under control. Hit again at 1.30 and 2.45, she finally went down at 3.26. No Japanese destroyer was hit or even badly damaged in these afternoon strikes.

26 Morison, *op. cit.*, p. 32,

Chapter 32: *Kamikaze Pilots in Leyte Gulf*

1 M. Ito, *The End of the Imperial Japanese Navy*, Jove Books, New York, 1986 (orig. 1962), p. 120.

2 D. M. Goldstein and K. V. Dillon (eds.), *Fading Victory: the Diary of Admiral Matome Ugaki*, University of Pittsburgh Press, Pittsburgh (Pa.), 1991, p. 449 and T. Koyanagi, 'The Battle of Leyte Gulf', in D. C. Evans (ed.), *The Japanese Navy in World War II*, Naval Institute Press, Annapolis (Md.), 1986, p. 380.

3 R. Inoguchi *et al.*, *The Divine Wind*, Four Square, 1961, p. 55.

4 Quote is from R. Inoguchi and T. Nakajima, 'The Kamikaze Attack Corps', in Evans, *op. cit.*, p. 432.

5 E. Hoyt, *The Kamikazes*, Panther, 1985, p. 28.

6 B. Millot, *Divine Thunder: the Life and Death of the Kamikazes*, Macdonald, 1971, p. 26.

7 Inoguchi *et al.*, *op. cit.*, pp. 37–8. See also Hata and Y. Izawa, *Japanese Naval Aces and Fighter Units in World War II*, Airlife, Shrewsbury, 1990 (orig. 1970), p. 111.

8 Quoted in Inoguchi and Nakajima, *op. cit.*, p. 422.

9 Quoted in *ibid.*, p. 421.

10 Quoted in *ibid.*, p. 424.

11 Quoted in Inoguchi *et al.*, *op. cit.*, p. 66.

12 *Shinfu* was a high-toned Chinese rendering of the Japanese characters for 'wind' and 'fire'. The more demotic version was *kamikaze*. A different Japanese source says the corps was called the *Kamikaze Tokubetsu Kogakitai*, though the English equivalent is exactly the same. Just for maximum confusion, *Shinfu* is sometimes rendered as *Shimpu*.

13 "*Shikishima no Yamatogoroko wo hito towaba Asaki ni nion Yamazakura-bana*", which means "The Japanese spirit is like mountain cherry blossoms, radiant in the morning sun."

14 Quoted in Millot, *op. cit.*, p. 43.

15 Hata and Izawa, *op. cit.*, Translator's Note, p. xi.

16 Inoguchi and Nakajima, *op. cit.*, pp. 429–30.

17 Quoted in Inoguchi *et al.*, *op. cit.*, p. 52.

18 Quoted in Inoguchi and Nakajima, *op. cit.*, p. 429.

19 Inoguchi *et al.*, *op. cit.*, pp. 63–4.

20 This attack remains something of a mystery and is ignored in some accounts. 'Judys' were naval aircraft but 201 Air Group, the focus of organised kamikaze tactics, contained only fighters. Perhaps news of Onishi's experiment had spread to other 'conventional' units and some pilots decided to make their own impromptu contribution.

21 Morison, *op. cit.* (pp. 301 and 305) shows that there were two separate attacks on Taffy-1; Hoyt, *op. cit.* (p. 83) claims that they were Army planes; T. Nakajima, in Inoguchi *et al.*, *op. cit.* (pp. 56 and 60) says both that three of the four kamikaze units were based at Mabalacat, and that the Cebu unit did not operate until the 26th.

22 Quoted in T. J. Cutler, *The Battle of Leyte Gulf 25–26 October 1944*, HarperCollins, New York, 1994, p. 269.

23 Quoted in Inoguchi *et al.*, *op. cit.*, pp. 64 and 67.

Chapter 33: *Leyte Island*

1 G. Perrett, *Old Soldiers Never Die: the Life of Douglas MacArthur*, André Deutsch, 1996, p. 203.

2 This account follows Perrett, *op. cit.*, pp. 427–8. Another book agrees that MacArthur originally said that he wished to experience his first sea battle but adds, with no further explanation, "He later changed his mind." See G. E. Wheeler. *Kinkaid of the Seventh Fleet*, Naval Institute Press, Annapolis (Md.), 1996, p. 396.

3 Perrett, *op. cit.*, p. 428.

4 In the normal course of events my distinction between Third/Fifth Fleet and Seventh Fleet would be an oversimplification; for while TF 38/58 was the core of the former, it did also possess its own amphibious element, III/V Amphibious Force (commonly III/V 'Phib') which was used to support the numerous landings along Nimitz's Central Pacific axis of advance, most recently in the Palau Islands. For the Leyte operation III 'Phib was on loan to Seventh Fleet and the troops and supplies for the cancelled Yap landings were simply redirected to the Philippines.

5 M. H. Cannon, *Leyte: the Return to the Philippines (U.S. Army in World War II)*, G.P.O., Washington, 1954, p. 184.

6 Quoted in *ibid.*, p. 36.

7 Quoted in *ibid.*, p. 187.

8 *Ibid.*, p. 111.

9 R. G. Martin, *The G.I. War*, Little Brown, Boston, 1967, p. 311.

10 Cannon, *op. cit.*, p. 167.

11 Quoted in *ibid.*, p. 49.

12 Quoted in R. L. Eichelberger, *Jungle Road to Tokyo*, Odhams, 1951, p. 177.

13 Quoted in Cannon, *op. cit.*, p. 94.

14 This reference to the first Japanese landings is an attempted resolution of two contradictory paragraphs in Cannon, *op. cit.*, pp. 94 and 99. The suggestion that decision-making about reinforcements was rather fragmented derives from E. J. Drea's account in *MacArthur's Ultra: Codebreaking and the War Against Japan*, Kansas University Press, Lawrence, 1992, pp. 166–7.

15 S. E. Morison, *Leyte* (*History of U.S. Naval Operations in World War II*, vol. XII), Oxford University Press, 1958, p. 65.

Chapter 34: *U.S. Naval Logistics in the Pacific*

1 S. E. Morison, *New Guinea and the Marianas* (*History of U.S. Naval Operations in World War II*, vol. VIII), Little Brown, Boston, 1953, p. 344.

2 Almost incredibly, all U.S. ammunition ships were named after volcanoes.

3 Morison, *op. cit.*, vol. XII (*Leyte*), p. 77.

4 Even so, S. E. Morison felt it necessary to chide the U.S. Navy for its continuing tendency to undervalue logistics at the expense of fast carrier derring-do. "It is an interesting commentary on World War II promotion policies in the Navy that the command of the At Sea Logistics Group was not considered worthy of flag rank, although an aviation rear admiral had to be temporarily removed from command of the escort carriers in order to permit them to operate under the command of a captain [J. T. Acuff] from the Service Force!" (Morison, *ibid.*, p. 75, ftnte.)

Chapter 35: *The Japanese Merchant Fleet*

1 Royal Institute of International Affairs, *Raw Materials*, Oxford University Press, 1939, p. 31.

2 United States Strategic Bombing Survey, *The War Against Japanese Transportation*, G.P.O., Washington, May 1947, p. 45.

3 *Ibid.*, pp. 54, 103 and 118 and USSBS, *The Effects of Strategic Bombing on Japan's War Economy*, G.P.O., Washington, December 1946, p. 13.

4 USSBS, *Effects*, *op. cit.*, pp. 111 and 189–93 and *Transportation*, *op. cit.*, p. 109.

5 Quoted in USSBS, *Transportation*, *op. cit.*, p. 48.

6 Quoted in P. Padfield, *War Beneath the Sea: Submarine Conflict 1939–45*, John Murray, 1995, p. 437.

7 Quoted in *ibid.*, p. 388.

8 United States Strategic Bombing Survey, *Summary Report (Pacific War)*, G.P.O., Washington, July 1946, p. 25.

9 Derived from USSBS, *Transportation*, *op. cit.*, p. 183.

10 *Ibid.*, p. 33.

Chapter 36: *U.S. Submarines in the Pacific*

1 T. Roscoe, *Pig Boats*, Bantam, New York, 1967, pp. 447–9.

2 See especially C. Blair, *Silent Victory: the U.S. Submarine War Against Japan*, Bantam, New York, 1985, pp. 722–86, and for valuable maps to be found on pp. 957–63.

3 P. Padfield, *War Beneath the Sea: Submarine Conflict 1939–45*, John Murray, 1995, p. 385.

4 Roscoe, *loc. cit.*

5 The packs comprised, respectively, *Sawfish, Icefish, Drum, Snook*; and *Shark II, Blackfish, Seadragon. Shark II* was lost with all hands, probably to a Japanese escort, on 24th October.

6 Quoted in Blair, *op. cit.*, pp. 767–8.

7 E. Beach, *Submarine!*, Heinemann, 1953, p. 162.

8 Quoted in S. E. Morison, *Leyte: History of U.S. Naval Operations in World War II*, vol. XII, Oxford University Press, 1958, p. 405.

9 C. Solberg, *Decision and Dissent: With Halsey at Leyte Gulf*, Naval Institute Press, Annapolis (Md.), 1995, p. 93.

10 *Ibid.*, p. 94.

11 C. Vann Woodward, *The Battle for Leyte Gulf*, Norton, New York, 1965 (orig. 1947), p. 159.

12 Morison, *op. cit.*, p. 334.

13 *Loc. cit.*

14 See Blair, *op. cit.*, pp. 959–62.

15 Beach, *op. cit.*, pp. 105–6.

16 G. Grider and L. Sims, *War Fish*, Pyramid Books, New York, 1964 (orig. 1958), pp. 128–9.

Chapter 37: *I-56 and the Japanese Submarine Fleet*

1 H. P. Willmott, *The Barrier and the Javelin: Japanese and Allied Pacific Strategies February to June 1942*, Naval Institute Press, Annapolis (Maryland), 1983, p. 528. See also M. Ito, *The End of the Imperial Japanese Navy*, Jove Books, New York 1986 (orig. 1962), p. 196. Estimates of the number of submarines actually deployed off the Philippines vary between 11 and 16 according to the source.

2 P. Padfield, *War Beneath the Sea: Submarine Conflict 1939–45*, John Murray, 1995, p. 407.

3 Quoted in N. Polmar and D. B. Carpenter, *Submarines of the Imperial Japanese Navy 1904–45*, Conway, 1986, p. 68.

4 M. Hashimoto, *Sunk: the Story of the Japanese Submarine Fleet 1942–45*, Cassell, 1954, p. 184.

5 Quoted in Padfield, *op. cit.*, p. 35.

6 Quoted in C. Blair, *Silent Victory: the U.S. Submarine War Against Japan*, Bantam, New York, 1985, p. 742.

7 Hashimoto, *op. cit.*, p. 114.

Chapter 38: *Mopping up on Pelelieu and Guam*

1 The following table shows the distribution of Allied and Japanese divisions in the Pacific on 25th October 1944. The figure in brackets shows the number of which belonged to the U.S. Marine Corps.

| | Number of Divisions | | |
	U.S.	'Anzac'	Jap.
Hawaii	3 (2)	–	–
New Hebrides	2	–	–
Solomon Islands and			
Bismark Archipelago	4 (1)	3	3
New Guinea and Biak	8	1	5
Dutch East Indies	1	–	6
Marianas	3 (2)	–	2
Palau Islands	2 (1)	–	1
Philippines	4	–	9 (one at sea)
Formosa	–	–	3
Ryukyu Islands	–	–	4
TOTAL	27 (6)	4	35

2 Another landing was staged to provide air cover for the southern flank of the Leyte assault. This was on Morotai, off Halmahera, where one of General MacArthur's own divisions, 31 U.S. Infantry, came ashore on 15th September. They faced some 500 Japanese and the only resistance of note was a 'pathetically feeble banzai attack that same night. By 4th October fighter planes were operating from a brand-new airfield and on the 13th they began to be joined by bomber units.

3 H. A. Gailey, *Peleliu 1944*, Nautical and Aviation Publishing Co., Annapolis (Md.), 1983, p. 20. The Rupertus remark is quoted in S. E. Smith (ed.), *The United States Marine Corps in World War II*, Random House, New York, 1969, p. 666.

4 Quoted in Smith, *op. cit.*, p. 727 and R. H. Spector, *Eagle Against the Sun: the American War with Japan*, Free Press, New York, 1985, p. 421.

5 Gailey, *op. cit.*, p. 44.

6 *Ibid.*, p. 45.

7 *Ibid.*, p. 176.

8 R. R. Smith, *The Approach to the Philippines (The U.S. Army in World War II)*, G.P.O., Washington, 1953, p. 566.

9 S. E. Smith, *op. cit.*, p. 731.

10 Quoted in Spector, *op. cit.*, p. 320.

11 A. M. Josephy Jr., *The Long and the Short and the Tall: the Story of a Marine Combat Unit in the Pacific*, Zenger, Washington, 1979 (orig. 1947), pp. 95 and 137.

12 *Ibid.*, p. 114.

13 *Loc. cit.*

14 *Ibid.*, pp. 138, 146 and 145.

Chapter 39: *First Australian Army in the Pacific Mandates*

1 In October 1944, MacArthur also committed to paper some preliminary ideas for using Australian troops to re-occupy the Dutch East Indies once the Philippines were secure.

2 G. Long, *The Final Campaigns (Australia in the War of 1939–45*, vol. 7), Australian War Memorial, Canberra, 1963, p. 23.

3 Quoted in *ibid.*, p. 608.

4 Quoted in *ibid.*, pp. 610 and 26.

5 Quoted in *ibid.*, p. 26.

6 The first formation to arrive was a brigade from 3 Infantry Division. Its two other brigades were also under orders as were two independent brigades that were to take over in Green, Emira and Treasury Islands.

7 S. E. Morison, *Breaking the Bismarks Barrier (History of US Naval Operations in World War II*, vol. vi), Little Brown, Boston, 1954, p. 409.

8 Quoted in Long, *op. cit.*, p. 276.

9 Quoted in *ibid.*, p. 275.

10 The Americal Division was formed in New Caledonia in May 1942, from Task Force 6814, an assortment of Army units rushed to defend the island from the rampaging Japanese. The name is simply an abbreviated amalgamation of 'America' and 'New Caledonia'.

11 Quoted in H. A. Gailey, *Bougainville: the Forgotten Campaign 1943–45*, University Press of Kentucky, Lexington, 1991, pp. 122–3.

12 Quoted in R. G. Martin, *The G.I. War*, Little Brown, Boston, 1967, p. 280.

13 Quoted *loc. cit.*

14 Quoted in *ibid.*, p. 129.

15 Quoted in *ibid.*, p. 135.

16 *Ibid.*, p. 185. The Australian perspective is given in Long, *op. cit.*, p. 103.

17 For some similarly improbable stories about the Marianas, told with a seemingly straight face, see E. Pyle, *Last Chapter*, Henry Holt, New York, 1945, p. 25.

Chapter 40: *Pacific Stepping-Stones*

1 J. M. Foster, *Hell in the Heavens*, Charter Books, New York, n.d. (orig. 1961), p. 341.

2 S. Birdsall, *Flying Buccaneers: the Illustrated Story of Kenney's Fifth Air Force*, David & Charles, Newton Abbot, 1978, p. 203.

3 S. Smith, *The Battle of Leyte Gulf*, Belmont, New York, 1961, p. 28.

4 R. H. Spector, *Eagle Against the Sun: the American War with Japan*, Free Press, New York, 1985, p. 301.

5 E. G. Love, *The 27th Infantry Division in World War II*, Battery Press, Nashville (Tenn.), 1982 (orig. 1949), p. 521.

6 *Ibid.*, p. 322.

7 Quoted in A. Tappert (ed.), *Lines of Battle: Letters from American Servicemen 1941–45*, Times Books, New York, 1987, pp. 211–12.

8 D. T. Brown, *Marine from Virginia*, University of North Carolina Press, 1947, p. 64.

9 S. E. Morison, *Breaking the Bismarks Barrier (History of US Naval Operations in World War II*, vol. VI), Little Brown, Boston, 1954, p. 97, and B. Davis, *Marine: the Life of Lt.-General Lewis B. Puller, USMC*, Bantam, New York, 1964, p. 184.

10 S. E. Smith (ed.), *The United States Marine Corps in World War II*, Random House, New York, p. 663.

11 E. B. Sledge, *With the Old Breed at Pelelieu and Okinawa*, Presidio, Novata (Cal.), 1981, p. 31.

12 R. Davis, *Marine at War*, Scholastic Book Services, New York, 1965, pp. 119 and 120.

13 S. M. Kahn, *Between Tedium and Terror, a Soldier's World War II Diary 1943–45*, University of Illinois Press, Chicago, 1993, pp. xx–xxi.

14 *Ibid.*, p. 187.

15 *Ibid.*, p. 180.

16 *Ibid.*, p. 189.

Chapter 41: *The War in China*

1 T. H. White and A. Jacoby, *Thunder Out of China*, Gollancz, 1947, pp. 66–7.

2 Stilwell was only chief-of-staff to Chiang Kai-shek in the latter's capacity as Supreme Commander in an Allied theatre, China. Chiang also had his own chief-of-staff, Ho Yin-chin, for the Chinese armed forces as a whole.

3 White and Jacoby, *op. cit.*, p. 172.

4 Also one division had been transferred each to Sumatra, Burma and Indo-China.

5 F. Owen, *The Campaign in Burma*, HMSO, 1946, p. 117. The uninformative Chinese account, especially about the month of October, is Hsu Long-hsuen and Chang Ming-kai, *History of the Sino-Japanese War (1937–45)*, Chung Wu, Taipei, 1971.

6 6th Area Army also included Thirty-fourth Army which conducted a subsidiary drive westwards from Changsha into Kweichow province. It threatened especially the city of Kweiyang, on the Kumming–Chungking railway that carried most of China's Lend-Lease aid.

7 131 and 170 Chinese Divisions facing 3, 13, 37, 40 and 58 Japanese, these forming the larger part of Eleventh Army. (See Hsu Long-hsuen and Chang Ming-lai, *op. cit.*, p. 430.)

8 H. H. Arnold, *Global Mission*, TAB Books, Blue Ridge Summit (Pa.), 1989 (orig. 1949), p. 427.

9 Li Tsung-jen and Te-Kong Tong, *The Memoirs of Li Tsung-jen*, Westview, Boulder (Col.), 1979, p. 428.

10 F. F. Liu, *A Military History of Modern China*, Princeton University Press, 1956, p. 129.

11 Li Tsung-jen and Te-Kong Tong, *op. cit.*, p. 417.

12 White and Jacoby, *op. cit.*, p. 129.

13 Lin Yutang, *The Vigil of a Nation*, Heinemann, 1946, p. 256.

14 *Ibid.*, p. 256. See also White and Jacoby, *op. cit.*, p. 129; and R. Alley, *Fruition: the Story of George Alvin Hogg*, Caxton Press, Christchurch (New Zealand), p. 114.

15 White and Jacoby, *op. cit.*, pp. 178–9 and 67–8.

16 *Ibid.*, pp. 182 and 181.

17 S. Gelder (ed.), *The Chinese Communists*, Gollancz, 1946, pp. xvi–xvii.

18 B. W. Tuchman, *Sand Against the Wind: Stilwell and the American Experience in China 1911–45*, Futura, 1981, p. 582.

19 T. H. White (ed.), *The Stilwell Papers*, Macdonald, 1949, pp. 185–6; quoted in Tuchman, *op. cit.*, p. 583.

20 White and Jacoby, *op. cit.*, pp. 35–6.

21 *Ibid.*, pp. 29–30.

22 H. Forman, *Report from Red China*, Robert Hale, 1946, p. 215.

23 The other key members of the Party's Politbureau in October 1944 were Chu Teh, the military commander, Chou En-lai, the ambassador to Chungking, and Liu Hsiao-chi, the General Secretary.

24 E. L. Dreyer, *China at War 1901–49*, Longman, 1995, p. 297.

25 *Ibid.*, p. 291.

26 Zhu De, *Selected Works*, Foreign Languages Press, Beijing, 1986, pp. 139–40.

27 P. Vladimirov, *The Vladimirov Diaries: Yenan China 1942–45*, Robert Hale, 1976, p. 274.

28 White and Jacoby, *op. cit.*, pp. 196 and 198; quoted in Dreyer, *op cit.*, p. 293.

29 Forman, *op. cit.*, p. 148.

30 Israel Epstein quoted in Gelder, *op. cit.*, pp. 70–1.

31 Forman, *op. cit.*, p. 218.

32 White and Jacoby, *op. cit.*, pp. 196 and 197.

33 Forman, *op. cit.*, pp. 166 and 201.

34 Quoted in Tuchman, *op. cit.*, p. 318.

35 *Stilwell Papers*, *op. cit.*, p. 318.

Chapter 42: *B-29 Bombers in China*

1 C. Berger, *B-29: the Superfortress at War*, MacDonald, 1971, p. 57. The Wichita plant had been built from scratch and the first ground had not been broken until June 1941.

2 W. H. Morrison, *Point of No Return*, Playboy, New York, 1980, p. 30.

3 Quoted in S. Birdsall, *Saga of the Superfortress*, Sidgewick & Jackson, 1981, p. 44.

4 Quoted in *ibid.*, p. 54.

5 W. F. Craven and J. L. Cate, *The Army Air Forces in World War II*, University of Chicago Press, 1954, vol. 5, p. 29.

6 J. Pimlott, *B-29 Superfortress*, Arms and Armour Press, 1980, p. 34.

7 Quoted in M. Caidin, *A Torch to the Enemy*, Ballantine, New York, 1960, p. 35.

8 Craven and Cate, *op. cit.*, vol. 5, pp. 4 and 175.

9 Quoted in Birdsall, *op. cit.*, p. 71.

10 Morrison, *op. cit.*, p. 128.

11 *Ibid.*, p. 96.

12 E. Larrabee, *Commander in Chief*, André Deutsch, 1987, p. 615.

13 Quoted in D. A. Anderton, *B-29 Superfortress at War*, Ian Allan, Shepperton, 1978, p. 72.

14 M. Caidin, *A Torch to the Enemy*, Ballantine, New York, 1960, pp. 50–1.

15 Quoted in C. Berger, *B-29: the Superfortress at War*, MacDonald, 1971, p. 97.

16 M. Schaffer, *Wings of Judgement: American Bombing in World War II*, Oxford University Press, New York, 1985, p. 109. Chapter Six of this book has been my main source on the origins of fire-bombing in the USAAF.

17 Quoted in Berger, *op. cit.*, p. 106.
18 Quoted in Schaffer, *op. cit.*, p. 121.

Chapter 43: *Fourteenth Army in Burma*

1 According to one recent source, 15 and 31 Divisions were in such a bad way that pursuing them was regarded as too much of a health risk. (See I. L. Grant, *Burma: the Turning Point*, Zampi, Chichester, 1993, p. 210.)
2 Quoted in R. Lewin, *Slim: the Standardbearer*, Leo Cooper, 1976, pp. 197–8.
3 These other divisions were 11 E. African, 81 and 82 W. African, and 5, 19, 20, 25, and 26 Indian Divisions. Technically speaking, one of the British divisions, 36 Infantry, was not part of Fourteenth Army but was attached to Stilwell's Northern Combat Area Command, which was directly under Mountbatten and SEAC.
4 A. Brett-James, *Report My Signals*, Hennel Locke/Harrap, 1948, p. 198.
5 G. Hanley, *Monsoon Victory*, Collins, 1946, pp. 141 and 49.
6 *Ibid.*, p. 109.
7 G. Evans and A. Brett-James, *Imphal: a Flower on Lofty Heights*, Macmillan, 1965, p. 331. During October 1944 the Allied Combat Cargo Task Force carried 9,000 tons of supplies, 12,000 personnel and 5,200 casualties.
8 Quoted in W. E. Duncan (ed.), *The Royal Artillery Commemoration Book 1939–45*, Bell, 1950, p. 122.
9 Hanley, *op. cit.*, p. 69.
10 A. Draper, *Dawns Like Thunder: the Retreat from Burma*, Leo Cooper, 1987, p. 253. Although this book deals with the events of 1942, the route taken then was just the same as that of late 1944 in reverse, and so I have made use of Draper's particularly graphic description.
11 F. Owen, *The Campaign in Burma*, HMSO, 1946, p. 116.
12 *Loc. cit.*
13 R. McKelvie, *The War in Burma*, Methuen, 1948, p. 185.
14 The Arakan could only serve as a depot for the main Rangoon thrust because it is essentially a coastal corridor that leads nowhere, the only access to Burma proper being via two narrow and easily defended passes at An and Tangup. Nevertheless XV Corps had completed plans for its forthcoming offensive by 18th October and passed them on to divisional commanders on the 25th. Operation ROMULUS, as it was known, envisaged a drive down the coast by 25 Indian and 82 W. African Divisions and an amphibious assault just south of Akyab by 26 Indian Division and 3 Commando Brigade. Ultimate objectives were the islands of Akyab and Ramree.
15 J. Callenach, *The Jeep Track: the Story of the 81st West African Division Fighting on the Arakan Front in Burma*, Regency Press, 1990, pp. 35–6.
16 S. Butterworth, *Three Rivers to Glory*, Arrow, 1958, p. 155.
17 *Ibid.*, p. 89.
18 *Ibid.*, p. 96.
19 *Ibid.*, p. 94.
20 W. Slim, *Defeat into Victory*, Cassell, 1956, p. 359.
21 Not that Bose had given up. A second INA division was already forming in northern Malaya, and on the 25th itself Bose had just arrived in Tokyo to petition

for a third. His favourite recruiting slogan was the slightly demotivating "Give me blood and I will give you freedom."

22 B. Oatts, *The Jungle in Arms*, New English Library, 1976 (orig. 1962), pp. 151 and 159. For another description of widespread homosexuality among Indian soldiers, this time Sikhs in Fourteenth Army, see J. Mellors, *Shots in the Dark*, London Magazine Editions, 1974, p. 126.

23 Brett-James, *op. cit.*, pp. 240–1.

Chapter 44: *Inventing the Secrets*

1 F. Knebel and C. W. Bailey, *No High Ground*, Weidenfeld & Nicolson, 1960, pp. 82 and 83.

2 S. Birdsall, *Saga of the Superfortress: the Dramatic Story of the B-29 and the Twentieth Air Force*, Sidgewick & Jackson, 1981, p. 288.

3 A frequent cover story for the uninitiated was that the modifications were for a plane suitable for ferrying top politicians. 'Thin Man' was Roosevelt and 'Fat Man' Churchill. Which of them became 'Little Boy', and by what logic, I have been unable to ascertain. 'Little Boy' was expected to weigh about 9,000lbs and be 10 feet long and over 2 feet in diameter. 'Fat Man' would be 5 feet in diameter, almost 11 feet long, and weigh 10,000lbs.

4 Quoted in R. Clark, 'Manhattan Project', in *History of the Second World War*, Purnells, 1968, vol. 6, no. 15, pp. 2638, 2639 and 2640.

5 In such a bombardment the atoms that are hit do not split but are 'enriched', absorbing the neutrons and shooting out two of their electrons, and thus transmuting into atoms of the new element plutonium.

6 S. Groueff, *Manhattan Project: the Untold Story of the Making of the Atomic Bomb*, Bantam, New York, 1968, p. 266.

7 *Ibid.*, p. 267.

8 *Ibid.*, pp. 189 and 269.

9 R. Rhodes, *The Making of the Atomic Bomb*, Touchstone, New York, 1988, p. 554.

10 L. R. Groves, *Now It Can Be Told: the Story of the Manhattan Project*, André Deutsch, 1963, p. 111.

11 In typical bravura Manhattan Project style, because it was not known on what frequency the gas-diffusion process would operate, the generating plant was built to be adaptable to five different cycles, an unprecedented and fantastically expensive project.

12 At one stage research into creating the submicroscopic holes had involved the use of a unique Chambard press which the American Chicle company used to print their chewing-gum wrappers. Also involved had been the Chrysler Corporation which had helped devise a corrosion-resistant method for electro-plating steel with nickel, essential if barrier production by itself was not to swallow up the total American supplies of the metal.

13 Groueff, *op. cit.*, p. 315.

14 Workable gaseous-diffusion still required the solution of various other problems which there is no space to deal with here. They included the anti-corrosion nickel-plating of the steel diffusers and the 570 miles of steel piping, the air-tight welding

of this piping, the design of leak-proof seals for the compressors, to tolerances of one millionth of an inch, and the development of mass spectrometer techniques to detect and monitor leakage.

15 Groueff, *op. cit.*, pp. 334–5.
16 The 'canning' of the slugs had been an enormous headache, comparable to the ongoing barrier crisis at Oak Ridge. It had only been solved in August 1944 after two years of experimentation with different soldering methods.
17 Rhodes, *op. cit.*, p. 498.
18 Groueff, *op. cit.*, p. 352.
19 Quoted in *ibid.*, p. 353.
20 *Ibid.*, p. 338.
21 Rhodes, *op. cit.*, p. 561.
22 Groueff, *op. cit.*, p. 366. This author and General Groves (*supra.*, p. 158) seem to confuse the original discovery of Pu-240, in November 1943, with the realisation of its consequences the following July.
23 Quoted in Rhodes, *op. cit.*, p. 479.
24 Groves, *op. cit.*, p. 158.
25 Rhodes, *op. cit.*, p. 549.
26 P. Goodchild, *J. Robert Oppenheimer*, BBC Publications, 1980, p. 113.
27 *Ibid.*, p. 123.
28 Rhodes, *op. cit.*, p. 561.
29 Quoted in S. Terkel, *The Good War: an Oral History of World War Two*, Penguin, Harmondsworth, 1986, p. 518.
30 Quoted in Rhodes, *op. cit.*, pp. 600 and 499.
31 Quoted in J. Newhouse, *The Nuclear Age: from Hiroshima to Star Wars*, Michael Joseph, 1989, pp. 27–8.
32 Rhodes, *op. cit.*, p. 565 and quoted in Terkel, *op. cit.*, pp. 510–11.
33 Quoted in Goodchild, *op. cit.*, p. 75 and Terkel, *loc. cit.*
34 Quoted in Groueff, *op. cit.*, p. 329 and Rhodes, *op. cit.*, p. 499.
35 Groueff, *op. cit.*, p. 228.
36 Groves, *op. cit.*, p. 168 and quoted in Goodchild, *op. cit.*, p. 79.
37 Quoted in Newhouse, *op. cit.*, p. 29.
38 Quoted in Rhodes, *op. cit.*, p. 563.

Select Bibliography

Not all the hundreds of sources consulted in the writing of this book are listed here as they can be found in the detailed Notes and References. So this Bibliography is confined to the titles which offered especially illuminating insights, statistical detail, and invaluable eye-witness testimony about various aspects of this one day at war. Publishers are in London unless otherwise indicated.

Adleman, Robert H. and George Walton, *The Champagne Campaign*, Leslie Frewin, 1973.

Altes, A. Korthals and N. K. C. A. In't Veld, *The Forgotten Battle: Overloon and the Maas Salient 1944-45*, Spellmount, Staplehurst, 1995.

Axworthy, Mark, *Third Axis, Fourth Ally: Romanian Armed Forces in the European War 1941–45*, Arms & Armour Press, 1995.

Birdsall, Steve, *Saga of the Superfortresses*, Sidgwick & Jackson, 1981.

Blair, Clay, *Silent Victory: the U.S. Submarine War Against Japan*, Bantam, New York, 1985.

Blaxland, Gregory, *Alexander's Generals: the Italian Campaign 1944–45*, William Kimber, 1979.

Bonn, Keith E., *When the Odds Were Even: the Vosges Mountain Campaign October 1944–January 1945*, Presidio, Novato (California), 1994 .

Brett-James, Antony, *Report My Signals*, Hennel Locke/Harrap, 1948.

Burns, John Horne, *The Gallery*, Secker & Warburg, 1948.

Cannon, M. Hamlin, *Leyte: the Return to the Philippines (U.S. Army in World War II)*, G.P.O., Washington, 1954.

Clarke, Jeffrey J. and Robert R. Smith, *Riviera to the Rhine (U.S. Army in World War II)*, G.P.O., Washington, 1993.

Currie, Jack, *Lancaster Target*, Goodall, 1981.

Cutler, Thomas J., *The Battle of Leyte Gulf 25–26 October 1944*, HarperCollins, New York, 1994.

Dawidowicz, Lucy, *The War Against the Jews 1933–45*, Penguin, Harmondsworth, 1977.

Doubler, Michael D., *Closing With the Enemy: How GIs Fought the War in Europe 1944–1945*, University Press of Kansas, Lawrence, 1994.

Ellis, John, *The World War II Databook*, Aurum Press, 1993.

Erickson, John, *The Road to Berlin: Stalin's War with Germany (vol. 2)*, Weidenfeld & Nicolson, 1983.

Forman, Harrison, *Report from Red China*, Robert Hale, 1946.

Freeman, Roger, *The Mighty Eighth War Diary*, Jane's, 1981.

Gailey, Harry A., *Bougainville: the Forgotten Campaign 1943–45*, University Press of Kentucky, Lexington, 1991.

———, *Peleliu 1944*, Nautical and Aviation Publishing Co., Annapolis (Maryland), 1983.

Garbett, Mike and Brian Goulding, *The Lancaster at War*, Ian Allan, Shepperton, 1971.

Gilbert, Martin, *The Dent Atlas of the Holocaust*, J. M. Dent, 1993 (2nd. ed.).

Gill, A., *The Journey Back from Hell: Conversations with Concentration Camp Survivors*, Grafton, 1988.

Groueff, Stephane, *Manhattan Project: the Untold Story of the Making of the Atomic Bomb*, Bantam, New York, 1968.

Hanley, Gerald, *Monsoon Victory*, Collins, 1946.

Hinsley, F. H. *et. al.*, *British Intelligence in the Second World War*, vol. 3 (parts 1 and 2), HMSO, 1984–88.

Inoguchi, Rikihei and Tadashi Nakajima, 'The Kamikaze Attack Corps', in David C. Evans (ed.), *The Japanese Navy in World War II*, Naval Institute Press, Annapolis (Maryland), 1986.

Ito, Masanori, *The End of the Imperial Japanese Navy*, Norton, New York, 1962.

Jones, William E., *Bomber Intelligence: 103, 150, 166, 170 Squadrons Operations and Techniques 1942–45*, Midland Counties, Leicester, 1983.

Josephy, Alvin M. Jr., *The Long and the Short and the Tall: the Story of a Marine Combat Unit in the Pacific During World War II*, Knopf, New York, 1946.

Kemp, Anthony, *The Unknown Battle: Metz 1944*, Frederick Warne, 1981.

Kennedy, Gregory P., *Vengeance Weapon 2: the V-2 Guided Missile*, Smithsonian Institution Press, Washington, 1983.

Lamb, Richard, *Montgomery in Europe 1943–45*, Buchan & Enright, 1983.

———, *War in Italy 1943–45*, John Murray, 1993.

de Lattre de Tassigny, Jean, *The History of the French First Army*, Allen & Unwin, 1952.

Lewis, Norman, *Naples '44*, Collins, 1978.

Long, Gavin, *The Final Campaigns (Australia in the War of 1939–45)*, vol. 7, Australian War Memorial, Canberra, 1963.

Longmate, Norman, *The Bombers: the RAF Offensive against Germany 1939–45*, Hutchinson, 1983.

MacDonald, Charles B., *The Battle of the Hürtgen Forest*, J. B. Lippincott, New York, 1963.

McInnes, Colin, *To the Victors the Spoils*, MacGibbon & Kee, 1950.

Middlebrook, Martin and Chris Everitt, *The Bomber Command War Diaries: an Operational Reference Book 1939–45*, Viking, 1985.

Ministry of Defence (Navy), *The U-Boat War in the Atlantic*, HMSO, 1989.

Morison, Samuel Eliot, *Leyte (History of U.S. Naval Operations in World War II)*, vol. XII, Oxford University Press, 1958.

Morrison, Wilbur H., *Point of No Return*, Playboy, New York, 1980.

Moulton, J. L., *Battle for Antwerp*, Ian Allan, Shepperton, 1978.

Orgill, Douglas, *The Gothic Line: the Autumn Campaign in Italy*, Heinemann, 1967.

Pisar, Samuel, *Of Blood and Hope*, Cassell, 1979.

Price, Alfred, *Battle over the Reich*, Ian Allan, Shepperton, 1973.

———, *Last Year of the Luftwaffe*, Arms & Armour Press, 1991.

Pyle, Ernie, *Last Chapter*, Henry Holt, New York, 1946.

Rhodes, Richard, *The Making of the Atomic Bomb*, Touchstone, New York, 1988.

Shaw, James C., 'Fast Carrier Operations 1943–45', introduction to Samuel Eliot Morison, *Aleutians, Gilberts and Marshalls (History of U.S. Naval Operations in World War II)*, vol. VII, Little Brown, Boston, 1951.

Shtemenko, S. M., *The Last Six Months: Russia's Final Battles with Hitler's Armies in World War II*, William Kimber, 1978.

———, *The Soviet General Staff at War 1941–45*, Progress Publ., Moscow, 1970.

Smith, Stan, *The Battle of Leyte Gulf*, Belmont, New York, 1961.

Solberg, Carl, *Decision and Dissent: with Halsey at Leyte Gulf*, Naval Institute Press, Annapolis (Maryland), 1995.

Starr, Chester G., *From Salerno to the Alps: a History of the Fifth Army 1943–45*, Battery Press, Nashville, 1979 (orig. 1948).

Stewart, Adrian, *The Battle of Leyte Gulf*, Robert Hale, 1979.

Streetly, Martin, *Confound and Destroy: 100 Group and the Bomber Support Campaign*, Janes, 1985.

Tarrant, V. E., *The Last Year of the Kriegsmarine May 1944–May 1945*, Arms & Armour Press, 1994.

Taylor, J. C., *German Warships of World War II*, Ian Allan, Shepperton, 1966.

Thompson, R. W., *The 85 Days*, Hutchinson, 1957.

Tillman, Barrett, *Hellcat: the F6F in World War II*, Patrick Stephens, Cambridge, 1979.

Weighley, Russell F., *Eisenhower's Lieutenants: the Campaigns of France and Germany 1944–45*, Sidgwick & Jackson, 1981.

Whitaker, W. Denis and Shelagh, *The Battle of the Scheldt*, Souvenir Press, 1984.

White, Theodore H. and Annalee Jacoby, *Thunder Out of China*, Gollancz, 1947.

White, W. L., *Report on the Russians*, World Publishing Co, New York, 1946.

Whitley, M. J., *Destroyer! German Destroyers in World War II*, Arms & Armour Press, 1983.

Woodward, C. Vann, *The Battle for Leyte Gulf*, Macmillan, New York, 1947.

Young, Richard A., *The Flying Bomb*, Ian Allan, Shepperton, 1978.

Ziemke, Earl F., *Stalingrad to Berlin: the German Defeat in the East (Army Historical Series)*, G.P.O., Washington, 1968.

Zorns, Bruce, *I Walk Through the Valley: World War II Infantryman's Memoir of War, Imprisonment and Love*, McFarland, Jefferson (N. Carolina), 1991.

Index

577